COMMUNICATING

COMMUNICATING

Consulting Authors
Warren T. Schimmel
*President,
The Berkeley School
of Westchester*
Carolyn Beth Camp
*Linn-Benton
Community College*

John Wiley & Sons
*New York   Chichester
Brisbane   Toronto   Singapore*

Developed and produced by Visual Education Corporation, Princeton, New Jersey

Project Editor: Susan Joan Gordon

Editor: Karen Wunderman

Writers: Barbara Daniels, David Daniels, Alice Delman, Sheila Furjanic, Cynthia Mooney, Judith Peacock, Mark Schaeffer, Robert Weisser

Chief Copy Editor: Susan J. Garver

Copy Editors: Alice Calaprice, Albert McGrigor, Susan Mayer, Susan Meyers, Joan Poole

Production Editors: Paula Harris, Sheera Stern

Cover and Text Design: Arthur Ritter, Inc.

Cover/Part Opening Photos: Tornberg/Coghlan

Photo Research: Judith Burns

Acknowledgments

The publisher would like to thank the board of reviewers for their guidance in commenting upon the manuscript for this book:

Dr. Bob F. Thomas
Roane State Community College
Harriman, Tennessee

Frankie T. Davis
Palm Beach Junior College
Palm Beach Gardens, Florida

Pamela A. Patey
Riverside City College
Riverside, California

Sarah S. Weber
Lansdale School of Business
Lansdale, Pennsylvania

Sharon Miles
Clackamas Community College
Oregon City, Oregon

Shelley Scher
Stone School
New Haven, Connecticut

Bonnie Rae Taylor
The Williamsport Area Community College
Williamsport, Pennsylvania

Contents

COMMUNICATING

PART ONE
INTRODUCTION

1

The Communication Process

"Communication is very important in my life, both at home and at work," says June Michaels. "My husband and I both think that one of the reasons our marriage is strong is that we're good at communicating—talking about what's on our minds and really listening to each other. Without that bond between us, I don't think we'd be as happy as we are. I really make a point of staying in touch with family members and friends too.

"I can't take communication for granted at work, either. I'm the unit supervisor for customer information systems at a savings and loan association. I suppose you could say that I spend my day communicating—speaking, listening, reading, and writing.

"Right now we have a new product—a new kind of mortgage—so I have to explain the new procedures to the people who work for me. So far, there is nothing in writing that tells them what to do. Later, after I'm sure about the best way to do the job, I'll write down the instructions and be sure that everybody has a copy.

"Listening is important to me too. As a supervisor, I have to listen to people's problems. For example, some time ago, a member of my department came to me complaining that there was too much background noise in the department. I questioned several other employees who agreed and who also had some ideas for solutions. Just last week we installed sound-deadening partitions around each desk. Not only do they solve the noise problem, but they also give each individual a little more privacy.

"Of course, I have to read at my job—not just read, but understand what I'm reading and react to it. I know my supervisors do a lot more reading than I do, and I'm already trying to read some of the same periodicals they do so I'll be ready for my next job when I get another promotion. That's why I always read the business section of the newspaper on the bus in the morning and subscribe to some specialized savings and loan magazines. And of course, I read the daily newspaper and a weekly news magazine because keeping up with world events can help me at work—and make me a more interesting person in general."

THE NATURE OF COMMUNICATION

June Michaels spends most of her day communicating, which means that she is constantly sending and receiving ideas, sharing meaning with other people. Communication always requires at least two people. You may not think that you communicate very much with others, but without realizing it, you are communicating almost constantly. You can even convey an idea without speaking or writing. Let's say, for instance, that you are preoccupied with a problem and want to be alone, so you sit at a cafeteria table by yourself, looking down. Other people are likely to sense that you want to be alone because that is exactly what your actions communicate. Thus, it is hard *not* to communicate with others, whether you are communicating deliberately or not.

Of course, most of the time your communication is more active. You probably like to share breaks from work or school with other people so that you can talk about the day's events or common interests. In fact, the desire to express ideas and feelings is natural and universal. The urge to speak and write is so strong that people are likely to feel frustrated, or even angry, if they are unable to communicate with others.

VERBAL COMMUNICATION

Verbal communication means using words to exchange ideas, whether it involves listening, speaking, reading, or writing. Verbal communication, on the job and off, takes up about 70 percent of a person's waking time. At home, people talk with friends or family members, read books and magazines, watch TV, and write letters. All of these activities involve using words to communicate.

At work, people spend an average of 45 percent of their communicating time listening to others—their managers, their co-workers, and the people they supervise, as well as salespeople and customers. Approximately 30 percent of the time spent communicating at work is spent talking. On a typical day, a worker may explain the office system to a new employee, persuade a customer to buy a new oven, and analyze the approach of an ad campaign. About 16 percent of people's time on the job is spent reading. Employees may read business magazines, as June Michaels does, and they almost certainly read letters, memos, and reports as well. For the remaining 9 percent of the time, workers are writing their own letters, memos, and reports. Obviously, good communication skills can make a big difference in how successful people are in their working lives.

NONVERBAL COMMUNICATION

Even though people spend so much of their time using words, experts believe that more than 90 percent of all messages are communicated nonverbally. Body language, facial expressions, tone of voice, and dress can supplement verbal messages or even contradict them. All behavior sends messages, even though people are often unaware of what they are doing.

We all began sending and interpreting nonverbal messages long before we learned to talk. As toddlers on shaky legs, we looked to our parents for reassurance. Their smiles encouraged us to take another halting step. As we grew up, we learned more about our society's code of nonverbal behavior. We learned to hear anger in a person's voice, even though we may not have understood what the words meant. We learned that how we were dressed could affect a person's attitude toward us for better or for worse. Mastering these signals, and many more, gradually improved our ability to communicate with others.

THE GOALS OF COMMUNICATION

Sometimes the point of communicating is not to say anything important, but merely to make contact with someone. For example, someone who says to you, "Nice day, isn't it?" is not communicating any new information. Instead, that person is acknowledging you as a person and reinforcing the relationship between you.

Most of the time people have one of four main purposes when they communicate: to inquire, to inform, to persuade, or to establish goodwill. Often, the goal of speaking or writing is to ask for information or for someone else's opinion. This may mean finding out where you should meet your friends after class. At work it could mean asking for information in order to coordinate tasks and solve problems. Asking the right questions is likely to be one of the keys to success at work.

Providing information to others is another important goal of communication. You might have to tell someone who repairs televisions exactly what has gone wrong with your TV set. In a community meeting, you could speak up to clarify or repeat important information. At work, instructions, memos, and progress reports are only a few of the ways to communicate information.

Even seemingly factual information is often intended to persuade other people to follow a certain course of action. Simply mentioning to a friend that a particular movie is playing nearby does more than communicate that information; it also suggests that going together to the movie might be a good idea. Business communication often has the important goal of persuading a potential customer to buy a product. Communication between employees is often meant to interest people in an idea. You should be alert for the intent to persuade in much of what you read and hear at work.

Establishing goodwill is also an important goal of business communication. Goodwill is made up of trust and confidence. It is a contributing factor both to productive interactions within a company and to fruitful relationships between the company and the public. Feelings of goodwill among employees translate into an increased willingness to support company objectives. Motivated employees contribute to company success and also experience feelings of personal accomplishment. All thriving businesses must also promote goodwill toward their present and potential customers. A positive company image and obvious concern help the public feel trust and confidence in a company. As an individual employee, you may not see an immediate payoff in sales from your efforts to be courteous toward customers. Because of your graciousness, however, customers may develop loyalty to your company, resulting in future purchases or favorable recommendations to their families and friends.

Communicating is a complicated process—far more complicated than it appears at first glance. Experts have divided it into six elements: sender, message, channel, receiver, perception, and feedback. All six must work effectively for proper communication to take place.

THE SIX ELEMENTS IN THE COMMUNICATION PROCESS

The Sender. The sender is the person speaking or writing. Although the sender may be responding to a previous message, he or she is usually the one who decides to communicate. The sender's appearance and reputation can influence the success of the communication process. People listen more carefully to someone who has an air of authority or to someone they know they can trust. The sender's primary goal is to get a response, preferably a favorable one. To do so, the sender tries to create a favorable impression and to prevent distractions—any circumstances that may draw the receiver's attention away from the message.

The Message. The message consists of whatever is said or written. The message should be as clear as possible to ensure that the intended message is actually received. Creating a message usually involves putting ideas into words. A message can also be nonverbal, such as a wave of the hand to mean "good-bye."

The Channel. The channel is the way a message moves from one person to another. Often, there will be a choice of channels. You might ask yourself, "Should I go see Mr. Bogart in person, or should I call him? Maybe I should write to him." Each of these channels has its advantages and disadvantages. After you have decided what channel to use, related questions might arise. Should your communication be formal or informal? Is there anything, such as a picture or a diagram, that can make your message clearer? The choice of the proper channel not only determines the form of the message but can also have a decisive influence on how successfully it is received.

The Receiver. The receiver is the person listening to or reading the message. The burden of communicating does not rest entirely on the sender; the receiver must, in turn, interpret what has been said or written. When you are the receiver, giving your full attention to a speaker or reading a message as carefully as possible means that you are doing your part to achieve good communication.

Perception. Perception is the receiver's understanding of the message. The sender's message must first be sorted out from surrounding noise and confusion and must then be interpreted. Perception involves taking into account both the verbal and nonverbal elements of the message. In general, the more willing you are to receive a message, the better you will understand it.

Feedback. Feedback is the receiver's response to the message. Until the receiver says or does something in reply, the sender has no way of knowing whether the message has been communicated successfully. Feedback can be as simple as a nod or shake of the head or as elaborate as a whole new verbal message in reply to the previous one. As a sender, you should watch for a response which shows that your communication has been successful. As a receiver, you should make sure your feedback shows that you have done your best to understand the message correctly.

Barriers to communicating can disrupt any stage of the process. Obviously, some barriers, such as a breakdown in the telephone line that interferes with the channel, are beyond the communicators' control. Others, however, such as lack of concentration or lack of knowledge, are determined by the communicators. Both sender and receiver have their own responsibilities to see that their roles are carried out as clearly and as efficiently as possible.

THE IMPORTANCE OF GOOD COMMUNICATION IN DAILY LIFE

You can strengthen important relationships by improving communication in your daily life. Communication is central to almost everything you do. Good communication skills can break down barriers between you and other people. These skills help build good friendships and a satisfying family life.

Knowing how to say what you mean and how to interpret the messages other people communicate to you will help you in every area of life. For example, if you are sick, you should be able to tell a doctor exactly what your symptoms are. If you are dissatisfied with a product, you should be able to complain effectively to a salesperson or, write a letter of complaint.

THE VALUE OF GOOD COMMUNICATION ON THE JOB

June Michaels is very aware of the value of communication at work. "It's up to me to explain how the goals of the company affect everybody's job," she says. "For example, we're trying to market our products to people in a certain age group who have salaries in a specific range. Therefore, it is very important that my employees record accurate birth dates and occupation codes. Before I explained why this was significant, some of them were not paying enough attention to those details."

Some of the people who work for June Michaels are very effective communicators. "One of the women writes very well," June notes. "Her memos to the branch offices are so clear that anybody could understand them, even someone unfamiliar with the savings and loan industry.

"On the other hand, I have one woman working for me who does not have very good reading skills. When I give her written instructions, she just doesn't understand them. So I've started explaining every new procedure to the group as a whole, in order to avoid singling her out. She's thinking about going back to school. Maybe that will help."

When June Michaels is asked to recommend a worker for a better job, she will of course select the person with good communication skills.

As a supervisor, June explains company goals and helps her workers see where they fit in. June's workers realize the importance of taking telephone messages accurately, gaining a thorough understanding of what they read, writing clear memos to co-workers, and writing effective letters to customers and branch offices. Like them, you will find that communicating on the job is very important.

DID YOU KNOW?
Cultural Differences in Communicating

Have you ever found yourself backing away from someone else? You may feel friendly toward the person, but he or she has moved so close to you that you feel uncomfortable, and you find yourself automatically stepping back. The reason? Your sense of personal space has been violated.

The sense of personal space that people develop varies greatly from culture to culture. In the United States, people are comfortable talking to each other at a distance of two to five feet. However, in Latin American and Middle Eastern countries, people get used to standing much closer to each other when they talk. In some cultures, people even want to smell each other's breath as they converse.

What constitutes appropriate physical contact during conversation also differs around the world. People in a number of countries punctuate their conversations by touching each other, even when talking to strangers. Americans, in contrast, are unlikely to touch each other, especially if they don't know the person.

Even the arrangement of office furniture is affected by different ideas about personal space. In at least one European country, you would be considered rude if you moved your chair closer to the desk of the person you were talking to. Office doors, too, send a message. In some countries, office doors are kept closed as a matter of course; to Americans, a closed door suggests unusual circumstances.

Time is treated differently in different cultures too. Americans arrive slightly early for appointments as a sign of respect, but in some other cultures waiting an hour for a meeting to begin is not at all unusual. Complaining about an hour's delay would offend someone who has a more flexible sense of time. Thus, rather than assuming that your views are the only natural ones, you are more likely to be successful in business if you make allowances for different perceptions of space and time when dealing with people from other countries.

THE DEVELOPMENT OF COMMUNICATION SKILLS

Learning how to communicate well is an ongoing process. Think about how much more effectively you communicate today than you did ten years ago. Ten years from now, you should be an even better communicator because communication skills improve with practice. Using this book will help you begin to make some important improvements in your ability to communicate.

Caring about becoming a more effective communicator is vital to sharpening your skills. Considering June Michaels' experience will help you realize the value of working on your communication skills now. As she explains, "I'm doing a job now that did not exist when I was in school. I couldn't have trained for this specific job, but the communication skills I learned in school—and am still learning—help make me flexible enough to adapt to the demands of new jobs. So whatever the future holds, I feel confident about my ability to deal with it."

PROBLEMS

A. Explain how communication could be blocked in the following situations, as well as how it might be improved.

1. "Wait! Don't move the paper forward with that knob," shouted Don. "You'll strip the gears and ruin the printer."

2. "You entered these age codes wrong, Franny," said Mrs. Myers. "You can just stay late and redo them."

3. "Get me that report by 8 o'clock tomorrow morning, Doug," said Sandra River. "I've got to have it by then."

4. "Cindy, you're always late," said Mr. Schwab. "Get here on time from now on or else."

B. List five to ten qualities you think a good communicator should have. Include qualities such as the ability to give instructions clearly and the willingness to listen to another person's point of view. Number your list in order of importance.

PROJECTS

A. Observe three situations in which people are communicating. For each situation, make notes identifying the sender, message, channel, receiver, and feedback. Also note any distractions and nonverbal communication you observe. How successful was the communication in each case? Why?

B. Make a plan for improving your communication skills. Start by identifying your strengths and weaknesses as a speaker, listener, reader, and writer. Then, for each weakness you have identified, list at least one specific method for improving the way you communicate. Keep a record of your progress.

2
Communicating on the Job

On a typical workday, the employees of Inverness Industries can be found at their usual places, doing their jobs. Today, Frank Fuller, the company's best salesperson, is on the telephone talking to a customer. Julie Schwartz, who handles customer relations, is preparing a brochure that describes the company's newest products. At a desk in the corner, a small group of employees is holding an informal meeting. Ellen Lehey, a company vice president, is in her office reading a long report about next year's sales projections. Elsewhere, people are writing memos and answering the day's mail at typewriters and word processors.

Each employee is doing a different job, but all are taking part in the same process—they are communicating. The list of office tasks that involve communicating is almost endless.

Many business people take communicating for granted and become aware of it only when it starts to break down. A sales representative who cannot explain the advantages of a product will lose sales. A word processing supervisor who does not give company procedures manuals to new employees will cause them to make unnecessary errors.

A company that improves communication can boost both its profits and the morale of its employees, as you will see in the following section. At the same time, individual workers who improve their communication skills can increase their chances for advancement.

The goal of any business is to make a profit. Effective communicating, both between the company and its customers and within the company itself, plays a vital part in achieving that goal.

The best salespeople are aware that communicating means both speaking *and* listening. Mark Cunningham, an outstanding salesperson at the Hanover Furniture Store, has won many awards for his work. He is friendly and courteous

HOW COMMUNICATING AFFECTS PROFITS

toward customers and takes the time to make them feel comfortable. When they have comments and questions, he listens closely so he can provide them with the information they need.

Ralph Chaska, on the other hand, has a poor sales record at Hanover, and he cannot understand why. He worries that he will lose his job and is trying hard to make sales. Only yesterday, a customer came in and asked Ralph to show her some wicker porch furniture. Instead, Ralph showed her a cedar picnic table that was on sale. Ralph was so busy pointing out how beautiful and practical the cedar table was that he never even heard the customer protest that she had asked about a wicker table. In the end, the customer left the store and bought her porch furniture at Albright's, Hanover's chief competitor. Ralph dismissed the customer as "just another browser," not realizing that he had lost a sale because he had talked a lot more than he had listened.

Communicating within a company is just as important as communicating with customers and suppliers. Many employees never face the public directly. Nevertheless, they affect company profits by the way they communicate with each other. Productivity—a company's ability to produce goods and services—depends in large part on communicating. When supervisors give sketchy instructions, workers will make mistakes that can slow down production. Workers can also make costly errors when they do not pay attention to instructions or fail to understand directions.

HOW COMMUNICATING AFFECTS MORALE

Successful communicating not only helps people do their jobs better, but also makes them happier with their work. Ruth Sabatino checks the accuracy of application information for a mortgage company. Ruth's supervisor has made it clear that the company's success depends largely on mortgage holders' submitting their payments regularly. Ruth knows that her thoroughness in checking application information will help the company choose its clients wisely. Understanding her company's goals and knowing she has an important role to play in achieving them makes Ruth feel that she is a member of a team.

On the other hand, when communication breaks down, hard feelings usually follow. Because the word processing supervisor mentioned earlier failed to give procedures manuals to his new employees, they were criticized for not typing correspondence according to company style. They felt resentful about taking the blame for their supervisor's oversight. People who are told clearly what is expected of them and why their work is important will feel happier about their jobs and more in command of their own lives than people who are not given that information.

HOW COMMUNICATING AFFECTS ADVANCEMENT

The top executives at Inverness Industries often find themselves representing the company, both to customers and to the executives of other companies with which they do business. They are all good communicators, in part because they realize that whenever they write a letter or make a speech, the reputation of Inverness Industries is at stake.

These executives expect employees at all levels in the company to be skillful communicators. The company leadership realizes that lower-level workers often have extensive contact with the public and thus very strongly influence people's perceptions of the company.

Jennifer Tilden has better academic qualifications than any other person in her office. She has a college degree and has taken additional courses in management and sales. Despite her education, Jennifer has never received the promotion she has been working for because she is a poor communicator.

When Jennifer writes a letter, she feels her time is too valuable to be spent making revisions. If the message is not clear, she expects the person who receives it to figure out what she means. Jennifer used to be selected to give sales presentations to important clients, but she never gave these presentations much thought. She just assumed that if she knew the company's products well

ON THE JOB
Coping With Communication Problems

Carol Butler had been working for the financial services firm of Kramer & Norton for nearly a month. Although she felt that she was doing her work accurately, efficiently, and promptly, her supervisor, Mr. Diamond, never seemed satisfied. He didn't give her much guidance, Carol felt, and his instructions were rarely clear.

Mr. Diamond told Carol that he would be out of the office for one week. He said that he would talk to her about what had to be done in his absence before he left on Friday.

Carol knew that there was a big stockholders' meeting coming up and that the company's quarterly report had to be ready at that time. In fact, most of the people in Carol's department had been told to put aside their routine work in order to work on the report.

Mr. Diamond was busy in meetings throughout most of Friday. He didn't get a chance to talk to Carol until 5 p.m., just as she was getting ready to leave the office. "This quarterly report is a top priority," he told her. "But we need to get these sales letters out next week." He handed her an envelope marked "Names/Addresses for Sales Letter" and then walked away.

The following Monday Carol was still confused about what she was supposed to be doing. She asked Valerie Lerner, another person in the department, what she thought. "Mr. Diamond told me not to work on the sales letters," Valerie said. "He said that getting the quarterly report done was our first priority."

Carol figured that Valerie knew what she was talking about, since she had worked at Kramer & Norton for ten years. Carol decided to work on the report for three days and then send out the letters on Thursday and Friday.

Mr. Diamond phoned her on Wednesday afternoon. "Did you send out the sales letters?" he asked. "No, I've been working on the quarterly report since Monday," replied Carol. "I thought you said it was a priority."

"It *is* a priority—but you were supposed to get the sales letters out!"

Carol felt extremely frustrated. Why couldn't Mr. Diamond have made his instructions clear to begin with? Was Valerie partly to blame for giving Carol misleading information? Why were there so many communication problems at Kramer & Norton?

enough, her presentations would work out fine. When clients asked her questions during a presentation, she became annoyed, thinking that they were not bright enough to understand what she had said.

Jennifer now finds that someone else is being asked to make the presentations that had been her responsibility. She is stuck in a dead-end job and feels resentful about it. Jennifer has never asked her supervisor why she has not been promoted, thinking only that "someone upstairs" does not like her. Better communication skills would help Jennifer, but first she must become aware of their importance. Her future with Inverness Industries—or any company— depends on it.

THE EFFECT OF SPECIALIZATION ON COMMUNICATION

Until recently, many workers performed a variety of tasks within a company. It was not unusual for people to understand an entire manufacturing process, from start to finish. Today, however, jobs are becoming increasingly specialized, so the words used to describe certain tasks are known to only a few people in the organization.

Although specialized language is necessary so that people doing the same work can talk among themselves, it can cause problems when those people communicate with someone who does not share their expertise. Then they must be careful to explain their ideas in more familiar words. Even office workers must try to remember that the words and phrases they use to describe their work (*cash flow*, for example) may not be clear to people in a different line of work. Specialization requires an increased sensitivity to the barriers that language can create.

THE INFORMATION EXPLOSION

In the past, recording and sending information were difficult tasks. Every time a letter was sent out, it first had to be copied by hand, a laborious process. All other documents had to be copied in longhand too. Today, technology has made it so easy to transmit and copy information that there has been a vast increase in the amount of information sent and received. (Think, for example, how many people copy magazine articles to send to friends. Do you think they would send the same article if they had to write it out by hand?)

It was once thought that computers and electronic communication would replace paper communication entirely. Instead, computer printers and quick copiers have increased the flow of paper. Too much information, though, can be as bad as not enough. It is difficult to find and remember the most important pieces of information when the total volume is so high.

It has become more important than ever to achieve quality, not quantity, in business communication. When you write a business letter, aim for as much clarity as possible in as few words as possible. Remember that the person to whom you are writing must read hundreds of letters besides your own. When you, in turn, read a business letter, look for the key ideas first and avoid getting bogged down in detail.

Learning how to use the new information processing technologies can also help you deal with the information explosion. The more experienced you become at using technology to locate vital information quickly, the better you will do your job and the more valuable you will be to your company.

Listening is the most neglected aspect of the communication process. Within two weeks of listening to an oral presentation, most people have forgotten 75 percent of what they heard.

People listen poorly for a variety of reasons, ranging from distraction caused by a speaker's appearance to daydreaming. Sometimes people listen carefully, but they still do not understand what they hear. This can happen when they do not have enough knowledge or experience to follow what a speaker is saying. In this case, a poor background in a subject leads to poor listening.

Listening skills, however, like reading, writing, and speaking skills, can be learned. Improving your listening skills (as you will discover in Part Ten of this book) will produce positive results both in your personal life and in your job.

LISTENING ON THE JOB

Someday your job may require you to speak to large groups of customers or co-workers. When you do, you should prepare carefully and speak formally. You will probably do far more informal speaking, however, to provide information, explain a process, introduce people, or welcome someone to your office.

Regardless of whether you must speak formally or informally, your goal should be to make a favorable first impression. The first judgments people make about you establish a framework on which their later impressions are built.

Even more important is that you be familiar with your subject. Regardless of how good you look and sound, if you do not know what you are talking about, you will not win the respect of the people to whom you speak.

In Part Ten of this book, you will learn more about speaking effectively. Speaking well involves, most importantly, practice, as well as sensitivity to your audience's goals and needs and constant attention to making your ideas vivid and memorable. People who speak effectively are likely to advance in their careers.

SPEAKING ON THE JOB

At work, good writing means effective writing. Whether you are writing a memo, a sales letter, or a formal report, you should be able to organize your ideas and emphasize the points that are most important.

A good business letter makes your company look good, and it makes you look good. To write an effective business letter, you need to understand your

WRITING ON THE JOB

reader's goals and needs. Thus, you cannot merely imitate a model letter and assume that it will be effective. Rather than emphasizing what *you* think or want, you should focus on your reader's interests and concerns.

This book will help you make a good impression through your writing. It explains the steps you can take to produce effective business writing, from well-conceived planning to careful editing and proofreading.

READING ON THE JOB

At work, you will be reading not only memos from co-workers and letters from people outside your company, but also instructions, policy manuals, and reports that can vary in length from a single page to several volumes. You will need to be able to skim quickly to get an overview of main ideas and to read carefully and slowly when you are reading something difficult or important. You should also be able to skim to locate specific information in a reference book or report.

Reading is useful to you on the job only if you know how to remember what you have read. Thus, you should develop ways to fix key facts and ideas in your mind so that you can use them when you need them.

A special kind of reading that is crucial on the job is proofreading, which is examining copy in order to find and correct errors. Mistakes in correspondence could make your company seem careless and unprofessional, resulting in plunging profits and loss of goodwill. This book will help you develop a wide range of reading skills.

In all the ways you communicate at work—listening, speaking, writing, and reading—increased effectiveness will mean not only success for your business, but improved morale and possibly a better job for you as well.

PROBLEMS

A. Explain how you would solve the following communication problems.

1. A supervisor has been leaving notes for people who have made mistakes in their work, but a few employees would prefer being told about their errors rather than getting notes. What should they do?

2. A new salesperson is afraid of speaking to important clients. What should she do?

3. Communication with top executives is blocked, so workers find out about company policy through the grapevine, resulting in rumors that have a bad effect on morale. Who could solve the problem? How?

4. A supervisor has told one worker that he is pleased with her work but that he is unhappy with the work one of her friends is doing. Should the worker tell her friend?

5. People who work together in an office have begun to believe that an unidentified co-worker is taking money from unattended wallets and pocketbooks. Trust among the workers is breaking down. What should they do?

B. Choose two descriptive passages of approximately the same length from books or magazine articles. Select a classmate to act as your partner, and read one passage while your partner just listens without taking any notes. After you have finished reading, ask your partner to tell you as much as she or he remembers about the passage. Then read the second passage while your partner takes notes. How good were your partner's listening skills with the first paragraph? Did taking notes help the person retain the material in the second passage?

PROJECTS

A. Analyze communication in a group or an organization to which you belong, such as a club, class, or work group. How does communication help the group meet its goals? Give one example of a communication breakdown or problem within the group, and describe a member of the group who is an effective communicator. In what ways does communication affect the group's morale?

B. Interview someone to find out which reading, writing, speaking, and listening skills he or she uses on the job. Find out how important good communication skills are in the interviewee's type of work. What advice about improving communication skills would this person give to people who are beginning their careers?

3

Using Information Processing Technology to Communicate Effectively

In recent years, millions of business people in the United States and in other parts of the world have had to make an important decision: Should they enter the computer age by investing in the latest electronic technology? Many business people were reluctant at first—after all, typewriters and filing cabinets had been providing good, reliable service for nearly 100 years. Still, other companies were buying computers and doing very well with them.

THE COMPUTER REVOLUTION

Now the debate is over. The value of computers has been proved; experts now predict that the success of a business in the 1990s will depend on its decisions about automation in the 1980s.

In a way, computers are only the latest products in a march of technology that began with the invention of the printing press. Some people think that word processors are only improved typewriters and that data bases are only filing cabinets brought up to date. Others believe, however, that computers will alter our ways of looking at work and at the world in general, since they provide access to new information and suggest new ways to analyze it.

How Computers Have Changed the Business World

New ways to use computers in business have developed so rapidly that it is hard to keep up with all the changes that are taking place. One field in which computers have made an enormous difference is in telecommunications—the electronic transmission of messages. Most mail, for example, used to take days or even weeks to reach its destination. Now, by means of electronic mail, in which written communications are sent over telephone lines or by laser beams or space satellites, messages can travel thousands of miles in seconds. Even pictures, diagrams, and maps can be sent electronically through new techniques of facsimile transmission.

Formerly, people often traveled considerable distances for face-to-face meetings. Now, teleconferences—meetings by telephone and television—make it possible for people in several different locations to discuss problems and reach agreements without ever leaving their offices, thus eliminating travel time and expense.

Word processing is another way in which computers have revolutionized office work. Word processors are computer systems for writing and editing letters, memos, and other messages. This new technology both saves time and decreases costs.

Information processing, which enables people to manipulate data electronically, is the computer's answer to the information explosion. Electronic filing systems, called data bases, enable companies to keep track of vast quantities of information at relatively low cost. Data banks are another information processing development. These electronic libraries offer companies access to news and financial information, thus allowing business people to make more informed decisions than ever before. Even graphics design—creating graphs, charts, and other visual aids to help make memo and report writing clearer and more concise—can be performed automatically by the computer.

The capability of working electronically, without paper, brings businesses many advantages. The new methods are faster than the old, yielding greater efficiency throughout the office. Costs are lower, not only because paper is saved but also because expenses for storing, filing, and retrieving information are lower. Most businesses rapidly make up the initial costs of computerizing their operations through subsequent savings of time and money.

Some people, however, feel threatened by computers, thinking that these new machines will make them and their hard-earned skills unnecessary. In fact, the quality of what comes out of a computer depends on the quality of what human beings put into it. Good communication skills are more necessary now than ever; while computers have opened new channels of communication, the quality of the messages they convey still depends on the knowledge and intelligence of the people who use them.

FEATURES OF WORD PROCESSORS

The look of offices today is very different from that of only a few years ago because so many computers used for word processing have replaced typewriters. The keyboard of a computer looks like a typewriter keyboard, except that there are more keys. Near the keyboard is a video display screen that looks like a television screen. As something is typed on the keyboard, it is displayed on the screen. Changes can be made easily on the screen. After all corrections have been made, a printed copy is produced on a computer printer, which is attached to the computer. Within the computer is a small central processing unit that is the "brain" of the word processor.

Some computers are used only to edit writing and arrange it on pages. These computers are called dedicated word processors. They are usually easy to learn to use, but they are limited just to word processing. Other office computers are more versatile. Besides acting as a word processing system, these computers are also capable of creating charts and graphs and keeping track of payroll, as well as many other tasks.

Learning to use a word processor is exciting because it can help you at each stage in the writing process. Since you can easily change your wording on the screen before you print a corrected copy, planning a memo or letter is easier than ever before. You can list your ideas on the screen and keep rearranging and refining them as you decide exactly what you want to say.

Later, if you find an error in something you have written, you can bring your writing to the screen again, make a quick change, and print a perfect copy. With word processing, you can avoid the time-consuming, repetitive tasks of retyping the entire piece again and again or using correction fluid or tape; you can concentrate on what you have to say. Have you ever reached the point where you know you should retype something to make a small change, but you just do not have the time or patience to do so? With word processing, well-written, error-free writing is much easier to produce, using the capabilities described here.

Typeover

If you have ever written a rough draft at a typewriter, you may have corrected an error quickly by typing over it. Of course, merely typing over an error creates copy that looks sloppy and is hard to read, which is not appropriate for business writing.

However, when you use a word processor to type over an error, the wrong letter disappears, and the right one replaces it on the screen. With a few keystrokes, you can type over errors, and no trace of your mistakes will remain.

Insert and Delete

When an incorrect word has the same number of letters as the correct word has, it can be fixed rather easily on a typewriter with correction tape or fluid. However, traces of the correction can detract from the appearance of the typed page. Corrections that involve adding or subtracting characters are more difficult on a typewriter. Usually, a line or an entire page has to be retyped.

At the word processor, however, when you replace a word with one that has fewer letters, the extra space automatically closes up. If you are adding more letters, the words that follow slide over to make room for your addition.

You can move anywhere within your memo or letter to insert words and letters. If you wish, you can easily delete words and letters that have been mistyped or that you decide you do not want. The ability to insert and delete gives you much more flexibility as you write.

Word Wraparound

Word wraparound is another useful feature. When there is not enough room for a word at the end of a typewritten line, you must use the carriage return to start a new line. On a word processor, the word is automatically moved down to the beginning of the new line.

Word wraparound saves time and helps you concentrate on your writing. You can keep on entering information at the keyboard without being distracted by a bell or concerned about when to start a new line.

Not only does the computer automatically place words on the lines where they belong, but it can also make an even right-hand margin, a process known as justifying. As you work at a word processor, you can experiment with different kinds of page formats to see which you prefer. For example, you could try adding extra line spaces to move a letter farther down on the page or experiment with wider margins or double-spacing. If you wish, you can leave decisions about format to the computer, which will automatically set up pages according to a predetermined format.

Block Move

You can also move a sentence, a paragraph, or a whole page from one place to another within the document you are writing. The part that you choose to move is known as a block. With a few keystrokes, you can indicate exactly where your block begins and ends and move it to its new location. You can also copy a block so that it appears in two places in your document at once, which saves retyping. Likewise, you can delete an entire block at once.

Search and Replace

Imagine you discover that you have misspelled a word throughout a long typewritten report. Correcting that error each time it occurs would be very time-consuming. At a word processor, you can use a special command to search for every occurrence of the misspelled word and replace each one with the correctly typed word, instantly.

You can use the same process to replace one phrase with another throughout a long document. For example, you could be sending the same long report to two clients, Central Soya Corporation and Emax Industries. By using the search-and-replace command, you could automatically change the words *Central Soya Corporation* to *Emax Industries* each time they occurred within the report. Then at a touch of a key, you could print a second copy of the report, avoiding repetitive retyping.

Boilerplate

Boilerplate is identical wording that is used repeatedly in different documents. The passage is held in storage in the word processor. In the past, people had to painstakingly retype the same phrases again and again in certain kinds of legal and business writing. Today, boilerplate can be brought to the screen and reused without any retyping. Boilerplate saves both typing time and proofreading time. Because the boilerplate is carefully proofread when it is first written, it does not need to be proofread again when it is reused. Each time it is reused, it is exactly the same, word for word and letter for letter.

Optional Features

Some word processors can do even more for you. A spelling checker will help to correct the spelling of many words in your document. You can also use programs that check your punctuation and grammar for common errors.

USING YOUR WORD PROCESSOR
Making the Transition to Word Processing

If you are used to the typewriter, the word processor may seem at first to be difficult to use and hard to control. Try following the steps in this list to make the transition to word processing easier.

1. Have a positive attitude. A computer can do many different things, but so can a pencil. Relax and look forward to the benefits of word processing, such as fewer repetitive typing tasks and easier error correction.

2. Arrange for some free time to experiment. Don't begin by working on a long, important document that must be completed in a short time. Instead, start with the rough draft of a shorter, less crucial task.

3. Concentrate on important commands first, leaving the others for later. Any good word processing program is complicated, but all you really need to know at first is how to insert and delete. Don't assume that you have to master everything at once. In fact, you may never need to learn some of the commands.

4. Take notes on crucial steps, such as how to start and end a session of word processing.

5. Study the printed materials that explain your word processing program. These materials may take a while to understand, but they may also reveal easier, better ways to perform certain tasks.

6. Find a partner. Get the name and telephone number of someone who is working with the same equipment you are using so you can contact that person if you can't find the answer to a question.

The range of tasks computers can perform in an office is wide and growing wider. Three such tasks are creating graphics, setting up and using data bases, and drawing on data banks. The three together are part of the rapidly growing field of information processing, which is concerned with making information easier to find and use.

INFORMATION PROCESSING

Graphics Design

Because business people must read many letters, memos, and reports each day, business writing should be as easy as possible to read and understand. Writing that contains a great many statistics will usually be difficult to read.

Such information would be much easier to comprehend if it appeared in the form of a graph or chart. One of the most valuable functions of a computer is that it can produce charts, graphs, and other visual aids quickly and easily. When statistical information is fed into the computer, a good graphics program can turn it into an appropriate visual aid automatically. Not only are reports containing visual aids easier to read, but they also look more professional and more appealing than those that do not. Many consecutive pages of prose appear to be difficult to read, even if the subject matter is fairly simple. A few well-placed charts and graphs can make a report appear more manageable and help arouse the reader's curiosity and interest. Most computer graphics programs can reproduce visual aids in color, making them even more attractive to the eye.

Computer graphics are also helpful to designers, engineers, and research scientists as they plan new products and test new theories. New uses for computer graphics, both in and out of the office, are being discovered all the time. Computers can be used to produce maps, drawings, blueprints, artwork for advertising, sheet music—almost anything.

Data Bases

Before computers, almost every office had at least one filing cabinet and usually more. Filing cabinets, however, are very heavy and take up an enormous amount of space. Sometimes they are also difficult to use. If a file folder is misfiled—placed in the cabinet out of its normal alphabetical order—it might be days or even weeks before anyone finds it.

In a computerized office, filing can be done electronically, with the use of data base programs. These programs enable the computer to store information, often on floppy disks, and then to find the information when needed. The disks hold a lot of information, are very light, and take up little storage space. A small box of them can replace a whole bank of filing cabinets.

These electronic files are called data bases. They are very flexible; information can be added, deleted, or rearranged at any time, and the whole file or part of it can be printed out on paper at the touch of a few keys. Disks can also be duplicated easily, making it possible for several people to work with the same file at the same time.

Data bases help simplify many office tasks. For example, a mailing list is one type of data base. The computer can be instructed to sort the mailing list into any one of a number of categories—perhaps all the customers who live in the same city or those who have not placed an order in the past three months. The selected list can then be printed out, which will produce a mailing label for each customer, all in a few minutes. Mailings that used to take days can now be finished in a few hours.

Many forms of record keeping have benefited from this new technology. Inventory control—knowing how much merchandise is in stock and which products are in short supply and need to be reordered—becomes much easier if the records are in a data base. The computer can print out not only the quantities of merchandise in stock, but also a separate list of items that are in short supply. Ordering then becomes routine.

Cost analyses can also be performed quickly and accurately by combining a data base with a program known as a spreadsheet. This tool is used to calculate how changes in one factor, such as the prices of raw materials, will influence other factors, such as the wholesale and retail prices of a product. Planning that used to take weeks can now be accomplished in hours.

Writing reports can become much easier when using a data base. Instead of rummaging through old-fashioned files to find needed information, you can summon it up in seconds on the same computer you use for word processing. A split screen—one half used for information from the data base and the other half for the text you are writing—can enable you to write knowledgeably about your subject without ever leaving your word processor.

Data Banks

A data bank is an electronic library. Information is stored in a large computer linked by telephone lines to many smaller computers. (The device that enables an office computer to reach a data bank by telephone is called a modem.) When subscribers to a data bank want to use any of the information it contains, they place a telephone call directly to the large computer—a procedure called accessing. Within seconds, the required information appears on their computer screen. Subscribers have, in effect, gone to the library without ever leaving their offices.

Data banks provide information on varied subjects. Many data banks are highly specialized, such as the ones that offer the latest stock prices or financial reports. Others cover news, providing either up-to-the-minute news bulletins from around the world or summaries of newspaper articles. More general data banks offer access to magazine or encyclopedia articles.

The number of data banks in this country is growing rapidly. Some services offer access to many data banks at once. A subscription to the main service entitles a computer owner to telephone any one of a number of data banks containing different sorts of information.

Business decisions require up-to-date information. Memos and reports that influence a company's long- and short-range planning must contain concise, accurate data from a wide variety of sources. Access to one or more data banks can help provide this information and save hundreds of worker-hours. As with other uses of computers in businesses, the use of data banks will continue to increase in the future.

EDITING EXERCISES

Assume that you are working at a word processor. Among the keys you can use are those marked "Delete," "Insert," and "Replace." Select the key you would use to correct each of the following sentences.

1. Thank you for your recnt order.

2. We are delighted that you are one of our knew customers.

3. Please let us known whenever you have speciail requests for product modifications or changes in delivery schedules.

4. Our salespeople are eagel to serve you.

5. Every month a sales representative will bring display materials you may use to advertis Iowa Office Supply products in your windows or within your store.

PROBLEMS

A. Can you predict the future? Picture yourself working in an office 20 years from now. Write a description of what you might do during a typical day, emphasizing the technology you would use to receive and send mail, gather information, and communicate with co-workers.

B. This chapter describes many of the advantages of using word processing and information processing technologies. What are some possible disadvantages of the new technologies? For example, will older workers lose their jobs because they find it hard to adapt to new approaches? Will office work become too impersonal because of the increased use of telecommunication? Brainstorm a list of possible disadvantages of the new technologies. Then number your list in order from the most serious disadvantage to the least serious one.

C. How will word processing and information processing affect the six parts of the communication process (sender, message, channel, receiver, perception, and feedback)? Briefly explain which parts of the communication process you think will be changed by each of the following technologies:

1. word processing

2. telecommunications

3. electronic mail

4. teleconferences

5. facsimile transmission

6. computerized graphics

PROJECTS

A. Ask someone to demonstrate a word processor for you. Take notes on how to delete letters, add letters, move from place to place within a document, and print a copy of what you see on the display screen. Ask the person demonstrating the word processor how its use has changed work habits. Also, ask the demonstrator how long it took to learn word processing and what the person likes best about it.

B. There are two types of computer printers—letter-quality and dot-matrix. Collect several samples of items (such as sales letters and address labels) prepared on each type of printer. Then answer the following questions: How similar is each sample to items produced on a typewriter? Do you prefer either of the two types of computer-printed materials to those done on a typewriter? If so, why? What business uses do you think might be appropriate for each type of print?

C. Evaluate a magazine devoted to computers or word processing. Consider the following questions in your evaluation.

1. Does the magazine cover one brand of computer or several brands?

2. What kinds of topics are covered in the articles?

3. Does the magazine seem to be for beginners, for advanced users, or for both?

4. What kinds of equipment and computer programs are advertised in the magazine?

Briefly summarize one of the articles in the magazine, and conclude by explaining whether or not you recommend that people buy the magazine.

D. The terms in the following list are used in word processing and information processing. Write brief definitions of as many of the words as you can. To find out what the words mean, consult computer books and magazines and ask computer users about them.

saving	disks
loading	program
default settings	cursor
function keys	menus
backup copy	scrolling
justification	bug
control key	character
compatible	hard copy
fanfold paper	memory
operating system	modem
spelling checker	mouse

E. Look through a news magazine or newspaper for examples of different kinds of graphs, charts, and diagrams. Describe three of the examples, and tell why they communicate more effectively than words alone would. Then explain how one type of graphic aid you found could be used in a memo or business report.

PART TWO
APPLYING THE RULES OF GRAMMAR

4

The Parts of Speech and the Sentence

Which came first—words or grammar? In your personal history, as in the history of human communication, words came first. You used individual words to communicate before you learned any rules of grammar,for tying those words together.

What, then, is grammar? Grammar is the structure of rules and conventions that underlie a language. By now, you have a good working knowledge of the structure of English, since you use the language every day. You know, for example, that in the sentence "Mailed letter the I," the rules for word order in English have not been followed. Why study grammar, then?

There are at least two reasons. First, you may have a few grammatical trouble spots that interfere with your ability to communicate effectively. Second, although you now have an overall picture of the language, examining the structure behind it will increase your awareness of how the various parts fit together.

The chapters in this part will help you review the structure of English and strengthen your communication skills.

THE PARTS OF SPEECH Words have particular functions. A word is only a noun, verb, or other part of speech because of how it functions in any given sentence. For example, the word *comb* can be a noun or a verb, depending on how it is used. This section of the chapter will examine the eight specific ways words can function in a sentence. It will include definitions of each part of speech and give several examples of how each fits into a sentence. Subsequent chapters will discuss each part of speech in more detail.

Nouns

Nouns serve the function of naming; they designate people, places, or things. The word *things* includes a diverse array such as qualities (ambition), actions (assistance), and states of being (illness). Notice how the italicized words in the following sentences identify people, places, or things.

> *James Lin* came by to display several new *products*.
>
> He showed us an *organizer* that fits on the *desk*.
>
> "*Organization* is the *key* to *success,*" he says.
>
> He feels that our *company* can benefit from the *File-Away*.

Pronouns

Pronouns replace nouns in certain situations. A pronoun acts as a substitute for a noun when it would be awkward to repeat the noun. For example, you would not write, "George is planning a holiday party. George called the Sly Fox about their facilities." Instead, in the second sentence you would write, "He called the Sly Fox. . . ." The pronoun *he* substitutes for the noun *George*.

The noun that a pronoun refers to may be in the same sentence or in a previous sentence. This noun is called the antecedent. In the following sentences, the pronouns are italicized. Their antecedents are underlined.

> <u>Department members</u> discussed the date for a long time before *they* finally came to a decision.
> We really should thank <u>Art Rayburn,</u> *who* agreed to make the reservation.

Verbs

Verbs are often called action words, but such an identification is only partly accurate. Many verbs *(send, open, write)* do express action. Yet others *(be, feel, have)* express conditions or states of existence. Examine how the italicized verbs in the following sentences reflect either actions or states of being.

> We *will publish* the volume on occupational safety this month.
>
> Please *write* a press release about our latest publication.
>
> We *believe* that the book has a good chance of success.
>
> It *is* the most up-to-date book available on the subject.

Adjectives

Adjectives modify nouns and pronouns. To modify is to give more information about—to describe, refine, or limit the meaning of a word. For example, the word *accountant* could indicate any accountant anywhere. *The new, red-*

haired accountant limits the meaning of *accountant* to a specific individual. Note how the italicized adjectives in the following sentences tell more about the nouns or pronouns they modify.

> We are offering *20 new* items.
>
> One is a *miniature* doll.
>
> The doll is *hand-painted*.
>
> It is of *French* manufacture.
>
> We have received *many* orders already.

Adverbs

Like adjectives, adverbs serve to modify other words in a sentence. But instead of affecting the meanings of nouns and pronouns, adverbs modify verbs, adjectives, or other adverbs. They answer such questions as, Where? When? How? How much? How often? In the sentences that follow, the adverbs are italicized. What question does each one answer?

> Twelve hundred gauges were sent *today*.
>
> Their arrival will make Edwards and Corelli, Inc., *very* happy.
>
> So far, we have been doing *extremely* well with order fulfillment *there*.

SHARPENING YOUR SKILLS 1

Identify the italicized word in each of the following sentences as a noun, pronoun, verb, adjective, or adverb.

1. We *regularly* contribute to several charities.
2. Good *management* is a major component of business success.
3. He was an *accurate* typist.
4. Our firm *is* the oldest in the city.
5. This model has been doing well ever since *it* came on the market.
6. We followed a *conservative* policy.

Prepositions

Prepositions connect nouns and pronouns to other words in a sentence to show relationships. The words *in, of,* and *for* are prepositions. See what happens when a preposition is left out of a sentence:

> We plan to place several word processing stations the reception area.

Without a preposition between *stations* and *the reception area,* the reader wonders where the word processing stations will be located in relation to the reception area. Will they be *in* it, *behind* it, *over* it, *under* it, or *around* it? Each of the italicized words you just read is a preposition. A preposition tells how the noun or pronoun that follows it relates to some other word in the sentence. By inserting the word *behind* in the example, you know where the word processing stations will be located in relation to the reception area.

A preposition is always followed by a noun or pronoun in a complete sentence. Together they form a prepositional phrase. In the following sentences, note the nouns that follow the italicized prepositions.

> Employees will be working *throughout* the night to take your orders. We have branch offices *around* the country.

Because prepositional phrases modify the verb or noun they follow, they function as adverbs and adjectives. Reread the sample sentences above to see how the prepositional phrases modify the verbs or nouns that precede them.

Conjunctions

The word *junction* within *conjunction* should give a clue to its meaning. A conjunction joins and shows the relationship between words or groups of words. Most conjunctions are single words such as *and, but, or, yet, although,* and *because.* Some conjunctions include several words *(in order that, as soon as).* Still others consist of sets of words that must be used in pairs *(either. . .or, both. . .and).* Study the way the italicized conjunctions in the sentences that follow connect words or groups of words.

> We publish *both* fiction *and* nonfiction books.

> Unsolicited manuscripts are read *but* are rarely accepted for publication.

> A contract is drawn up *as soon as* the marketing manager approves the outline.

Interjections

Interjections are exclamatory words that function apart from the grammatical construction of a sentence. Interjections often express emotion *(Hurray! Wow! Help!).* They may also convey greetings *(Hello, Good-bye, Happy Thanksgiving),* requests *(Please),* gratitude *(Thanks),* and feelings such as hesitation or relief *(Well, Whew!).* The following examples demonstrate how interjections function independently:

> *Hurray!* The Design Department finally landed the Haynes contract!

> *Well,* where do we go from here?

> *Congratulations!* Your franchise has had a splendid first quarter.

SHARPENING YOUR SKILLS 2

Identify the italicized word in each of the following sentences as a preposition, conjunction, or interjection.

1. Desmond Surgical Supplies is located *near* the airport.

2. That book review was very negative. *Ouch!*

3. While you are here, please visit our recreational facilities *and* our company park.

4. Please write your account number on your check *or* money order.

5. Efficiency experts hope to improve working conditions *throughout* the plant.

6. The Personnel Department posted the new position, *but* no one from within the company applied.

THE SENTENCE

As you have seen, words have meaning only because of their relationship to other words in a sentence. Sentences are the basic units of expression in the English language. In some ways, a sentence is like a jigsaw puzzle. Various pieces fit together to create a word picture that communicates meaning. Like a puzzle, a sentence is complete only when all the pieces are put together correctly.

Completeness

A sentence must be able to stand on its own; it must be complete. Can you see why the following groups of words are considered fragments or incomplete sentences?

Spoke to me about the plans.

Because they are meeting today.

Each of these fragments forces the reader to ask a question: Who spoke about the plans? What is affected by their meeting? Fragments require other words in order to make sense.

Subjects and Predicates

For the moment, think of a sentence as a word puzzle with only two pieces— a complete subject and a complete predicate. The complete subject is the person(s) or thing(s) that the sentence is about. It includes not only the person or thing but also any other words that describe or limit the qualities of that person or thing. Read the following sentences. In each, the complete subject has been italicized.

> *Oscar Mendez, your sales representative*, will return from vacation on June 30.

> *The name of his assistant* is Janet Carson.

> *You* may call her with questions or problems.

> *Janet* will quickly process your requests.

Within each complete subject is the simple subject of the sentence. The simple subject is the nucleus, or heart, of the complete subject. It is always a noun or a pronoun. When there are no words to describe or limit the simple subject, it is the same as the complete subject.

Following are the sentences from the previous example, this time with the simple subject underlined. Notice that in the last two examples, the simple subject is also the complete subject.

> *Oscar Mendez,* your sales representative, will return from vacation on June 30.

> The *name* of his assistant is Janet Carson.

> *You* may call her with questions or problems.

> *Janet* will quickly process your requests.

In some sentences, the subject does not appear at all—it is understood rather than stated. What, for example, is the subject of the following sentence?

> Ask for her by name.

You is the subject. The word *you* is understood, even though it does not appear.

The complete predicate—the second piece of the puzzle—is the rest of the sentence. The complete predicate tells you what the subject does, should do, or is. Look back to the sample sentences given above. The complete predicate in each sentence is the part that is *not* italicized.

The simple predicate, which is the nucleus of the predicate, is always a verb. In the following listing of the same group of sentences, the simple predicate of each sentence has been italicized.

> Oscar Mendez, your sales representative, *will return* from vacation on June 30.

> The name of his assistant *is* Janet Carson.

> You *may call* her with questions or problems.

> Janet *will* quickly *process* your requests.

The simple predicate may be interrupted, as in the last sample sentence.

Locating Complete Subjects and Complete Predicates

You can check your sentences for completeness by first reading them aloud to see if they make sense and then looking for the complete subject and complete predicate.

You can find the complete subject by asking yourself whom or what the sentence is about. The answer to this question forms the complete subject. (Be sure you include all the words that describe or limit the subject.)

After finding the subject, check to see if the rest of the sentence tells you clearly what the subject does, should do, or is. If so, the rest of the sentence makes up the complete predicate.

In many sentences, the subject comes first, followed by the predicate. Often, however, the subject is surrounded by the predicate. In the following sentence, the subject is italicized. Notice how the predicate surrounds it.

Several years ago, *board members* voted to institute a profit sharing plan.

SHARPENING YOUR SKILLS ③

Some of the following groups of words are fragments and others are sentences. If the group of words does not form a sentence, write the word *fragment*. If it is a sentence, underline the complete subject once and the complete predicate twice.

1. Greg Rafferty will handle customer relations.
2. Noiselessly, KleenAir filters remove smoke and odors. *fragment*
3. Many employees who work in the building. *fragment*
4. By installing a Colton organizer, you can save office space.
5. This word processing program allows us to check for errors.
6. Since there are three possibilities. *fragment*

KINDS OF SENTENCES   Business writers use sentences in many different ways to accomplish a variety of goals. Every sentence, however, can be placed in one of four categories. Each category serves a different purpose.

Declarative Sentences

If you write to a co-worker, "Your report is excellent," you have written a declarative sentence. Declarative sentences are those that state facts or opinions—they declare something. The great majority of sentences in written communication, including those in this paragraph, are declarative. Declarative sentences end with a period.

Interrogative Sentences

Interrogative sentences ask questions, as the following sentences demonstrate:

> When can we meet to go over the plans?

> Is 10 a.m. on Thursday convenient?

Interrogative sentences end with a question mark.

Imperative Sentences

Imperative sentences are strong sentences—they give orders or make requests.

> Lock your office door when you go home.

> Be careful on the ice!

> Please tell the security guard if you are the last to leave.

(Note that it is simply the addition of "please" that turns an order into a request.) Imperative sentences usually end with a period, but they may also end with an exclamation point when the writer wants the sentence to have extra emphasis.

Exclamatory Sentences

Exclamatory sentences express emotion, often strong excitement. These sentences always end with an exclamation point, the only form of punctuation that conveys emotion.

> Our profits are up 25 percent this year!

> I got a promotion *and* a raise!

> This layout is sensational!

Sometimes an imperative sentence expresses emotion: *Leave me alone!* Such a sentence can be classified as either imperative or exclamatory.

SHARPENING YOUR SKILLS 4

Identify each of the following sentences as declarative, interrogative, imperative, or exclamatory.

1. How nice of you to say so! exclamatory
2. Every order must be accompanied by a deposit of $100. imperative
3. Inform all department heads of the policy change. imperative
4. How can we cut costs without sacrificing quality? interrogative
5. Company morale is very high. declarative

6. Did the product meet with your approval? *interrogative*

7. This is bad news! *exclamatory*

8. Please make this change in your files. *imperative*

EDITING EXERCISES

Transform each of the following sentence fragments into a complete, business-related sentence.

1. The brochure you requested.

2. Ten cartons of textbooks.

3. Because the office is closed on Monday.

4. Met to discuss new product strategies.

5. Mark Gorman, your service technician.

6. Unless you cancel the order before June 9.

7. Our products, which are of the highest quality.

8. Until further notice.

9. Arrived in the mail today.

10. The shipping costs you incurred.

11. You cordially invited.

12. Will meet with consumer representatives.

13. Mr. Schlegel, who was away on business.

14. Proudly announces a major breakthrough in communications technology.

15. In the years to come.

PROJECTS

Using the four different kinds of sentences when you write makes your writing more interesting to read. Use all four kinds of sentences to write a piece of business correspondence explaining why you erroneously shipped 200, instead of 20, Halloween costumes to your best client, Rite-Mart Department Store.

5
Nouns

As the preceding chapter explains, sentences are about nouns. You may speak or write a unit of thought about a *contract* or the *marketplace* or *efficiency*. Nouns are the words used to designate or name the things of the entire world, which includes the business world. Analyzing how nouns function in sentences can help you avoid errors in grammar by increasing your understanding of the unique characteristics of nouns. A large portion of this chapter is devoted to the rules for forming noun plurals, the source of many spelling errors. Emphasis is also given to the distinction between plurals and possessives, which can cause confusion because they sound alike but are written differently.

RECOGNIZING TYPES OF NOUNS

Nouns are that large group of words that name people, places, or things. Nouns can also be subdivided into different classes depending on their meanings and the way they are formed. Nouns are proper or common, concrete or abstract, simple or compound. Some nouns are collective.

Proper Nouns and Common Nouns. Every noun is either proper or common. A common noun names a class of persons, places, or things. A proper noun names a specific person, place, or thing and is always capitalized.

Common	Proper
man	David Silverstein
country	France
company	Jefferson & Kibble
book	*Communicating*

Portable computers make communicating possible in many settings.

Concrete Nouns and Abstract Nouns. Every noun is also either concrete or abstract. A concrete noun names an object that you can see, hear, touch, smell, or taste. The word *orange,* which affects the senses, fits into this category. In contrast, a word such as *honesty* is an abstract noun—something that cannot be experienced directly through the senses. Such a noun may be a concept, an idea, or a quality.

Concrete	Abstract
book	capitalism
eraser	integrity
typewriter	sympathy

Simple Nouns and Compound Nouns. *House* is a noun; so is *courthouse*. The difference between the two is that *house* is a simple noun, consisting of just one word. A compound noun, such as *courthouse,* is made up of two words that function as one. Many compound nouns are written as one word. Others are hyphenated. Still others are written as distinct words.

Simple	Compound
hand	handbook
father	father-in-law
word	word processor

Collective Nouns. A collective noun names a group of people or things that are considered as one. For this reason, it generally takes a singular verb, as shown in parentheses after each collective noun below.

group (meets)	council (votes)
team (wins)	association (convenes)

SHARPENING YOUR SKILLS 1

Underline each noun in the following sentences.

1. This camera will last a lifetime.

2. Does the appliance work well?

3. Next month I will attend a convention in Spain.

4. Our headquarters are in Wichita, Kansas.

5. Several employees plan to sue the company.

6. Check the printout for current prices.

RECOGNIZING NOUN FORMS

Nouns can also be recognized by the special endings that they take. Some of these endings, called suffixes, indicate number (how many) and possession. Others transform different parts of speech (such as verbs) into nouns. These suffixes, like the one that changes *prepare* into *preparation,* fall into specific categories.

Number

Most nouns are either singular or plural. Either they name one person, place, or thing, or they designate more than one. Plural nouns have characteristic endings—especially *s* and *es*.

s	*es*
disks	glasses
printers	businesses

Possession

Another characteristic noun ending is the one that shows possession. For most singular nouns, you add *'s* to indicate ownership. For most plural nouns, you add just the apostrophe.

Singular Possessive	Plural Possessive
the company's rules	the companies' merger
an applicant's credentials	five applicants' interviews
our director's office	several directors' decisions

Other Noun Endings

Certain suffixes, when added to other parts of speech (or even to other nouns), form nouns. A number of these suffixes indicate a state or condition. Others indicate the doer of an action. The list that follows shows many of these suffixes:

-ance/-ence	appearance, influence
-ation	preparation
-er/-or	treasurer, advisor
-ion/-sion	opinion, cohesion
-ism	capitalism, realism
-ity	activity, sensibility
-ment	contentment, equipment
-ness	carefulness, kindness
-ship	companionship, ownership

RECOGNIZING NOUN FUNCTIONS

Nouns perform specific jobs in sentences. As you already know, nouns can be subjects. They can also act as part of the predicate. In that role, they complete the predicate in a variety of ways. A noun may, for example, receive the action of the verb or rename the subject of the sentence.

Nouns as Subjects

Notice that in the following sentences, the italicized noun is the subject; it tells who or what is doing the action.

Our *company* is selling more pressure gauges than ever before.

Until recently, this *product* was exhibiting a sluggish sales record.

Nouns as Complements

Although the following sentence has both a subject and a verb, it does not make sense because the predicate is not complete.

We require immediate.

To make the predicate complete, you must add one or more complements. A complement is a word or a group of words that completes a predicate.

> We require immediate *payment.*

The noun *payment* acts as a complement in this sentence. There are several ways for a noun to complete a predicate.

Direct Object. When it acts as a direct object, a noun receives the action of the verb.

> We have now interviewed six *candidates.*

> Walter Molino prepared a sample *questionnaire* for the interview.

Indirect Object. A noun that acts as an indirect object in some way receives the direct object. The indirect object precedes the direct object and tells to or for whom or what the action is being done. An indirect object, then, is also affected by the action of the verb, but less directly.

> Please show *Pamela* the warehouse.

> On your way out, give my *door* a push.

To find an indirect object, you must ask questions such as, Show the warehouse (direct object) to whom? Give a push (direct object) to what?

Object of a Preposition. A noun can also be the object of a preposition in a prepositional phrase. In this role, the noun is related to other words in the sentence, a relationship explained by the particular preposition it follows.

> Arctic Outerwear protects you against the *elements.*

> You will be toasty inside an Arctic *parka.*

Objective Complement. When a noun follows a direct object and renames or further describes it, it complements the object.

> On Monday you can meet my assistant *Charles.*

> He jokingly calls this project "The *Titanic.*"

Subject Complement. A noun that further describes or renames the subject of a sentence acts as a subject complement. Also called predicate nominatives, subject complements are found only in sentences with linking verbs such as *be, appear, become, seem,* and *feel.*

Linking verbs do not describe action. They are called linking verbs because they connect, or link, the subject of a sentence with another word in the sentence, in this case, a noun. In the following examples, the subject is underlined and the subject complement is italicized.

> <u>Rufus</u> is a *collie.*

> The <u>book</u> is a *history* of Mexico.

(To understand the role a linking verb plays, study the difference between the sentences *Dan saw a dog* and *Dan is a dog.* In the second sentence, *Dan* and *dog* are the same thing.)

SHARPENING YOUR SKILLS 2

Identify the italicized noun in each of the following sentences as a subject, direct object, indirect object, object of a preposition, objective complement, or subject complement.

1. Copeland plans to renovate several offices during the *summer.*
2. Our company promises the *customer* satisfaction.
3. Poor management spells *disaster.*
4. *Children* love Small Farmer overalls.
5. The award recipient is *Joshua Rubin.*
6. The Marketing Department has named the new fiber *Wearall.*

FORMING COMPOUND NOUNS

The fact that compound nouns may be written in three ways—solid, hyphenated, or open—creates difficulties for many business writers. There are, however, some guidelines to help you. Still, in order to be certain, check an up-to-date dictionary when you are in doubt. Many compound nouns are treated differently in different dictionaries. The most important thing to remember is to be consistent.

Solid Compounds. Solid compounds are the most common type.

checklist	warehouse	workstation
software	paperwork	overtime
marketplace	salesperson	

Nouns ending in the prepositions *down, out, over, back, away, about, around,* and *by* are usually written solid.

drawback	standby	markdown
printout	giveaway	turnabout
runaround	turnover	

Hyphenated Compounds. Compound nouns ending in the prepositions *in, on, between, through,* and *together* are usually written with hyphens between the word elements.

come-on	stand-in	run-through
run-on	go-between	get-together
break-in		

Nouns ending in *up* and *off* are written solid or hyphenated, depending on the word.

flare-up	backup	runoff
start-up	trade-off	layoff
markup	show-off	

Until you are familiar with nouns in this category, you should check the spellings in a dictionary.

Open Compounds. Open compounds are written as two words. Many such compounds are made up of a noun and a gerund (the *-ing* form of a verb).

word processing	parking lot	finish line
decision making	time sheet	editor in chief
tape deck	paper clip	problem solving

SHARPENING YOUR SKILLS 3

Underline the compound nouns in the following sentences.

1. We would like to give Susan Vasquez a nice send-off, since she has been such a valuable employee.

2. We now have 277 employees on our payroll.

3. Please have all costumes ready Friday for a run-through of the show.

4. What is the timetable for the writers' conference?

5. Remind the maintenance supervisor to have the damaged hand truck repaired by Tuesday.

6. A poster in the warehouse illustrates safe lifting techniques.

FORMING BASIC NOUN PLURALS

When you write, you probably obey most of the rules for forming basic noun plurals without even thinking about them. You would probably find it difficult, though, to recite all these rules. This section will help you review the rules for forming basic plurals. In addition, remember that plurals are not generally formed by adding apostrophes.

When to Add *s*

To form the plural of most nouns, just add *s*.

book → books
catalogue → catalogues
profit → profits

privilege → privileges
statement → statements

When to Add *es*

For nouns that end in *s, x, ch, sh,* and *z,* add *es* to form the plural. Note that adding *es* adds another syllable to the word.

loss → losses
tax → taxes
telex → telexes
clash → clashes

blitz → blitzes
business → businesses
approach → approaches

SHARPENING YOUR SKILLS 4

Write the plural form of each of the following nouns.

1. rash
2. government
3. bus
4. corporation
5. reproach
6. wax
7. lunch
8. function

When a Noun Ends in *y*

When a noun ends in *y*, first check the letter that comes before the *y*. If a vowel precedes the *y*, just add *s*.

toy → toys
buy → buys

Monday → Mondays
journey → journeys

If a consonant precedes the *y*, change the *y* to *i*, and add *es*.

company → companies
story → stories
secretary → secretaries

frequency → frequencies
facility → facilities

How to Make a Proper Noun Plural

Do not change the spelling of a proper noun. Add *s* to form the plural of proper nouns unless the ending creates an extra syllable. Then add *es*.

s	*es*
Barnaby → the Barnabys	Ames → the Ameses
Clancy → the Clancys	Hess → the Hesses
Mahony → the Mahonys	Muntz → the Muntzes

SHARPENING YOUR SKILLS 5

Write the plural form of each of the following nouns.

1. city
2. malady
3. colony
4. bay
5. Rooney
6. copy
7. play
8. Jones

Some nouns do not follow the basic rules for forming plurals. If you are ever unsure of how to form the plural of a noun that fits into one of the special formats that are discussed in this section, consult a dictionary.

FORMING SPECIAL NOUN PLURALS

Nouns That End in *o*

If a noun ends in *o*, first check the letter that precedes the *o*.

Vowel Before the *o*. These nouns are the simplest. Just add *s* to form the plural.

duo → duos   cameo → cameos
zoo → zoos   studio → studios

Consonant Before the *o*. No one rule covers all the nouns of this type. Nouns borrowed from Italian and Spanish just take *s* to form the plural.

crescendo → crescendos   avocado → avocados
solo → solos   burrito → burritos
piano → pianos   pueblo → pueblos

Other Nouns That End in _o._ The following is a miscellaneous group of nouns ending in _o._ Some always form the plural with _s._ Others always form the plural with _es._

_s_	_es_
auto → autos	echo → echoes
ditto → dittos	hero → heroes
ego → egos	potato → potatoes
memo → memos	tomato → tomatoes
photo → photos	veto → vetoes

For still other nouns ending in _o,_ there are two possible plural endings. The _s_ form is preferred for those nouns in the left-hand column below. The _es_ form is preferred for those on the right.

_s_	_es_
flamingo → flamingos	cargo → cargoes
tuxedo → tuxedos	motto → mottoes
zero → zeros	mosquito → mosquitoes

Nouns That End in _f_ or _fe_

Most of the nouns that end this way merely add _s_:

safe → safes	cliff → cliffs
proof → proofs	belief → beliefs

For some nouns that end in _f_ or _fe,_ you must change the _f_ or _fe_ to _ve,_ then add _s._

half → halves	knife → knives
leaf → leaves	life → lives
shelf → shelves	wife → wives

SHARPENING YOUR SKILLS 6

Write the plural form of each of the following nouns.

1. two
2. zero
3. studio
4. taco
5. radio
6. leaf
7. veto
8. knife

Irregular Plurals

Some words have irregular plurals; that is, they do not follow any rules for forming plurals. Many of the nouns in this category form their plurals through internal changes. Some of the most common of these irregular plurals follow.

man → men	mouse → mice
foot → feet	goose → geese
woman → women	child → children

Nouns With One Form for Singular and Plural

Some nouns keep the same form in both the singular and the plural. In some cases, the singular acts as the plural too, as in these examples:

He caught one fish.

She caught three fish.

Below are some more nouns that are usually written in the singular form.

shrimp	fruit	corn
deer	sheep	aircraft

Still other nouns are always written in the plural form; they have no singular form.

athletics	pants	news	belongings
series	tongs	economics	thanks
civics	scissors	mathematics	trousers

Foreign Plurals

Plurals in other languages are often formed differently from English plurals. Some of the words the English language has borrowed from other languages have kept their original plurals; others have acquired English plurals. A few words have two alternate plurals—one foreign and one English. In these cases, however, one form is usually preferred.

The rules that follow show the preferred plural when there is an alternate.

Words That End in *um*. Most of these words use the foreign plural, which drops *um* and adds *a*. The English plural adds *s*.

Foreign	English
bacterium → bacteria	memorandum → memorandums
addendum → addenda	chrysanthemum → chrysanthemums
curriculum → curricula	
datum → data	

Note that *data* is acutally a plural form, and that *datum* is the singular. The use of *data* with a singular verb, however, is becoming accepted: *This data is difficult to interpret.* Other usages are changing too. For example, the plural of *memorandum* is often *memoranda.* As always, if in doubt, look it up.

Words That End in *is*. Form the plural of words that end in *is* by replacing the *is* with *es*.

basis → bases	diagnosis → diagnoses
crisis → crises	synopsis → synopses
analysis → analyses	parenthesis → parentheses
emphasis → emphases	hypothesis → hypotheses

Words That End in *on*. Many words that end in *on* form the plural by dropping the *on* and adding *a*.

criterion → criteria
phenomenon → phenomena

Words That End in *us* or *a*. Some words with these endings have retained their foreign plurals—*us* changes to *i*, and *a* becomes *ae*.

Other words that end in *us* or *a* take English plurals. The *us* words take the addition of *es*, and the *a* words take the standard plural *s*.

Foreign	English
alumnus → alumni	campus → campuses
nucleus → nuclei	census → censuses
stimulus → stimuli	prospectus → prospectuses
alumna → alumnae	agenda → agendas
vertebra → vertebrae	formula → formulas

Plurals of Compound Nouns

Making compound nouns plural can be a hit-or-miss operation if you are not sure what to pluralize. When you make open or hyphenated compounds plural, be sure to pluralize the main noun.

golf club → golf clubs	father-in-law → fathers-in-law
parking lot → parking lots	chief of staff → chiefs of staff
editor in chief → editors in chief	runner-up → runners-up

If neither element of the compound is a noun, just add *s* to the end of the word.

has-been → has-beens	drive-in → drive-ins
show-off → show-offs	go-between → go-betweens

Plurals of Titles

Titles such as *Mr.* and *Mrs.* have plurals, but they are rarely used.

Mr. → Messrs.   Miss → Misses
Mrs. → Mmes.   Ms. → Mses. or Mss.

These plurals, because they are used so infrequently, sound stilted. If you need to pluralize names with titles, do the following.

If the names of the persons are different, give each name separately:

Instead of	Use
Messrs. Fulton and Curran	Mr. Fulton and Mr. Curran
Mmes. Payne and Gray	Mrs. Payne and Mrs. Gray

When the names are the same, pluralize the name, not the title:

Instead of	Use
Misses Levine	the Miss Levines
Mss. D'Agostino	the Ms. D'Agostinos

Use the plural titles only in formal writing, such as on invitations. In such a case, avoid the mistake of pluralizing both the title and the name. (Do not use *the Mses. Brookses.*)

SHARPENING YOUR SKILLS 7

Correct any errors in noun forms in the following sentences.

1. Please have the costs analysises on my desk by Wednesday.

2. Recent tests showed a concentration of 4,000 bacterias per cubic centimeter of water.

3. Most of the local farmers raise either cows or sheeps.

4. The Messrs. Joneses request the honor of your presence at a formal dinner.

5. All childs will love the Rolling Rocker.

6. Both of my brother-in-laws have gone into the food processing business.

EDITING EXERCISES

A. Correct the errors in compound noun formation in the following sentences.

1. Employees are entitled to two weeks of sick-leave with pay.

2. The company news letter will be called *The Tattler*.

3. We plan to do a followup on the interview with the company president.

4. Come to Dunstan's for a better living-room.

5. Workers will be paving the parking-lot this week.

6. Pay roll delays create employee dissatisfaction.

7. Have you investigated the circumstances of last week's break in?

8. Company rules prohibit me from employing your brother in law.

9. Minetta's Meats is conveniently located just off the express-way.

10. Cavett Community College has many courses in wordprocessing.

B. Correct the errors in noun plurals in the following sentences. For nouns with two plural forms, select the preferred spelling.

1. The number on the carton contains three zeroes.

2. Please file all the memorandumes with information on the parkings lot.

3. How many annexs does the design committee propose to build?

4. Please send price information for the following: wood cabinets, metal typewriter tables, and plastic shelfs.

5. I plan to make journies to all the facilitys in November.

6. Did each of the censuss show a rise in population?

7. I wish to order the following items: 11 erasers, 5 dozen red pens, and 1 scissor.

8. The latest incidents have caused several flares-up of violence in outlying areas.

9. Our reporter took several photoes of the events.

10. Mistakes appear in several of the addendums to this document.

11. Tests show that there are irregularities in the nucleuses of the cells.

12. Musical crescendoes are often placed where emphasises are required.

13. Speeches by noted alumnas should end the day on a fine note.

14. Ships with cargos over a certain weight cannot unload at this port.

15. Please type both agendaes on plain paper.

PROJECTS

Write a letter to a real estate agent in another city explaining that you are moving there to take a new job. Tell the agent that you will need a place to live. Use as many nouns as you can to describe the characteristics you would like in an apartment. Use at least one of each of the following:

- common noun
- concrete noun
- compound noun
- collective noun
- plural of a noun that ends in an *o* preceded by a consonant
- plural of a noun ending in *f* or *fe*

In your letter, circle and label each of the nouns from this list.

6
Pronouns

Suppose that the English language did not have pronouns such as *I, me, he*, and *you*. Imagine how awkward ordinary conversations would become. You would have to use proper names every time you wanted to refer to a person.

Because pronouns substitute for nouns, they help improve communication in several ways. Pronouns can serve to increase clarity by showing the relationship between different parts of a sentence and between different sentences and paragraphs.

There are seven categories of pronouns, each serving a different function:

- personal pronouns
- reflexive and intensive pronouns
- demonstrative pronouns
- interrogative pronouns
- relative pronouns
- indefinite pronouns
- compound reciprocal pronouns

This chapter will emphasize personal pronouns, the most commonly used type.

PERSONAL PRONOUNS

Table 6-1 lists all the personal pronouns. They are called "personal" because they have different forms for the first person (the one talking), the second person (the one talked to), and the third person (the one talked about). Personal pronouns substitute for nouns that function as subjects, objects, and possessives. (Possessives will be discussed in Chapter 7.)

Note how three of these pronouns function in the following sentences:

Leonard Stefanic hired Linda Kraus for the position of head teller. *He* considered *her* the best candidate for *it*.

Table 6-1. Personal Pronouns

Person	Subject Pronouns		Object Pronouns	
	Singular	*Plural*	*Singular*	*Plural*
First	I	we	me	us
Second	you	you	you	you
Third	he she it	they they they	him her it	them them them

These sentences illustrate several important characteristics of pronouns:

- Pronouns must agree with their antecedents (the nouns they replace) in person. *Leonard Stefanic, Linda Kraus*, and *the position* are all being talked about, so the pronouns are all in the third person.
- Pronouns must agree with their antecedents in number. *Leonard, Linda*, and *the position* are all singular; so are the pronouns *he, her*, and *it*.
- Pronouns must agree with their antecedents in gender. Leonard is a man, and *he* is masculine; Linda is a woman, and *her* is feminine; *the position* is neuter—neither masculine nor feminine—as is the pronoun *it*.
- With just two exceptions, the form of a personal pronoun reflects its function in a sentence. *He*, a subject pronoun, is the subject of the second sentence. *Her*, an object pronoun, is the object of the verb *considered*. The forms of these two pronouns are determined by the fact that one is a subject and the other is an object. You will notice, however, if you look at Table 6-1 again, that *it* and *you* use the same form whether they are subjects or objects.

PERSONAL PRONOUNS AS SUBJECTS

Since pronouns substitute for nouns, they function in some of the same ways. Like nouns, subject pronouns can act as subjects and as subject complements. Most people automatically use the correct pronoun form for the subject of a sentence. Trouble often arises with subject complements. Studying the relationship between subjects and subject complements will enable you to select the correct form.

Subjects

Only a subject pronoun can serve as the subject of a sentence. As such, it must agree with its antecedent in person, gender, and number. In each of the following sentences, the antecedent is underlined, and the pronoun is italicized. Notice the agreement between them.

Marilyn Wilkie has been promoted. *She* is now head proofreader.

That machine is still under warranty. *It* will be fixed at no charge.

Elizabeth and Russell have switched offices. *They* are much happier now.

George read the report. *He* will comment today.

Subject Complements

Subject pronouns may also be used as subject complements, which rename the subject. After any form of the verb *to be* (including *am, is, are, was, were, been, being*, and *be*), use a subject pronoun rather than an object pronoun. The forms of the verb *to be* act as an equal sign, linking the subject and the pronoun (subject = pronoun).

Was it *she* who called you yesterday? (not *her*)

It has always been *he* who approved payroll checks. (not *him*)

It will be *we* who are responsible. (not *us*)

It is *I*. (not *me*)

Perhaps the most common error involving the use of pronouns as subject complements occurs when answering the telephone. When someone asks for you by name, respond by saying "This is *she*" or "This is *he*," not "This is *her*" or "This is *him*."

SHARPENING YOUR SKILLS 1

In each of the following sentences, fill in the blank with the correct subject pronoun.

1. If Anthony wants to discuss this order, ___*he*___ should call me this afternoon.

2. When she answered the telephone, Karen said, "Yes, this is ___*she*___ ."

3. Mr. Amundsen and Ms. Rodgers have made all the travel arrangements for the conference. ___*They*___ can answer any questions you have.

4. Since Jesse and I will attend the same seminar, ___*we*___ are planning to book the same flight.

5. Adelaide Parks did an excellent job as project coordinator. ___*she*___ worked well with both her supervisors and her staff.

Object pronouns, like the nouns they take the place of, serve as the direct and indirect objects of verbs and as the objects of prepositions. Like subject pronouns, these pronouns must also agree with their antecedents in person, number, and gender.

Direct Objects

When a pronoun acts as a direct object, it receives the action of the verb directly.

> I will send you a sample of our industrial cleaning solution. Please tell *me* how you like it.

> I have given Gloria Evans your name. Please call *her* if you are still interested in the job.

Indirect Objects

A pronoun acting as an indirect object can appear only in a sentence that has a direct object because the indirect object receives the action of the direct object.

> If you call on Thursday, speak to my secretary. Give *her* your name and number. (*Her* receives *your name and number.*)

> Jeff Atkins and Rita Eldridge will call for an appointment. Show *them* the outline we discussed. (*Them* receives *the outline.*)

Objects of Prepositions

A preposition shows how its object (the noun or pronoun that follows it) relates to other words in the sentence. Only object pronouns can act as the objects of prepositions.

> Cliff and I visited with the representatives from Bates Toy Company yesterday. Their mood was definitely less cordial toward *us* this time.

> Several consumer groups have objected to the safety of Annihilator dolls. Tests show that the dolls burst into flames when an electric heater is placed near *them*.

In most situations, writers have no difficulty choosing the appropriate subject and object pronouns. No one, for example, would write "Him is arriving soon" or "Mrs. Tucker asked I to do it." In three areas, though, many writers run into trouble. They are uncertain about which pronouns to use with compound objects, with nouns, and in comparisons.

Compound Objects

People often make the mistake of saying or writing "between you and I" instead of "between you and me." The difficulty occurs in this type of phrase because the preposition has *two* objects—in this case, *you* and *me*. The elements of this compound object function as a unit. Therefore, each separate element functions as an object.

When you are faced with this type of phrase, test the phrase by using each pronoun alone with the preposition.

Johnson's Aluminum Products gave key chains to *him* and *me*.

If you first ask, "Did Johnson's Aluminum Products give key chains to *he* or to *him*?" the object pronoun *him* is the obvious choice. Then ask, "Did Johnson's Aluminum Products give key chains to *I* or to *me*?" In this case, the object pronoun *me* is clearly the correct choice.

Pronouns Used With a Noun

Many people choose the wrong pronoun form when it is immediately followed by a noun. For example: *We supervisors should meet once a week*. How do you know to use *we* instead of *us*? Try using the pronoun alone without the noun. The sentence would read, *We should meet once a week. Supervisors* is the subject of the sentence; therefore, the pronoun must be a subject pronoun, in this case, *we*.

Similarly, if a pronoun is followed immediately by a noun that is the object of a sentence, you should use an object pronoun.

Management is going to present its findings to us workers.

Without the noun, the sentence would read, *Management is going to present its findings to us. Us*, the object pronoun, is the correct choice.

Comparisons

A number of business writers also have problems with sentences containing comparisons.

Janet Guzzardo has more confidence in the nearby chemical plant than *I*. Still, toxic chemical leaks worry Janet as much as *me*.

The key to choosing the correct pronoun lies in realizing that certain words are implied but not stated in sentences such as these. When the missing words are filled in, the proper choice becomes clear. In the following sentences, the implied words are added in italics.

Janet Guzzardo has more confidence in the nearby chemical plant than I *do*.
Still, toxic chemical leaks worry Janet as much as *they worry* me.

SHARPENING YOUR SKILLS 2

Choose the correct pronoun in each of the following sentences.

1. Mr. Wheaton frequently talks to (she / her) on the telephone.

2. I hope that this conversation will not go beyond you and (I / me).

3. (We / Us) secretaries should let our supervisors know that their smoking bothers us.

4. Luke implied that Merrill Products Company is more likely to offer the position to me than (he / him).

5. Roger has more problems than (I / me) with the new word processing equipment.

6. I am not sure why the same letter was sent to both Martin and (I / me).

INTENSIVE AND REFLEXIVE PRONOUNS

Table 6-2 lists the eight pronouns that end in the suffix *-self* or *-selves*. These pronouns serve two specialized purposes. When used as reflexives, they refer to a previous noun or pronoun in the sentence. When used as intensives, they emphasize a noun or pronoun in the sentence. Reflexive and intensive pronouns must agree in person, number, and gender with the nouns or pronouns they refer to or emphasize.

Ellen taught *herself* to use the coding machine. (reflexive)

I was concerned when I found out that we had locked *ourselves* out of the building. (reflexive)

You *yourself* said that Mr. Harrison would not be promoted. (intensive)

I had to hear the explanation *myself* to believe it. (intensive)

The pronouns *yourself* and *yourselves* sometimes refer to an understood antecedent.

Talk among *yourselves* until he returns.

Suit *yourself*.

In both sentences, *you* is the understood antecedent.

A reflexive or intensive pronoun, however, must refer to *some* noun or pronoun, either stated or implied. It cannot be used alone as a subject or object. The construction of the following sentences is incorrect although it is used often.

Ms. Murdoch and *myself* checked the faulty valve this morning.

Vanessa brought the valve to the attention of Mr. James and *myself*.

In neither case does *myself* refer to any noun or pronoun, stated or understood. The correct pronoun in the first sentence is *I*; in the second, it is *me*. One way to test such a sentence is to use *myself* on its own, as in *Myself checked the faulty valve this morning.* Clearly, *myself* is not correct. Also, remember that "hisself," "ourself," and "theirself" are incorrect forms and should *never* be used.

Table 6-2. Reflexive and Intensive Pronouns

Person	Singular	Plural
First	myself	ourselves
Second	yourself	yourselves
Third	himself herself itself	themselves

SHARPENING YOUR SKILLS 3

Choose the correct pronoun in each of the following sentences.

1. Last night thieves broke in and helped (himself / themselves) to several typewriters and calculators.
2. It was clear to both Ramon and (me / myself) that Baxter Filter Corporation has a superior product.
3. We do every repair (ourself / ourselves).
4. Make (yourself / you) at home until I return.
5. Wendell believes that if he wants something done right he must do it (himself / yourself).
6. Stephen and (myself / I) attended the seminar on videodisk technology.

OTHER TYPES OF PRONOUNS

Definitions for the other types of pronouns are given below. For examples of forms and uses, see Table 6-3.

- Demonstrative pronouns point out specific objects. They indicate closeness *(this, these)* and distance *(that, those)*.
- Relative pronouns introduce dependent clauses (groups of words which have a subject and verb but which cannot stand alone as a sentence). Relative pronouns relate the dependent clause to the rest of the sentence and may be either subjects or objects of verbs.
- Interrogative pronouns introduce questions.

- Indefinite pronouns refer to persons, places, or things, usually without being specific.
- Compound reciprocal pronouns indicate relationship between two or more persons or things.

Study Table 6-3 to determine the function of each type of pronoun.

Table 6-3. Other Pronouns

Type	Forms	Uses
Demonstrative	this, these, that, those	*This* is Barclay's finest jewelry. *Those* are not as well made as *these*.
Relative	what, that, which, who, whom, whose, whichever, whoever, whomever, whatever	I have a copy of the book *that* won the fiction prize. Give it to *whomever* you want. Tell me *what* you want.
Interrogative	what, which, who, whom, whose, whichever, whoever, whomever, whatever	*What* did Allen say? To *whom* did he say it?
Indefinite	another, anybody, anyone, somebody, nobody, no one, someone, each, many, much, one, several, few, most, more, some, and so on	*Nobody* expected you to do the impossible. *Few* have done so well.
Compound Reciprocal	each other, one another	Frank and José work well with *each other*. All our products complement *one another*.

SHARPENING YOUR SKILLS 4

Underline the pronoun in each sentence, and indicate which type it is.

1. Anyone could have left the door open.
2. The seminar, which began with a case study, showed how employee dissatisfaction can decrease profits.
3. Employees should help one another meet the sales quota.
4. These are the pictures of the fire in the maintenance office.
5. Which of these three dresses did Mrs. Payton return?

THE USE OF WHO OR WHOM

Do you say "Whom shall I say is calling?" or "Who shall I say is calling?" Deciding between the pronouns *who* and *whom* (and *whoever* and *whomever*) is a problem that is easy to solve. First, it is important to distinguish between the subject pronouns (*who, whoever*) and the object pronouns (*whom, whomever*). A good memory aid is the fact that four of the object pronouns include the letter *m—him, them, whom,* and *whomever.*

Interrogative Pronouns

The subject pronouns *who* and *whoever* act as the subject or subject complement in a question:

> *Who* wants to know?

> The applicant is *who*?

The object pronouns *whom* and *whomever* act as the direct object or the object of a preposition in a question:

> *Whom* are you hiring?

> To *whom* did you send the article?

Changing the order of the sentence so it is no longer a question can help you select the correct pronoun:

> You are hiring *whom*.

> You did send the article to *whom*.

Relative Pronouns

A relative pronoun introduces a dependent clause—a group of words which contains a subject and a verb but which cannot stand alone as a sentence.

To determine whether to use a subject pronoun or an object pronoun, analyze the function of the relative pronoun in the dependent clause that it introduces.

> I think they will give the job to *whoever* applies.

> Rosemary may hire the person *whom* she spoke to yesterday.

In each case, you must first consider the dependent clause on its own. In the first sentence, the dependent clause is *whoever applies.* Since *applies* needs a subject, the subject pronoun *whoever* is correct.

In the second sentence, the dependent clause is *whom she spoke to yesterday.* Since the preposition *to* needs an object, *whom* is the correct choice.

Look at the sentence presented at the beginning of this section: *(Whom / Who) shall I say is calling?* If you invert the sentence so that it is no longer a question, you find that *who* is correct because it functions as the subject of the dependent clause. The clause is italicized below:

I shall say *who is calling*.

SHARPENING YOUR SKILLS 5

Choose the correct pronoun in each of the following sentences.

1. (Who / Whom) received the check?

2. Has Ellen told you (who / whom) will be elected by the panel?

3. Today Rand's Camera Shop will announce (who / whom) will receive the photo contest prize.

4. (Who / Whom) sat next to Dr. Leon?

5. Send the package to (whoever / whomever) is in charge of returns.

6. I do not know (who / whom) will handle your complaint.

EDITING EXERCISES

A. Correct any pronoun errors in the following sentences. If a sentence has no errors, write the word *correct* next to it.

1. Whomever would have stolen an address book?

2. Treat yourself to a weekend at Twin Oaks resort!

3. Ms. Hooks feels that the client's hostility is directed at you and I.

4. It is me who designed the Three Corners Office Park.

5. Seth believes even more strongly than me that the Accounting Department must be reorganized.

6. Test results such as this are difficult to double-check.

7. The engineers himself assured us that the tank could withstand increased pressure.

8. No one knows the access code except you and me.

9. Ms. Lopez expressed her thanks to both Wendy and I.

10. Nearly everyone in this department has more seniority than me.

11. Who did you promote to assistant manager?

12. I would like to accept responsibility for the damage since it was I who checked the brakes in the truck.

13. Lee Inverso is the one whom the panel chose.

14. Would you object to a visit from Ms. Wu and me?

15. I agreed to meet whomever arrived on the bus.

B. In the sentences that follow, correct any nouns that have been pluralized incorrectly. (If a noun shows a pluralization that is not the preferred one, substitute the preferred spelling.)

1. The company's facilitys serve a tristate area.

2. We would like to distribute these calendars as mementoes of the trip.

3. Did the memoes state what time the celebration is to begin?

4. Advertising through several mediums—such as newspaper, radio, and television—will boost sales.

5. Unlike many city college campi, the grounds of Brand College are spacious.

6. Long journies always require extensive planning.

7. Has Mr. DeVries sent you the sales analysises yet?

8. Be sure you list all our charitable donations when you figure the income taxes.

PROJECTS

To gain a fuller appreciation of how much you rely on pronouns, write a letter to a friend about your recent activities using no personal, demonstrative, or interrogative pronouns.

Business and Technology

(*Top*) Computers, like other types of business equipment, are tools. Different businesses have adapted these tools to suit the needs of their particular field. For example, the financial community uses computers extensively because they allow banks and brokerage firms to process a large volume of information very quickly. Before computers were introduced on Wall Street in the late 1960s, all stock transactions had to be handled on paper. As a result, the stock exchanges and brokerage houses were almost drowning in paper.

(*Bottom*) Today more than 150 million shares of stock may be traded daily on the New York Stock Exchange alone. All these shares are bought and sold electronically through computers that link stockbrokers to the exchange floor.

(*Below*) Like brokers, commodity traders depend on computers for buying and selling. Computers used on the commodity market list up-to-the-minute prices and make predictions about future prices.

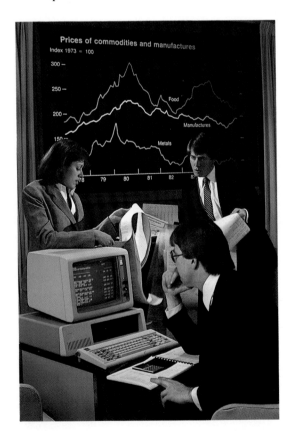

(*Above*) Investment bankers and economic analysts are especially interested in the ability of computers to predict economic changes. Many investment firms now buy and sell stocks, bonds, and commodities when their computer programs tell them the time is right.

(*Left*) Data processing is another important function of computers in banking and finance. Large and powerful computers are constantly updating financial data. The data center in your own bank, for example, keeps track of deposits and withdrawals, computes interest and service charges, and prints out monthly statements summarizing the status of each customer's account. While banks and other financial institutions were among the first private businesses to use computers, their use has since spread to many diverse industries.

(*Below*) Computers are now used throughout the airline and travel industries. Travel agents and ticket agents use computers to check flight schedules and to make reservations. Once travelers are on the plane, its takeoff, journey, and landing will be directed by air traffic controllers using computers that track the movements of the plane.

(*Top*) The airplane industry has still another use for computers—to help design and test airplanes. Using desktop computers like this, engineers and designers can develop and analyze new aircraft. Aircraft manufacturers use computers to thoroughly inspect new planes (*bottom left*). The Boeing 767 shown here is undergoing tests on its fuel gauges.

The auto industry also uses computers to design, manufacture, and inspect its products (*bottom right*). With computer-aided design (CAD), engineers can test designs on a screen rather than on the road.

(*Top left*) In order to produce cars efficiently, auto companies are turning to computer-aided manufacturing (CAM), as well as to CAD. Directed by computers, robots now weld, assemble, and paint cars.

(*Top right*) In addition, auto companies have installed a number of computers to inspect automobiles and keep track of inventory.

(*Bottom right*) The auto industry is not the only one putting computers on the factory floor. This steel manufacturing firm installed a computer-aided manufacturing system that helps mold loops of steel cable.

(*Above*) Other manufacturers are using computers to help manage inventory and shipping.

(*Left*) Even police precinct houses are turning to computers to cut down on paperwork and provide instant access to records.

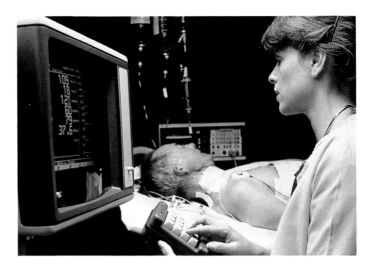

(*Above left*) Law firms are also depending on computers to obtain information and reduce routine typing. Many law firms subscribe to LEXIS, an electronic library of legal information. LEXIS can provide a lawyer in New York with transcripts of a particular case in Ohio, for example, or a list of all cases involving product liability. Access to a data base such as LEXIS can reduce the time law firms spend on research. Computers can also help law firms cut down on the amount of time needed to create and revise legal documents such as contracts and wills. Instead of having to retype a document every time a change is made, legal secretaries can update it electronically.

(*Above right*) Computer use has also spread to the medical profession. The health care industry is now using computers for a variety of tasks, including diagnosis. Computers will not replace doctors, of course, but they can help doctors diagnose and treat patients. One program now allows doctors to input information about a patient's medical history and symptoms. The computer compares that information with its preprogrammed knowledge of different diseases and makes an initial diagnosis. The computer may also suggest certain lab tests to confirm that diagnosis and may prescribe medication and treatment. Programs that use artificial computer intelligence are sometimes called expert systems. Another medical diagnostic tool is the CAT (computerized axial tomography) scan, which enables health care professionals to look inside the brain to detect tumors or other problems. Once a computer has diagnosed a patient, a hospital may rely on one to monitor the patient. This critical-care computer system checks the patient's vital signs from a bedside terminal and alerts the hospital staff to any significant changes.

(*Left*) Because of their expense, computer monitors, CAT scans, and expert systems are usually found only in hospitals. However, individual doctors are turning to computers to store patient records and handle billing.

(*Below*) Laboratories use computers to monitor and report lab tests. With computers, a laboratory can reduce paperwork and shorten the time it takes to get test results to doctors and patients. Computers are now being used in businesses across the country, appearing on the hospital ward and the factory floor, on the airport check-in counter and the engineering desk. More and more of the thousands of different industries in this country are putting computer technology to work to perform the myriad tasks needed to produce and deliver products and services.

7
Noun and Pronoun Possessives

The rules for forming noun and pronoun possessives are few, yet this is one grammatical element that causes many writers to stumble. Probably the main reason for confusion stems from the apparent similarity between words that are plural nouns and words that are possessive nouns. There are several techniques you can use to differentiate between them.

First of all, think carefully about the meaning of the word in question. If it is possessive, it will show ownership. Something in the sentence belongs to someone in the sentence. You will also find it useful to remember that an apostrophe is used to form a possessive—to show ownership. It is never used to form the plural of a noun or pronoun. Not all possessives use apostrophes, however, and a word can be both plural and possessive at the same time. Many writers have difficulty with these trouble spots. The rules in this chapter should help you use noun and pronoun possessives correctly.

POSSESSIVE FORMS OF NOUNS

In at least one sense, identifying the possessive of a noun is easy. A possessive noun must have an apostrophe. The trick is to know where to place the apostrophe and whether or not it should be followed by an *s*.

Singular and Plural Nouns That Do Not End in an *s* Sound

The possessive of all singular and plural nouns that do not end in an *s* sound is formed by adding *'s* to the word.

the bank's hours   a dozen women's dresses
Dr. Clark's office   Arkansas's governor
the children's department

Note that although *Arkansas* ends with the letter *s*, it does not end with an *s* sound. Thus, its possessive is formed with *'s*.

Singular Nouns That End in an *s* Sound

The possessive of singular nouns that end in an *s* sound is formed with *'s* if a syllable is added when the possessive is pronounced. Most singular nouns that end in an *s* sound take the *'s*.

    the boss's memo
    St. Louis's port
    Ms. Hicks's contract
    William Cox's report

Nouns that end in sounds related to *s*—*z*, *sh*, or *ch*—also take *'s* to form the possessive.

    the church's file
    Amy Welsh's job
    Mr. Gomez's computer

   You should use an apostrophe alone to form the possessive of singular nouns ending in an *s* sound if the addition of *'s* would make pronunciation awkward. There is no absolute rule on what is awkward and what is not; often, you will have to say the word aloud and decide for yourself how to spell it.

    Althea Philips' substitute (instead of Philips's)
    for goodness' sake (instead of goodness's)
    Moses' teachings (instead of Moses's)

   When forming the possessive of a noun that already ends in *s*, be careful to put the apostrophe after the word, not within it.

    Ms. Jones's desk (not Jone's)
    Maureen Higgins' report (not Higgin's)

Plural Nouns That End in an *s* Sound

Plural nouns that end in an *s* sound form the possessive by adding an apostrophe only. The rule here is to first form the plural of the noun and then form the possessive. For instance, to form the plural of the singular noun *referee*, add *s* (*referees*). To form the plural possessive, simply add an apostrophe (*referees'*). Notice the difference between the singular possessive (*referee's*) and the plural possessive (*referees'*).

    the Joneses' business
    the secretaries' typewriters
    the customers' accounts

Compound Nouns

The possessive of a singular compound noun, whether it is a closed, open, or hyphenated compound, is formed by adding 's to the end of the compound.

> the stockbroker's commissions
> the general manager's report
> my sister-in-law's firm

Forming possessives of plural compound nouns requires a little more care because the *s* that makes these nouns plural is not always at the end of the compound. Sometimes the *s* is placed after the first word in the compound. Remember that you pluralize the most important word in a compound noun. Once you have done that, you can form the possessive.

When the last word of a plural compound noun ends in *s*, form the possessive by adding an apostrophe only.

> the district attorneys' meeting
> the salesclerks' performance

When the last word does not end in *s*, form the possessive by adding 's to the end of the compound.

> our brothers-in-law's money
> the editors in chief's memos

If the possessive form of the compound noun sounds awkward to you when you pronounce it, rewrite the sentence so that you do not have to use the possessive. Instead of writing "Ms. Harrelson will attend the editors in chief's meeting," you could write "Ms. Harrelson will attend the meeting of the editors in chief."

Special Possessives

Names of organizations or companies often contain words that may or may not be possessives, according to individual style. Whenever possible, get the spelling of the organization's name from an official publication (such as an annual report) or letterhead, or call the company and ask for the correct spelling. If this is not possible, follow the guidelines below.

Use an apostrophe if the word in question is a singular possessive or a plural possessive that does not end in an *s* sound.

> Chesebrough-Pond's Inc.
> Pinkerton's, Inc.
> *Women's Wear Daily*

Do not use an apostrophe if the word is a common plural noun.

> Veterans Administration
> New York State Nurses Association

When the name of an organization ends in an abbreviation, form the possessive by adding *'s* to the end of the abbreviation.

> Levi Strauss & Co.'s order
> Commodore International Ltd.'s annual statement

You may be able to avoid this construction by using the organization's complete name in a prepositional phrase the first time it is mentioned, and then using a shortened form of the name for subsequent mentions.

> In reference to the order from Levi Strauss & Co., ... Levi Strauss's order ...

If the organization's name ends in a number or a prepositional phrase, add *'s* to the end to form the possessive.

> United Bank of New Jersey's account
> Computron-2's salespeople

When the name of a holiday contains a possessive, it is normally singular.

> New Year's Eve
> Washington's Birthday
> St. Patrick's Day

However, there are some cases in which this does not hold true.

> April Fools' Day
> Presidents' Day
> Veterans Day

There are many expressions of time and measurement that also are written in the possessive form. How they are formed depends on whether they are singular or plural.

> an hour's work
> two weeks' notice
> ten dollars' worth

SHARPENING YOUR SKILLS 1

Form the possessive for each of the following nouns.

1. attorney-at-law

2. secretary

3. partners

4. Sun-Diamond Growers of California

5. vice presidents

6. Wanda Smith

7. the Philipses

8. chief executive officer

9. Geraldo Rodriguez

10. committee member

11. masterpiece

12. Amalgamated Bank Corp.

Many people have problems with possessive pronouns because they think the pronouns should contain an apostrophe. Pronouns do not form the possessive by adding *'s*. Instead, there are special pronouns to show possession. You can review these possessive pronouns in Table 7-1.

POSSESSIVE FORMS OF PRONOUNS

Table 7-1. Possessive Pronouns	
Singular	Plural
my, mine	our, ours
your, yours	your, yours
his	their, theirs
her, hers	
its	
whose	whose

Some possessive pronouns in the table only have one form, such as *his* and *whose*. These pronouns remain the same, regardless of where they occur in the sentence. Other pronouns, however, have two forms. Which form you use is determined by the word's position relative to the noun it modifies.

This is *our* house.

This house is *ours*.

In the first example, the possessive pronoun *our* is being used as an adjective before the noun *house*. The second form of the pronoun (*ours*) stands alone, not followed by a noun. The following examples show the different uses for the first person singular possessive pronouns.

My office is at the end of the hall.

The office at the end of the hall is *mine*.

Mine is the office at the end of the hall.

SHARPENING YOUR SKILLS 2

Rewrite each of the following sentences so that it uses the alternate form of the possessive pronoun that is italicized. Remember that some pronouns have only one form regardless of where they are used in the sentence.

Example: That is *his* typewriter.   That typewriter is *his*.

1. *Their* memos are in the file.

2. Those shoes are *whose*?

3. We are supposed to use *your* plan.

4. *Ours* are the pens with the erasers on top.

5. The comments in green ink are *mine*.

PROBLEMS WITH PRONOUNS THAT SOUND ALIKE

The possessive pronouns *its, your, their, theirs,* and *whose* sound precisely the same as the contractions *it's, you're, they're, there's,* and *who's*. The context will always determine whether you should use a possessive pronoun or a contraction. Review the following pairs of words to be sure that you always use the right one. Remember: Possessive pronouns never need apostrophes, but contractions always do.

***Its* and *It's*.** The possessive pronoun *its* means "belonging to it." The contraction *it's* is a shortening of *it is*. You can substitute the words *it is* to see whether *its* or *it's* is appropriate.

The company is concerned that *its* stock will drop drastically. (*It is* does not fit here, so *it's* would be inappropriate.)

The company is concerned that *it's* the target of a takeover attempt. (*It is* does fit here, so *it's* is correct.)

***Your* and *You're*.** The possessive pronoun *your* means "belonging to you." The contraction *you're* is a shortened form of *you are*.

Louisa, did you bring *your* printout with you today?

You're sure that this is the latest printout, Louisa?

***Their, They're,* and *There*.** The possessive pronoun *their* means "belonging to them." The contraction *they're* is a shortened form of *they are*. The pronoun *there* is used to introduce a sentence; the adverb *there* indicates a certain place.

Sylvia and Ed forgot *their* badges.

Sylvia and Ed aren't sure if *they're* going to attend the seminar.

There are just two seats left at the table for Sylvia and Ed.

Sylvia and Ed placed the cartons over *there*.

***Theirs* and *There's*.** The possessive pronoun *theirs* means "belonging to them." The contraction *there's* is a shortened form of *there is*.

These brochures are ours, and those brochures are *theirs*.

Yes, *there's* another copy of this report if you need it.

***Whose* and *Who's*.** The possessive pronoun *whose* means "belonging to whom." The contraction *who's* is a shortened form of *who is*.

No, I don't know *whose* folder this is.

No, I don't know *who's* going to be the new manager of Customer Services.

SHARPENING YOUR SKILLS 3

Choose the correct word in each of the following sentences.

1. Please remember to bring (your / you're) inventory statement to the meeting.

2. Are you sure that these requisitions are (there's / theirs)?

3. Connie, do you know (whose / who's) briefcase this is?

4. The company's recent announcement of (its / it's) new product line generated much enthusiasm among the employees.

5. Ms. Berberick said that (theirs / there's) no reason for this shipment to be delayed.

6. (Whose / Who's) responsible for the McNamara account?

7. (They're / There) is no shortage of vice presidents in this company.

8. I need (you're / your) signature on this order.

POSSESSIVES BEFORE GERUNDS

A gerund is a verb form which ends in the suffix *-ing* and which is used as a noun. When a noun or pronoun modifies a gerund, it is in the possessive form.

We appreciated *Fred's* typing the entire report for us.

Ms. Svenson said that *our* speaking to the trainees was very helpful.

However, there are cases in which a participle is mistaken for a gerund. A participle is a verb form that, like the gerund, ends with *-ing*. However, participles are used as adjectives, and the noun or pronoun preceding them should not be in the possessive form. Whether the *-ing* word serves as a gerund or a participle often depends on the emphasis you want to give in the sentence.

> I heard *you* speaking at the conference.

> I admired your *speaking* at the conference.

In the first sentence, *you* is the important word. It is the object of the sentence, and *speaking* acts as a participle modifying *you*. In the second sentence, *speaking* is the important word, acting as a gerund; thus, the possessive form *your* is used.

POSSESSIVES IN APPOSITIVES

An appositive is a noun or noun phrase that identifies or renames the noun next to it in the sentence. Appositives that are not absolutely essential for identifying the nouns they follow are set off with commas.

> Ms. Ransome, our supervisor, is studying for a master's degree in business administration.

When you are putting the appositive into possessive form, you make certain changes to this comma rule. First, to form the possessive of an appositive, place an apostrophe or *'s* (whichever is appropriate) at the end of the appositive, not after the noun the appositive refers to. You must then drop the comma that follows the appositive.

> There is ample parking in Baltimore, Maryland's business district.

> Mel Shipley, the stock clerk's question was certainly valid.

You may wish to reconstruct a sentence if you feel that forming the possessive of the appositive sounds awkward. In such a case, you should use an *of* phrase.

> The business district of Baltimore, Maryland, offers ample parking.

> The question asked by Mel Shipley, the stock clerk, was certainly valid.

THE USE OF POSSESSIVES TO SHOW CO-OWNERSHIP

To indicate that two nouns share ownership, make only the second of the two nouns possessive.

> Jeanne and Donna's agency
> Mr. Wismer and Ms. Dallas's company
> Martin and Franklin's agreement

To indicate separate ownership, make each noun possessive.

> the seller's and the buyer's signatures
> Bill Smith's and Marilyn Eischer's sons

Sometimes, as in *the seller's and the buyer's,* the repetition of the word *the* may be used to emphasize separate ownership.

You may also need to distinguish between two nouns that share ownership of an item and one compound noun that includes the word *and* (for example, the name of a business). The context will decide the correct meaning.

Will and Mary's store will close for the summer.

Will's and Mary's stores will close for the summer.

Will and Mary's stores will close for the summer.

In the first sentence, Will and Mary own a store together. In the second sentence, both Will and Mary own their own stores. In the third sentence, the name of a chain of stores is *Will and Mary's.*

SHARPENING YOUR SKILLS 4

Correct any errors that you find in the following sentences. If a sentence has no errors, write the word *correct*.

1. The supervisor insisted on us checking the assembly again.

2. Emily and Rose's new office is small but bright.

3. Bill's, the maintenance manager, request is on your desk.

4. Vicki's helping us complete the study was appreciated deeply.

5. Spokane, Washington, setting is perfect for our planned factory.

6. Mr. Sampson and Ms. Baxter's departments will be reviewed this week.

7. Paul's and Marion's article made the monthly newsletter much more informative than usual.

8. We were grateful for Connelly handling of the job.

9. Barbara, the shop steward, demand was sent to the negotiating committee.

EDITING EXERCISES

A. Choose the correct word in parentheses in each sentence.

1. The (banks / bank's) officers met last week.

2. Arthur (Knox's / Knox') account is overdue.

3. The (Joneses' / Jone's) shop opens next month.

4. (My / Mine) territory includes the Southwest.

5. I appreciate (you / your) listening to my presentation.

6. (Fred and Sandy's / Fred's and Sandy's) store sells those replacement parts.

7. (There's / Theirs) going to be a rush for the fall fashions.

8. Take (your / you're) portfolio with you.

9. (Whose / Who's) covering the financial district for the *Chronicle*?

10. Saving failing small businesses is (they're / their) specialty.

B. Punctuate the possessive nouns in the following paragraph.

    The sisters-in-laws stockbrokerage has been growing rapidly. They are trading stocks for several pension funds, and their stockbrokers commissions are substantial. Their secretaries time is almost completely taken up processing new orders, and their customers accounts are profiting from their conscientious management.

PROJECTS

A. Using the groups of sound-alike words that follow, write one sentence for each word showing the difference between the words in each group.

its
it's

theirs
there's

your
you're

whose
who's

their
they're
there

B. Write a two-paragraph summary of a book you have recently read or a movie or TV show you especially liked. When you are finished, go back and underline each plural noun you used and circle each possessive noun you used. If you have nouns that are both plural and possessive, they should be underlined and circled.

8
Verbs I

Ms. Donovan the new word processor.

Are you confused? So you should be. You just read a group of words that do not make sense because they lack a verb to tell you what is happening between Ms. Donovan and the new word processor. Sentences are about nouns or pronouns. It takes verbs, though, to tell you the action or state of being of those nouns or pronouns. Look now at the ways various verbs perform those functions in regard to Ms. Donovan.

Ms. Donovan *will be fixing* the new word processor. (action)

Ms. Donovan *has returned* the new word processor. (action)

Ms. Donovan *is* the new word processor. (state of being)

Verbs also indicate the time of an action or state of being. They convey this sense of time by varying their tense. In English, verb tenses are grouped according to three kinds of time: present, past, and future. In addition to the simple present, past, and future tenses, there are several other tenses that are commonly used in speaking and writing.

THE PRINCIPAL PARTS OF VERBS

All the verb tenses are derived from five basic verb forms, called the principal parts. The first, the infinitive, consists of the word *to* plus the base verb, as in *to walk*. The other four forms—present, past, past participle, and present participle—involve changes within the verb.

The way the forms are created from the base verb determines whether the verb is regular or irregular. Thousands of verbs follow the regular pattern of formation (Table 8-1). Some common verbs do not; those will be looked at more closely in Chapter 9, as will some other aspects of verb usage.

8-1. Regular Verb Form Patterns	
Infinitive to charge to plan to request	*Examples* she wants *to charge* he is going *to plan* they need *to request*
Present charge(s) plan(s) request(s)	*Examples* I *charge*; he *charges** we *plan*; she *plans** you *request*; it *requests**
Past charged planned requested	*Examples* they *charged* Mel *planned* the client *requested*
Past Participle charged planned requested	*Examples* people have *charged* he had *planned* I should have *requested*
Present Participle charging planning requesting	*Examples* they are *charging* Sam will be *planning* I was *requesting*
*Note the change in the present tense for the third-person singular.	

The Past Participle

For all regular verbs, the past participle is the same as the past tense form. Both the past tense and the past participle are formed by adding *d* or *ed* to the present tense form, as explained later in this chapter. Since the past tense and past participle are identical, how can you tell these two forms apart when they are used in sentences?

Only the present tense form and the past tense form can be used alone as verbs. A participle can never be used alone as a verb. To serve as a verb, a participle must be part of a verb phrase. A verb phrase includes the verb and its helping verbs, or auxiliaries (*has hired, will be hired, was hired,* and so on).

> Ms. O'Donnell *assigned* Molly to the Anderson project. (*Assigned* is a past tense verb because it is not part of a verb phrase.)

> Molly *has been assigned* to the Anderson project. (Here, *assigned* is part of the verb phrase *has been assigned*. Therefore, *assigned* is a past participle.)

The Present Participle

To form the present participle of any verb, add *ing* to the present tense form.˜ (If the present tense form ends in *e*, drop the *e* before adding *ing*, as in *hire → hiring* and *replace → replacing*.)

Like the past participle, the present participle can be used only with auxiliaries and is therefore always part of a verb phrase.

> Jerome *may be assigning* these accounts to Francine. (The present participle *assigning* is part of the verb phrase *may be assigning*.)

> They *have been working* late every night this week. (The present participle *working* is part of the verb phrase *have been working*.)

It is useful to remember that the participle—both the present form and the past form—is always the last word in a verb phrase—the *main* verb in the phrase. For instance, in the phrase *have been working*, the main verb is *working* and the auxiliary is *have been*.

THE PRESENT TENSE

The present tense of a verb is used in several related ways. The present tense, which does not need auxiliaries, can describe an action that is taking place now or a state of being that exists now.

> I have no news about the project.

The present tense can be used to make a statement that is always true.

> The earth rotates on its axis.

In addition, the present tense can describe an action that takes place repeatedly or a state of being that exists continuously.

> All department heads meet once a month.

When using the present tense of a verb with a third-person singular noun or pronoun, follow these spelling guidelines.

- Add *es* to a base verb that ends in *s, x, z, ch,* or *sh*.

  miss → misses
  fix → fixes
  buzz → buzzes
  catch → catches
  push → pushes

- If the base verb ends in a *y* that is preceded by a consonant, change the *y* to *i*, and add *es*.

  apply → applies
  carry → carries
  defy → defies

- In all other cases, simply add *s* to the base verb.

  taste → tastes
  earn → earns
  delay → delays

THE PAST TENSE

Like the present tense, the past tense of a verb requires no auxiliaries. The past tense indicates an action that took place at a previous time or a state of being that existed at one time.

> Yesterday Ms. Gonzalez *hired* a new trainee.

> The speech about improving morale *was* fascinating.

Follow these guidelines for forming the past tense of regular verbs. Formation of the past tense of irregular verbs will be discussed in Chapter 9.

- Add *d* to a verb that ends in *e*, as in *placed*.
- Add *ed* to a verb that does not end in *e*, as in *flashed*.
- If a verb ends in a *y* that is preceded by a consonant, change the *y* to *i*, and add *ed*, as in *studied*.

THE FUTURE TENSE

To indicate that an action or a state of being will begin or will take effect at some future time, use the future tense. To form the future tense, add the auxiliary verb *will* to the base verb.

> The new branch *will open* next month.

> Rachael *will become* assistant vice president when George retires.

SHARPENING YOUR SKILLS 1

Rewrite each of the following sentences in the past and the future tenses.

1. Peter repairs office machinery.
2. The managers plan the schedule.
3. Winston and I face a challenging assignment.
4. The director explains every task thoroughly.
5. Sales climb during the holiday season.
6. Charles types with great accuracy.
7. Alphonse and Rita carry a heavy work load.
8. Rick and I erase the disk after every run.

Present, past, and future tenses offer three basic ways to express simple time. In addition to these basic tenses, the English language offers other ways to express the time of an action or a state of being. The perfect tenses allow writers and speakers more flexibility in treating time and the relationship of one action to another.

THE PERFECT TENSES

The Present Perfect Tense

The simple past tense describes an action that was completed in the past, as in *The director finished the ad campaigns last week*. Sometimes, however, you must convey the idea that an action happened at an unspecified time in the recent past or that an action began in the past but is not yet completed. The present perfect tense communicates these time elements.

The present perfect tense is formed by using the auxiliary *has* (or *has been*) or *have* (or *have been*) with the past participle.

> The director *has finished* the ad campaigns. (This sentence shows that the director completed the campaigns at an unstated time in the recent past. When, as above, the words *last week* are added, the simple past tense *finished* is correct.)

> Dana *has occupied* that corner office ever since he joined the firm. (In this sentence, the present perfect tense is used to show that Dana still occupies the corner office.)

The Past Perfect Tense

In speaking and writing, it is often important to distinguish between two past actions—specifically, to communicate clearly which of two past actions occurred first. To convey this relationship, use the past perfect tense for the action that occurred first and the simple past tense for the second action.

To form the past perfect tense, use *had* or *had been* with the past participle.

> Vernon *had mailed* the check before we *called*. (This sentence mentions two past actions. The past perfect tense *had mailed* makes the sequence of actions clear. First, the check was mailed. Then the call took place.)

The Future Perfect Tense

Whenever it is important to indicate that an action will be completed at a specific future time, use the future perfect tense. This tense is also used to show the sequence of two actions that will occur in the future. The future perfect tense is used to show the action that will occur first. The present tense is used to show the future action that will occur second.

To form the future perfect tense, combine *will have* or *will have been* with the past participle.

> By March 30 the parking lot *will have been repaved*. (It is not completed yet, but it will be finished in the future—specifically, by March 30.)

> By the time the new telephone system *arrives*, service *will have been interrupted* for a full week. (This sentence mentions two future actions. The future perfect tense *will have been interrupted* shows that the interruption of service will have occurred *before* the arrival of the system occurs.)

SHARPENING YOUR SKILLS 2

Identify the italicized verb phrase in each of the following sentences as the present perfect tense, past perfect tense, or future perfect tense.

1. By this time tomorrow, the letter *will have arrived*.

2. The job *has been completed* within the allotted time.

3. We *have waited* five weeks for acceptance of our proposal.

4. I called by 10 a.m., but the tickets *had been sold* already.

5. By the time the will is executed, the lawyers *will have devoted* three months to the project.

6. The trucks *have parked* in this pattern before.

7. By the time I complete this chore, I *will have carried* 50 cartons.

8. By the end of June, Margo *will have completed* the course work for her bachelor's degree in computer science.

THE PROGRESSIVE TENSES

The tenses you have just reviewed do not exhaust all the ways to express the time of a verb. Certain other tenses convey action that takes place over a period of time, action that is continuing, and action that is in progress. These tenses are called the progressive tenses because they convey a sense of the progress of an action over time.

In the following examples, note how the present participle is used with various auxiliaries to convey an action or a state of being that is in progress, was in progress, or will be in progress.

The Present Progressive Tense

The present progressive tense couples *am, is*, or *are* with the present participle to show action now in progress.

> I *am reviewing* the folders.

> Several orders *are waiting* for shipment.

The Past Progressive Tense

The past progressive tense describes action that was in progress at a specific time in the past. The present participle plus *was* or *were* transmits that meaning.

> Workers *were hammering* during the entire speech.

> The consultant *was leaving* when we arrived.

The Future Progressive Tense

The future progressive tense indicates action that will be ongoing at a particular time in the future. This tense is made up of *will be* plus the present participle.

> We *will be featuring* Sunbrite lawn furniture from June 28 to July 3.

> You *will be working* while we are on vacation.

The Perfect Progressive Tenses

The perfect progressive tenses resemble the perfect tenses, with one major difference: The present participle is used instead of the past participle to indicate ongoing action.

The present perfect progressive is composed of the auxiliaries *has been* or *have been* plus the present participle.

> The new model *has been selling* very well.

The past perfect progressive adds *had been* to the present participle.

> Customers *had been asking* for the previous model until the demonstration.

The future perfect progressive is formed with *will have been* and the present participle.

> By the end of next week, we *will have been selling* the new model for an entire quarter.

SHARPENING YOUR SKILLS 3

In each of the following sentences, identify the progressive verb phrase in parentheses.

1. The entire division (will be moving / will move) next week.

2. Francis and I (worked / were working) on the revisions throughout the day.

3. I (am reviewing / will review) your memo for documentation of the dispute.

4. Many customers (will wait / were waiting) for the January sales to begin.

5. Farmers (experienced / are experiencing) crop failures because of the drought.

6. Many employees (will be riding / will ride) the shuttle bus from now on.

7. You (stand / are standing) in the way of progress.

8. At the end of this hour, we (will have typed / will have been typing) for four hours.

EDITING EXERCISES

Correct any errors in the formation of verb tenses in the following sentences.

1. The product performd well in the stress test.

2. A flashing red light always indicate a problem in the system.

3. Any bank customer who applys for a loan this week will receive a free pocket calculator.

4. Mr. Davis hopes to influenced the Board of Directors with his letter.

5. My assistant worryed that you would not find your way to our office without a map.

6. Our small office party turning into a large celebration.

7. If we send for the parts now, we will avoided the price increase.

8. Joe will pick me up, since he pass my house on the way to work.

PROJECTS

Read three or four paragraphs in a newspaper or news magazine. Circle all the regular verbs you can find. (Be sure to include auxiliaries in verb phrases.) Divide a piece of paper into five columns. As headings for the columns, write the five principal parts of verbs: the infinitive, the present, the past, the past participle, and the present participle. Transfer each of the verbs or verb phrases you circled in the article to the appropriate column on your paper. How many of each type were there? Which was used most often?

9
Verbs II

When small children learn language, they begin with single words, such as *hi*. Later, they learn general rules that they try to apply to new words. Children sometimes make mistakes with verbs because they have not yet learned exceptions to these general rules.

One general rule in English is that the past tense of a verb is formed by adding *ed* to the base verb. Small children, knowing this rule but not the exceptions to it, might say "taked," "comed," or "buyed." These are intelligent errors: The vast majority of English verbs are regular and do work this way, as you studied in the previous chapter.

IRREGULAR VERBS

Gradually, children learn that many common verbs are irregular. The past tenses and past participles of such verbs are formed not by adding *d* or *ed*, but in various unpredictable ways. Often the spelling of the base verb itself changes. Sometimes the present, past, and past participle forms are identical. (Note, though, that the present participles of irregular verbs are formed regularly.)

Fortunately, people begin to master irregular verbs almost as soon as they learn to talk. Therefore, the purpose of studying them is to clarify those few forms that tend to cause difficulties. One kind of error results from trying to make an irregular verb conform to the regular pattern. For example, if you say "Mr. Armstrong drawed the money out of the bank," you are using an irregular verb (*draw, drew, drawn*) as if it were regular.

Another problem arises when the past participle of an irregular verb is confused with its past tense. In "I seen her yesterday at the meeting," the writer has mistakenly used the past participle of *see* instead of its past tense, which is *saw*. To avoid this type of error, remember that a past participle is always part of a verb phrase. It never stands alone without auxiliaries.

You can also avoid errors when using irregular verbs by looking up troublesome forms in a list, such as the one given in Table 9-1, or in a dictionary.

Table 9-1. Common Irregular Verbs

Base Verb	Past Tense	Past Participle	Base Verb	Past Tense	Past Participle
become	became	become	lend	lent	lent
begin	began	begun	lie	lay	lain
bite	bit	bitten	lose	lost	lost
blow	blew	blown	make	made	made
break	broke	broken	pay	paid	paid
bring	brought	brought	put	put	put
buy	bought	bought	read	read	read
catch	caught	caught	ride	rode	ridden
choose	chose	chosen	ring	rang	rung
come	came	come	rise	rose	risen
cut	cut	cut	run	ran	run
do	did	done	say	said	said
draw	drew	drawn	see	saw	seen
drink	drank	drunk	set	set	set
drive	drove	driven	shake	shook	shaken
eat	ate	eaten	shrink	shrank	shrunk,
fall	fell	fallen			shrunken
fight	fought	fought	sing	sang	sung
find	found	found	sit	sat	sat
fly	flew	flown	speak	spoke	spoken
forget	forgot	forgotten,	spring	sprang	sprung
		forgot	stand	stood	stood
freeze	froze	frozen	steal	stole	stolen
get	got	gotten, got	swear	swore	sworn
give	gave	given	sweep	swept	swept
go	went	gone	swim	swam	swum
grow	grew	grown	take	took	taken
hang	hung	hung	teach	taught	taught
hide	hid	hidden, hid	tear	tore	torn
keep	kept	kept	tell	told	told
know	knew	known	throw	threw	thrown
lay	laid	laid	wear	wore	worn
leave	left	left	write	wrote	written

SHARPENING YOUR SKILLS 1

Select the correct verb form in parentheses in each of the following sentences. Use your dictionary or refer to Table 9-1 if necessary.

1. Jessica said that by the end of next week she will have (wrote / written) the entire proposal.

2. We offered Bill Franklin the position, but he had already (took / taken) another job.

3. Over the years, these investments have (grew / grown) considerably.

4. Have your two assistants already (went / gone) to the airport?

5. By the time we arrived, the first session had (began / begun).

TRANSITIVE AND INTRANSITIVE VERBS

Transitive verbs are followed closely by direct objects—nouns or pronouns that receive the action of the verbs. Intransitive verbs are not followed by direct objects. There is no noun or pronoun to receive the action of the verb. Such verbs may be followed by other words or phrases that modify the verbs.

Most verbs can be either transitive or intransitive depending upon their use in a particular sentence. In the sentence *Rita called John*, *called* is a transitive verb because it is followed by a direct object. However, in the sentence *Rita called*, *called* has no object and is therefore intransitive. A good dictionary can tell you whether a verb is always transitive or always intransitive or whether it can be either depending on its use in a particular sentence.

Easily Confused Verbs

Understanding the distinction between transitive and intransitive verbs can enable you to use the troublesome verbs *lay/lie* and *raise/rise* with confidence. These verb pairs are related in meaning but not interchangeable in use because, in both pairs, one verb can take an object while the other cannot.

Lay / Lie. The verb *lay* means "to put or place something." All forms of the verb *lay*—the infinitive *(to lay)*, the present *(lay, lays)*, the past *(laid)*, the past participle *(laid)*, and the present participle *(laying)*—always take a direct object, as in *Karl lay the receiver down with care.*

The verb *lie*, on the other hand, means "to recline or place oneself in a horizontal position." The principal parts of the verb *lie*—the infinitive *(to lie)*, the present *(lie, lies)*, the past *(lay)*, the past participle *(lain)*, and the present participle *(lying)*—never take a direct object, as in *Karl lay down for a nap.* (Note that the base verb *lay* and the past tense of *lie* are spelled the same.)

One way to test for the correct verb is to see whether you can substitute a form of the verb *to put* for the word in question. If you can, you need a form of the transitive verb *to lay*; if you cannot, you need a form of the intransitive verb *to lie*. Since you can say "Karl always *puts* his coat down on the chair," the present tense form of *to lay* is correct. You cannot, however, say "Karl always *puts* down for a nap at 2 p.m."; thus, you need the present tense of the verb *to lie*.

Raise / Rise. A similar pattern exists with *raise* and *rise*. *Raise* means "to lift something." All forms of the verb *raise*—the infinitive *(to raise)*, the present *(raise, raises)*, the past *(raised)*, the past participle *(raised)*, and the present participle *(raising)*—take a direct object, as in *The bank has raised interest rates on loans.*

   Rise, which means "to stand up," "to get out of bed," or "to move upward," does not take a direct object to complete its meaning. The principal parts of *rise* are the infinitive *(to rise)*, the present *(rise, rises)*, the past *(rose)*, the past participle *(risen)*, and the present participle *(rising)*. As you can see, none of the following sentences has a direct object.

> The entire audience *rose* in unison.

> You must *rise* by 5 a.m. to catch the early train.

> Produce prices *rise* during times of drought.

SHARPENING YOUR SKILLS 2

Identify the italicized verbs in the following sentences as transitive or intransitive.

1. The elevator *rose* with dizzying speed.

2. Two reactors *exploded* at the same time.

3. Mr. Klein *laid* the report on the table.

4. Inflation is *raising* the cost of living.

5. The entire staff *donated* blood.

6. The president is *lying* down right now.

LINKING VERBS A linking verb connects a subject to a word that identifies or describes it. When a linking verb connects the subject to a word that identifies it, the pattern of the sentence is subject + linking verb + noun.

> Sharon *is* the instructor.

In such sentences, the linking verb states that the subject *is* something by linking the subject with an identifying noun.

   The sentence pattern subject + linking verb + adjective is followed when the linking verb connects the subject to a word that describes it.

> Richard *looks* happy.

Table 9-2. The Verb to Be

Tense	Singular	Plural
Present	I am you are he, she, it is	we are you are they are
Past	I was you were he, she, it was	we were you were they were
Future	I will be you will be he, she, it will be	we will be you will be they will be
Present Perfect	I have been you have been he, she, it has been	we have been you have been they have been
Past Perfect	I had been you had been he, she, it had been	we had been you had been they had been
Future Perfect	I will have been you will have been he, she, it will have been	we will have been you will have been they will have been
Progressive Tenses	*Present* Present tense of verb *to be* plus *being*	*Past* Past tense of verb *to be* plus *being*
Principal Parts	*Infinitive* to be *Present* am, is, are *Past* was, were	*Past Participle* been *Present Participle* being

A linking verb cannot connect the subject of a sentence to an adverb. For example, you would not say "Richard looks happily." *Happily* is an adverb. The correct word is the adjective *happy*.

The most common linking verb is *to be*. It is also the most irregular verb. Check Table 9-2 for a review of all the forms of *to be*.

Some common linking verbs give sense impressions: *feel, look, smell, sound,* and *taste*.

The proposal *sounded* good.

I *feel* wonderful today.

Other linking verbs include *appear, become, remain,* and *seem. Seem* and *become* always function as linking verbs, but the other verbs are sometimes linking verbs and other times not. For instance, *appeared* is a linking verb in *The sea appeared calm,* but it is not a linking verb in *The moon appeared on the horizon.*

Other words, such as *continue, prove,* and *grow,* are less commonly used as linking verbs. In *Mr. Blake grew tired, grew* is a linking verb; but it is a transitive verb in *Mr. Blake grew roses.*

SHARPENING YOUR SKILLS 3

Identify the linking verbs in the following sentences. Not every sentence contains a linking verb.

1. After 1986 Mr. Bertoli became the chief executive officer of the company.

2. Our adjustment manager is usually patient with customers who have complaints.

3. Hotcha Chili smells wonderful and tastes even better.

4. Every salesperson has a copy of the new price list.

5. Luke looked proud when the committee selected him.

AUXILIARIES   After studying Chapter 8, you know that verbs may be either single words or phrases made up of several words. Verb phrases always include auxiliaries plus a main verb. The most common auxiliary verbs are listed below.

Common Auxiliaries

am	can be
is	can have
are	might
was	might be
were	might have
has	might have been
have	must
had	must have
has been	must have been
have been	could
had been	could be
will	could have
will be	could have been
will have	should
will have been	should be
can	should have

do	should have been
does	would
did	would be
may	would have
may be	would have been
may have	

Some auxiliaries can be used alone as main verbs *(Dr. Penza is the speaker today)* as well as in verb phrases *(Dr. Penza is speaking today)*.

Auxiliaries are used to form certain future, perfect, and progressive tenses, as you learned in Chapter 8. They also perform other functions.

- They are used to show uncertainty:

  The program *might be* canceled.

- They are used to show necessity:

  We *must* meet our production quota this month.

- They indicate ability:

  Jan *can* type.

- They are used to emphasize base verbs:

  I *did* remember to copy the expense vouchers.

- Combined with *not*, auxiliaries are used in negative sentences:

  The drawer *does not* open easily.

Most auxiliaries combine with *not* to form contractions, as in *don't, wouldn't,* and *haven't.*

- Auxiliaries are used to form questions:

  Does he have a job?

  Should I begin?

To change a sentence with an auxiliary into a question, merely move the auxiliary verb to the beginning of the sentence. *We should send the order* becomes *Should we send the order?*

Ways to Avoid Errors With Auxiliaries

When you check your sentences to make sure they are complete, be sure you have used an auxiliary with the present participle when the participle is the only verb form in the sentence. The sentence *Fifty students studying word processing* is incomplete. Add an auxiliary to correct it: *Fifty students are studying word processing.*

Another pitfall to avoid is using *of* as an auxiliary. A sentence such as *We should've called earlier* may sound as if it contains the word *of*, but what you hear is the contraction of *have* in *should've*. Double-check your writing to be sure you have avoided mistakes such as "should of," "would of," and "could of."

SHARPENING YOUR SKILLS 4

Correct any mistakes in verb use in the following sentences. If a sentence has no errors, write the word *correct* next to it.

1. I could of become an expert typist.
2. Sean has close the door.
3. The president remembering the day she began her first job.
4. Our department will not be working on the new contract.
5. Vonnie should studied every night last semester.

ACTIVE VOICE AND PASSIVE VOICE

Sentences containing transitive verbs can be written in two ways, one in which the subject performs the action and the other in which it receives the action. *Voice* is the term used to indicate whether the subject of a verb acts or is acted upon. When the subject acts, the verb is in the active voice. When the subject is acted upon, the verb is in the passive voice.

In the sentence *Ms. Willard hired a new assistant*, Ms. Willard is described as performing the action, and the verb *hired* is in the active voice. The sentence *A new assistant was hired by Ms. Willard* communicates the same information, but in the passive voice. *A new assistant* is the subject of the second sentence although Ms. Willard, who is mentioned in a prepositional phrase, still performs the act of hiring. The sentence *A new assistant was hired* provides less information but focuses even more sharply upon the new assistant.

Because the object of the active sentence becomes the subject of the corresponding passive one, it follows that only transitive verbs can be used in the passive voice. A form of the verb *to be* is used with the past participle to redirect the action of the main verb: the passive version of *The designer solved the problem* is *The problem was solved by the designer*.

Which voice you use depends on whether you wish to call more attention to the person or thing performing the action or to the person or thing being acted upon. In *Mr. Dyer made the suggestion*, Mr. Dyer is being pointed out as the person responsible. In *The suggestion was made by Mr. Dyer*, more attention is being given to the suggestion than to the person who made it.

In general, the active voice is more forceful than the passive. For this reason, the passive voice is sometimes referred to as the voice of tact. It is a more gentle, less direct way of saying something. At the same time, because the passive voice is less direct, it can result in weakly stated or awkward sentences. *My trip to London will always be remembered by me* is wordy and sounds awkward. *I will always remember my trip to London* is more concise and easier to understand. Guidelines for choosing between the active voice and the passive voice are given in Chapter 35.

SHARPENING YOUR SKILLS 5

Change the passive voice to the active voice in each of the following sentences.

1. Specific goals should be set by managers.

2. All windows and doors must be locked by the night supervisor.

3. The minutes of the last meeting were read by the secretary.

4. The colors for the new office furniture were chosen by Don Powell.

5. Two new uniform styles will be selected by the flight attendants.

USING YOUR WORD PROCESSOR
Locating and Correcting Errors

With a word processor, you can easily locate and correct errors. First, keep a record of the most frequent errors you make at the word processor, and learn the commands that correct them most efficiently. For example, if you frequently reverse letters, look for a command that allows you to correct transpositions.

Use the search command to look for possible errors. If you sometimes confuse *there* and *their*, you can use the search command to locate those words. The search command can also be used to locate other possible trouble spots quickly.

If your word processing program has a command that tells the cursor to jump ahead one word at a time, use that command to help you proofread carefully. It will slow you down so that you can see each word clearly. As you jump from word to word, read silently to be sure that

what you have written makes sense. Jumping backward from word to word is another way to check spelling.

Are incomplete sentences a problem for you? Adding blank lines between sentences makes it easier to evaluate each sentence for completeness. Without the distractions of the preceding and following sentences, it is much easier to tell whether a sentence is correct. Later, you can easily remove the blank lines to put your sentences back into paragraphs.

Anytime you are unsure of something in your writing, try adding a code such as ** or + +. Once you have finished a draft, the search command will enable you to find the code marker—and the problem areas—quickly. After you have made your correction, you can easily delete the code marker.

EDITING EXERCISES

Correct the errors in verb use in the following sentences. If a sentence has no errors, write the word *correct* next to it.

1. Lesley has spoke with Ms. McNulty about the revised schedule.

2. I seen Albert this morning before he left for Los Angeles.

3. In the past two months, Dean has flew to the West Coast three times.

4. We quickly drunk our refreshments and rushed to the train station.

5. According to the attorney, the claimant had fell because of negligence on the part of the store owner.

6. Lowell has drove to the new plant several times.

7. Whom has Mr. Fredericks chose to replace Ms. Owens?

8. Yes, I had forgotten about the panel discussion until Marcia called to remind me.

PROJECTS

Locate two business documents (a letter, a memo, a page from a report, etc.). Underline every verb in each document; tell what tense it is in, whether it is in the active or the passive voice, and whether it is transitive or intransitive. Which tenses were used most often in your business documents? Which were rarely or never used? Which voice did the writers use more often—the active or the passive? Did you find any errors in the verb forms within the documents you chose?

10
Adjectives

"You did an outstanding job on the report, Tricia," Mr. Jackson said. That was exactly what Tricia Pace wanted to hear. After working for almost a week on the report, she was eager to learn what her manager thought of it. Through the use of an adjective, he was able to tell her.

Mr. Jackson did not merely say that Tricia had done the job; he chose the adjective *outstanding* to describe her work.

Like Mr. Jackson, you often use adjectives to give your opinions, develop ideas, or add information. You might refer to "the *old* office" or "a *better* plan." *Old* and *better* are adjectives that describe the nouns *office* and *plan*. *The* and *a* are articles, which are also adjectives. Together, these adjectives point out or identify the nouns and describe them or restrict their meanings.

Adjectives modify nouns, pronouns, or groups of words used as nouns. *Modify*, which means "to change," refers to the way words qualify, limit, or restrict the meanings of other words.

The Location of Adjectives

Adjectives are most often found just before the words they modify.

The *dynamic* speaker mesmerized the sales force.

If two or more adjectives are used together, they may follow the word they modify.

The speaker, *dynamic* and *convincing*, mesmerized the sales force.

An adjective may also be located after a linking verb such as *be, seem, look,* or *taste*. An adjective in this position is called a predicate adjective. In the following sentence, the predicate adjective *expensive* modifies the noun *products*.

> The new products looked *expensive*.

Because they complete the meaning of subject nouns, predicate adjectives are a type of subject complement.

DESCRIPTIVE ADJECTIVES

Descriptive adjectives name qualities of the nouns or pronouns they modify. *Profitable, green,* and *thick* are examples of descriptive adjectives. These are the kind of words most people think of when they refer to adjectives. Descriptive adjectives specify the quality, size, color, and condition of the words they modify. Words that tell how many and what kind are descriptive adjectives.

Another way to identify a descriptive adjective is to use the phrase *a ____ thing.* Any word, such as *natural, frozen,* or *U-shaped,* that fits in the blank is a descriptive adjective.

Some descriptive adjectives can also be recognized by their suffixes. Other parts of speech, especially nouns and verbs, can be transformed into adjectives by adding adjective suffixes.

> reason + able → reasonable
> hope + less → hopeless
> help + ful → helpful
> fool + ish → foolish
> instinct + ive → instinctive

Participles, proper adjectives, and compound adjectives are special types of descriptive adjectives.

Participles

Participles are verb forms used as adjectives. The present participle is the form of the verb that ends in *ing*. In the phrase *the falling prices, falling* describes *prices* and is therefore being used as an adjective rather than a verb.

Past participles, which are verb forms that usually end in *ed,* also commonly function as adjectives. In the phrase *an annoyed customer,* the past participle *annoyed* modifies the noun *customer,* so it is being used as an adjective.

Proper Adjectives

Adjectives derived from the names of people, places, and organizations are known as proper adjectives.

> a *Victorian* house
> a *Japanese* import
> a *Republican* fund-raiser

Some adjectives derived from proper nouns no longer depend on them for their meaning, so they are no longer capitalized. For example, venetian blinds are no longer associated solely with the city of Venice; thus the word *venetian* is not capitalized.

Compound Adjectives

Sometimes two or more words are used to form a compound adjective. These words work together to form a single modifier before a noun. Some compound adjectives are hyphenated. Others are written either as one word or as two or more separate words.

> a *well-planned* job
> a *forthcoming* promotion
> a *word processing* system

SHARPENING YOUR SKILLS 1

In the following sentences, identify each descriptive adjective and the noun or pronoun it modifies.

1. A growing business needs a computer system with multiuser capability.

2. The system must be flexible, with adequate software.

3. The Micro-Sota Company offers free, fast service and custom programming.

4. The basic hardware, easy-to-use and affordable, features the newest in American design.

LIMITING ADJECTIVES

Limiting adjectives point out or identify nouns. They include articles, possessive adjectives, and demonstrative adjectives.

Articles

The articles *a, an,* and *the* are among the most common words in the English language. Although they are adjectives, they are not used to describe or modify. Instead, they indicate or identify nouns.

The is known as a definite article because it is used to make things specific or definite: *the computer, the employer.* However, if any computer or employer is meant, rather than a specific one, an indefinite article is used: *a computer, an employer.*

A is used before consonants, but *an* precedes vowels and vowel sounds. Thus, *an* is used before the word *hour* because the first sound in *hour* is a vowel sound. *A* is used with words that start with a "yu" sound: *a uniform, a union.*

Possessive Adjectives

Possessive adjectives are possessive pronouns used as adjectives. They tell to whom something belongs, as in *his answer* and *my desk*. Possessive adjectives are *my, our, your, his, her, its,* and *their.*

Demonstrative Adjectives

Demonstrative adjectives *(this, these, that,* and *those)* are also pronouns used as adjectives. They clarify which noun is being discussed.

Do not confuse demonstrative adjectives with demonstrative pronouns. For example, both of the following sentences use the word *that.*

> *That* account earns thousands of dollars for the company.

> *That* is the company's most profitable account.

In the first sentence, *that* is a demonstrative adjective; it modifies *account.* In the second sentence, *that* is a demonstrative pronoun; it is the subject of the sentence.

Demonstrative adjectives are the only adjectives with plural forms. *These* is the plural form of *this,* and *those* is the plural form of *that.* Because plural forms for adjectives are uncommon, people sometimes use the wrong demonstrative adjectives. "Them pens" is wrong because the pronoun *them* can only be used as the object of a verb or a preposition (see Chapter 6). Instead, use *those pens* or *these pens.* "These kind" is also incorrect because *these* is plural, but *kind* is singular. The correct forms are *this kind* and *these kinds.*

Avoid using demonstrative adjectives when the nouns they modify have not already been mentioned, as in "I met this girl who gave me directions." The correct phrasing is *I met a girl who gave me directions.* Use demonstrative adjectives that clearly refer to people, things, or ideas you have already named.

> Mr. Wilson's proposal was accepted. *This* proposal was discussed Monday.

Using demonstrative adjectives in this way helps unify your writing because it shows how the ideas presented are related.

SHARPENING YOUR SKILLS 2

In the following sentences, identify each limiting adjective and the noun or pronoun it modifies.

1. Our company needs a regional sales director.
2. That position offers an excellent starting salary and significant bonus potential.
3. There are three basic requirements for the position: business degree, sales experience, and good health.

4. If you qualify, send us your résumé at once.

5. Those persons appearing most qualified will be interviewed later this month.

Most descriptive adjectives can be used to make comparisons. The degrees of comparison are based upon the positive form, which simply states a particular quality.

COMPARISON OF ADJECTIVES

> Pat McCormick gave a *short* report to the committee.

The comparative degree is used to compare two things.

> Pat's report was *shorter* than Mike Laven's report.

When three or more things are compared, the superlative degree is used.

> In fact, Pat's report was the *shortest* report the committee heard that day.

Regular Comparisons

Most adjectives form their comparative and superlative degrees in a regular way. To do so correctly, you must count syllables.

One-Syllable Adjectives. To form the comparative degree of one-syllable adjectives, add the suffix *-er* to the positive form. To form the superlative degree, add the suffix *-est.*

> small, smaller, smallest
> thin, thinner, thinnest
> fierce, fiercer, fiercest
> dry, drier, driest

Notice that some adjectives require a spelling change before adding the comparative or superlative suffix.

Two-Syllable Adjectives. Formation of the comparative and superlative degrees varies for two-syllable adjectives. For many such adjectives, the comparative is formed by adding the suffix *-er,* and the superlative is formed by adding *-est.*

> easy, easier, easiest

For others, the comparative is formed by putting *more* before the adjective; the superlative is formed by putting *most* before the adjective.

> special, more special, most special

For some adjectives, the comparative and superlative can be formed either way. For example, *more lovely* and *lovelier* are equally acceptable.

Adjectives of Three or More Syllables. Adjectives of three or more syllables form the comparative degree with *more* and the superlative degree with *most.*

> interesting, more interesting, most interesting
> reasonable, more reasonable, most reasonable

The words *less* and *least* can also be used to form comparisons.

> reliable, less reliable, least reliable

Irregular Comparisons

A small number of the thousands of adjectives in the English language have irregular comparative and superlative forms. These adjectives are listed in Table 10-1. As you can see, these adjectives are among the most common in English, so it is important to master their comparative and superlative forms.

Table 10-1. Adjectives With Irregular Comparative and Superlative Forms

Positive	Comparative	Superlative
well, good	better	best
bad	worse	worst
much, many	more	most
little	less	least
Also:		
little	littler	littlest
far	further	furthest
Also:		
far	farther	farthest

COMMON ADJECTIVE ERRORS

A number of common adjective errors involve comparisons. Writers may overcompare two things by using a double comparison, undercompare them by using an incomplete comparison, or attempt to create a comparison by using a word that does not make sense in a comparative form. Writers also need to distinguish between coordinate and subordinate adjectives so they know when a comma is needed—and when it is not.

Double Comparisons

An error you may sometimes encounter is a double comparison, in which both the suffix *-er* or *-est* and the word *more* or *most* are added, as in "most easiest," "more better," or "most cruelest." You can avoid this error by remembering to use just one of the ways to form a comparative or superlative, but not both at once.

Incomplete Comparisons

In advertising, comparisons are often left unfinished to give a vague promise of superiority. "Frippo Maintenance cleans offices better" sounds positive, but it could mean that Frippo gets offices cleaner than using no maintenance service at all. To be sure that readers or listeners understand your comparisons, make an effort to complete them. Rather than saying "The new intercom is louder," you could finish the comparison by explaining what the new intercom is louder than. Also, it is much more informative to say "Peony is the fastest program we tested" than to say just "Peony is the fastest program."

Comparison of Absolute Adjectives

Adjectives that cannot be compared are known as absolute adjectives. These adjectives, such as *perfect* and *unique,* do not have comparative and superlative forms because, logically, something is either flawless or one-of-a-kind, or it is not. Thus, comparatives such as "more perfect" or "most unique" are meaningless.

Some absolute adjectives cause more problems for writers than others. For example, you will probably not be tempted to say that one room is "more unlocked" than another. However, words such as *matchless, round,* and *equal* are sometimes compared. Rather than identifying something as *more matchless, roundest,* or *more equal,* you should describe it as *more nearly matchless, most nearly round,* or *more nearly equal.*

Confusion Between Subordinate and Coordinate Adjectives

More than one adjective may precede a noun. In the sentence *Tonia has a bright, colorful office,* the words *bright* and *colorful* are coordinate adjectives because they are in the same general category. Coordinate adjectives are separated by commas.

In contrast, the adjectives *small* and *vocational* in the phrase *a small vocational school* are not equal because *vocational* is more important than *small* in describing the school. *Vocational* and *school* function as a unit, with *small* modifying the entire concept. *Small* is subordinate to *vocational.* Because the two adjectives are not coordinates, they are not separated by a comma.

Two tests will help you determine whether or not adjectives are coordinate. First, if they make as much sense when they are reversed as in their original order, they are coordinate. *A colorful, bright office* has essentially the same meaning as *a bright, colorful office.* It sounds wrong, however, to say "a vocational small school."

The second test is to try to insert the word *and* between the adjectives. If it is reasonable to insert *and,* the adjectives are coordinate. *A bright and colorful office* is acceptable. You would not say "a small and vocational school," though.

Notice that a comma is never used between the last adjective and the noun it modifies.

SHARPENING YOUR SKILLS 3

Correct the adjective errors in the following sentences.

1. Model 437 produces a sharper faster copy than the less expensive machine.

2. Gregory Heller made a concise, interesting, presentation at the board meeting.

3. The striped fabric is a more better choice for the office windows than the floral pattern.

4. Stan's typing was more flawless than Maggie's.

5. You're sure to agree that Stomer file cabinets last longer.

EDITING EXERCISES

Correct the adjective errors in the following paragraph.

Shoplifting is a increasing problem for BabCo. Recent figures show a loss of $543,000 because of shoplifting this year. Furs, jewelry, and television sets are rarely stolen because extra security is provided for them kinds of items. Less expensive goods, such as french perfume and italian shoes, are more easier to steal. It might be more better to increase security for these type of product. Also, newly hired salespersons should not work alone because of their limited experience with detecting theft. Sales teams would be effectiver at preventing shoplifting.

PROJECTS

Investigate the use of adjectives in business writing. Select a business letter you have received or, if you have a job, select a letter written by someone whose work you admire. First, count the number of nouns and the number of adjectives in the letter. Next, identify and count the adjectives that follow nouns or linking verbs. Then, count the number of nouns that are preceded by more than one adjective. Are adjectives frequently used in this piece of business correspondence? Are they used before nouns, after nouns, or after linking verbs? What changes might you make in your own use of adjectives to make your writing style more businesslike?

11
Adverbs

Elaine Valdez works in a secretarial pool and frequently hears requests such as these:

"Please type this report *today.*"

"Please type this report *upstairs.*"

"Please type this report *very carefully.*"

"Please type this report *again.*"

Each speaker requests the same action—typing. However, each speaker qualifies the time, place, manner, and extent of the action with words such as *today, upstairs, very carefully,* and *again.* Adding these words makes the instructions more precise.

THE ROLE OF ADVERBS

Words that modify action verbs are called adverbs—they "add to" the meaning of verbs. Like adjectives, adverbs are not essential to sentences, but they do provide extra information and vividness.

Besides modifying action verbs, adverbs can modify an adjective, another adverb, a group of words, or even a whole sentence. *Bitterly cold* is an example of an adverb modifying an adjective, and *very angrily* is an example of an adverb modifying an adverb. In *Rhonda's desk was almost in the hallway,* the adverb *almost* modifies the group of words *in the hallway.* In the following example, the adverb *unfortunately* modifies the whole sentence:

Unfortunately, our company overbid on the project.

IDENTIFICATION OF ADVERBS

Adverbs have so many uses that they can be difficult to identify. One way to recognize them is to assume that any one-word modifier that is not an adjective is an adverb. However, more exact ways of determining adverbs do exist.

Function

How a word is used in a sentence is your best guide to determining its part of speech. Adverbs tell when *(now, yesterday),* where *(here, there),* how *(easily, quietly),* or to what extent *(extremely, slightly)* about a verb, an adjective, or another adverb.

Structure

The majority of adverbs end in the suffix *-ly,* and the most common way to form an adverb is to add *-ly* to an adjective. Usually, the *-ly* is merely added to the word without any change in spelling *(rapid → rapidly).* However, note these three exceptions:

- Change final *y* to *i* if it is preceded by a consonant *(easy → easily).*
- Add *al* to words ending in *ic (basic → basically).*
- Drop the final *le* when a word ends in *ble (legible → legibly).*

Although many adverbs end in the suffix *-ly,* the ending is not a guarantee that a word is an adverb. Some adjectives, such as *deadly, homely, costly,* and *friendly,* end in *-ly,* while many common adverbs, such as *there, then, often,* and *already,* do not. A number of words, such as *early, fast, more,* and *better,* can be either adjectives or adverbs, depending on how they are used.

> Rick Owen worked the *early* shift.

> The shift started *early.*

In the first sentence, *early* is an adjective modifying *shift.* In the second sentence, *early* is an adverb modifying *started.*

Other Adverb Affixes. A few adverbs are formed by adding the prefix *a-* to adjectives and nouns *(anew, aloud, aside).* Adverbs can also be formed by adding the suffixes *-where (somewhere, nowhere), -ward (homeward, afterward),* and *-wise (lengthwise, crosswise).*

Adverbs With Two Forms. Some adverbs have two forms: a form that ends in the suffix *-ly* and a form that is the same as the adjective.

> slowly, slow
> quickly, quick
> loudly, loud

Generally, the short form of this type of adverb is more common in commands and in informal situations. The expressions "Get rich quick" and "Drive slow" sound less formal than "Get rich quickly" and "Drive slowly."

Location

Another way of identifying adverbs is by their location in sentences. Adverbs are movable, and they can be found in almost any position in a sentence—at the beginning, in the middle, or at the end. Shifting them from place to place can change the emphasis or the meaning of a sentence.

> *Only* Nick writes proposals. (No one else writes proposals.)
>
> Nick *only* writes proposals. (Nick writes proposals but does nothing else with them.)
>
> Nick writes *only* proposals. (Nick does not write anything but proposals.)

If an adverb such as *unfortunately* modifies an entire sentence, it can be located anywhere in the sentence. Usually, however, adverbs should appear close to the words they modify. Often they are found just before the words they modify.

> We *easily* found the solution.

They may also come just after the words they modify.

> Mr. Wilson replied *quickly.*

In sentences with a verb phrase, a common location for an adverb is between the elements of the phrase.

> We had *never* used a simpler program.

SHARPENING YOUR SKILLS 1

In the following sentences, identify each adverb and the word or group of words it modifies.

1. Mr. Harvey almost always stops at Mickey's Diner for lunch.
2. Very few clients have complained recently.
3. Our office is now located downstairs.
4. Ms. Cohen must type the monthly report tonight; tomorrow will be too late, unfortunately.
5. Although Tom Sims doesn't have much money, he contributes generously to the company's charity drives.

COMPARISON OF ADVERBS

Like adjectives, adverbs can be compared. The degrees of comparison are based upon the positive form, which simply states a particular quality.

> I type *fast.*

The comparative degree is normally used to compare one thing with another.

> Sam types *faster* than I do.

When three or more items are compared, the superlative degree is used.

Compared with Sam and me, Marie types *fastest.*

Regular Comparisons

For most one-syllable adverbs, the comparative degree is formed by adding the suffix *-er;* the superlative degree is formed by adding the suffix *-est.*

hard, harder, hardest

The comparative degree of longer adverbs is usually formed with *more;* the superlative degree of such adverbs is formed with *most.*

quickly, more quickly, most quickly
efficiently, more efficiently, most efficiently

Like adjectives, adverbs can also form comparisons with *less* and *least.*

frequently, less frequently, least frequently

Avoid using the comparative or superlative form of an adjective when an adverb form is needed. In the following example, the comparative form of the adverb *easily* is needed to modify the verb *works.* The comparative form of the adjective *easy* should not be used.

INCORRECT: Rafael's method works *easier* than Peter's.

CORRECT: Rafael's method works *more easily* than Peter's.

The adjective form can be used only to modify a noun. In the following sentence, *easier* is a predicate adjective modifying the noun *method.*

Rafael's method seems *easier* than Peter's.

Irregular Comparisons

Like adjectives, some adverbs have irregular forms for comparisons. Here are the two most common adverbs with irregular comparison forms:

Positive	Comparative	Superlative
well	better	best
badly	worse	worst

The ABN photocopier works *well;* the Schiff works *better;* the Merex, though, works *best* of all.

In the softball tournament, the Accounting Department performed *badly,* Purchasing performed even *worse,* and Shipping performed *worst* of all.

SHARPENING YOUR SKILLS 2

For each sentence, write the correct form of the word given in parentheses.

1. I worked (*long*) _____ on Monday than I did on Tuesday.

2. Synthetic fabrics usually pack (*neat*) _____ than those made of natural fibers.

3. Which of the three computers performs calculations (*rapid*) _____ ?

4. The company hopes to do (*well*) _____ in the second quarter than it did in the first.

5. The mail is (*early*) _____ than usual today.

Adverbs appear often in the English language. Along with their frequency come many opportunities for errors. Using double negatives and putting adverbs in the wrong place are the most common errors.

Double Negatives

Not, never, nothing, no, and *nobody* are examples of negative words. Using two negative words at once for extra emphasis is common in other languages, and it appeared commonly in English 400 years ago. Today, however, double negatives, as used in "I don't want no paper," brand speakers and writers as uneducated. This sentence actually states that you *do* want paper. Technically, double negatives cancel out each other. Avoiding double negatives can be difficult when one of the negatives is hidden in a contraction such as *don't*.

Though not as obvious as some negative words, *hardly* and *scarcely* are also negatives. Do not mistakenly combine either of these adverbs with another negative word, as in "There wasn't scarcely time to do the job." *There was scarcely time to do the job,* which avoids a double negative, is correct.

Misplaced Adverbs

Sometimes the word or phrase an adverb modifies is hard to identify. This difficulty can occur if the adverb is too far from what it modifies or if it can possibly modify either of two words or phrases. Consider this example:

The speaker whom the conventioneers were waiting for *eagerly* bounded on to the stage.

The adverb *eagerly* could modify either the action of the speaker or that of the conventioneers. Were the conventioneers waiting eagerly or did the speaker bound on to the stage eagerly?

Your goal should be to place adverbs so that their role is clear. Depending on your intent, you could state the sample sentence in one of these ways:

The speaker whom the conventioneers were *eagerly* waiting for bounded onto the stage.

The speaker whom the conventioneers were waiting for bounded onto the stage *eagerly.*

SHARPENING YOUR SKILLS 3

Correct the adverb errors in the following sentences.

1. The bookkeeper couldn't find the ledger nowhere.

2. The receptionist who fractured a rib recently returned to work.

3. I agreed yesterday to help him.

4. The electric vegetable peeler didn't do nothing when it was plugged in.

CONFUSING MODIFIERS

Because, as mentioned in the section on comparisons, many people confuse adverbs and adjectives, this error is given special attention.

Using Adjectives for Adverbs

Using an adjective instead of an adverb to modify an action verb is a frequent error. In the first sentence that follows, the adjective *serious* is used incorrectly to modify the verb *takes.* The adverb *seriously* is correct.

INCORRECT: He takes his job *serious.*

CORRECT: He takes his job *seriously.*

In addition, an adjective cannot modify an adjective.

INCORRECT: Mr. Tanner has a *reasonable* secure future with the company.

CORRECT: Mr. Tanner has a *reasonably* secure future with the company.

In informal usage, some adjectives are widely accepted in place of adverbs. However, you should use the standard form in business communication.

Almost/Most. *Almost,* which means "nearly," should be used before *all, every,* and *any,* as well as before all compounds beginning with these words. *Most* is incorrect before these words because it means "to the greatest degree." If you can substitute *nearly,* you know that *almost* is the correct choice.

INCORRECT: *Most* all the assistants were promoted.

CORRECT: *Almost* all the assistants were promoted.

Good/Well. *Good* is an adjective, as in *a good client* or *The report looks good. Well* is an adjective when it follows a linking verb and means "healthy": *He felt well.* With that meaning in mind, you can easily understand that it is incorrect to say "That dress looks well on you." When *well* follows an action verb, it is an adverb, as in *They worked well together.*

INCORRECT: He spoke *good.*

CORRECT: He spoke *well.*

Real/Really. Using *real* as an adverb, as in "Dylan did *real* well," is considered too informal for most business communication. The sentence should be changed to *Dylan did really well.* A good test is to see whether *very* can be substituted. If so, *really,* not *real,* is needed.

Sure/Surely. Writing "The Legal Department *sure* worked hard" is too informal for business situations. The sentence *The Legal Department surely worked hard* is more appropriate. Look to see whether *certainly* can be substituted in place of sure or surely. If it can, *surely* should be used.

Using Adverbs for Adjectives

Remember to use adverbs to modify only action verbs, not linking verbs. It is incorrect to say "It tastes *wonderfully*" when you mean something tastes very good. The correct way of stating this idea is, "It tastes *wonderful.*" Especially check to be sure that you are using adjectives, not adverbs, after sensory linking verbs *(feels, looks, tastes, smells).* "The food smelled *badly*" is incorrect because food cannot smell anything. No action is taking place. Instead, say "The food smelled *bad.*" *Bad* describes *food.*

In referring to their state of being, people sometimes say "I feel *badly.*" In writing, though, you should substitute "I feel *bad.*" Because *feel* is a linking verb in this sentence, an adjective is needed rather than an adverb.

SHARPENING YOUR SKILLS 4

For each sentence, choose the correct form of the word in parentheses. Be able to explain your choice.

1. The accountant said she could (easy / easily) finish by noon.

2. The fumes coming from the factory car smell (terrible / terribly).

3. Jack looked (wistful / wistfully) as the installer replaced his manual typewriter with a computer.

4. Bright colors look (good / well) on him, but his clothes seldom fit him (good / well).

5. No matter how (good / well) Barbara did the work, her supervisor always complained.

6. A secretary must spell (good / well) enough to catch errors in drafts.

7. This machine was working so (bad / badly) last week that I had to call the Service Department three times.

8. Miss Soderlund felt (bad / badly) about missing the meeting.

9. Why does this sandwich taste so (peculiar / peculiarly)?

10. I (sure / surely) don't blame him for feeling (nervous / nervously) about the interview.

EDITING EXERCISES

A. Correct the adverb errors in the following paragraph. Be sure that the adverbs are formed correctly and that they are in the most appropriate positions in the sentences.

To choose the right career, you should be real alert to business trends and understand your own values and abilities. If you don't never listen to or read business news, you can't hardly make the right job choice. Recognizing business trends is only not enough, however. You should take yourself serious too. Knowing what matters to you should sure help you decide on a career. Carefully also, consider your skills and abilities. Do you work together good with others? Do you learn new skills quicklier than other people? Do you, on the other hand, look badly when compared with other workers? Efficiently try to find ways to use your abilities and gradually to improve the skills you will need for the jobs you would like eventually to have.

B. Correct the adverb errors in the following sentences.

1. I sure am busy this week.

2. Most all the defective pieces have been replaced.

3. I feel badly that I didn't finish the report on time.

4. Three applicants did good on the test the Personnel Department gave.

5. The vice president is real happy about the results of the survey.

PROJECTS

The parts of speech of the nonsense words in the sentences below can be identified by their structure and position. Mark the words you think are verbs, nouns, and adverbs using the abbreviations V, N, and ADV.

He latiated glapishly and dorely and then glooded the graches with cutitation. "I bridiately gorform my gricks after I gonflet them," he said.

Based on the way the nonsense words are used in the passage, which of the forms below seem possible to you? Be ready to explain why.

latiating	bridiate	cutiationing
dorelies	grick	gorforming
grach	glooding	gonflets

Write a passage of your own containing ten nonsense words whose parts of speech can be identified by their structure and position. Then create possible alternate forms for five of your nonsense words. Be ready to identify the part of speech of each of your nonsense words.

12
Prepositions

After arriving at his sales meeting, Mr. Deener realized that he had forgotten an important report. He telephoned his assistant to send it to him. To help her locate the report quickly, Mr. Deener said it was *in* a manila folder *under* the dictionary *on* the shelf *behind* his desk. Mr. Deener used the prepositions *in, under, on,* and *behind* to describe the position of the report in relation to other objects in the office. Prepositions are valuable words for indicating location and other characteristics.

Prepositions are connecting words. They connect nouns and pronouns to other words in a sentence to show relationships and add information.

Compared with some other parts of speech, prepositions are limited in number; there are fewer than 150 in all. Some of them, such as *via* (which means "by way of") and *sans* (which means "without"), are uncommon; however, most prepositions are used often. In fact, studies of word frequency show that the prepositions *in, on,* and *to* are among the ten most commonly used words in written and spoken English. Although it is possible to write sentences without prepositions, all but the simplest sentences contain at least one. Many prepositions, such as *above* and *below*, have core meanings that deal with space. Others, such as *since* and *until*, are concerned primarily with time. Still others, such as *around* and *following*, encompass both space and time. In addition to their basic meanings, most of these prepositions have additional meanings that do not relate specifically to time or space. There are also a number of prepositions that communicate different kinds of meanings, such as cause (as in *because*). A list of common prepositions appears in Table 12-1.

THE FUNCTION OF PREPOSITIONS

Table 12-1. Common Prepositions		
aboard	despite	outside
about	down	over
above	during	past
across	except	plus
after	excluding	regarding
against	following	since
along	for	through
among	from	throughout
around	in	till
as	including	to
at	inside	toward
before	into	under
behind	like	underneath
below	minus	until
beneath	near	up
beside	of	upon
besides	off	versus
between	on	with
beyond	onto	within
by	out	without
concerning		

Compound Prepositions

Sometimes two or more words form a compound preposition, in which the words work together as a unit. The following is a list of some common compound prepositions:

according to	due to	on account of
along with	except for	out of
apart from	in addition to	together with
as well as	in front of	with regard to
because of	in spite of	
by means of	instead of	

PREPOSITIONAL PHRASES

A group of words that starts with a preposition is called a prepositional phrase. The preposition links a noun or a pronoun in the phrase to the rest of a sentence. Such phrases are used to expand basic sentences, often by indicating location (*at the bank, in my desk*) or time (*after work, before class*).

Structure

At the end of each prepositional phrase is a word or group of words known as the object of the preposition; the object is either a noun or a pronoun. The preposition shows the relationship between its object and another word in the sentence.

> The folders *on* that desk were filed *in* the wrong order.

In this sentence, the preposition *on* shows the relationship between the noun *folders* and the noun *desk*. The preposition *in* indicates the relationship between the verb phrase *were filed* and the noun *order*.

Modifiers, such as adjectives and articles, may be included in a prepositional phrase between the preposition and its object. The modifiers are italicized in the examples below.

> in *early* April
> after *the devastating* tornado
> to *our best* customers

The object of the preposition may be compound; one preposition is followed by more than one object. For example, in the prepositional phrase *for increased growth and profits, growth* and *profits* together make up the object of the preposition *for*. In the phrase *to restaurants, hotels, or institutional customers,* the words *restaurants, hotels,* and *customers* are all objects.

Sometimes the object of a preposition is a verb form *(after finishing)* or a group of words that includes a verb *(from what you tell me)*. In these examples, *finishing* and *what you tell me* function as nouns.

Prepositions and Other Parts of Speech. Many of the words in Table 12-1 can be used either as adverbs or as prepositions. If the word, in this case *behind,* has an object and functions as a connective, it is a preposition.

> Your folder is *behind* that pile of books.

However, if the word acts as a modifier and has no object, it is an adverb.

> I left my folder *behind.*

Some words, such as *for, since,* and *as,* can be either prepositions or conjunctions. To identify them as prepositions, look for the object. (Conjunctions, which also connect sentence elements, are described in Chapter 13.)

Function

Each prepositional phrase is a unit that functions as a single part of speech, usually as an adjective or adverb and occasionally as a noun. The preposition connects the phrase to the word it modifies or to the sentence as a whole.

Adjective Phrase. Prepositional phrases are often used as adjectives, to modify nouns. Most adjective phrases follow their nouns.

> Mrs. Jenkins was the manager *of the division.* (The prepositional phrase modifies *manager.*)

Like one-word adjectives, prepositional phrases can follow linking verbs.

The letter is *about the McClellan account.* (The prepositional phrase describes *letter.*)

Adverb Phrase.   Prepositional phrases can also function as adverbs to modify verbs, adjectives, or other adverbs. When they do, they occur in the same positions as ordinary adverbs.

Like other adverbs, adverb phrases tell when, where, how, or to what extent.

The sales trainee went *to Miss Dowd's office.* (The adverb phrase modifies the verb *went.*)

The employees seemed glad *about their raises.* (The adverb phrase modifies the adjective *glad.*)

The committee worked far *into the night.* (The adverb phrase modifies the adverb *far.*)

Like one-word adverbs, prepositional phrases can be used as sentence modifiers. Among the more common ones used in this way are *for instance, for example, on the other hand,* and *in short.*

Adjective and adverb phrases can appear in the same sentence, frequently following one another.

The company's revenues rose *in the first nine months of the fiscal year.* (The first phrase modifies the verb *rose,* and the second phrase modifies the noun *months.*)

Noun Phrase.   Prepositional phrases occasionally function as nouns. A prepositional phrase may, for example, act as the subject of a sentence.

By the back door is best.

Misplaced Phrases

Prepositional phrases should be placed wherever they seem most natural. In general, closely connected words should be kept as near one another as possible. A misplaced prepositional phrase may result in unintentional humor.

He sold the cup to a new customer *with missing handles.*

Any sentence that offers a possibility for misreading needs to be rewritten. Notice how much clearer the sentence is when the prepositional phrase is in the right place.

He sold the cup *with missing handles* to a new customer.

A related problem occurs when the word that a phrase should modify is missing from the sentence.

At the age of four, his father died.

The introductory prepositional phrases appear to modify *father,* but this arrangement does not make sense. The sentence needs to be rewritten.

When the boy was four years old, his father died.

SHARPENING YOUR SKILLS 1

In the following sentences, identify each prepositional phrase and the word it modifies.

1. You will find Miss Polacki in the main office down the hall.

2. In spite of protests, the contract negotiations were postponed for a week.

3. Three people behind my assistant and me whispered throughout the entire speech.

4. At the computer exhibition, two salespeople from a rival company came over to discuss the business market.

5. Without explaining, Steve Barnhart got up and left the meeting.

CHOOSING THE RIGHT PREPOSITION

In the English language, the choice of prepositions is not a matter of personal preference. Definite patterns and rules exist. Correct preposition choice can depend on the meaning of the sentence or on common usage.

People who speak English as their native language usually make the right preposition choices, but some choices are troublesome.

According to Meaning

Sometimes the choice of preposition depends on how words are used in a sentence. The same word can require different prepositions in different sentences. In other cases, you may need to choose between two prepositions that are similar, and therefore often confused. This section offers guidelines for choosing the correct preposition according to sentence meaning.

Agree With / Agree To. Use *agree with* when the object of the preposition is a person. Use *agree to* when the object is not a person.

I *agreed with* Margaret.

I *agreed to* the plan.

Angry With / Angry At. Use *angry with* when the object of the preposition is a person. Use *angry at* when the object is not a person.

I am *angry with* Sandy for being late.

I am *angry at* the proposal for reducing employee benefits.

Beside / Besides. *Beside* means "at the side of," as in *I sat beside the new client.* *Besides* means "in addition to" or "other than," as in *Besides a trust fund, he has an inheritance too.*

Between / Among. *Between* is the correct preposition when two possibilities are being considered. In general, when three or more choices are available, use *among.*

> Choose *between* the morning and afternoon shifts.

> Choose *among* the morning, afternoon, and evening shifts.

Compare To / Compare With. Use *compare to* to show a likeness. Use *compare with* to analyze similarities and differences.

> Mr. Huss *compared* the company's financial condition *to* a sinking ship.

> Mr. Huss *compared* this quarter's figures *with* those from last quarter.

Due To / Because Of. Use *due to* following a linking verb. Use *because of* for sentences requiring an adverb phrase.

> The billing error was *due to* our carelessness.

> Sales increased *because of* the special promotion.

From / Off. Use *from* when the object of the preposition is a person. Either *from* or *off* is correct when the object is a thing.

> Our department borrowed the video equipment *from* John.

> Edwin took his name *off* the committee list; Sue removed her name *from* the list too.

In Regard To / With Regard To / As Regards. All three phrases are correct. Remember, though, that it is incorrect to use the phrase *in regards to* or *with regards to.*

> *in (with) regard to* your letter

> *as regards* your letter

Wait For / Wait On. Use *wait on* meaning "to serve." Use *wait for* meaning "to stay in one place until someone or something comes."

> The clerk *waited on* the customer.

> The clerk *waited for* the customer to make up his mind.

According to Common Usage

Certain verbs, nouns, and adjectives are associated with specific prepositions through common usage. The correct preposition that follows these words does not vary from sentence to sentence. For example, common usage calls for *interfere with* rather than *interfere to* and *superior to* rather than *superior than. Different from* is always correct, but opinions differ on *different than.* (Some people never use *different than;* others use it only when it introduces a clause, a group of words containing a subject and a verb.) The following common words require specific prepositions because of custom:

averse to (*not* averse against)
capable of (*not* capable to)
comply with (*not* comply to)
dispense with (*not* dispense of)
identical with (*not* identical to)
independent of (*not* independent from)
inferior to (*not* inferior than)
plan to (*not* plan on)
retroactive to (*not* retroactive from)
substitute for (*not* substitute to)

SHARPENING YOUR SKILLS 2

Insert the correct preposition in each sentence.

1. All pay raises are retroactive _____ the first of the year.

2. Emissions from factory smokestacks must comply _____ federal regulations for air quality.

3. The personnel committee had to choose _____ five well-qualified candidates.

4. _____ me, others on the committee were Doris, Marion, and Hal.

5. The Board of Directors agreed _____ Ms. Applebaum's plan for increasing production.

6. I've been waiting _____ these figures.

7. The employees were angry _____ management for proposing a pay reduction.

8. The United States would prefer being independent _____ foreign oil.

9. Our company's product is superior _____ that of our competitor.

10. The man seated _____ Mr. Cannon is the new public relations director.

**COMMON
PREPOSITION
ERRORS** Although prepositions are often small words, using them incorrectly can make sentences sound rough and awkward. Misplacing, omitting, or repeating a preposition is a common error.

Misplaced Prepositions

"Never end a sentence with a preposition" is one of the few grammatical rules nearly everyone remembers. This rule has been attacked so often and so cleverly that no recent grammar book dares to include it.

It is true that clumsy sentences can result from blindly following this rule. Nevertheless, prepositions have their proper places in sentences, just as other parts of speech do. Most prepositions, in fact, do not fit well at the end of a sentence.

Perhaps a better rule to follow is to put the preposition in the most natural place. Prepositions often occur at the ends of questions. It is more natural to say "What are you looking for?" than "For what are you looking?" although the second version is also correct.

On other occasions, as in the sentence *The results will depend on what you ask for*, there is no comfortable place for the preposition except at the end of the sentence. Because the preposition *for* follows the verb *ask* so naturally, it would sound strange placed anywhere else in the sentence.

Missing Prepositions

Sometimes people omit prepositions in casual conversations, as in "I bought a couple tires." Listeners realize that what is meant is "a couple *of* tires." In formal speech and writing, though, be sure to include the prepositions. In a formal report or business letter, write "that type of problem" rather than "that type problem."

People also often incorrectly omit a preposition when separate nouns or verbs refer to the same word. Such a construction often requires two different prepositions.

INCORRECT: I have no aptitude or interest *in* management.

CORRECT: I have no aptitude *for* or interest *in* management.

Extra Prepositions

If a preposition has already appeared once with its object, be careful not to repeat it at the end of the sentence.

INCORRECT: This is the chance *for* which I have been waiting *for*.

CORRECT: This is the chance *for* which I have been waiting.
OR
This is the chance I have been waiting *for*.

Some verbs, adverbs, and adjectives do not require any prepositions.

INCORRECT: Where is he *at*?

CORRECT: Where is he?

Extra prepositions should be cut from expressions such as *off of, outside of, inside of*, and *near to*; *off, inside*, and *near* are simpler, as well as correct.

INCORRECT: The chart fell *off of* the wall.

CORRECT: The chart fell *off* the wall.

You can also improve your style by avoiding the awkward use of two or more prepositions together.

INCORRECT: The temperature will rise *to from* between 500 and 625 degrees Fahrenheit.

CORRECT: The highest temperature will be *between* 500 and 625 degrees Fahrenheit.

SHARPENING YOUR SKILLS 3

Correct the preposition errors in the following sentences.

1. Mr. Prescott stepped off of the plane in Dallas and met with company officials inside of the airport terminal.

2. Our company does not do that type work.

3. Mr. Maddox proudly declared, "By honesty is what we live!"

4. They disagreed and laughed at his proposal.

5. The receptionist showed Mrs. Werket where to sit at.

6. This is the project for which I hope to be remembered for.

EDITING EXERCISES

A. Correct the misused prepositions in the following list. If the item does not contain a preposition error, write the word *correct* next to it. Consult a dictionary if necessary.

1. capable to	5. devoted on
2. object to	6. restrain from
3. justified in	7. superior than
4. interfere on	8. similar to

B. Move the misplaced prepositional phrases in the sentences below. If necessary, revise the sentences to make them clearer.

1. We took the new computers to the office in the truck.

2. At the company picnic, children must be with an adult under 12 years of age.

3. The telephone is constantly ringing on my desk.

4. Jake found the lost part after lunch under the rug.

5. The receptionist offered to place the call with a friendly smile.

6. She wrote the sign on the wall of the office with a red pen.

C. Correct the errors and improve the style in the following passage.

Thank you for your order. We hope to be capable to filling it at an early date. The mat-cutting system, along with the picture frame clamps, is sure to please you. That type of product should be superior than that with which you have been working with.

Beside these excellent products, you can choose between our high-quality glass, glass cutters, and miter boxes. Between you and I, I may be able to arrange on a special discount for additional orders. I hope to hear from you soon.

PROJECTS

Circle the prepositional phrases in a document you have written. Then answer the following questions: Which preposition did you use most often? What is the average length of your prepositional phrases? How many sentences begin with prepositional phrases? Choose one of your sentences to revise. Change it by moving the prepositional phrases to alternative locations. If possible, find a prepositional phrase that can be condensed or eliminated.

13
Conjunctions

Look closely at the letter below. Can you think of ways to improve it?

Dear Valued Customers:

We appreciate your business. We are sending you our new catalogue of values. We offer new products. The designs have been improved. We offer high-quality extras. Our prices are as low as ever.

Did you notice how short and choppy the sentences are? The individual sentences are not hard to read, but the letter is difficult to follow because the relationships between the ideas have not been made clear. The missing words, those that show how ideas are related to each other, are conjunctions, words such as *and* and *because*.

This chapter explains how to use conjunctions to link words, word groups, and entire sentences so that you can move smoothly and logically from one idea to the next.

With conjunctions added, the letter is much smoother and clearer.

Dear Valued Customers:

Because we appreciate your business, we are sending you our new catalogue of values. We offer new products, improved designs, *and* high-quality extras, *but* our prices are as low as ever.

Because conjunctions point out the relationships between ideas, learning how to use these connectives effectively will help you improve your communication skills. Conjunctions can express a variety of relationships. Words such as *and* signal addition; words such as *but*, contrast; and words such as *or*, alternatives. Other groups of conjunctions come in pairs. *Whether . . . or* expresses alternatives; *if . . . then*, cause and effect.

CONJUNCTIONS TO JOIN EQUAL ELEMENTS

Two kinds of conjunctions join sentence elements that are similar in form and function. Coordinating conjunctions such as *and* can link one word to another, one phrase to another, and one clause to another.

pens *and* pencils

on the floor *and* on the stairs

We keep the cutting machines running all day, *and* we often use them all night.

Correlative conjunctions, such as *not only... but also,* are matched pairs of conjunctions that also join similar sentence elements.

The new machine is *not only* timesaving *but also* cost-effective.

Conjunctive adverbs, such as *however* and *therefore,* are not, strictly speaking, conjunctions. They are, however, like conjunctions in that they provide a link between similar sentence elements. They join two independent clauses (clauses that can stand alone as sentences). They also provide a transition between two sentences.

The company did not meet its production goals for the first quarter; *therefore,* adjustments in purchasing will be necessary.

The company did not meet its production goals for the first quarter. *However,* the employees are not at fault.

Coordinating Conjunctions

Coordinating conjunctions link sentence elements which are of the same kind and which function in the same way. Although there are only seven coordinating conjunctions, they are among the most common words in English.

and	for
but	yet
or	nor
so	

And, but, or, and *so* are frequently used to join words, phrases, and clauses. In addition, each conjunction has a special meaning that helps it express the particular relationship between the elements it connects. *And* shows a succession of elements.

Megan wrote the report, Barry typed it, *and* Arlene presented it to the board.

But expresses contrast.

Susan asked for a raise, *but* she didn't get one.

Or indicates cause and effect or an alternative.

> You must finish your work, *or* you will not get paid.

> He left the report at the office *or* at home.

So indicates a result or a consequence.

> We did not hear from you, *so* we will leave the conditions of your account the same.

For, yet, and *nor* are less common coordinating conjunctions. *For* is usually used as a preposition.

> I went to the newsstand *for* the latest issue of the magazine.

When *for* is used as a coordinating conjunction, it means "because" and joins two independent clauses.

> Mr. Gormley was upset, *for* he had lost the firm's largest account.

Yet has the same meaning as *nevertheless*. *Yet* is often preferable to *nevertheless* because it is shorter and clearer.

> I worked with Danette for a year, *yet* I never got to know her.

Nor has the same meaning as *or*, but it is negative. *Nor* must follow a grammatically negative word, such as *no, not, never,* or *neither*.

> He liked neither typing *nor* filing.

To emphasize a negative idea, *nor* can replace *or* in sentences containing negative words. *Cindy would not answer the telephone, nor would she work late* is stronger than *Cindy would not answer the telephone or work late.*

Punctuating Sentences With Coordinating Conjunctions. You have probably noticed that a comma is not used when a coordinating conjunction joins two words or phrases. However, when a coordinating conjunction joins two independent clauses, a comma is placed before the conjunction. Refer to Chapter 19 for more about punctuation with coordinating conjunctions.

Beginning Sentences With Coordinating Conjunctions. Coordinating conjunctions are normally used to join two similar parts of the same sentence and are therefore found within the sentence. Sometimes, however, they are used at the beginning of a sentence, linking it with the previous sentence. Such positioning of a coordinating conjunction gives it extra emphasis.

> We have not yet begun. *But* we must start soon.

Violating the general rule of placing conjunctions within sentences attracts the reader's attention. Remember, though, that starting a sentence with a coordinating conjunction is informal and can make your writing choppy if overused.

To start a sentence in a more formal way, use a word such as *also* or a phrase such as *in addition* instead of *and*. Try substituting *however* or *on the other hand* for *but*.

Correlative Conjunctions

Correlative conjunctions are matched pairs of conjunctions used to link ideas and emphasize them. The following are the most common correlative conjunctions:

both . . . and	not only . . . but also
either . . . or	whether . . . or
neither . . . nor	

Correlative conjunctions always come in pairs. Thus, whenever you use *not only*, you must also use *but also* later in the same sentence.

> *Not only* does this lawn mower do a superior job, *but* it *also* costs less than the competing model.

The words in correlative conjunction pairs are not interchangeable; avoid using *neither* with *or* and *either* with *and*.

Conjunctive Adverbs

Conjunctive adverbs link independent clauses that are in the same sentence; they also provide a transition between two separate sentences. Conjunctive adverbs that join two independent clauses are usually preceded by a semicolon and are sometimes followed by a comma. See Chapters 19 and 23 for a further discussion of how to punctuate these transitional elements within sentences and between sentences.

The appropriate conjunctive adverb is determined by the relationship between the two clauses or sentences. For example, if the second clause or sentence is a result of the first, you might use the conjunctive adverb *therefore*.

> Business has been bad this year; *therefore,* the employees' annual bonuses will be smaller than usual.

The adverb *however* does the opposite. It suggests that the event in the second clause or sentence is occurring in spite of what the first one says.

> Business has been bad this year. *However,* the employees' annual bonuses will be the same size as usual.

Conjunctive adverbs can show many other relationships as well. Table 13-1 lists some of the more common conjunctive adverbs, arranged in groups according to the kinds of relationships they express.

Table 13-1. Conjunctive Adjectives	
Function	Examples
Addition	also, besides, furthermore, likewise, moreover, similarly
Emphasis	indeed, obviously
Conclusion	consequently
Exception	conversely, however, nevertheless, nonetheless, otherwise
Time	finally, first, next, second, then

Placement of Conjunctive Adverbs. Conjunctive adverbs can occupy any of several positions within a sentence or clause. For example, the conjunctive adverb *however* can be located in several places in the sentences that follow. In each case, the positioning of *however* affects the emphasis of the sentence.

My new office is bright and quiet. *However,* not everyone else was as fortunate.

Our new building is very large. My office, *however,* is very small.

The new conference room is very large. The remodeled offices are, *however,* very small.

My new office is very spacious. Jonas's quarters are not, *however.*

SHARPENING YOUR SKILLS 1

Identify each coordinating word in the following sentences as a coordinating conjunction, correlative conjunction, or conjunctive adverb. Tell what part of speech or sentence part each coordinating word joins (nouns, verbs, prepositional phrases, clauses, and so on).

1. I need white, yellow, or blue paper.

2. Earl Davin has worked for Wallen Tool and Die for only three years; consequently, he is not fully vested in the pension fund.

3. Both he and I signed up for the workshop.

4. The secretary typed the letter, but he forgot to photocopy it.

5. Miss Fleming will arrive either today or tomorrow and will go straight to the conference.

6. Registrants were standing not only in the aisles but also in the hallway.

7. Jack Messer said he'd never leave the company. Obviously, he changed his mind.

8. Everyone was glad about Jan's promotion, yet we were sorry to see her leave the department.

9. Leona Hamlin had to quit her job, for her health was failing.

10. Neither jeans nor shorts would be appropriate dress for the office.

SUBORDINATING CONJUNCTIONS

Both coordinating and correlative conjunctions and conjunctive adverbs connect sentence elements that are similar in form and function. Another set of conjunctions exists to link independent clauses to subordinate clauses—clauses that cannot stand alone as sentences. These conjunctions—called subordinating conjunctions—both create subordinate clauses and show the relationship of the subordinate clause to the independent clause. Such a relationship can be one of cause, effect, time, place, condition, exception, or alternative. Note in what manner the subordinating conjunction in each of the following sentences relates the subordinate clause to the independent clause:

Although I worked at the Ajax Company for two years, I never received a promotion. (exception)

As soon as I realized my predicament, I resigned my position. (time)

I then accepted a job with a young company *so that* I might have a better chance to advance. (result)

Table 13-2 lists the most common subordinating conjunctions.

Table 13-2. Subordinating Conjunctions	
after	now (that)
although	once
as	on condition that
as far as	provided (that)
as if	seeing (that)
as long as	since
as soon as	so that
as though	such that
because	supposing (that)
before	than
considering (that)	that
even if	though
even though	unless
even when	until
except (that)	when
how	where
if	wherever
in case	whether
in order that	while
in that	why

SHARPENING YOUR SKILLS 2

Identify the subordinating conjunction in each of the following sentences.

1. The new manager is more efficient than Mr. Daley ever was.
2. As far as I'm concerned, we can start the project anytime.
3. Frank was hired because Mr. Latimer recommended him.
4. If sales do not improve, the store will be closed.
5. Supposing I don't finish, what will happen then?

COMMON CONJUNCTION ERRORS

Two main errors that occur when using conjunctions are joining nonparallel sentence elements and mistaking various parts of speech for conjunctions or using the wrong conjunction.

Lack of Parallel Structure

The words joined by a coordinating conjunction should be in the same form and have the same function. For example, a noun should be linked with a noun, a prepositional phrase with a prepositional phrase, a clause with a clause, and so on. When similar sentence elements are linked in this way, they have parallel structure.

When the elements joined by coordinating conjunctions are not in parallel form, the result is a sentence that is misleading and awkward.

> In Jim's opinion, the new manager was a *dictator, snobbish,* and *she never spent a penny.*

This sentence is difficult to read because a noun, an adjective, and a clause have been incorrectly joined. In the corrected version, all the elements have been changed to nouns.

> In Jim's opinion, the new manager was a *dictator,* a *snob,* and a *miser.*

The sentence elements being joined by correlative conjunctions must also be parallel. In the following sentence, *both* is misplaced.

> She was *both* unhappy with the salary *and* the hours.

Moving *both* so that each conjunction is followed by a noun results in a smoother, clearer sentence.

> She was unhappy with *both* the salary *and* the hours.

Mastering parallel sentence structure is a vital grammatical skill. You will read more about it in Chapter 35.

SHARPENING YOUR SKILLS 3

Revise these sentences so that the elements are parallel.

1. Jane was neither in her office nor eating lunch.

2. Mrs. Chin wanted an assistant who was cheerful, in good health, and efficient.

3. Every night the custodian emptied the wastebaskets, and the floor was swept by her too.

4. We wondered whether to send the letter or should we wait.

5. Typing and to file are my preferences.

Mistaken Conjunctions

Another common error is using other parts of speech as conjunctions.

Using *Like* Instead of *As, As If,* or *As Though.* In informal speech, the word *like* is sometimes used as a subordinating conjunction. *Like,* however, is actually a verb, preposition, or noun. Formal usage, then, requires *as, as if,* or *as though.*

> INCORRECT: He acts like he knows what he's doing.

> CORRECT: He acts *as if* he knows what he's doing.

Using *Being That* or *Being As* Instead of *Because.* *Being that* and *being as* cannot be used as conjunctions in formal usage.

> INCORRECT: *Being that* it is late, we should begin the program.

> CORRECT: *Because* it is late, we should begin the program.

Using *Because* Instead of *That.* Many people object to starting a sentence with *The reason is because.* They consider the phrase redundant since *because* means "for the reason that." Instead, use *The reason is that* or *The reason is.*

Using *Plus* Instead of *And.* Do not use the preposition *plus* as a coordinating conjunction between independent clauses. Instead, use *and.*

> INCORRECT: Richard wrote the report, *plus* he prepared the illustrations.

> CORRECT: Richard wrote the report, *and* he prepared the illustrations.

Then *or* Than? These two words are easily confused. *Than,* a subordinating conjunction, is always used in comparisons.

> I am older *than* you are.

Then, a conjunctive adverb, indicates time or sequence.

> I got to work early; *then* I remembered that I had forgotten my lunch.

EDITING EXERCISES

A. Revise the following passage to correct errors that involve conjunction usage.

Our new hikers' jacket is very versatile. The reason is because with the sleeves removed, it becomes an attractive vest. Nevertheless, it both offers the protection of a jacket and the freedom of a vest. This down-filled jacket has a roll-up hood, plus it has ten pockets. The pockets can be used to hold film and for carrying maps.

B. The following sentences are short and choppy. Use conjunctions to combine them so that the line of thought is clear and smooth. Cut unnecessary words.

Many people look at want ads. They want to find job openings. Newspaper articles can provide clues to job openings. An example is a story about a popular new product. It is a clue to a business. The business is expanding. It will probably need new workers. Newspaper articles also report on industries. Sales are increasing in these industries. Earnings are also increasing. This is a clue to new jobs. News stories about promotions can also alert people to job openings. So can stories about retirements..

C. Identify the correlative conjunctions in the following sentences, and underline the parts of the sentences that should be, but are not, parallel. Then correct the sentences.

1. Whether you use computers at work or to enjoy yourself, you should handle computer disks carefully.

2. Both dust and lying in the hot sun can damage disks.

3. Neither magnetic fields nor when you touch the shiny part of a disk with your fingers should be allowed.

4. You should not only avoid bending computer disks but also not write on the disks with ballpoint pens.

5. You can store your disks either in plastic cases or get a ring binder with storage pockets.

PROJECTS

Find a short article or piece of business communication that contains a variety of conjunctions. Retype it, leaving blank spaces for the conjunctions. Then have a classmate try filling in the missing conjunctions. Compare your classmate's work with the original. How many conjunctions were the same words or were from the same group of conjunctions? Did your classmate's choice of conjunctions substantially change the meaning of the article?

14
Phrases

A phrase is a group of related words that lacks a subject and/or a predicate. Therefore, a phrase cannot express a complete thought. Instead, it functions as a single unit—adding information, color, and variety to a sentence. Good writers, therefore, make extensive use of phrases.

Phrases are named according to the type of word around which they are built. You have already studied two main types of phrases: the verb phrase and the prepositional phrase. This chapter will explain verbal phrases.

KINDS OF VERBAL PHRASES

A verbal is a verb form used as another part of speech. A verbal phrase is made up of a verbal and its modifiers, complements, and objects. Three types of verbal phrases are gerund phrases, participial phrases, and infinitive phrases.

Gerund Phrases

A gerund, which always ends in *ing*, is a verb form used as a noun. In the following sentences, the word *typing* is a gerund because it functions as a noun.

Typing is a secretarial skill. (subject noun)

Jack's favorite class was *typing*. (subject complement)

Jack enjoys *typing*. (direct object)

The office manager gave him some tips on *typing*. (object of the preposition)

A gerund, with its modifiers, complements, and objects, forms a gerund phrase, which also functions as a noun.

Running a small business requires long hours and hard work. (subject noun)

Karen's first mistake was *arriving late for work.* (subject complement)

I hate *eating my lunch fast.* (direct object)

My supervisor objected to *my having a radio at my desk.* (object of the preposition)

Notice that while a verbal does not function as a verb, it still retains some of the characteristics of a verb. Thus, a verbal can be completed by direct objects and complements, and it can be modified by adverbs and adverb phrases.

SHARPENING YOUR SKILLS 1

In the following sentences, identify each gerund phrase, and tell how it functions as a noun (as a subject, as a subject complement, and so on).

1. The committee was intent on completing the agenda and did not notice the time.
2. Part of Kim's job is keeping the supply room in order.
3. Going against company policy would be foolish.
4. The company tried sending out sample products to potential customers.
5. Ms. Beckley didn't mind taking dictation or filing the correspondence during the recent crunch.

Participial Phrases

To function as verbs, present participles such as *working* and past participles such as *hired* must be used with one or more auxiliary verbs, as in *was working* and *had been hired.*

Without auxiliaries, participles can function as adjectives. Then they are a type of verbal.

A *pounding* headache kept Charles home from work. (The present participle *pounding* modifies the noun *headache.*)

The proofreader rubbed her *tired* eyes. (The past participle *tired* modifies the noun *eyes.*)

A participial phrase includes the present or past participle and its modifiers, complements, and objects. A participial phrase, like a participle, functions as an adjective.

Rewriting sections of the report, Miguel worked hastily. (The participial phrase modifies the proper noun *Miguel.*)

The office, *painted a dull gray and green,* depressed everyone. (The participial phrase modifies the noun *office.*)

Meanwhile, Alicia sat at the next desk, *listening to a tape of the meeting.* (The participial phrase modifies the proper noun *Alicia.*)

Notice that participial phrases can appear before or after the words they modify, or they can be separated by several words.

Distinguishing Between Gerunds and Present Participles. By themselves, the words *telephoning* and *working* could be either present participles or gerunds. The only way to tell which role they play is by examining how they are used in sentences.

Telephoning ahead for reservations saved time and money.

Telephoning ahead for reservations, I saved time and money.

In the first sentence, the phrase is the subject of the verb *saved,* so it is a gerund phrase. In the second sentence, the phrase is modifying the pronoun *I,* so it is a participial phrase.

Now examine these sentences:

The woman *working overtime* is one of our best employees.

The woman earned a bonus for *working overtime.*

In the first sentence, the phrase is modifying the noun *woman,* so it is a participial phrase. In the second sentence, the phrase is the object of the preposition *for,* so it is a gerund phrase.

Unlike gerunds, introductory participial phrases and nonessential participial phrases are set off from the rest of the sentence by commas.

Solving difficult problems is his job. (gerund phrase)

Solving difficult problems, he advanced quickly in his job. (introductory participial phrase)

Distinguishing between a present participle and a gerund also enables you to control the emphasis in a sentence.

The staff watched him demonstrating the new equipment.

The staff watched his demonstrating the new equipment.

In the first sentence, the writer wanted to emphasize the person doing the demonstrating. *Him* is the direct object of the verb *watched,* and *demonstrating the new equipment* is a participial phrase modifying *him.* In the second sentence, the writer, who wanted to emphasize *demonstrating,* used the word as a gerund that is the direct object of the verb *watched.* As a gerund, *demonstrating* must be preceded by the possessive form *his.*

SHARPENING YOUR SKILLS 2

Decide whether each italicized phrase is a gerund phrase or a participial phrase.

1. *Repairing the telephone system* took the man two days.

2. The man *repairing the telephone system* took two days.

3. *Having finished his part of the work,* Roger left.

4. After *having finished his part of the work,* Roger left.

5. Evelyn's job was *keeping track of inventory.*

6. Evelyn's job, *keeping track of inventory,* was important to the company's financial success.

7. Jake remembered *having seen Sara at the conference.*

8. Jake signed Sara's expense account, *having seen her at the conference.*

ON THE JOB
Making Choices

Tyler Wilson works for the small public relations firm of Carrick & Fergus in his hometown. The president, Mr. Carrick, thinks highly of Tyler and often compliments him for his fine work.

Although Tyler likes his job, he doesn't think that it pays as much as he should be making. He has been looking around for another job.

A large public relations company, Medina & Stein, has just offered Tyler a job. The firm is located in a city about an hour's commute from Tyler's home. The new job would be similar to what Tyler is doing now, but it pays a much higher salary.

Still, Tyler isn't sure whether to take the job. He would prefer to work for a small company rather than a large one, and he really doesn't want to commute to the city. He has a few days to think it over before he has to give Medina & Stein his decision.

Tyler thinks that this is a good opportunity to ask Mr. Carrick for a raise. He has decided to tell Mr. Carrick that he has been offered another job at a higher salary. He also plans to tell the president that he enjoys working at Carrick & Fergus and that he would like to stay with the company. He is going to add, however, that Medina's offer proves that he is worth more money, and that unless Mr. Carrick gives him a raise, he will have to accept the other job. In summary, he plans to say that he hopes Mr. Carrick appreciates him and his work enough to offer him a raise so that he can stay at Carrick & Fergus.

Is this a wise course of action? What if Mr. Carrick tells him to go ahead and take the new job? If Mr. Carrick says that he can't give Tyler a raise right now, should Tyler stay in his present job and hope that he'll get a raise later? Suppose he accepts the new job and then decides that he really doesn't like it?

Infinitive Phrases

An infinitive is the base verb with the word *to* in front of it. Used this way, *to* is called the sign of the infinitive and should not be confused with the preposition. An infinitive can function as a noun, an adjective, or an adverb.

> *To succeed* was his only ambition. (subject noun)

> Mr. Miller was the first executive *to retire.* (adjective modifying the noun *executive*)

> After work, I'm too tired *to exercise.* (adverb modifying the adjective *tired*)

An infinitive phrase is made up of the infinitive and its modifiers, complements, and objects. Like an infinitive, an infinitive phrase can function as a noun, an adjective, or an adverb.

> I forgot *to complete my time card.* (object noun)

> It became her goal *to break the all-time sales record.* (adjective modifying the noun *goal*)

> Bob seems happy *to be on a new job.* (adverb modifying the adjective *happy*)

Splitting the Infinitive. You may be familiar with the term *split infinitive.* A split infinitive occurs when another part of speech, usually an adverb, comes between the sign of the infinitive and the base verb. An example is "to completely revise." In the past, grammar rules forbade splitting the infinitive. Now this rule has been relaxed. If the sentence seems more natural with the infinitive split, it is all right to do so. Your ear will be the judge.

SHARPENING YOUR SKILLS 3

Identify each infinitive phrase, and tell whether it functions as a noun, an adjective, or an adverb.

1. The main purpose of the exhibit is to attract customers.

2. It would have been more practical to start over.

3. To talk about clients behind their backs is not the best way to do business.

4. The receptionist offered to get coffee for the visitors.

5. To avoid being questioned by the employees, Mr. Weller went out the side door.

6. Jeanette Carte went back to her office to phone for a reservation.

7. Walt went to the meeting but didn't dare make his suggestion.

8. The chairperson turned to Felicia to give her a chance to explain her proposal.

Two types of errors are common when verbal phrases function as modifiers. One is the misplaced modifier, and the other is the dangling modifier.

Misplaced Modifiers

A misplaced modifier is a descriptive phrase that has been placed in a sentence in such a way that the wrong word is modified.

> Mr. Draper seemed unaware of the secretarial staff *pacing back and forth in his office.*

In this sentence, the secretarial staff appears to be pacing. The writer meant, however, that Mr. Draper was pacing. The phrase needs to be moved closer to the word it modifies.

> Mr. Draper, *pacing back and forth in his office,* seemed unaware of the secretarial staff.

Misplaced modifiers can sometimes result in humorous or ridiculous statements.

> *Lying in the top drawer of the filing cabinet,* Ms. Prohaska found the Faber file.

In this sentence, the participial phrase modifies *Ms. Prohaska.* It is unlikely, however, that Ms. Prohaska was in the top drawer. The phrase needs to be moved so that it modifies the correct word.

> Ms. Prohaska found the Faber file *lying in the top drawer of the filing cabinet.*

Dangling Modifiers

A dangling modifier is a phrase that cannot logically modify any word in the sentence. The phrase is left hanging, or dangling. Dangling modifiers occur most often when the phrase is used to introduce the sentence. To correct the error, the writer cannot simply move the phrase, as with a misplaced modifier. Instead, the sentence must be revised and the missing noun or pronoun supplied.

> On *entering the auditorium,* the size of the crowd surprised us.

In the sentence you just read, the gerund phrase is dangling, and the sentence appears to state that the size of the crowd entered the auditorium. To correct the error, the writer must supply a word that the phrase can modify.

> On *entering the auditorium,* we were surprised by the size of the crowd.

Infinitive phrases can also dangle.

> *To run efficiently,* proper maintenance is needed.

After reading this sentence, the reader wonders, What needs proper maintenance to run efficiently? A revised sentence might read:

> *To run efficiently,* the photocopying machine needs proper maintenance.

Here is an example of the most well-known dangling modifier—the dangling
participial phrase:

> The two-day conference was pleasant, *visiting associates and exchanging
> information.*

Who was visiting associates and exchanging information? Surely it wasn't the
conference! The sentence has to be revised.

> The delegates had a pleasant time at the two-day conference, *visiting asso-
> ciates and exchanging information.*

SHARPENING YOUR SKILLS 4

Correct the dangling or misplaced modifiers in the following sentences.

1. After spending two weeks on the road, Rich's desire to be a salesman
   was lost.
2. Rushing to the airport, the flight still took off.
3. Perched on the telephone wire beneath her office window, Miss Angelo
   saw a cardinal.
4. To manage well, personality traits must be considered.
5. Hank and I saw an amusing sign driving down the freeway yesterday.
6. Discouraged by this series of setbacks, the promotion was abandoned.

VERBAL PHRASES IN WRITING

Verbal phrases are useful for combining short, choppy sentences. For example,
the following two sentences can be combined into one, using an infinitive
phrase.

> Many employees came to the banquet. They honored Nick Jolson's achieve-
> ments.

> Many employees came to the banquet to honor Nick Jolson's achievements.

A gerund phrase can be used to combine these sentences:

> Jenny acts in a theater group in her spare time. It is a form of relaxation.

> Acting in a theater group in her spare time is a form of relaxation for Jenny.

A participial phrase can be used for a smoother sentence here:

> Alex brought a carton from the storeroom. It was filled with books.

> Alex brought a carton filled with books from the storeroom.

Combining sentences so that one sentence becomes a phrase within another sentence is known as embedding. You will learn more about sentence-combining techniques in Chapter 35.

SHARPENING YOUR SKILLS 5

Combine each pair of sentences by using the type of verbal phrase indicated in parentheses.

1. Many interruptions happened. They delayed the project. (infinitive)
2. Ms. Aronson asked for express mail service. With express mail service, she could get overnight delivery. (infinitive)
3. Mr. Diehl sells cars. It is his occupation. (gerund)
4. Ms. Lund plays a fine game of tennis. It is her latest achievement. (gerund)
5. I was sitting at my desk. I could see a bird on the window ledge. (participial)

EDITING EXERCISES

Correct the errors related to phrases in the following sentences. Be ready to explain your corrections.

1. I cannot bring myself to like really him.
2. Mr. Barnes had spoke before that committee many times.
3. Ms. Wilker gave the report to Tina and I for word processing.
4. I would of been here on time, but my bus was late.
5. After making the telephone call, the outcome pleased Vinnie.
6. It had something to do with him being an engineer.
7. When Mr. Flanagan retired, he had earned the respect of his associates, the admiration of his friends, and his employees loved him.
8. From his file cabinet, Mr. Mann gave me a copy of the annual report.

PROJECTS

Using articles from business magazines or the business section of your local newspaper, find examples of different types of phrases. Examine how skilled writers use phrases. Business articles can serve as a model for your own writing. They can also keep you informed on what is happening in the business community.

15
Clauses

Ned Fallon knew it was time to do something about his writing. Every time he read over a proposal or a letter he had written, he almost became seasick because his sentences were so choppy.

> Our company sells small word processors. We sell them to homes and small businesses. The cost is low. The service is excellent. The warranty for all components is two years.

To improve his writing, Ned needs to master the use of both phrases and clauses. Like a phrase, a clause is a group of related words. Unlike a phrase, a clause has a subject and a predicate. There are two types of clauses—independent and dependent.

INDEPENDENT CLAUSES

An independent clause, also called a main clause, expresses a complete thought and can stand by itself as a sentence.

> Since he had trained on a well-known word processing system, *Frank received several job offers.* (*Frank received several job offers* could be a sentence by itself.)

There may be more than one independent clause in a sentence, as in the following example:

> *Corporations are willing to invest millions of dollars in word processing systems*; however, *they will spend these sums only for products that greatly improve office production.*

High-speed printers produce letter-quality documents very quickly.

Even though a dependent clause has a subject and a verb, it does not express a complete thought. Notice how something seems to be missing from the following dependent clauses:

DEPENDENT CLAUSES

> until those products were introduced
>
> while word processing is one of the major uses of the computer
>
> because small businesses cannot afford expensive systems

A dependent clause, also called a subordinate clause, begins with an introductory word, such as *until, while,* or *because.* This introductory word limits the clause so that it cannot stand by itself and must rely on an independent clause to complete its meaning. Like a phrase, a dependent clause functions as a single part of speech—as an adjective, an adverb, or a noun.

> Small businesses can now purchase single-purpose computers for writing and editing *that are relatively inexpensive.* (adjective modifying *computers*)
>
> *Because many home and small business users have difficulty with personal computers,* these single-purpose word processors are finding a market. (adverb modifying *are finding*)

A sentence can have more than one dependent clause.

> *Although computer salespeople may disagree,* home and small business users *who type only memos, manuscripts, and letters* don't need high-performance personal computers. (The second dependent clause is part of the independent clause.)

Sometimes writers will incorrectly capitalize and punctuate a dependent clause as though it were a sentence. Although it may look like a sentence, it is not. This type of error is known as a sentence fragment or an incomplete sentence.

> Since Olseth took over as chief executive officer and chairman of the board.

> That gave the report.

Sentence fragments are discussed in more detail in Chapter 37.

SHARPENING YOUR SKILLS 1

Identify each of the following groups of words as a complete sentence or as a fragment composed of a dependent clause.

1. Although the staff worked late. *dependent*
2. As the work continued. *dependent*
3. A supervisor who directs our work. *depent*
4. The staff works late. *c*
5. Once while they were working late. *dependent*

Adjective Clauses

Like one-word adjectives and adjective phrases, adjective clauses modify nouns and pronouns. They usually begin with a relative pronoun: *what, which, who, whom, whose, that.* The pronoun connects the dependent clause to the independent clause and serves as a subject or object within the dependent clause.

In the following sentence, the adjective clause modifies the noun *manager* in the main clause. The relative pronoun *who* is the subject of the dependent clause.

> Mrs. Jackson was a manager *who always praised her staff's good work.*

In the next example, the adjective clause modifies the noun *report.* The relative pronoun *that* is a direct object in the dependent clause *that she had ordered.*

> The staff cheerfully completed the report *that she had ordered.*

In the next sentence, the adjective clause modifies the noun *Mrs. Jackson.* The relative pronoun *whom* is the object of the preposition.

Mrs. Jackson, *of whom I speak so highly,* has been with the company for 20 years.

Notice that the relative pronoun can sometimes be omitted.

The president received the report [*that*] Mrs. Jackson's staff had prepared.

She is an employee [*whom*] other companies would like to hire.

Adjective clauses can also be introduced by the relative adverbs *where, why, when,* and *how.*

Lisa didn't know the reason *why she hadn't been promoted.* (The adjective clause modifies the noun *reason.*)

She went to the file *where her records were kept.* (The adjective clause modifies the noun *file.*)

Which or That? Selecting the correct relative pronoun to introduce an adjective clause can sometimes be a problem. In Chapter 6, you studied the distinction between the relative pronouns *who* and *whom.* Writers must also pay attention when choosing *that* or *which* for sentences.

One way to decide is to look at the word the adjective clause modifies. Do not use *which* or *what* to refer to people. *Who* is used to refer to individuals, and *that* is used to refer to groups of people.

Mr. Newman was the man *who* helped me.

Another way to decide between *that* and *which* is to determine whether the adjective clause is essential or nonessential to the meaning of the sentence. *That* is used to introduce essential clauses only.

A company *that* manufactures inferior products will not be successful.

Which should generally be reserved for nonessential clauses.

The A. C. Spring Company, *which* advertises discount prices all the time, manufactures inferior products.

However, in several cases, *which* is preferable to *that* for introducing essential clauses. Use *which* when a sentence has several parallel essential clauses.

This position is one *which* will provide a challenge and *which* will lead to advancement.

Which is also preferred when *that* appears previously in the sentence. This usage avoids confusion.

That is the book *which* you will need.

You will also need to use *which* when an essential clause is constructed with one of the following expressions: *this . . . which, that . . . which, these . . . which,* or *those . . . which.*

> We are looking for *those* suspense stories *which* will thrill readers of all ages.

Notice that nonessential clauses are set off by commas, but essential clauses are not.

Adverb Clauses

Another type of dependent clause is the adverb clause. A subordinating conjunction such as *where, when, why,* or *how* introduces an adverb clause and connects it to an independent clause.

Like one-word adverbs and adverb phrases, adverb clauses modify verbs, adjectives, and adverbs.

> Phil took a typing test *when he applied for the job.* (The adverb clause modifies the verb *took.*)
>
> Phil's typing was excellent *as far as the examiner could determine.* (The adverb clause modifies the adjective *excellent.*)
>
> Phil typed faster *than any of the other applicants typed.* (The adverb clause modifies the adverb *faster.*)
>
> *Because Phil was the best typist,* he got the job. (The adverb clause modifies the verb *got.*)

Also, like one-word adverbs and adverb phrases, most adverb clauses can be moved around in a sentence. Occasionally starting sentences with adverb clauses is one way of providing variety in your writing and speaking.

> *When Phil applied for the job,* he took a typing test.
>
> *As far as the examiner could determine,* Phil's typing was excellent.

Notice that introductory adverb clauses are set off from the rest of the sentence by a comma. When an adverb clause appears at the end of the sentence, a comma is generally not used.

Noun Clauses

Noun clauses function in sentences in the same way as one-word nouns. Noun clauses can be introduced by relative pronouns such as *who, which, that,* and *what* (and by variant forms of these pronouns—*whoever, whichever, whatever*). They can also start with subordinating conjunctions such as *where, when, why,* or *how.*

> *Whoever collated this report* lost page 19. (The noun clause is the subject of the verb *lost.*)

Our supervisor asked *that we check our work more carefully.* (The noun clause is the direct object of the verb *asked.*)

The seriousness of the error depends on *what was on page 19.* (The noun clause is the object of the preposition *on.*)

No one knew *where the page was.* (The noun clause is the direct object of the verb *knew.*)

As with adjective clauses, the word *that* in noun clauses can sometimes be omitted. When it is simply subordinating a clause (and not performing a function within it), *that* can usually be dropped.

She hoped [*that*] we would never make the same mistake again.

That can also be omitted before indirect quotations.

The manager said [*that*] he didn't even know [*that*] the page was missing.

SHARPENING YOUR SKILLS 2

Identify the italicized words in each sentence as an adjective clause, an adverb clause, or a noun clause.

1. The Stanley Corporation has installed a testing program *that assesses the risk of heart disease.*

2. Right now, the program is testing only executives; in the future, it will be available to *whoever wants it.*

3. The executives receive a computerized analysis of their heart condition *after they do push-ups, pull-ups, sit-ups, and other exercises.*

4. Company executives say *the test is an ordeal.*

5. *Although each test costs $250,* it would cost far more to replace a key executive *who had had a heart attack.*

Clauses can be combined to form different types of sentences: simple, compound, complex, compound-complex, and elliptical. Knowing how to construct different types of sentences will make your writing and speaking smoother and more interesting.

CLAUSE COMBINATIONS

Simple Sentences

A simple sentence consists of one independent clause. The number of words in the sentence is not important as long as the sentence contains a verb and its subject. A sentence may contain just two words.

Secretaries type.

There are even one-word sentences.

> Begin! (The subject here, *you,* is understood.)

The following sentence has been made longer by adding modifying words and phrases and a direct object.

> Sitting at her workstation, the efficient-looking secretary with black hair typed the addresses for the form letters.

A simple sentence may have compound parts—a compound subject, a compound verb, or a compound direct object.

> *Corporations* and *small businesses* send out sales letters. (compound subject)

> They *mail* them directly to consumers and *encourage* a response. (compound verb)

> Sales letters promote various *products, services,* and *opportunities.* (compound direct object)

In these examples, the sentence parts share elements with each other; thus, these are still simple sentences. In the first example, the compound subject (*corporations* and *small businesses*) shares the verb *send out.* In the next sentence, the compound verb (*mail* and *encourage*) shares the subject *they.* In the third example, the compound direct object (*products, services,* and *opportunities*) shares the subject and verb (*letters* and *promote,* respectively). Notice that a comma is not used between compound parts unless they form a series.

Compound Sentences

A compound sentence consists of two or more independent clauses. The most common way to join independent clauses is to use a coordinating conjunction: *and, but, or, so, nor, for,* or *yet.* A comma is placed before the conjunction, unless the clauses are extremely short.

> We talked and we ate.

> Our competitors will enter a bid, but we have the right of first refusal.

> Businesses use mass mailings, or they send direct-marketing letters.

> Many businesses now use personalized direct-marketing letters, and they get the attention of potential customers much more quickly than form letters.

> Mass mailing campaigns flood the market with computer-processed sales materials, but direct-marketing letters take a more selective approach.

In the following sentence, three independent clauses are joined using commas and the coordinating conjunction and.

> The stationery is a good-quality colored bond, the letter is printed on a letter-quality printer, and the envelope carries a real stamp.

Independent clauses can also be joined by a semicolon or by a semicolon and a conjunctive adverb (*however, nevertheless, moreover, therefore,* and others).

> Mass mailing campaigns flood the market with computer-processed sales materials; direct-marketing letters take a more selective approach.

> Businesses address direct-marketing letters to specific individuals; *furthermore,* the letters appear to be personalized. (Notice the comma following *furthermore.*)

Be careful not to join two or more independent clauses with just a comma (called a comma splice) or with no punctuation at all (called a fused sentence). Errors in joining independent clauses are quite common in writing.

> INCORRECT: First comes the direct-marketing letter, then comes the in-person call.

> CORRECT: First comes the direct-marketing letter; then comes the in-person call.

> OR

> CORRECT: First comes the direct-marketing letter, and then comes the in-person call.

Complex Sentences

A complex sentence consists of one independent clause and one or more dependent clauses. The dependent clauses are italicized in the following examples.

> *Since the envelope suggests quality,* the letter usually gets past the secretary's desk.

> The letter, *which is limited to one page,* informs the prospect about the product or service.

> The writer says *that he or she will call in a few days to discuss the proposal.*

> *Because direct-marketing letters discuss a real problem that the prospect is facing,* they are more likely to receive consideration.

Compound-Complex Sentences

A compound-complex sentence consists of two or more independent clauses and at least one dependent clause. In the following sentences, the dependent clauses have again been italicized.

> *When the owner of a foreign-car repair shop wrote to owners of luxury cars,* she promised lower hourly rates and free pickup and delivery, and the letter generated a tremendous response.

> *Since banking has changed drastically in the last few years,* a newspaper publisher wrote to bankers, and he offered a wide range of current information *that could help them stay competitive.*

Elliptical Sentences

An elliptical sentence leaves out one or more words that the listener or reader can be expected to supply mentally. For example, the words *can achieve* have been left off after *bulk mailings* in the complex sentence *Direct-marketing letters can achieve a greater response than bulk mailings.*

Elliptical sentences are not fragments. In fact, they are useful for avoiding tiresome repetition. Elliptical sentences, however, are open to various kinds of errors. One of the most common is choosing the incorrect pronoun for the dependent clause. For example, this sentence is phrased incorrectly: "No one writes direct-marketing letters better than me." If you finish the comparison, you can hear that the pronoun *me* is incorrect: "No one writes direct-marketing letters better than me writes direct-marketing letters." The correct pronoun to use here is *I.*

SHARPENING YOUR SKILLS 3

Identify each of the following sentences according to its type: simple, compound, complex, or compound-complex.

1. Two tire companies plan to merge forces and operate jointly under one name. *Simple*

2. One company has a chemical division, which it plans to sell; nonetheless, it would continue making coated fabrics. *Comp. Complex*

3. Last year, one company earned $2 billion; the other earned $44 million. *Compound*

4. Although the boards of both companies have approved the merger, it won't be completed until midyear. *Complex*

5. One company is strong in retreaded tires, and the other is strong in new tires; thus, they are a perfect fit for a merger. *Compound/complex*

EDITING EXERCISES

A. Correct the errors in the following sentences. Be ready to explain your corrections.

1. Employees failing to report to work.

2. The report was not true, however, it was interesting.

3. Because sales for the last four months have been lower than projected.

4. This photocopying machine isn't working like it should.

5. That is a pen that will please the most discriminating taste.

6. The worker-suggestion program replaced the suggestion box in many companies, it has led to fruitful innovations.

7. Tanya has better communication skills than him.

8. Whomever walks in that door first will get the job.

9. Whom should I say is calling?

10. Bill wrote the grant proposal, and the summary of the pilot project.

B. Combine each pair of sentences into a single sentence, using a variety of sentence types.

1. Stan worked on the project. Al worked on the project.

2. Vandals broke into the office last night. They sprayed graffiti on the walls.

3. Marie searched the archives for the document number. She could not locate it.

4. Mr. Phillips came to the meeting. Everyone disliked him.

5. Ms. James discovered the fire in the storeroom. She called the fire department.

6. She is the woman for the job. That is obvious to us.

7. Our supervisor opened her mouth to speak, but she did not say anything. She seemed angry and upset.

8. What will you do about the project? I would like to know.

9. The computer was down. We had to write the article by hand.

10. You can make the sale. You will be promoted.

PROJECTS

Select a letter, report, or other message you have written recently. Analyze your sentence structure. Count how many simple sentences, compound sentences, complex sentences, compound-complex, and elliptical sentences you used. Did you use a variety of sentence structures? Try changing the structure of some of your simple sentences through the use of different kinds of clauses.

16

Agreement Principles

Grammatical agreement means a correspondence between words that is vital to clear communication. It means, for example, matching a singular noun with a singular verb or making all the pronouns in a sentence conform with their antecedents. Where grammatical agreement does not exist, readers might have a difficult time interpreting the meaning of a sentence.

PRONOUN AGREEMENT

Pronouns are used in place of nouns to avoid repetition. The sentence *The man had forgotten the man's time card* sounds awkward and is unclear. A clearer sentence would be *The man had forgotten his time card. His* is the correct pronoun in this sentence and agrees with *man,* the word for which it stands. Pronoun agreement means that pronouns must correspond to their antecedents in person, in number, and in gender.

Agreement in Person

Person refers to the point of view of the pronoun. Agreement in person means that pronouns have the same point of view as their antecedents. If, for example, you were talking about a group of employees, you would use the pronouns *they* or *them* to replace *employees,* rather than *I* or *you.* Most people can make pronouns agree in person without having to stop to think about it. Here is a review of the grammatical meaning of the term *person.*

1. First-person pronouns are used by a person or persons to talk about themselves.

   I lost *my* keys.

2. Second-person pronouns are used to refer to the person or persons to whom someone is talking.

   Do *you* have *your* folder?

3. Third-person pronouns are used to refer to the person(s) or thing(s) being talked about.

   The *trainees* have *their* manuals.

As you know, the same form is used for second person in both the singular and the plural. Using *you* in business communication is often effective since it clearly and directly refers to the reader or listener. On the other hand, when you use second person, be sure you do in fact mean the reader or listener rather than people in general. If you habitually use *you* to refer to people in general, you might unintentionally offend a reader who thinks that *you* refers to him or her specifically. For example, the sentence *If you are found guilty of a felony, you will be dismissed from the force* could offend police officers. The sentence *If a police officer is found guilty of a felony, he or she will be dismissed from the force* makes the same point, but in a more diplomatic way.

Once you start a sentence in one person, you should not shift to another unless you have an important reason for doing so. Such shifts can be disorienting to listeners and readers alike. Often, shifts are made from third-person pronouns (such as *he* and *they*) to those in the second person (*you*).

   A *clerk* should work hard if *you* want to be successful

Switching from *clerk* to *you* in that sentence is an agreement error. Who should work hard, the clerk or the reader? To fix this sentence, put both the pronoun and its antecedent in the third person:

   A *clerk* should work hard if *he or she* wants to be successful.

SHARPENING YOUR SKILLS 1

Correct the pronoun agreement errors in the following sentences.

1. A student must study if you want to pass this course.
2. As we inspected the grounds, you could not help noticing safety violations.
3. If anyone finds the key, you will get a reward.
4. I worked hard, but you need more time to do a good job.
5. When our manager is on vacation, she expects you to take over her responsibilities.

Agreement in Number

Pronouns should agree in number with their antecedents. Singular antecedents require singular pronouns, whereas plural antecedents require plural pronouns. For example, in the sentence *The guards patrol in their cars,* the plural pronoun *their* agrees with *guards,* the plural subject of the sentence.

An unnecessary switch in number is a common error. You probably hear people make agreement errors such as this every day: "A *person* should practice what *they* preach." The problem here is that *person* is singular, yet the speaker has selected the plural pronoun *they* to refer to the singular antecedent.

Remember that the phrase *he or she* is singular, not plural. It refers to one person only.

> INCORRECT: *Each supervisor* should choose *their* best workers for the project.

> CORRECT: *Each supervisor* should choose *his or her* best workers for the project.

Indefinite Pronouns. Indefinite pronouns are words that refer to people in general. A common grammatical error consists of using a plural possessive pronoun to refer to a singular indefinite pronoun. This error occurs frequently with the indefinite pronouns *everybody* and *everyone,* which are singular even though they may seem to refer to more than one person. You can test the fact that these pronouns are singular by putting a verb with them. You would not say "everybody are" or "everyone are." Instead, you would use a singular verb. You also need to use a singular possessive pronoun when it refers to *everybody* and *everyone.*

> INCORRECT: Does *everybody* have *their* training manual?

> CORRECT: Does *everybody* have *his or her* training manual?

If repeating *his or her* becomes awkward, you can revise a sentence like this by eliminating the pronoun.

> Does everybody have a training manual?

In speech, people do use plural possessive pronouns to refer to singular indefinite pronouns, but in formal writing, it is better to use singular pronouns with them. Below is a list of the most common singular indefinite pronouns.

anybody	nobody
anyone	no one
anything	nothing
another	somebody
everybody	someone
everyone	either
everything	neither
each	

Bear in mind that some indefinite pronouns, such as *several, few,* and *many,* are plural.

_____ left *their* folders in the conference room.

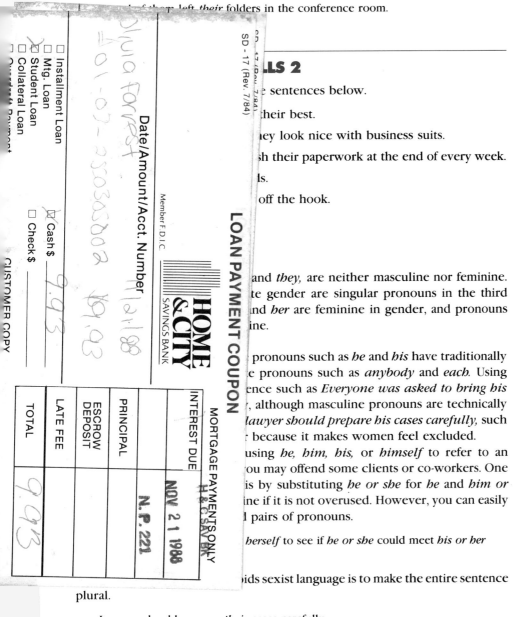

LS 2

e sentences below.

their best.

ey look nice with business suits.

sh their paperwork at the end of every week.

ls.

off the hook.

and *they,* are neither masculine nor feminine. te gender are singular pronouns in the third nd *her* are feminine in gender, and pronouns ine.

pronouns such as *he* and *his* have traditionally e pronouns such as *anybody* and *each.* Using ence such as *Everyone was asked to bring his* , although masculine pronouns are technically *lawyer should prepare his cases carefully,* such because it makes women feel excluded. using *he, him, his,* or *himself* to refer to an ou may offend some clients or co-workers. One is by substituting *he or she* for *he* and *him or* ine if it is not overused. However, you can easily l pairs of pronouns.

herself to see if *he or she* could meet *his or her*

ids sexist language is to make the entire sentence plural.

Lawyers should prepare *their* cases carefully.

Sometimes the pronoun can be omitted completely.

Lawyers should prepare cases carefully.

However, using *they* or *their* with a singular antecedent is not an acceptable solution.

> INCORRECT: A lawyer should prepare *their* cases carefully.

Your company may have a policy on how to avoid sexist language. If so, follow that policy. If not, choose the pronouns that are most likely to make you seem fair-minded without requiring awkward wording.

SHARPENING YOUR SKILLS 3

Change the wording in the sentences below to make them nonsexist.

1. Any successful person must rely on his secretary.
2. A taxpayer should prepare his return carefully.
3. Each surgeon should ensure that his instruments are sterile.
4. A secretary should keep her desk as clear as possible.
5. A client appreciates having his requests answered promptly.

VERB AGREEMENT
Just as pronouns must agree with their antecedents, verbs must agree with their subjects. Gender is not a problem in verb agreement because no English verb has different forms for male and female subjects. Likewise, agreement in person presents few problems for native speakers.

Verb agreement in number—matching a singular subject with a singular verb and a plural subject with a plural verb—does need more attention. Fortunately, most verbs have only a few forms. A typical verb, such as *work,* has only one form in the past tense—*worked*—for all three persons and for both the singular and the plural. The present tense has only two forms: *works* for subjects in the third-person singular and *work* for every other person and number.

In practice, therefore, questions of verb agreement in number generally come up only in the third-person present tense. The verb requires a final *s* when the subject is *he, she, it,* or any singular noun, but not when it is *we, you, they,* or any plural noun. Even irregular verbs such as *does, is,* and *was* end in *s* in the third-person singular. Thus, *he doesn't,* rather than *he don't,* is correct. As a quick system of proofreading for subject-verb agreement, make sure that either the subject or the verb ends in *s:*

> The company operate*s* on a tight budget.

> The companie*s* operate on a tight budget.

Certain types of subject nouns and pronouns and certain sentence constructions, however, can make choosing the correct verb a problem. The following section presents common errors in subject-verb agreement.

Agreement With Indefinite Pronouns

When the subject of a sentence is an indefinite pronoun, some problems can arise because plural pronouns do not end in *s*. Singular indefinite pronouns, as listed on page 148, take singular verbs.

> Everybody always *comes* to the meetings with a pad and pencil.

Plural pronouns take plural verbs.

> Several *come* to the meetings with a pad and pencil.

Uncertainty can arise, however, with those indefinite pronouns that are sometimes singular and sometimes plural: *all, most, some, none.*

In such a case, you need to look at the rest of the paragraph to decide whether the pronouns are being used in the singular or in the plural. Look, for example, at the following paragraph:

> Managers are required to take notes at the meetings. Most of them bring a pad and pencil. Some bring tape recorders.

In this paragraph, the plural noun *managers* and the prepositional phrase *of them* are clues that *most* and *some* are plural indefinite pronouns that take plural verbs.

The indefinite pronoun *none* needs special attention. When it means "not one," *none* is treated as singular.

> None of the women *has* retired.

When it means "not any," *none* is treated as plural.

> None of the chemicals in our product *are* harmful.

Agreement With Compound Subjects
Joined by *And*

Compound subjects are composed of two or more nouns or pronouns joined by coordinating or correlative conjunctions. Compound subjects joined by *and* take plural verbs.

> Management and most of the staff *were* willing to go.

The *and* in this sentence is the signal to use a plural verb. An exception to this rule is a sentence in which the two subjects form a single unit. In such a case, use a singular verb.

> Bacon and eggs *is* my favorite breakfast.

When both of the subjects refer to the same person or thing, a singular verb is used.

> My teacher and coach *was* Jane Wilk.

Agreement With Compound Subjects Joined by *Or* or *Nor*

Verb agreement can become confusing when subjects are joined by *or* and *nor.* The basic rule is to make the verb agree with the subject that is nearer to it. When you are deciding whether to use a singular or plural verb in such a sentence, consider only the closer of the two subjects. If both subjects are plural, the verb is plural.

> Neither the secretaries nor the administrators *accept* the proposal.

If both subjects are singular, the verb is singular.

> Either Dyan or Cindy *writes* the sales letters.

If one of the subjects joined by correlative conjunctions is singular and one is plural, the verb still agrees with the closer subject.

> Either the receptionist or the secretaries *open* the mail.

Reversing the subjects results in this sentence:

> Either the secretaries or the receptionist *opens* the mail.

Although this construction is correct, it may seem odd to you. If it does, you can revise the sentence to put the plural subject second.

Agreement When Subjects and Verbs Are Separated

When choosing verbs, be careful not to be distracted by phrases or clauses appearing between subjects and their verbs.

> INCORRECT: The complexity of the new programs *are* creating problems.

> CORRECT: The complexity of the new programs *is* creating problems.

Since subjects and verbs are never in prepositional phrases, you can simplify the task of choosing the right verb by circling or crossing out prepositional phrases and reading your sentence aloud without them.

> The complexity *is* creating problems.

Be especially careful when a prepositional phrase beginning with a compound preposition comes between a subject and verb.

> The president, *together with the vice presidents,* establishes company policy.

The correct verb is *establishes* because the prepositional phrase does not affect the number of the verb. (See Chapter 12 for more examples of compound prepositions.)

Clauses can cause similar problems. In the sentence *The train that runs on the weekends arrives late,* the verb *arrives* is correct since *train* is the subject of the sentence. The clause *that runs on weekends* does not affect the number of the subject, which is singular.

Agreement When Linking Verbs Follow Subjects

Problems can also arise with linking verbs. In the sentence *Complaints about working conditions are the fifth item on the agenda,* the subject is *complaints,* not *item.* Therefore, a plural verb is required.

SHARPENING YOUR SKILLS 4

Correct the verb errors in the following sentences.

1. Mr. Michaels and Ms. Jerome has the most seniority.
2. Neither the employees nor the union are satisfied with the agreement.
3. The broadcast that is heard on Fridays attract the most listeners.
4. The dispute about employee benefits are first on the agenda.
5. A task force made up of both older and younger employees are more likely to succeed.
6. His main support are his vice president and his accountant.
7. Neither of them were late for work.
8. He don't have the right attitude.
9. The solution to many of our problems are better guidelines.
10. Questions about the operating system is most important.

EDITING EXERCISES

A. Revise the passage below to eliminate pronoun errors.

Many business people use public libraries in his or her work. Employers expect carefully researched reports; he will not like mistakes and guesses in your work. Thus, each employee should be sure they know how to use the library. Reading the most important business magazines would help anyone to do their job better. Also, business people should be familiar with the special encyclopedias, dictionaries, and abstracts available in his or her field. If a business person wants to be successful, they should also become familiar with government documents. Most libraries keep other useful booklets and materials in its vertical files.

B. In the following passage, choose the correct word in each set of parentheses.

In recent months, several employees have asked the Payroll Department to mail their checks directly to their banks. While the idea of direct deposits (is / are) a good one, we cannot mail 1,500 checks to several different banks every two weeks. Although the convenience of all employees (is / are) important to us, neither the Payroll Department nor the mailroom (is / are) presently equipped to perform this service.

Therefore, everybody who for whatever reason (wishes / wish) to have (his or her / their) paycheck mailed directly to a bank must pay a fee to cover costs. Starting next month, all employees who so (requests / request) may have their paychecks mailed to the bank of their choice for $10 per year. Note: Under this plan both an employer who is paid biweekly and one who is paid monthly (pays / pay) the same fee.

PROJECTS

Examine a business document, such as an insurance policy or a contract for a credit card, to see how pronoun gender has been handled. Does the document avoid sexist language? If so, what technique is used? If the document does contain sexist language, fix it.

17
Common Agreement Problems

Agreement, as you reviewed in the previous chapter, is a matter of matching the gender, person, and number of certain words in sentences and paragraphs. Subjects must agree with their verbs, and pronouns must agree with their antecedents.

Usually, you can determine the correct verb or pronoun to use because it sounds right in a sentence. Sometimes, however, the correct word sounds wrong at first. This chapter will help you solve such agreement difficulties.

Occasionally, after finding the subject of a sentence, you may not be certain whether it is singular or plural. Some words can be singular sometimes and plural other times. The following sections will discuss such words.

SUBJECTS THAT CAUSE PROBLEMS

Collective Nouns

Collective nouns are words that are singular in form, even though they refer to a group of people or things. Some examples of collective nouns are *crowd, class,* and *team.* A team, for example, is composed of individuals, but you can say that a team, as a whole, *works* together. A corporation is said to expand *its* product lines. Even though a corporation is made up of hundreds or even thousands of people, a corporation is referred to as a single unit.

The grammatical question remains: Are *team* and *corporation* singular or plural? When the sentence focuses on actions performed by a team or corporation as a whole, these nouns are singular.

The creative team *is* in the midst of designing a new logo.

The corporation made *its* biggest profits this past year.

Sometimes, however, a collective noun is used to refer to each member of the group, taken individually. Usually, a committee is thought of as acting together.

> The committee *meets* every Tuesday afternoon.

But, if the members act as individuals, a plural verb is used.

> The committee *are* having their portraits painted.

Some people, however, find a sentence like this awkward (perhaps because they are so accustomed to thinking of a committee as acting together). They may prefer the sentence *The members of the committee are having their portraits painted.* This sentence is also correct because the subject of the plural verb *are* is *members*, a plural noun.

SHARPENING YOUR SKILLS 1

Correct the agreement errors in the sentences below.

1. The company have begun their fall advertising campaign.
2. The training class meet in room 217.
3. An audience of top managers are more difficult to talk to than an audience of salespeople.
4. The crowd are getting out of control.
5. All the members of the committee is not present.

Number Words

Several words referring to numbers, including the word *number* itself, can be either singular or plural, depending on whether the speaker or writer is thinking of the group as a whole or of the individuals it contains. These two sentences show the difference:

> The number of workers in this plant *has* decreased in the past three months.

> A number of workers in this plant *were* late last Tuesday.

In the first sentence, the writer is thinking of the workers as a whole—how large the number of workers was three months ago and how large the number is now. In the second sentence, each individual worker was late. The writer is thinking of how many were late; the phrase *a number of workers* means about the same thing as "some workers."

Fortunately, there is an easy rule to cover this situation. Whenever you use the phrase *the number*, use a singular verb. Whenever you use the phrase *a number*, use a plural verb. The rule applies even when modifiers come between the article and the word *number*.

The very large number *was* surprising.

A very large number *were* surprising.

Words such as *majority* and *minority* follow the same patterns as collective nouns. If you are thinking about the group as a whole (*The majority agrees),* use the singular. If, however, you are thinking of the actions of separate members of the group (*The majority were divided*), use the plural.

Time and Distance Words. Sentences in which the subject is a length of time or a measure of distance can be puzzling. Words that indicate time or distance are usually singular. *Three months is a long time to wait for an order* is correct because the time described is being thought of as a whole. In *The first three months of the year are the busiest,* the months of January, February, and March are being thought of individually; that is, there is much work to be done in each individual month.

When adding numbers, you have a choice: Either a singular or a plural verb is correct. *One plus one is two* and *One plus one are two* are equally correct.

SHARPENING YOUR SKILLS 2

Correct the agreement errors in the sentences that follow.

1. The number of complaints have decreased since we began the new quality-control procedures.
2. A number of customers has complained about our billing system.
3. The majority of the executives think we are on the right track.
4. The first three years of a business is the hardest.
5. Two miles are too far to walk just for lunch.

Nouns Ending in *s*

Many nouns that end in *s* have a deceptive appearance. Words such as *news, measles,* and *economics* look plural, but they are actually singular.

The financial news from Europe *is* encouraging lately.

Measles *is* no longer a common childhood disease.

Economics *is* often a valuable course for business students.

See Table 17-1 for more examples.

On the other hand, some nouns ending in *s* are usually treated as plural, even though they name only one object: *scissors, slacks, tongs.* You cannot therefore have "a scissor" or "a tong." Note also that these words are commonly used with "a pair of." Some abstract nouns, such as *riches* and *means,* also

Table 17-1. Nouns Ending in *s*		
Singular	Plural	Singular or Plural
checkers	acrobatics	acoustics
civics	athletics	headquarters
economics	belongings	politics
gallows	credentials	sports
genetics	falls (waterfalls)	statistics
horseshoes	goods	
mathematics	means	
measles	riches	
mumps	scissors	
news	series	
physics	slacks	
	thanks	
	tongs	
	trousers	

have only a plural form. Words such as *athletics* and *acrobatics,* although they may seem similar to *mathematics* or *economics,* are usually treated as plural.

> The scissors *are* on my desk.

> His means of obtaining control of the company *were* deceptive.

> Amateur athletics in this community *are* receiving financial support from our company.

See the middle column of Table 17-1 for more examples of nouns ending in *s* that are treated as plurals.

An additional group of nouns ending in *s* are sometimes singular and sometimes plural. Words such as *politics* and *sports* fall into this category. Treat them as singular or plural, depending on your intended meaning. *Politics is a very popular topic of discussion in our office* is correct because politics is being thought of as a whole. *Her politics are too conservative for me* is also correct because here the sentence subject is the many opinions on different issues that together make up a person's political viewpoint.

Nouns Borrowed From Foreign Languages

Nouns that have retained their original plural forms from other languages are another source of agreement headaches. Many of these words are borrowed from Latin and have retained their Latin endings (*um* in the singular and *a* in the plural).

Singular	Plural
addendum	addenda
datum	data
medium	media

Other nouns come from Greek, bringing their endings (*on* in the singular and *a* in the plural) along with them.

Singular	Plural
criterion	criteria
phenomenon	phenomena

Because final *a* is such a rare plural form in English, many people have difficulty remembering that such words as *data* and *phenomena* are really plural. In fact, popular usage has now made it acceptable to treat *data* as a singular form.

Irregular Nouns

Some very common nouns such as *men, women, children,* and *feet* are irregular in the plural. Nouns that are the same in the singular and the plural are another possible source of confusion. Again, some common nouns fall into this category: *fish, deer,* and *moose* are good examples. With these words, only the sentence as a whole can tell you whether they are singular or plural. *The fish I caught were delicious* tells that you caught more than one fish. *Was* might have been the correct verb form if you had been less lucky. In the usage of hunters and fishers, the plural and the singular of most animals, birds, and fish are the same.

SHARPENING YOUR SKILLS 3

Correct the agreement errors in the sentences that follow.

1. The news from Florida are that the citrus crop will be excellent this year.

2. My scissors is missing. Has anyone seen it?

3. Although this is an excellent idea, the means for carrying it out is not available right now.

4. Politics offer an opportunity for public service.

5. The criteria for judging this product is well known to everyone in the industry.

SENTENCE TYPES THAT CAUSE AGREEMENT PROBLEMS

Agreement problems are usually easier to identify when the subject and verb occur in the expected order: the subject first, then the verb. When this usual order is reversed, you may need to look at a sentence more closely.

Sentences with relative clauses, in which the relative pronoun (such as *who, which,* or *that*) is sometimes widely separated from its antecedent, also require careful thought.

Inverted Sentences

Any time the usual order of a sentence is reversed, the sentence receives special attention. Inverting the subject and verb in a sentence can be an effective means of achieving emphasis. When inverting ordinary word order, however, pay particular attention to make sure no agreement errors creep in.

A sentence such as "Into each speaker phone goes more than 200 specially made parts" can seem effective in sales literature because it emphasizes the product by naming it first. However, rewriting the sentence in the usual order ("More than 200 specially made parts *goes* into each speaker phone") reveals an agreement error. It now becomes clear that the subject of the verb is not *speaker phone* but *parts*. The verb *go,* therefore, must be plural.

Sentences beginning with the expletives *there is, there are, here is,* and *here are* also invert the usual order of subject and verb. In the sentence *There was a sale on office supplies at the Ajax Company yesterday,* the subject of the verb *was* is *sale*, not *there*. In such sentences, the subject is always located *after* the verb.

Many questions invert the usual order of subject and verb. In the question *Where are the files on the Henderson case?* the subject *files* follows the verb *are*. In other questions, the subject comes between parts of the verb phrase.

> Why has the penalty for overdue payments been increased?

In this question, the subject is *penalty* and the verb phrase is *has been increased*.

SHARPENING YOUR SKILLS 4

Correct the agreement errors in the sentences that follow.

1. In the history of all businesses come a turning point.

2. Into all good marketing decisions go a great deal of hard work.

3. There are no better way to solve these problems.

4. There was many discussions among the top executives before they expanded the product line.

5. Where is the scissors?

Relative Pronoun Clauses

In Chapter 16, you looked at the problem of subject-verb agreement when a dependent clause separates the subject and verb in the independent clause. This section examines the problem of subject-verb agreement within the dependent clause itself.

When a relative pronoun such as *who, which,* or *that* is the subject of a dependent clause, the verb may be singular or plural. The correct choice depends on whether the antecedent of the pronoun is singular or plural. Because the same relative pronouns are used for both singular and plural antecedents, agreement problems often arise in sentences of this type.

In the sentence *The woman who gives me these instructions is very knowledgeable*, the relative pronoun *who* plainly refers to *woman*—the subject of the main clause. Since *woman* is singular, the pronoun used (*who*) is also singular, and the singular verb *gives* is needed.

Sentences with relative clauses can usually be broken down into two simpler sentences.

> The woman is very knowledgeable. The woman gives me these instructions.

The first of these two simple sentences is the main clause in the original version. The second simple sentence is combined with the first by substituting the relative pronoun *who* for the subject *woman*.

Many sentences with relative clauses are longer and more complicated than this one. In such sentences, it is sometimes hard to tell which noun is the antecedent of the relative pronoun. Consider this sentence:

> Triet Nguyen Tran is one of the men who solve problems quickly.

The name *Triet Nguyen Tran*, a proper noun, looks like the antecedent of *who*. If it were, the verb in the relative clause should be singular *(solves)*. A closer examination, however, shows that the sentence really works like this:

> Triet Nguyen Tran is one of the men. The men solve problems quickly.

The two sentences were combined in the original version by substituting the relative pronoun *who* for the subject of the second sentence. When you break down the sentence this way, you see clearly that the relative pronoun *who* is plural and requires a plural verb.

People can also be misled by a particular word in the relative clause itself. In the sentence *Personnel problems, which are his specialty, take up most of his time,* the antecedent of *which* is *personnel problems*, not *specialty*. Therefore the verb is plural. The sentence works like this:

> Personnel problems take up most of his time. Personnel problems are his specialty.

Rather than break every sentence with a relative clause into two separate sentences, check carefully for the antecedent of the relative pronoun.

SHARPENING YOUR SKILLS 5

Correct the agreement errors in the sentences below.

1. The person in the office who are responsible for these accounts is Mary Clark.

2. All packages which comes through the front door are inspected by the security guard.

3. Back orders, which is a real problem this time of the year, must be shipped as soon as possible.

4. Each of the executives who has their own expense accounts must submit receipts for his or her meals.

5. All of the trucks that is not in service must be repaired immediately.

EDITING EXERCISES

A. Correct the agreement errors in the following passage.

There is several stages in a typical career. The group of employees at the first stage is beginning their jobs. A majority of the work at this stage are routine. The criterion for advancement to the next stages are the ability to lead and the desire for more responsibility. The news are good for people at this stage. With advancement comes higher salaries and more independence. The datum show that only a few people advance further and are able to shape the future of their companies. At the top of any business is those few people who makes decisions about the company's goals. The person who reaches the top and provide leadership for all employees understand how to move successfully from each career stage to the next.

B. Correct the agreement errors in the following sentences.

1. Everybody have their book.

2. A quick decision on these questions are necessary.

3. Mr. Brubaker, together with his assistants, have chosen their new office furniture.

4. Either Chip or Derek choose the time and place of the meetings.

5. Each of the women have their application forms.

6. Our team has their game next week.

7. A number of people was late.

8. Thirty dollars a week are a good raise.

9. Physics are my favorite subject.

10. Neither books nor magazines contains the answer to my question.

The words in the following list are either always singular, always plural, or sometimes singular and sometimes plural. Look up the words in a large dictionary or other reference book. Then write sentences illustrating the correct use of five of the words.

binoculars	forceps
civics	graphics
economics	jeans
ethics	optics
eyeglasses	statistics

18
Proofreading for Grammatical Errors

Errors in the messages a company sends out can greatly damage its image. When people receive letters, reports, or proposals riddled with errors, they begin to form low opinions of the company—or individual—that cannot control errors in matters such as grammar, punctuation, and typing. Their low opinions can translate into lost business, which in turn means lost revenue—something every business wants to avoid.

Errors can also cost money in more direct ways. Suppose your company quotes a customer a price of $105.50 instead of $1,050.50. By the time the mistake is discovered, it may be difficult or impossible to recover the many dollars the error cost.

Clearly, producing error-free messages is a goal toward which all businesses should strive. One way to achieve that goal is through effective proofreading. Proofreading is the critical reading of a message and the careful marking of any errors that require correction. Accurate proofreading is an important part of the total process that produces accurate communication.

A SHARED RESPONSIBILITY

Producing accurate business communications should be the concern of every worker who participates in the communication process.

- The writer of a message is responsible for writing clear, coherent communications. He or she must pay attention to grammar and punctuation rules during the writing phase. A writer also has the responsibility of presenting a clear message to whoever will put the message into final form. A sloppy or unreadable original can cause mistakes further down the line.

• Word processors, secretaries, typists, and other support personnel have a responsibility to transcribe precisely messages created by others. People who keyboard or type documents must have a good working knowledge of grammar and punctuation in order to reproduce a written message in correct business format.

Errors During Keyboarding or Typing

This chapter is concerned primarily with proofreading for grammatical errors. Of course, a number of purely mechanical mistakes may occur during keyboarding or typing. These, too, are the concern of the proofreader, since such mistakes can alter a message. They also suggest to the reader that the company sending the message is careless and unprofessional. Review the following basic types of mechanical errors.

Transpositions. Transpositions occur when characters or words are reversed, such as keyboarding *fo* rather than *of* or *4593* rather than *4953*. Sometimes, entire words or groups of words may be transposed in a sentence. The resulting sentence usually makes no sense.

Omissions. Another common type of error consists of leaving out individual characters, whole words, or even lines or paragraphs from a message. When a letter is omitted, the mistake is usually obvious, but the omission of a number may not be noticed immediately.

Repetitions. Repetitions occur when a keyboarder or typist repeats a character, word, or line. Although this type of mistake is fairly obvious to readers and is unlikely to cause confusion, it will annoy readers and distract them from the message.

Spacing Errors. There are many spacing errors, including incorrect paragraph indention, improper spacing around punctuation or between words, and addition of space where it does not belong (such as within a word or number). Spacing errors can be merely annoying (*present ly* for *presently*), or they can garble a message (*a long side* for *alongside* or *10 25* for *1025*).

Skilled word processors, secretaries, and typists not only type accurately but also know the kinds of errors they are most likely to make. They proofread their work with these weaknesses in mind.

Proofreading is a skill that anyone can learn. Developing the following abilities can help you become a good proofreader.

THE PROCESS OF PROOFREADING

The Ability to Concentrate. To be a competent proofreader, you must read slowly and concentrate on what you are reading. It is easy to miss a mistake, especially one that you yourself have made. By concentrating on each character and each space, you will find every error.

The Ability to Read Against an Original. Often, you will proofread your typed or keyboarded copy of a message against an original. The copy must match the original letter for letter, number for number, space for space. Sometimes, proofreaders read backward when they read against an original. In this way, they are able to ignore the meaning temporarily and concentrate on each character. Other proofreaders work with a partner; one person reads the original aloud as the other checks the copy for errors.

The Ability to Read for Sense. Most proofreaders read a document at least two times—once for mechanical errors and once for sense. You must develop the ability to spot incomplete thoughts, illogical sequences, and other communication problems.

A Knowledge of the Mechanics of the Language. Effective proofreaders have an adequate grasp of the rules of grammar and punctuation. They can spot an error when they see one.

A Mastery of Proofreading Symbols. Good proofreaders know all the symbols that indicate where errors are and what corrections need to be made. These symbols, which are a type of shorthand, allow corrections to be indicated clearly and understandably.

This chapter will concentrate on proofreading for grammatical errors—the errors involving the rules you have learned in this part of the book. In Chapter 30, you will learn to proofread for punctuation and stylistic errors.

Proofreading Symbols

Proofreading symbols, also called revision marks, are the marks used universally by people who correct printed or typed copy. These symbols are designed to show—in the smallest amount of space possible—where a correction should be made and what it should be. You must practice making these marks precisely and using them accurately. Table 18-1 provides a list of the most commonly used proofreading symbols. The Appendix gives a complete list. (Refer to the Appendix if you come upon any symbols in this chapter with which you are not familiar.)

When there is room, write corrections above the errors. However, in a single-spaced document, make the symbols on the line and put the corrections in the margin, as shown in this example:

e/to be/can/s   twic/ as often a/s seems necessary₀we avoid thi/ problem by merely scheduling

plant/   trips to the ~~building~~

Here is the corrected version:

> twice as often as seems to be necessary. We can avoid this problem merely by scheduling trips to the plant

Notice that some corrections (such as transpose, delete, and close up) are complete with nothing written in the margin. Where there are marginal notations, they are shown in order of appearance in the line, and they are separated by slashes.

Table 18-1. Commonly Used Proofreading Symbols

Correction	Symbol	Example of Marked Copy	Example of Corrected Copy
Insert character	‸	th‸re (e)	there
or word		it‸true (is)	it is true
Insert space	# ‸	How‸can (#)	How can
Insert period	⊙	to me⊙	to me.
Add on to word	‿	present‿s	presents
Delete letter	ℓ	why ~~o~~not	why not
or word	—ℓ	now ~~now~~ or	now or
Delete and close up space	ℓ with close-up marks	plain~~e~~ly	plainly
Delete space	⁐	on‿to	onto
Capitalize letter	≡	twice (≡ under t)	Twice
or word		danger (≡ under word)	DANGER
Lowercase letter	/	/White	white
or word	/‾‾‾	/CAUTION	caution
Transpose letters	⌴⌐	hte	the
or words		of process	process of
Change word	— or ‸—ℓ	~~two~~ three	three
		~~two~~ three	three
Change letter	/	afflu/nt (e)	affluent
Align vertically	‖	‖Raymond Joseph	Raymond Joseph

SHARPENING YOUR SKILLS 1

Write the symbol that indicates each of the following corrections.

1. Capitalize letter or word.

2. Delete space.

3. Insert character or word.

4. Insert period.

5. Transpose letters or words.

COMMON NOUN PLURAL ERRORS

The noun errors you should be watching for fall into two broad categories, both involving plurals: plural formation errors and confusion between the possessive and plural forms.

Most plural formation errors occur when plurals are formed in some way other than by the addition of *s*—as when the noun ends in *s*, *x*, *ch*, *sh*, or *z* or when the plural is irregular or foreign. Only familiarity with plural forms will allow you to proofread effectively for these errors.

Many writers confuse plural and possessive forms. When you see a word ending in *s*, *'s*, or even *'*, ask yourself whether the plural or the possessive is required.

The paragraph that follows includes several noun plural errors that have been marked for correction.

Our ~~companies~~ *company's* study shows that word processor's have many advantages over electronic typewriters. We used a number of criterions *a* in evaluating the efficiency of the machines we tested. Our study shows that in every one-to-one test, a word processors capabilitys *ies* are infinitely superior to an electronic typewriters.

PRONOUN PROBLEMS

Like noun errors, grammatical problems involving pronouns fall into two major categories. Writers generally have trouble choosing between a subject pronoun and an object pronoun or distinguishing between pronouns and other words that sound like them.

The problem of choosing the correct pronoun most often occurs when two pronouns follow a preposition (as in *between you and me*) or when a comparison is being made (as in *Who knows better than I?*). The pronouns *who* and *whom*, along with *whoever* and *whomever*, also give many writers problems.

Pronoun sound-alikes that cause the most trouble are the following:

its / it's
your / you're
their / there / they're
theirs / there's
whose / who's

When you proofread, scrutinize your message for such errors. The paragraph that follows has been marked for correction of pronoun errors.

The friendship between him and ~~I~~ me goes back a long time; it's beginning was

in our college days when we would spend long nights together studying. He

was always a harder worker than ~~me,~~ I and his grades proved it. ~~They're~~ There was

never any doubt in my mind that he would be a great man someday.

SHARPENING YOUR SKILLS 2

Use proofreading symbols to correct the following noun plural and pronoun errors. Then rewrite the sentences in correct form.

1. Loretta generally proofreads better than me.
2. Mr. Valencia does not know whom is chairperson of the committee.
3. All bank branchs will be open on Monday.
4. They're is really no reason to postpone the president's luncheon.
5. How many employee's will attend the seminar?

ERRORS IN VERB USE

The most common errors writers make when using verbs fall into two categories. The first error involves subject-verb agreement. Subjects and verbs, of course, must agree in number. When the subject is a collective noun, a foreign noun, an indefinite pronoun, or a compound subject, choosing between singular and plural verb forms may cause problems.

The second category of errors involves choosing between a transitive verb and an intransitive verb. Examples would be the choices between *lie* and *lay* and *rise* and *raise*. In each case, one verb is intransitive (*lie, rise*) and takes no object. The other is transitive (*lay, raise*) and takes an object.

The paragraph that follows includes several verb errors. They have been marked for correction.

The committee believes that the root of employee dissatisfaction ~~lays~~ lies in

the comparatively low salary levels at Morgan Products. Unless we allow salary levels to r̂ise to current market levels within five years, we may find that most of our best workers ~~has~~ *have* resigned.

SHARPENING YOUR SKILLS 3

Use proofreading symbols to correct the folllowing verb use errors. Then rewrite the sentences in correct form.

1. Lie the cloth on the table before trying to cut it.
2. Every one of the products have a defect.
3. The marketing team have come up with a very promising campaign.
4. Three typists and one manager is needed for this project.
5. Parentheses is always used around part numbers.

DID YOU KNOW?
Proofreading With a Partner

Proofreading at work often means working with someone else to check for errors. If possible, find a partner so that one of you can read the original document while the other person proofreads the copy. With this technique, proofreading will be both quicker and easier. When you proofread with someone else, try the following tips:

1. If you are proofreading, keep your place with a finger or with the end of a pencil. Aim for 100 percent accuracy.

2. If you are reading the original document, read slowly and carefully, grouping related words together in phrases that make sense. Speak in a clear voice, and pronounce words carefully.

3. Spell out difficult words, such as people's or companies' names or words that could easily be misspelled. To do this, you must proofread letter by letter. rather than word by word. Read numbers in the same way, one number at a time.

4. Both you and your partner should place a blank sheet of paper under each line as you read or proofread it. Then you can concentrate on one line at a time.

5. If you are proofreading a word-processed copy, make your corrections in a bright, contrasting color so that you will not miss any corrections when you type them in.

6. Trade tasks midway through a long proofreading job so that one person does not have to read or find errors for too long at a time. Varying the tasks helps improve accuracy.

Writers frequently misuse an adjective for an adverb and vice versa. The most commonly confused adjective-adverb pairs are *bad / badly, good / well, real / really,* and *sure / surely.* Comparison of adjectives also causes problems, which include double comparisons (*more better* or *least happiest*) and comparison of absolute adjectives (*less final* or *more entirely*).

    The paragraph that follows shows some adjective and adverb errors, marked for correction.

ADJECTIVE AND ADVERB PROBLEMS

    All of us at Mason Electronics feel very bad~~ly~~ about your uncle's untimely

death. Had he been a~~more~~ older man (inserted: *n*), his death would not have come as

such a shock. ~~Most~~ (Few) of us ~~thought~~ (realized) that the illness he had was ~~less fatal than it~~

~~proved to be.~~ We all mourn the death of this ~~most~~ unique man.

Notice that correcting an error involving the comparison of an absolute adjective may require the reconstruction of the sentence.

SHARPENING YOUR SKILLS 4

Use proofreading symbols to correct the following adjective and adverb errors. Then rewrite the sentences in correct form.

1. Trevor was sure relieved to discover that no harm had come to the building.

2. That double-breasted suit looks well on men with broad shoulders and narrow waists.

3. Mr. Pratt is real impressed with the report Alex Maxwell prepared.

4. People usually find it more easier to talk on the telephone than to write a letter.

Common writing mistakes include using the wrong preposition in certain constructions and adding prepositions where they do not belong. The most commonly confused preposition pairs are *between / among, beside / besides,* and *from / off.* Watch for these prepositions as you proofread to be sure you have used them correctly.

    Some writers add prepositions such as *at, from, of, to,* and *with* where they are not needed. When you see "The strike is finally over *with*" or "Our building is opposite *to* the bank" (and similar constructions), delete the unnecessary preposition.

PREPOSITION ERRORS

The paragraph that follows shows several preposition errors, marked for correction.

The proposed building site has caused quite a stir ~~between~~ *among* the five members of the committee. Beside~~s~~ the problem of the distance from the present site, some question exists about whether adequate transportation is available. The site is a vacant lot ~~among~~ *between* two factories and opposite ~~to~~ a high school. It is not near ~~to~~ the train station or any public bus route.

MISUSE OF CORRELATIVE CONJUNCTIONS

Correlative conjunctions come in pairs—*both / and, either / or, neither / nor, not only / but also,* and so on. Because these conjunction pairs compare like items, the elements that follow them should be parallel. When you see correlative conjunctions, make certain that a word is compared with a word, a phrase with a phrase, and a clause with a clause.

The paragraph that follows includes several errors involving correlative conjunctions, marked for correction.

Operating this machine is not difficult, but it takes some time to learn the procedure. Keep the enclosed instructions handy at all times. Remember that when the fluid light goes on either you must add fluid or turn the machine off. Letting it run dry will damage the motor. Fortunately, ~~not only do~~ you have *not only* a light to remind you but also a buzzer. Either call Clarice or me if you need any further assistance.

Notice that for the last correction you must not only transpose words but also change the capitalization, since a different word begins the sentence.

SHARPENING YOUR SKILLS 5

Use proofreading symbols to correct the following preposition and conjunction errors. Then rewrite the sentences in correct form.

1. The problem is caused not only by poor communication but also laziness.
2. Beside Elton and Frances, who was promoted this year?
3. Where will the new branch be located at?
4. Either we must cut costs or raise prices.
5. There are differences of opinion between the 11 members of my department on how to increase productivity.

EDITING EXERCISES

A. Proofread each of the following sentences, using the proper proofreading symbol to mark each grammatical error. Then rewrite the sentences in corrected form.

1. If we rise the height of the windows six inches, we will achieve a more balanced effect.

2. You can obtain the figures for the 1988 budget off Robert Decatur.

3. We at Chang Purification Systems can do the job good for you.

4. The news media has been thoroughly briefed on the current status.

5. We neither have the time nor the money to pursue this project further.

6. We will hire whomever is best for the position.

7. The accommodations for the industrial show were real comfortable.

8. When you arrive, give you're name to my assistant, Ms. Roberts.

9. Hearing of your retirement, I both felt happy and sad.

10. Beverly Shultz was sure glad that the Board of Directors agreed.

B. Proofread the following paragraphs, using the proper proofreading symbols to mark each grammatical error. Then rewrite the paragraph in corrrected form.

1. Nistok Shoes is having a Labor Day Sale on September 1. A number of shoes and boots in our inventory is going on sale. Accessorys such as socks, laces, and shoe care products will be on sale as well. You won't find a more better deal in the metropolitan area—come and save at our Labor Day Extravaganza!

2. Reading over the annual report, I am beginning to wonder if we have kept in mind where our priorities should be at. This company was founded by two men who believed in equal opportunity for all. The Board of Directors have to meet—soon—to discuss the future direction of this firm.

PROJECTS

Locate a fairly long document that you have written. Rewrite it, adding grammatical mistakes that fall into the categories discussed in this chapter. Try to vary the errors, and do not make them too obvious. When you have finished, retype the document with the errors. Exchange documents with a classmate, and proofread each other's work for grammatical errors. When you think you have found all of them, exchange papers again and check each other's work. Did either of you miss any errors? If so, what kinds? Did either one of you find an error that the other person did not even know was there?

PART THREE
APPLYING THE RULES OF PUNCTUATION AND STYLE

19
Commas

Jerry Dowdell, the manager of a small chain of shoe stores, wanted to know the sales figures for blue shoes, suede shoes, and athletic shoes. He sent the following memo to the stores:

> Please send me March sales figures on blue suede and athletic shoes.

The responses came back this way:

> blue suede: 144
> athletic: 327

Jerry had to call the stores to explain what he wanted, and his salespeople had to spend extra time retallying. The problem would have been avoided if the sentence had been punctuated correctly.

> Please send me March sales figures on blue, suede, and athletic shoes.

The problem was not that Jerry did not know management; he did not know commas.

The comma is the most important punctuation mark used within the sentence. The comma has two basic functions: (1) to break down a complicated sentence into simple components so that the reader can understand the sentence more easily; and (2) to separate items in a series (as in Jerry Dowdell's memo).

Many students learn that a comma is used whenever there is a pause in the sentence. This guideline, while helpful, is not quite accurate. A comma is used in specific situations to separate the sentence into its parts. Remember that all sentences are built around a simple sentence consisting of a subject and a verb. As a sentence becomes more complex, commas are needed to keep the meaning of the sentence clear.

Consider the simple sentence below (which will be used throughout the chapter as a building block):

> Our company doubled its profits last year.

Here is a second simple sentence:

> We expect to do better this year.

These two simple sentences can be made into a compound sentence by joining them with a conjunction.

> Our company doubled its profits last year, *and* we expect to do better this year.

When two simple sentences are joined by a conjunction, a comma is placed before the conjunction, but never after it.

In joining two simple sentences, be sure to use both the comma and the conjunction. A comma by itself is not sufficient. If there is no conjunction joining two sentences, the appropriate punctuation mark is a semicolon, a colon, or a period.

> Our company doubled its profits last year; we expect to do better this year.

WITH INDEPENDENT CLAUSES IN A COMPOUND SENTENCE

Computer storage makes it easy to access information about individual customers.

WITH AN INTRODUCTORY ELEMENT

When an introductory word, phrase, or clause is added to the sentence, it is usually separated from the main part of the sentence by a comma. Look again at the basic simple sentence:

> Our company doubled its profits last year.

The following examples show how various introductory clauses, phrases, or words may be added to the sentence:

> *Although costs rose,* our company doubled its profits last year. (a subordinate clause)

> *Under its new management,* our company doubled its profits last year. (a prepositional phrase)

> *Happily,* our company doubled its profits last year. (an introductory word)

As with the compound sentence, the best way to identify an introductory element requiring a comma is to locate the basic sentence and see whether anything is added on at the beginning. If the added word, phrase, or clause is not essential to the meaning of the sentence, use a comma.

Another way to recognize an introductory element quickly is to be alert to the words often used in this way. Some of the most common ones are listed below.

accordingly	now
actually	nevertheless
consequently	obviously
finally	otherwise
first	originally
fortunately	so
however	theoretically
meanwhile	then
moreover	therefore
naturally	thus
next	

However, before adding a comma, make sure that the word is used in an introductory capacity and is therefore nonessential.

> *Originally,* our store sold only photographic equipment. (nonessential)

> *Originally* selling only photographic equipment, the store recently began to sell video cameras as well. (essential)

In the first sentence, *originally* stands alone as an introductory word that is not essential to the meaning of the sentence. In the second sentence, *originally* is the first word of an entire introductory phrase.

When an introductory word does not require a pause after it in speech, the commas may be omitted.

Finally we got here!

Then the motor started.

Introductory clauses often begin with subordinating conjunctions. Whenever you use a word such as *although, because,* or *unless* to start a sentence, it is likely that you are creating a subordinate clause that must be separated from the rest of the sentence by a comma.

Unless disaster strikes, we expect to do better this year.

Notice that there is a natural pause at the end of the subordinate clause, which alerts you to the need for a comma.

Verbal Phrases

Be sure to distinguish between a participial phrase and a gerund phrase at the beginning of a sentence. In that location, the participial phrase takes a comma.

Using new production methods, our company doubled its profits last year.

The gerund phrase at the beginning of the sentence takes no comma.

Using new production methods resulted in a 40 percent increase in worker output.

In the first sentence, the subject is *company*. The verbal phrase provides added information to the basic sentence, so the phrase is set off with a comma. In the second sentence, however, the verbal phrase is a gerund and is the subject of the sentence, so no comma is used. Another way to distinguish between participial and gerund phrases in this situation is to see whether the introductory verbal phrase is followed by a verb, a noun, or a pronoun. If it is followed by a verb, as in the second sentence, the phrase is a gerund acting as the subject and should not be set off by a comma. A noun or pronoun indicates a participial phrase.

Infinitive Phrases

If an infinitive phrase is added to a simple sentence, a comma is used to separate the two sentence parts.

To prove that investment in new technology can pay off, our company doubled its profits last year.

However, if the infinitive phrase is the subject of the sentence, no comma is used. (Note that an infinitive phrase that acts as a subject is followed by a verb.)

To prove that investment in new technology can pay off is one of our goals.

Remember, if you locate the simple sentence first, you can spot an added introductory element more easily. You can then make a decision about whether the introductory element requires a comma.

SHARPENING YOUR SKILLS 1

Insert the missing commas in the following sentences. If a sentence does not require any commas, write the word *correct* next to it.

1. Our company doubled its income last year so we are optimistic about future growth.

2. Mr. Reynolds has scheduled a meeting at 10 a.m. Thursday and all department heads should attend.

3. All employees are expected to sign in when they arrive but it is not necessary to sign out at lunchtime.

4. Benefiting from its new advertising the music store sold 3 trombones and rented 15 instruments to students from Lakewood High School.

5. Because our videocassette recorders have been highly rated by experts our company was able to double its profits last year.

6. Nevertheless we will continue to use the SFX-123 copier.

7. Under the new system the four administrative assistants will rotate tasks daily.

8. To write an effective memo you should use the fewest words necessary to communicate your idea.

WITH A SUBORDINATE CLAUSE AT THE END OF A SENTENCE

Like a subordinate clause at the beginning of a sentence, a subordinate clause at the end of a sentence is usually set off with a comma.

   Our company doubled its profits last year, *although costs rose.*

However, if the subordinate clause is necessary to complete the meaning of the sentence, no comma is used.

   The new sales figures will be distributed *before the month ends.*

Note that in sentences like the two above, natural pauses help you determine whether or not to use a comma. The first sentence calls for a pause, indicating that the clause is nonessential. In the second sentence, there is no natural pause before the subordinate clause, which helps you determine that the clause is an essential element.

Elements that interrupt a sentence in the middle and are not essential to its meaning are also set off from the main part of the sentence. Two commas are necessary, however, to set off interrupters.

Words

A single word may interrupt a sentence.

> Our company, *consequently*, doubled its profits last year.

The following words are among those commonly used as interrupters:

accordingly	moreover
consequently	nevertheless
however	therefore

Be sure to use two commas, not one, to set off such words completely from the main part of the sentence.

Phrases

Similarly, a phrase may interrupt the sentence. Such elements are often called "parenthetical," a slightly misleading name since they are not placed in parentheses. However, they do give extra information that is not essential to the meaning of the sentence.

> Our company, *though only a few years old*, doubled its profits last year.

You can see that when the phrase *though only a few years old* is omitted, the basic meaning of the sentence is unchanged. Some typical phrases that often occur as interrupters are listed below.

after all	as a matter of fact
for instance	on the other hand
for example	so to speak

All such phrases in a sentence should be set off by commas.

Be careful always to use two commas, one before and one after the phrase. One comma would have the effect of separating the subject from the predicate.

Clauses

The same rule applies to clauses that interrupt the sentence with extra information.

> Our company, *if the present trend continues*, will more than double its profits this year.

Clauses beginning with the following conjunctions are often interrupters:

as	before	since
because	if	when

However, make sure that a clause set off by commas really contains nonessential information. If the clause changes the meaning of the basic sentence, it should *not* be separated from it by commas.

> The secretaries, *when the new typewriters arrive*, will be able to do their jobs better. (nonessential)

> Please inform Mr. Brooks *when the new typewriters arrive* so he can inspect them. (essential)

Omitting the clause *when the new typewriters arrive* from the second sentence would render the sentence almost meaningless. The clause, therefore, is essential.

SHARPENING YOUR SKILLS 2

Insert the missing commas in the following sentences. If a sentence does not require any commas, write the word *correct* next to it.

1. Our company, can triple its profits this year, if the new development in microchips is successful.

2. Municipal bonds may be a good investment, since they are tax-exempt.

3. The supervisor, reports that frequent rest periods, make workers more productive, because fatigue is lessened.

4. Unfortunately, we will not be able to fill your July 12 order, because the item requested has been discontinued.

5. The new timetable, although it is shorter than the old one, provides enough time for testing the product.

6. The months of June, and July, therefore, are expected to account for the largest volume of sales.

7. Please, do not leave the office while the machine is running.

8. The X-100 fan, if my figures are correct, uses only 59 cents worth of electricity per week.

WHO, WHICH, AND *THAT* CLAUSES

What is the difference between the *which* and *that* clauses in the two sentences below?

> Our company, *which makes food processors*, doubled its profits last year.

> The company *that makes food processors* doubled its profits last year.

In the first sentence, the clause is parenthetical. It is not essential to the meaning of the sentence. Therefore, it is set off from the sentence with commas. In the second sentence, the clause is necessary; it identifies the company as the one "that makes food processors." Because the clause is essential, it is not separated from the rest of the sentence.

Clauses beginning with *that* always contain essential information, so they are never set off with commas. Clauses beginning with *which* are usually nonessential, which means they require commas.

Clauses beginning with *who* can function either way.

> Ms. Jensen, *who works in the budget office*, is an accountant. (nonessential)

> The woman *who works in the budget office* is an accountant. (essential)

In the first sentence, the *who* clause simply provides extra information, which means that it should be set off from the rest of the sentence. In the second sentence, the *who* clause identifies a particular woman, making it necessary to the meaning of the sentence.

SHARPENING YOUR SKILLS 3

Insert the missing commas in the following sentences. If a sentence does not require any commas, write the word *correct* next to it.

1. The letters that I dictated yesterday should be mailed this morning.
2. Our new fee schedule, which goes into effect on October 31, will simplify the computation of freight charges.
3. A few part-time employees who are not eligible for the company health plan, are seeking higher wages as compensation.
4. Our store, carries a large selection of men's and women's sportswear, which will be on sale this week.
5. Ms. O'Connor, who is in charge of customer relations, has been with Mason's for three years.

WITH APPOSITIVES

As you have already learned, an appositive is a noun or noun phrase that renames the noun it follows. Appositives are usually separated from the rest of the sentence by commas.

> The 1200-Z, *our finest quadraphonic receiver*, sells for $1,500.

However, a one-word appositive, if it identifies the noun preceding it, is not set off by commas.

> My brother *Ted* just received a promotion.

> The year *1985* held few surprises for the oil industry.

SHARPENING YOUR SKILLS 4

Insert the missing commas in the sentences below. If a sentence does not require any commas, write the word *correct* next to it.

1. Our company, the Johnson-Weller Corporation, doubled its profits last year.

2. Please send copies of the report to Mr. Baxter in sales and to Ms. Peres the director of advertising.

3. Ms. Lewis, the attorney for the defendants, would like to set up a meeting of all parties involved in the lawsuit.

4. We arranged to rent the film *Bananas* for one week beginning on June 9.

5. Consumer groups have rated our portable vacuum cleaner, the Light Touch, as one of the best in its price range.

WITH A SERIES OF WORDS, PHRASES, OR CLAUSES

The term *series* is used to refer to three or more words, phrases, or clauses which have the same form and which follow each other consecutively. In the following examples, the series are italicized:

We *inventoried the shelves, reported the results,* and *ordered new supplies.* (verb phrase series)

The new copying machines are *faster, cheaper,* and *more versatile.* (adjective series)

Be sure that the machine is unplugged *when it is being cleaned, as new ink is added,* and *while the paper tray is being refilled.* (clause series)

For clarity, the items in a series, whether single words, phrases, or clauses, should be separated by commas. Commas are placed after each item in the series except the last.

Watch out for the following problems when punctuating a series:

• Place commas only after items in the series, not after the conjunction.

INCORRECT: The jacket is available in brown, black, red, and, plaid.

CORRECT: The jacket is available in brown, black, red, and plaid.

• Do not place a comma after the last item in the series.

INCORRECT: We have received the books, magazines, and cassettes, that you ordered.

CORRECT: We have received the books, magazines, and cassettes that you ordered.

- When conjunctions are repeated between items in a series, do not use commas.

  INCORRECT: We have received the books, and magazines, and cassettes that you ordered.

  CORRECT: We have received the books and magazines and cassettes that you ordered.

- When commas appear within phrases or clauses in a series, use semicolons to separate the items in the series. The semicolons provide a visual aid to help the reader group and separate the items in the sentence.

  INCORRECT: We will hold fashion shows this month at our stores in Albany, New York, Chicago, Illinois, and Dallas, Texas.

  CORRECT: We will hold fashion shows this month at our stores in Albany, New York; Chicago, Illinois; and Dallas, Texas.

- When a series concludes with the abbreviated term *etc.*, put a comma before *etc.* If *etc.* does not end the sentence, it should also be followed by a comma.

  Make sure that all classrooms are supplied with paper, pencils, erasers, chalk, etc., on the first day of school.

A Series of Adjectives Without a Conjunction

When two or more adjectives modify the same noun and are not joined by conjunctions, commas should be used to separate the adjectives.

  This new, small, fuel-efficient automobile should sell well.

There are two instances in which this rule does not apply. If the order of the adjectives cannot be reversed without a change in meaning, no comma is used.

  The first spring fashions will arrive on January 15.

In this sentence, reversing the order of the adjectives *first* and *spring* would result in a group of words that makes no sense: *the spring first fashions.* The adjective *spring* is far more closely attached to the meaning of the noun *fashions* than is the adjective *first.* No comma is used in such cases.

Another way to check whether commas should be used between adjectives is to see what the sentence would sound like if you inserted the word *and* between the adjectives. If *and* sounds right between the adjectives, use a comma. If it does not sound right, do not use a comma.

In some instances, an adjective and the noun following it form a single idea. Some examples are *swimming pool, maple tree, income tax*, and *cough drop.*

In such cases, the adjective is not preceded by a comma.

> Anyone purchasing an oven this week will receive a one-quart baking dish free.

In this sentence, the phrase *baking dish* is a single idea, so no comma is placed before the adjective *baking*.

SHARPENING YOUR SKILLS 5

Insert the missing commas in the sentences below. If a sentence does not need any commas, write the word *correct* next to it.

1. Telecommunication systems have improved as a result of computers laser technology, and competition in the marketplace.

2. The new Omicron Home Computer can be used to keep records of household expenses, to do complex mathematical calculations, and even to play popular word games.

3. Plans to renovate the old apartment building call for a modern self-service elevator, a well-insulated computer-operated heating system, and new energy-saving appliances in all kitchens.

4. Among those attending the conference are Andrew di Matteo who will speak on new types of software, Dr. Mary McCormack who will speak on the computer of tomorrow, and Phillip Brown, editor of *Bits and Bytes*.

5. Please report any problems to your supervisor or to the project coordinator or to Mr. Standish.

6. We have found that the large rectangular oak tables sell best to younger more affluent customers.

EDITING EXERCISES

 A. Punctuate the following sentences correctly. If a sentence is correct as written, write the word *correct* next to it.

1. We have the white all-cotton shirts that you requested but will have to order the cotton trousers.

2. The Portable Business Computer is small enough to fit in a briefcase, but it can use a wide variety of business-oriented software.

3. We have installed the new telecommunication system at our offices in Atlanta, Georgia, Orlando, Florida, and Houston, Texas.

4. Construction of the new municipal center is already one month behind schedule, and further delays are expected.

5. All applicants for the typing position should be asked to submit a résumé, to provide the names of references, and to take a typing test.

Homework for 1/6/89

6. The Minuteman watch includes such features as a built-in calculator, an automatic digital calendar, and an alarm.

7. The continental breakfast comes with coffee or tea or milk, and costs $2.95 per person.

8. Fruit and vegetable seeds, fertilizer, fencing, garden tools, etc., are all available at discount prices.

B. The following sentences contain interrupting words, phrases, and clauses. Place commas where needed in the sentences. If a sentence does not need any commas, write the word *correct* next to it.

1. Dr. Martin Fleiry, an expert on agriculture in developing countries has joined the staff of the World Food Exchange.

2. Durolux carpeting, which is made of 100 percent nylon, comes with a five-year guarantee.

3. Office personnel using the floppy disks, however, should keep the disks in their own offices.

4. Employees who wish to obtain coverage for dental care should sign up for the ToothGuard program.

5. An inexpensive filter system, although it removes most industrial chemicals from tap water may not filter out lead, metals, and bacteria.

6. A new feature on our credit cards a built-in computer chip will make it easier for sales clerks to detect counterfeit cards.

7. The new chairs that we have ordered for, example, should reduce backaches and neck problems among typists.

8. The boutique Charlie's, which specializes in fashions for business women, will hold a fashion show on April 12.

PROJECTS

There are different schools of thought regarding the correct usage of commas in a series. You have learned in this chapter that a comma should be placed after each element in a series except the last one. In most journalistic writing, however, you will find that the comma is omitted from the next-to-last item in a series. (For example, *She didn't have enough time to write the memo, the letter and the report.*)

Look through various kinds of materials—newspapers, magazines, textbooks, trade books, and so on. Find examples of both styles, and copy them onto a separate piece of paper. Which type of publication used which style? Which style was used more often?

20
Special Comma Uses

Eric Larsen wrote a letter to the personnel director of a large company asking for a job as a word processor. Read his letter to discover why Eric did not get the job.

> Dear Ms. Watanabe,
>
> Since July 6 1986 I have been employed as a word processor with Kean Kean & Gorwitz, attorneys-at-law. I am seeking a new position, because the firm is moving to Minneapolis Minnesota. If you would like a reference, I'm sure that Mr. Harold Kean Esq. would speak on my behalf. Please write to him at 1070 First Avenue Cleveland Ohio 43,198. I am eager very eager to meet with you about a position at your firm.
>
> Sincerely
>
> Eric Larsen

The problem, of course, is missing and misused commas. In this short letter, there are 11 commas missing and 2 used incorrectly. You may have noticed many of the errors, particularly those concerning the date and address.

In Chapter 19, you studied how commas are used to separate the parts of a sentence. Other uses of the comma are conventional rather than structural, such as the comma placed after the day in a date, as in July 6, 1986. This chapter will cover all standard uses of commas in dates, names, numbers, and addresses, as well as the use of commas to improve clarity in three situations: where a phrase might be misread, where words are repeated, and where words are omitted.

Scheduling is greatly simplified through the use of computer software.

One special use of the comma is in dates, numbers, and addresses. The purpose of commas used in this way is to separate different elements of the unit.

DATES, NUMBERS, AND PLACES

Dates

When the month, day, and year are written out, a comma follows the day.

June 30, 1989

If the date comes in the middle of a sentence, a comma follows the whole date, as well.

The dividends recorded on June 30, 1989, were the largest of the past decade.

However, if the date is written in European fashion, with the day first, no commas are used.

The dividends recorded on 30 June 1989 were the largest of the past decade.

If a date includes only the month and year, commas are usually omitted altogether.

Our sales figures for December 1986 show an increase over the same month in 1985.

When the day of the week is included with the date, a comma is placed after the day of the week. For the remainder of the date, apply the rules just presented.

The current quarter ends Friday, January 22, 1988.

Numbers

In any number of four or more digits, it is customary to use commas to separate thousands, millions, billions, and so on. Beginning at the right side of the number, put a comma after every three digits.

Last year, we sold 1,058,791 copies of *Fishing* magazine.

As you can see from the following sentence, without the commas the number might easily be misread.

Last year, we sold 1058791 copies of *Fishing* magazine.

In the following types of numbers, however, commas are never used:

Telephone numbers: (212) 466-2222
Zip codes: New York, NY 10222
Serial numbers: Account #7936428
Addresses: 25298 Kennedy Boulevard
Dates: 8000 B.C.
Page numbers: page 1039
Numbers *after* a decimal point: 3.6514

Finally, no commas are used between parts of a weight or measure when they express a single total.

The new portable Minivac weighs only 1 pound 3 ounces.

Flight time to O'Hare Airport is 3 hours 15 minutes.

Places

When an address has more than one element (street, city, state, country, and so on), use commas to separate the parts of the address.

> Our new offices will be located at 17 Main Street, Oshkosh, Wisconsin.

> These hand-knit sweaters can be obtained by writing to O'Malley and Company, 23 Kilkenny Road, Dingle, County Kerry, Ireland.

The next exception to the rule requiring commas after each element in the address is the zip code. No comma comes between the state and the zip code.

> Please order ten copies of "Probate in Simple Terms" from Legal Writes, 16 Crescent Street, Boston, Massachusetts 02154.

When an address, or a place name of more than one element, appears *within* the sentence, the last element in the address is also followed by a comma.

> Our new factory outlet at 1551 Magnolia Street, Jackson, Mississippi, will open on May 15.

> Dr. Justine Small of Ann Arbor, Michigan, will act as consultant to the Lewis Chemical Co.

SHARPENING YOUR SKILLS 1

Insert the missing commas in the following sentences. If a sentence does not require any commas, write the word *correct* next to it.

1. During the month of October 1986 our store in Baltimore Maryland had approximately 10800 customers.

2. Ms. Rhonda Smith of 12235 Washington Avenue Cambridge Massachusetts 02138 was the winner of this month's contest.

3. On 12 December 1984 the newborn panda weighed 10 pounds 12 ounces.

4. Since March 1 1986 our shipping department has been located at 1716 First Avenue Minneapolis Minnesota 55414.

5. Electric hair dryer No. 32300 can be found on page 1131 of the catalogue. To order, write to Meyer & Sons P.O. Box 15 Chicago Illinois 60637.

NAMES OF PEOPLE AND COMPANIES

The best general rule to follow in writing people's names and titles and the names of companies is this: Copy the name exactly as the person or firm writes it, with the punctuation each prefers. However, in the case of common abbreviations (such as *Jr., Ph.D.,* and *Inc.*), use the following guidelines when individual preferences are not known.

A Title or Degree. When a person's name is followed by a title or degree, the title or degree is set off from the sentence with two commas.

> Mr. Lawrence Riesman, *Ph.D.,* has been hired to give a series of workshops.

Of course, if the title or degree ends the sentence, only one comma is needed.

> Please send a copy of the contract to Belinda Jones, *Esq.*

Jr. or Sr. When a person's name is followed by *Jr.* or *Sr.,* no comma is used in most cases.

> We are pleased to announce that Julio Salazar *Jr.* is joining the firm as marketing director.

However, when individuals write their names with a comma preceding *Jr.* or *Sr.,* follow their style. Again, if the title appears in the middle of a sentence, be sure it is set off with two commas.

> At today's conference, Frank Cillo, *Jr.,* will give a talk on investment tax credits.

DID YOU KNOW?
Punctuation Has Changed

Although there has been written language since ancient times, there hasn't always been punctuation. The first system of standard punctuation was devised by Greek scholars in Alexandria, Egypt, around 300 B.C.

Development of a system for punctuating English did not begin until the 1500s. The King James Bible, published in 1611, and the First Folio of Shakespeare's works, published in 1623, were among the first printed works in English to have the standard punctuation marks that we take for granted today, including periods, question marks, commas, colons, semicolons, dashes, and hyphens. Moreover, the editors of these works made a conscious effort to use punctuation consistently.

In the 1700s, writers used punctuation marks much more heavily than writers do today. At that time, punctuation was used more to reflect the rhythms of actual speech than to clarify the meaning for a silent reader by indicating the relationships among the various words in a sentence. Also, people then wrote longer sentences, with more verbs per sentence; they also wrote more compound sentences.

Writers continued to punctuate their sentences heavily throughout the 1800s. For example, a nineteenth-century writer might have written, "First, call the client, then, please,—before the end of the day,—contact Mr. Dickens, Dr. Meredith, and, Mrs. Travis."

The general rule today is to use punctuation only when it is necessary to avoid confusion in a sentence and to clarify meaning. A modern writer, then, would be more likely to write: "First call the client; then please contact Mr. Dickens, Dr. Meredith, and Mrs. Travis before the end of the day." Many newspapers and magazines have even made it their style not to separate the last two items in a series: ". . .the river, the town and the field. . . ." In business writing, with its focus upon speed and efficiency, there is now a letter style that dispenses with the punctuation usually used after the salutation and complimentary closing.

Roman Numerals. The same rules apply to roman numerals following a person's name. If you know that an individual's name is written with commas, follow that style. In general, though, do not set off the numeral with commas.

> Inquiries should be addressed to Nicholas Quill *III* at our Mill Valley office.

When roman numerals appear after the names of public or historical figures, no commas are used.

> We are preparing a series of filmstrips on Queen Elizabeth *I* for use in high schools.

Company Names. When writing the name of a company, copy the name exactly as it appears on the company letterhead, if available. Styles of punctuation may vary from firm to firm.

> The Campbell Group, Inc.
> Boomerangs Inc.
> Judson, Weller, Smith, and Mays
> Fink, Thomas & Green
> The Perry-Farb Organization, Ltd.

Remember, if a comma precedes the abbreviation *Inc.* or *Ltd.,* a second comma should follow it when the abbreviation occurs in the middle of a sentence.

> As of June 1, we will be sending all film stock to Colortronics, *Inc.,* for processing.

If you do not know the company's style, follow these guidelines:

- Use *no* comma with common abbreviations, such as *Inc.* and *Ltd.*

- Use no comma before the ampersand sign (*&*) in company names, but *do* use commas between other names in a series.

- To write a shortened form of a company name that consists of a series, use the first two names with one comma between them.

SHARPENING YOUR SKILLS 2

Insert the missing commas in the following sentences. If a sentence does not require any commas, write the word *correct* next to it.

1. Martha Knox Ph.D. of Hartley Motors Ltd. has invented a new device for reducing automobile emissions.

2. We are pleased to announce that Lydia Wong Esq. has joined the Litigation Department of Landis Field Bates and Stern.

3. Please send a copy of our catalogue to Richard Costello Jr. of Books Inc.

4. Malcolm White III of Robbins Ryan & Fox has recently been elected president of the West Milford Chamber of Commerce.

5. Father Daniel Estok S.J. will give a talk on Pope John Paul II and his writing.

OTHER USES OF THE COMMA

There are four special situations in which commas are used. In these situations, the commas set off the name of a person being spoken to, two parts of a letter, or details in a reference.

With Terms of Direct Address. When a sentence names the person spoken to, that name is set off from the rest of the sentence with commas. Terms of direct address are set off by one comma when they are at the beginning or end of the sentence, by two commas when they are within the sentence.

Ms. Brooks, I hope you will attend the meeting on Monday.

I have appreciated the opportunity to meet with you*, sir.*

Are you sure, *Bob,* that these figures represent the total sales for May?

After Salutations. In an informal or friendly letter, the salutation is followed by a comma.

Dear Frank,

Your letter came at just the right time....

However, in a formal or business letter, the salutation is followed by a colon.

Dear Ms. Weaver:

I enjoyed our interview. ...

After Closings. In all letters, except those written in open punctuation style, the closing is followed by a comma. (Refer to Chapter 38 for a full treatment of letter formats.)

Sincerely yours,
Cordially,
Affectionately,

With References. In references to literary and legal works, commas are used to separate smaller units from larger units.

The famous speech occurs in *Hamlet,* Act III, Scene 1, lines 56–88.

An interesting legal precedent is cited in Weems' *Torts,* Volume II, Chapter 9, page 321.

Commas are used for clarity in three special situations. Without the added commas in these instances, the word arrangement would be confusing, and the information could be misunderstood.

To Show Omissions. Sometimes, a comma stands in for a missing word, much as an apostrophe stands in for missing letters in contractions, such as *can't.*

> In the seminar on computer languages, Ms. Dietrich spoke on COBOL; Mr. Stockton, on FORTRAN.

In the second clause the word *spoke* is omitted and its meaning is understood. Words omitted in this way are usually verbs.

> Jeri Woods will head the entertainment committee; Bill Fuchs, the fund-raising committee; Margery O'Neal, the membership committee; and Alan Royce, the entertainment committee.

In this sentence, notice that commas appear wherever the verb phrase *will head* has been omitted. A comma must be used for each omission.

To Show Repetition. When words are repeated for emphasis, commas separate the repeated words.

> *Please, please* remove all programs from the computer when you have finished using them.

Sometimes, a repetition may involve a phrase that expands upon, but basically repeats, a word or phrase in the sentence.

> Video-Tech was *impressed, very impressed,* with your presentation.

Although *very* is added, the phrase *very impressed* is basically a repetition of *impressed.* Notice that the repeated phrase is set off completely from the rest of the sentence with two commas.

To Prevent Misreading. Use a comma in any sentence where the reader would be likely to join parts of the sentence that do not belong together. Read the following sentence:

> Under the new law review of safety measures is required every month.

You probably read *law review* as one phrase and had to start over when that reading proved incorrect. In sentences like this, a comma is necessary to prevent misreading.

> Under the new law, review of safety measures is required every month.

Misreading is most likely to occur in sentences beginning with infinitives, prepositions, or adverbs.

> INCORRECT: To conclude the conference will discuss new marketing techniques.

> CORRECT: To conclude, the conference will discuss new marketing techniques.

In general, use a comma in any sentence where it is needed to prevent misreading—even if none of the other rules requiring a comma applies.

SHARPENING YOUR SKILLS 3

Insert the missing commas in the following sentences. If a sentence does not require any commas, write the word *correct* next to it.

1. The eight-cylinder engine gets only 12.miles a gallon; the six-cylinder engine 17.

2. According to the official government regulations prohibit the use of asbestos in children's toys.

3. Savings savings savings—our new sale is the biggest ever.

4. Still a conscientious firm should deal with consumer complaints promptly.

5. It is obvious, John, that you are not suited for this position.

EDITING EXERCISES

Insert the missing commas in the following sentences.

1. Margaret Fitzgerald, D.D.S., of Baltimore, Maryland, highly recommends our new line of flavored dental floss.

2. On September 5, 1985, Darryl Jones, Esq., joined the staff of Bernstein, Brooks, and Turben.

3. During the week of 12 May 1985 we ordered 2,175 books from Paperback Sales Inc., at 12775 Mountain Road, Millburn, New Jersey 07041.

4. Tax preparer, Deborah Rahv, C.P.A., helped save clients over $100,000 last year.

5. In October 1984 I consulted Melvin Josephson, M.D., of Los Angeles, California, about a work-related injury.

6. We are being represented in the lawsuit by Nancy Wong, Esq., of Stoddard, Stoddard, Berger & Weiss.

7. Rodney Mitchell III, will be joining the staff of China Imports, Ltd. as a sales representative.

8. The film is 1 hour 45 minutes long and can be rented from Flix Distribution 112 First Avenue Alexandria Virginia 22302.

9. Walter Johnson Jr. of 1797 Bonnie Brae Road Tucson Arizona 85719 should receive a complimentary toaster.

10. More than 9000000 people have visited our theme park in Baton Rouge Louisiana since its opening on May 31 1979.

PROJECTS

Compose a letter that you might send to a credit card company requesting a credit card. In your letter, give your full address, date of birth, salary, and assets (all information can be fictitious). Include a salutation and closing. Be sure to use commas correctly throughout your letter.

21
Periods

The marketing director of a wholesale carpet firm received the following memo from one of his salespeople:

> TO: Mr Lopez
>
> FROM: Bob Wright
>
> I've asked my customers whether they like the new line of Oriental rugs? The ones that sell for $99. are most popular. The least popular rugs are ... the high-priced ones! I think our stores in New Jersey and New York should advertise the inexpensive rugs. Please let me know if you agree? I'll give you more specific data tomorrow. At the 9 am meeting.

Although Mr. Lopez understood Bob's memo, he had a vague sense that Bob did not quite know what he was talking about. The reason? A number of mistakes in punctuation, all involving the use of the period. A memo like this, which lacks needed periods and contains unnecessary ones, makes the writer less effective in getting across ideas.

Like the comma, the period is used in two ways. The first use is structural: A period is used to mark the end of a sentence, the basic unit of thought in writing. The second use is conventional; a period is used, for example, with abbreviations and sums of money.

In this chapter, you will learn when to use a period and when *not* to use a period. The text will also focus upon special problems with periods, such as periods in lists and in sentences that end with abbreviations.

Before continuing, you might find it helpful to take a quick look back at Chapter 4 to refresh your memory about the four types of sentences.

There are three main uses of the period.

1. A period is used to end a declarative or imperative sentence.

2. A period is used after abbreviations.

3. Three spaced periods are used to mark an omission in a quoted passage. The omission is called an ellipsis.

Periods to End Sentences

The most important use of the period is to end a sentence. The declarative sentence, which makes a statement, ends with a period.

> A lunchtime exercise program for employees will begin on Monday.

An imperative sentence, or command, is also followed by a period.

> Do not enter a new program into the computer without Mr. Ming's authorization.

Similarly, a sentence making a request that is basically a command is followed by a period. This holds true even when the request is phrased in the form of a question. Compare the following two sentences:

> Richard, would you advise us to buy zero-coupon bonds or municipal bonds?

> Richard, would you make sure that all salespeople turn in weekly reports by noon on Monday.

The first sentence is a question; an answer is expected, so the sentence ends with a question mark. The second sentence, although similar in structure, is a request for the person to perform a specific action. No answer is expected, so the sentence ends with a period.

An indirect question also ends with a period instead of a question mark. For example, look at the following two sentences:

> Will the Montgomery Township store carry designer suits?

> Mr. Tucker would like to know whether the Montgomery Township store will carry designer suits.

The first sentence is a question and ends with a question mark. The second is an indirect question in the form of a statement; therefore, it ends with a period.

SHARPENING YOUR SKILLS 1

Place the correct punctuation mark at the end of each sentence.

1. Would you please order the new software for the Advertising Department

2. Would the National Hotel in Honolulu be able to accommodate our 1990 convention

3. Ms. Gillette would like to know why the invoice was filed before the items were checked off

4. Tim, why haven't we sent a representative to Fuller Diamonds as Mr. Fuller requested

5. Let me know whether the construction of the Baltimore plant is proceeding on schedule

Periods With Abbreviations

Most common abbreviations are followed by a period.

Frost-Jameson Inc.
Dr. Ruth Kawabata
9 a.m.
600 B.C.
Benjamin Mitchell, Ph.D.

The period is used whether the abbreviation stands alone or occurs within a sentence.

The Kite Co. was founded in 1979.

However, if the abbreviation occurs at the end of a sentence, only one period is used.

The meeting will begin at 7 p.m.

Linens, Ltd., manufactures sheets, towels, draperies, etc.

Some words that began as abbreviations of longer words are now considered words in their own right. Some examples are *exam, gym,* and *memo.* Such words are *not* followed by periods.

You'll find those questions answered in my *memo* of January 12.

When using less common abbreviations, you should be aware that some are followed by periods and others are not. It is always a good idea to check if you are not sure of the correct usage in a particular case. Many dictionaries have a separate list of established abbreviations; others include abbreviations in the main body of the dictionary. For specific guidelines regarding formation and usage of abbreviations, see Chapter 29 of this book.

SHARPENING YOUR SKILLS 2

Place periods where needed in the following sentences.

1. Ms Hart has been named vice president of Pine Products Ltd

2. Please order markers, pencils, erasers, etc

3. Roberts & Steele Inc had third-quarter profits that were 12 percent higher than those of Wemrock, Bolton, and Co

4. At 10 a m Mr Ravitch has a meeting with the head of the university, Dean Roland Winslow, Ed D , Ph D

Periods for Ellipses

Three spaced periods are used for an ellipsis—the omission of a word, words, or sentences from a quotation. For example, suppose you wanted to quote from the following passage in a newsletter called *Market News:*

> The technology sector, according to our stock market forecast, has the largest potential for growth. Therefore, in spite of the recent recession, we are recommending investment in technology stocks, such as CTI and Sync Systems. Once the economy improves, they will come roaring back like gangbusters.

If your quotation omits a word or words within a sentence, use three spaced periods to mark the ellipsis.

> *Market News* says, "The technology sector ... has the largest potential for growth."

If you omit words at the beginning of a quotation, it is not necessary to indicate an ellipsis. If the quoted material can stand as a sentence, it should begin with a capital letter.

> *Market News* says, "We are recommending investment in technology stocks, such as CTI and Sync Systems."

When words are omitted at the end of a quoted sentence, four periods are used (three for the ellipsis and one to end the sentence).

> *Market News* says, "We are recommending investment in technology stocks. ..."

Similarly, when one or more complete sentences are omitted after a quoted sentence and the text is picked up again to be quoted, four periods are used (one to end the sentence and three for the ellipsis).

> *Market News* says, "The technology sector ... has the largest potential for growth. ... We are recommending investment in technology stocks, such as CTI and Sync Systems."

The use of the ellipsis to shorten quotes is a good idea, because it results in tighter writing. Keep in mind, however, that the ellipsis is used only when you are changing the actual structure of a quoted sentence or paragraph by eliminating some part of the beginning, middle, or end. It is not necessary to use an ellipsis to indicate that entire sentences, paragraphs, or pages of material follow the material you have quoted.

Another problem people sometimes have with ellipsis marks is using them in place of other punctuation, especially the dash.

INCORRECT: The new Torero is the car that has everything ... the look of a sports car, and the price tag of an economy car.

CORRECT: The new Torero is the car that has everything—the look of a sports car, and the price tag of an economy car.

Although ellipsis marks are occasionally used as a stylistic device in creative writing, their use in business writing should be confined to marking omissions from quotations.

WHEN NOT TO USE A PERIOD

You have already reviewed some of the situations in which a period is not used: A period is not used after shortened words that are not abbreviations, such as *memo*. When an abbreviation occurs at the end of a sentence, a second period is not used after the abbreviation. There are additional constructions in which no period is used.

Titles and Free-Standing Headings. Headings set off from the text, as well as titles of chapters, books, poems, and songs, are not followed by periods—even if the title or heading is a complete sentence.

The book *Anyone Can Invest in Real Estate* should be required reading for all agents at Weiner Realty.

Roman Numerals. No period follows roman numerals, except in a numbered outline, where a roman numeral *is* followed by a period.

We have a large selection of Louis XV furniture.

Letters or Numbers in Parentheses. No period is used after letters or numbers in parentheses; however, a period *is* used to end the sentence, even if the sentence ends with a number or letter in parentheses.

There are three reasons that the X-100 has not sold well: (1) it is too expensive, (2) it has not been advertised, and (3) it is not compatible with other systems.

Similarly, no periods would be used if the points were lettered *(A), (B), (C).*

Dollar Amounts in Whole Numbers. No period is used after whole numbers of dollars.

The *$99* airfare will be in effect until April 1.

SHARPENING YOUR SKILLS 3

Using the correct proofreading symbol, delete all the periods that do not belong in the following sentences.

1. Mr. J. W. Nash will address the meeting with a speech entitled "Twelve Ways to Higher Productivity.".

2. Please check at least once a week to see that your desk is well supplied with pens, pencils, paper, staples, etc..

3. The book *You Can Make a Million Too.* had advance sales of over $56,000 as of last week.

4. To get into the editing mode with this program, follow these steps: (1). turn on the computer, (2). enter the date and time, and (3). press "E" for edit when the main menu is displayed.

5. The latest version of this machine, the Copymate II., can turn out 40 copies a minute.

Lists occur frequently in business. Confusion over when to use periods—or whether to use periods at all—occurs just as frequently. A few guidelines will help you use periods correctly in lists. These guidelines are based in large part on the length of the elements in the list.

WHEN TO USE PERIODS IN LISTS

Short Phrases in Lists. If a list consists of short phrases, the phrases do not end with periods.

Topics for Today's Meeting
A. Office reorganization
B. Use of new computer codes
C. Overtime authorization

However, if the phrases in a list are essential to complete a statement introducing the list, periods *are* used.

At today's meeting, we will discuss:
A. reorganizing the office.
B. using the new computer codes.
C. authorizing overtime.

Each phrase, when added to the introductory statement, forms a complete sentence; for example, *At today's meeting we will discuss reorganizing the office.* Therefore, a period is used after each item, and each item begins with a lowercase letter.

Complete Sentences in Lists. If the items in a list are complete sentences, each should be followed by a period.

> I'd like to discuss the following topics at today's meeting:
> A. The office should be reorganized.
> B. Computer operators will need instruction on the new codes.
> C. Overtime must be authorized in advance by department heads.

Long Clauses in Lists. If the items on the list consist of long clauses, each should be followed by a period—even if none of the above rules applies.

> Items to Discuss at Today's Meeting
> 1. Reorganizing the office so orders can be filled more quickly.
> 2. Setting up seminars to acquaint computer operators with the new codes.
> 3. Making sure overtime is authorized in advance by department heads.

In general, the use of periods in lists should be consistent; either all or none of the items should end with periods.

SHARPENING YOUR SKILLS 4

Place periods where needed in the lists below.

1. All job applicants should have:
   1. at least two years' experience
   2. working knowledge of COBOL
   3. familiarity with state tax laws

2. Goals for week of May 2:
   a. Finish inventory of all stock in clothing department
   b. Revise and get final approval on June newspaper ads
   c. Begin training program for new cashiers

3. Complaints by Tele-Serv Customers
   A. People often have to dial a number several times to get through
   B. Poor connections are frequent, especially during business hours
   C. Credit card calls usually require a 3- to 5-minute wait

EDITING EXERCISES

A. Place the correct punctuation at the end of each of the following sentences.

1. Ms. Otero would like to know whether all employees have received information on the company pension plan

2. Theo, would you please find out who will be attending Gerald Goldberg's retirement dinner on March 4

3. Many owners of small businesses wonder whether a savings bank or a commercial bank can better serve their needs

4. Ellen, will you be able to finish editing *Do-It-Yourself Solar Heat* by Friday

5. Please let me know right away if you would like to make a bid on the Fremont Street house

B. Place periods where needed in the sentences below.

1. James L. Batson II, former vice president of the National Coalition for Progress, has been named general counsel of the Small Business Foundation

2. Wanda Robinson, who has her M A in business administration, can give you all the information you need on depreciation, tax shelters, investment tax credits, etc

3. J. L. Griffith will give a talk entitled "Retirement Planning" at 7 p m on Monday at the youth center

4. Some of the most exciting tours from Safari Ltd include (1) Fox Hunting in Ireland, (2) Rafting in Colorado, and (3) Hiking in Switzerland

5. Copies of *Women Can Succeed in Business* are available from the Anthony Press, P O Box 17, Chapel Hill, North Carolina 27514

6. I was wondering whether Dr Saunders will be attending this year's medical convention

PROJECTS

Write a business letter to a fictitious company about a problem you have had with one of their products. Do not use any periods or capital letters correctly in your letter. You might even throw in a few misplaced periods and capital letters for confusion's sake. Exchange your letter with someone else in the class. Try to determine how the sentences should read, and insert periods and capital letters as needed, deleting those that are incorrect.

22
Question Marks and Exclamation Points

Suppose that you have submitted a proposal to improve the health of workers in your company by setting up a small gym in the building. The vice president to whom you have submitted the plan sends back the following memo:

Do you have any idea what that would cost?

The memo clearly asks you to supply more information, and you would reply with estimated figures. Suppose, on the other hand, you received this reply:

Do you have any idea what that would cost!

In this case, the message is a definite "No." Yet, the only difference between the two sentences is the final punctuation mark.

The meaning of a sentence often changes entirely when a question mark or exclamation point, rather than a period, ends the sentence.

Murray and Co. ordered 50 dwarf apple trees.

Murray and Co. ordered 50 dwarf apple trees!

There is no oil on the property.

There is no oil on the property?

As you can see, an exclamation point or question mark suggests a different tone of voice than does a period, which denotes a simple statement of fact. The exclamation point conveys emotion; the question mark indicates uncertainty. Although the choice of a period or exclamation point can be a subjective one, there are general rules to follow for using these punctuation marks.

A telephone linked to a computer system is used to obtain data—and to discuss it.

WHEN TO USE A QUESTION MARK

You already know that a question mark is used at the end of an interrogative sentence, or question. But there are times when a sentence that looks like a question really is not a question. You must be able to distinguish between these types of sentences in order to correctly use the question mark. Use the guidelines discussed in the following sections to sort out which situations call for a question mark.

Direct Question

Always use a question mark after a direct question.

> When will we receive the new shipment from Davis Brothers?

Notice that direct questions often begin with, or contain, the words *who, what, where, when, why,* or *how.*

> Angela, how many people are expected to attend the programming class?

A question mark is also used when a short question comes at the end of a statement. Compare these two sentences:

> A copy of the Waste Disposal Project report has been sent to Ms. Okawa.

> A copy of the Waste Disposal Project report has been sent to Ms. Okawa, hasn't it?

The first sentence, a statement, ends with a period. In the second sentence, the short question *hasn't it*? has been added to the original statement. The entire sentence, therefore ends with a question mark.

Question Worded as a Statement

Use a question mark to end any sentence intended as a question—even if it has the word order of a statement. Compare the word order of the following two sentences.

> Mr. Hernandez will be staying at the Diamond Hotel in Miami Beach.

> Will Mr. Hernandez be staying at the Diamond Hotel in Miami Beach?

The first sentence is a statement and has the word order typical of a statement: subject + verb. The second sentence is a question and has the word order typical of a question: auxiliary + verb + subject + main verb. However, the first sentence could be intended as a question. If so, it would end with a question mark instead of a period—despite the word order.

> Mr. Hernandez will be staying at the Diamond Hotel in Miami Beach?

Series of Questions

A series of questions may be structured in two possible ways.

- Several questions may be asked in a single sentence.

  > Rob, have you met with Ms. Tufaro, shown her the sketches, and received her approval?

Three questions here are written as one sentence, requiring just a single question mark. Such a sentence always has commas and a coordinating conjunction to join the parts of the series.

- More informally, a single-sentence question may be followed by phrases asking other questions.

  > Rob, have you met with Ms. Tufaro? shown her the sketches? received her approval?

In this type of sentence, the added phrases have the same structure as the concluding phrase in the sentence. The added phrases are not capitalized because they are alternate endings for the sentence.

Question Within a Question

When a sentence contains a question within a question, only one question mark is used.

> Why did you ask, "Who will write the progress report?"

The part of the sentence in quotation marks is a question; the sentence as a whole is another question. One question mark at the end of the sentence is all that is needed.

Estimated Figure or Date

Use a question mark to indicate a doubtful or estimated figure or date. Put the question mark in parentheses immediately after the date or figure.

> Researchers recommend that this chemical not be used in manufacturing because concentrations as low as 15(?) parts per 1,000 may be harmful.

This use of the question mark is an efficient method of indicating uncertainty.
   When the estimated date or figure is already in parentheses, the question mark goes immediately after the number.

> The rising value of the works of Rogier van der Weyden (1399?–1464) is the subject of this month's Art Investment Society lecture.

SHARPENING YOUR SKILLS 1

1. Combine the following two sentences into one, changing the punctuation accordingly.

   The Misiguchi computer is the best one for our purposes. Don't you agree?

2. Change the following statement into a question in two different ways.

   The membership of Local 512 will elect new officers on April 15.

3. Punctuate the following sentence to indicate that the date and figure are questionable.

   The founder of the airline company, Albert Gidding (b. 1886), made his first flight of 1,000 feet in a glider.

4. Combine the following two sentences into one, changing the punctuation accordingly.

   "Can we buy a helicopter for less than $100,000?" What did you have in mind by asking that?

5. Rewrite the following sentence so that it is a single-sentence question followed by phrases asking other questions. Capitalize and punctuate correctly.

Have our stores been successful in selling the Persian rugs, the dhurries from India, and the Afghan wall hangings?

WHEN NOT TO USE A QUESTION MARK

There are four situations in which question marks are often used incorrectly. The first three are covered in greater detail in Chapter 21, but they are listed here for reference. See the preceding chapter if you need to review the material.

Indirect Question

Do not use a question mark after an indirect question.

Ms. Simon wonders whether the computer can be programmed to delete repeated names from the mail list.

This is an indirect question because it is merely reporting that a question has been asked. The sentence itself does not ask a question, so no question mark is used.

Polite Request

Do not use a question mark after polite requests. These are imperative sentences (commands) phrased in question form for the sake of politeness.

Roger, will you arrange for Mr. Parker to tour the plant on Friday at 10 a.m.

A polite request is easy to distinguish from a question. The speaker does not expect an answer, but expects the listener to *do* something in response.

Exclamation

Do not use a question mark after an exclamation that is phrased as a question.

How can you be so irresponsible as to continue selling this hazardous product!

As with a polite request, a sentence such as this is not really asking a question — even though it is in question form. Again, a good test is whether an answer is expected. In the example above, no answer is expected, and the sentence ends with an exclamation point to show strong emotion.

Sarcastic or Humorous Statement

Do not use a question mark to call attention to a sarcastic or humorous statement.

INCORRECT: We can have a new heating system installed for only (?) $3,000.

This informal use of the question mark is inappropriate in business writing.

SHARPENING YOUR SKILLS 2

Place the correct punctuation mark at the end of each sentence.

1. Would you please make a copy of the contract and send it to Ms. Martha Flynn

2. Will Representative Dickson be able to address the Executives Club next month

3. Who will be responsible for ordering the new software

4. Who could have expected that all of our sorting machines would break down on the same day

5. The advertising director would like to know whether the magazine ads will be full-color or black-and-white

6. Does Mr. Richardson know when the Appleby Chemicals case will be coming to trial

WHEN TO USE AN EXCLAMATION POINT

An exclamation point is used to give special emphasis to a sentence—to intensify its effect. Writers employ this punctuation mark to convey strong feeling or excitement.

Congratulations! Sales of your album have just passed the 1 million mark!

The exclamation point is often used after interjections, where added emphasis is desired.

No! Do not send me any more information about your condominiums in Alaska.

Exclamatory sentences often begin with the question words *who, what, why,* and *how.*

What a disappointing sales drive!

Who could have predicted a 20 percent rise in that stock!

Notice that the second sentence, although phrased in the form of a question, is an exclamatory sentence. If the intention of a sentence is exclamatory, always use an exclamation point—even if the sentence is in question form.

Jim, how did you ever think up this ingenious system!

As you can see, the exclamation point is an unusual kind of punctuation in that its use depends on subjective judgment rather than clear-cut rules. It is often a matter of personal choice whether or not to emphasize a statement by putting an exclamation point at the end. Compare these two sentences:

Where are the supplies I ordered last week?

Where are the supplies I ordered last week!

The first sentence is simply asking a question. The second is more emphatic, suggesting that the speaker is annoyed or angry. The choice to use an exclamation point is up to the writer. As a general rule, however, exclamation points should be used very sparingly to ensure that they will have full impact when they are used.

WHEN NOT TO USE AN EXCLAMATION POINT

As with the question mark, do not use the exclamation point to indicate humor or sarcasm.

INCORRECT: The most recent candidate for the secretarial job types a speedy (!) 30 w.p.m.

Another informal practice that has no place in business writing is the use of more than one exclamation point at the end of a sentence.

INCORRECT: The budget for the next quarter is incredible!!

Similarly, do not combine the exclamation point with the question mark at the end of a sentence.

INCORRECT: You call this a report?!

Although this sentence is in the form of a question, it is intended as an exclamation. Therefore, the exclamation point should be used alone.

CORRECT: You call this a report!

SHARPENING YOUR SKILLS 3

Decide whether the exclamation points in the following sentences are used correctly. If a sentence has no errors, write the word *correct* next to it. If a sentence contains errors, correct the punctuation.

1. What kind of computer should we buy!

2. Treat Foods, Inc., makes various healthy (!) snacks like cupcakes and cheese-flavored chips.

3. Why didn't Laura take her vacation in June!?

4. What an impressive résumé!

5. Do you seriously expect me to authorize a fact-gathering trip to Hawaii?!

6. Why can't your company make a copy machine that doesn't break down twice a week!

7. Good work!

8. We made the sale!!

EDITING EXERCISES

A. Correct the punctuation errors in the following paragraph.

Theresa, I received your memo suggesting that we invite local players to challenge the Omicron V in a chess tournament. What an intriguing way to promote our new computer. Both Ms. Reynolds and I discussed the proposal with various staff members. One person wondered whether there are enough chess players in the area to ensure a high turnout? Ms. Reynolds asked if Scrabble might not be a better choice? Of course, we'd also need an estimate of the costs involved. We don't want to turn this into the chess Olympics, do we?! Would you work up a detailed list of the expenses for such a promotion? We'd also like to know, will the tournament be for adults only, teenagers, children? Did Ms. Reynolds already tell you that Joe asked "What will be the prize for the winner?"? Obviously, we can't afford to give away a computer! However, we might make up a package of game-related software, don't you think. Will you please send me a memo expanding your ideas by Monday? Keep these brainstorms coming!

B. Decide whether the end punctuation marks in the following sentences are used correctly. If a sentence has no errors, write the word *correct* next to it. If a sentence contains errors, correct the punctuation.

1. What do you expect from a $99 computer!

2. Mr. Matthieson, would you please give me all the information you have on Databits, Inc.?

3. The new furniture in the lobby is a big improvement, don't you think.

4. Why did we ever decide to manufacture a line of disposable bathing suits?!

5. Ms. Cox would like to know whether the contracts will be ready by June 3?

6. Can we add the European market reports to our data bank without getting a new computer? without getting new software? without hiring additional personnel?

7. The photocopying machine is *not*, I repeat *not*, for personal use!!

8. Is it Mr. O'Casey who asked "When will we meet with Dawson Associates?"?

9. Congratulations on a job well done!

10. The people at Farber and Farber phoned to ask if the new directory has been published yet?

PROJECTS

A. Career counselors often give the following advice about making a good impression in a job interview. The job applicant should not only answer questions, but also ask them. The applicant's questions about the job and the company can convey his or her knowledge of the field, as well as displaying intelligence and assertiveness.

   Suppose that you are about to go on a job interview. Decide what the job title is and what the company does. Then list ten questions you might ask at the interview.

B. Advertising in the print media sometimes overuses the exclamation point. Copy such as "GIANT SALE!!!" defeats its purpose by relying too much on the exclamation point. Using magazines and newspapers, select two advertisements—one that misuses the exclamation point and one that uses it effectively.

23
Semicolons and Colons

Semicolons are sometimes called "strong commas" while colons are called "weak periods." These names refer to the way semicolons and colons separate clauses and make the reader pause or take special notice of certain words. There are guidelines for the use of semicolons and colons, but their use is often determined by the emphasis the writer wants to give a statement. If a comma is not strong enough, a semicolon might be better. If a period is too abrupt, a semicolon may be appropriate.

SEMICOLONS

The semicolon is often used to separate major ideas in a sentence. It is also used to add clarity to a sentence that is lengthy and heavily burdened with commas. You will learn about these and other uses of the semicolon in this section.

Between Independent Clauses

A compound sentence is ordinarily formed by joining two independent clauses with a comma and a conjunction.

> The Wechsler group did the analysis, and it deserves full credit for the cost savings.

A compound sentence can also be formed without a conjunction. However, a comma alone would not be strong enough to separate the two clauses; therefore, a semicolon is called for.

> The Wechsler group did the analysis; it deserves full credit for the cost savings.

Note that joining two independent clauses this way is effective only if the ideas expressed in the clauses are closely related. If they are not, you should write the clauses as two sentences.

Before Transitional Words

Clauses are often joined by transitional words such as these:

accordingly	nevertheless
besides	on the contrary
consequently	otherwise
for example	so
furthermore	that is
hence	then
however	therefore
moreover	thus
namely	yet

In such cases, a semicolon is used after the first clause as long as the second clause is independent and thus can function alone as a sentence.

> Martina recommended Mrs. Mendez highly; therefore, we hired her as a consultant.

If one clause is dependent, use commas to set off the transitional word or phrase.

> If the shipment arrives more than two days late, however, we will not accept it.

Ordinarily, a comma is placed after a transitional word or phrase. However, a comma is not necessary after the single-syllable words *hence, so, then, thus,* or *yet,* unless you want a special pause for emphasis.

The transitional words *so* and *yet* can be preceded by either a comma or a semicolon. When the two independent clauses are short and closely related, a comma may be used. When the clauses are long and complicated, a semicolon is necessary.

> We have given them several chances, yet they have not paid the bill.

> There have been an increasing number of requests for uniform filing procedures from the sales, marketing, and customer service departments; nevertheless, our files remain in the same state of disorganization they have been in for the last five years.

In a Series of Phrases and Clauses

Ordinarily, commas are used to separate the elements of a series.

> We need to order paper clips, pencils, and notepads.

However, semicolons are used when the elements of the series are phrases or clauses that contain internal commas. Semicolons prevent misreading in such cases.

> We need to order paper clips, pencils, and notepads for the office; clipboards and strapping tape for the warehouse; and adhesive tape, ink, and rollers for the packer.

> The committee includes George Jackson, head of engineering; Maya Dietrich, head of production; and Jim Wright, head of distribution.

Common Semicolon Errors

Be careful not to overuse the semicolon. Because the semicolon causes the reader to take a long pause, too many semicolons tend to disrupt the flow of your writing.

Be sure, also, that you place semicolons correctly, especially when you use them with quotation marks and parentheses. The semicolon is always placed *after* these two punctuation marks.

> The lawsuit accuses the company of "illegal restraint of trade"; later on, it describes several incidents of such actions.

> Nearly 75 percent of our 1986 QR-400 television sets have been returned (all with the same channel-selector defect); therefore, we are discontinuing production.

Do not use a semicolon to link a phrase with a clause or a dependent clause with an independent clause. A comma should be used in these cases.

> Although learning quickly, Geri still has problems with the new order system.

> Despite all our careful planning, the increase in the cost of raw materials cut our profits.

Do not use a semicolon to introduce a list of items or a statement. A colon or a comma is best in such cases.

> The committee reviewed the following indicators of job satisfaction: employee performance, morale, overtime, and sick leave.

> In his closing remarks, Mr. Addison said, "We must all pull together if we are to meet the deadline, as I know we will."

SHARPENING YOUR SKILLS 1

In the following paragraphs, correct any errors in the use of semicolons.

1. The committee's findings are as follows; overtime will be restricted; early retirement will be encouraged; and management will take a 10 percent

cut in pay. Although drastic; these measures should help the company's competitive position.

2. Kwon Li's probation period is not yet complete; nevertheless, her performance deserves recognition. I recommend that she be retained because her work is consistent, efficient, and fast, her attendance is excellent, and her effect on the other employees has been extremely positive.

3. Model TC-15 is our latest copier; it joins our other successful machines in satisfying customer needs for reliable, economical copying. The TC-15 beats its nearest competitor in price; service interval; and ease of operation.

COLONS

The colon is a specialized form of punctuation that is used to indicate a significant break in a sentence. The guidelines below will help you learn when it is appropriate to use a colon.

Between Independent Clauses

A colon can be used between two independent clauses if the second clause explains or illustrates the first clause and if there is no transitional word or conjunction between the two clauses.

> The salespeople in that region are remarkable: each one has sold more than $1 million of insurance this year.

Note that if the second clause is not an anticipated explanation of the first clause or if there is a transitional phrase between the clauses, you should use a semicolon.

> The salespeople in that region are remarkable; therefore, they have earned certain privileges.

For Special Emphasis

A colon is a strong punctuation mark: it makes readers pause, and it gives special emphasis to what follows. This emphasis is especially helpful for drawing attention to rules or other important statements.

> This is the first safety rule: Disconnect the power source before servicing the machine.

> Notice: There will be a test of the fire alarm system today at 2 p.m.

The independent clause after the colon in such sentences begins with a capital letter. The colon causes the reader to stop, and the capitalization of the first letter in the second clause indicates the beginning of the statement introduced in the first clause.

Before Lists

A colon may be used when listing items. Very often, writers introduce a list with a word or term such as *the following, as follows, thus, this,* or *these,* followed by a colon.

> Our newest employees are the following: Mary Kalvia, Tony Esposito, and Joan Murphy.

An introductory word or term is not always needed, especially if the listed items are anticipated in the opening clause.

> We welcome three new employees: Mary Kalvia, Tony Esposito, and Joan Murphy.

The listed items do not have to be written on the same line as the colon; they can be written in list form.

There are instances in which a colon should not be used before a list. For example, if the phrase that anticipates the list is separated from the list by another sentence (called an intervening sentence), no colon is used:

> Trainees will need the following supplies. The items can be requisitioned in the mailroom.
> | | |
> |---|---|
> | 1 portfolio | 2 expense booklets |
> | 1 appointment book | 100 business cards |

A colon is not used if the listed items follow a verb or a preposition.

> The committee members are Jacobs, Cooney, and Frazier.

> The set consists of two decanters, six glasses, and an ice bucket.

Other Uses of Colons

There are many other instances in which colons are used to separate certain elements. Colons are used in expressions of time and proportion.

> I caught the 6:45 train this morning.

> The ratio of stocks to bonds in the pension fund is now about 2:1.

Salutations in business letters are often followed by colons.

> Dear Sirs:
> Dear Ms. Sexton:

When a book or other published work has a subtitle, it is often set off from the main title with a colon.

> *Managing Real Estate: Twelve Pitfalls on the Road to Profits*
> *Disk: The Magazine of EDP*
> "The Most Important Part of Your Job: Closing the Sale"

If you wish to draw special attention to a direct quotation, place a colon before it. If no special attention is needed, a comma is appropriate. (Commas are used far more often than colons to introduce direct quotations.)

> The president proclaimed to the stockholders: "This has been the best year in this company's history!"

> Senator Morris replied, "If the tax bill gets through Congress, hundreds of jobs will be saved."

It is also standard practice to use a colon to introduce a long piece of quoted material.

> The Fourth Amendment to the Constitution reads:
> > The right of the people to be secure in their persons, houses, papers, and effects, against unreasonable searches and seizures, shall not be violated, and no Warrants shall issue, but upon probable cause, supported by Oath or affirmation, and particularly describing the place to be searched, and the persons or things to be seized.

The quoted material is usually indented from the main text to further set it off from its introduction. No quotation marks are necessary when material is quoted in this way.

Capitalization Following a Colon

In most cases, capitalization after a colon follows general grammatical rules. If a colon is followed by a proper noun, a proper adjective, or the pronoun *I*, the first letter is capitalized. The first letter after a colon is also capitalized when the colon is followed by one or more complete sentences which make a statement that is introduced by the material preceding the colon.

> The manual says this: Make on-the-job safety your priority.

> The main point of the report was the following: The cost of fringe benefits is almost one-third of our expenses.

> There are two benefits to this program: First, employee morale should improve. Second, productivity should increase.

A direct quotation that follows a colon always begins with a capital letter. Therefore, if you wish to use a colon to draw attention to a quotation, make sure the beginning of the quotation forms a complete sentence. See the first example on this page.

Do not capitalize the first letter after a colon if the material that follows could not stand alone as a sentence.

> We need to order cover papers in three colors: green, red, and yellow.

> The following divisions will be represented at the trade fair: chemicals and medical technology.

Do not capitalize the first letter after a colon when the material that follows explains or illustrates the first part of the sentence. This rule holds whether or not the material can stand alone as a sentence.

The Western Region is proud of Bob Stanion: he has been the top salesperson for the last three quarters.

Remember to place all colons outside quotation marks and parentheses.

SHARPENING YOUR SKILLS 2

In the following sentences, correct any errors in the use of colons. Capitalize letters as necessary.

1. Research has found several new uses for the product; this discovery will make it more marketable.

2. The budget has not been approved yet; therefore, we cannot hire any new staff.

3. Make this your motto; I always wear my safety equipment.

4. These are your duties; first, clean off the old grease. Second, check for any cracked pistons. Third, make any repairs. Fourth, regrease the engine.

5. The new models are: the KR-9, the SR-9, and the XR-9.

6. I recently read *The Fortune-Makers; Ten Who Rule the Market.*

7. I quote Benjamin Franklin: "early to bed and early to rise makes a man healthy, wealthy, and wise."

8. John is our newest employee, he just began in August.

9. We have reserved booths for: Wilson & Co., Petroproducts, and Oil Management Inc.

10. I never would have made the 930 a.m. meeting if you hadn't typed that report for me.

EDITING EXERCISES

A. Correct any errors in the use of semicolons and colons in the following passages. Capitalize letters as necessary.

1. The feasibility study has shown three things, first, that the sales regions are too large for one person to cover, second, that Region 3 is growing faster than the others, third, that Region 1 has had no growth in the last two quarters. We recommend the following steps, Region 1 should be split into three regions, Regions 2, 4, and 5 should be restructured into four regions, and Region 3 should become two regions.

    2. Here is the most difficult part of your job, you must keep a positive state of mind. You will be working on several projects at once, therefore, a problem on one can affect your work on another. You must not allow this to happen, otherwise, your entire work load will be backed up. Remember to do the following, whistle while you work, ask for advice before a problem becomes overwhelming, and realize that everyone is here to help you.

B.   Revise the following sentences, placing semicolons and colons where they are needed and deleting those that are not necessary. Capitalize as necessary.

    1. In the past year, fuel costs have dropped, allowing us to cut prices, however, labor costs have risen, so the price cuts were moderate.

    2. There will be two speakers at the lunch meeting. We urge everyone to attend: the first speaker will be Mary Josephson, followed by Karl Thompson.

    3. The recipients of the Outstanding Employee award for this month are: Miriam Mokala, Sam Smith, and Lester Howard.

    4. The company sponsors an exercise class during lunch, moreover, it provides bonuses for keeping fit and not taking sick leave.

    5. The new printer had to be redesigned, there were too many customer complaints about its performance.

PROJECTS

A.   Choose a letter or other message you have written. Read through the message, and look for ways in which you can improve your writing by using semicolons and colons. Are there any short, related sentences that can be joined with a semicolon and a transitional word? Do you need to separate the elements of a series with a semicolon? Can you combine several sentences into a list that is introduced by a colon? Circle the sentences you can revise, and then rewrite the message.

B.   In order to become comfortable using semicolons and colons, read through an article in a business magazine or newspaper. Study how the writer has used these punctuation marks, and relate the examples to what you have learned in this chapter.

24

Dashes and Parentheses

"I'm sorry, Steve," said Mrs. Hughes, "but you'll have to revise this brochure. It looks as though you wrote it in Morse code. There are just too many dots, dashes, and parentheses."

It was true. Steve Dempsey was fond of using dashes and parentheses in his writing. Whenever his sentences became tangled, Steve depended on dashes to find his way out. He also enjoyed using parentheses to make breezy asides to his readers.

Dashes and parentheses can add variety, clarity, and lightness to writing, but they need to be used appropriately and sparingly. Otherwise, they lose their effectiveness, and the writer seems flighty and disorganized.

Careless writers insert dashes and parentheses whenever and wherever they feel like it. These marks of punctuation, however, do have a special function. Like commas, they are used mainly to set off parenthetical elements. Parenthetical words, phrases, and clauses provide additional information or explanatory material. They are nonessential—a sentence can survive without them.

Dashes break into sentences abruptly. They attract the reader's attention and emphasize the additional information.

> Sales for September were $1 million—an alarming decrease of 20 percent from August sales!—according to these reports.

Parentheses, on the other hand, slip into sentences quietly. They deemphasize the additional information and can more easily be omitted and replaced by commas. With commas, the additional information seems to flow more smoothly into the main thought. Commas are mild separators; the parenthetical element seems more closely related to the rest of the sentence.

DASHES VERSUS PARENTHESES

223

The cost of insurance rose by $1,000 (a 10 percent increase over the last premium).

The cost of insurance rose by $1,000, a 10 percent increase over the last premium.

In some situations the use of one kind of punctuation is clearly more appropriate than another. In other situations, however, the choice of punctuation depends on the writer's purpose.

The future of the company—as our chief executive officer has said—depends on our marketing strategy.

The writer of the previous sentence wants to call attention to the person who made the statement.

The future of the company (as our chief executive officer has said) depends on our marketing strategy.

The writer of this sentence wants to minimize the fact that the chief executive officer made this statement.

The future of the company, as our chief executive officer has said, depends on our marketing strategy.

The writer here feels that this would be a natural statement for the chief executive officer to make.

SHARPENING YOUR SKILLS 1

Identify the parenthetical element in each sentence. Would you use commas, dashes, or parentheses to set it off? Be ready to defend your choice.

1. I constantly receive promotional material from Passport a major credit card company.
2. There was only one task she disliked taking dictation.
3. Larry's idea which, in fact, he had borrowed from Peter captured the boss's imagination.
4. Miss Dawson who speaks both French and German fluently volunteered for an overseas position.
5. Dick Miller whose squeaky voice irritated everyone gave the after-dinner speech at the company banquet.

DASHES   Because of their size—twice as long as a hyphen—dashes command attention. They can set off single words, phrases, or clauses. They can appear within a sentence or at the end of a sentence.

Dashes are strong marks of punctuation, and they can replace commas and parentheses in setting off parenthetical elements such as nonrestrictive modifiers and appositives. In doing so, they stop the reader forcefully and give more impact to what follows. Compare, for instance, the effects of punctuation in the following sentences.

Mr. Hoff, the personnel manager, is sarcastic with employees.
Mr. Hoff—the personnel manager—is sarcastic with employees.

Maxwell Frank (who is a well-known stockbroker) was fooled by the scam.
Maxwell Frank—who is a well-known stockbroker—was fooled by the scam.

In both sets of sentences, the dashes cause the reader to pause, adding emphasis to the parenthetical element. When commas or parentheses are used, the information contained within them is interpreted by the reader as an aside: it is inconsequential to the meaning of the sentence. With the dashes, however, the information becomes important to the meaning of the sentence.

Special Uses

Besides setting off parenthetical elements, dashes have a number of other uses.

- Dashes can be used to indicate a break in thought, an interruption in conversation, or a change in tone.

  "I was thinking—now I forget what I was going to say."

- Dashes can be used to separate an afterthought from the main sentence. An afterthought can provide variety to writing style, soften a statement, give emphasis, and arouse curiosity.

  I hope to see you at next year's trade fair—perhaps even before then.

  Your sales of snowblowers this winter were down by 20 percent—of course, you couldn't control the warm weather we had in January.

  Send your order in now—you may receive a bonus.

- Dashes can be used to present a contrasting idea.

  Revenues were $4 million—compared to expenditures totaling $4.5 million—for the last fiscal year.

- Dashes can be used to signal a repetition or a restatement.

  You did a super job on this proposal—just super.

  Make an appointment with my secretary for the week after next—that's the week of February 10.

- Dashes can be used to signal a summary statement. When the words *these, they,* and *all* are used as subject pronouns and a list of details precedes them, a dash is used.

  A pleasant speaking voice, good communication skills, an ability to think clearly—these are the desired qualities of a telemarketing specialist.

- Dashes can be used to introduce words, phrases, or clauses. In this case, a dash takes the place of a colon and provides a stronger, but less formal, break.

   All employees have the following responsibilities—to do their job well, to obey company rules, and to be loyal to the firm.

- Dashes can be used to separate independent clauses in a compound sentence. In this case, a dash replaces a semicolon or a comma. More attention is drawn to the second clause.

   He ran to catch his bus—but it sped past him.

   Sally does the work—the manager gets the credit.

- Dashes can be used to prevent confusion with internal commas. When words that are set off contain internal commas, dashes can replace the parenthetical comma(s) for easier reading.

   Sheila noted the stopovers on her boss's itinerary—Seattle, Portland, San Francisco, and Las Vegas—and made hotel reservations in each city.

- Dashes can be used to call attention to individual words.

   A free parking space, a company car, a lounge area, and other pleasant job features have a special name—perks.

- Dashes can be used to indicate faltering or hesitant speech.

   "Well—I—uh—don't think I can make a decision on that."

SHARPENING YOUR SKILLS 2

Insert dashes where appropriate in the following sentences.

1. A schedule of events, a name tag, a map of the city, a list of restaurants and nightclubs all of this and more will be provided when you register for the workshop.
2. I'll see you at the meeting oh, and don't forget the blueprints.
3. Three members of the staff the copy editor, the art director, and the business manager deserve special credit.
4. I'll be up for promotion in five years if I don't get fired first.
5. My plane arrives at 6 p.m. that's 6 p.m. Central Daylight Time.

Punctuation and Capitalization With Dashes

The use of dashes requires careful attention to other punctuation and to capitalization.

The first word of the word group that is set off is not capitalized. This is true even if the words form a sentence.

> Maintaining a costly inventory—prices had risen to an alarming point—became one of the company's most serious problems.

Of course, there are exceptions. If the first word of the word group is a proper noun, a proper adjective, the pronoun *I*, or the beginning of a quotation, capitalization is maintained.

> The newspaper story began with a startling announcement by E. H. Dobson— "After 50 years of doing business in the downtown area, our store will close its doors in June."

Using dashes correctly with other punctuation marks can be tricky. It depends on where the words to be set off are placed in the sentence.

Within a Sentence. When the words to be set off appear within the sentence, two dashes are used. No punctuation is used before the first, or opening, dash, unless it is preceded by a quotation or by an abbreviation that ends with a period.

> The opening session begins at 9 a.m.—not 9:30 a.m. as previously announced—and continues until noon.

Similarly, no punctuation appears before the second, or closing, dash, unless the words that are set off form a question or an exclamation, as in the following example.

> Frank Anders—do you remember how shy he used to be?—is now a computer salesman.

If the second dash occurs where a comma would normally be placed (as in a compound sentence or following an introductory clause), retain the dash and omit the comma.

> While you may object to his business methods—I'll agree they're bizarre— you must admit he's successful. (Normally, there would be a comma separating the dependent clause from the independent clause.)

If the second dash occurs where a semicolon or a colon would normally be placed, drop the dash and use the required sentence punctuation.

> Here is what the report had to say—or at least the essence of it: the Abercrombie Company is on the verge of bankruptcy. (The second dash is not used following the word *it*.)

Within the group of words that are set off, commas are used in the regular way.

> Three assistant managers—James Palmer, Betsy Kraft, and Terry Miller—were up for promotion.

At the End of a Sentence. When the words to be set off appear at the end of the sentence, only an opening dash is used. The closing dash is replaced by the regular end punctuation.

> At the end of his probationary period, Jack received an unfavorable evaluation—a very unfavorable evaluation.

> This is a tremendous job opportunity—don't you agree? (Notice that the question mark, while belonging to *don't you agree*, ends the entire sentence.)

SHARPENING YOUR SKILLS 3

Correct any errors in capitalization or punctuation in the following sentences.

1. Accounting, business law, marketing, management,—these are some of the courses Marlene took for her business degree.

2. It took the Maintenance Department only two minutes to discover the cause of the trouble—a paper jam in the cylinder—!

3. Please deliver this paper supply to Apsco Printing—The company is at 5th and Grand.—before 2 p.m.

4. Our Omaha branch—have you heard—has been very innovative?

5. Try to finish the report by Wednesday—Certainly by Friday—otherwise, we won't have time to review it before the meeting.

PARENTHESES

Unlike dashes and commas, parentheses almost always appear in pairs: There is an opening parenthesis and a closing parenthesis. (Notice the spelling of the singular form.) Parentheses can enclose single words, phrases, and clauses. The parenthetical elements they set off can be part of a sentence, or they can stand alone as independent sentences.

Unlike dashes, parentheses do not shout at the reader. Instead, they quietly add the explanatory or illustrative material.

> Many career opportunities exist in the field of merchandising (for instance, wholesale and retail buying).

Special Uses

Besides setting off parenthetical elements in general, parentheses are also used for special kinds of material.

• Parentheses can be used to give cross-references. A cross-reference refers the reader to another part of the book or document for more information. It can also refer the reader to another resource.

The author of this study toured 25 facilities around the country. (Their names and locations are listed in Appendix A.)

As I have said repeatedly (see my memos of January 10, February 6, and March 10), I am opposed to this project.

- Parentheses can be used to give brief facts. Parentheses are useful for providing a variety of short, quick details, such as dates, abbreviations, definitions, publishing information, pronunciations, and statistics.

Horace Moses (1862–1947) founded Junior Achievement, an organization that teaches young people how to run a business.

The book *How to Make a Million Dollars With Your Small Business* (New York: Phillip Sands & Sons, 1986) has become a best-seller.

- Parentheses can be used to give directions. In certain situations, the use of parentheses can provide clarity or prevent confusion.

Please complete and submit these forms (print or use a typewriter).

- Parentheses can be used with city-state expressions used as adjectives. In this instance commas might be confusing, and dashes would be too emphatic.

I visited our Kansas City (Kansas) branch office in July.

- Parentheses can be used with internal commas. When the words being set off already contain commas, parentheses are clearer than adding more commas.

I visited other branch offices (Seattle, Milwaukee, Hartford, Roanoke) earlier in the year.

- Parentheses can be used with the repetition of dollar amounts in legal writing.

In the event of hospitalization, the company agrees to pay the insured a sum not to exceed three hundred dollars ($300) per day for medical services.

- Parentheses can be used with enumerated items. Within a sentence, parentheses are used to enclose numbers or letters that signal items in a series.

First National will soon implement two new policies: (1) a monthly service charge on all low-balance, 5 percent daily interest savings accounts; and (2) a change in the way interest is accrued on your account.

When letters or numbers appear on separate lines (called a display list), parentheses are not used.

1.
2.
3.

An exception would be the subdivisions of an outline. Note that at the lower levels only one parenthesis is used.

1.
  a.
   (1)
     (a)
       1)
         a)

SHARPENING YOUR SKILLS 4

Identify the material that should be enclosed in parentheses in the following sentences.

1. Kearny Construction submitted a bid of $5,000 for the remodeling project see attached itemized statement.

2. When we meet next Tuesday at the weekly personnel meeting, we'll rate each employee's performance.

3. The small town of Laurelton pop. 3,000 is trying to attract new business.

4. The receptionist's duties include 1 answering the telephone; 2 greeting visitors; 3 making appointments.

5. We've received several out-of-town orders Fort Dodge, Dodge City, New Haven, and East St. Louis.

Punctuation and Capitalization With Parentheses

As with dashes, the use of parentheses requires careful attention to punctuation and capitalization. The rules depend on where the words in parentheses appear.

As Part of a Sentence. When the words in parentheses are part of a sentence, the first word is not capitalized.

> The messenger service delivered the package to Mr. Wilson's law office (on the fifth floor of the Baker Building).

Exceptions would be a proper noun, a proper adjective, the pronoun *I,* or the beginning of a quotation.

> Messenger services (John's is the best) are a must for busy offices.

No punctuation is used before the first, or opening, parenthesis, unless it is preceded by a quotation or by an abbreviation that ends with a period.

> The gross national product (GNP) is expected to decline by one percentage point next year.

No punctuation is used before the second, or closing, parenthesis, unless the words set off form a question or an exclamation.

> If Ann accepts the position with the Willard Agency (Jack thinks it's possible), she will have to relocate.

> If Ann accepts the position with the Willard Agency (do you think it's possible?), she will have to relocate.

If the parenthetical phrase takes a question mark or exclamation point, the end-of-sentence punctuation must be different. If the parenthetical phrase and the sentence each take the same punctuation mark, use only one to end the entire sentence.

> INCORRECT: I finally finished typing the manuscript (hallelujah!)!

> CORRECT: I finally finished typing the manuscript (hallelujah)!

If the last word before the closing parenthesis is an abbreviation that ends in a period, retain the period. If the words set off are a quotation, quotation marks are called for.

> Please be certain all personal belongings (umbrellas, coats, purses, etc.) are hung up or concealed at all times in the event that a client pays us an unexpected visit.

> The company motto ("Quality comes first") is imprinted on all company stationery.

If a punctuation mark would normally occur in a sentence before the parenthetical expression, place it after the parenthetical expression instead.

> Tony first refused the job (do you blame him?), and then he expressed disapproval of the company's ethics.

Standing Alone. When the words in parentheses stand apart as an independent sentence, the words are written as a full sentence set off in parentheses. The first word is capitalized, and regular end punctuation is used before the closing parenthesis. No punctuation follows the closing parenthesis.

> Orange Computers, Inc., controls the market in personal computers. (Nearly 2 million were sold nationwide last year.) The profits have been enormous.

SHARPENING YOUR SKILLS 5

Correct any errors in capitalization or punctuation in the following sentences.

1. Bob MacDougall joined our law firm in 1974 (He was then a junior partner.) he has since left for a position in Washington, D.C.

2. May I leave work early (and may I have tomorrow off?) since there's not much work to do?

3. Although Charlie Hoffman seemed to be the logical choice for vice president, (he's been with the company for twenty years), management hired someone from outside.

4. If you have questions, please call our customer service representative (863-2503, between 8 a.m. and 5 p.m.)

5. Last year I gave $50 to the alumni foundation (I graduated in 1978) and the company matched my contribution.

EDITING EXERCISES

A. Correct the errors in punctuation and capitalization in the following sentences.

1. Here it is!—The sweepstakes prize that can make you super rich—!

2. Order now and get great free gifts, (you don't pay a penny extra!

3. Here's how to order: (1.) Paste the magazine stamps in the space below; (2.) Paste your address label to the left; (3.) Place a postage stamp on the front of the card; (4.) Mail today. If we don't hear from you by April 30,—just four short weeks from now, we must drop your name from our mailing list.

4. Why not take advantage of our generous offer right here and now?—(You'll find savings up to 50 percent!).

5. Send in your order now—along with your grand prize numbers—; you could be the next lucky winner!

6. Listen to what Steve Kramer, last year's winner of $10 million, has to say—"my family and I never thought we'd be winners. You can be a winner, too!"—

7. Wouldn't you like to buy the car of your dreams perhaps a (Cadillac, Lincoln Continental, or Mercedes-Benz?)

B. Following each sentence is a parenthetical element. Insert the parenthetical element into the sentence, using correct punctuation and capitalization.

1. Your health premium is payable on a quarterly basis. *Every three months*

2. List below all hospitalizations: *If none, write "none"*

3. Your doctor can call on other physician and nurse specialists within the same center, and you'll have access to sophisticated lab and X-ray departments. *Internal Medicine, Family Practice, Children's Medicine, Ob/Gyn, Surgery, and others*

4. All the other services to keep you well are covered, too. *Or to get you better*

5. An effectively managed Health Maintenance Organization offers an alternative to skyrocketing medical costs. *HMO*

6. Choose one of the family medical centers as your clinic. *See the medical center brochure.*

7. We think our quality care and cost control make our HMO your best choice. We think you'll agree!

8. If you have any questions or concerns, contact Doug Forest at 343-6080. *He's our marketing representative.*

C. Rewrite the following paragraphs, inserting correct capitalization and punctuation. You should use at least one question mark, exclamation point, semicolon, colon, and dash, and one set of parentheses.

like most other policyholders in the state you'll probably be paying more for car insurance with this renewal the reason we're paying more for claims particularly claims involving bodily injury is simple liability cases are higher with each passing year insurance companies are not to blame medical costs keep escalating court settlements for bodily injury if they continue to escalate at the current rate soon the average person will not be able to afford to have insurance also did you know that the number of claims paid has increased significantly in the last couple of years by practicing defensive driving habits and using seat belts policyholders can help

rest assured we'll keep doing our best to make the most efficient use of your premium dollars so you can continue enjoying the best car insurance value around

If you have any questions please contact your agent

continued on reverse side

PROJECTS

A. Advertisements often make use of parentheses and dashes for special effects—to call attention to a particular phrase, to emphasize a point, and so on. In a newspaper or magazine, find three printed advertisements that make use of these punctuation marks. Rewrite the sentences using more conventional punctuation (periods, commas). What effect did this have on the ad? Did it lose some of its punch? Was it less interesting or less persuasive?

B. Write a one-paragraph memo that you would give your supervisor to explain why progress on a particular project is behind schedule. Use parentheses and dashes at least once in your memo.

25
Quotation Marks and Underscores

The editor of the company newsletter asked Katherine Delmont to write an article about the company's recent open house. To get the reader's attention, Katherine decided to open her article with reactions from the employees.

> "My family thought the open house was great. They got a chance to see where I work and what I do. Now when I talk about my job it means more to them."
> —Rita Lufkin

> "I found out a lot about the company I never knew before. I met some people I'd never seen before. It makes me feel important to be part of this organization."
>
> —Jack Murphy

Katherine used quotation marks to indicate the employee's exact words. In fact, the most common function of quotation marks is to set off direct quotations. They are also used to indicate titles and occasionally to give special emphasis to words.

Quotation marks usually appear in pairs, either as double quotation marks (" ") or as single quotation marks (' '). Single quotation marks are used mainly for quotations within quotations.

Like quotation marks, italics are used to indicate titles and to give emphasis to words. Since italics are not available on standard typewriters or in handwriting, underscores, or underlines, are used instead. If what you are writing will eventually be typeset, underscores tell the typesetter to set the material in italic type.

Although quotation marks and underscores have similar functions, they are never used together for the same words. Thus, indicating the title of a company newsletter with both quotation marks and underscores would be incorrect.

A quotation tells what someone said. You can quote another person's written or spoken words. Sometimes you may even quote yourself. There are two kinds of quotations: direct and indirect.

QUOTATIONS

Direct Quotations

In a direct quotation, you use quotation marks to indicate the speaker's exact words. By doing this, you make the words stand out and give credit to the speaker. Usually, an identifying expression such as *he said* appears with the quotation, but it is not enclosed in quotation marks.

> Mr. McCabe said emphatically, "I am totally opposed to the merger with AM & M." (A sentence is quoted.)

> Mr. McCabe still professes "strong feelings of loyalty" for his company. (Only a phrase is quoted.)

Indirect Quotations

In an indirect quotation you only paraphrase, or give the sense of, what the person said; you do not use the speaker's exact words. Indirect quotations are usually introduced by the words *that* and *whether*. (The word *that* can often be omitted.) Do not enclose an indirect quotation in quotation marks.

> Mr. McCabe said that he was totally surprised by the proposed merger with AM & M.

Quotations Within Quotations

Sometimes the person you are quoting will, in turn, quote another person, forming a quotation within a quotation. Use single quotation marks within double quotation marks for this situation.

> Mr. McCabe sighed, "Our late president always said, 'Never sell out! Never sell out!' "

Single quotation marks are also used when titles or words needing special emphasis appear within double quotation marks.

> Mr. McCabe told his secretary, "Write 'Confidential' on this envelope and hand-deliver the letter to Miss Putnam's office."

No Quotation Marks Necessary.   Quotation marks are not used to enclose proverbs or other well-known sayings.

> Don't jump out of the frying pan and into the fire really fits this situation.

> Mr. McCabe said, "The company may be in trouble, but we shouldn't jump out of the frying pan and into the fire." (Quotation marks are needed here to set off Mr. McCabe's words—not the proverb.)

No quotation marks are used with unspoken thoughts or questions.

> I really don't know what to do, thought Mr. McCabe.

> What am I doing here? he wondered.

SHARPENING YOUR SKILLS 1

Tell whether or not quotation marks are needed for each of the following sentences.

1. Miss Mann asked whether or not we could work late.

2. I told her that I had an appointment after work today, but that I could stay late tomorrow night.

3. I don't know how they expect me to finish this report by Thursday, Sam remarked to his colleague.

4. Sally said she could help Sam.

5. You did an excellent job on this report, Jean, remarked Miss Mann. I'm going to write a letter about this for your personnel file.

6. Miss Mann believes that when the cat's away, the mice will play.

7. A month later I reminded Miss Mann, You said you'd write a letter for me. Have you written it yet?

8. Sam is not very well organized, Sally thought to herself.

TITLES   Depending on the circumstances, either quotation marks or underscores are used to set off titles. Quotation marks indicate minor titles (usually titles of shorter works), while underscores indicate major titles (usually titles of longer works).

Quotation Marks

Use quotation marks to enclose the titles of parts of complete published works, such as units and chapters in books and columns and articles in newspapers and magazines. Use quotation marks to enclose the titles of complete unpublished works: reports, studies, dissertations. The titles of lectures, conference themes, curriculum courses, sermons, and essays are also set off by quotation marks.

"Know Your Marketplace," Mark Juran's column, appears in most major newspapers.

Donna typed her report, "Prime Office Locations in the Metropolitan Area," for presentation at the board meeting.

The titles of short stories, songs, short musical compositions, and poems are enclosed in quotation marks, as are the titles of individual programs in a radio or television series.

Underscores

Use underscores for the titles of complete published works, such as books, magazines, newspapers, pamphlets, and newsletters.

Maggie Lewis reads the business section of the New York Times regularly.

I read an interesting article in Forbes magazine last week.

The titles of long poems, plays, movies, musicals, long musical compositions, operas, and radio and television series are also underscored.

No Quotation Marks or Underscores

Some titles use neither quotation marks nor underscores. The names of the standard book parts—preface, table of contents, appendix, and index—do not get special treatment, although they may be capitalized.

The Preface to the best-seller Managing Your Money reveals how the author did his research. (The word *preface* is capitalized in this example because it is part of a certain book.)

Previewing the table of contents gives you a good idea of the book's organization. (A specific table of contents is not referred to here, so the term is not capitalized.)

The titles of catalogues and directories, political documents, and sacred writings are not underscored or put in quotation marks.

the New York Yellow Pages
the National Zip Code Directory
the Constitution of the United States
the Treaty of Versailles
the Bible
the Koran

When you type or write the title of a composition at the top of the page, do not underscore it or put it in quotation marks. The same is true if you are typing a report on the job.

SHARPENING YOUR SKILLS 2

In the following sentences, add quotation marks or underscores where necessary.

1. A free seminar, "Managing Your IRA," will be held today from 9 a.m. to 1 p.m. at the <u>Regency Hotel downtown</u>.

2. Our corporation ran a full-page ad in the March 3 issue of <u>BusinessWeek</u>.

3. My teacher assigned Unit 1, "Learning the Keyboard," in <u>Fundamentals of Typing</u> for the next class session.

4. Did you see the office equipment advertised in the J. C. Penney Catalogue?

5. KUSA-TV won a broadcast journalism award for its news segment The "Insurance Crisis."

SPECIAL EMPHASIS

Sometimes a writer may want to call attention to a certain word, or the writer may want to use a word in an unusual way. In these situations, quotation marks and underscores can be useful.

Quotation Marks and Underscores

Quotation marks and underscores can work together to provide special emphasis. One example is a formal definition. Another is the translation of a foreign word.

> One meaning of the verb <u>interface</u> is "to interact or communicate harmoniously."

> The French term <u>carte blanche</u> means "blank document."

In these examples, the underscoring distinguishes the term from its definition or translation in quotation marks.

An informal definition does not need special emphasis.

> An intrapreneur is someone who advances within a company by suggesting new products or ideas.

Either quotation marks or underscores can be used to call attention to words as words. Such expressions usually begin with *the word* or *the term*.

> The term "user friendly" refers to computer technology that is relatively easy to use.

> OR

> The term <u>user friendly</u> refers to computer technology that is relatively easy to use.

When too many quotation marks might be distracting to the reader, some writers use quotation marks for one term and underscores for a series of terms.

> Add the names <u>Grayson Development</u>, <u>B & F Wholesalers</u>, and <u>Hawkinson Insurance Co.</u> to our list of potential customers.

Underscores

Underscores are used to set off foreign words and phrases that have not become part of the English language. For example, use underscores for <u>wie geht's?</u> but not for résumé. A dictionary will help you determine which foreign words have become familiar.

Quotation Marks

For special emphasis in some situations, quotation marks are more accepted usage than underscores. For example, use quotation marks to enclose expressions introduced by the words *marked, known as, labeled, signed,* and *entitled.*

> Even though the package was marked "Fragile," the shipping clerk threw it on the truck.

Quotation marks can also be used to indicate a word that has been coined by a speaker.

> Jeff calls the computer's cursor a "whatchamadoodle."

No Quotation Marks or Underscores

Avoid putting well-known expressions such as *pros and cons* in quotation marks. Nor should you use quotation marks to draw attention to puns or humorous remarks. Trust your reader to catch your play on words without such aids. In the following sentence, for example, no quotation marks are necessary to point out the pun on *builds.*

> This housing contractor builds self-respect.

Do not use quotation marks for signs or familiar nicknames.

> Eric posted a No Smoking sign in the storeroom.

Especially avoid overusing quotation marks for special emphasis in more formal writing, such as annual reports or proposals. Rephrase any slang expressions to avoid quotation marks—and inappropriate informality.

> INCORRECT: The sales department was getting a lot of "heat."

> CORRECT: The sales department was under pressure to improve its performance.

SHARPENING YOUR SKILLS 3

In the following sentences, add quotation marks or underscores as necessary.

1. Mary typed a list of employee dos and don'ts.

2. Jake didn't know that modus operandi means a method of procedure.

3. Mrs. Barnes uses the word really too much in her business communication.

4. The document was signed Harry T. Peterson.

5. All he does is fool around with computers—he's definitely a hacker.

CLOSING QUOTATION MARKS AND OTHER PUNCTUATION

Closing, or second, quotation marks usually appear with other punctuation. This occurrence frequently bewilders writers: Does the punctuation go inside or outside the quotation marks? The rules that follow apply to both single and double quotation marks.

With Periods and Commas

Always place a period or comma inside the closing quotation mark.

Last semester I took "Fundamentals of Accounting."

At a salary of $60,000 per annum, meaning "for each year," Blake still felt underpaid.

With Semicolons and Colons

Place a semicolon or colon outside the closing quotation mark.

Read the chapter entitled "Merge Operations"; then practice the skills described.

The following applications were labeled "Credit Approved": Reid Johnson, Nadine Jones, Karen Rudd.

With Question Marks and Exclamation Points

If the question or exclamation applies only to the quoted material, place the question mark or exclamation point inside the closing quotation mark. A period is not necessary to end the sentence.

I read an article on software prices entitled "Are They Heading for a Fall?"

The manila envelope was marked "Photos, do not bend!"

If the question or exclamation applies to the entire sentence, place the question mark or exclamation point outside the closing quotation mark.

> Did you know that <u>CAI</u> means "computer-assisted instruction"?

> I can't believe he labeled that junk "First class"!

If the quoted material and the entire sentence require the same mark of punctuation, use only the mark that comes first.

> Did you read the article on software prices entitled "Are They Heading for a Fall?"

SHARPENING YOUR SKILLS 4

Correct any errors in punctuation in the following sentences.

1. The topic of the meeting is "If I Can't See It, How Can I Sell It"?

2. In computer terminology the verb <u>debug</u> means "to check and correct errors in a program".

3. Please bring me the following items from the folder labeled "Comco:" business plan, financial outlook, independent analysis.

4. Have you read Chapter 10, "Where Do We Go From Here?"?

5. Chapter 1 is titled, "Making the Most of Your Coffee Break;" Chapter 2 is called, "Getting Along With Your Co-Workers."

Correct punctuation and capitalization of direct quotations require careful thought. Since several punctuation marks appear in a row, writers must take special note of the proper order for the marks. Writers must also be aware of where one sentence in a direct quotation ends and another begins. Three situations especially need attention: direct quotations with identifying expressions, long quotations, and dialogue.

PUNCTUATION AND CAPITALIZATION OF DIRECT QUOTATIONS

Identifying Expressions

An identifying expression such as *she replied* can come before or after a quotation. It may also interrupt a quotation. Knowing how to use other punctuation with closing quotation marks helps in handling these expressions.

Quotation at Beginning of Sentence Followed by Identifying Expression. Use a comma to separate the quotation from the identifying expression.

> "All the departments have submitted their budgets," said the controller.

If the quotation is a question or an exclamation, use a question mark or an exclamation point in place of the comma.

> "How many departments have not submitted their budget requests?" Mr. Mattson asked.

Quotation at End of Sentence Preceded by Identifying Expression. Use a comma to separate the identifying expression from the quotation. Always capitalize the first word of the quotation.

> Mr. Mattson asked, "Have all the departments submitted their budget requests?"

Notice that the identifying phrase can include an additional description.

> With a sigh of relief Mr. Mattson said, "All the departments have submitted their budget requests."

You may use a colon instead of a comma to introduce a quotation of two or more sentences.

> Mr. Mattson made the following announcement at the board meeting: "All the departments have submitted their budget requests. They appear to be reasonable."

Quotation Interrupted by Identifying Expression. When the identifying expression interrupts a quotation, place a comma and closing quotation mark before the expression. Place a comma after the expression. When the quotation starts in again, use an opening quotation mark. Do not capitalize the first word.

> "All the departments," announced Mr. Mattson, "have submitted their budget requests."

When the identifying expression ends a sentence and the quotation continues in a new sentence, place a period after the expression. Start the new sentence with an opening quotation mark and a capital letter.

> "All the departments have submitted their budget requests," Mr. Mattson announced. "They appear to be reasonable."

Long Quotations

There are two ways to handle a quotation that will take four or more typewritten lines. The preferred way is to type it as a single-spaced extract. Skip a space before and after the extract. Indent the extract five spaces on each side. Do not use quotation marks. (The indention and single spacing take the place of quotation marks.) The extract might be introduced in this way:

> In the June 9 issue of BusinessWeek, Mr. Devries states:

The other way is to type the quotation with the same line length and spacing as the rest of the material. Put quotation marks at the beginning and ending of the paragraph. If the quotation is more than one paragraph long, place opening quotation marks at the beginning of each paragraph. However, place a closing quotation mark only at the end of the last paragraph. Change any double quotation marks within the quoted material to single quotation marks.

SHARPENING YOUR SKILLS 5

Correct any errors in punctuation and capitalization in the following sentences.

1. "If you work for our firm," Mrs. Storm said, "You will need good typing and organization skills."

2. "We offer a complete array of benefits." "We also offer competitive salaries," Mrs. Storm stated.

3. "Have you had any experience," asked Mrs. Storm?

4. "Mrs. Storm added," "of course, we expect a professional manner from our employees."

5. "You mean I get the job" exclaimed Cyndy!

EDITING EXERCISES

Correct any errors in punctuation or capitalization in the following sentences. If there are no errors, write the word *correct* next to the sentence.

1. The envelope was marked "Urgent! Read contents immediately!"

2. "Did you read the "Preface" to 'Ahead of the Bottom Line' " asked Gilbert?

3. I listen to the feature *Getting the Most for Your Money* every week on the Ruth Slater Show.

4. The title of my report is "Change-making Systems."

5. Some friend you are—telling lies about me behind my back!"

6. Becky listed all the "pros" and "cons" of her job.

7. Please hand me the box marked Handle With Care.

8. The district manager was just "thrilled to pieces" when I showed him the July sales figures.

9. "As the saying goes, don't count your chickens before they are hatched," Juan warned Ms. DeQuincy.

10. David suggested that his brother read the column called Insider's Report in the Wall Street Journal.

PROJECTS

A. In a comic strip, the cartoonist generally uses conversation balloons to show what the characters are saying. For practice in punctuating quotations, write the conversation from a comic strip as it would appear in regular paragraph style. You will need to add identifying expressions. Include a description of the setting for the conversation. If possible, find a comic strip that shows an office situation. For example, you might punctuate a conversation between Dagwood Bumstead and Mr. Dithers in the comic strip "Blondie."

B. A newsletter is an example of in-house business communication. In-house publications are for the employees rather than for the public. Discuss the importance of company newsletters with your classmates. Collect samples of newsletters from local businesses.

C. The following terms of foreign origin often appear in business communications. Look up the meaning of each one. Since these terms have become more common, they are generally not put in quotation marks or underscored—unless attention is being called to them in a definition or a translation.

ad hoc	laissez-faire
ad infinitum	per annum
bona fide	per se
de facto	pro rata
et al.	pro tem
ex officio	quid pro quo
ibid.	vis-à-vis

26
Apostrophes and Hyphens

Dan had just finished typing a ten-page report for his supervisor. He asked Chris, a co-worker in the Internal Finance Department, to proofread it for him.

Chris found that Dan's typing was very accurate. The only errors he had made involved misplaced apostrophes and hyphens. Such errors, however, can greatly change the meaning of a message. Note what the omission of an apostrophe does in the following sentences.

Mr. Waldoch called the employees' names.

Mr. Waldoch called the employees names.

Likewise, without a hyphen, the phrase *new-employee forms* might be interpreted to mean "new forms for employees to fill out" rather than "forms for new employees to fill out."

APOSTROPHES

Apostrophes are used often in writing, but they do not always mean the same thing. Depending upon the context in which they appear, they can show possession or ownership, replace missing letters and numbers, and form special plurals.

Possession

If you want to indicate that the office next to yours belongs to the manager, you might say "the office of the manager." To show the relation of a cafeteria to a group of employees, you might say "the cafeteria for employees."

Such phrases, however, become awkward, especially if there are several of them close together. A more direct way to show ownership or to express a relationship is to use a possessive noun or a possessive pronoun, followed by the object owned.

> the manager's office
> their cafeteria

Sometimes the object of ownership is not stated, but implied.

> Is this Sue's desk or Carrie's? (The object of ownership is omitted after the possessive noun *Carrie's.*)

Missing Letters and Numbers

An apostrophe is used to take the place of a missing letter or letters. You are familiar with the use of apostrophes in contractions, such as *aren't* and *I'm.* Sometimes writers confuse a contraction with a possessive noun.

> The cleaning crew's been here.

In the above sentence, the word *crew's* is a contraction of *crew* and *has* and should not be mistaken for a possessive noun.

Individual words can also have missing letters.

> ma'am (madam)
> snackin' (snacking)

Manufacturers often omit letters in the names of their products. This practice is meant to give the product a livelier image and make its name easier to say. For example, the name of a salad dressing might be Sweet 'n' Spicy. Note that there is an apostrophe both before the *n* (to take the place of the *a* in *and*) and after the *n* (to take the place of the *d*). The first apostrophe is incorrectly omitted in many brand names, however.

An apostrophe is also used to mark the omission of the century number in dates.

> the class of '68
> an '86 Mercedes-Benz

This usage is inappropriate in formal writing and when the century number might be mistaken, as would happen if the writer meant the class of 1868.

Special Plurals

A letter, symbol, numeral, or abbreviation can be made plural. For the plural of a lowercase letter or an abbreviation followed by a period, add *'s.* The apostrophe prevents misreading.

> Mr. Wallin's *i*'s look like *e*'s.

> Miss Wood has two Ph.D.'s: one in business and the other in education.

> Evan is processing acct.'s 234A and 246B.

For the plural of a capital letter, an abbreviation not followed by a period, a numeral, a symbol, or a word referred to as a word, an apostrophe and *s* are not necessary—unless there would be confusion without them.

> these *D*s OR these *D*'s
> YMCAs OR YMCA's
> three 8s OR three 8's
> #s OR #'s
> too many *and*s OR too many *and*'s
> 1980s OR 1980's

Notice the italics for words referred to as words and for letters referred to as letters. The *s* or *'s,* however, is not italicized.

Common Problems With Apostrophes

Misuse of the apostrophe is one of the most common errors in writing. Some writers mistakenly add apostrophes to simple plurals.

> INCORRECT: The manager needs volunteer's to work on the Henderson project. (The volunteers do not own anything.)

> CORRECT: The manager needs volunteers to work on the Henderson project.

Inserting apostrophes within the objects of ownership, rather than after the possessive word, is another frequent error.

> INCORRECT: Jack followed the managers direction's carefully.

> CORRECT: Jack followed the manager's directions carefully.

Many writers also incorrectly insert apostrophes in possessive pronouns.

> INCORRECT: After considering all the bids, the company accepted their's.

> CORRECT: After considering all the bids, the company acccepted theirs.

Reviewing the rules in Chapter 7 for forming possessives can help you avoid apostrophe errors.

SHARPENING YOUR SKILLS 1

For each sentence, write the correct form of the word in parentheses.

1. The cashier put all the (IOU) _____ in the left compartment of the cash drawer.

2. Electric typewriters usually have repeating (*x*) _____ .

3. Jane Gephart and Gary Migday received their (M.A.) _____ in finance.

4. The company was in financial trouble, but the board paid no attention to the auditor's (SOS) _____ .

5. If you work for Ms. Godunov, you must watch your (*p* and *q*) _____ .

6. The stock clerk counted off the items by (two) _____ .

HYPHENS   Like other punctuation marks, the hyphen has specific functions: It unites words divided between two lines, holds together compound words, and clarifies words, especially those with prefixes and suffixes.

Word Division

You know that it is not always possible to fit every letter of the last word on a line of type or writing. Space limitations require the word to be broken. A hyphen is used to indicate that the word continues on the next line.

Words are not divided according to the whims of each writer. There are definite guidelines to follow. The basic guideline is that words are divided— as much as possible—according to their pronunciation. Since syllables are the units of pronunciation, words are divided by syllables.

Dictionaries, of course, show correct word division. You can follow the syllabication of the boldface entry word. However, it would be time-consuming to look up every word that needs hyphenation. Besides, simply knowing what the syllables are does not always tell you the best place for the hyphen. Knowing a few simple rules of hyphenation can save you time and trouble.

- Do not divide a one-syllable word.

    should, work, plant

    Note that adding *ed* to a word does not always add a syllable.

    typed, filled

- When two consonants come between two vowels, divide between the consonants.

    in-voice, of-fer, per-son-nel

    However, some words cannot be divided this way because the division violates the pronunciation.

    de-cline, work-ers

- When the base form of a word ends in a double consonant, divide after the double consonant.

    bill-ing, dress-ing, small-est, call-ers

- When the final consonant in a word doubles before a suffix is added, divide between the double consonant.

    thin-ner, forget-ting

- Divide between two vowels only if they are sounded separately.

   reli-ant, co-operating

- If a word contains a one-letter syllable, divide after the syllable.

   poli-cy, tabu-late, organi-zation

In addition to these rules, appearance can also be a guideline in word division. A hyphenated word should not look odd to the reader's eye, nor should the division interfere with the reader's comprehension of the word. Ease of reading is the underlying reason for the following rules.

- Do not set off a one-letter syllable.

   INCORRECT: i-dentify, criteri-a

   CORRECT: iden-tify, cri-teria

- Avoid dividing words of five or fewer letters.

   INCORRECT: ar-ea

   CORRECT: area

- In dividing a word, have at least three characters on the upper line and on the lower line. The hyphen counts as one character, as do other punctuation marks such as periods and commas.

   faint-ed.   mark-up?

- Do not hyphenate at the end of a paragraph or at the end of a page.
- Avoid overhyphenation. Having too many hyphens down the right-hand margin looks worse than an uneven margin.

Special Word-Division Situations. Certain kinds of words receive special treatment. Do not divide abbreviations, acronyms, contractions, numerals, abbreviations with numerals, or personal names.

Incorrect	Correct
ac-ct.	acct.
CE-TA	CETA
does-n't	doesn't
$1,356,-000	$1,356,000
500-A.D.	500 A.D.
A. J. Fish-burn	A. J. Fishburn

Divide solid compound words between the words that make them up. Divide hyphenated compounds at the hyphen.

   INCORRECT: hand-lebar, time-shar-ing

   CORRECT: handle-bar, time-sharing

Divide after a prefix and before a suffix.

    INCORRECT: in-terchange, spe-cialize

    CORRECT: inter-change, special-ize

SHARPENING YOUR SKILLS 2

Choose the word that shows correct treatment at the end of a line of type or writing. Be able to explain your choice.

    1. salespeo-ple, sales-people

    2. around, a-round

    3. econo-mies, econ-omies

    4. stopped, stop-ped

    5. begin-ning, be-ginning

    6. every, eve-ry

    7. rent-al, ren-tal

    8. fil-ling, fill-ing

    9. trespas-sing, trespass-ing

   10. super-visor, su-pervisor

   11. re-ality, real-ity

   12. manage-ment, man-agement

Compound Words

Spelling a compound word is sometimes a problem. Should it be written open, solid, or hyphenated? Many compound words, especially those new to the English language, are in a constant state of change. For example, if you looked up the following compound word in three different dictionaries, you might find three different spellings. All of them are correct.

    life style, lifestyle, life-style

For some compound words you will need to choose the spelling given in a particular dictionary and then stick with it. The important thing is to be consistent. Other compound words are definitely either solid, open, or hyphenated. The following information will help you determine which words need hyphens.

Compound Nouns. Use a hyphen between two nouns that refer to one person or thing that plays two roles.

    secretary-treasurer, producer-director

Hyphenate family relationships.

> brother-in-law, great-uncle

Compound nouns ending in prepositions form a mixed bag. Some are solid; others are hyphenated. The following hyphenated compounds are especially useful in business.

In words:	break-in	stand-in
	check-in	trade-in
	drive-in	walk-in
Off words:	drop-off	spin-off
	lift-off	trade-off
	send-off	write-off
Up words:	close-up	touch-up
	follow-up	wrap-up
	mock-up	write-up

Compound Adjectives. Many compound adjectives made up of particular word patterns are hyphenated before the noun but not after it.

* Adverb + participle (except adverbs ending in *ly*)

a *well-done* steak	The steak turned out *well done.*
the *much-discussed* merger	The merger was *much discussed.*
long-lasting shoes	These shoes are *long lasting.*
Exception:	
a *wholly owned* subsidiary	The subsidiary is *wholly owned.*
a *poorly designed* plant	The plant was *poorly designed.*

* Participle + adverb

a *lived-in* look	The house looked *lived in.*
worn-out ideas	His ideas are simply *worn out.*
the *warmed-up* engine	Make sure the engine is *warmed up.*

* Phrases

off-the-record remarks	The senator considered her remarks *off the record.*
up-and-down career	His career has certainly been *up and down.*
a *six-year-old* edition	This edition is now *six years old.*
on-the-mend budget	The budget is *on the mend.*

* Number + unit of measurement (except with *percent* or a dollar sign)

a *two-inch* margin	a margin of *two inches*
a *15-year* record	a record of *15 years*
Exceptions:	
a *10 percent* increase	
a *$12* markup	

A number of compound adjectives are hyphenated whether they appear before or after the noun.

- Noun + participle

  Computer-aided design offers exciting possibilities.

  We now offer *interest-bearing* accounts.

  Every product is *market-tested* before release.

  The convention offers a *mind-boggling* display of software.

- Adjective + participle

  A *half-baked* idea is better than none.

  Our *smooth-spreading* paints contain latex.

  The director wants a name that is *sweet-sounding*.

  The project is still only *half-finished.*

- Adjective + noun + *ed*

  The *low-priced* line is the least popular.

  These suits are extremely *old-fashioned.*

  Light-colored fabrics make sense in summer.

Numbers. When two-digit numbers from twenty-one to ninety-nine are spelled out, they are compound words and require hyphens. This is true whether the numbers appear alone or as a part of a larger number.

> forty-nine
> five thousand and forty-nine

Fractions that are spelled out are hyphenated.

> two-thirds   one twenty-fifth

Some writers prefer to hyphenate fractions only when they appear as modifiers. Contrast these two examples:

> The contract needs a *three-fourths* majority for approval. (The fraction is an adjective modifying *majority.*)

> *Three fourths* of the employees voted for the contract. (The fraction is a noun.)

Compounds With Letters or Numerals. When one of the parts of a compound is a letter or a numeral, a hyphen is used.

> System-7000
> A-line

Prefixes and Suffixes

With certain prefixes and suffixes hyphens are almost always used. Use a hyphen with the prefixes *ex-, self-, all-, quasi-,* and *quarter-.* Use a hyphen with the suffixes *-elect* and *-odd.*

ex-manager	president-elect
self-employed	thirty-odd

Hyphens are occasionally used with other prefixes and suffixes to prevent confusion or misreading For example, a hyphen in *re-creation* ("to create again") distinguishes it from *recreation* ("leisure-time activity").

Hyphens are also used to avoid doubling or tripling letters.

non-native (*not* nonnative)   quill-like (*not* quilllike)

A prefix with a proper name or adjective is hyphenated.

anti-American   pre-Columbian

SHARPENING YOUR SKILLS 3

Insert hyphens where necessary in the following sentences.

1. My exmanagers attended a two day seminar on problem solving.
2. John's greatgrandfather, a highly intelligent man, founded the company.
3. This factory is ill-equipped for producing high-quality merchandise.
4. All able-bodied employees should try out for the company's slow-pitch softball team.
5. J. D. Metal Products, a well-known manufacturer, is located in a semiindustrial part of the city.

EDITING EXERCISES

A. The following paragraphs are from a letter written in response to a customer complaint. The letter contains several errors in the use of the apostrophe and hyphen. Find and correct the errors.

We are sorry to hear that your dis-satisfied with our childrens puzzle's. Thank you for pointing out the safety hazard of the yellow pegged pieces. This has been brought to the attention of our product development specialist.

Enclosed is our check for three dollars and ninety five cents ($3.-95). This is the refund of your purchase price for "Beginners Basic Puzzle." In addition, we will give you a one dollar rebate on any of our toys you might purchase from now through '88. Just send us the sale's receipt and the proof of purchase from the box.

B. The following paragraphs are from a letter advertising an electric tooth-
    brush set. Correct all punctuation errors.

>   Were offering you a fabulous five piece electric toothbrush for only
> $5.00, add $2.00 shipping and handling per order. This famous cordless
>   toothbrush set has been nationally-advertised in magazines such as
>   "Time" and "Newsweek". It comes complete with all accessorie's four
>   individually-colored, dental approved toothbrushes, sturdy, hand-
>   some display or storage base, and contour control handle module. Just
>   push the starter button and it brushes your teeth "like magic!"
>
>   Why such a bargain. We want you as a customer—when you order
>   youll also receive our catalogue filled with new and novel money
>   saving items—Were sure youll buy something else from our cata-
>   logue—Thats the reason—Take advantage and order now.

C. Rewrite each of the following word groups to create a hyphenated com-
    pound adjective.

    1. a secretary who is 18 years old

    2. an office building with nine stories

    3. debates that last all night

    4. a program that trains managers

    5. desks covered with papers

    6. papers stained with coffee

D. Rewrite these phrases using possessive nouns.

    1. the demands of the union

    2. suggestions made by product research

    3. the calculators belonging to the clerks

    4. the book that Margaret brought

PROJECTS

A. Using newspaper and magazine ads as well as packages, make a list of
    product names that use apostrophes. Do any product names use apos-
    trophes incorrectly? Can you find names of products that should include
    apostrophes but do not?

B. Make a list of apostrophe errors that you come across in your daily life.
    Posters on community, school, or church bulletin boards or signs in shops
    would be good sources.

C. With your classmates make a list of compound words commonly used in
    business. After consulting several dictionaries, decide how each word should
    be spelled (open, solid, or hyphenated). Make a style sheet to show your
    agreed-on spellings.

27
Capitalization

Al Grazzini was startled to receive an envelope addressed in the following manner:

> Mr. al grazzini Sr.
> National tile & terrazzo co.
> 1560 industrial blvd.
> hanover, pa 17333

"Look," Al said to his partner. "The person who addressed this envelope either doesn't know anything about capitalization or is trying to get my attention. Well, I'm paying attention, but I'm not impressed. I wonder what the letter inside this envelope looks like."

Correct capitalization is important, not only for getting addresses right, but also for many other business purposes. Like rules for punctuation, capitalization rules aid clear communication in business correspondence.

Although you are familiar with most of the rules of capitalization, in some instances the rules may be complicated or have exceptions. For example, should you capitalize the first letter of a question within a sentence? Which words should be capitalized in the title of a report or conference? This chapter will give you some useful guidelines for correct capitalization.

FIRST WORDS

A basic rule of capitalization is that the first word of every sentence is capitalized.

> The first-quarter report showed a slight dip in earnings.

This rule also holds true for sentences contained within other sentences.

> Rona said, "The Western Region led the company in sales again."

The first word of an interrogative sentence contained within another sentence is usually capitalized.

The question the board needed to decide was, Should sales be expanded?

A sentence following a colon is also capitalized if it states a rule or completes an introduction.

This is the new slogan: You're never too old to have fun.

In the example, the first sentence introduces the second. (Refer to Chapter 23 for exceptions to capitalizing after a colon.)

The rule for capitalizing sentences also applies to outlines. When creating an outline or a list, capitalize the first word of each item.

    I. Old business
       A. Appropriation for playground
       B. Hiring of speech teacher
       C. Retirement of Mr. Synge

PROPER NOUNS

As you know, common nouns are words that name classes of persons, places, or things: *artists, buildings, streets.* Proper nouns designate specific persons, places, and things: *Georgia O'Keeffe, Broadway, Trump Tower.* Although there are a few exceptions, proper nouns should be capitalized.

Names of People

Most people feel insulted when they see their names misspelled. Correct spelling includes correct capitalization. The general rule is to capitalize all names and initials. Also capitalize prefixes to surnames, such as *O', Mc, Mac,* and *Fitz.* Terms that follow surnames, such as *Jr., Sr.,* and *Esq.,* are also capitalized.

    Joan Carney
    Margaret J. Smith
    Tom O'Grady Jr.
    Randy McPherson

The letter following the prefixes *O'* and *Mc* is normally capitalized. Because the rule is less consistent for *Mac* or *Fitz,* it is important to check individual spellings.

    Ramsay MacDonald
    George Macdonald
    Ella Fitzgerald
    John FitzWilliam

Other name prefixes include *du, de, d', le, la, van,* and *von.* Capitalization often depends on the family's preference. Whether or not the prefix is retained if the surname stands alone may also vary. If the prefix is retained, capitalize it to show that it is part of the surname. The name prefix is always capitalized if it begins a sentence.

For the correct capitalization of names of famous persons, consult a reference book, such as a dictionary or encyclopedia. For the correct capitalization of name prefixes in business communication, consult a telephone directory or previous correspondence. In some instances, you may simply have to ask individuals for the correct spelling of their names. You should not feel self-conscious about asking for this spelling. People prefer to be asked and see their name spelled correctly to not being asked and seeing it incorrect.

Titles of People. Capitalize a person's title if it appears directly before the name. Do not capitalize the title if it is used alone or if it is written after the person's name, unless the title is part of a postal address or refers to an important national or international official.

Controller Wilson	Secretary of State Shultz
Henry Wilson, the controller	George Shultz, Secretary of State
the controller	the Secretary of State

Mr. Henry Wilson, Controller
Scene Publications
506 Sixth Avenue
St. Paul, MN 55164

In legal documents such as deeds, wills, and contracts, custom dictates that certain words should be capitalized throughout. These words are usually specified at their first appearance.

Gene and Sandra Barry, hereinafter called "Purchaser," agree to pay a monthly sum of three hundred dollars ($300).

Consult a law dictionary for questions regarding capitalization of legal terms.

Academic Degrees. Academic or honorary degrees that are placed after a person's name are capitalized whether they are spelled out or abbreviated. When names of degrees are spelled out but do *not* follow a person's name, they are not capitalized.

Laura Dey, B.A.
Amanda Kearns, M.D.
Ronald Degan, Doctor of Law
David Gunter, D.D.S.
bachelor's degree, master's degree, doctorate

Names of Companies and Organizations

The first letter of each major word in the name of a company or organization is capitalized.

> Winston's Hardware Store
>
> Fayetteville Savings and Loan
>
> National Association for the Advancement of Colored People
>
> The Arts Council of Princeton

Many businesses or groups are also known by their initials. In general, each letter is capitalized.

> AFL–CIO (American Federation of Labor–Congress of Industrial Organizations)
>
> NOW (National Organization for Women)
>
> ROTC (Reserve Officers Training Corps)

When a common noun such as *bank* or *company* is part of the name, it is capitalized. However, if the common noun refers to two or more separate companies, the word is not capitalized. Similarly, the name of a union is capitalized only when it is the official name; otherwise, the word *union* is not capitalized.

> The Prudential Insurance *Company* is now located in the mall.
>
> The Aetna and Prudential insurance *companies* have both opened offices in the mall.
>
> Our company has a good working relationship with First National *Bank*.
>
> The First National, Amalgamated, and Northeast *banks* have all adopted unified customer-account reporting forms.
>
> The employees are represented by the International Chemical Workers *Union*.
>
> The chemical workers' *union* offers insurance and other benefits to its members.

When referring to a specific department in your own company, follow company style. Generally, a department name is capitalized if it is preceded by *the*, but not if it is preceded by *our* or another possessive. Names of departments in other companies are usually not capitalized, except for special emphasis or for addresses.

> The *Personnel Office* has posted the company's job openings.
>
> Our *personnel office* has posted the company's job openings.
>
> I would like to get information from Wilson Corporation's *accounting department*.

Names of Political and Government Groups

The full names of legislative, judicial, administrative, and military departments, bureaus, and offices are capitalized. When words such as *service, bureau, department, office,* and *court* are part of the complete name, they are capitalized as well. Incomplete names are not capitalized.

> Minneapolis City Council, city council
> Hennepin County District Court, district court
> Department of Commerce (or Commerce Department), the department
> United States Navy, the navy

When citing an announcement, regulation, or ruling issued by a government agency, you do not need to use a formal name, such as *Office of the Mayor; the mayor's office* is correct.

> The *mayor's office* announced today that Emma DeLac has been appointed chief administrative aide.

Names of political parties are capitalized, as are words such as *committee* and *caucus* when they pertain to a group within a party.

> Republican Party
> Republican National Committee
> Women's Caucus of the Democratic Party
> Democratic–Farmer–Labor State Central Committee

SHARPENING YOUR SKILLS 1

Use proofreading symbols to correct any errors in capitalization in the following sentences.

1. The chairperson said, "the company needs new direction from the top."

2. Theresa O'malley compiled the report.

3. da Vinci had one of the greatest minds our world has ever seen.

4. Deregulation of many businesses began during president Carter's term.

5. Samantha earned a Doctorate from Wharton Business school.

6. The editorial raised the question, should government bail out big business?

7. The letter carriers' Union is negotiating a new contract with the United States postal service.

8. The Democratic Party has a close relationship with the Afl–Cio.

9. If Resident does not pay rent when due, management may evict Resident.

10. No one can resist our new slogan: you'll move faster in Quix.

PLACE NAMES

The names of particular places are proper nouns and should be capitalized. These include public places, buildings, streets, cities, states, countries, continents, oceans, or any other geographic designation.

> Central Park
> Atlanta International Airport
> Golden Gate Bridge
> State Street
> Interstate 295
> New Brunswick, New Jersey
> United States
> Antarctica

The words *the, city,* and *state,* as well as others designating a particular type of geographic or political division, should be capitalized only when they are actually part of the place name.

> The Hague
> New York City
> Vatican City
> Washington State

Geographic terms such as *river, lake,* and *mountain* are capitalized when they are part of a place name. Terms such as *building, canal, bridge,* and so on are capitalized if they are part of the names of structures. Note that such terms are also capitalized when they refer to several places or structures.

Singular	Plural
the Red *River*	the Red and Columbia *Rivers*
the Pacific *Ocean*	the Atlantic and Indian *Oceans*
the Hampton Road *Tunnel*	the Holland and Lincoln *Tunnels*

When writing about specific geographic features, check to be sure that terms such as *mountains* or *river* are truly part of the name. In some cases, such identifying terms are not used.

> the Himalayas (*not* the Himalaya Mountains)
> the Rhine (*not* the Rhine River)
> the Rio Grande (*not* the Rio Grande River)

TITLES OF LITERARY AND ARTISTIC WORKS

The titles of published and unpublished works, television and radio programs, movies, speeches, and many others follow the same capitalization rule: Capitalize the first and last word and all important words. Important words are nouns, pronouns, verbs, adjectives, adverbs, and subordinating conjunctions. Unimportant words are coordinating conjunctions, the sign of the infinitive (*to*), and short prepositions (generally fewer than four letters). The articles *a, an,* and *the* are not capitalized unless they are the first word of the title or follow a colon or dash.

> *What Color Is Your Parachute?*
> *How to Master the Art of Selling*
> "Coping With Change on the Job"
> "Trends Among the Rich and Famous"
> *In Search of Excellence*
> "Women in the Business World: A Growing Trend"

Many newspapers include *the* as part of their titles. When the full title of the newspaper is written out, capitalize *the.* However, when the newspaper's name is incorporated into a sentence, *the* can usually be lowercased.

> Sam Walton follows the marketplace news as reported in the *Boston Globe.*

The word *magazine* is not capitalized unless it is part of the official title.

> *Forbes* magazine
> *Home Magazine*

Be careful that what you are capitalizing is actually a title.

> Joseph Grebowski presented a report on business trends.

In this sentence, *business trends* is a topic and not a title.

Hyphenated Compounds in Titles. How to capitalize a hyphenated word in a title or heading is sometimes a problem. Always capitalize the first element of a hyphenated compound. Capitalize the second element if it is a noun or a proper adjective or if it equals the first element in importance.

> "How to Find the Right Stock in the Post–Industrial Economy"
> "The Need for Better City–State Relationships"

Do not capitalize the second element if it modifies the first element or if the two elements form a single word.

> "Medium-sized Companies in the Metropolitan Area"
> *The Self-made Millionaire*

SHARPENING YOUR SKILLS 2

Use proofreading symbols to correct any errors in capitalization in the following sentences.

1. The Allegheny and Monongahela rivers meet in Pittsburgh to form the Ohio river.

2. O'hare international Airport is one of the busiest air terminals in the world.

3. The article on personal computers in Sunday's issue of The *New York Times* has information that can help the accounting department.

4. The pilot took a longer route to avoid flying over the rocky mountains.

5. The cargo should be arriving in Boston Harbor tonight on the freighter *Hamburg express*.

6. I recently read the book *Robots In The Workplace: the Future is Now*.

7. Please make sure this package is delivered to Johnson & company, 245A Lewiston avenue, Bartlett, georgia 31905.

8. Have you see the article on Oil Prices in *Time* Magazine?

9. The himalaya mountains have always been barriers to trade.

10. Our truckers can use either interstate 95 or U.S. route 1.

NAMES OF DAYS, MONTHS, AND HOLIDAYS

The names of the days of the week and the months of the year are always capitalized. The words *day, week,* and *month* are capitalized only when they are part of a holiday or specially designated occasion.

Monday
January
Martin Luther King Day
Professional Secretaries Day
National Education Week
National Soup Month

Capitalize the names of religious, ethnic, and commemorative holidays.

Christmas
Passover
Thanksgiving

The names of seasons—*winter, spring, summer, fall*—are not capitalized.

Our fiscal year begins in late *spring.*

Most employees take their vacation in the *summer.*

TRADEMARKS AND PRODUCT NAMES

By law, certain products and their names are the sole property of the companies that produce or market them. The names of these products must be capitalized, even though they are used so often in everyday conversation and writing that they seem to be common nouns. Check a competent authority for names with which you are not familiar. Following is a list of trademarks with generic names that can be used in their place.

Alka-Seltzer (antacid)
Chap Stick (lip balm)
Coca-Cola, Coke (cola)
Fiberglas (fiber glass)
Frigidaire (refrigerator)
Jell-O (gelatin)
Kleenex (tissues)
Levi's (jeans)
Ping-Pong (table tennis)
Sanka (decaffeinated coffee)
Saran Wrap (plastic wrap)
Scotch tape (cellophane tape, tape)
Styrofoam (plastic foam)
Teflon (nonstick coating)
Xerox (photocopier or photocopy)

If a trade name is used with the generic term, only the trade name is capitalized.

Lipton soup
Dannon yogurt
Chrysler station wagon
IBM typewriter

Trade names are protected for only a certain number of years. When the protection period is over, the names no longer have to be capitalized. As a result, many trade names eventually become common product names.

aspirin
escalator
kerosene
linoleum
mimeograph
nylon
zipper

Since there is no general publication that lists the dates when protection runs out for trademarks, always check an up-to-date dictionary to be sure of the correct spelling and capitalization.

Proper adjectives, you recall, are adjectives derived from proper nouns.

PROPER ADJECTIVES

Noun	Adjective
America	American
Victoria	Victorian
Europe	European

Almost all proper adjectives are capitalized, including those that derive from names of ordinary people or places. Proper adjectives that are not capitalized are those that, through long use, have lost their association with the proper nouns from which they came.

brussels sprouts
french fries
manila envelopes
roman numeral
turkish towels
venetian blinds

COMPASS POINTS

The words *northern, southern, eastern, western,* and so on derive from the names of the points of the compass. Do not capitalize an adjective indicating direction unless it is part of the name of a political unit or a recognized region: *southern France,* but *Southern Hemisphere.*

The names of the points of the compass—*north, south, east, west,* and the points in between—are not capitalized when used merely to indicate direction.

north of the river
southeast of St. Louis

However, when a compass direction is used to indicate a part of the world or a definite section of a country, it is capitalized.

the Far East
the North and the South (during the American Civil War)
the Midwest
the West Coast

In writing, be careful to note the difference between a compass direction and a geographic area.

The company is located *southwest* of Highway 101. (compass direction)

The A. S. Tandy Company will move its headquarters to the *Southwest*— probably Arizona. (geographic area)

SHARPENING YOUR SKILLS 3

Use proofreading symbols to correct any errors in capitalization in the following sentences.

1. The Xerox machine was fixed the day before Labor day.

2. I am going out West this Fall.

3. Sonya would like a glass of coca-cola with her lunch.

4. Our company has technology contracts with four Central American Countries.

5. Sales have been surprisingly strong in the south.

6. Many of the Jeans sold in the United States today are imported.

7. Mr. Kemper had Roman shades installed in his office.

8. The dental clinic ordered two cases of kleenex.

9. The Northern part of the state is economically depressed.

10. Mark keeps a supply of band-aids in his desk.

EDITING EXERCISES

A. Use proofreading symbols to correct any errors in capitalization in the following sentences.

1. The article entitled "managing a small company" was written with the entrepreneur in mind.

2. Our company won the colgate toothpaste account last Spring.

3. the Orientation included a visit to the plant in New York city.

4. In 1986, capital cities corporation merged with and gained control over the much larger american broadcasting company.

5. mary s. walker will become Junior Vice President next May.

6. The Asian Branch Office has had a profitable Summer season.

7. The title of his speech was "english-speaking countries and foreign economies."

8. We are looking forward to the seminar on Corporate Finance taught by professor Townsend.

9. Our main plant is in philadelphia, but Western Pennsylvania is increasingly favorable for our operations.

10. Although Montreal is Canada's largest city, the canadian Government has its offices in ottawa.

B. Use proofreading symbols to correct any errors in capitalization in the following paragraphs.

(1) thomas alva edison was born into a wealthy ohio family in 1847. (2) he was educated at home, because Schools were not prepared for his questioning Intellect. (3) By the time he was 16, he had edited, written, and produced a Newspaper, and had begun his career as america's Greatest Inventor.

(4) edison's first inventions had to do with improving the Telegraph, because he was a Telegraph Operator and wanted more time to read. (5) he then built a Sophisticated Stock Ticker. (6) With the profits from his sale of the patent for the Stock Ticker, he opened an "Invention Factory" in menlo park, new jersey.

(7) from this Factory, edison and his crew of inventors created Hundreds of inventions. (8) In 1877, edison unveiled the Phonograph, and in 1879, the Incandescent Light Bulb. (9) Interestingly, the great Electric Utility, con edison, was not founded by the man whose name it bears. (10) That utility, and others like it, used Alternating Current to provide power, whereas edison believed that Direct Current was much better. (11) edison died in 1931, two years after the Fiftieth Anniversary of the invention of the Light Bulb.

C. Use proofreading symbols to correct any errors in punctuation and capitalization in the following sentences.

1. Our company's three leading products, paper napkins, paper towels, and paper plates, have been on the market for only five years.

2. The latest National figures show these trends, a drop in personal savings, a rise in consumer debt, and increased sales of durable goods.

3. The late joan mathis who was treasurer of the Corporation was a visionary business person.

4. According to the Union Rules Management cant change our holiday's without notice.

5. Mr. Beckwith inquired why arent we getting those parts"?

6. Marie Jastrow is in charge of wilson's Accounting Department the whole department is computerized.

7. During national library week Bobs going to read the best-seller the one minute manager.

8. The ambassador to italy has sought to gain a trade agreement with the italian wine industry which competes with american wine makers.

9. I read an interesting article titled the art of self-defense.

10. The supply of gasoline along the east coast this summer should be adequate.

PROJECTS

A. Write a proper noun for each of the following common nouns. If possible, use examples from your own community. Do not repeat examples from this chapter.

1. highway

2. community organization

3. dentist

4. small business

5. bank officer

6. bridge

7. government agency

8. park

9. newspaper

10. union

28
Numbers

Numbers play a major part in business communication. They appear in invoices, contracts, bids, profit and loss statements, addresses, payroll checks, inventory lists, tax statements, and many other situations. Numbers must be expressed clearly and correctly. If they are not, revenue could be lost or employee time could be wasted.

There are certain rules for writing numbers that will give your business communication a consistent style. Perhaps the greatest source of concern is whether to write them out or use numerals. Both forms appear in business documents. This chapter explains when each form is preferable.

In general, numbers from one through ten are spelled out when they appear in sentences.

> There are *five* processors in stock.
> We took *seven* orders yesterday.
> She sent all *11* invoices.

When the numeral *0* would stand alone, words such as *no* or *none* are used instead.

> *No* orders were taken yesterday.

In all correspondence but the most informal notes, ordinal numbers (numbers ending in *st, d,* or *th*) are spelled out.

> our first convention
> the fourth quarter
> Third Avenue
> the thousandth customer

NUMBERS EXPRESSED IN WORDS

In Dates

Although numerals are generally used for writing dates, words are used on some occasions. In legal documents, proclamations, or invitations, the complete date, including the year, is often spelled out.

> Contract of sale made as of the third day of June, nineteen eighty-five . . . .

A date is also spelled out if it is used as an ordinal.

> The fiscal year begins on the fifteenth of April.

However, this sentence can also be stated as such:

> The fiscal year begins on April 15.

Note that writing *April 15th* is incorrect.

At the Beginning of a Sentence

Any number that begins a sentence should be spelled out.

> One hundred and sixty-three people attended the conference this year, compared with 137 last year and 125 the year before.

However, for maximum clarity, the number should be moved to another position in the sentence, especially if the sentence contains other numerals.

> This year 163 people attended the conference, compared with 137 last year and 125 the year before.

NUMBERS EXPRESSED AS NUMERALS

For clarity, numerals are the preferred style when dealing with technical matters, measurements, or any written material that involves many numbers.

As noted before, numbers above ten are generally written as numerals. When three or more related numbers appear close together and some of the numbers are above ten, write *all* the numbers as figures.

> There are 5 seniors, 15 juniors, and 22 sophomores in the program.

However, if the numbers are not related, their style can be mixed.

> There are 15 juniors and 22 seniors in the five programs.

When dealing with numbers in the millions or above, you can combine figures and words.

> West Germany has a population of 62 million.

However, if related numbers above and below a million are grouped together, use numerals for all the numbers.

> Last year's volume of 850,000 accounts grew to almost 2,000,000 this year.

With approximate values, usage varies depending on the exactness of the estimate. Use figures to suggest a more exact estimate.

Thousands of people attended.

Almost 20,000 people attended.

Money

Amounts of money are almost always expressed in numerals. In general, you can use numerals to express amounts in any currency.

United States Currency	Foreign Currency
$50.89	DM5,000 (German deutsche mark)
a bill for $790	Y 2,400,000 (Japanese yen)
a deficit of $15,000,000	£12 (British pound)

For round amounts in the millions and above, you can use the following style:

$140 million   £10 billion

Remember, though, that when grouping amounts both above and below a million, all numbers should be in figures.

Divisional profits were $490,000, $685,000, and $2,035,000.

For amounts of more than a million that include fractional amounts, use the following style:

$10.3 billion (*for* $10,300,000,000)
$154.25 million (*for* $154,250,000)

However, for amounts that would not produce a simple decimal, write out the whole number or, if possible, round to a simpler decimal.

$10,377,000 (*not* $10.377 million)
almost $5.5 billion (*from* $5,497,900,000)

Ordinarily, you would not use a decimal point and zeros with whole-dollar values that appear in running text.

Our company is submitting a bid of $295.

In tables or lists, however, decimal zeros are almost always included.

April	$4,098.75
May	2,480.00
June	657.16
July	6,109.00
Total	$13,344.91

Note that in a table or list, only the first and last elements have a dollar or cent sign.

Dollar and Cent Signs. When writing an amount of less than a dollar, use numerals (when the amount is above ten) and the word *cent(s)*:

> The book costs 79 cents.

> The sales tax is six cents.

However, if the amount is grouped with amounts of a dollar or more, use a decimal point and a dollar sign.

> The total fee is $1.50: $.50 for the child and $1.00 for the accompanying adult.

In general, you should not use the cent sign unless you are writing a technical report that uses many other symbols:

> The price is now 5.5¢/doz., which is an increase of 2¢ during the last month.

Use the dollar sign when the dollar amount appears in figures: $25, $103.56. Use the word *dollars* when the dollar amount is spelled out: *two dollars, nine dollars.* Spelling out whole-dollar amounts generally follows the rule of spelling out the numbers one to ten when they appear in sentences. For large amounts, it is generally preferable to write *$12 billion* rather than *12 billion dollars.*

When using dollar and cent signs with a range or series of numbers, the signs should be used with each number.

> $100–$200   50¢ to 85¢

When using *million, billion,* and so on, the terms should also be used with each number.

> $40 million to $60 million

Note the confusion that could result were the term not used with each number:

> $40 to $60 million

However, when using the words *dollars* and *cents* with ranges or series, write them only at the end.

> 17, 19, and 21 cents

Monetary Amounts. There are cases in which you should spell out monetary amounts. For example, certain phrases would be awkward with numerals.

> We spent hundreds of dollars on this set.

General amounts of money should be spelled out.

> We received an estimate of a quarter of a million dollars.

The same applies for money amounts at the beginning of a sentence.

> Twenty-five dollars seemed like a lot to pay.

SHARPENING YOUR SKILLS 1

Correct any errors in expressing numbers in the following sentences.

1. We sold nine policies in the 1st week, twelve the 2nd week, and eight so far this week.

2. The price ranges from 100 to $200.

3. We took in 0 money today.

4. The company has liabilities of $2.754 million.

5. Tickets cost three dollars, five dollars, and nine dollars.

6. 546 graduates received their master's degrees.

7. The feasibility study cost 1,000s of dollars.

8. We are lowering the price from $1.09 to 79 cents.

9. 100s of shoppers walk through our doors each day.

10. Total attendance for the season was 845,000, for a six-year total of 2 million.

Quantities and Measurements

Numbers that represent quantities or measurements are written as numerals.

> 55-gallon drum
> 14 feet by 10 feet
> 24 grams

When the units of measurement are abbreviated, as in *lbs, rpm, sq m,* numerals are always used.

If a measurement is used in a nontechnical sense or in informal correspondence, the number can be spelled out.

> I lost two pounds last week.

Fractions and Decimals

Fractions that would not create long compound words should be spelled out.

> One half of the shipment was fine; the other half was damaged.

> The fuel gauge indicated that the tank was one-fourth empty.

Fractions that would create a long compound word and mixed fractions are written as numerals.

> Nancy bought a 5/16-inch bit for her drill.

> The carpenter installed a $4\frac{1}{4}' \times 3\frac{1}{8}'$ panel in the cafeteria.

Convert fractions, especially mixed fractions, into decimal form if they do not need to be fractions and can be converted easily:

This process uses 1.5 times as much energy. (*not* 1½ times)

Express all decimals as numerals. When a decimal stands alone, place a zero before the decimal point, as in 0.63. The zero helps to alert the reader that the numeral is a decimal. However, drop zeros at the end of a decimal, unless the decimal is in a table with longer decimals or unless you need to show that the decimal has been rounded.

Tolerances
0.0150
0.1000
0.0005

No commas appear in decimals.

Percentages

Express all percentages in numerals, and, unless your writing is for a scientific or technical publication, write out the word *percent*. Of course, when a percentage begins a sentence, it is spelled out.

Our tax rate was 28 percent.

Thirty-five percent of our employees graduated from college.

After drying for 15 min. the specimens were sprayed with a 2% iodine solution.

Percentages that include fractions or decimals should be expressed in figures.

0.5 percent (*not* ½ percent)
9.625 percent (*not* 9⅝ percent)

In a series or range of percentages, the word *percent* follows the last value only. When using the % symbol, however, the symbol must follow each value.

10, 20, and 30 percent   50–75 percent off
10%, 20%, and 30%   50%–75% off

Roman Numerals

Roman numerals are normally used to designate historical events, parts of books, and legislation.

World War II   Article I
Unit III

They are also used to indicate sequels, recurring events, and descendants with the same name.

Rocky IV   Frank Jordan III
Super Bowl XX   Pope John Paul II

Small roman numerals are used to paginate the frontmatter of books (table of contents, copyright page, and so on).

i, ii, iii, iv, v

SHARPENING YOUR SKILLS 2

Correct any errors in expressing numbers in the following sentences.

1. The dealership offered 7,8% financing on a new car.
2. My lawyer found a loophole in Article v of the contract.
3. This steel skin is capable of withstanding a pressure of forty psi.
4. We have three-thirty-second-inch bits in the store.
5. Each box of floppy disks has been marked down five percent.
6. The package weighed three lbs.
7. The interest rate has jumped .75 percent in the last month.
8. The new copying machine is $1\frac{1}{2}$ times faster than the old one.
9. The program takes $\frac{1}{4}$ hour to run.
10. 45% of our customers use credit for their purchases.

NUMBERS EXPRESSED IN WORDS AND NUMERALS

When it comes to expressing time or writing addresses, both words and numerals are used.

Time

Numbers are used to express the time of day and periods of time.

Time of Day. The time of day can either be expressed in numerals or spelled out: 6 a.m. or six in the morning. The abbreviations *a.m.* and *p.m.* or phrases such as *o'clock, in the morning,* or *last night* help to express the time.

The time of day is usually spelled out in formal writing (for example, reports, letters), especially when only even, half, and quarter times are given.

Employees report to work at eight o'clock in the morning.

I will meet you at a quarter to five.

A hyphen is used between the hour and minute *(seven-thirty),* unless the minute part itself is hyphenated *(seven thirty-five).*

Figures are used for more informal writing (for example, memos) or when the exact moment is to be emphasized.

The meeting starts at 8:30 a.m.

Do not use zeros with the hour *(7 a.m.)*, unless they are part of a time schedule. Notice that *a.m.* and *p.m.* are generally reserved for figures. They are not used when numbers are spelled out.

Do not use *a.m.* or *p.m.* with a time phrase. Since *a.m.* means "in the morning" and *p.m.* means "in the evening," you would be repeating yourself if you also used a time phrase.

INCORRECT: 6:00 a.m. in the morning

CORRECT: 6 a.m. OR six in the morning

Periods of Time. There are several ways in which you can write periods of time. If the time period is included in a technical piece or is part of an instruction, write it with numerals.

a 4-month guarantee
a 15-year mortgage
50-minute baking time
a cooling-off period of 30 days

When used in a nontechnical sense, spell out the time period.

I waited twenty days for the part.

The mechanic didn't come for eleven hours.

Dale worked at Tiller & Family for fifteen years.

Write decades and centuries as follows:

the 1970s	the nineteen-seventies
the '70s	the seventies
the 1900s	the nineteen hundreds
the twentieth century	

Addresses

When addressing a letter to a company or institution, always determine the exact address that the company uses. You may be able to obtain the address from a telephone book, but because of space requirements, it will usually be abbreviated. In addition, offices often have suite or floor numbers that are not included in the telephone book. You may, therefore, need to call the company to obtain the complete address.

In street addresses, numerals should be used for the building number and the floor and suite numbers.

267 Elm Street
1095 Broadway, Suite 4014
15-05 Mutton Lane, 7th Floor

When the name of the street is a number, the number is usually spelled out. This makes it easier to read with the house or building number.

516 First Avenue
1006 Thirty-third Street

However, if space is limited, use a numeral for numbers above ten.

Zip code numbers are always in numerals. An important point to remember is that the United States Postal Service is currently switching from five-digit codes to nine-digit codes. Note the use of a hyphen in the nine-digit code.

Newark, NJ 07101
Newark, NJ 07101-1270

Consult a zip code index, a telephone book, or the post office to get exact zip code information.

Using numbers in written communication raises two common questions: What should you do with a range of numbers, and what should you do when two numbers appear together?

COMMON NUMBER PROBLEMS

A Range of Numbers

In expressing a range of numbers or years, you may delete certain digits of the second numeral. For example, if a report concerns the years from 1983 through 1986, you may write *1983–86*. If you are referring to page numbers in the hundreds, you may write *pages 316–44,* instead of *pages 316–344.* Numbers below 100 do not follow this style. You should not, for example, write *pages 73–9.* Instead, you must write *pages 73–79.*

When numbers are part of a *between . . . and* or a *from . . . to* construction, never use a dash to indicate a range.

Between 5 and 7 p.m., we will be home. (*not* 5–7 p.m.)

From 15 to 20 managers will attend. (*not* 15–20)

Two Numbers Together

Occasionally, you will have a sentence where two numbers appear next to each other. To avoid confusion, you can either place a comma between the numbers or spell out one of the numbers.

On March 21, 15 houses will be started.

On March 21 fifteen houses will be started.

SHARPENING YOUR SKILLS 3

Correct any errors in expressing numbers in the following sentences.

1. Their mailing address is Two-Oh-Six Franklin Avenue, Staten Island, NY 10314.
2. Ship 30 2-gallon containers by Friday.
3. They are open from 8 a.m.–'7 p.m.
4. Deliver this package to 55-09 60 Street, Suite Nineteen.
5. In the evening I catch the 6:33 p.m. commuter train.
6. This contract requires a response in 15 days.
7. Our office is located at 307 3rd Avenue.
8. The dealership has 10 300s, 5 280s, and 17 240s.
9. The picture tube came with a written, two-month warranty.
10. This is to notify you that the annual meeting of stockholders will be held on Thursday, June 19, 1986, at 10 a.m. in the morning.

EDITING EXERCISES

A. Correct any errors in expressing numbers in the following sentences. If the sentence has no errors, write the word *correct* next to it. Be able to explain your answers.

1. The price of oil has dropped to about fifteen dollars a barrel.
2. This price drop contributed to millions·of dollars in deficits for some oil-producing countries.
3. The delegates will reconvene at 9 a.m. tomorrow morning.
4. The company's stock traded at 22.00 dollars a share today.
5. 200,000 shares were traded today.
6. Our counselors are Jason & Rowe, Fifteen Park Place, Suite Sixty, Merrifield, VA 22116-1404.
7. The company rewarded its top salespersons with trips to Super Bowl 21.
8. The Consumer Affairs Department takes calls between 9 a.m.–5 p.m.
9. There were four shop stewards, 12 line workers, and 20 drivers at the meeting.
10. Revenues topped $2.5 million while expenses stayed below $875000.

B. Correct any errors in expressing numbers in the following sentences. If the sentence has no errors, write the word *correct* next to it. Be able to explain your answers.

1. The price of gold went up 25¢ to $345.89.

2. Twenty-two patients were hospitalized for a longer time than Medicaid guidelines allow.

3. Total profits were up 25%.

4. The two-pound box of candy retails at fifteen dollars and seventy-five cents, while the five-pound box costs only twenty-five dollars.

5. The previous ad campaign brought only a $\frac{1}{4}$ of a $1,000,000 in sales.

6. We will need 600 three- × three-inch beams and 1000 eight-foot lengths of one- × four-inch planks.

7. The new addition will cost between $6 million and $8 million.

8. Pages 20–3 of the employee manual describe the pension fund.

9. This die maker can meet your specifications to within 22 hundredths of an inch.

10. The concert tour was planned for 20 cities in six states.

C. Correct any errors in punctuation or capitalization in the following sentences. Be able to explain your answers.

1. We have sizes 28; 30; 32; and 34 in stock, but not size 36.

2. 20 percent of the respondents have never heard of Continental Life insurance company.

3. Six people (out of one hundred asked knew the jingle for Tonys burger hut.

4. The Hall hosts 100s of receptions every year.

5. The arbitrator asked, "is twelve-fifty an hour your last offer."

6. We have been guaranteed a $1,000,000-dollar loan.

7. The building fund topped it's goal of $2.356 million dollars by more than 400,000 dollars.

8. Since you have been a faithful customer we're sending you a special money saving book.

9. The coupons are valid now through December, 1988 on all types of automotive service for Summer and Fall maintenance.

10. The law, that senator Sieff introduced, is intended to make the Federal Government balance the budget.

PROJECTS

Find examples of business documents that use numbers. Discuss how numbers have been used in these documents. Are there situations similar to those discussed in this chapter? Are there variations in how numbers have been treated? Do you see any additional uses of numbers?

29
Abbreviations, Contractions, and Symbols

Abbreviations, contractions, and symbols are used to save space and time in writing. They can make writing clearer because they are easier to read than the words they stand for. Your use of them will depend on the type of writing that you do. Contractions, for example, are generally acceptable in interoffice memos but not in formal letters.

ABBREVIATIONS

Abbreviations are the shortened form of words or phrases. Business communication makes use of a number of abbreviations. These include titles, state names, and quantities and measurements. In addition, certain business terms and names for companies, organizations, and government agencies are often abbreviated.

Titles

Perhaps the most common abbreviations are titles appearing before or after a person's name.

Mr.	Esq.
Mrs.	LL.D.
Ms.	R.N.
Dr.	M.D.
Jr.	M.S.W.
Sr.	

Abbreviations of civil, religious, and military titles *may* be used if the person's full name follows.

Rep. Donald Miller
Rev. Timothy Lawrence
Maj. Gen. Constance Bennett

However, the title should be written out if only the last name follows or if *the* is used with the title.

Representative Miller
the Right Reverend Timothy Lawrence
the Honorable Mayor Marilyn Harris

The abbreviations *Jr., Sr.,* and *Esq.* are used with the person's *full* name. (Notice that no comma is used with the name)

INCORRECT: Mr. Kastler Jr.

CORRECT: Mr. Lyle Kastler Jr.

Since *Jr.* and *Sr.* are considered part of a person's name, other titles can be used with them.

Robert Luxford Sr., Ph.D.

Esq., however, is a courtesy title. Thus it is never used with any other titles, either before or after the name.

INCORRECT: Mr. Edward Pouti, Esq.

CORRECT: Edward Pouti, Esq.

Similarly, do not use *Mr., Mrs.,* or *Ms.* with academic degrees that appear after the name.

INCORRECT: Ms. Paula Schaap, J.D.

CORRECT: Paula Schaap, J.D.

In addition, do not use *Dr.* with an academic degree following a name; the two together would be repetitive.

INCORRECT: Dr. Robin Ananicz, M.D.

CORRECT: Dr. Robin Ananicz

Company, Organization, and Government Names

Some companies use abbreviations in their names, and others do not. Therefore, you should make every effort to determine the correct spelling—if possible, from the company's letterhead or official publication. Following are some common abbreviations that appear in company names. Note their spellings.

Co. (*for* Company)
Corp. (*for* Corporation)
Inc. (*for* Incorporated)
Ltd. (*for* Limited)
Bro. (*for* Brother)
Bros. (*for* Brothers)
Mfg. (*for* Manufacturing)
Mfrs. (*for* Manufacturers)

When addressing letters, use the company's complete name. However, you generally do not have to use *Co.* or *Inc.* (and very often, initials or other unimportant words) in running text. Exceptions to this style are company names that require *Co., Inc.,* or another abbreviation to prevent confusing the name with other businesses bearing similar names. There is, for example, Time Inc. as well as *Time* magazine.

Many well-known companies, organizations, and government agencies, as well as certain business terms, are known by their initials. In such cases, periods are not used between the letters.

IBM (International Business Machines Corp.)
RCA (Radio Corporation of America)
ASMA (American Society of Marine Artists)
YMCA (Young Men's Christian Association)
FCC (Federal Communications Commission)
IRS (Internal Revenue Service)
GNP (gross national product)
CD (certificate of deposit)

The names of radio and television stations and broadcasting systems are usually written this way too: *KNBC-TV, WXRK-FM, the CBS television network.* It would be repetitive to write "the CBS broadcasting system" because *CBS* means "the Columbia Broadcasting System."

If the name of a federal agency is written out, *United States* can be abbreviated to *U.S.;* if the name of the agency is given in initials, *United States* can be abbreviated to *US.*

U.S. Information Agency, *or* USIA

Some or all of an organization's initials may make up a pronounceable word, or acronym.

NATO (North Atlantic Treaty Organization)
NOW (National Organization for Women)
OPEC (Organization of Petroleum Exporting Countries)

As with company names, be sure that you do not use redundant words with acronyms; for example, never write "the NOW organization."

Other Business Abbreviations

When the word *number* is required before a number, you can use *No.* (or *Nos.* if more than one number will follow). At the beginning of a sentence, however, you should spell out the word *number*.

You can omit *No.* when using words such as *Invoice, Room,* and *Check,* but keep it following words such as *License, Order, Social Security,* and *Patent.*

The change affects engine No. 154.

Number 1087 is the only check missing.

Check 1087 is missing.

We sent you Invoice 540717.

Table 29-1 lists other abbreviations used in business correspondence.

Table 29-1. Business Abbreviations

Abbreviations	Definitions	Abbreviations	Definitions
acct.	account	FY	fiscal year
AP or A/P	accounts payable	incl.	inclusive
AR or A/R	accounts receivable	LCL or l.c.l.	less-than-carload lot
ASAP	as soon as possible	LIFO	last in, first out
Attn.	Attention	misc.	miscellaneous
BS or B/S	bill of sale	n/30	net in 30 days
CEO	chief executive officer	NA	not applicable,
c.i.f. or CIF	cost, insurance,		not available
	and freight	nt. wt.	net weight
COD or C.O.D.	cash, or collect,	OTC	over the counter
	on delivery	PO	purchase order
CPA	certified public	POE or p.o.e.	port of entry
	accountant	ppd.	prepaid, postage paid
cr.	credit	recd.	received
dist.	district	SASE	self-addressed,
distr.	distributor		stamped envelope
dr.	debit	shtg.	shortage
EOM or e.o.m.	end of month	SO	shipping order
FAS or f.a.s.	free alongside ship	vs. or v.	versus
FIFO	first in, first out	whsle.	wholesale
FOB or f.o.b.	free on board		

Place Names

For city and place names, spell out the entire name, unless an abbreviation is part of the official name. Also, spell out words such as *Fort, Mount, Point,* or

Port, except when space limitations require abbreviations. Abbreviate *Saint* in American place names; in foreign place names, follow the style given in a geographical dictionary or other authoritative source.

> Los Angeles
> Port Mansfield
> Mount Vernon
> St. Louis
> Sault Ste. Marie

When addressing envelopes or packages, and when writing the inside address of a business letter, always follow the official style of the United States Postal Service for the abbreviation of state names. In this style, each state name is represented by two capital letters, without any periods.

When writing informal communications, such as memos or lists, you may abbreviate state names using the traditional abbreviations. Both the traditional and postal abbreviations are shown in Table 29-2; note that some states do not have a traditional abbreviation.

In the text of a formal letter, you should always spell out state names.

Foreign Expressions

A number of foreign expressions are commonly used in place of their longer English counterparts. Some of the words in these foreign expressions are abbreviations and require a period. For example, *ibid.* is an abbreviation for *ibidem.* Below is a guide to some of the more common foreign expressions used in business communication. Note that because these terms have become familiar in English, they are not italicized.

Foreign Term	Definition
ad hoc	for a particular purpose
ca.	approximately
cf.	compare
e.g.	for example
et al.	and others
etc.	and so forth
ibid.	in the same place
i.e.	that is
N.B.	note especially
re	concerning
viz.	namely

Use commas with these expressions as you would if you were using the English equivalent.

> Please contact sales, accounting, R&D, etc.

> In evaluating the report, consider several factors (e.g., the number of respondents).

Table 29-2. United States and Territories

State or Territory	Traditional Abbreviation	Postal Service Abbreviation	State or Territory	Traditional Abbreviation	Postal Service Abbreviation
Alabama	Ala.	AL	Missouri	Mo.	MO
Alaska	—	AK	Montana	Mont.	MT
Arizona	Ariz.	AZ	Nebraska	Nebr.	NE
Arkansas	Ark.	AR	Nevada	Nev.	NV
California	Calif.	CA	New Hampshire	N.H.	NH
Canal Zone	C.Z.	CZ	New Jersey	N.J.	NJ
Colorado	Colo. or Col.	CO	New Mexico	N. Mex.	NM
Connecticut	Conn.	CT	New York	N.Y.	NY
Delaware	Del.	DE	North Carolina	N.C.	NC
District of Columbia	D.C.	DC	North Dakota	N. Dak.	ND
			Ohio	—	OH
Florida	Fla.	FL	Oklahoma	Okla.	OK
Georgia	Ga.	GA	Oregon	Ore. or Oreg.	OR
Guam	—	GU	Pennsylvania	Pa.	PA
Hawaii	—	HI	Puerto Rico	P.R.	PR
Idaho	—	ID	Rhode Island	R.I.	RI
Illinois	Ill.	IL	South Carolina	S.C.	SC
Indiana	Ind.	IN	South Dakota	S. Dak.	SD
Iowa	—	IA	Tennessee	Tenn.	TN
Kansas	Kans.	KS	Texas	Tex.	TX
Kentucky	Ky.	KY	Utah	—	UT
Louisiana	La.	LA	Vermont	Vt.	VT
Maine	—	ME	Virgin Islands	V.I.	VI
Maryland	Md.	MD	Virginia	Va.	VA
Massachusetts	Mass.	MA	Washington	Wash.	WA
Michigan	Mich.	MI	West Virginia	W. Va.	WV
Minnesota	Minn.	MN	Wisconsin	Wis.	WI
Mississippi	Miss.	MS	Wyoming	Wyo.	WY

Quantities and Measurements

If your writing is nontechnical or you are using isolated measurements, spell out units of measure. Abbreviate the units in technical writing, in a table or other place where space is at a premium, or in sentences containing several measurements.

> The copier's height is 25 in., its width 49 in., its depth 25 in., and its weight 194 lbs

Following are some common abbreviations for standard and metric units of measure. In current usage, periods are not used with abbreviations for units of measurement, except to prevent confusion. For example, the abbreviation for *inch (in)* may be read as the word *in*; the abbreviation for *gallon (gal)* may be read as the word *gal*. In such cases the period should be used.

in (inch)	mm (millimeter)
ft (foot)	cm (centimeter)
yd (yard)	m (meter)
mi (mile)	km (kilometer)
oz (ounce)	g (gram)
pt (pint)	kg (kilogram)
qt (quart)	ml (milliliter)
gal (gallon)	cl (centiliter)
lb (pound)	l (liter)

Common abbreviations used in scientific, mathematical, astronomical, and other fields are listed in dictionaries and similar references.

When giving a range of measurements, place the abbreviation after the last value unless the range involves different units.

3–12 g   1 in × 2 ft
21–33 ft of wire

SHARPENING YOUR SKILLS 1

Correct any errors in the use of abbreviations in the following sentences.

1. We called Rep. Hansen's office to check the regulations.
2. Mrs. Renata King, M.D., will be speaking on occupational health and safety.
3. Label the file "L. Winslow & Broths., Incorp."
4. I'm staying in Room No. 1606.
5. Wkst is an affiliate of the NBC Broadcasting Company.
6. The L.A. Parks Department is taking bids on fencing materials.
7. Our main office is right in downtown Rocky Pt.
8. Dr. Clayton Robbins, Ph.D., will deliver the keynote address.
9. The reception area measures 20 ft × 30 ft.
10. We are negotiating similar arrangements with our Canadian subsidiaries (i.e. Josten Canada, Ltd., and Josten Credit Canada).

Common Abbreviation Problems

Thus far, this chapter has shown you abbreviations acceptable for business communication. Some familiar abbreviations, including abbreviations for names of the months and days, are not normally used in formal correspondence.

In addition to knowing which abbreviations are acceptable, you may also find it helpful to know which abbreviations use periods and how abbreviations are made plural.

Periods With Abbreviations. As you have seen, many common abbreviations are followed by a period. The period may come at the end of the abbreviation (Bros., Nebr.), after every letter (e.g., D.C.), or after every abbreviated element (S. Dak., nt. wt).

You have also seen that some abbreviations—especially those composed of capital letters—do not use periods. The names of some companies, government agencies, and organizations fit this category, as do certain business terms.

> IDS (Investors Diversified Services)
> FBI (Federal Bureau of Investigation)
> NEA (National Education Association)
> CRT (cathode-ray tube)

The abbreviations for the time zones for the continental United States do not use periods.

> EST (Eastern Standard Time)
> CST (Central Standard Time)
> MST (Mountain Standard Time)
> PST (Pacific Standard Time)
> EDT (Eastern Daylight Time)

Plural Forms of Abbreviations. Abbreviations form their plurals in several ways. The most common way is to simply place an *s* after the abbreviation and before the period (if there is one).

> Gens. Benjamin Yates and Bradley Powell
> Accts. 234A and 246B
> several YWCAs

Some abbreviations form their plurals by adding an apostrophe and *s* (see Chapter 26).

> M.A.'s
> Ph.D.'s

A few abbreviations change their whole form when made plural.

> Messrs. (plural of *Mr.*)
> Mmes. (plural of *Mrs.*)

Other abbreviations, such as those for measurements, are the same in both singular and plural.

> 1 lb   20 lb
> 1 qt   320 qt

SHARPENING YOUR SKILLS 2

Add periods as necessary to the following abbreviations.

1. Calif	11. US Department of Justice
2. LLD	12. AT & T Communications
3. cm	13. Rev
4. IA	14. acct
5. Attn	15. Ms
6. AFL–CIO	16. etc
7. radio station WCCO	17. No
8. re	18. ft
9. Mfrs	19. &
10. UNESCO	20. CST

CONTRACTIONS

A contraction is a combination of two words either spoken or written. Ordinarily, when a contraction is formed, one or more letters or sounds are dropped, and an apostrophe replaces them. Although contractions are appropriate for internal memos and conversation, they should be avoided in formal correspondence.

Contractions can be formed from several types of words, including joining a verb and *not*, a pronoun and an auxiliary verb, or a subject noun and an auxiliary verb.

Verb + *Not*

For some of the most common contractions, the word *not* is shortened to *n't* and is joined to a verb.

aren't	hasn't
can't	haven't
couldn't	isn't
didn't	shouldn't
doesn't	wasn't
don't	won't
hadn't	wouldn't

Pronoun + Auxiliary Verb

Instead of using the words *I would have,* you might shorten *would* and form the contraction *I'd*, as in *I'd have*. This sort of contraction is usually formed with a pronoun and some form of the verb *be, have, had, will,* or *would*.

BE: I'm, you're, he's, she's, it's, we're, they're, who's, there's.

HAVE: I've, you've, he's, she's, it's, we've, they've, who's, there's.

HAD: I'd, you'd, he'd, she'd, we'd, they'd, who'd.

WILL: I'll, you'll, he'll, she'll, it'll, we'll, they'll, who'll.

WOULD: I'd, you'd, he'd, she'd, we'd, they'd, who'd.

Subject Noun + Auxiliary Verb

A contraction can be made with any subject noun.

The *shop's* been closed since Friday. *(shop has)*

The *shop's* closed. *(shop is)*

Mary'd better check the ledger. *(Mary had)*

Mary'd like to check the ledger. *(Mary would)*

Common Contraction Errors

Remember to use an apostrophe with all contractions. Without one, many contractions would look like other words: *we'll* would look like *well, she'll* would look like *shell*, and so on. Another common error with contractions is placing the apostrophe in the wrong place, as in "does'nt" instead of *doesn't*. Remember that the apostrophe stands in for a missing letter or letters, so it must be placed where the letters have been omitted.

SHARPENING YOUR SKILLS 3

Correct any errors in the use of contractions in the following sentences. If a sentence does not contain any errors, write the word *correct* next to it.

1. Wo'nt you wonder how shell take her dismissal?
2. Last month's figures show that it's not our best-selling line anymore.
3. Well need the addresses for Messrs. Wilson and Barnston.
4. Did you know that were going to merge with Landow Corp.?
5. Carol Wilcox we'd Marty Montagu in a civil ceremony.
6. Freemont Industries closed its deal with Piedmont Corp.
7. The jobs scheduled for this month.
8. I'll health forced him to retire.

SYMBOLS   In business communication, symbols are used only in tables, bills, or orders, or in formal correspondence that requires technical language. Certain symbols used in business are universally recognized as standing for specific words. The following list contains some of the most common business symbols:

$	dollar(s)	×	by multiplied by
¢	cent(s)	#	number (before a figure)
%	percent	#	pounds (after a figure)
@	at	¶	paragraph
&	and	§	section
'	foot (feet)		
"	inch(es); ditto		
°	degree(s)		

ON THE JOB
Conducting International Business

Nancy McGuire works for an international import-export company. In her position as assistant to the vice president, she deals directly with a number of foreign companies by letter, telex, and telephone.

When she first started her job, Nancy was puzzled by many of the expressions and abbreviations she saw on letters and telexes from foreign countries. For example, on June 29 she opened a letter to her company from a company in England. The first sentence read, "Thank you for your letter of the 12th inst." Nancy had no idea what "the 12th inst." meant. She showed the letter to Mick Meadows, an Englishman who worked in her office. Mick explained that *inst.* is an abbreviation for the word *instans*, which means "in the present month." The writer was referring to a letter that Nancy's company had sent on June 12. Mick also explained that the abbreviation *ult.* (for *ultimo*) means "in the previous month" and that *prox.* (for *proximo*) means "in the next month." Thus, if the message had read "your letter of the 12th ult.," the writer would have been talking about May 12.

Nancy has also learned that in Germany, Spain, and Italy, street numbers are written after street names in addresses. Thus, when writing to companies in these countries, she would write "Via Veneto 2861" or "Ludwigstrasse 75," for example.

One morning, the vice president asked Nancy to call a company in Lagos, Nigeria, to check on a cargo shipment. She decided to make the call after lunch. However, even though she was able to get a transatlantic line, there was no answer. After trying several times, she called the overseas operator to find out if there was something wrong with the telephone system. "There's nothing wrong," the operator told her. "But if you're trying to reach a company in Lagos, they will already have been closed for several hours. It's after 9 p.m. in Nigeria. Their time zone is seven hours ahead of ours." If Nancy had remembered to check the time difference, she would have made the call in the morning, when her superior had asked her to. Now she would not be able to contact the Nigerian company until the following day.

SHARPENING YOUR SKILLS 4

Insert the correct symbol in each blank space.

1. The customer ordered a 50- _____ sack of fertilizer.

2. We should pay no more than _____ 10,000 a month for that 40- _____ 50-ft loft.

3. The package said to preheat the oven to 375 _____ .

4. Sell 2,500 shares _____ $17.40.

5. Please refer to order _____ 26301.

A. Correct any errors in abbreviations, contractions, or symbols in the following sentences. If the sentence contains no errors, write the word *correct* next to it.

1. Mr. Ralph Jones, Esq., will be our consultant.

2. Sampson&Broths., Incd., has won the contract.

3. The price of a barrel of oil has dropped since O.P.E.C. lost power.

4. The company's income before taxes is larger than the gross GNP of many countries.

5. Our manufacturing center is in Pnt. Lookout, but our home office is in Prt. Jefferson.

6. Ive heard that Beckley, WV, is a good place to do business.

7. The gauge has to be able to measure a difference of 2 mms.

8. The project requires 14 ft.–28 ft. of wire.

9. I paid Invoice Number 45630 with Check Number 234.

10. We could'nt pick up the package at customs without the proper i.d.

11. The convention will be held in Saint Paul this year.

12. Rev. Chilstrom will give the invocation.

13. Send that to the ad. hoc. committee.

14. Order a 55-gall. drum of floor wax and 25 two-quart bottles of cleanser.

15. The SALT II treaty discussions were delayed.

B. Correct any errors in punctuation, style, and the use of abbreviations and symbols in the following sentences.

1. Mrs Morris, the vice president is visiting our Fargo office next week.

2. The costs are as follows; three dollars, seven dollars, and 80 dollars.

3. Preston said, "I want the I.B.M. sales rep immediately"!

4. We cant afford to pay for a 15,000,000-million-dollar advertising campaign.

5. Please figure our profits with markups of 24%.

6. Send the letter to Mmes. Francis, and Falcone.

7. Our company uses the L.I.F.O. inventory system.

8. Meredith asked how much does the 20-mms-diameter tube cost.

9. The order came back marked N.A.

10. The C.E.O. has requested a meeting with the heads of manufacturing sales and advertising.

PROJECTS

A. Find examples of abbreviations, contractions, and symbols in business documents. Discuss their appropriateness for the particular piece of writing.

B. Compile a list of business acronyms. Include business terms and the names of companies, organizations, and government agencies. A new area for acronyms is computer hardware and software (e.g., BASIC, FORTRAN, COBOL).

30
Proofreading for Punctuation Errors

Charlie Young looked puzzled as he began to read a memo from a co-worker:

> Please provide me with updated evaluations on Wanda Franklin and Leo (pho-tocopies are sufficient, also, please indicate whether their jobs are code sis or sas. Thanks.

After a second and third reading, he realized that the message should have looked like this:

> Please provide me with updated evaluations on Wanda, Franklin, and Leo (photocopies are sufficient). Also, please indicate whether their jobs are code si's or sa's. Thanks.

Errors in punctuation such as the ones in this memo can be confusing for readers and embarrassing for writers. This chapter will help you review the most common types of punctuation errors.

COMMON COMMA MISTAKES

Some business writers have more trouble with commas than with any other type of punctuation. Generally, errors fall into one of four categories:

- Misuse of a comma to separate the subject and predicate of a sentence

  INCORRECT: The package from Wilson Graphics, arrived three days late.

- Misuse of a comma to separate two items in a series or to separate three items all joined by *and, or,* or *nor*

  INCORRECT: Send it on May 12, or May 14.

  INCORRECT: Sand City offers sun, and ocean, and fun.

- Misuse of a comma where a period is appropriate

  INCORRECT: We will expect you at six, dinner will be served at six-thirty.

- Misuse of commas in place names

  INCORRECT: Our office in Mobile Alabama is completed.

  INCORRECT: Our office in Mobile Alabama, is completed.

  In both cases *Alabama* should be set off by two commas.

The following paragraph contains a number of comma errors that have been marked for correction:

Megan Johnson comes to us from Seattle, Washington where she spent five

years as a computer analyst with Thorndyke Systems. Megan will head our

new software design department, a position that will utilize both her man-

agement and her data processing skills. The plans she has for the department

are very exciting we are looking forward to seeing them develop. Please join

us in welcoming Megan to Adams, Inc. We know she will bring innovation

and ingenuity and a breath of fresh air to our company.

SHARPENING YOUR SKILLS 1

Use proofreading symbols to correct the following comma use errors. Then rewrite the sentences in correct form.

1. We will have it ready by Thursday, or Friday.
2. We will have a representative waiting, she will take you to your hotel.
3. Our first choice for production assistant, turned us down.
4. The proposed site is in Portland Oregon.
5. The material is neither flexible, nor heat-resistant.

PROBLEMS WITH PERIODS Most of the time, periods do not give writers any trouble. Occasionally, however, a writer may mistakenly substitute another mark of punctuation (such as a question mark) for a period or have trouble with periods in abbreviations and initials.

Remember that a period, not a question mark, belongs at the end of a direct question, as in *Orlando Martinez wonders if the suits will be ready next week.*

Be sure you know how to use periods with abbreviations: whether at the end of the abbreviation *(Corp., Inc.)*; after every letter *(a.m., i.e., U.S.A.)*; after every abbreviated element *(N. Dak., loc. cit.)*; or not at all *(AMA, IRS, cm, mm)*. When initials stand for personal names *(Lorraine M. Arthur, C. E. Martinelli)*, they are always followed by periods.

The paragraph that follows includes some common period errors, marked for correction.

This morning M. I. Jones Jr. asked me if the order for Masterson Corp. had

gone out. I told him that as far as I knew it had gone out in the a.m. on Tuesday,

via UPS. To my embarrassment, I have since discovered that it never went

out at all. Please see that it goes out this p.m.

Question marks and exclamation points have very specific functions. Used incorrectly, they will be misleading or ineffective.

Problems with question marks usually involve either placement or choice between a question mark and a period. A question mark belongs at the *end* of an interrogative sentence, never in the middle.

INCORRECT: How could you say? "Our products are second-rate."

When you make a polite request or command, end it with a period, not a question mark.

Will you please see that my wishes are honored.

Use exclamation points only at the end of statements that express strong feeling. When an interjection expresses milder feeling, use a comma or a period instead.

INCORRECT: Oh! It doesn't really matter!

CORRECT: Oh, it doesn't really matter.

The following paragraph contains several errors involving question marks and exclamation points that have been marked for correction.

Well, I knew your perfect record couldn't last forever. Does this sound familiar?

"10 rolls of gift wrap to 'Gifts n' Stuff.'" Our order was for 10 rolls, but you

sent us 100. I am returning the 90 extra rolls in a separate package. Will you

see that they get back to your stockroom.

SHARPENING YOUR SKILLS 2

Use proofreading symbols to correct errors in the use of periods, question marks, and exclamation points in the following sentences. Then rewrite the sentences in correct form.

1. Please attend the meeting on April 15 at 10 am.

2. Several customers wanted to know if the beef was chemical-free?

3. Which is correct? 1 cm or 1.5 cm?

4. Yes! It is hard to wait for such a long time.

5. May I suggest that you call Mr. Chan directly, since I no longer handle complaints?

MISTAKES INVOLVING PARENTHESES AND DASHES

One of the points to remember about parentheses is that they always come in pairs—sometimes writers forget to add the final parenthesis in a sentence.

The use of other punctuation with dashes may also be a source of confusion. Be aware of the following rules:

• Do not include a comma, semicolon, colon, or period before an opening dash.

INCORRECT: As usual,—if anything can be called usual here—we will begin at 8 a.m.

• Do not include a period before a closing dash.

INCORRECT: Immediately—do it right away.—cancel the order.

• Do not include a dash before an end mark.

INCORRECT: We have a goal—to serve you best—!

When proofreading punctuation with parentheses, remember these rules:

• Do not precede a parenthesis with a comma, semicolon, or dash. In the sentence that follows, the comma should follow the closing parenthesis:

INCORRECT: Clearly, (at least I hope it is clear) we need a new distributor.

• Avoid using double punctuation—the same punctuation within the closing parenthesis and at the end of the sentence. In both sentences that follow, the punctuation in the closing parenthesis should be deleted.

INCORRECT: Are you sure (*can* you be sure?) that Al stole the money?

INCORRECT: These proofs had better be perfect (I'm not kidding!)!

• Do not omit necessary punctuation within a closing parenthesis. In the sentence that follows, a question mark should precede the closing parenthesis:

INCORRECT: I am never sure how to spell Ms. Csikszentmihalyi's (is that it) name.

The paragraph that follows includes a number of errors involving dashes and parentheses, marked for correction:

Our year is off to a good start (for a change)! For the first time in five years,

(weren't they long years?) we began with money in the bank. Of course, we

should not be too self-assured—a few slow months could hurt us badly.

However, let's not dwell on the negative. Congratulations to all of you (even

you, Dave) for a great year!

MISTAKES INVOLVING QUOTATION MARKS AND UNDERSCORES

Some of the problems that occur with dashes and parentheses also occur with quotation marks. Like parentheses, quotation marks must always be used in pairs. Many writers are unsure where to place punctuation around quotation marks. The rule is that periods and commas always go inside and that semicolons and colons always go outside. The placement of other punctuation marks depends on whether they apply only to the quoted material (in which case they go inside) or to the whole sentence (in which case they go outside).

An additional problem with quotation marks involves indirect quotations: Remember that quotation marks are used only when something is quoted directly, not when it is restated.

Punctuating the title of a literary or artistic work requires choosing between quotation marks and an underscore. When you proofread, check to be sure that titles of complete works (books, magazines, and so on) are underscored and titles of parts of larger works (chapters, articles, and so on) are placed in quotation marks.

The paragraph that follows includes a number of errors involving quotation marks and underscores, marked for correction:

The meeting was called to order by Sibyl Jerome, who noted that we barely

had a quorum. Hannah Medeiros introduced the first item of business, a

discussion of new products. Hannah noted that we need to produce what she

called "magnet products. These would sell well and introduce customers to our name, drawing them to our other products as well. At this point Steven

Italiano interjected, "Great—but we haven't come up with one idea so far."

The group agreed that creativity seemed at a low ebb. Hannah suggested that

everyone get a copy of the book _Creative Energy_ by Joseph McClellan and

read it before the next meeting, especially the chapter entitled "Idea People."

Several people grumbled good-naturedly about "assigned reading," but every-

one agreed to give it a try.

SHARPENING YOUR SKILLS 3

Use proofreading symbols to correct mistakes involving dashes, parentheses, quotation marks, and underscores in the following sentences. Then rewrite the sentences in correct form.

1. We have a firm price on the swimming goggles ($7.95 per pair.).

2. Wayne says the client thinks our services are "pricey.

3. Unless you indicate otherwise,—by November 20—we will cancel the order.

4. Emilio Sorora's "Employment Skills Handbook" won a prestigious book award last year.

5. "It takes skill", said Nick Masterson, "to anticipate the tastes of the American public".

HYPHEN ERRORS   Hyphens are used primarily in compounds _(well-known, labor-management)_ and in word division. Writers sometimes have trouble remembering whether a particular compound is hyphenated or not. Learn to recognize which common compounds and compound patterns should be hyphenated, which are solid, and which are open. Look up the word in a dictionary if you are not sure.

Word division is another potential problem area. Word division rules (such as the one prohibiting division of one-syllable words or contractions) must never be ignored. Word division guidelines (such as the one suggesting division of words after rather than within prefixes) should be followed whenever possible.

The following paragraph adds some hyphens where they are not needed, fails to add others that are needed, and violates word division rules. All these mistakes are marked for correction.

Enclosed with this letter is a sample of our market̿tested decal plastic. You

will notice that the sheet accepts print easily and provides an invisible back̿

ground for the imprinted message. I believe that we should go ahead w-

ith this product as soon as possible.

Apostrophes are used in forming possessives, contractions, and a few special plurals. Business writers sometimes have trouble deciding when to use an apostrophe and where to place it in a word.

Problems with possessives often occur when a name already ends in *s*, and the writer must choose between adding *'s* or just *'*. On the one hand, pronunciation guides the writer to write *Prince Charles's*, rather than *Prince Charles'*. On the other hand, pronunciation also guides the writer to write *Frank Aristides'* rather than *Frank Aristides's*. In this case, be sure the apostrophe is placed at the end of the name *(Aristides')*, not before the end *(Aristide's)*.

Another problem with possessives occurs when writers use an apostrophe with possessive forms of personal pronouns. These forms should never take an apostrophe (*yours, hers, theirs,* not *your's, her's, their's*).

Generally, problems with apostrophes in contraction involve forgetting them entirely (*cant* for *can't*) or putting them in the wrong place (*were'nt* for *weren't*). Remember that the apostrophe represents the missing letter(s) and should appear where the letter(s) normally would.

Plural forms rarely use apostrophes. The business writer must recognize when an apostrophe is needed for clarity, as in the following examples:

dot all the *i*'s
a.m.'s rather than p.m.'s

The paragraph that follows includes a variety of errors involving apostrophes, all marked for correction:

Today the proofs for Warren Bridges' book came in; when I looked over

them I was appalled. Something is amiss in the printing house—throughout

the proofs *b*s, *d*s, *g*s, *o*s, *p*s, and *q*s are smudged. I don't understand why these

mistakes were'nt caught by the printing house proofreaders. I'm just glad that

MISTAKES IN USING APOSTROPHES

the proofs didn't go out to the author this way—Warren Bridges overreactions to unclear type are legendary. Please look into this and get back to me as soon as possible.

SHARPENING YOUR SKILLS 4

Use proofreading symbols to correct the following mistakes involving hyphens and apostrophes. Then rewrite the sentences in correct form.

1. Unfortunately, the supplier would'nt give a cash refund.
2. Whose keys were stolen—your's or Woody's?
3. The manufacturer provides a safety check-list for use with the machine.
4. Denise says that the mistake was not her's.
5. Please provide me with an uptodate report on your project.

CAPITALIZATION ERRORS

Capitalization errors most commonly occur with generic forms of nouns, titles of persons, and titles of works. Generic forms—words that are used in the place of a full name—are not usually capitalized (*the river* for *the Delaware River* and *the corporation* for *Jadney Corporation*).

Proper capitalization of titles of persons involves looking at both placement and function. Generally, when a title precedes a name *(Chairperson Molarz)* capitalization is necessary. When a title follows a name, however, it generally needs no capitalization *(Ms. Molarz, our chairperson)*. Be sure you know the capitalization rules concerning titles, since they are frequently used in business writing.

Capitalization in titles and headings is a third potential trouble spot. Remember to capitalize the first word, the last word, and all major words. Give special attention to the capitalization of hyphenated words in titles.

The following excerpt from an article includes several capitalization errors, marked for correction.

President Goode Gets a Musical Goodbye

Dr. Harland Goode, president of Weatherby College, was honored at a dinner held last night to celebrate his 40 years of service. Attended by both faculty and students at the college, the event featured a sumptuous dinner followed by a "roast" of president Goode. At the end of this night of celebration of dr.

Goode, the college glee club sang "Goodbye to our Goode-hearted President"

and "For He's a Jolly Goode Fellow."

The difficulties that business writers have with numbers center on one decision: whether to write numbers as figures or as words.

Watch to be sure that numbers that begin sentences are always written in words. (Whenever this style is awkward, rewrite the sentence to reposition the number.) Check to be sure that all related numbers within a sentence are treated alike and that series or ranges of numbers are expressed clearly (*50, 60, and 70; pages 25–32; from 1990 to 1995*).

The paragraph that follows contains many number errors, including some of those just mentioned. Each error is marked for correction.

ERRORS IN WRITING NUMBERS

The results of our consumer survey have finally been compiled. An over-

whelming ~~seventy~~ *70* percent of the people who buy our coffee would not buy

another brand. ~~18~~ *Eighteen* percent had tried it for the first time. The remaining 12~~%~~ *percent*

bought our brand because it was on sale that week. As I see it, we need to

work primarily with our new buyers, aiming to convince 10, 12, or even 15

percent of these people not to buy any other brand. At the same time, we

will try to draw as many new buyers to our product as possible. With an

aggressive marketing strategy, I think we can expect to double sales in ~~twelve~~ *12*

to 15 months.

Errors in writing abbreviations generally fall into two categories: abbreviation of dates and incorrect plural forms. Always check to be sure that within a date the name of the month is spelled out (*January,* not *Jan.*) and that the date is a figure, not an ordinal (*12*, not *12th*). Be sure all days of the week are also spelled out, except within a chart.

Watch for incorrect plural forms of abbreviations. Remember that many abbreviations merely add *s (vols., POs)*, others add *'s (Ph.D.'s, p.m.'s)*, some double the letter *(pp.)*, and still others do not change form *(in, mm, cm)*.

ABBREVIATION ERRORS

The excerpt that follows includes a number of abbreviation errors, all marked for correction.

A written confirmation of the vinyl flooring measurements I dictated over the

telephone on (Feb.) 6th follows:

56 × 45cms (Color No. 65)

104 × 45 cms (Color No. 36)

(If No. 65 and 36 are out of stock, give me 68 and 39 respectively.)

We accept your terms regarding c.i.f.s.

Thank you.

SHARPENING YOUR SKILLS 5

Use proofreading symbols to correct the following mistakes involving numbers and abbreviations. Then rewrite the sentences in correct form.

1. 12 of our employees have received civic awards.
2. Will president Samski speak at the annual meeting?
3. How long has Andrew been with the Company?
4. You will find the cleaning instructions on ps. 16 through 20 of the manual.
5. The reports ranged in length from eight to 20 pages:

EDITING EXERCISES

A. Proofread each of the following sentences, using the proper proofreading symbol to mark each error in punctuation or capitalization. Then rewrite the sentence in corrected form.

1. Unless I hear from you before May 12, (by letter or telephone) I will assume you want to go ahead with the project.
2. Cathy's proposed slogan is "Give me Liberty Cleaning, or death."
3. Is it true? that the company picnic will be held at the president's house.
4. Last Friday professor Angelo Carrera resigned.
5. A failure of the cooling equipment could lead to the injury of 15 20 or even 30 workers.
6. Once the seminar is over, the rest of the day is your's.

7. Feel free to use my office telephone at any time (you may wish to call your office.).

8. Either my assistant, or my secretary, or I, will meet you at the airport.

9. After the meeting Jay said, "Everyone seemed to be in favor of the office remodeling.

10. Ian McManus has accused us of plagiarism in Chapter 15 of "Honest to Business."

11. The road crew should consist of no less than 12 and no more than fifteen people.

12. Both Major Plastics and Eskin Machines hire C.P.A.'s.

13. If possible, please schedule the meeting for the afternoon of April 5th.

14. In her letter, Louise Crowley asked if we still wanted to bid on the Hutchinson job?

15. Apparently Nicole made those remarks "off the record;" unfortunately, they were printed in the morning paper.

B. Proofread the following paragraphs, using the proper proofreading symbol to mark each error in punctuation. Then rewrite the paragraph in corrected form.

1. There are several good reasons for choosing A. N. Griffin Construction, I.n.c, as our builder. First, the company has an excellent reputation for constructing office buildings of good-quality. Second, its quotation (although not the lowest was in my opinion the lowest realistic quotation. Finally, A N Griffin has a policy of guaranteeing the proposed completion date; the company deducts $1000 a day from the price for every day completion is delayed. Will you please get back to me with your comments immediately?

2. 40 years ago Mankowski Enterprises began handling advertising campaigns for several small businesses. Today those "small businesses" (although we wo'nt mention any names here), are among the most wellknown in the country. Mankowski Enterprises specializes in matching the right campaign with the right company—success guaranteed or your money back—. Call Mankowski Enterprises today. Find out why we are called "The Road to Success".

PROJECTS

Collect a number of pieces of direct mail advertising that you, your parents, or your friends have received. Proofread the written material and mark any errors for correction. After you have gone through all the pieces of mail, categorize the errors you have found.

PART FOUR
BUILDING BASIC WORD SKILLS

31
Strengthening Business Vocabulary

William Carroll's co-workers don't mean to be unkind, but they cannot help smiling at some of the things he says, such as "physical year" for *fiscal year* and "deprecate" for *depreciate*. Even his manager laughed at first when she heard some of William's mistakes. Now she is beginning to feel less amused and more concerned that William's errors will make a bad impression on other companies and lead to financial losses. William's incorrect use of words is making him appear unqualified for his job; a poor vocabulary causes poor communication, which can be costly for a business.

THE VALUE OF A GOOD VOCABULARY

Having a good vocabulary helps people avoid embarrassment and therefore feel more confident. It does much more, however. If you improve your vocabulary, you will be a better communicator in every way—a better speaker, writer, listener, and reader. These skills can help you function more effectively both on the job and in your personal life. You can learn to expand your vocabulary independently, so that when people at work use words such as *aftermarket* and *expertise*, you can determine what the words mean and add them to your own vocabulary.

Good communicators need to learn not only the meanings of new words but also ways to use the words appropriately. By following the simple program that is described in this chapter, you can build your working vocabulary.

A Poor Vocabulary Can Cause Problems at Work

An inadequate vocabulary can lead to confusion at work; it can even limit your chances for advancement. For example, if your knowledge of words and how to use them correctly is not as good as it should be, you could find yourself adding errors when you process other people's words—using "irregardless" rather than *regardless* or "notorious" rather than *notable.* Unfamiliarity with accepted ways of using words could also prevent you from noticing your own mistakes when you proofread. A poor vocabulary could, in addition, cause you to misunderstand directions.

The Business Writer Needs a Good Vocabulary

A good vocabulary is essential for those who give as well as take directions. It may work out just fine to say "Now all you do is wiggle that knob" when you are standing beside someone and can point to the knob you mean. However, in written directions, careful word choice is crucial to clarity: "If the copied image is too high on the page, turn the vertical adjustment knob to the left."

To be successful as a business writer, you need to avoid overused expressions such as *the bottom line* and repetitive wording such as *mutual cooperation.* (The word *cooperation* implies that all parties are contributing, making *mutual* unnecessary.)

Another way to improve your business writing is to occasionally substitute specific alternatives for common descriptive words such as *good, bad, interesting,* and *important.* If you have already used the term *interesting* when writing about a co-worker's memo, you can choose *thorough* or *informative* when you mention the memo again. A thesaurus, which provides lists of alternate words for expressing a thought, is a valuable resource for any writer. Chapter 32, on reference books, gives more information on using a thesaurus.

When beginning a new job, you must master the concepts that are basic to the job. If people at work use words such as *productivity, inventory,* and *proposal,* you will have to learn what these terms mean. Some words may be familiar to you but will have different, specialized meanings at work.

WAYS TO INCREASE WORD POWER

Some books promise to improve your vocabulary in 30 days or in 12 easy lessons. These books appeal to many people because they suggest that vocabulary growth is a matter of following a few simple steps. Unfortunately, although people can learn new words from such books, they usually forget them quickly because they often learn words that they cannot use in their daily lives. They would be better off learning words they have already heard or seen but do not fully understand.

Master Words You Recognize

A good way to increase your word power is to learn to use the words you already recognize when you see or hear them.

When building vocabulary, you may be tempted to concentrate on rare words that few people use. A more practical goal would be to move into your active vocabulary words you already recognize. These words have a proven value; you have already encountered them in books, magazines, and other sources.

Read to Increase Your Vocabulary Skills

Almost any reading you do can help increase your word power. You can start by reading whatever you find enjoyable: mysteries, Westerns, romances, or nonfiction books about your hobbies or other interests. Reading newspapers or magazines can also help you build your vocabulary. Then "read your way up" by choosing books that contain unfamiliar words. They will be far more useful in reaching your goal of increased word power than books that do not ask your mind to stretch.

Learn Words in Context

When you encounter an unfamiliar or difficult word, try to guess its meaning from context, which is the environment in which words are used. The same word may have a number of different meanings, and only the context can reveal which one is intended. Learning new words in context is easier than learning them in isolation because remembering how they were used makes them easier to understand.

Check the Definition of Unfamiliar Words

Some people might be content with guessing the meaning of a word. Others might want to check their guess in the dictionary. Guessing before looking in a dictionary will make the word easier to remember because guessing involves active reading.

Always keep a dictionary close at hand while reading. As a practical matter, though, do not look up every unfamiliar word, because doing so too often would interrupt the flow of your reading. Try to look up only the key words, the ones the author considers the most important. Many key words are printed so that they stand out; they may appear in the title or in subheadings, or they may be highlighted in the text itself. An author may also provide assistance by defining terms.

Try putting a check next to the entry in your dictionary every time you look up a word. That way you will know when a word is especially important to you; if you have had to look up the same word two or three times, you might want to make an extra effort to memorize its meaning.

Build Your Vocabulary in School and at Work

One of the best sources of new vocabulary is the classroom. Every time you take a course in a new subject, such as accounting or small business management, you will probably add 300 to 500 words to your vocabulary. Learning new concepts in such courses is inseparable from learning the words that describe those ideas. Because the new terms are closely related to each other and to the subject matter of the course, they are easier to learn than if you were trying to master them separately. Most textbooks include glossaries at the end; these easy-to-use aids allow you to learn the definitions of new words as you read.

Seeing new words in textbooks, however, is not the only way to increase your vocabulary while taking a course. Often, your instructor will use words that are new to you; if you underline those words in your notes and look them up as soon as class is over, you can add them to your vocabulary with a minimum of effort. The same technique can be used on the job: whenever someone uses an unfamiliar word or corrects a word you have misused, write down the word and look it up later. At that time, make a word card by writing the word on the front of a note card and the definition (along with a sentence or phrase that illustrates the word) on the back. Put the cards in a place where you can see and review the words several times a day—on a mirror at home or in a drawer at the office.

When you are working, you will need to learn the technical terms associated with your type of job. Ask for brochures, pamphlets, and magazines that deal with your company's products or services. You can also do an effective job of building your vocabulary by reading company memos and reports when you are on the job.

DENOTATIONS AND CONNOTATIONS

A large vocabulary enables writers to make their communications more interesting—and more effective. They can choose the exact words for each situation. Look, for example, at the following sentence: "The children wept because of the death of their female parent." What is wrong with this sentence? Even though *mother* and *female parent* mean the same thing, *mother* would be more appropriate in the sentence. One word works and the other does not because the ideas associated with each word are different. What a word suggests—its flavor—is called its connotation.

A word's denotation is its dictionary definition, or its literal meaning. Even when a word has several different denotations, readers are rarely confused by them. For example, the word *foot* refers to the part of your body at the end of your leg as well as to the unit of measurement equal to 12 inches. Despite the two meanings, context (the entire sentence or passage in which the word appears) always makes it easy to decide which meaning is intended.

DID YOU KNOW?
The Selection of Trade Names

Have you ever wondered how the name for a new product is chosen? Manufacturers spend a lot of time and money to develop a name that makes people want to buy and use the product. The name must, therefore, be a word with positive connotations.

Charles Inman has begun the process of choosing a trade name for a new pine-scented jewelry and silverware cleaner his company has developed. Charles has hired a consultant who specializes in trade-name creation to produce a list of possible names.

Charles marks the first two names on the list, Blithe and Glee, with question marks. They're positive, but he thinks potential consumers would be unlikely to associate these names with his product. He is looking for a name that is both memorable and easy to say, so he circles Dip 'n' Shine for further consideration. On the other hand, he crosses out No-Rub, which could suggest other kinds of products, such as floor waxes. Besides, he thinks the name is dull.

Charles is especially interested in a name for which he can secure a trademark, so that no one else can use it. From a legal standpoint, the easiest names to protect are invented names, such as Biv and Daz. However, such names require large advertising budgets because consumers learn to associate the name with the product only after seeing and hearing many ads for it.

Blends of familiar word parts, such as Magifresh and Softsolve, do a better job of suggesting products. Respelling words also makes them easier to trademark. Charles notices one respelling on the list that doesn't suit him: SaniKleen. He believes that shine, rather than sanitation, is the main selling point of the new cleaner.

Charles decides to have another discussion with the consultant about the connotations the name for the new product should have. He knows that the wrong name can spell failure for even the best new products.

Shaping Attitudes With Words

Connotations cause many more communication problems than denotations. Often, feelings are associated with words. For instance, if you are reporting a strange smell to a co-worker, you must decide what to call it. Is it a scent or an odor? *Scent* suggests that the smell is pleasant, but *odor* makes it sound like something that should be eliminated.

Controlling Connotations

As you write, you need to remember that most words bring with them associated meanings that can either make your message more effective or detract from it. In a business communication, the sudden intrusion of a word or phrase with informal connotations can distract and confuse readers. For example, "If the data in the final report are not clarified, we're up the creek" starts in a formal, impersonal way but shifts abruptly to an informal conclusion.

Most business writing is factual, so business people often choose words with neutral connotations rather than highly charged, emotional words. For example, no one likes to lose a job, but being "dismissed" sounds more neutral, and somehow less painful, than being "fired." When emotions are unavoidable, make sure that your wording is as positive as your meaning allows.

Suppose you are working hard one day and your supervisor, Ms. Peltz, interrupts you with the welcome words, "Take a short break." You go down to the cafeteria and return to your desk after about 20 minutes. When you step back into the office, your supervisor asks, "Where were you? I said a *short* break, didn't I?"

To you, the 20 minutes seemed short enough. How were you to know that Ms. Peltz thought *short* meant only five minutes? If she had been more precise in her choice of words, she would have avoided a tense situation.

DESCRIPTIVE WORDS

Abstract Words Versus Concrete Words

Abstract words name qualities, ideas, or concepts: *courtesy, value,* and *productivity* are examples of abstractions. Concrete words describe things that can be experienced through the senses: sight, hearing, touch, smell, or taste. *Paper, brown,* and *ridged* are concrete words.

Concrete words are very vivid and help a reader understand what is being talked about; yet they are not appropriate for every writing situation. Good writers understand the power of each type of word. For example, in the following excerpts from advertisements, the first, with its use of concrete terms, is much more effective than the second one, which uses abstract words.

> With Rainbow detergent your blues are bluer, your greens are greener, and your whites are brighter. Your whole wash smells like a spring breeze!

> Flash detergent makes colors more vivid—and your wash will smell fresh too.

In a memo discussing work habits, on the other hand, abstract terms such as *diligence* and *promptness* would be appropriate.

Vague Words Versus Specific Words

Although both abstract and concrete words have a place in effective writing, vague words rarely aid communication. In the story at the beginning of this section, Ms. Peltz's use of *short* was vague, and thus open to varied interpretations. Whenever possible, replace vague terms with specific ones. *Soon,* for example, gives less information than *by July 12. Inexpensive* is vague, while *99 cents* is specific. Substituting specific terms for vague ones helps your writing communicate the message you intend.

SYNONYMS Because no two words have exactly the same denotations and connotations, part of the challenge of using synonyms is learning the precise shades of meaning that words have. A thesaurus will help you find synonyms, and a dictionary will help you distinguish one from another. Only wide reading, however, will develop your feeling for the subtle similarities and differences between words.

Choosing Among Synonyms

Studying synonyms will help you build your vocabulary. You will also learn to make the right choice from among similar words. For example, an advertising copywriter describing the effect of a new coat style on the wearer would choose from among the terms *slender, slim,* and *trim.* The ad writer would certainly avoid the more negative words *skinny* and *scrawny.* An executive who has decided against a co-worker's proposal must choose whether to say that he "declines" the offer or "rejects" it. In such situations, the broader the range of words you know, the greater the chance you have of choosing the right word.

Often, one synonym is clearer and more appropriate than another. For example, someone running from a burning building shouting "Conflagration! Conflagration!" would do better to shout "Fire! Fire!"

Avoiding Monotony

Many people have been taught to avoid monotony by using synonyms rather than repeating a word. In a memo reminding office workers to be polite to clients, the terms *considerate, concerned for others, courteous,* and *thoughtful* could be used, avoiding the sameness of repeating the word *polite* five times. However, this practice can be overdone. Some people go to great lengths to avoid repeating words, which can result in unnecessary wordiness and confusion.

Using Synonyms to Unify Writing

Repeating important concepts strengthens writing, providing the help readers often need to recognize and remember key ideas. A short memo reminding workers of the importance of not being late for work might use the terms *on time, prompt,* and *punctual.* These synonyms help readers see that the memo has one main idea: getting to work on time. Without the synonyms, readers might not realize that all the details in the memo support that main idea.

ANTONYMS Understanding antonyms, which are words that are opposite in meaning, can also help you communicate better. To sharpen your understanding of a word, use a thesaurus to find antonyms for the word. Then check the definitions of these antonyms in a dictionary. You could also examine the synonyms for the original word as well as for the antonyms.

Learning antonyms will increase your vocabulary. Realizing, for example, that the opposite of *diligent* is *lazy* clarifies its meaning. Recognizing opposites that are often used together, such as *profit* and *loss,* also helps you choose wording that makes your meaning clear.

Antonyms can also allow you to stress the positive. Try using antonyms to rephrase negative ideas in more positive terms. A statement such as "We hope not to fail in this venture" can be made more positive by using an antonym: "We hope to succeed in this venture." Reminding people to "be more careful" is more positive than cautioning them to "avoid being careless."

JARGON AND OVERUSED LANGUAGE

Jargon is the special language used by people in a trade, profession, or other group. If a trade or field of study calls for special skill or knowledge, those who are involved in it soon develop a vocabulary that applies to the field. Members of this "in" group find it more convenient to use jargon than to express complicated, technical ideas in ordinary language. They also find it more precise, because ordinary language often lacks the necessary words to express these ideas. Learning the terms used in any new field, from carpentry to astrophysics, is part of the beginner's task in mastering that field.

Remember Your Audience

Technically trained people who use jargon when speaking with or writing for nonspecialists risk confusing and annoying their audience. A field need not be technical to acquire jargon of its own. Business people use jargon such as *career path, cash-flow problem,* and *fiscal year.* Outsiders, and even some customers or clients, may not fully understand these phrases. On the whole, it is better to avoid business jargon when writing for a nonbusiness audience, even if it means taking a little extra care to explain an idea in ordinary language. The extra effort will pay off in improved communication.

Avoid Overblown Language

Jargon may sometimes be appropriate, but overblown language never is. Some people use the longest words they know just to sound impressive, and their letters and reports are stuffed with complicated phrases such as *feasible expedient* (possible solution) or *efficacious refutation* (good argument). Rather than sounding impressive, however, they only succeed in bewildering their readers.

Other writers choose overblown language because they are too rushed or too lazy to express themselves more concisely. The following phrases, once common in business letters, are now used only by people who want a ready-made way of saying something, even if it makes them sound old-fashioned or pompous:

> Please find attached hereto a copy of our invoice.

> We trust that this proposal meets with your approval.

A skillful business writer chooses words to express, not to impress. Such a writer also takes the time to cut words, phrases, and even whole sentences that make a letter or report longer than necessary.

The best way to avoid overblown language is to read a message aloud to see if it sounds as natural as possible. Good writing is different from speech—it is more precise, more concise, and sometimes more formal. However, it should never be pompous or artificial.

CLICHÉS

Since ancient times, poets have been using figurative language—"O, my Luve is like a red, red rose," for example—to make their writing more interesting. Figurative language is nonliteral; it conveys meaning through powerful images. When a figurative expression is used too many times, however, it loses its ability to interest the reader and sometimes becomes almost meaningless. Conventional phrases used so often that most of their meaning is lost are called clichés.

When a phrase becomes a cliché, only the first few words of it need to appear on the page before the reader knows how it will end. Every reader would fill in the blanks in the following examples in the same way:

> as pretty as a _____
> as old as the _____
> as light as a _____

When readers know exactly what is coming, their attention begins to wander, and they may not even bother to finish the letter or memo in which the cliché appears. No business writer can afford to give a reader this kind of excuse to stop reading.

A phrase need not be poetic to seem tired. Some literal phrases, such as *at your earliest convenience, last but not least,* and *in this day and age,* can become just as uninteresting through overuse. Whether we call them clichés or merely tired language, successful writers avoid worn-out phrases.

EDITING EXERCISES

A. Assume that you are working on a report that will be sent to the stockholders of your company. The word processing program you are using includes a thesaurus that, at your request, has suggested alternative ways to complete the sentences below. Consider the connotations of each of the words suggested, and choose the clearest, most appropriate word in each case.

1. After nearly a century as the undisputed (director/leader/chief) of the aluminum industry, Alumino Company has (inaugurated/kicked off/begun) testing a plastic (carbonated beverage/nonintoxicating liquid/soft drink) can.

2. Earnings fell 2.3 percent in the last quarter due to (declining/degenerating/repudiating) oil prices and the cost of (prefacing/introducing/insinuating) new products.

3. Hiring temporary workers is (more miserly/less costly/less dear) than depending on (permanent/invariable/perpetual) staff members.

4. Corporate (top brass/executives/czars) can make paper (counterparts/copies/replications) of whatever they write on the new electronic boards.

B. Revise the following words and phrases in a sales letter to make them clearer and easier to understand.

1. in today's society

2. for a period in excess of two months

3. commence

4. have a dialogue with

5. in lieu of

6. at an early date

7. instigate

8. prior to

9. pursuant to your request, here is

10. herewith, please find

C. Suppose you have realized that some sentences in a memo you wrote contain clichés that are also slangy. Rewrite the following sentences to make the wording both more original and more formal.

1. We blew our competitors out of the water.

2. The vice president of our division has bigger fish to fry.

3. Every cloud has a silver lining.

4. Let's grab the bull by the horns.

D. Choose a paragraph from a textbook or magazine. Rewrite the paragraph, making five changes in word choice. For example, you could change "short-term" to "brief" and "be more productive" to "work harder." Briefly explain how each of your changes weakens or strengthens the paragraph.

PROBLEMS

A. Study the words in each of the following groups until you are confident you understand the shades of meaning that distinguish the words in each group. Then choose the word in each group that you think has the most positive connotation and the word that has the most negative connotation. Be ready to explain your choices.

   1. a draw, a standoff, a stalemate, a deadlock
   2. histrionic, dramatic, theatrical, melodramatic
   3. flagrant, glaring, monstrous, obvious
   4. careless, inadvertent, thoughtless, heedless
   5. clumsy, crude, untrained, awkward
   6. harmful, detrimental, pernicious, unfavorable
   7. peculiar, strange, unique, outlandish

B. Choose a job you would like to have someday. List as many tasks as you can think of that you would perform if you had the job. Then circle the tasks on your list that you would perform more effectively if you had a wider vocabulary.

C. Suppose you are responding to a classified advertisement for a job that ends with the following directions: "Accurately describe yourself in 25 words." Plan your description by listing all the words and phrases you can think of that describe you. Since you want the job, stress your most positive qualities. Then condense the ideas to 25 words by choosing words that most briefly and effectively describe those qualities.

PROJECTS

A. Suppose that as a member of the new-product division of a corporation you have been asked to suggest names for new products. Choose one of the following products: a credit card, a motorcycle, a soft drink, a breakfast cereal, or a shampoo. Choose five real-life products that compete with the product you have chosen, and write explanations of the connotations their names have. Then choose a new name for your company's product, and explain the connotations you think your choice has.

B. Search a business magazine or the business section of a newspaper for ten words you cannot define although you have seen or heard them before. Copy the sentences or headlines containing the words, find their definitions in a dictionary, and rewrite the definitions in your own words to show that you understand them. Then use each of the words in a sentence.

32
Using Dictionaries and Reference Materials

There was once a character in a book who announced to another character, "When *I* use a word, it means just what I choose it to mean—neither more nor less." As a result, it was nearly impossible to understand what he was saying.

The point of the story was that word usage cannot be arbitrary. If we use words differently from the way most people do, we will run into trouble. At best, others will need to take extra time to determine what we mean. At worst, they will completely misunderstand us, and communication will be impossible.

Fortunately, we know what most words mean. Everyone who speaks English uses the vast majority of common words in the same ways; that is in part what "speaking English" means. For unfamiliar words, we have at our disposal one of the most valuable tools for communicating: the dictionary.

In 1747, when the English writer Dr. Samuel Johnson announced that he was going to make a dictionary, some of his friends wondered why. They were accustomed to using dictionaries when reading foreign languages, but a dictionary for their native tongue seemed unnecessary.

Nevertheless, when Dr. Johnson published his dictionary eight years later, it became a best-seller. Many people discovered that a dictionary could help them use words precisely, which in turn enabled them to communicate better. A good dictionary could assist them in many other ways too.

Language is a form of human behavior. Like other human activities, it changes over the years, although so slowly that we are often unaware of it. Some of the words in the first dictionary have since changed in meaning; others have **A CHANGING LANGUAGE** completely disappeared from the language. New dictionaries contain many words that did not even exist in the eighteenth century. Some changes, in fact, have happened very recently.

Language changes because the world changes. Every new thing needs a new name, and in this age of high technology, our language must constantly add new words to keep up. The computer revolution of the last 20 years has introduced a new language called computerese, which has hundreds of new terms, such as *software* and *input*. Other terms, such as *hardware* and *output*, are older words that have taken on new meanings.

Hardware once referred primarily to hammers and nails and other things sold in a hardware store. Now it has the additional meaning of "computer machinery"—CRT screens, disk drives, and the like. *Output* used to mean only what a worker or machine produced; now it usually means the work produced by a computer. *Software* and *input* were coined according to the patterns suggested by the other two. When a new need arises, users of the language find a way to meet it.

Slang is an area of language in which changes occur rapidly. Slang terms current 20 years ago, such as *cool* and *groovy,* seem strange to us today. The phrase *generation gap* (much more popular in the 1960s than today) meant partly that parents felt they were no longer speaking the same language that their children were.

Words and Feelings

Words have the power to make people feel good or bad about themselves. For example, someone new on the job often feels self-conscious about a lack of knowledge or skill. Referring to this individual as a "trainee" (which emphasizes the positive process of training) rather than a "beginner" (which focuses on the negative aspect of the person's inexperience) will give the new employee more confidence.

Some words that originally suggested no offense have become insults over the years. *Villain,* for example, once meant simply "boy." Keeping track of these changes is one of the many tasks performed by dictionary makers (formally called lexicographers). Taking note of such changes can make using the dictionary an informative and interesting experience.

THE ROLE OF THE DICTIONARY

A good modern dictionary describes how English words are pronounced and used by well-educated speakers and writers. Many people, however, expect a dictionary to do something more—to settle disputed questions about how English should be used. For example, is it acceptable to use *transpire* to mean "to happen" or "to occur"? Some people feel that if a dictionary can't tell them, no one can. Even dictionaries, however, may disagree with one another on such questions.

Prescriptive or Descriptive?

In former times, lexicographers were only too happy to answer questions about usage. They believed that their role was to prescribe what was correct and to censor what was incorrect. Today, however, they feel that the usage of the best speakers and writers is the only authority and that their primary job is to describe accurately what that usage is. In other words, lexicographers now explain what is, rather than what they think should be.

This approach does not mean, however, that anything goes. Although usage may change, in which case a future dictionary may accept usage now considered substandard, there are definitely degrees of acceptability in word usage. The safest procedure is to follow the guidance of an *up-to-date* dictionary.

Usage Labels

An up-to-date dictionary is particularly important when you are trying to determine the usage of words. Dictionaries use a number of labels to describe acceptable usage. Words not otherwise marked in a dictionary are considered suitable for use in all kinds of speaking and writing, from the most casual to the most formal. Words marked "colloquial" or "informal" can be used in speech but should be avoided in more formal situations, such as business letters and reports. For example, you might refer to an unsuccessful project as a "flop" in informal conversation, but in a report you would use the word *failure*. Words marked "slang" are acceptable only in the most informal situations. Other kinds of usage labels found in dictionaries include "dialectal" (words used only in one region of the country) and "obsolete" (words no longer in use). To be safe, use only unlabeled words in business writing.

INFORMATION IN A DICTIONARY

Many people use a dictionary only to check spelling and/or to look up the meanings of unfamiliar words. A dictionary, however, can provide much additional information and can be useful in a surprising number of ways.

How a Word Looks and Sounds

Pronouncing a word correctly is obviously useful in speaking, and sometimes provides a clue to spelling as well. The word *athlete*, for example, is sometimes misspelled by people who pronounce an *e* between the first and last syllables. Using the pronunciation key in the dictionary can help avoid such errors.

Sometimes the dictionary will show alternate forms of spelling or pronunciation. (The word *judgment*, for example, can also be spelled "judgement," although the former spelling is preferred.) For such words, the dictionary will tell whether the two forms are equal variants or whether one form is more accepted than the other.

A dictionary can also provide information about how to form the plurals of nouns, whether or not to use capital letters (should you use *french fries* or *French fries?*), and how to divide a word into syllables. Such information is especially valuable when typing business correspondence.

How Words Are Used

The primary function of a dictionary is to tell what words mean. Only a small percentage of words have a single definition, however. Most words have more than one meaning, and a dictionary will list the different possibilities and explain them as clearly as possible. The word *business*, for example, usually means "commerce," but it can also mean a firm that carries on commerce, or even a place where commerce is carried on ("Their business was located in the center of town") . The word *business* can also mean "doings of any kind," as in "She was tired of the whole business." In the theater, *business* refers to the movements with which actors accompany their lines. It can also mean "right," as in "You have no business being here." A good dictionary will catalogue all the meanings of a word. Some dictionaries provide synonyms and antonyms for words, which further clarify the shades of meaning of a term.

The part or parts of speech to which a word belongs are important to its meaning. A dictionary shows that some words, such as *gross* or *net*, can be nouns, verbs, or adjectives as the context demands. The following examples show *gross* used as three different parts of speech in three different contexts:

Please order a *gross* of blue pens. (noun, meaning "12 dozen")

Next year we will *gross* over $2 million. (verb, meaning "to earn as a total before deductions")

Your accident was a case of *gross* negligence. (adjective, meaning "outright")

Where Words Come From

Good dictionaries also show how words came into the English language. This part of an entry, called the derivation or etymology, can help fix the meaning of the word in your mind. For example, the word *corporation* comes from the Latin word *corpus*, meaning "body," and a corporation is a body of people who have come together for the purpose of carrying on a business.

Other Valuable Information

In addition to explaining words, dictionaries contain a wealth of other information. Most dictionaries identify a great many names of both people and places. Dictionaries also often include the meanings of common abbreviations and symbols. Larger dictionaries provide tables of weights and measures, maps, and even such surprising items as lists of colleges and universities. This so-called encyclopedic material can greatly enhance the value of a dictionary.

Although all modern dictionary makers explain that their dictionaries are descriptive rather than prescriptive, many people still want to think of the dictionary as a flawless authority. Their idea reflects misconceptions about how languages change and how dictionaries are made.

CORRECTING MISCONCEPTIONS ABOUT DICTIONARIES

Not All Dictionaries Are Alike

Dictionaries that have different copyright dates will offer different definitions of words whose usage has changed. Using an old dictionary may give people outdated notions about words. For example, until recently, the word *network* meant either "a group of radio or television stations" or "a netlike arrangement of veins, passages, or conducting wires." Only a dictionary published during the last few years would contain a new meaning of the word—"a system of business and professional contacts." Knowing this meaning is of great importance to anyone in the business world.

Dictionaries published at the same time also differ in many ways. Judgments about spelling, pronunciation, and meaning may vary. Different dictionaries also emphasize different aspects of language. *The American Heritage Dictionary*, for example, contains more usage labels than *Webster's New Collegiate Dictionary* because of differences in the editorial policies of the scholars who compiled the two.

USING YOUR WORD PROCESSOR
The Value of Spelling Checkers

Are you a less than perfect speller? If so, a computerized spelling checker can help. It quickly compares all the words in your word-processed document with those in an electronic dictionary that contains thousands of frequently used words. (Most spelling checkers allow you to add a personal list of words as well.) The spelling checker works by indicating any words not included in its word bank. These words are either misspelled or correctly spelled but missing from the dictionary's programmed list of words. You can find out which is the case by referring to a standard dictionary.

Spelling checkers are powerful tools, but they do not replace careful proofreading. Since spelling checkers have no way of knowing what you mean, they accept *the* for *then* and *by* for *my*. You need to check homonyms such as *their* and *there* especially carefully. Try using your word processor's search function to locate the words you sometimes confuse so that you can check them in context.

Take care when adding new words to the spelling checker's dictionary. A good print dictionary is still essential so that you do not add misspelled words. You will also need to refer to other resources to check proper nouns, such as brand names and customers' names, before adding them to the electronic dictionary.

The best way to use a spelling checker is to put it to work to help you identify the kinds of spelling errors you make. Keep a record of the errors your spelling checker locates, and work to eliminate them from all your writing, whether or not you are working at a word processor.

Noah Webster was an eighteenth-century American lexicographer who compiled the finest American English dictionary of his time. This work is still available in revised form and remains one of the most respected and popular dictionaries. Nevertheless, believing that a dictionary which carries the name *Webster's* is the ultimate authority can be misleading. Since the word *Webster's* is not copyrighted, any dictionary publisher can use it in the title, and many do. You will need to look further than the title to learn about a particular dictionary.

No Dictionary Contains Every Word

The English language has the richest vocabulary of any language—it contains more than 800,000 words, far more than are compiled in any one dictionary. Paperback dictionaries typically contain about 55,000 words; hardcover college dictionaries contain between 100,000 and 200,000. Makers of unabridged dictionaries aim to be more inclusive, but even their more than 450,000 entries still do not include the very specialized vocabularies of technical fields. No dictionary can include the most recent additions to the language since English is constantly growing and changing.

The First Meaning Is Not Necessarily the "Right" Meaning

Each dictionary maker must decide upon a method for putting meanings in order within each entry. *Webster's New World Dictionary* and the much larger *Oxford English Dictionary* list entries in chronological order, with the earliest meanings first. Other dictionaries give the most concrete or the most common meaning first, following that with more abstract or less common meanings. However, no dictionary is organized so that the first meaning is the most acceptable one. The introduction to a dictionary will explain how the meanings of the words are arranged.

SELECTING A DICTIONARY

When you buy a dictionary, check the copyright date to be sure you are not purchasing one that is merely a reprint of an outdated edition. Look for a few recently coined words, such as *skyjacker*, *panty hose*, and *biodegradable*, to be sure the dictionary is up to date.

A paperback dictionary is easy to carry, but it contains far fewer words than a hardback college dictionary and is likely to fall apart much more quickly. A hardback dictionary should stand up well under constant use, and it is likely to contain illustrations and be easy to read. Thumb indentations, another feature often found in large dictionaries, make finding words easier. Also, when selecting a dictionary, be sure the type is large enough, the printing clear, and the paper quality good. Look to see whether the illustrations help you understand words at a glance and whether the key to pronunciation is conveniently

The High-Tech Office

(*Left*) A series of technological developments has revolutionized American business. Technologically advanced equipment has spread to offices around the country and changed the way people work and the amount of time it takes them to get their work done. The computer is at the heart of this revolution.

Computers were first put to work by private business in 1954. The first computers contained thousands of vacuum tubes; each computer took up a large room.

A second generation of computers was introduced at the end of the 1950s. These computers used solid-state transistors instead of vacuum tubes, which meant they were smaller, faster, and more powerful than those of the first generation. A third generation of computers, which appeared in 1964, was based on tiny microcircuits that allowed computers to become still smaller in size while gaining speed and power. By the 1970s the third generation had produced the personal computer (also known as the microcomputer), a powerful machine small enough to fit on top of a desk. The comparatively low prices of personal computers put them in reach of small- and medium-sized companies that previously could not afford computer equipment. Sales of personal computers shot up as companies began introducing them into the workplace.

(*Right*) The key to the personal computer is the microprocessor, a part so tiny it can fit on a dime with room to spare. The microprocessor contains more than a half million miniaturized transistors and circuits on a tiny chip made of silicon. The chip is programmed in advance by the manufacturer to perform a particular function such as running a computer. Because microchips are small and inexpensive, microcomputers are too.

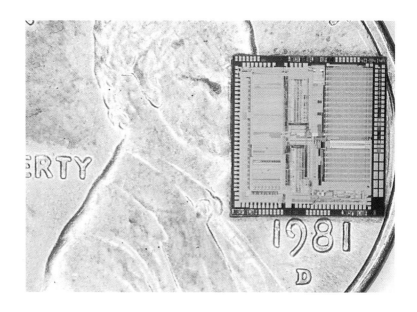

Despite the advantages of the microcomputer, big computers are still needed to do big jobs. The largest and fastest computers, called supercomputers, are generally used for scientific and military applications. The next-largest computers are mainframe computers (*left*), used primarily for data processing, payroll, accounting, and record keeping. Financial institutions, insurance companies, and hospitals are among the biggest users of mainframe computers. Smaller companies generally do not own mainframes because of the high costs of buying and operating them. The least expensive mainframe computer costs hundreds of thousands of dollars; many cost millions. Mainframe owners also need a large, temperature-controlled facility to house the computer and an experienced staff to run it and maintain it. Costs and space are not the only factors that prevent smaller businesses from owning a mainframe computer: not every business has a volume of work that requires a mainframe.

(*Left*) Mainframe computers are capable of handling huge amounts of information with great speed. They can also run a large number of peripheral input/output devices. These pieces of equipment, sometimes referred to as peripherals or i/o devices, feed information into the computer for processing and store information after it has been processed. Very often this information is kept on magnetic, reel-to-reel tapes, similar to the kind used on a music tape deck. Mainframe users generally store their tapes in a tape library.

(*Above*) When a business needs the information stored on a tape, the tape will be sent from the library to the mainframe area, where it is placed on a tape deck that can read the magnetic information stored on the tape and send the information to the computer's brain, the central processing unit. Blank tapes can be written on; that is, they can accept and record information sent from the computer.

(*Top right*) Another input/output device associated with mainframe computers is the disk drive. Like magnetic tapes, hard magnetic computer disks store information that can be fed into the computer's central processing unit. These disks look somewhat like phonograph records and are stacked on top of one another in sealed disk packs. Like a tape drive, the disk drive can write data onto the disk and read that data back at a later date. However, there is one important difference between tape and disk storage. Information stored on tape is in sequential order and must be read that way, from beginning to end. Information stored on disk is stored randomly and does not have to be read in order. This difference means that it is usually faster to access information stored on disks than that which is stored on tape.

(*Bottom right*) In order to instruct, direct, and monitor a mainframe computer and its input/output devices, mainframe operators use a console and video display terminal. Together, the console, central processing unit, and peripheral devices make up the mainframe system.

4

One step below the mainframe system is the minicomputer (*top*). Minicomputers are smaller, less powerful, and less expensive than mainframes; but they are larger, more powerful, and more expensive than micros. This minicomputer is small enough to fit under a desk. Its peripherals include a disk drive, which is also stored under the desk; a keyboard; a terminal (or screen); and a printer.

(*Bottom*) The microcomputer system, or personal computer, is compact enough to fit on top of any desk. This system consists of a keyboard, disk drive, terminal, and printer. The price of a complete system depends on the memory capability of the computer and the type of disk drive. Letter-quality printers, color monitors, and modems will also increase the price of a PC system.

(*Top left*) A smaller version of the personal computer is the portable computer. Portables usually consist of a central processing unit, keyboard, and screen. Some fit into a briefcase. The portable in the bottom photo runs on battery power and weighs less than ten pounds. Because portables are so light, many business people use them while they are away from the office or traveling on business.

(*Top right*) The use of personal computers is spreading quickly. Today Japan is one of the principal manufacturers of computers and microchips. Besides making computers, the Japanese are using them; so American manufacturers have created keyboards in English and Japanese.

6

(*Top left*) How do businesses around the world use computers? One of the primary uses is number-crunching — performing mathematical calculations at lightning speed. Calculations that once took hours to perform manually can now be processed electronically in seconds.

(*Top right*) Creating graphics such as bar and pie charts is another use for the computer in today's high-tech office. By adding a color printer, businesses can put handsome computer-generated graphics on paper for use in sales presentations and business meetings.

(*Bottom*) Word processing is an extremely popular computer application. Some computers are dedicated word processors, specifically designed and programmed to do word processing. Other computers are not specifically manufactured as word processors, but can perform a number of different functions including word processing. Word processing computers allow businesses to customize mass mailings and make changes to text with ease. The word processing operator can make sure a letter contains no errors before having the computer print it. If the operator wants to make any changes after printing, all he or she needs to do is correct the disk and have the computer make a new printout.

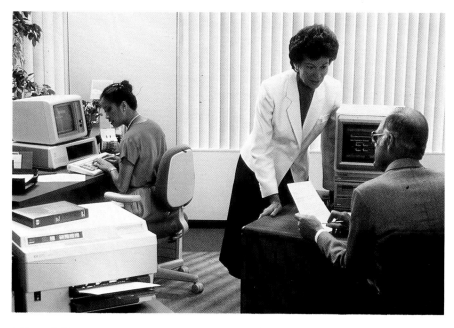

7

(*Above*) Management information systems (MIS) are another business application for the computer. These systems give business people access to information and allow them to manipulate and juggle that information to make various predictions and forecasts. Many business managers use these systems to make a number of basic business decisions—how to price a product, where to assign the sales force, how much to spend on advertising, and so on.

(*Right*) Along with the computer revolution has come a revolution in telecommunications. The range and quality of mobile telephone transmission and reception have increased greatly. At the same time, the cost of mobile telephones has declined. A number of businesses have begun providing their sales force and managers with mobile telephones so they can communicate with their office and their clients while on the road.

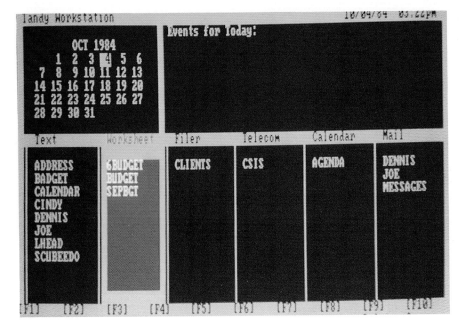

Events for Today:

OCT 1984
        1 2 3 4 5 6
7 8 9 10 11 12 13
14 15 16 17 18 19 20
21 22 23 24 25 26 27
28 29 30 31

Text   Worksheet   Filer   Telecom   Calendar   Mail

ADDRESS   6BUDGET   CLIENTS   CSIS   AGENDA   DENNIS
BADGET   BUDGET   JOE
CALENDAR   SEPBGT   MESSAGES
CINDY
DENNIS
JOE
LHEAD
SCUBEEDO

[F1]   [F2]   [F3]   [F4]   [F5]   [F6]   [F7]   [F8]   [F9]   [F10]

(*Above*) When the desktop computer was first introduced, many people predicted that a paperless office would emerge—one that did away with typewriters, paper, pens, and pencils, and provided a computer station for every employee. While the paperless office will probably never come to be, many businesses today are using computers as calendars, appointment books, and file cabinets. Some computers even allow users to mail information electronically from one computer terminal to another.

Electronic mail can be sent through computers that are linked together in a network or to any computer with a modem, a device that transmits and receives computer data via telephone lines.

(*Right*) Teleconferencing is another innovation in telecommunications. Teleconferencing uses television cameras and telephone lines to enable business people in different locations to see and hear each other and conduct meetings without actually meeting in person. Teleconferencing equipment is very expensive and, as yet, few businesses can afford it. Like the computer, however, teleconferencing equipment may one day be within reach of many small businesses.

located and easy to interpret. Abbreviations used within entries should also be easy to understand.

Recommended Dictionaries

Good college dictionaries to consider include the following:

- *The American Heritage Dictionary*
- *Funk & Wagnalls Standard College Dictionary*
- *The Random House College Dictionary*
- *Webster's New Collegiate Dictionary*
- *Webster's New World Dictionary*

When you decide to buy a dictionary, go to any good bookstore and do some comparison shopping. Examine the dictionaries, keeping in mind the points mentioned in the previous section. Decide which dictionary seems easiest to use and is the most appealing to you. You might also ask a teacher or librarian (or even a bookstore employee) for additional advice.

Developing the habit of using your dictionary will make you a better communicator, whether you are reading, writing, speaking, or listening. An important first step in building the dictionary habit is to read the introduction, which will explain the principles your dictionary is based upon. This approach is far more effective than using the trial-and-error method to interpret entries.

USING A DICTIONARY

All dictionaries provide guide words at the top of each page that indicate the first and last words on that page. By using these words, you will be able to find the word you want quickly and easily.

The sample shown in Figure 32-1 identifies the parts of a dictionary entry.

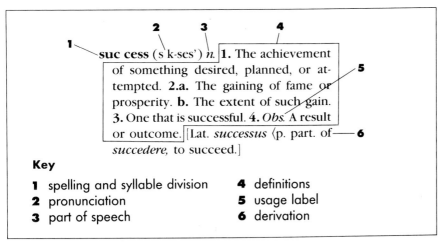

Key

1 spelling and syllable division
2 pronunciation
3 part of speech
4 definitions
5 usage label
6 derivation

Figure 32-1 A dictionary entry.

USING A THESAURUS

If you are looking for another way to describe an employee who is efficient, try turning to a thesaurus. *Effective, capable, competent, skillful*, and *proficient* are among the words you will find. Unlike a dictionary, a thesaurus does not include definitions of words. Instead, it provides lists of synonyms and related words that can jog your memory if a specific word has slipped your mind. A thesaurus can introduce you to new words as well.

Entries in a thesaurus are usually arranged in one of two ways: alphabetically or topically. Alphabetical entries are arranged like those in a dictionary, but instead of information about the meaning of the word, there is a list of synonyms for the word. When entries are arranged topically, you must first look up the word you want in an alphabetical index, which directs you to the entry you want in the body of the thesaurus. Figures 32-2 and 32-3 show thesaurus pages arranged both ways.

The words in a thesaurus entry are not necessarily interchangeable. No two words mean *exactly* the same thing. If you are planning to use a word you have found in a thesaurus, be sure to look it up in a dictionary to find out whether its shade of meaning is appropriate. That way you will avoid the kind of mistake one student made when she was looking for a way to describe someone who was economical. After selecting a word from her thesaurus, she wrote about "our parsimonious controller." She did not realize that *parsimonious* means "stingy."

A dictionary of synonyms will also help you avoid this problem. It gives you synonyms for a particular term *and* discusses their various shades of meaning.

OTHER KINDS OF DICTIONARIES

If your job requires that you use and recognize unusual words, an ordinary college dictionary may not contain the ones you need. Specialized dictionaries are available for different fields. The following is a list of some specialized dictionaries that may help you on the job:

- Dictionaries of abbreviations and acronyms, for example, the *Abbreviations Dictionary* (Elsevier Science Publishing Company, 1986) and the *Acronyms, Initialisms, and Abbreviations Dictionary* (Gale Research Company, 1985)
- Dictionaries of legal, medical, technical, and business and financial terms, such as the *Dictionary of Legal Words and Phrases* (Gould Publications, 1983), *Black's Medical Dictionary* (Barnes & Noble Books, 1984), *McGraw-Hill Dictionary of Science and Engineering* (McGraw-Hill, 1984), and the *Dictionary of Business and Management* (John Wiley & Sons, 1983)
- Dictionaries of foreign words and phrases or modern American usage, such as the *Dictionary of Foreign Words and Phrases in Current English* (Routledge & Kegan Paul, 1983) and the *Harper Dictionary of Contemporary Usage* (Harper & Row, 1985)

---

finish *vb* **1 syn** CLOSE 3, complete, conclude, determine, end, halt, terminate, ultimate, wind up, wrap up
rel accomplish, achieve, effect, fulfill
idiom have done with
2 syn GO 4, consume, exhaust, expend, run through, spend, use up, wash up
3 syn KILL 1, carry off, cut off, destroy, dispatch, down, put away, scrag, slay, take off
4 syn MURDER 1, assassinate, ‖bump off, cool, do in, ‖dust off, execute, knock off, liquidate, put away

---

Figure 32-2 An alphabetical thesaurus entry.

---

nouns end 70.1
    symmetry 247.1
    texture 350.1
    elegant style 587.1
    perfection 675.1
    completion 720.2
    skill 731.8
verbs end 70.5
    kill 408.13
    refute 505.5
    use up 664.2
    perfect 689.10
    destroy 691.12
    complete 720.6

6. complete, perfect, finish, finish off, **conclude, terminate, end,** carry to completion, prosecute to a conclusion; **get through, get done,** get through with, get it over, get it over with; **finish up,** clean up [coll.], wind up [coll.], close up [U.S.], button up [coll.], put the lid on it [slang], call it a day [slang]; **round out; top off,** crown, cap; **give the finishing touches,** put the finishing touches on, finalize; break the back *or* neck of.

Figure 32-3 A topical thesaurus index and entry.

There are even special dictionaries (such as *The Bad Speller's Dictionary,* Random House, 1967) that include a word spelled incorrectly (the way many think it is spelled), followed by the correct spelling. These dictionaries help individuals who have trouble checking spelling because they do not know where to look.

STYLE MANUALS

Dictionaries provide a great deal of information about words, but they do not answer all the questions people have about language. To answer specific questions about word usage, punctuation, and capitalization, you will need to turn to a style manual. There are a number of style manuals available that provide both basic and comprehensive information for business offices. One of the most widely used is *The Gregg Reference Manual*.

Lengthy, detailed style manuals include *The Chicago Manual of Style* and *Words Into Type. The Elements of Style,* written by William Strunk Jr. and E. B. White, is a brief, popular guide to rules of usage and principles of composition that are often violated.

Organizations such as the American Medical Association and the Modern Language Association have their own style manuals, and the Government Printing Office puts out a style manual especially useful for people preparing documents in government offices. The company you work for may have its own manual as well. Company style manuals ensure that corporations present a consistent picture to the outside world. They may include rules for the wording and capitalization of the names of company divisions and products and may designate styles to be used for letters and memos.

EDITING EXERCISES

A. Suppose that your manager has asked you to comment on a report she has written. As you study the report, you find some words that you are unsure about:

beneficiary	consignment
monetary	arbitration
liquidity	debit

To prepare to discuss the report with your manager, look up each word in the dictionary. Copy the pronunciation of the word. Then define the term in your own words, and use it in a sentence.

B. Assume that you have just written a proposal to make some changes in the hiring procedures of the company where you work. The word processor you used to write the report provides tentative word divisions based on general theories about hyphenation, but you have often found it to be incorrect. Use a dictionary to check the following word divisions, and correct words that are not divided between syllables:

promo/tion	acknow/ledgments
object/ive	qualifi/cations
refer/rals	recommend/ation
exper/ience	corres/pondence
refe/rences	respons/ibilities

C. The president of your company is giving an important speech. Before copies are sent to local newspapers and television stations, you have been asked to check the spelling of the words in the speech. You have used a good computerized spelling checker to verify the spelling of most of the words in the document, but the following words are not included in the spelling checker:

Pitsburgh

Charles A. Lindburgh

Kuwate

Apollo

Franklin Deleno Roosevelt

Aleksei Kosigin

Frankfort, Germany

Use college, unabridged, or specialized dictionaries to check the spelling of these words. Correct any errors you find.

PROBLEMS

A. Use a dictionary and a thesaurus to find two synonyms and an antonym for each of the following words:

believable	acquit
persevere	enormous
helpful	disapprove
imaginative	excellent

Circle the words on your list that you would use if you were trying to vary the wording in a sales letter to potential subscribers to a news magazine.

B. Study the pronunciation key in your dictionary. A short form of the key probably appears at the bottom of every page or every other page, but you should examine the longer key provided at the front of the dictionary. After you understand the symbols in the key, use them to indicate the pronunciation of each of the following words:

audit	gross
balance	insurance
credit	lease
depreciate	merger
equity	promote
fiscal	trust

Check your versions of the pronunciations against those printed in your dictionary, and correct any errors you find.

C. Look through a thesaurus to find an entry that interests you. From that entry, select five words that are synonyms or that are closely related in meaning. Look them up in a dictionary, and write a paragraph in which you distinguish among the meanings of the words. Include phrases or sentences that illustrate the varying shades of meanings.

PROJECTS

A. Look up one of the following words or phrases in three different dictionaries:

lien	collateral
shareholder	list price
proxy	direct mail
inventory	power of attorney
franchise	merger
beneficiary	portfolio

Describe the similarities and differences you find in the entries. Examine elements of the definitions such as the way pronunciation is indicated, the meanings, usage labels, related forms, examples of usage, synonyms and antonyms, cross-references, and derivations. Choose the entry you like best, and explain why you like it.

B. Compile a mini-dictionary of five current slang terms. Use the entries in a college dictionary as models. Show how to pronounce each term, using pronunciation symbols. Write clear definitions organized by parts of speech, and include phrases that illustrate the terms. Add synonyms and antonyms, along with your guesses about the derivations of the words.

33

Avoiding the Most Common Word Errors

As Marc Chernow sorted the mail Thursday morning, he came across an envelope marked "Attn: Personal Department." He shook his head because he had seen the same thing several times that week. The company Marc worked for was advertising for a new secretary, and candidates had been instructed to address their applications to the Personnel Department. Marc knew that this was one of the applications that would never be opened because the person who wrote it had confused a basic business word, *personnel*, with *personal*. Marc's company could not afford to hire a secretary who could not distinguish between similar words.

More than 2,000 sets of words in English—such as *buy*/*by* and *great*/*grate*—sound the same but have different spellings and meanings. Almost everyone has trouble with at least a few of these many sets of homonyms. In addition, there are sets of words, called confusables, that look or sound enough alike to cause problems. *Personal* and *personnel* are two commonly confused words from this group. Misusing homonyms and confusables can obscure the meaning of a message—and make the writer look unprofessional.

Examining the context in which a homonym or a confusable is to be used is the most important way to avoid choosing the wrong word. In addition, there are a number of techniques you can use to distinguish between two confusing words. Circling or enlarging the parts that cause problems is a good way to start. Also, be sure you know what the words mean, how to pronounce them, and what part of speech each word is. Then look for letter similarities that can help you relate the spelling of each word to its meaning. For example,

MASTERING CONFUSING WORDS

stationERy and *papER* both contain *er,* while something that is *stationAry* stAnds still. Such reminders may seem funny at first, but if they help you choose the right words, they are well worth your time. In fact, the more amusing they are, the better, because humor makes them easier to remember. Reminders you yourself create are often the most helpful.

Word cards (discussed in Chapter 31) can also help you master confusing words. To make a word card, put the word on one side and the definition (with an example sentence) on the other. Try to guess the correct spelling of the word by looking at the side with the definition. Using cards rather than writing the words on sheets of paper simplifies your study because it allows you to shuffle the cards to prevent learning the words in only one order. You can also easily select the words that are giving you extra trouble rather than spending the same amount of time on all the words. Remember to place these cards in convenient spots (on a mirror at home, in a desk drawer) where you can easily glance at them while doing something else.

POSSESSIVE PRONOUNS VERSUS CONTRACTIONS

Commonly used possessive pronouns and contractions such as *your/you're* and *its/it's* can easily be confused with each other. The confusion arises because nouns show possession with the use of apostrophes: *boy/boy's, dogs/dogs'.* However, possessive personal and relative pronouns never use apostrophes. *It's,* therefore, never indicates possession. *It's* most often is a contraction of *it is;* the apostrophe indicates the missing letter. (In informal writing, *it's* may be a contraction of *it has,* as in "It's been a good year for Hempstead Enterprises.")

In the same way, *you're* means "you are," *they're* means "they are," and *who's* means "who is." The related words *(your, their, whose)* show possession. To use these confusing words correctly, mentally substitute *you are, they are,* and *who is* to be sure that the contractions are required.

You're the winner of the brand-name contest! (You are the winner . . . .)

Please send your payment to the address below. (*Not:* Please send you are payment . . . .)

Who's in charge of the coffee fund this quarter? (Who is in charge . . . .)

Please provide the name of any employee whose attendance record is perfect. (*Not:* Please provide the name of any employee who is attendance . . . .)

ONE WORD OR TWO?

Some words are confusing because they can be written as one word or as two separate words. Often, the words have different meanings when they are separated. For example:

• *All together* means "all in one place" or "all acting together," but *altogether* means "entirely."

- *All ready* means "completely prepared," but *already* means "previously."
- *Everyday* means "ordinary," but *every day* means "each day."
- *Maybe* means "perhaps," but *may be* is a form of the verb *to be.*
- *Sometime* means "at an unstated time," but *some time* means "a period of time."

All right and *a lot* do not have acceptable one-word spellings. Many people consider "alright" to be an error, and no one accepts "alot." To eliminate confusion, remember that the word "alwrong," like "alright," is not acceptable.

The words in the groups that follow sound the same but have different spellings and meanings. Each word is followed by one or more sentences that show its use. Some of the groups include reminders to help tell the words apart.

HOMONYMS

ad (noun) shortened form of *advertisement*

Our ad in Sunday's paper increased sales.

add (verb) to find the sum; to join or unite to increase size, quantity, or importance

Add this column of figures, please.

If you add a transmittal letter to your proposal, the Board of Directors will take it more seriously.

Reminder: Add a *d* when you find the sum or increase the quantity.

allowed (verb) permitted

Writing personal letters on company letterhead is not allowed.

aloud (adj.) loudly enough to be heard

Talking aloud disturbs the people at the other workstations.

Reminder: When you say something ALOUD, you say it out LOUD.

capital (noun or adj.) money or property used for investment; the city where a state or national government is located; an uppercase letter

He could not raise enough capital to open the new store.

Des Moines is the capital of Iowa.

capitol (noun) the building where a legislature meets

The dome of the capitol is covered with gold leaf.

The Capitol is located in Washington, D.C. (Note the use of uppercase letter *c* for the building where the federal legislature meets.)

Reminder: A capitOl has a dOme.

cite (verb) to quote

> Cite the sources you used when you prepared the final report.

sight (noun) something to look at; the power of seeing

> It was quite a sight to watch Martha as she tackled the malfunctioning sorter.

> His sight improved greatly after the surgery.

site (noun) location

> The tenth-floor banquet room is a better site for the conference.

council (noun) group of advisors, such as a governing board

> The mayor and council meet on the second Tuesday of every month.

counsel (noun) advice; a lawyer; (verb) to give advice

> We have never regretted following Bill's counsel.

> Larry Gross is the new counsel for the Acme Corporation.

> Ms. Wexler counsels the employees who want to retrain for new jobs.

Reminder: A counCIl is a CIrcle of advisors.

do (verb) to perform an action; to accomplish

> What are we going to do about the Morgan account?

due (adj.) owed

> The bill is due on June 15.

Reminder: Something that is duE is owEd.

know (verb) to understand; to be acquainted with

> Do you know the company's policy on vacations?

> Do you know the new supervisor?

no (adj.) not any; (adv.) not so

> There is no reason to refuse their offer.

> No, Mr. Pratt is not resigning.

lessen (verb) to reduce

> Making a backup disk lessens the risk of losing data.

lesson (noun) something to be studied

> Before the next training session, please study the lesson on using a spelling checker.

passed (verb) went by; handed to

> We passed our new office building on the way to the factory.

> Sarah passed the memo to John.

past (noun) time before the present; (adj.) gone by; (prep.) beyond; (adv.) by or beyond

> This is not the fanfold paper we used in the past.

> The time is past when we could have made that sale.

> I walked right past the window display without seeing it.

> Stop for me when you go past.

principal (adj.) chief, most important; (noun) the person in charge of a school; invested funds

> The principal problem is the amount of data required.

> Dr. Benjamin Farkas has been appointed principal of the new high school.

> We spend the interest on this investment, but we never touch the principal.

principle (noun) a basic truth or general law; ethics

> The principle is a good one, but it is hard to put into practice.

> We can trust him because he is a man of principle.

Reminders: The principAl part is the mAin part.
The princiPAL of the school is your PAL.
A principLE is a ruLE.

their (possessive pronoun) belonging to them

> The architects presented their plans for the new offices.

there (adv.) at that place; also used with forms of *to be*; to introduce new ideas

> Please put the new desk over there.

> There are several other problems that should be solved quickly.

they're (pronoun + verb) they are

> They're planning to attend the committee meeting.

Reminders: THERE tells wHERE and is the opposite of *HERE*.
HEIRs inherit tHEIR possessions.

threw (verb) tossed

> Vandals threw paint on one of the company cars.

through (prep.) from one side to another; by way of; (adj.) finished

> We can't see through the windows of this office.

> To get to the Accounts Receivable Department, just walk through this corridor.

> We are through with this part of the report now.

Reminder: Only one letter separates the past tense *thrEw* from the present tense *thrOw*.

Note: Never write *through* as *thru* except when abbreviating personal or very informal notes.

to (prep.) toward, until; sign of the infinitive, as in *to buy, to study*

> Please take the cash bag to the bank.

> Robert Elkins would like to apply for the job.

too (adv.) also; more than enough

> Sam Miller is skilled at word processing too.

> Patricia is too busy to accept another assignment now.

two (adj. or noun) the number 2

> Two candidates are competing for the position.

Reminder: If *also* or *overly* can be substituted, *too* is correct.

waiver (noun) the act of giving up a right or privilege; the document that abandons a right

> Radway Enterprises has agreed to a waiver of the contract provision.

waver (verb) to vary; to totter from side to side

> Tyler wavers between lax supervision and rigid control of the people in his department.

Reminders: A waiver gIves something up.
Relate *WAVEr* to WAVEs, which move back and forth.

weather (noun) atmospheric conditions

> The company picnic will be held on Friday if the weather is good.

whether (conjunction) word that introduces choices

> Decide whether to take a break now or later.

Reminders: The wEAther is clEAr.
Relate *WHether* to question words such as *WHere* and *WHat*.

The spellings, meanings, or pronunciations of the words below are so close that they are often confused. Rhyming words are given to help you pronounce some of these troublesome words. Parts of speech are included when they will help you distinguish between words.

CONFUSABLES

accept (verb) to receive willingly; to approve of

> I am happy to accept the promotion.

> Virginia accepts this plan in principle, but she wants to make some changes.

except (prep.) with the exclusion of, but

> Everyone except Mr. Dana has approved the proposed changes.

Reminder: The *ex* in *EXcept* means "out," as it does in *EXclude.*

access (noun) permission to enter or use; (verb) to retrieve information from a computer file

> We do not have access to that information.

> You cannot access the file without using the password.

excess (noun or adj.) surplus

> Because of excess overtime charges, the budget must be adjusted.

Reminder: EXcess amounts are EXtra amounts.

advice (noun) a recommendation

> Ms. Medica's advice proved useful.

advise (verb) to make a recommendation

> The technician advised us to replace, rather than repair, the typewriter.

Reminder: Advice rhymes with *mice*; advise rhymes with *wise.*

affect (verb) influence

> Lower temperatures affect productivity in our Alaska plant.

effect (noun) a result; (verb) to bring about

> The new flextime policy has had a positive effect on morale.

> Upper management effected a change that should greatly increase profits.

Reminders: Think of the concept of causE and Effect.
If you can put *thE* in front of the word, use *Effect.*

among relates more than two people, places, or things

> The research team chose among three methods of soil analysis.

between relates two people, places, or things

Mrs. Rischer will decide between the two best applicants for the job.

Reminder: Use the two *e*'s in *betwEEn* as a reminder that it relates *two* things.

anecdote a story

Miss Wilson's anecdote will help me remember to treat customers more courteously.

antidote a remedy that counteracts a poison, disease, or other harmful influence

Careful proofreading is the antidote to typing errors.

Reminder: The *ANTI* in *ANTIdote* means "against," so an ANTIdote works against harmful influences.

appraise to set a value on

The warehouse must be appraised before we set a selling price.

apprise inform

Mr. Metcalf neglected to apprise us of the rate changes.

Reminder: When you apprAise, you set a vAlue.

casual informal

Casual dress is acceptable for overtime shifts on Saturday.

causal responsible for

Absenteeism was a causal factor in increasing expenses.

Reminder: CAUSal factors are CAUSes.

choose to select (present tense) (rhymes with *clues*)

Ralph must choose between the day shift and the night shift.

chose selected (past tense) (rhymes with *hose*)

Yesterday we chose a title for the report.

complement something that completes

Dan's creativity complements Ellen's attention to detail.

compliment praise

Thank you for the compliment.

Reminders: A complEment complEtes.
A complIment praIses.

conscience (noun) moral sense

My conscience would bother me if I did not give my best effort.

conscientious (adj.) honest; careful

A conscientious candidate does not try to buy votes.

Angela was promoted because she is a conscientious worker.

conscious (adj.) aware

The committee is conscious of the need for a larger parking lot.

formally not casually; in the proper way

You usually write more formally than you speak.

formerly at an earlier time

She was formerly an account executive for Willis and Ross, Inc.

Reminder: Note the word FORMAL in FORMALly and the word FORMER in FORMERly.

later (adv.) afterward; (adj) after the usual time

Finish the report later.

Paul took a later train to work this morning because he had no meetings scheduled.

latter (adj.) the second one of two things mentioned

I have used both the Easytype program and the Whizzwrite, and I prefer the latter.

loose (adj.) not fastened or restrained (rhymes with *goose*)

The technician found a loose wire.

lose (verb) to misplace or be deprived of something (rhymes with *dues*)

We do not want to lose the Gemco account.

loss (noun) damage; an amount or thing that is lost (rhymes with *toss*)

We are insured against loss due to fire or flood.

The loss of the government contract means we must close the Oakland office.

Reminder: If you lose something, you lOse an *o*.

moral (adj.) ethical; (noun) principle or maxim

We have a moral objection to using the information leaked to us by a government worker.

The moral of the story is: Don't make promises you can't keep.

morale (noun) mood or spirit

> Morale has improved since employees began participating in decision making.

personal (adj.) private, individual

> Rick resigned from the committee because of personal problems.

> Sharon has a personal style of dressing.

personnel (noun) employees, staff

> All personnel will receive checks on Friday.

Reminders: Anything personAl is privAte.
PersonnEl are Employees.

quiet (adj.) silent; calm (rhymes with *riot*)

> Peter was quiet after being reprimanded for his boisterous behavior.

> The store was noticeably quiet after the holiday rush.

quit (verb) to stop (rhymes with *fit*)

> James has to quit his job because he's moving to Colorado.

quite (adv.) totally, completely; very (rhymes with *bite*)

> Glenn arrived quite late to the meeting.

> She is quite interested in developing a new product line.

respectfully in a courteous or respectful manner

> I respectfully request to be removed from this project.

respectively in the order named

> First, second, and third prizes go to Martin Waites, Ariel Jordan, and Betsey Pastore respectively.

Reminder: RespectFULLy means "FULL of respect."

than (subordinating conjunction) compared to

> Jeanne is more concerned about meeting the deadline than including the lab reports.

then (adv.) at that time; next

> I wish I had known then what I know now.

> Open a new file; then name it.

Reminders: Use *thAn* to compAre.
THEN tells wHEN.

A. From the words given in parentheses in the following sentences, choose the words that correctly complete each sentence. Each sentence contains more than one group of choices.

1. If an administrative assistant must (advice / advise) an employer, a reminder system will help that individual (know / no) what to (do / due).

2. (Choose / Chose) (among / between) a computerized calendar and one you can keep on (your / you're)) desk or wall.

3. Computerized reminder systems store (alot / a lot)) of information (all together / altogether) in a small amount of space.

4. A reminder system (appraises / apprises) office workers of business obligations and (lessens / lessons) the chances that people will forget (their / there / they're) appointments.

5. Good reminder systems give (personal / personnel) (access / excess) to important deadlines so that everyone is (conscience / conscious) of them.

6. A daily "to (do / due)" list (complements / compliments) a weekly or monthly calendar and is a useful (anecdote / antidote) to forgetfulness.

7. A four-week schedule is an (affective / effective) reminder system, (accept / except) for managers (who's / whose) schedules include appointments made more (than / then) a month in advance.

B. Correct the misused words in the following paragraph.

Office workers can save alot of time by improving there filing techniques. First, be sure you no the principals upon which you're company's files are based. Than learn how two use filing equipment and supplies. Tables with rollers or trays improve excess to material too be filed. Sorting racks and color-coded files also make filing easier. (The latter decrease the chances of loosing a file.) Be sure to organize the files so that all personal aloud to use them can due so quite easily. Use a system that makes it easy to ad files. Choose between pressure-sensitive file labels, preprinted labels, and continuous-feed labels. Experts advice using the largest possible type of drawer labels and guide tabs. Keep stationary and other frequently used material at you're fingertips and put seldom-used materials in higher or lower drawers. File every day rather then allowing large stacks of filing to undermine your moral. Finally, when going threw a file, use both hands to avoid spilling it's contents.

C. Find the clichés, overblown language, and misused words in the following paragraph. Use a dictionary to verify your guesses about word meanings. Then revise the paragraph to improve word choice.

If you make a business trip to Washington, D.C., your principle goal
will be, needless to say, to due your job conscientiously. You will no
doubt want to be fresh as a daisy for your business meeting or conference. However, after your threw, don't forget to see the cites that
commemorate the American passed. We, the people of the United
States, need to cogitate on our heritage. Seeing the Capital building
or the monuments to the great men who formally led our nation should
inspire us not to waiver despite the difficulties we face.

PROBLEMS

A. Match the definitions on the left to the words on the right.

1. atmospheric conditions	a. quit
2. group of advisors	b. already
3. afterward	c. weather
4. completely prepared	d. latter
5. not casually	e. respectively
6. in a respectful manner	f. council
7. stop	g. casual
8. in the order named	h. counsel
9. responsible for	i. later
10. silent	j. quiet
11. very	k. all ready
12. previously	l. quite
13. the second of two	m. respectfully
14. advice	n. formally
15. informal	o. causal

B. The following spellings indicate the pronunciation of ten of the easily
confused words explained in the chapter. Underlining shows the syllables
that are stressed. The /ə/ stands for an unstressed vowel (pronounced like
the *u* in *but*). Write the correct word for each phonetic spelling:

<u>ĕk</u>·sĕs	<u>lāt</u>·ər
əd·<u>vīz</u>	looz
ə·<u>prīz</u>	<u>mōr</u>·əl
chōz	pər·sən·<u>ĕl</u>
<u>kahn</u>·chəs	kwĭt

Prepare word cards for the following easily confused words: adverse/averse, allusion/illusion, climactic/climatic, deference/difference, deposition/disposition, deprecate/depreciate, detract/distract, disburse/disperse, elicit/illicit, eligible/illegible, eminent/imminent, explicit/implicit, foreword/forward, liable/libel, partition/petition, persecute/prosecute. Write a different word on each card, and give its definition, a sentence illustrating its meaning, and a reminder on the other side. Use the cards to help you learn the words.

34
Developing Spelling and Proofreading Skills

Ellen McCoy has been a poor speller ever since grade school. She remembers being embarrassed by her low scores on spelling tests back in the fourth grade.

By the time Ellen entered high school, however, she had accepted her spelling weakness as a fact of life. When her English teachers returned her themes with words circled in red, C grades, and remarks such as "An A paper, except for the spelling," she merely shrugged. She was just a poor speller, she thought, in the same way some other people were tall or had green eyes.

Now that she is at work, however, the old feelings of embarrassment have returned. She is afraid her supervisor, Ms. Blake, will think she is not very intelligent if she continues to submit letters with basic spelling errors. Despite her concern, Ellen still thinks there is little she can do about her problem.

Ellen is wrong. People can improve their spelling, even if they have been labeled "poor spellers" all their lives. You, too, can improve your spelling. After all, you already spell the vast majority of words correctly. Even in the words you misspell, most of the letters you choose are the right ones. By learning just a few spelling patterns and mastering a short list of troublesome words (short compared to the enormous list of words you already spell perfectly), you can greatly improve your own spelling. Also, by learning to proofread better, you can eliminate those exasperating errors in familiar words— errors overlooked through carelessness.

SPELLING PROBLEMS ON THE JOB

When you write a letter, memo, or report, you are communicating information to your readers. They should be able to understand that information, and anything that distracts them can reduce their understanding. Sometimes readers will be so distracted by a spelling error they will have to reread the sentence, or even the entire paragraph, in which the error occurs. As a result, they may feel that your communication is wasting their time and take it less seriously, or even refuse to read it.

In business, you may often find yourself writing to customers or co-workers who have never met you. Their only way of judging your capabilities is through your writing. It makes sense, therefore, to make your writing reflect your abilities accurately—even down to such basic details as spelling.

WHAT YOU CAN DO

To improve your spelling, you should first make a list of the words you either have misspelled in the past or feel uneasy about whenever you write them. Add to this list words that give you trouble on the job—both those you misspell and those you must look up in the dictionary. Write these words down as soon as you encounter them; if you neglect to do so, you may forget them. Pay special attention to common words, because they occur frequently and therefore are the ones readers are most likely to notice if they are misspelled.

There are several good techniques for learning the words on your list. One is to try to find smaller words inside larger ones. The word *government,* for example, contains the core word *govern.* Remembering this could help you include the *n* that is silent in some people's pronunciation. Once you find a smaller word, make up a sentence to connect the two words in your mind: "There's IRON in the envIRONment" is an example of a helpful reminder.

Studying the pronunciation of a word may help you remember how to spell it. For example, knowing that a vowel is usually shortened when it is followed by a double letter should help on words such as *compassion,* where the double *s* makes the *a* short, and *occasion,* where the long *a* suggests that you need only one *s.* Exaggerating the pronunciation of a word to yourself as you write it on your list may help. Pronounce *February* with a distinct *r* sound, for example, or *Wednesday* in three syllables: "Wed-nes-day."

Make word cards for unfamiliar words, preferably with the troublesome parts omitted so you can supply them for practice: write "for _ _ gn," for example, or "s _ _ ze," to review exceptions to the "i before e" rule. Writing difficult words several times may help. Above all, use all your senses: say the word aloud as you write it so you can *hear* the word as well as see it.

Some people try to disguise poor spelling by writing illegibly, exchanging one problem for another. A much better method is to write as clearly as possible, so you can spot your errors more easily when you proofread. Proofreading with great care is perhaps the best way to improve spelling because it helps you pay close attention to the spelling of *all* the words you write.

SOME BASIC SPELLING PATTERNS

Most words follow regular patterns. You may not be aware of these patterns, but you follow them whenever you write. When a word looks wrong to you, it is often because it violates a general pattern or rule that you know but may not be able to explain. For example, the general rule for adding an ending that starts with a consonant is to add it without changing the spelling of the word:

> approximate + ly → approximately
> sincere + ly → sincerely

Because you have seen many words that follow this rule, the misspelled word "immediatly" should look wrong. Checking the dictionary reveals that an *e* is, in fact, missing before the *ly*.

Becoming more aware of some basic spelling patterns will enable you to avoid many spelling errors without referring constantly to the dictionary. As you build your own spelling list, examine each word to see whether it follows or violates the general patterns. For example, the words *truly* and *argument* are difficult to spell because they violate the general rule about adding endings. Some people misspell these words because they do not realize that they are exceptions to the regular pattern.

Is It *ie* or *ei*?

Confusion over whether to use *ie* or *ei* can be reduced if you learn the saying that explains how these letters are used:

> *I* before *e*
> Except after *c*
> Or when sounded as *a*
> As in *neighbor* and *weigh*.

This saying will help you decide between *ei* and *ie* for words with a long *e* or long *a* sound.

Words With the Long *e* Sound.   Most of the words with a long *e* sound follow the regular pattern with the *i* before the *e*.

achIEve	fIEld
belIEve	pIEce
cashIEr	nIEce

If the letter *c* comes just before the *e* sound, then the *e* comes before the *i*.

cEIling	percEIve
recEIve	concEIvable
decEIve	

A few words are exceptions to these guidelines, even though they are pronounced with the long *e* sound:

codEIne	EIther
nEIther	sEIze
protEIn	specIEs
financIEr	shEIk
caffEIne	wEIrd

Some of these words keep the spellings of the languages from which they were borrowed. Others used to be pronounced with a long *a* or long *i* sound. Their pronunciations have changed, but their spellings have not. *Sheik* can still be pronounced with a long *a,* and *either* and *neither* with a long *i.* It may be helpful if you memorize these few exceptions.

Words With the Long *a* Sound.   The long *a* sound is spelled *ei:*

> Elght   frElght
> vEln

Because the word *their* is pronounced with an *a* sound that is very close to a long *a,* you can consider that it belongs to the *ei* pattern.

Words With Other Vowel Sounds.   The long *i* sound is also spelled *ei:*

> hElght   slElght

Words that have other vowel sounds show both spellings:

> consclEnce   forElgn
> frIEnd   forfElt
> revIEw

Final *y* Before a Suffix

The core of a word is called its root. Some roots stand alone, as in the word *form.* A prefix may be added at the beginning of a root to modify its meaning *(inform).* Sometimes a suffix is added at the end of a word to change its meaning or its part of speech *(forming).* Many words have both prefixes and suffixes added to their roots *(informing).* Adding a prefix does not change the spelling of the root, but adding a suffix sometimes does. When you are adding a suffix to a root that ends in *y,* be aware of the following rules.

When *y* Follows a Consonant.   When the final *y* in the root word follows a consonant, change the *y* to *i* in most cases before adding the suffix.

> study → studies
> copy → copied
> lovely → loveliest
> beauty → beautiful

There are exceptions to this rule. When the ending starts with an *i,* the *y* remains. A common misspelling occurs when people forget to keep the *y* before the suffix *-ing:*

> study → studying
> carry → carrying
> try → trying

You also keep the *y* when adding the suffix *-ly* or *-ness* to a one-syllable word ending in *y*:

> shy → shyly
> shy → shyness
> dry → dryly
> dry → dryness

When *y* Follows a Vowel.   When the final *y* follows a vowel, you do *not* change the *y* to *i* before adding a suffix:

> obey → obeys
> turkey → turkeys
> annoy → annoyed
> joy → joyous
> boy → boyish

A few common words are exceptions to this rule:

> day → daily
> slay → slain
> lay → laid
> pay → paid
> say → said

Doubling Final Consonants

These rules will help you decide whether to double a final consonant when adding a suffix that begins with a vowel. You probably already know that you should double a final consonant before adding such an ending to one-syllable words with short vowel sounds. This spelling keeps the vowels short:

> hop → hopped
> rag → ragged
> scar → scarring

If you do not double the consonant, you get entirely different words: *hoped, raged,* and *scaring.*

You do *not* double the final consonant before a suffix that begins with a vowel in these two cases: when the root word has two vowels before the final consonant or when the root word ends in two consonants.

> need → needing
> brick → bricked

(These last two rules apply to both single- and multiple-syllable words, such as *congealed* or *distinguished.*)

Most writers have a greater amount of trouble adding suffixes to words of more than one syllable that end in a single vowel and consonant. For example, *refeRRing* has two *r*'s, but *refeRence* has only one. How can this difference be explained?

The secret to deciding whether or not to double the consonant is to determine where the stress falls in the newly formed word. In *reFERring*, the syllable before the ending is emphasized, but in *REFerence*, the first syllable is stressed. The pattern, then, is: If the second syllable of a two-syllable word is stressed, double the final consonant when adding a suffix. If the stress shifts to the first syllable when the ending is added, do not double the final consonant.

Examples of words that require doubling of the final consonant are the following:

beGINner
occCURring
conTROLled

Some words that do not require doubling when a suffix is added are:

OFfered   BENefiting
DIFference   PREFerence

For this rule, your ears are as important as your eyes. By saying the word aloud, you will know where the stress falls.

ON THE JOB
The Importance of Being Accurate

Carla Walters knew the prices of all the ABC Company's products—she had been their chief sales representative for three years. When she dictated the letter to the purchasing agent at Value Stores, she knew the wholesale price of the X10 without having to look it up: $22 a gross.

After Ellen, her secretary, typed the letter, she brought it to Carla for her to sign. Carla was on the telephone at the time and signed the letter without reading it. Ellen had always been a reliable typist, and Carla trusted her completely.

A week later, however, Carla's supervisor, George Costas, called her into his office. "I've just been on the phone with Dave Frey at Value Stores," he said. "Dave wanted to know if we were really selling the X10 at $2 a gross, as you told him in your letter. When I came in to work this morning, I thought we were still in business for profit. What's going on?"

Carla remembered the letter well enough. She knew she had dictated the correct price of $22 a gross. But what price had Ellen typed? Carla had no way of knowing since she had signed the letter without proofreading it. What should she do now? Honor the ridiculous price of $2 a gross or admit she had made a careless mistake? Wouldn't Dave Frey think she was incompetent regardless of her choice? Who was more to blame—Ellen for mistyping or Carla for not proofreading the letter before she signed it? Most important, what can be done to make certain such a mistake never happens again?

Most spelling errors occur in the middle of a word or in its ending. People learn to read rapidly by training themselves to see just as many letters of a word as they need to guess what the word is. They usually notice the letters that begin words, but they can easily miss some common trouble spots farther along in the words.

Silent Letters

The following words contain silent consonants.

deBt   eiGHth
gHetto   morTgage

They must be learned one at a time. Work on visualizing the words to fix the silent letters in your memory. Writing the words with the silent letters enlarged to three or four times the size of the other letters can help you create a mental picture of them.

Many words end in a silent *e,* which is used to make an earlier vowel long, as in *hope* and *tape.* The silent *e* is unchanged when a suffix that begins with a consonant is added.

achievE → achievEment
forcE → forcEful
lonE → lonEly
onE → onEness

The silent *e* is dropped, however, before a suffix that starts with a vowel.

rate → rating
guide → guidance
become → becoming

The silent *e* is kept in a few words in order to ensure that a *c* or a *g* maintains a soft sound.

noticE → noticEable
couragE → couragEous
changE → changEable

Carefully reading aloud what you have written should help locate this exception to the general rule.

Double Letters

Double consonants can also be confusing. Be sure to look closely for letters that are doubled in words like the following:

embaRRaSS   aCCoMModate
recoMMend   poSSeSSion

Dividing the words into syllables can also help you remember which letters to double:

iR Rel e vant   pro feS Sion

Remember that when you add a prefix, you merely add it to the word.

un + paid → unpaid
mis + used → misused
dis + appoint → disappoint

What sometimes appear to be doubled consonants are merely the result of a prefix that ends with the same letter that begins the root:

un + named → unnamed
mis + spell → misspell
dis + satisfy → dissatisfy

The spellings of the original word and of the prefix are not changed.

Sounds Lost in Speech

Many sounds in the English language are slurred in speech and, as a result, can easily be overlooked in writing. For example, the *ed* in phrases such as *an old-fashionED style, what the department usED to do,* and *a prejudicED witness* is sometimes wrongly omitted because it is not clearly pronounced.

Even careful pronunciation will not help you distinguish among certain vowels in unstressed syllables. For example, the vowels in the last syllables of *attendance* and *deference* are pronounced the same, as are those in the last syllables of *taxable* and *collectible.* The sound in each case is an indefinite sound (like an "uh") that can be spelled with an *a, e, i, o,* or *u.* If you examine the words you frequently misspell, you will probably find this sound in many of them.

There are helpful rules for deciding whether to use the suffix *-able* or *-ible.* If you can add another suffix beginning with an *a* (such as *-ate, -ation,* or *-ative*), use *-able.*

imagine → imaginative
imagine → imaginable

tax → taxation
tax → taxable

If you can add another suffix beginning with *i* (such as *-ive* or *-ion*), use *-ible.*

collect → collection
collect → collectible

suggest → suggestive
suggest → suggestible

When deciding between using the suffixes *-ance* and *-ence,* use the following rules. If a word uses the suffix *-ent (independent, diligent),* it will also use the suffix *-ence (independence, diligence).* If it uses the suffix *-ant (attendant, reliant),* it will also use the suffix *-ance (attendance, reliance).* This rule never varies.

To spell other words with this indefinite sound, you must visualize the actual spelling rather than linking sound and spelling as you usually do when you write.

Commonly Misspelled Words

The following business-related words are notorious for causing difficulties even among good spellers. For this reason, they are often called spelling demons. The parts of the words that are most commonly misspelled are capitalized. Making up personal reminders can be a great aid in mastering these problem words.

absenCe	definITEly	indispensAble	quanTity
aCCoMModate	dependEnt	iRRelevAnt	recEIving
achievEment	despErate	judGMent	reCoMMend
aCQuaintAnce	develOP	lIEUtenant	relEvAnce
aCQuire	disaSTrous	lonELIness	repEtition
allEGE	dOEsn't	maintEnance	restAUrant
amatEUr	eigHTH	manEUver	rHYthm
analYZe	embaRRaSS	mathEmatics	rIdiculous
apparEnt	envIRONment	miSCeLLaneous	sEIze
approximatEly	equiPPed	morTgage	sepArate
argUMent	exaGGerate	noticEable	simiLAr
articLE	excEEd	occaSionally	sincerEly
aTHlete	existEnce	occuRRence	suBPoena
basicALLY	extremEly	offeRed	superSEDE
begiNNing	FebRUary	optImism	survEIllance
benefiTed	finanCIaLLy	paraLLel	thorOUGH
burEAUcracy	forEIgn	permanEnt	traGedy
buSINess	forfEIt	persistEnt	truLY
calEndAr	fORty	poSSeSSion	undoubtEDly
cashIEr	fulfiLL	precEDE	uNNeCeSSary
catEgories	goverNment	prEJudiceD	vacUUm
concEIvable	grammAr	privilEGE	wEIrd
condemN	guarantEE	procEED	whoLLy
convENience	hEIght	proFession	wriTing
critiCism	humorOUS	prominEnt	
deBt	iMMediatEly	PSYchology	

The most common spelling errors are those which people should be able to avoid but which they overlook in their hurry to complete a task. Good proofreading skills are vital to good spelling.

You may already be accustomed to the idea of proofreading what you write, but you may not be in the habit of proofreading a separate time just to catch spelling errors.

To proofread successfully, you must slow down and examine your work word by word and letter by letter. Touching each letter with the eraser end of a pencil helps locate errors. Knowing the trouble spots in your personal list of spelling demons comes in handy here: pay special attention to words with *ie* and *ei,* double letters and silent letters, and other combinations that have caused difficulties for you in the past. Keeping a log of errors you make can alert you to the kinds of words you need to proofread with an extra measure of attention.

Seeing your work line by line can also help. Take a straightedge (a ruler or the top of another sheet of paper) and cover all but the first line of your text. After reading that line carefully, bring the straightedge one line down and read the next line. Reading your work aloud can also help, especially with words often mispronounced. *Athletics,* for example, and *nuclear* are often misspelled by people who do not say them correctly.

As you continue to proofread for spelling, you will develop a sense of which words you need to check in the dictionary. Words with alternate spellings should be looked up to see if one spelling is preferred. For instance, you should use the American rather than the British forms of words. Words with unusual plurals *(knives, heroes, women)* are also a possible source of error.

Apostrophes, both in contractions and in possessive endings, need to be examined very carefully. Make sure the apostrophe in a contraction is in the place where the omitted letter or letters would have been (and make sure the word is a contraction—writing *it's* for the possessive *its* is an extremely common error). Possessive endings can also be tricky; be sure that apostrophes are in the right places.

Typographical Errors

In business, you will often find yourself proofreading a typewritten or word-processed document—either your own work or someone else's. Some people have a casual attitude toward errors in typewritten texts: "Oh, that's just a typo" is a common excuse. The reader, however, has no way of knowing whether the word was mistyped or misspelled; either error makes a bad impression.

Transposed letters are a common form of typographical error. Even words you would never actually misspell can contain them: "fo" for *of* and "nad" for *and.* It is also possible to repeat a letter inadvertently: "oof" and "annd" look odd and may cause difficulties for your readers. Poor spacing can also hurt: "an d" is clearly a typo, but "with out" could be seen as a spelling error.

By far the most common typographical errors, however, come from simply striking the wrong key ("any" for *and*) or failing to strike a key at all ("ad" for *and*). Letter-by-letter proofreading can catch these and many other errors.

EDITING EXERCISES

A. Identify and correct the misspelled word in each group.

1. a. approximatly   b. irrelevant   c. bureaucracy   d. tragedy
2. a. allege   b. psychology   c. cashier   d. begining
3. a. subpoena   b. occurence   c. rhythm   d. prejudiced
4. a. separate   b. lonliness   c. surveillance   d. mortgage
5. a. repetition   b. definitely   c. indispensible d. permanent

B. Identify and correct each misspelled word in the following passage. Use a proofreading technique you have not tried before, such as touching each letter or syllable with the eraser end of a pencil, putting a ruler or second sheet of paper beneath each line and moving it down as you read, or reading the passage aloud. Use a dictionary to check spellings you are unsure of. Note that the passage includes words from the last chapter as well as from this one.

Does your judgmeant about what to wear ever embarass you in a business setting? If some of you're clothing makes you look rediculous, a thourough evaluation of your wardrobe is extreamly important. Undoubtably, careful selection and maintainance of your clothing will imporve your appearance at work. Experts reccommend that you aquire simple, conservative clothes for work. Basicly, you should develope a look that is similar to that of your co-workers. However, forfiting your individuality is unecessary. There is know guaranty that an artical of clothing that looks attractive on an aquaintance will wholely suit you if your heighth, weight, or coloring is different. The quality of your purchases is more important then the quanity, but dressing well dosen't require you to excede your budget.

PROBLEMS

A. Insert *ie* or *ei* in each word below. Then identify the words using the following code:

1. The long *e* sound is spelled with *ie,* following the regular pattern.

2. The long *a* sound is spelled with *ei.*

3. A sound other than *e* or *a* is used, so the *ie/ei* rule does not apply.

4. The letters follow *c,* so *ei* is used.

5. The sound is long *e* or long *a,* but this word is an exception to the *ie/ei* rule.

f ___ ___ ld	c ___ ___ ling	l ___ ___ utenant
rec ___ ___ ve	surv ___ ___ llance	w ___ ___ rd
s ___ ___ ze	consc ___ ___ nce	hyg ___ ___ ne
ach ___ ___ ve	bel ___ ___ ve	gr ___ ___ ve
for ___ ___ gn	___ ___ ghth	prot ___ ___ n
y ___ ___ ld	rel ___ ___ f	dec ___ ___ t
ch ___ ___ f	th ___ ___ f	

B. Form new words by following the rules for adding the suggested suffixes to the following words. A few of the words are exceptions to the general rules.

happy + est	plenty + ful	advance + ment
obey + s	valley + s	fate + ful
lovely + er	gratify + ing	admire + able
study + ing	notice + able	argue + ment
imply + s	excite + ment	explore + ation
envy + ous	impulse + ive	true + ly
tyranny + cal	separate + ing	

C. Add the suggested endings to the following words. Then circle the syllable that is stressed in each newly formed word. Be sure you double the final consonant only in stressed syllables.

begin + ing	marvel + ous	profit + able
prefer + ed	benefit + ed	submit + ed
commit + ed	refer + ence	
occur + ence	confer + ing	

PROJECTS

A. From the list of commonly misspelled words in the chapter, choose 20 that are difficult for you. Circle, enlarge, or underline the parts of the words that are troublesome, and write a sentence illustrating the use of each word. Invent reminders for as many of the words as you can. Tape-record your list or have someone read it to you to check your mastery of the words you chose.

PART FIVE
WRITING EFFECTIVE SENTENCES AND PARAGRAPHS

35
Achieving Effective Sentences

When you are driving on an expressway, you can be lulled into drowsiness by the constant speed of the car and the sameness of the scenery. This condition, known as highway hypnosis, is very dangerous. As a writer, you must take care not to induce a similar type of hypnosis, one that is deadly to communication. Just as constant speed and monotonous scenery can cause a driver to doze, sentences of the same length that plod along in the same style will put your readers to sleep. This chapter will give you tips on how to bring vitality to your writing.

THE QUALITIES OF A GOOD SENTENCE

Effective sentences have three qualities: clarity, variety, and appropriate emphasis. This chapter will present suggestions on how to introduce these elements into your writing. Be aware that these qualities are not mutually exclusive. That is, a technique to achieve one quality may enhance another quality as well.

Clarity

Clarity is the one absolutely essential quality of good sentences. Without clarity, the reader must take extra time to decipher what you mean. Some readers may simply stop reading.

You can achieve clarity in several ways: include only relevant details, use parallel structure, and omit unnecessary words.

Variety

As already noted, a stream of sentences that are all the same can lead to a form of hypnosis that hinders communication. You can make your writing interesting by varying word choice, word order, sentence length, and sentence type.

Appropriate Emphasis

A good sentence leads the reader to its most important idea and directs attention away from less important ones. Readers should not have to sift through your sentences to discover what you mean. They should be able to pick out the main ideas with one reading. Using the active voice and combining sentences are effective tools for achieving appropriate emphasis.

DID YOU KNOW?
The Personal Nature of Writing Style

Suppose someone presented you with unlabeled excerpts from one of Ernest Hemingway's novels and from one of the works of William Faulkner and asked you to identify which was which. If you had a strong background in literature, you could identify each immediately upon reading it, even if you had never read the works from which the excerpts were taken. You would be able to identify authorship just on the basis of each author's distinctive style. Hemingway's style is terse, whereas Faulkner's is complex. Hemingway often tells a story through dialogue and action; Faulkner frequently uses perceptions of one or more characters to develop his plot.

Good business writers also develop a personal writing style. Business writing, though it is practical, does not have to be mechanical. It can, and generally should, reflect the style of the person who produces it.

Take a look at these three sales messages, each presenting the same information effectively, but in a different style.

This Fourth of July there will be a celebration of savings at every A-1 Home Center in the Delaware Valley. Our Garden Center is bursting with sale prices on every item. Come to your nearest A-1 Home Center on Independence Day for All-American Savings!

Every year George Dunlap's garden gets bigger and better. But he always spends the same amount of time on it. How does he do it? By purchasing the newest laborsaving equipment at A-1 Home Center during the Annual Fourth of July Sale.

The Fourth of July. Parades. Picnics. Family get-togethers. Garden-supply sales. Garden-supply sales? This Fourth of July, take time out from holiday activities to visit an A-1 Home Center during the spectacular Fourth of July Sale.

The rules you will learn in this book can be applied by writers with widely different styles. If you strive to develop your own methods, your writing will be lively and interesting.

HOW TO ACHIEVE CLARITY Clear sentences are unified; every word contributes to a single effect. Clear sentences are also balanced. Their elements work well together, and the relationships between elements are obvious. Clear sentences do not confuse readers with unnecessary words.

Unified Ideas

A well-written sentence produces a single effect. Instead of being crammed with unrelated details, it includes only the words that convey and clarify its primary message. Take a look at the two sentences that follow. Which has a more unified effect?

> The Permawood finish looks like fine-grained wood, although it is actually synthetic material; the cost is lower than that of actual wood, although some people prefer actual wood, of course.

> Natural wood, though it has some advantages over synthetic wood, can fall prey to termites, dry rot, mildew, and fire; Permawood cannot.

Finding a unifying theme in the first sentence is difficult; the sentence seems to just run on and on. A description of Permawood, a remark about its cost, and a comment on what some customers prefer are all crowded into one overburdened sentence. The second sentence, however, presents one theme clearly: the disadvantages of natural wood as compared with Permawood. Each part of the sentence works toward that effect.

When you are writing, shape each sentence around one main point. As you revise, be on the lookout for details that do not belong. Be careful not to go too far, however; you may end up creating a sentence that is missing important facts.

> I rented a car for the trip and therefore was late for my appointment.

The reader may not understand why renting the car made the writer late. The following sentence states the situation more clearly.

> My rental car broke down, making me late for my appointment.

Parallel Structure

As a child, you probably played on a seesaw at the playground. If so, you will remember that both children using it had to be of fairly equal weight, or the equipment would not work. If the children were of unequal weight, the heavier child would weigh down one end and stop all movement. Like a seesaw, a sentence must be balanced to work. In other words, it must have parallel structure.

Parallel structure involves the use of the same grammatical structure for sentence elements that function in the same way. Study the following examples and their explanations.

> The Toasty Space Heater is clean, operates safely, and you do not have to pay much for fuel.

In this sentence, the series begins with an adjective *(clean)*, continues with a verb and an adverb *(operates safely)*, and ends with a clause *(you do not have to pay much for fuel)*. To make this sentence parallel, all items in the series might be adjectives.

> The Toasty Space Heater is clean, safe, and economical.

In the next example, the writer mixes a gerund phrase *(answering the telephone)* with an infinitive phrase *(to greet customers)*.

> His duties are answering the telephone and to greet customers.

The corrected sentence might use two gerund phrases.

> His duties are answering the telephone and greeting customers.

Individual words, phrases, or whole clauses can be parallel. When a sentence lacks parallel structure, it sounds awkward and is confusing. The reader expects like elements to be treated in the same way. When they are not, the reader may not understand the intended meaning. The use of parallel structure eliminates extra words and makes the meaning of a sentence—even a very long one—clear.

Conciseness

Good gardeners prune the trees in their care. Pruning involves cutting off dead, and even some living, branches to aid growth. Otherwise, these branches will sap strength from the rest of the tree.

Writers must be somewhat like gardeners—they must eliminate unnecessary words in order to strengthen their writing. Wordiness weakens communication. Extra words mean more for the reader to read; they can also hide key information by creating clutter.

> As I see it, the clearance sale we as a company held in the month of January proved to be quite a success. Things really worked very well indeed. The sale went far beyond our fondest expectations and hopes.

These sentences are wordy. The same thoughts could be expressed much more succinctly.

> The January clearance sale was such a success that it far exceeded our expectations.

When you write, strive to be concise. Say what you need to say in as few words as possible. Usually, writers concentrate on pruning deadwood (unnecessary expressions) when they revise a document rather than when they are composing the first draft. Common types of deadwood are redundant expressions, empty expressions, unnecessary repetition, and inappropriate adjectives.

Redundant Words, Phrases, and Clauses. To be redundant is to repeat an idea unnecessarily. The phrase *attractive in appearance* is redundant because the word *attractive* implies appearance. Here is just a small sample of common redundancies. Can you think of others?

circle around	expert in the field of
green in color	new innovation
refer back to	restate again
true facts	each and every

Empty Expressions. Some writers fill their writing with expressions that add words without clarifying meaning. Here are just a few of the expressions to avoid.

there is	it is a fact that
there are	for the reason that
tend to	I am of the opinion that
proceeded to	what I mean to say is that

The sentence *It is a fact that our increased sales were partly due to good weather* contains unnecessary phrases. The statement *Good weather contributed to our increased sales* expresses the same idea more concisely. Also, a sentence such as *This company employs 250 people* is preferred to *There are 250 employees in this company.*

Unnecessary Repetition. Repeating the same word more than once in a sentence can be an effective way to emphasize a point or key idea. Yet, such repetition can also be boring, implying that your vocabulary is inadequate. Notice how repetition is effective in the first sentence but not in the second.

> The *safety* of the worker, the *safety* of the product, and the *safety* of the consumer are all important at Chapman Industries.

> Pam made an *important* point; it is *important* to stress safety constantly, or workers will not see it as *important.*

In the second sentence, repeating the word *important* actually hides the main idea of safety.

Unnecessary repetition usually becomes obvious as you revise your first draft. You may have to look more closely for empty expressions and redundancy.

Inappropriate Adjectives. Adjectives usually make sentences stronger. Some writers, however, tend to use too many adjectives, which weakens writing and obscures meaning. Resist the temptation to automatically add one or more adjectives to every noun.

Do not use the wrong adjective in an attempt to evoke an immediate response to a letter or memo. An "urgent message," for example, should rightly concern some danger to life or property. A person who refers to a message about the office Christmas party as "urgent" is obviously misusing the word.

You make your adjectives count by being specific. Vague, overused adjectives such as *incredible* and *fantastic* are not likely to serve a useful purpose; they make overstatements that can cause readers to doubt the truth of what you are saying. If you are not certain about whether an adjective is working to make your meaning clearer, you should probably eliminate it.

When you write, concentrate on making your sentences varied. With practice and experience, this skill will come automatically.

HOW TO ACHIEVE VARIETY

Word Choice

Good writers avoid using the same words repeatedly. They choose synonyms—different ways to say the same thing. For help finding appropriate synonyms, use a thesaurus. Chapter 32 explains how this special dictionary can be used effectively.

Word Order

The order of words in a sentence is not fixed. In fact, you can usually arrange the words in a sentence in several ways, some of which are more effective than others.

The most common word order in sentences is subject + verb + complement.

> You will find these accommodations superb.

Another order is possible, however.

> These accommodations you will find superb.

Note how different the rhythm of the second sentence is and how it also emphasizes the word *accommodations.*

Other word-order variations are possible.

> Don finally arrived for his appointment at 12:30 p.m.
>
> Finally, at 12:30 p.m., Don arrived for his appointment.
>
> Mr. Melvold's voice boomed over the intercom.
>
> Over the intercom boomed Mr. Melvold's voice.

Sentence Length

Too many long sentences in a row cause readers to lose track of your main idea. Too many short sentences produce a choppy effect and obscure relationships between ideas; all sentences appear equally important. Effective writing makes use of sentences of different lengths.

Sentence Type

Perhaps the best way to achieve variety is to use different types of sentences. In Chapter 15 you learned that sentences can be classified according to the number and kind of clauses they contain. A simple sentence contains one independent clause. A compound sentence consists of two or more independent clauses. A complex sentence has one independent clause and one or more dependent clauses.

Sentences can also be grouped according to how they treat their main ideas. Does the main idea come first, or does the sentence lead up to it?

Loose Sentences. In loose sentences, the main idea of the sentence leads the way, followed by supporting or modifying details. In the following example, the main idea is italicized.

> *Employees must park in the rear parking lot* because the front lot is being repaved this week.

Readers expect to find the main idea presented first, and this method is used most often by writers, particularly in business.

Periodic Sentences. By reversing this order, you get a periodic sentence—one in which the main idea, or the completion of the main idea, is saved until the end. Periodic sentences create a feeling of suspense, since the reader must wait until the end to see how the main idea comes out. Note the position of the main idea, which has been italicized, in each of the following periodic sentences:

> Although many products—from oils to creams to black magic—have claimed to cure baldness, *no remedy has been truly effective—until now.*

> During the months of January through April, *this project,* despite emotional protests from my family, my friends, and even my cocker spaniel, *demanded that I work 16 hours a day 6 days a week.*

Notice how much more forceful this periodic sentence is than a loose sentence using the same words:

> This project demanded that I work 16 hours a day 6 days a week during the months of January through April, despite emotional protests from my family, my friends, and even my cocker spaniel.

Periodic sentences can be effective, especially when used to sum up or conclude a series of thoughts. Used too often, however, periodic sentences sound stilted and overdramatic. In fact, any technique loses its effectiveness if overused.

Mixed Sentences. A mixed sentence is neither wholly loose nor wholly periodic. The main idea is sandwiched between slices of explanatory detail. In the mixed sentence that follows, the main idea is italicized.

Despite icy conditions, *we drove to Chicago,* the site of the industrial show.

This sentence would be less clear if all the explanatory details were lumped together at the end of the sentence.

We drove to Chicago, the site of the industrial show, despite icy conditions.

Use of the Three Formats. By intermingling loose, periodic, and mixed sentences, you will make your writing clearer and more interesting. To prove this point, read the two short paragraphs that follow. The first is composed entirely of loose sentences. The second uses almost exactly the same words, but varies the sentence structure.

You will begin your tour at the information desk in the main lobby. Look over the pictorial history of Kendall Corporation as you wait for your guide. Winston Kendall built an electronics empire with a staff of one and an all-encompassing vision from a modest basement apartment in the Bronx.

You will begin your tour at the information desk in the main lobby. As you wait for your guide to arrive, look over the pictorial history of Kendall Corporation that is on display. From modest beginnings in a basement apartment in the Bronx, Winston Kendall built an electronics empire with a staff of one and an all-encompassing vision.

Skillful writers know how to call attention to or stress a word or an idea. Two techniques you can use to achieve appropriate emphasis are writing in the active voice and combining sentences.

HOW TO ACHIEVE EMPHASIS

Use of the Active Voice

The following two sentences say the same thing, but not in the same way.

Three models for a new sales structure were presented by Marty.

Marty presented three models for a new sales structure.

The second sentence, which is in the active voice, conveys the message more strongly and more concisely than does the first sentence, which is in the passive voice. In general, sentences in the active voice are more emphatic than those in the passive voice because the active verb and its subject are closely connected. The passive voice often weakens your writing—and may even make it less clear—because someone or something is being acted upon rather than performing the action.

For this reason, try to avoid the passive voice when writing, unless there is a compelling reason for using it. When is the passive appropriate?

- Use the passive voice when you want to minimize the importance of the doer of the action—or emphasize the receiver. In the sentence *Albert was given the sales award at the meeting,* the emphasis is on Albert, not on the company, which gave the award.
- Use the passive voice when the doer of the action is unknown. In the sentence *This policy was changed years ago,* the person who changed the policy is probably not known.
- Use the passive voice when the doer of the action is unimportant or irrelevant, as in *The letters were mailed yesterday.* The important fact concerns when the letters were mailed, not who mailed them.
- Use the passive voice to minimize negative information, as in *The Hopkins report was finished three weeks late.* In this example, the person who prepared the report is not important. Using the passive voice allows you to present negative information neutrally.

Methods of Changing to the Active Voice. Suppose, then, that you are revising a document, and you come upon a passive verb that needs to be changed. How do you change it to the active form? First you need to decide who the doer of the action is, which is easy to determine if there is a *by* phrase following the verb.

The meeting was called to order by Ms. Chong.

Ms. Chong is the subject of the verb *called.* To put the sentence in the active form, just make *Ms. Chong* the subject.

Ms. Chong called the meeting to order.

Sometimes there is no *by* phrase to guide you. Once you discover the subject, you may have to restructure the sentence more extensively.

When you return the defective merchandise, your money will be promptly refunded.

Who is doing the refunding? In this case, the company is the implied subject.

When you return the defective merchandise, we will promptly refund your money.

What is the implied subject of the following sentence?

According to a survey of buyers, sports cars were bought on impulse in three out of five cases.

As the revision that follows shows, the respondents to the survey are the implied subject.

Three out of five people surveyed bought sports cars on impulse.

Be on the lookout for the passive voice in your writing, and restructure as necessary to replace it with the stronger, more interesting and more effective active voice.

Sentence Combining

A particularly effective way of achieving emphasis is to use sentence-combining techniques. Depending on the relationship of the ideas in adjoining sentences, you can choose one of several sentence-combining techniques. The three major types are coordination, subordination, and embedding. If you want to give equal emphasis to ideas, use coordination. Use subordination or embedding when you decide that one idea is more important than another.

Coordination. Coordination is nothing more than joining related words, phrases, and clauses with coordinating words, such as *and, but,* and *or.* Besides helping to make choppy sentences smoother and repetitious sentences more streamlined, coordination indicates that certain ideas have equal rank.

In each of the following examples, two sentences are combined through coordination.

The secretary did not know what to do with the excess inventory. Her supervisor did not know either.

Neither the secretary nor her supervisor knew what to do with the excess inventory.

Jill walked across the street. She went into the bank.

Jill walked across the street and into the bank.

The desks should be in the center of the room. The file cabinets should be against the wall.

The desks should be in the center of the room, but the file cabinets should be against the wall.

Many words can coordinate ideas; the following is a partial list. Refer to Chapter 13 for a complete list of coordinating and correlative conjunctions.

and	either . . . or
but	neither . . . nor
or	not only . . . but also
nor	whether . . . or
yet	both . . . and
for	such . . . as
so	if . . . then

You can also use punctuation, namely a semicolon, to coordinate independent clauses.

> Our customers have reached their limit; they refuse to pay more for this product.

Sometimes a semicolon is used before a transitional expression such as *however* or *in addition*.

> Perhaps the market will improve; however, I doubt it.

> Perhaps the market will improve; in addition, the percentage of income transferred to savings accounts may increase.

The key to effective coordination lies in linking ideas of equal weight. If the ideas are not of equal importance, you should consider using subordination.

Subordination. When you link ideas of unequal significance, subordinate the less important idea by putting it into a dependent clause. Remember, to make a clause dependent, put a subordinating word such as *although, because,* or *since* in front of it.

With subordination, you draw attention to the main idea. First, of course, you must realize that the ideas have different levels of importance and decide which is the main one. Two related ideas are presented in the following two sentences.

> The new computer has been installed. No one has used it yet.

The writer decides that the first sentence includes the main thought. To subordinate the second sentence, the writer puts the word *although* in front of it. The two clauses are then joined in a complex sentence.

> The new computer has been installed, although no one has used it yet.

Of course, the writer could also place the dependent clause at the beginning of the sentence.

> Although no one has used it yet, the new computer has been installed.

In each of the following examples, notice how subordination shows the relationship between ideas in the sentence. First the ideas are given separately; then they are combined. (The main idea or independent clause is italicized in each combined sentence.)

> Few people returned the questionnaire. We can assume there is little interest in a company van pool.
> Since so few people returned the questionnaire, *we can assume there is little interest in a company van pool.*

> I had planned to drive home. I did not have a drink at the reception.
> *I did not have a drink at the reception* because I had planned to drive home.

Be sure you know how you want to relate ideas before you subordinate. Sometimes either idea could be subordinated, depending on your purpose, audience, or circumstances.

> Some word processors can do amazing things, although none are able to think. (emphasis on what word processors can do)
>
> No word processor is yet able to think, although some can do amazing things. (emphasis on what word processors cannot do)

Embedding. Embedding is similar to subordination, except that the subordinated idea usually becomes a phrase and is enclosed within or attached to the independent clause. Sometimes the sentence being embedded can be condensed to just one word. Some examples will help you understand this sentence-combining technique.

> That woman is my assistant. She is tall.
>
> That tall woman is my assistant. (The adjective *tall* simply becomes embedded in the first sentence.)
>
> Michael wrapped the package and tied it with heavy string. He took it to the post office.
>
> After wrapping the package and tying it with heavy string, Michael took it to the post office. (The first sentence has been embedded as a phrase in the second sentence.)

Use of Sentence-Combining Techniques. Naturally, you will want to use all three sentence-combining techniques since a string of coordinated or subordinated sentences is as tedious as a string of choppy ones. The first paragraph that follows includes short, loose sentences. The second utilizes sentence combining.

> Bob arrived at his hotel at 6 p.m. He checked into his room. Bob did not have a chance to unpack. He received a telephone call from the conference director, Morris Ames. Mr. Ames wanted to take Bob to dinner and to a movie. Bob had just spent the last ten hours on an airplane. He could not think of sitting in a movie theater for two hours. He politely declined the invitation.
>
> Bob arrived at his hotel at 6 p.m. and checked into his room. Before he had a chance to unpack, he received a telephone call from the conference director, Morris Ames. Mr. Ames wanted to take Bob to dinner and to a movie. Having just spent ten hours on an airplane, Bob could not think of sitting in a movie theater for two hours. He politely declined the invitation.

Through coordination, subordination, and embedding, choppiness is eliminated, the flow of ideas is improved, and the relationship between ideas is clarified. The important result is that the reader continues to read and communication is improved.

EDITING EXERCISES

A. For each of the following numbered items, combine the sentences into one sentence with parallel construction.

1. I could not have made it without your financial support. You supported me emotionally too.

2. This snack is delicious. It also has high nutritive value. Also, it does not cost much.

3. Our plan was to send out the questionnaire. Then we would study the responses. Finally, we planned to draw conclusions.

4. At the safety seminar, we learned to recognize danger signals immediately. After that you get help quickly. Then one should give first aid effectively.

5. When I arrived, the fittings were already cleaned, and they had been painted. Someone had stacked them too.

B. Prune the deadwood from each of the following sentences.

1. By way of answering the letter you recently sent to me, I have prepared this true fact sheet that I have here.

2. The persons who are most likely to use a great number of our products are those persons who are not presently being reached by our advertisements, in my opinion.

3. The test served the purpose to which we had assigned it, and we saw no reason to repeat it again.

4. I arrived late for the meeting due to the fact that my watch had ceased to run.

5. We have arranged to have a technician on hand at all times of the day and night in order that we may serve you in a better fashion.

C. Each of the following sentences is written in the passive voice. Rewrite it in the active voice unless there is a good reason for using the passive. If so, state the reason.

1. Will the tests be administered by you?

2. Last night the Sales Clerk of the Year award was presented to Celia Piotrowski.

3. After the pressure was checked by Vance, the system was put into full operation by me.

4. In the April meeting, a report on the new building was given by Lamont Owens.

5. The asbestos insulation in the building was removed years ago and replaced with safer material.

A. Identify each of the following sentences as loose, periodic, or mixed. Then underline the main idea in the sentence.

1. Until the security guard came to turn out the lights, I had no idea it was 10 p.m.

2. Sharon will bring the minutes of the last meeting so that we can refer to them.

3. The Komfychair is selling well, despite a slow start.

4. In the last year, several suppliers have eliminated key services, making it difficult to meet production deadlines.

5. The furniture, the equipment, the files—all were destroyed in the recent fire.

6. No one is able to explain how the data was lost, not even the computer expert.

B. Each of the following sentences includes unrelated details. Rewrite the sentence so that it contains only relevant information.

1. On my recent business trip, which was my twelfth for the company, I helped install a data processing system in a small accounting firm that once audited our company.

2. In reseaching this report, I interviewed many of our customers, and I typed every page of the report myself.

3. Odell Medical Supplies Company has been providing hospitals and clinics with high-quality equipment for over 50 years; several of my relatives work there.

4. Our technical advisor, who wears contact lenses, suggests that we test the high chair for several months before putting it on the market.

5. The tour of your facility was interesting, ten minutes long, and informative.

Analyze for clarity the sentences in a piece of business communication. You may use a newsletter from a public utility, a letter from a charitable organization, a brochure from a department store, or any other similar item. Are there errors in parallel structure? Do any sentences stray from presenting just one main idea? Can you find examples of wordiness? You might also analyze the sentences for variety and emphasis.

36
Developing Paragraphs

You may have heard the expression "They can't see the forest for the trees." That means people are so caught up in details that they fail to see the overall picture. If your writing consisted only of a series of individual sentences, your readers would probably have a similar problem. They would read sentence after sentence without being able to find a direction in the writing—its ultimate message.

By grouping sentences revolving around each idea into paragraphs, you help the reader discern the forest (the meaning of the passage) from the trees (the individual sentences). By arranging sentences in a particular order, you also help the reader make sense of the whole message.

In this chapter, you will learn more about the purposes of paragraphs and their basic structure. You will examine in detail the qualities of a good paragraph and ways of developing paragraphs to achieve these qualities.

PARAGRAPH PURPOSE AND STRUCTURE

A paragraph can be defined as a group of sentences representing a unit of thought. It usually includes a topic sentence that states the main idea.

In addition, paragraphs have other important functions:

- Paragraphs provide "rest stops" for the reader. A page without paragraphs is very uninviting. Paragraphs make your writing more readable by breaking up the page. They provide places for the reader to breathe mentally.
- Paragraphs help focus the reader's attention on particular ideas. Without paragraphing, all your ideas flow together. Paragraphs separate and organize main ideas so that the reader can focus on them.
- Paragraphs help clarify the structure of a message. By indicating the divisions between ideas, paragraphs provide a physical framework for them.

In this way, they help you, the writer, organize your message, as well as assist the reader in comprehending it. Paragraphs show how your thoughts are introduced, supported or analyzed, and summarized or concluded.

Paragraphs, then, are both individual units within themselves and elements of a larger whole. They have an internal structure built around a key idea but are also woven into the larger structure of a letter, memo, report, or other document.

The Topic Sentence

A topic sentence states the main idea of a paragraph. It helps the reader identify what the paragraph is about. It reminds you, the writer, of the idea you are shaping. A topic sentence may appear in one of three positions in a paragraph: at the beginning, in the middle, or at the end.

At the Beginning. Introducing the topic at the start is straightforward and clear. You prepare the reader for the related ideas that follow. For this reason, you will use the beginning position most often in writing. In the following paragraph, the topic sentence is italicized. Notice how it gives the reader a preview of what is to come.

> *An attractive benefits package is as important to a prospective employee as a high salary.* Questionnaire respondents frequently pointed to major medical coverage, a good pension plan, and profit-sharing opportunities as key factors in their decision to join our company. When questioned, several people pointed out that these benefits act to increase their salaries in ways that save them tax dollars.

In the Middle. Sometimes writers will need to place the topic sentence in the middle of a paragraph. In this case, the topic sentence usually follows transitional material or descriptive elements that act to introduce the topic. The topic sentence relates the ideas that come before it to those that follow it.

> I saw smiles and bright eyes and laughter. Hands shot up when the teacher asked a question. No notes were being passed, no bored smirks exchanged, and no mindless doodles drawn. *No one needed to tell me that these students were fully involved in the learning process.* They seemed eager to hear and eager to share their points of view. Challenge, excitement, and pride were in the air. It was obvious that this teacher had created a remarkable atmosphere that nurtured rather than stifled a child's natural desire to learn.

At the End. Occasionally, you may want to place the topic sentence at the end of the paragraph. Doing so adds emphasis and drama to the passage. In this position, the topic sentence acts as a summary of the details in the paragraph.

> There were hints on keeping ice sculpture intact through a long summer party. Several pages were devoted to choosing the right liqueur for kiwi fruit flambé. But where were the directions for making a simple white sauce? Could I find a recipe for pound cake? I am sure there are uses for this book. *But if you want a basic cookbook with useful recipes, stay away from* Cook's Tour.

Paragraph Length

Proper paragraph length is, of course, dependent on many factors. Paragraph lengths differ according to subject matter and audience. For example, technical reports for a general audience tend to use shorter paragraphs for easier reading, especially as the material becomes more complex.

Average paragraphs run between 100 and 200 words. They usually include between three and ten sentences, which take up between six and eight lines. On a double-spaced typewritten page, this measures up to one half of the page. However, nearly all business writing is single-spaced to save time and photocopying costs.

These guidelines are just that—guides. As you write, and especially as you revise, look at what you have written and ask yourself if your paragraphing mirrors your organization. Look for paragraphs that need to be combined and for others that need to be divided.

Rarely will you have to write paragraphs longer than those described in this chapter. Sometimes, however, you may want to write extremely short paragraphs of only one or two sentences. Such a paragraph might serve to emphasize an idea.

> We had become complacent, sure that we had the most trusted name in oven manufacture. We studied ways to reduce heat loss, insulate the oven door, and create a self-cleaning appliance. We had a palette of colors, single- and double-door models, and designer touches.
>
> But while we were perfecting the conventional oven, our competitors were working on a revolutionary concept in cookery.

A short paragraph might also be used for transition.

> When I began as a printer, I thought that my job would be to take what people wrote, set it up well on a page, and print it for them. I expected that I might need to run a proof and that I might discover I had made an error. But I always assumed that what was given to me by the client would be the finished product, the final word.
>
> Boy, was I wrong!

You will find that such short paragraphs are appropriate only occasionally in your writing. Use them wisely.

A good paragraph can be thought of as one that satisfies readers' expectations. Readers expect three things from a paragraph: coherence, unity, and completeness. They sense that something is wrong if any one of the three is missing. Take an overview of these qualities before examining them in detail.

THE QUALITIES OF A GOOD PARAGRAPH

Coherence involves the way sentences in a paragraph relate to one another. A coherent paragraph is clear and easy to follow. One sentence leads logically to the next, which leads to the next, and so on. The writer does not jump back and forth in time or place or between the logical steps of an argument.

Unity, the second quality of a good paragraph, is the result of careful shaping around a single idea. An effective paragraph has a focus and stays within that focus. Grammar and word choice also contribute to unity. Paragraphs without unity are confusing.

Completeness is the third quality of a good paragraph. The central theme of the paragraph should be fully developed—the reader should not feel that something has been left out. A complete paragraph leaves the reader satisfied and ready to move on to the new idea in the next paragraph.

Techniques for creating coherent paragraphs fall into two broad categories: mechanical methods, such as the choice of particular words and structures, and presentation of thoughts in a logical order.

ACHIEVING COHERENCE

Mechanical Methods

This section will examine several mechanical aids to coherence: transitional expressions, linking pronouns, repetition, and parallelism.

Transitional Expressions. As you know, one of the problems with a series of loose sentences is choppiness. Each idea seems isolated. By using certain expressions, especially combined with proper coordination and subordination, you can connect the ideas in one sentence to those in the next. These words and phrases are called transitional expressions. In the paragraph that follows, the transitional expressions are italicized.

> Several situations acted together to hide the problem until it was almost too late. *First,* two out of three supervisors were involved in special assignments, leaving the third swamped with daily tasks. *Second,* weekly reviews, the framework for communication, had been allowed to lapse. *Finally,* plant records were poorly kept and sometimes falsified. *As a result,* decreases in production went unnoticed until early in the fiscal year.

The expressions *first, second,* and *finally* move the reader from point to point. The expression *as a result* tells the reader that the consequences of these actions are about to be stated. Table 36-1 lists the most common transitional

Table 36-1. Common Transitional Expressions	
Function	Examples
Sequence	finally, first, next, second, then, third
Time	after, after that, afterward, before, before that time, during, earlier, later, meanwhile, now, simultaneously, since then, so far, until now
Place	above, behind, below, beyond, elsewhere, here, in the background, opposite, there
Emphasis	actually, chiefly, especially, indeed, in fact, most important, surely, without a doubt, yes
Concession	admittedly, although, granted that, it is true, of course, to be sure
Example	as an illustration, for example, for instance, in the following manner, in this case, namely, specifically, such as, that is
Comparison/Contrast	but, conversely, however, likewise, nevertheless, on the other hand, similarly, still, yet
Amplification	again, also, and besides, further, furthermore, in addition, in the first place, moreover
Result/Consequence	as a result, consequently, hence, therefore
Conclusion/Summary	all in all, in conclusion, in other words, in short, so, then, to sum up

expressions, grouped according to the concepts they convey. Transitional expressions such as these can be used to create coherence not only within paragraphs but also between them.

Linking Pronouns. Linking pronouns are pronouns substituting for nouns. You probably use this method of achieving coherence without thinking about it. Read the following sentences:

Seven hundred pairs of jeans arrived today. The jeans were delivered almost three weeks late.

Instead of that, you would probably write:

Seven hundred pairs of jeans arrived today. *They* were delivered almost three weeks late.

The pronoun *they,* referring to *jeans,* links the second sentence to the first. Always be sure, however, that the antecedent of a pronoun is clear.

Repetition. In addition to aiding coherence, linking pronouns help you eliminate unnecessary repetition; yet, sometimes, repetition is an effective aid to coherence. In the following paragraph, key phrases have been repeated to add emphasis and bring the paragraph together as a unit.

> We need *a training program* for all new employees. *A training program* will acquaint employees with proper procedures, allow them to become familiar with equipment before using it on the job, and build worker confidence. Most important, *a training program* will decrease injuries from accidents caused by inexperience and carelessness.

You do not always have to repeat an entire phrase. In some cases, you can achieve coherence through repetition of ideas rather than words.

Parallelism. Parallel structure within a paragraph involves placing similar ideas in similarly constructed sentences. Emphasis, as well as coherence, results. The reader's attention is drawn to the similarity of ideas by the similarity in sentence structure.

The paragraph in the previous section uses parallelism effectively. Notice how sentences beginning with the same element and having similar structure place ideas side by side for the reader. Repetition of words, however, is not necessary in parallel structure.

> Many questions need to be asked about the recent accident. Who were the team supervisors when the accident occurred? Why weren't they on the plant floor? What types of protective clothing would have lessened the injury? When can we expect answers, and what can be done to prevent future accidents?

These parallel questions bind the paragraph together and move the reader from one point to the next.

LOGICAL ORDER

The other way to achieve coherence is by arranging your thoughts in a logical or sensible order. Together with the mechanical aids described in the last section, the internal logic of a paragraph brings your message home to the reader. There are many ways to arrange your thoughts logically, each appropriate for a different type of subject matter and setting. Several of the most useful are discussed here.

Chronological Order. Chronological order is the order in which a series of events took place. It is especially helpful to use chronological order when you are describing the steps in performing a procedure or discussing the background of a situation.

> Maurice Douglass came to work for us in June of 1984 as a teller. After exhibiting accuracy, honesty, and responsibility in that job, he was promoted the following summer to head teller. He fulfilled his duties well and showed exceptional promise as a manager. When the position of office manager opened up in December of 1987, there was no doubt in our minds that Maurice was the prime candidate.

Here the sentences are ordered according to the occurrence of the events: in June of 1984, then the summer of 1985, and finally the end of 1987. This paragraph could be confusing arranged in another way.

Spatial Order. Spatial order, instead of organizing information by time, is based upon place. Thoughts are arranged sequentially according to a physical location, such as left to right, right to left, top to bottom, bottom to top, near to far, or far to near. Spatial order is especially useful when you are describing a physical object or a place.

> On the bottom floor of Lambert's, we sell clothing—men's, women's, and children's. The second floor is devoted to beauty and health items such as makeup, medicines, and sports equipment. On the third floor we sell toys exclusively, and on the top floor of the store, we carry automotive supplies, tools, and housewares.

The writer describes the store from bottom to top because that is how the customer would experience it. Whenever you decide to use spatial order, think of the point of view of the reader as you plan the paragraph.

Deductive Order. Deductive order is a completely different type of development that is useful for persuasive writing. Deductive order moves from the general to the particular. It applies basic principles to specific examples. Before looking at a deductive paragraph, examine how such reasoning works.

> BASIC PRINCIPLE: Serious athletes care more about high quality and comfort in their clothing than they do about low prices.
>
> SPECIFIC EXAMPLE: The Antelope 5E running shoe is constructed well and is very comfortable. It is more expensive than most other running shoes.
>
> CONCLUSION: Serious athletes will buy the Antelope 5E.

Notice that when you use the deductive method, the reader must be convinced that the basic principle is true and that your example applies to the principle. Here is a paragraph based on this logical framework.

> Both industry studies and our experience have shown that serious athletes care more about the quality and comfort of their clothing than about low prices. They realize that good materials and construction are expensive, but they are willing to pay more in order to avoid injuries and discomfort during training. Therefore, I believe that the Antelope 5E shoe, with its superior construction and maximum comfort, will sell well even though it is priced higher than most running shoes.

Inductive Order. Inductive logic is just the opposite of deductive logic— it moves from the particular to the general. An inductive paragraph presents a number of specific examples as evidence before drawing a conclusion from these examples. When using the inductive approach, you can never discuss every possible example. You must be sure, therefore, to choose examples that are representative and provide convincing evidence for your main point.

> I interviewed several groups of employees regarding their experience with the leased word processing equipment. The typists reported that their productivity almost doubled, since they no longer had to retype documents, only to edit them at the screen and print them out. Editors said that the equipment increased their output, as well, since editorial changes could be made quickly and cleanly. They didn't need to worry about losing manuscripts, since every file was saved. Production department workers reported widespread satisfaction, explaining that precoding design features eliminated the need to mark up the manuscript by hand. On the strength of this evidence, I propose the purchase of this equipment.

Notice how the writer gives three representative examples of workers who found the equipment to be time- and cost-efficient. Notice, too, how the writer states the conclusion at the end of the paragraph. A paragraph using inductive logic usually leads to a final topic sentence. However, to establish the context for the reader, a paragraph organized inductively may still require an introductory sentence. In the sample paragraph, the first sentence explains the situation to the reader.

Climactic Order. Climactic order involves ranking ideas by importance, from least to most important. Like inductive and deductive order, climactic order is a good choice when you are writing to convince or justify. Careful ranking is very important. Notice how distracting a paragraph seems when the ideas are not arranged from least to most important.

> We need to remodel to create a conference room for several reasons. First, our office meetings (currently held in the reception area because it is the only place large enough) would benefit from a more comfortable, meeting-oriented room. We also need the conference area for meetings with clients. For these meetings we require a place that is away from phone interruptions, out of office traffic, and equipped with a large table for displaying material. It will add to our company's image to have an attractive conference area for client meetings. Finally, it would give us a place to hold office social functions, such as holiday and birthday parties.

The last point sounds anticlimactic coming after the discussion of client meetings and company image. A more coherent order would place the office parties first, followed by office meetings, and end with the discussion of client visits and company image.

In business communication, paragraphs following deductive order are generally expected. They deliver the message efficiently and are easier to write. However, for variety consider using inductive and climactic order from time to time. Like periodic sentences, they will keep the reader in suspense.

ACHIEVING UNITY   Unity in a paragraph is achieved partially through controlling the ideas in the sentences—they must all lead to, comment on, or expand the main idea of the paragraph. In this way, each sentence contributes to paragraph unity. The italicized sentences in the following paragraphs do *not* contribute to unity because they have no relationship to the central thought of the paragraph.

> Nick Perez is presently a sales representative for Armbruster Plastics. He has experience with both telephone and outside sales, as well as management from a two-year period as office manager at Armbruster. *Mr. Perez's hobbies include photography, antique cars, and camping.* His qualifications make him the prime candidate for the sales manager position.

> I visited Central Power Company on Wednesday. A company representative explained operational details to me and showed me how Central Power uses the equipment we supply. *We had lunch in the company cafeteria.* The trip was very informative, and I thank you for the opportunity to make it.

Unity Through Grammar

As you know, grammar is the structure and arrangement of words. Another way to bind paragraphs together into meaningful wholes is through correct grammar. Observe these grammar rules in all your writing:

- Make sure your subjects and verbs agree.
- Make sure your pronouns and antecedents agree.
- Maintain a consistent point of view. (If you begin the paragraph in the third-person singular, you must continue using it throughout the paragraph.)
- Use consistent verb tenses that reflect the timing of the actions they describe.
- Place modifiers near the words they modify.
- Use coordination and subordination appropriately.

Lack of correct grammar hinders unity and confuses the reader.

Unity Through Diction

Diction means "the choice of words." (Think of the word *dictionary.*) Your choice of words can contribute to paragraph unity. Choose your words carefully, searching for ones that are in keeping with your subject matter.

You also need to keep a consistent tone throughout. If you are writing a formal letter, memo, or report, use formal language—and only formal language. If you are writing something that is informal, do not inject formal language, because it will sound stilted in contrast.

Inconsistent diction can be jarring, as in the following example.

> We are saddened to announce the retirement of Margaret Ching, head of
> the Public Relations Department. Margaret has been with the company for
> over 40 years and is a well-respected member of the Mornay Cosmetics family.
> A farewell luncheon will be held on Friday, September 18, which all employees
> are encouraged to drag their carcasses to.

The choice of *drag their carcasses to,* an informality at best, destroys the
unity of the passage. The word *attend* would be a better, if less colorful, choice.

A complete paragraph is one that is fully developed. Underdeveloped paragraphs, like incomplete sentences, leave your reader with questions. These
questions block communication and weaken writing.

**ACHIEVING
COMPLETENESS**

This section discusses four basic methods of paragraph development to
achieve completeness: development by specific detail, by definition, by com-
parison/contrast, and by cause and effect. (The various types of logical order
might also be considered methods of paragraph development.)

ON THE JOB
Constructive Criticism

Suppose your friend and co-worker, Caroline
Roselli, has just written a letter explaining your
company's manufacturing process to a client.
Before sending the letter out in today's mail,
Caroline asks you to proofread it for typographical errors. As you do, you notice that the organization of the letter is very poor—you have
to read it several times to understand what Caroline is saying, even though you are thoroughly
familiar with the manufacturing process.

Should you tell Caroline about the poor organization, even though she asked you only to
proofread for typographical errors? Should you
forget it, since she wants the letter to go out
today? If you do tell her, how should you go
about it?

Although a prompt letter is important, a clear
letter is crucial. You have a responsibility to tell
Caroline about the problem—but how? Here
are some tips:

- Be as positive as possible. Avoid saying,
  "Caroline, this letter doesn't make any sense!"
  Instead, say, "Caroline, I found only one
  typo—this transposition on line 5 of page 2.
  But I think the organization is a bit confusing. Reworking the sequence of the letter
  would make it clearer to the client."
- Help the writer reorganize. Don't merely
  criticize the letter and leave it at that. Make
  a short outline or number the existing sentences to show a clearer order. With this
  help, Caroline will probably still be able to
  get the letter out today.
- Let the writer make the final decision. Present your suggestions to Caroline, but don't
  force them on her. Rely on the logic of your
  reorganization, rather than pressure, to
  convince her.

Development by Specific Detail

Using this method, you would begin with a central idea, expressed in a topic sentence, and then develop this idea through specific details. These details illustrate the truth of the central idea. Development by specific detail is common and useful in a variety of settings.

> *You Two* bridal service will aid you in planning your perfect wedding from start to finish. Our bridal consultant can help you discover exactly what type of wedding you want, whether small or large, simple or lavish, traditional or contemporary. Let our consultant assist you in making up the guest list, selecting an invitation style, and planning every detail of your day. We will even arrange to have your special occasion recorded on videotape so that you can enjoy it again and again in years to come.

This paragraph begins with the central idea that *You Two* bridal service can create the perfect wedding. Then it develops the idea to show in specific detail exactly what services *You Two* provides.

Development by Definition

To define something is to state its exact meaning. When you develop a paragraph through definition, you use the paragraph to explain in detail the meaning of a term. Often, defining a term means limiting it; that is, you must tell not only what a term means, but also what it does *not* mean. You may want to give examples showing what it is or is not. Before deciding to use this form of development, be sure that the term deserves it. Do not use a whole paragraph to define a term that could be just as easily described in several words.

The following paragraph uses this method to specify how the term *leave of absence* will be used in a report.

> The term *leave of absence,* as discussed in this report, means "a predetermined period of time when an employee is not at work but after which it is understood that he or she will return." Therefore, a preset maternity leave of six months, after which the woman intends to return to full-time work, is a leave of absence. Time spent on education, whether a semester, a year, or more, after which the employee expects to come back to full-time work, is a leave of absence. On the other hand, if an employee leaves the company with no intention of returning but is reemployed several months or years later, this interim period is *not* considered a leave of absence. The period of time was not predetermined, and the employee had not stated at the outset a desire to return.

Development by Comparison/Contrast

Comparing and contrasting two or more ideas or objects is another effective method of paragraph development. With this method, you concentrate on the ways things are alike (comparison) and the ways they differ (contrast). Generally, you state the similarities first and then show the differences.

> Both cleaning products we tested cleaned ceramic and tile surfaces well. Both were easy to use and had step-by-step cleaning directions that were clearly displayed. Here, however, the similarity ended. Product A had a child-safety cap and specific directions on what to do if accidental poisoning occurred. Product B had a screw cap and included only the words *HARMFUL IF SWALLOWED*, omitting even the warning that a physician should be called. Product A cautioned against use with any other product containing bleach, noting that toxic fumes could result from the mixture. Product B contained no such warning, although laboratory tests showed that use with bleach products produced noxious vapors. Finally, Product A came in an unbreakable bottle that was difficult to tip over. Product B's brittle plastic container tipped easily and shattered upon contact with a tile floor or ceramic tub.

In this paragraph, the writer has compared the products feature by feature. The reader gets a clear idea of how the two products compare.

Another way to compare and contrast is to discuss Product A's features, then Product B's. With this method, it might be better to use a separate paragraph for each product discussed. This method is more appropriate when information about each product is lengthier and more involved.

Development by Cause and Effect

A final pattern of development traces which causes bring about which effects. It draws connections between events. For example, you might show how an office rearrangement led to a quieter atmosphere.

Although this method can be very effective, you must take care to choose logical cause-and-effect relationships. If your audience is not convinced that the links are genuine, your argument is lost.

> Oddly enough, it seems that a simple weather forecast began the chain of events that led to the recent milk shortage. On December 6, radio stations predicted heavy snowfalls of 10 to 12 inches by nightfall. Local residents flooded neighborhood grocery stores to stock up on basics such as eggs, butter, and milk. Because of the unexpected influx of customers, several stores depleted their regular supply of milk. Seeing this, shoppers wrongly interpreted it as a general shortage, and a wave of panic buying made their fears a self-fulfilling prophecy.

EDITING EXERCISES

A. Each of the exercises that follow includes a group of sentences that can be arranged into a coherent paragraph. The sentences are in a jumbled order, however. Construct a paragraph from the sentences, and then tell if it is developed through chronological, spatial, deductive, inductive, or climactic order.

1. (a) The entrance hall opens into a large reception area with fireplaces at either end. (b) At the extreme west end of the building is a glass-enclosed patio opening onto a spacious, tree-shaded lawn. (c) Note that the entrance to the building is located at the extreme east wing. (d) West of the office complex are six conference rooms arranged in a circular pattern, all opening onto a central hall. (e) Moving farther west from the reception area, you will find a central hallway flanked by offices on either side.

2. (a) Every section of the store, from toys to clothing to accessories, showed increases equal to or greater than this, ranging from 17 percent to a full 50 percent. (b) During the storewide Summer Super Sale, lawn and garden departments increased their sales by 17 percent. (c) These new accounts mean increased business for years to come. (d) From all the evidence, the Summer Super Sale was a success. (e) In addition to increased sales, a number of new charge accounts were opened.

3. (a) A profit-sharing plan is one way to help employees link their own efforts with company success. (b) For these reasons, I see a profit-sharing plan as a method for improving product quality. (c) With such a plan, employees see that the harder they work, the more the company profits. (d) The more the company profits, the more they see their personal profits grow. (e) Most management experts agree that the more closely employees identify with their company, the better the quality of their work will be.

B. Study each of the following sentence pairs as if they were part of a paragraph. In each case, a transitional expression would help the reader move from one idea to the next. Choose an appropriate expression, and rewrite the sentences. You need not combine the sentences into one.

1. Funds for continuing education have been available for two years. No one told the employees of the funds' existence.

2. Employees were insured privately until last year. Last year we presented a comprehensive health plan to our employees.

3. Volume of sales was down last year by 4 percent. Profits were up by 7 percent.

4. I have observed many instances of poor communication. As of yesterday, none of the print shop employees had heard of the new lateness policy that went into effect earlier in the week.

5. My flight to Detroit arrived 15 minutes ahead of schedule. I arrived at RPM Motors earlier than I had expected.

Locate the topic sentence in each of the following paragraphs.

1. Requests for a continuing education program have come from employees at all levels. Production line workers are interested in safety courses. The clerical staff wants to learn more about the capabilities of our word processing system. Middle-level managers have requested efficiency seminars. Finally, upper management is interested in long-range planning skills.

2. Some test solutions cleaned well but had an unpleasant odor. Consumer testers said they liked the cleaning power but did not want their kitchen smelling this way. Another group of solutions had a pleasant minty smell but scored low on grease-cutting ability. Testers commented that it would not take users long to discard the product once it proved useless. We need to strike a balance between an appealing scent and effective cleaning power.

3. Warren Van Doren is the best choice for the position of shop foreman. He has been working for the company for five years and has proved to be a dependable and ambitious worker. He is well liked by the other employees and, during several shop emergencies, has revealed strong leadership abilities. Warren recently expressed interest in this position and would be willing to assume responsibilities immediately.

Write a paragraph for each of the following methods of development. You may choose your subject from those provided.

1. A paragraph developed through specific detail on (a) the kinds of people who attend your college, (b) the atmosphere of the town or city where you grew up, or (c) the impression made upon you by a recent event

2. A paragraph developed through definition that describes (a) leadership, (b) efficiency, (c) resourcefulness, or (d) effective communication

3. A paragraph developed through comparison and contrast on (a) your taste in clothes or music as compared to a friend's, (b) the relative merits of two jobs you have held, (c) the similarities and differences between what you thought post-high-school education would be and what it is

4. A paragraph developed through cause and effect on (a) stiffer drunk driving laws, (b) bilingual elementary education, or (c) dress codes in business

37
Avoiding the Most Common Writing Errors

In Chapters 35 and 36, you looked at ways to write effective sentences and to develop good paragraphs. Now it is time to warn you about the most common pitfalls for writers so you can avoid them as you compose various kinds of messages.

PROBLEM SENTENCES

Good sentences—sentences that accurately communicate the writer's message—possess clarity, emphasis, and variety. Both beginning and experienced writers sometimes have trouble writing effective sentences. Sentences that fail to communicate usually have one of six problems:

- incompleteness
- faulty punctuation
- excessive detail
- unrelated ideas
- faulty coordination or subordination
- grammatical errors

This section examines these common errors in detail.

The Incomplete Sentence

To be a sentence, a group of words must contain a complete subject and predicate and express a complete thought. A group of words that does not meet these qualifications is a sentence fragment. A common error is capitalizing and punctuating fragments as though they were sentences.

Writers occasionally use fragments on purpose for emphasis or dramatic effect, especially in advertising. In most business writing, however, a fragment is an error that distracts the reader. For example, a fragment in the following paragraph leaves the reader confused:

> Insurance rates are climbing higher than ever before. *Lawsuits brought by injured workers.* Even winning cases costs us money in legal fees, court costs, and wasted time.

The phrase *lawsuits brought by injured workers* contains a subject but no predicate. You could create a complete sentence by writing *Lawsuits have been brought by injured workers.* You could also join the fragment to the sentence that precedes it: *Insurance rates are climbing higher than ever before, in part because of lawsuits brought by injured workers.*

The Run-on Sentence

Another common sentence-writing error is the run-on sentence. In a run-on sentence, two or more sentences are joined as though they were one sentence.

> We will hold the board meeting on Monday morning if Mr. Matson approves we will adjourn by noon.

Sometimes writers use a comma to separate the sentences (called a comma splice), but they still form a run-on sentence. A comma is not strong enough to separate complete thoughts.

> Lynn photocopied the report, then she gave the original back to Ms. Slossen.

The easiest way to correct a run-on sentence is to put a period at the end of the first sentence and to capitalize the first word of the second.

> Lynn photocopied the report. Then she gave the original back to Ms. Slossen.

If you want to emphasize the close relationship between the two thoughts, change the run-on sentence into a compound sentence. To do this, use either a semicolon or a comma and a coordinating conjunction.

> Lynn photocopied the report; then she gave the original back to Ms. Slossen.

> Lynn photocopied the report, and then she gave the original back to Ms. Slossen.

If you want to emphasize one thought more than the other, change the run-on sentence into a complex sentence by using a subordinating conjunction.

> After she photocopied the report, Lynn gave the original back to Ms. Slossen.

The Overburdened Sentence

Some sentences are simply overburdened with too many ideas or too much information. When too many details—no matter how interesting—are crammed into one sentence, communication suffers. The sentence seems to go in several directions at once.

> Memo forms with attached carbons, which come in yellow, green, and white as well as yellow, blue, and white, are available at a unit price of 68 cents, or $6.80 per thousand.

The details about carbon color and price per thousand are indeed related to the main point of the sentence, but they create a confusing clutter. Two sentences would be clearer.

> Memo forms with attached carbons are available at a unit price of 68 cents, or $6.80 per thousand. Carbons come in two color combinations: green, yellow, and white, or yellow, blue, and white.

The Unfocused Sentence

A sentence should include only one central thought; all other ideas in the sentence should work to clarify that thought. Remember that this kind of focus is what the reader expects. Including two different thoughts in a sentence may make the reader try to find some link between the two—a link that may not exist.

> The Management Institute, which has ample parking facilities, is once again offering three seminars in long-range budgeting this semester.

The clause about ample parking facilities is unrelated to the main thought of this sentence—the offering of seminars. Attempting to link the two can make the reader lose the main point of the message.

The Illogical Sentence

You know that sentence combining is a way to achieve emphasis and variety. Sometimes, however, writers combine sentences in ways that do not seem to make sense.

Faulty Coordination. Faulty coordination involves trying to coordinate too many ideas at once, trying to group unrelated ideas, or trying to coordinate ideas that should be subordinated instead. Each of the following sentences illustrates one of these aspects of faulty coordination:

> We arrived at the convention center and parked the car and walked to the building but found the front door locked so we stopped a security guard and he told us how to get in.
>
> I set up our display, and the convention was held in Phoenix.
>
> I had been too busy to eat lunch and was ravenous by dinnertime.

In the first sentence, the ideas are not really coordinated, but simply strung together. At least two sentences, perhaps three, are needed. In the second sentence, there is no relationship at all between the ideas. The third sentence requires subordination, not coordination.

Faulty Subordination.   Too many subordinated ideas can also pull apart the central thought of a sentence and bewilder the reader.

> Our treasurer, Marcia Levitt, who has been with Ace Equipment for 25 years and who has guided us through many financial trouble spots, is retiring on March 20, despite the fact that our president has asked her to stay until we finish the building program.

Although each idea is properly subordinated to another idea, there are too many dependent clauses. It would be clearer to use both coordination and subordination.

> Our treasurer, Marcia Levitt, is retiring. She has been with Ace Equipment for 25 years and has guided us through many financial trouble spots. Ace's president has asked Marcia to stay until we finish the building program, but she has decided to leave on March 20.

Another type of faulty subordination involves confusing the main and subordinated ideas in a sentence. The result is illogical.

> Because we succeeded in meeting the deadline, we assigned overtime hours.

The above sentence reverses the true cause-and-effect relationship, which is expressed logically below.

> We succeeded in meeting the deadline because we assigned overtime hours.

The Ungrammatical Sentence

An ungrammatical sentence is a little bit like a puzzle with all the pieces available but none in the right place. The picture is not clear because the parts do not fit together correctly. At least six factors can contribute to ungrammatical sentences:

- ambiguous use of pronouns
- shifts in voice, tense, person, or number
- lack of parallel structure
- faulty comparisons
- misplaced modifiers
- dangling modifiers

Ambiguous Use of Pronouns.   Pronouns stand in the place of nouns. A pronoun is useful only if you know exactly what noun it is replacing—in other words, its antecedent. In the following sentences, the use of pronouns is ambiguous or unclear:

> Gabrielle informed Lena that she had now earned two weeks of compensatory time.

The personal pronouns *she* and *her* might logically refer to either Gabrielle or Lena. In this case, Lena has the time coming to her. The following would be a better way to write this sentence:

> Gabrielle said that Lena had now earned two weeks of compensatory time.

In the next example, the pronoun *it* is too far from its antecedent, *hallway.* Repeating the word *hallway* in the second sentence would make the meaning clear.

> Several offices open into the hallway, including Dan Pacini's, Kathy Pollack's, and mine, and there are desks, chairs, and filing cabinets lining the walls. It had not been painted for at least five years.

The antecedents of demonstrative and relative pronouns, such as *this, that,* and *which,* frequently are unclear.

> Russell told me he was bored with his job, which was no surprise.

The pronoun *which* appears to refer to *job,* but that makes no sense. *Which* actually refers to the whole preceding clause. Here is a clearer version:

> I was not surprised to learn that Russell was bored with his job.

Shifts in Verbs. A sudden shift of gears in a car can cause discomfort for the riders. Shifts in verb tense and voice can have a similar effect on readers.

> Before the slide show began, I turned out the lights; after it was over, they were turned on.

Here the writer both turned the lights off and turned them back on. Yet the shift to passive voice makes it appear that someone else turned them on. A more coherent sentence reads this way:

> Before the slide show began, I turned out the lights; after it was over, I turned them back on.

In the following sentence, the writer incorrectly shifts from the past tense to the present:

> As soon as the test animal successfully completed the maze, he receives a reward.

Either the writer should keep both verbs in the past tense (*completed. . . received*) to report what happened in the past, or the writer should use the present tense (*completes. . . receives*) to describe the way the maze works.

Shifts in Pronouns. Pronoun shifts also weaken communication. Most commonly, writers tend to shift to second person from first or third.

> I cannot be sure if I am getting through to my staff; you get the feeling they misunderstand you.

There is no reason to switch from *I* to *you*. The second clause should read, *I get the feeling they misunderstand me.*

Some writers also have trouble staying with the singular or plural, as in this sentence:

> If a person wants to get ahead, they must be willing to sacrifice.

This writer should either stay in the singular (*person . . . he or she*) or use the plural throughout (*people . . . they*).

Lack of Parallel Structure. Parallel structure is achieved by using similar grammatical structures to discuss similar elements within a sentence. Whether the similarity is brought about by coordination, subordination, listing, or some other method, you must be sure to keep like elements parallel.

Faulty Comparisons. Faulty comparisons may occur in elliptical sentences, or sentences that have missing words.

> Our price was higher than the competitor.

Such a sentence tempts the reader to ask how high the competitor is. The price should not be compared to the competitor, but to the competitor's price.

> Our price is higher than the competitor's.

Another problem with comparisons occurs when an interrupting phrase causes the writer to forget how he or she began the comparison.

> Honesty is as important, if not more important, than skill.

To check such a sentence, remove the interrupting phrase to see if the sentence still makes sense. *Honesty is as important than skill* sounds odd. The writer should have written the sentence this way:

> Honesty is as important as, if not more important than, skill.

Misplaced Modifiers. Modifiers should be placed as close as possible to the word they modify. Otherwise, they may appear to refer to a different word, with confusing or humorous results.

> The illustrations were studied by the client spread out on the conference room table.

It is unlikely that the client was spread out on the table; more likely, the illustrations were.

> The client studied the illustrations spread out on the conference room table.

Dangling Modifiers. Dangling modifiers differ from misplaced modifiers in that the word they modify does not appear in the sentence at all.

> Having welcomed our guests, dinner was served.

Clearly, *dinner* was not responsible for welcoming the guests. The writer has forgotten to include a word that would clarify the evening's events.

> Having welcomed our guests, we served dinner.

A dangling modifier is almost always found at the beginning of a sentence. When you begin a sentence with a modifier, make sure you include all necessary words.

PROBLEM PARAGRAPHS

Learning to write a good paragraph takes practice. To communicate effectively, paragraphs must demonstrate coherence, unity, and completeness. At least five types of paragraphing errors can lead to communication problems:

- lack of sentence variety, transitions, or linking pronouns
- too many ideas or excessive detail and repetition
- no topic sentence or central focus
- illogical ordering of ideas
- inconsistencies in point of view, diction, or grammar

This section examines these common errors in more detail.

USING YOUR WORD PROCESSOR
Checking for Problems in Writing Style

Government workers have long been notorious for writing in bureaucratese, a complicated, jargon-filled writing style that generally confuses rather than enlightens the reader. Recently, a government official ordered the workers in his department to write in plain English instead. To help these officials change their writing style, the department's word processing software was programmed so that writers could not use jargon.

Software that assists writers in word selection is an example of the greatly expanding range and sophistication of word processing programs. Some of the simplest programs let the word processor function as a sophisticated typewriter. Others now take the word processor far beyond what a typewriter can do.

While there is still no program that can actually compose a letter or document on its own, some programs are able to analyze what you have written. These programs do not merely point out spelling errors or correct basic grammatical mistakes; they can also suggest possible improvements to your writing style.

For example, one program can command the computer to measure the reading level of a document. The program picks out words that might be unfamiliar to most readers.

The program also flags long sentences—those that are most likely to be unclear. You can then review these sentences and break them into shorter, simpler sentences. This program even spots clichés and recognizes the use of passive voice.

No matter how advanced any word processing program may be, however, it is no substitute for a writer with a clear command of language. The writer, in the end, is responsible for every word, sentence, paragraph, and punctuation mark that is put down on paper.

The Choppy Paragraph

Chapter 35 discussed the need to vary sentence structure. The exclusive use of loose sentences works against communication by isolating each idea. If you fail to establish relationships through sentence structure, you imply that none exist. In the following paragraph, notice the monotonous, fragmented effect made by a series of loose sentences:

> We need to arrange for a time-and-motion study of the production process. Waste occurs on every level. Managers do jobs that should be assigned to their employees. Clerical workers retype documents needlessly. Document originators constantly change their minds. Plant floor workers waste time walking from one station to another. A different arrangement of equipment would save steps for the workers. We must study plant operations with a view to efficiency.

By varying sentence types, adding transitions and linking pronouns, and combining sentences, the writer could make this paragraph a unified whole that promotes communication.

> We need to arrange for a time-and-motion study of the production process. Waste now occurs on every level. Managers, for example, frequently do jobs that should be assigned to their employees. Because document originators constantly change their minds, clerical workers retype documents needlessly. Finally, a poor equipment arrangement on the plant floor causes workers to waste steps and, therefore, time. To remedy these problems we must study plant operations with a view to efficiency.

The Overloaded Paragraph

There are no hard-and-fast rules governing paragraph length. The guidelines in Chapter 36 are just that—guidelines. A paragraph that is too long is not too long because it has 225 words rather than 200 or because it covers 12 lines instead of 8. Generally, an overly long paragraph includes more than one main idea, excessive detail, or repetition.

By including more than one idea, the writer has overloaded the following paragraph:

> This report will discuss the precarious balance between plant safety and production-quota demands. I would like to thank Palmer Jacobi, Rosanna Robinson, and Jeffrey Huang for their help with this report. Although safety and high production levels are not mutually exclusive goals, each must work to shape the direction of the other. This study concerns plant operations at the Chemico Company only. Both interviews with workers and industry studies were used in the preparation of this report. No attempt should be made to apply these findings to other industries.

This paragraph begins by describing the scope of the report. In the second sentence, however, the purpose shifts to thanking those who helped with report preparation. The next two sentences go back to defining the scope of the report. Then, in the fifth sentence, the writer once again comments on report sources. The final sentence shifts back to the main purpose (the reader assumes) of the paragraph—to describe the scope of the report.

To unload this paragraph, the writer would need to remove the second and fifth sentences and include them in another paragraph—a paragraph focused upon sources of help.

The Unfocused Paragraph

As a business writer, you should always state your point clearly and display it effectively in a topic sentence. A paragraph without a topic sentence has no apparent direction.

> Customers have submitted complaints ranging from faulty tea bags to foreign material in the tea itself. A spot check of several flavors of tea in my local supermarket confirmed the truth of these reports. Production errors account for at least 90 percent of the problems. Typical tea drinkers are finicky, and there are many other brands to lure them away.

This paragraph discusses several subjects: customer complaints, a spot check made by the writer, the tracing of problems to production errors, and the personality of tea drinkers. There is no apparent focus. The reader must invent a unifying idea—which may or may not match the writer's main idea.

Read the paragraph again, but this time place the following sentence at the beginning as the topic sentence: *Unless we act quickly to control the production process, sales of the Tea-Amo line of beverages will decline rapidly.* Once you know the point of the paragraph, you can see how the sentences work together to support that point.

The Illogical Paragraph

You know how puzzling a familiar word can look when the letters are out of sequence. Your paragraphs will be just as mysterious if your sentences fail to follow a logical order. Chapter 36 discussed five logical orders: chronological, spatial, deductive, inductive, and climactic. Notice how violating even the simplest of these orders—chronological—results in an incoherent paragraph.

> In its more than 30 years in business, Gillespie Corporation has become the primary name in financial management on the East Coast. Gillespie Corporation was founded in 1955 by Miles Gillespie, Sr., whose dream was to build a financial management firm that would serve both businesses and families. By 1957, the firm had expanded to include four financial advisors and ten office workers. In 1955, the company consisted of Miles and his partner, Walton Ignatius. By 1965, the Gillespie Corporation had mushroomed to a payroll of 150.

The paragraph is much clearer if the events are discussed chronologically.

> Gillespie Corporation was founded in 1955 by Miles Gillespie, Sr., whose dream was to build a financial management firm that would serve both businesses and families. In 1955, the company consisted of Miles and his partner, Walton Ignatius. By 1957, the firm had expanded to include four financial advisors and ten office workers. By 1965, the Gillespie Corporation had mushroomed to a payroll of 150. In its more than 30 years in business, Gillespie has become the primary name in financial management on the East Coast.

The Inconsistent Paragraph

Another error in paragraph writing is inconsistency in point of view, diction, or grammar. Switching these elements back and forth confuses and distracts the reader. In Chapter 36, you read a paragraph that lacked consistent tone. Here is one that lacks consistent structure among similar sentence elements. In other words, the paragraph contains faulty parallel structure.

> When workers are careless during the production process, unfortunate events follow. Improperly cut boxes receive inadequate glue. Before they are filled, boxes without enough glue break apart. The machinery becomes jammed because of boxes that are broken. Work stops and workers are frustrated.

Although these items are in logical order, lack of parallelism hides the fact that all these actions—cutting, gluing, and filling—are consecutive steps in one process. Parallel structure makes this clear.

> When workers are careless during the production process, an unfortunate chain of events follows. Improperly cut boxes receive inadequate glue. Inadequately glued boxes break apart before they are filled. Broken boxes jam the machinery, causing work stoppages and worker frustration.

EDITING EXERCISES

Identify the problem in each of the following paragraphs. Then edit to improve communication.

1. In some individuals caffeine causes nervousness and jumpiness. Others complain of sleeplessness. Still others say that even small amounts of caffeine upset their stomachs. Yet many persons claim that caffeine helps them stay alert and concentrate better. Others report that the drug lessens headache pain.

2. We have found that our most competent employees all showed exceptional promise as business school students. Phyllis Graziano was in the top 5 percent of her class of 250. Student body president at his business school was Jackson Choudhri. Valedictorian Rosemary Mercer is another

example. Each of these individuals displayed promise as a student that continued in his or her work with our company.

3. We cannot place all the blame for the fire on the workers present when the fire happened. The conditions that led to the fire were present hours before the fire started. Rags soaked in volatile chemicals had been allowed to pile up in the corner. Faulty wiring had not been reported. Machinery was allowed to run for days on end without cleaning or checking. Everyone must accept some blame for this tragedy.

4. The bookshelves are sturdy, attractive, and low-priced. They hold over 800 books. These books may be hardcover or softcover. The books may be up to 12 inches tall. The shelves are made of solid oak. The oak is varnished. The shelves are priced very reasonably. The price is far below that of any comparable bookshelf. Consumers will buy these bookshelves.

PROBLEMS

A. Identify the problem in each of the following sentences. Then rewrite it to improve communication.

1. Khan's Auto Parts boasts speedy delivery, a money-back guarantee, and a warehouse in Lexington, Kentucky.

2. Until the next board meeting.

3. White Graphics, Inc., has been in business for ten years, located in a painted brick building with double glass doors and an attractive reception area.

4. Environmental experts gave our plant a top rating and last year we had a poor rating.

5. Harold, whose wife's name is Lucille after the comedienne Lucille Ball, was promoted to shop foreman yesterday.

6. I waited for Mr. Kovak to arrive as I completed my expense report.

7. The instruction manual was lost and I was forced to rely on my common sense.

8. It became clear who was at fault when I saw the shift supervisor leave early at which time discipline relaxed that led to poor work habits.

9. Our interior decorators used wallpaper instead of paint, insisting that it gave a warmer feeling; the building has three stories.

10. Unless the work is finished by Tuesday.

11. Mrs. Goldberg would not give up the project meant everything to her.

12. Thirty years ago only 10 percent of our employees had college degrees, now 87 percent have them.

B. Identify the grammatical error in each of the following sentences. Then rewrite it to improve communication.

1. Each team supervisor has specific instructions to follow in case of illness, injury, or if someone dies.
2. Craig's sales record is almost as good as me.
3. Please remember to turn down the heat and have the door locked when you go.
4. We need to budget time more carefully; after the annual meeting we will have to get to work on it.
5. Standing behind a grove of trees, I found a small building.
6. I made my way to the corporate center and ask for Mr. Moses Fox.
7. Our visitors observed the experimental rats talking among themselves.
8. Whenever any employee has a grievance, they should tell me.
9. This evaluation is as bad as, if not worse, than the last one.
10. After you finish looking around the facility, one can have lunch in the cafeteria.
11. To get to the warehouse a car is necessary.
12. The marketing department is always disagreeing with the production department; this makes us all confused.
13. The camera was returned to the man crushed beyond recognition.
14. You will find the reports either in the file cabinet or they will be on my desk.
15. The report was typed while eating lunch.

PROJECTS

Choose one of the following topics for a paragraph:

- a job or jobs I've had
- how to look for a job
- what I look for in a job
- the skills necessary for a certain job
- why a certain job is important

Write a topic sentence for your paragraph. Before writing the paragraph, make a list of the points you want to include, and decide on a logical order. Be sure to include transitional words and linking pronouns in your paragraph.

PART SIX
WRITING EFFECTIVE LETTERS

38
Letter Formats and Uses

When you go on a job interview, you try to present yourself in the best possible way to your prospective employer. Perhaps you plan in advance what you want to say—why you are interested in the position and what qualifies you for it. At the same time, you try to look your best because you know that an unprofessional appearance can create a negative first impression.

In the same way, a business letter represents a company to the person who receives it. How the letter looks will make an impression, good or bad. It is crucial, therefore, to take special care in preparing business letters to create a positive first impression.

Throughout this chapter, generally accepted directions for letter preparation are provided. Each company, however, sets its own guidelines for written correspondence, and you will need to adapt to the customs of your workplace. When you enter a new job, check a company procedures or style manual for information, or ask your supervisor what guidelines should be followed.

LETTERS THAT LOOK PROFESSIONAL

Before the recipient reads one word of a letter, that individual receives an initial impression by looking at the letter itself. When you prepare correspondence, think of the whole letter as a picture in a frame. To make the letter pleasing to the eye, place the text on the page with generous, even margins at the left and right and at the top and bottom.

On printed stationery, type the first line (the date) on line 12, 13, 14, or 15. Leave a bottom margin of 6 to 12 lines. Side margins will vary depending on the size of the stationery. A 5-inch line is customary on standard-size stationery. Some writers use a 6-inch line for longer business letters. Remember when choosing margins to avoid making the letter look poorly placed.

In addition, the typing must be perfect. Do not send out a letter with noticeable erasures or corrections; obvious mistakes give correspondence a messy, unprofessional look.

THE STATIONERY

Business leaders realize that a company's choice of stationery can help to create a positive first impression—before the recipient even reads the message that the stationery contains. Stationery reflects a company's image.

Weight

Stationery appeals to touch as well as to sight. That is why 16- to 20-pound bond paper is commonly used for business correspondence. Poundage indicates the thickness of the paper; the term *16-pound bond* means that 500 sheets of that paper, known as a *ream*, weigh 16 pounds. Sheets lighter than 16-pound bond feel flimsy. Sheets heavier than 20-pound bond are hard to handle and feel more like cardboard than paper.

Color

White or off-white stationery is standard for business correspondence. Pastel shades are sometimes used, however, especially by less traditional firms. Some companies distinguish their stationery with a watermark, a design impressed onto the paper during its manufacture. This design is visible only when the paper is held up to the light. The company logo is often used as a watermark.

Size

Standard stationery size is $8\frac{1}{2}$ by 11 inches. The metric standard size is designated A4 and measures 210 by 297 millimeters. Some executives use slightly smaller sheets, called monarch, which measure $7\frac{1}{4}$ by $10\frac{1}{2}$ inches. (There is no equivalent metric-sized sheet.) A third size of stationery, called half-sheet or baronial, is $5\frac{1}{2}$ by $8\frac{1}{2}$ inches. (As metric A5, it measures 148 by 210 millimeters.) These note-sized sheets are usually used for personal notes or very brief letters, as well as for short memos or other interoffice correspondence. Some physicians and lawyers also use baronial stationery.

THE LETTERHEAD

If you placed a typical personal letter beside a typical business letter, one difference would be obvious. The business letter would be typed on paper with a printed letterhead. A printed letterhead gives a business letter a professional identity.

Designs for letterheads vary greatly. (Look at Figures 38-2, 38-6, and 38-8 for examples.) Yet, effective letterhead designs share certain characteristics:

They are attractive and easy to read and frequently designed to reinforce a company's identity, sometimes through the use of a slogan or logo. A letterhead usually occupies about two inches at the top of the page, although some companies use side letterheads that appear in the top portion of the left margin. Certain information must be included:

- the company name
- the company address, including the zip code

Most companies also include their main telephone number in the letterhead. Special addresses (such as those for cablegrams) or telephone numbers (for telecommunications equipment) also appear if they apply.

When a letter takes up more than one page, most firms use a blank sheet of paper—not a sheet with a printed letterhead—for succeeding pages. This paper matches the letterhead sheet in size, color, and quality. Some businesses provide printed second sheets. The company name appears on the printed second sheet, at the bottom of the page, but in much smaller type than on the letterhead.

THE ENVELOPE

A company's envelopes should be of the same paper quality and color as its stationery. In the upper left corner, the return address should be printed in a style like that of the letterhead. On a printed envelope, the typist sometimes places the name of the letter writer above the printed company name (see Figure 38-1).

If you use envelopes without a printed return address, type the name of the sender, the company name, and the company address in the upper left corner.

Size

Table 38-1 shows the envelope sizes that correspond to the three most popular stationery sizes. These sizes call for you to fold letters in thirds before placing them in envelopes.

Table 38-1. Standard Business Stationery

Stationery Size	Dimensions	Envelope Size	Dimensions
(Customary)			
Standard	8½″ × 11″	No. 10	9½″ × 4⅛″
Monarch	7¼″ × 10½″	No. 7	7½″ × 3⅞″
Baronial	5½″ × 8½″	No. 6¾	6½″ × 3⅝″
(Metric)			
A4	210 × 297mm	DL	220 × 110mm
A5	148 × 210mm	C⅞	162 × 81mm

Address Format

When you type an address on an envelope, use the format preferred by your company. The following is a widely accepted format:

- Single-space the address.
- Use all uppercase letters.
- Block all lines at the left.
- Place the recipient's name on the first line and the street address on the next line(s).
- On the last line, type the city followed by a comma and one space, then the state abbreviation. (Using the two-letter abbreviations provided by the Postal Service, type the state abbreviation in uppercase letters with no periods.) Separate the zip code from the state abbreviation with one space.

On a No. 10 envelope, begin the address on line 14, four inches from the left edge (40 pica spaces, 48 elite spaces). For smaller envelopes, begin the address on line 12, two inches from the left edge (20 pica spaces, 24 elite spaces). Figure 38-1 shows a No. 10 envelope with the address printed correctly. Note that it shows the nine-digit zip code. The format for this code consists of the usual five-digit zip code followed by a hyphen and four more digits, which identify the addressee more precisely.

When typing an address for a window envelope, be sure there is at least ⅛-inch margin between the edges of the window and each side of the address, no matter how much the letter shifts within the envelope.

Special Notations

You may need to type special notations on an envelope.

Mailing Notations. Special mailing notations, such as *CERTIFIED MAIL, REGISTERED MAIL,* and *SPECIAL DELIVERY,* go below the postage stamp. This positioning makes it easy for postal employees to see the notation. Make the notation entirely in uppercase letters on the ninth line from the top of the envelope. (See Figure 38-1.) Some companies use stamps or stickers that give this information, making typing it unnecessary.

Other Notations. Place a *Personal* notation, a *Confidential* notation, or an attention line three or four lines below the return address or on line 9, whichever is lower. Capitalize the first letter of each main word, and underscore the entire notation. Position the notation so that it is even with the left margin of the return address. Figure 38-1 shows an attention line correctly typed.

You may also include an attention line in the address. Place it between the company name and the street address.

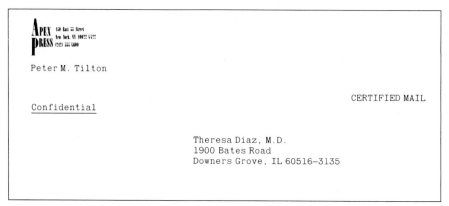

Figure 38-1 Envelope with attention line.

THE PARTS OF A BUSINESS LETTER

No two business letters are the same, because each is tailored to the needs of both the sender and the recipient. Business people, however, have come to expect information in letters to be presented in a standardized way. A standard format means that the reader can concentrate on content, knowing that certain format conventions have been followed. For example, the recipient of a business letter can expect to find a printed or typed letterhead that provides the sender's address. Upon opening the letter, the recipient can concentrate immediately on what it says rather than spend time searching for a return address.

In this section, you will look at the eight standard parts of a business letter, as well as six optional parts.

Standard Letter Parts

Figure 38-2 shows the standard letter parts, labeled for easy identification.

Letterhead or Return Address. Most correspondence will be prepared on printed letterhead paper. Occasionally, however, you may type a business letter on plain paper. In this case, you need to create a typewritten letterhead. Begin the first line of the return address on line 4. Double-space between lines, and triple-space before the date. Center each line horizontally.

Dateline. The dateline reminds both sender and recipient when a letter was prepared. Without a dateline, the recipient has no idea how recent the information in the letter is. On the third line below the letterhead (line 12, 13, 14, or 15), indicate the date on which you type the letter. The most common form is the following: *January 12, 1988.* Some military offices and offices outside the United States use this format: *12 January 1988.* No matter which format you use, never abbreviate the name of the month or use an ordinal ending with the numeral, as in "Jan. 12th, 1988."

Inside Address. The inside address is the recipient's address typed on the letter. Begin the inside address on the fifth line below the date, and type it single-spaced. When you are addressing the letter to an individual, be sure to include a courtesy title, such as *Mr., Mrs., Miss,* or *Ms.* Some individuals require special courtesy titles. For example, in writing to a member of Congress, you would use the title *The Honorable.* For a full list of courtesy titles, consult an office style manual.

Salutation. The salutation of a letter acts as a greeting. The most common salutation is *Dear* (name). Unless you are writing an informal letter, which addresses the individual by first name, you will use the appropriate courtesy title with the name. When the addressee's gender is not known (*R. M. Jessup,* for example), you must repeat the entire name: *Dear R. M. Jessup.* Type the salutation at the left margin on the second line below the inside address. Capitalize each noun and title. Whenever possible, use an individual's name rather than an impersonal salutation such as *Ladies and Gentlemen.*

Body. The body of a letter is its message. Begin the body on the second line below the salutation. Single-space within paragraphs, but double-space between them. Only when you are typing a very short letter should the body be double-spaced (in which case paragraphs must be indented). This situation happens rarely; but when it does, monarch or baronial stationery can be used.

Complimentary Closing. Just as a salutation serves as a greeting, a complimentary closing acts as a farewell. Some complimentary closings (*Very cordially yours, Respectfully yours*) are more formal than others (*Sincerely, Best regards*). The complimentary closing should match the salutation, and the message, in tone and degree of formality. To create a uniform tone, some companies set guidelines on salutations and closings for all letters.

Type the complimentary closing on the second line below the last line of the body. Capitalize the first letter of the first word only.

Signature Block. The signature block, which identifies the author of the letter, includes the following components:

- the writer's signature
- the writer's name, typed
- the writer's position or title, typed

Type the writer's name on the fourth line below the complimentary closing. The three blank lines allow room for the signature. Type the writer's title either on the same line as the name or on the line below.

Some companies include a company signature in the signature block, which emphasizes that the letter is from the business as a whole. If you work for a firm that uses a company signature, type the company name in uppercase letters on the second line below the complimentary closing. Align the name on the left with the first letter of the closing. Type the writer's name on the

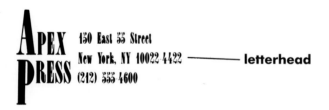

letterhead

**inside
address**

dateline

January 12, 1987

Mr. Philip O'Leary
4050 Swiss Avenue
Dallas, TX 75204–1256

salutation　　　　**body**

Dear Mr. O'Leary:

Thank you for your interest in our new Healthwise book series on total fitness. Within the next several years, we will introduce five fully illustrated volumes on exercise, nutrition, disease prevention, mental health, and environmental health. We have gathered an impressive panel of consultants who are experts in these fields. They will ensure that the information in the series is accurate and up to date.

Because of your interest, we are placing you on our mailing list for our monthly newsletter, To Your Health. This up–to–the–minute report includes articles on health concerns as well as periodic updates on the progress of the Healthwise series. We hope that this and all our health publications will help health care consumers like you live healthier, happier lives.

**complimentary
closing**

Sincerely yours,

Lance Brower

**signature
block**

Lance Brower
Director, Marketing Department

klr

**reference
initials**

Figure 38-2 Parts of a business letter.

fourth line below the company signature. (Figure 38-6 shows a company signature.)

Reference Initials. Reference initials identify the typist who prepared the letter. As typist, place your initials at the left margin on the second line below the last line of the signature block. Reference initials are most commonly typed in lowercase letters, but may also be typed in uppercase. Use either uppercase or lowercase letters for both sets of initials. The writer's initials need not appear, since the writer's name is in the signature block. If, however, the writer wants initials to be included, type them first, separated from yours by a slash (for lowercase initials) or a colon (for uppercase initials).

Optional Letter Parts

The following optional parts of a business letter are used in specific situations. Use them when appropriate.

Personal or Confidential Notations. Sometimes letters contain material that should be read only by the individual to whom the letter is addressed. A notation indicating this restriction should appear on both the envelope and the letter itself.

To make such a notation, type the word *Personal* or *Confidential* at the left margin on the second line below the date. (The salutation begins on the third line after this notation.) To draw attention to the notation, either type it in uppercase letters or use uppercase and lowercase letters and underscore them as follows:

PERSONAL or Personal
CONFIDENTIAL or Confidential

See Figure 38-5 for the proper placement of this notation.

Attention Line. It is always best to address a letter to an individual and to use that person's name in the inside address and salutation. Yet sometimes it is necessary to address a letter to a department or to a particular position. In these situations, an attention line will direct the letter to the necessary department or individual. Type an attention line on the second line below the inside address. Begin at the left margin, and use one of the following terms:

Attention: Advertising Department
ATTENTION: ADVERTISING DEPARTMENT

You may underscore the line, although it is not necessary. Never abbreviate the word *Attention.* Figure 38-6 shows the proper placement of this line.

As explained on page 399, an attention line may also appear within an address. Place it between the company name and the street address in the inside address. Choose this location if you plan to use electronic equipment to print the envelope address from the inside address. This way the attention line will automatically be printed on the envelope, saving the time that would be required if it were a separate step.

Subject Line. A subject line tells the reader at a glance what the letter is about. There are several acceptable formats:

> Subject: Healthwise Series
> SUBJECT: HEALTHWISE SERIES
> HEALTHWISE SERIES

You may underscore this element, but you need not do so. Begin the subject line at the left margin on the second line below the salutation. For extra emphasis it may be centered, unless you are using a letter style that blocks all lines at the left. (See the section titled "Letter Formats" on page 406.) Figure 38-7 displays a correctly typed subject line.

Notations. There are four types of notations. Some or all may be used in a letter.

1. *Enclosure Notation.* An enclosure notation indicates that one or more additional documents, such as a brochure, a form, or a check, accompany the letter. The word *Enclosure* or the abbreviation *Enc.* is most often used for this purpose. If more than one item is enclosed, list the enclosures or tell how many there are. Type the notation at the left margin on the line below the reference initials. Figures 38-5 and 38-6 show enclosure notations.

2. *Mailing Notation.* If a letter or package will travel by special mail service (Express Mail, Certified Mail, etc.), type the appropriate notation at the left margin on the line below the reference initials (or enclosure notation). Figure 38-5 shows this notation. This notation informs the recipient that the letter had special handling.

3. *Copy Notation.* If one or more individuals are to receive a copy of the letter, put a copy notation at the left margin, following the reference initials (or previous notation). Type the abbreviation *c* followed by a space, or the notation *Copy to:* or *Copies to:* followed by two spaces. Then list vertically the names of the persons who will receive a copy. You may use a colon after *c*, but it is not necessary. Figures 38-6 and 38-7 show copy notations.

4. *Blind Copy Notation.* Use a blind copy notation when the writer does not want the recipient to know who will get a copy of the letter. A blind copy notation goes on one or more copies of the letter, but not on the original. On the appropriate pages, type *bc* or *Blind copy (copies) to:*

USING YOUR WORD PROCESSOR
Writing Letters With Ease

Word processing equipment allows the business writer to concentrate on the message to be conveyed. Available software can standardize format, provide for editing at the keyboard, and even correct some stylistic errors automatically.

The operator of a word processor can preselect a letter format and be assured that all elements (such as the inside address, salutation, and complimentary close) will appear in the right place. The letter will also be centered on the page. A letter that seems too short can be reprinted double-spaced or with a shorter line length at the touch of a button, without retyping.

The editing capabilities of a word processor allow the writer to rewrite and rearrange parts of the letter at the keyboard. When appropriate, boilerplate paragraphs can be inserted, eliminating the need for extra typing. A justification program evens the right margin automatically,

and a hyphenation program hyphenates words according to accepted rules and guidelines. Some processors will even put the current date on a letter according to an internal calendar. With a search-and-replace program, any word or phrase used repeatedly in a letter can be replaced automatically. In addition, spelling and grammar checkers can aid the individual in proofreading the final copy.

Most word processors will automatically create subsequent page headings and even produce mailing labels for envelopes. All these features save writers time and allow them to concentrate on communicating clearly.

Today's word processors help business writers create accurate correspondence quickly. Of course, a word processor is only a tool—you, the writer, are ultimately in control of and responsible for the final product.

on the seventh line from the top of the page at the left margin. Be sure that this matches the format of the copy notation when one is included. Vertically list the names of the recipients. This notation may also be typed on the second line below the final line of the letter.

Postscript. A postscript is a final thought typed after the message of the letter. Only rarely in business letters are postscripts actual afterthoughts. More often, writers use postscripts to emphasize a point or to make reference to a subject that is not directly related to the content of the letter. Type a postscript on the second line below the reference initials or the final notation. Type *PS:* or *PS.,* leave two spaces, then type the postscript. If a blind copy notation appears at the bottom of the letter with the postscript, type the blind copy notation last, separated from the postscript by a blank line.

Continuation Pages. When a letter runs longer than one page, each subsequent page needs a special heading. Keeping the same horizontal margins, type the following heading information on the seventh line from the top of each new page:

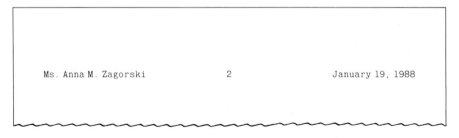

Ms. Anna M. Zagorski   2   January 19, 1988

Figure 38-3 Single-line continuation page heading.

An alternate style is the following:

```
Ms. Anna M. Zagorski
Page 2
January 19, 1988
```

Figure 38-4 Block-style continuation page heading.

Begin the body of the letter on the third line after the last line of the heading.

PUNCTUATION STYLES

Salutations and complimentary closings require special punctuation. There are two styles for punctuating these letter parts. The traditional style uses a colon after the salutation and a comma after the complimentary close. Figures 38-2, 38-6, and 38-7 show the traditional style.

The open style of punctuation omits punctuation after both the salutation and the closing. Figure 38-5 shows this style.

LETTER FORMATS

Most business letters are arranged in one of four basic formats. On the job, you will need to discover which format your employer prefers.

Block Style

The block letter is so named because all lines begin at the left margin, giving each element a rectangular appearance. Only items such as quoted material (which is indented five spaces from each margin), charts, and the like are not blocked at the left. Figure 38-5 shows a block style letter.

APEX
PRESS

150 East 55 Street
New York, NY 10022 4422
(212) 555 4600

January 19, 1988

CONFIDENTIAL

Theresa Diaz, M.D.
1900 Bates Road
Downers Grove, IL 60516-3135

Dear Dr. Diaz

Thank you for agreeing to review the manuscript for the Healthwise volume on
nutrition. The enclosed Consultant Review Sheet will help you understand the
type of review we are seeking. Please be sure to bring this sheet with you,
along with any questions you have, when you arrive at the Richmond Hotel for
the consultants' conference during the week of February 8 through 13.

I am also happy to enclose with this letter a check for $1,000, the initial
installment of your fee for this work.

I look forward to seeing you at the conference.

Sincerely yours

Peter M. Tilton

Peter M. Tilton
Health Editor

rft
Enclosures:
1. Consultant Review Sheet
2. Check 56834
Certified Mail

Figure 38-5 Block-style letter.

Modified Block Style—Standard

In the standard modified block style, all lines begin at the left margin except for the following three:

- the dateline
- the complimentary closing
- the signature block

These three items begin at the center point and extend to the right. Figure 38-6 shows this style.

Modified Block Style—Indented Paragraphs

The modified block style with indented paragraphs is the same as the standard modified block except that the first line of each paragraph of the message is indented, usually five spaces. Figure 38-7 shows this style.

Simplified Style (AMS Style)

A special style of letter has been developed by the Administrative Management Society. Follow these guidelines to type a letter following this format, which is called the simplified style:

- Begin all lines at the left margin.
- Omit the salutation. In its place, type a subject line in uppercase letters on the third line below the inside address. Do not use the word *SUBJECT* or a colon; type only the actual topic.
- Omit the complimentary closing.
- Within the signature block, type the writer's name and position all on one line, in uppercase letters. Separate the name from the title by typing a hyphen, preceded and followed by a space. Place this on the fifth line below the final line of the body.
- Use the recipient's name in at least the first sentence to make the letter more personal.

Figure 38-8 shows the simplified style of letter.

TYPES OF BUSINESS LETTERS

Most of the business letters you write will fall into one of four categories: routine, diplomatic refusal, sales, and social-business.

Routine letters enable a business to conduct many of its day-to-day operations and to function successfully. They include requests for information, appointments, reservations, products, and services, as well as responses to requests. Other kinds include letters accompanying documents and letters

700 West 184 Street New York, NY 10033-5000 (212) 555-7000

January 26, 1988

Apex Press
150 East 55 Street
New York, NY 10022-4422

Attention: Administrative Assistant, Book Department

Ladies and Gentlemen:

We have received your request for the reservation of a suite of rooms for
February 8 through 13. We are setting aside the 7th floor of the hotel for 34
guests, as well as Meeting Room B from 8 a.m. to 10 p.m. from February 9 through
13.

Please look over the enclosed description of hotel meal plans. One of the most
popular with conference groups is Plan B-1, which provides the following:

• A continental breakfast in the Sunflower Room
• A diner's-choice lunch in the Sunflower Room
• A full-course dinner, with choice of three entrées, in the Executive Dining
  Room
• Coffee, soft drinks, juice, and snacks in the meeting room throughout the
  day

Thank you for choosing the Richmond Hotel for your conference. We are sure
that the friendly staff and pleasant atmosphere will contribute to the success of the conference. Please let us know if any of your guests have special
needs for which we can provide. Your comfort is always our concern.

Very cordially yours,

RICHMOND HOTEL

W. Marshall Saunders, Manager

Enclosure
C: L. Fogle
   E. Poitras

Figure 38-6 Modified block-style letter—standard.

APEX PRESS 150 East 55 Street
New York, NY 10022-4422
(212) 555-4600

January 29, 1988

Ms. Laura MacGill
344 West 49 Street
New York, NY 10019-6869

Dear Laura:

Subject: Copyediting for the Healthwise Series

    It was good to talk with you yesterday. You must know how glad I was to
hear that you will copyedit the Healthwise manuscripts on a free-lance basis.
Your precise attention to details of grammar, punctuation, and style as well
as your accurate fact-checking will make this a valuable resource for our
audience.

    The enclosed information sheet gives you an overview of the project as
well as a tentative editorial schedule. Do the turnaround times seem reasonable to you?

    I am looking forward to our 10:00 meeting on Wednesday morning, February
4, to discuss the details of the project.

                    Cordially,

                    Peter M. Tilton

                    Peter M. Tilton
                    Health Editor

cem
Enc.
c M. Ashley

PS. Would you mind bringing some pictures from your recent trip to France?
Perhaps you could fill me in on your adventures over lunch.

Figure 38-7 Modified block-style letter—indented paragraphs.

100 Middle Street   Bridgeport, CT 06604-4009

February 23, 1988

Mr. Raymond Guerra
Apex Press
150 East 55 Street
New York, NY 10022-4422

TYPESETTING BY LETTER PERFECT PRESS

As the production manager for a large publisher, Mr. Guerra, you are faced
with important considerations when choosing a typesetter. You need a press
that you can depend on for ''letter perfect'' results that are on time and
competitively priced.

We believe that Letter Perfect Press is the answer to your typesetting needs.
One of our sales representatives, Meredith Ankram, will call within the next
few days to explain the advantages of typesetting the Letter Perfect way.

Paul Chiang

PAUL CHIANG — PRESIDENT, LETTER PERFECT PRESS

dl

Figure 38-8 Simplified-style letter.

conveying information to customers and clients. In Chapter 39, you will learn and practice the techniques for developing a routine business letter.

Diplomatic refusals, or "bad-news letters," are sent when a company cannot honor a customer's request. These letters must be written tactfully, using a positive approach, to not alienate the recipient. Their purpose is to retain goodwill by helping the reader understand the reason for the company's refusal. You will learn and practice the techniques for writing diplomatic refusals in Chapter 40.

Although every letter sent by a company should contribute positively to business, the primary purpose of certain letters is increasing profits. They are written with a very specific audience in mind and with the purpose of persuading this audience to buy a product or service or to accept an idea. In Chapter 41, you will find out more about writing sales letters.

Because there is no longer a strong dividing line between business and social life, many business messages actually have a social purpose as well. These social-business letters include thank-you notes for such things as gifts, courtesies, and business referrals; letters of congratulation for promotions, honors, and births; letters of sympathy; and formal invitations and replies. Social-business letters will be covered in Chapter 42.

PLANNING A BUSINESS LETTER

As you have learned, a business letter represents you and your company to the person who receives it. A hastily written letter that omits important details, presents ideas in a disorganized fashion, or has an inappropriate tone can have a negative impact on the recipient. This can in return, rebound against the company.

In planning a business letter, it will help you to remember the following five basic steps:

1. Know your purpose.

2. Become informed.

3. Organize your information.

4. Write a rough draft.

5. Make it easy for your reader to respond.

Know Your Purpose

Your first step is deciding on the purpose of your letter and the type of letter you need to write. Your goal may be to announce an upcoming meeting, to ask a customer to pay an overdue account, or to clarify the details of a contract. Generally, you should let the reader know the purpose of the letter in the first paragraph. In Chapters 39 to 42, you will learn more about how to state your purpose in various types of letters.

Become Informed

Your next step is to gather all the information you need. Find out all the facts and be specific about them. As you gather your information, you may find it helpful to make a list of the facts you plan to include. A list can help you check facts and figures for accuracy and give you a head start on the next step in planning, which is organizing information.

Organize Your Information

You will accomplish your purpose most efficiently if you present all the points in a logical order. One way to ensure that your presentation will be logical is to consider your reader's needs as you organize. Generally, your letters should be organized in the following manner.

- Tell the reader the purpose of the letter and present the main idea.
- Support the main idea by presenting explanatory details.
- Summarize the main idea and close the letter in a pleasant and positive way.

As you arrange the facts for a letter, look for logical groupings of ideas. Put the basic facts in the first paragraph. In two or more body paragraphs, you can provide supporting details. Depending on your topic, you may arrange these details in order from most to least important, from least to most important, or sequentially. In the concluding paragraph, you can restate your main idea and bring the letter to a satisfying close.

It may help to draw up a simple outline to use as a basis for your rough draft.

Write the Rough Draft

Now, working from the notes you made in the previous step, write a rough draft of your letter. Once your ideas are on paper in draft form, you can take the time to edit thoroughly. As you reread your letter, consider the following questions:

- Does your letter use an appropriate tone? Is it tactful and courteous?
- Is the letter expressed in positive terms that will create goodwill?
- Is the letter free of sexist language, such as "businessmen" instead of *business people*?
- Does the letter focus on the reader? Does it use *you* and *your* more often than *I*, *we*, *my*, and *our*?
- Are the spelling, grammar, and punctuation correct?

As you make necessary changes in your rough draft, use the proofreading symbols you studied in Chapter 18 to correct it. This rough draft, marked for correction, will be the basis for your final draft.

Make It Easy for the Reader to Respond

If you want an individual to respond in some way to your letter, make sure that person can respond easily. One way to do this is to attach a return slip. Another is to prepare a section of the letter so it can be torn off and mailed. A third response technique is to provide a telephone number. Some companies provide toll-free numbers; others simply list their regular business numbers.

EDITING EXERCISES

Retype the following business letter parts, correcting any format errors. If a letter part has no mistakes, write the word *correct* next to it.

1. Feb. 19, 1988
   (dateline)

2. Carl DenBleyker
   400 South 15 Street
   Philadelphia, PA
   19107-2824
   (inside address)

3. dear Ms. Skenon:
   (salutation)

4. Sincerely Yours,
   (complimentary closing)

5. January 23d, 1988
   (dateline)

6. Very cordially yours,
   William Francione, Credit Manager
   (signature block)

7. Apex Press
   (company signature)

8. Attn: Ms. Beverly Espenshade
   (attention line)

PROBLEMS

A. Suppose that another typist has finished a letter to Dr. Yolanda Washington in Encino, California, but has gone home sick before typing the envelope. Type the following address in the proper format on a No. 10 blank envelope. Put Peter M. Tilton's name and the Apex Press address where the return address should go. Type the attention line separate from the address.

1. Attention line:
   Attention: Dr. Yolanda Washington

2. Address:
   Encino Medical Associates
   17421 Ventura Boulevard
   Encino, CA 91316-5555

3. Mailing notation:
   SPECIAL DELIVERY

B. Type a short letter addressed to one of your classmates, describing the kind of position you would like to hold in a company. Use one of the four basic letter styles, and use any two optional letter parts correctly.

C. Use the following information to compose a letter in each of the four letter styles. Within the letters, use each punctuation style at least once. You do not need to use all the possible letter parts in every letter.

1. Letterhead:
   Apex Press
   150 East 55 Street
   New York, NY 10022-4422
   (212) 555-4600

2. Dateline:
   February 16, 1988

3. Inside address:
   Mr. Jeremy Levin
   85 East Elm Street
   Brookline, MA 02144-5678

4. Subject line:
   CONSULTANTS' CONFERENCE

5. Salutation:
   Dear Mr. Levin

6. Message:
   Thank you for participating in our recent conference for the Healthwise book series. I feel that much was accomplished and that together we will create a valuable resource for the health consumer.

   Please feel free to call me with any questions or comments as we continue this project.

7. Complimentary closing:
Sincerely

8. Signature block:
Peter M. Tilton
Health Editor

9. Reference initials:
(your initials)

10. Copy notation:
M. Ashley
L. Rothberg

11. Postscript:
If you have any suggestions that might improve future conferences of this type, please jot them down and send them to me. I would appreciate your comments.

PROJECTS

Collect 10 to 12 copies of actual business letters. For each, do the following:

1. Identify the letter arrangement format and punctuation style.

2. Identify each part of the letter (letterhead, dateline, etc.).

3. Note any format errors.

In addition, study the letterhead style(s) carefully. Does the letterhead contain a logo or slogan? Does it project a particular image?

39
Writing Routine Business Letters

Routine letters make up the major portion of the correspondence that is received and sent by most business offices. These letters include requests, responses to requests, cover letters used to transmit documents, and acknowledgment letters.

Though routine letters are very common, this does not minimize their importance. Look, for example, at one routine piece of correspondence. A short time ago Susan Welman wrote to the guest relations office of WXCZ Television. She asked if her seven-year-old niece would be allowed to use one of the tickets she had obtained for the taping of a television quiz show called *Dollar Dynamics*. Today she received the following answer from the station:

Yes, she can.

Ms. Welman's first reaction might be "Who is 'she,' and what can she do?" After Ms. Welman had a chance to recall her request, she would probably be pleased with the affirmative answer but unsettled by the brevity of the response.

When John Suneski, an administrative assistant at WXCZ, was assigned the task of answering Ms. Welman's inquiry, he took the easy, but unacceptable, way out. He answered her question without taking the time to write a letter. In doing so, he compromised the reputation of the television studio.

Although routine letters are not difficult to write, they deserve as much attention as letters that are more of a challenge. In this chapter, you will learn the basic rules for organizing and writing routine letters. Then you will learn and practice specific techniques for writing requests, responses to requests, letters of transmittal, letters of acknowledgment, and printed responses.

THE NATURE OF A ROUTINE LETTER

You have already learned that routine letters are those that conduct many of the day-to-day operations that enable a business to function successfully. Letters requesting information, appointments, reservations, products, and services are typical of the everyday letters written by businesses. Other examples include responses to requests; letters accompanying documents; and letters acknowledging orders, appointments, and oral agreements.

Each of these common business letters is considered routine because it is intended to have a neutral effect on the reader. Routine letters do not address special problems such as persuading the reader to take a specific course of action or refusing to grant the reader's request. Instead, they enable the business to communicate in an efficient and professional manner with its customers about the many details of day-to-day operations.

Many businesses rely on secretaries or administrative assistants to draft much of the routine correspondence that is signed by the management. In other business offices, secretaries and administrative assistants both write *and* sign most routine correspondence. Still other offices ask their secretaries or administrative assistants to produce routine boilerplate letters, using paragraphs that have been programmed into word processing systems. An assistant at WXCZ Television, for example, might use this method for acknowledging the program suggestions that often come from viewers. The acknowledgment would be called up, and such information as the viewer's name, address, and program idea would be added. Information commenting on the idea might also be added.

By assigning this responsibility to support personnel, managers gain more time to devote to other activities. Routine correspondence, however, represents the company in a very important way. Even a very short, routine letter can help a reader retain confidence in a company or, conversely, doubt its business competence. The next section will help you understand how to organize and write routine letters.

PLANNING ROUTINE LETTERS

As you plan a routine letter, you should follow a basic outline that arranges the information so that the reader can quickly and easily understand it. You will also need to use sound letter-writing skills that include considering who your audience is, what your purpose is, and how to express your ideas briefly, completely, and courteously.

Organizing Routine Letters

The following basic outline will help you to structure most routine letters.

1. Begin with a statement of purpose.
2. Provide any details necessary to clarify the purpose.
3. Close with a statement of goodwill.

The following letter is an improved version of the one-line letter John Suneski wrote to Susan Welman. Notice how each of the paragraphs within the letter expands on one of the subpoints of the basic outline just given.

The first paragraph clearly informs Ms. Welman that she will be able to bring her seven-year-old niece to the taping of *Dollar Dynamics*. The second paragraph clarifies the guest relations policy by indicating that children must be at least six years old and that Ms. Welman's niece must be accompanied by an adult in order to attend the taping. These added details ensure that Ms. Welman will not change her plans and ask her nephew, who is only five years old, to join her on the visit to WXCZ. John's first letter to Ms. Welman left out this important information.

The final paragraph of the letter is a simple goodwill statement indicating that the studio hopes Ms. Welman enjoys her visit. It demonstrates WXCZ's interest in a continuing relationship.

Drafting Routine Letters

As you prepare the rough draft of your routine letter, take special care to be brief, complete, tactful, and courteous. Try to compose the letter to give it a personal touch.

Be Brief. When John Suneski wrote his letter to Susan Welman, he was much too brief. But many beginning writers have just the opposite problem: They write in a style that is too wordy. Needless information merely distracts the reader.

Be Complete. Brevity is important, but not at the expense of completeness. If the second paragraph of the letter in Figure 39-1 merely said that Ms. Welman's niece met the requirements without saying how—let alone that an adult should accompany her—important information would have been missing. John's actual response is an extreme example of completeness sacrificed to brevity.

Before drafting a routine letter, be sure to jot down the information you need to convey, and check your list for completeness. This list will help you avoid leaving out necessary information.

Be Tactful and Courteous. Although you may not intend to offend your reader with your letter, you may do so if you concentrate only on your message and not on the receiver of that message.

Some readers will be offended if your letter is too impersonal. Others will feel that you are being discourteous if you fail to comment on friendly remarks they have made in their letter to you. In both cases, keeping a "you" focus and responding to specific points in the message will maintain goodwill.

A viewer has written to WXCZ complimenting the station on its complete and interesting tour of the broadcast facilities. In addition, she has asked about

Guest Relations Office
126 Pierre Avenue
New Orleans, Louisiana 70116-7575

July 1, 1988

Ms. Susan Welman
555 Lockman Circle
Zwolle, LA 70058-2797

Dear Ms. Welman:

You will be pleased to know that your seven-year-old niece will be welcome
to attend the taping of <u>Dollar Dynamics</u> on August 1, using one of the tickets you obtained for the show.

Your niece meets the qualifications of our guest relations policy, which
specifies that children in the audience be at least six years of age. We do
ask, however, that you or some other adult accompany your niece to the taping.

We hope you enjoy your visit to our studio and continue to be pleased with
WXCZ programming.

Cordially,

John Suneski

John Suneski
Administrative Assistant

Figure 39-1 A routine letter.

tickets for the *Noon in New Orleans* show. John has written the following answer:

> We have received your letter of August 15. Pursuant to your request, free tickets are available for the *Noon in New Orleans* show on a first-come, first-served basis. Write to WXCZ TICKETS at this address, and specify a first and second choice of ticket dates.
>
> At this time the earliest available tickets are for the September 15 show.

Although John included the necessary details about *Noon in New Orleans,* he neglected to thank the writer for her kind comments about the studio tour. It appears from John's letter that the studio did not appreciate her taking the time to write.

In addition, the tone of John's letter is inappropriate for its purpose. In the first place, the tone is too formal. The legal-sounding expression *pursuant to* will not help John maintain goodwill. Secondly, John has not included a "you" emphasis. Thanking the viewer specifically for her appreciative remarks would be an effective way to focus on the reader. John might open his letter in the following way:

> Thank you for your very kind words about the studio tour. It is always good to know that our efforts to please you are appreciated.

The guidelines you have just learned for organizing and drafting routine letters apply to a variety of routine correspondence situations. In the next sections, you will learn useful techniques for writing various kinds of everyday correspondence.

WRITING REQUESTS

Four of the most common types of request letters written in business offices ask for information, orders, appointments, and reservations.

Requests for Information

A letter requesting general information, literature, or free services can be very short, but it must also be complete. The letter need only include a description of the information or service required and a brief goodwill statement. Sometimes a short explanation of why you are making the request is appropriate. The inclusion of a return address is not necessary if the letter is typed on company letterhead, but it is essential if the letter is typed on plain bond paper.

For example, an employee of the guest relations office at WXCZ might request the following literature from the Apex Novelty Company.

> Please send me a copy of your *Guest Relations Specialty Catalogue.* I would also like to receive a brochure describing your new training manual titled *Treasured Techniques for Tour Guides.*
>
> We have been pleased with your products and training publications in the past and look forward to using them again this year.

Requests for Orders

If you work in a small company, you may be asked to order merchandise by writing an order letter. Although larger companies usually use specially designed purchase order forms, many small companies write letters that carefully spell out the items they wish to order. Figure 39-2 shows an order letter that Andrea Cohen of WXCZ has prepared after examining the *Guest Relations Specialty Catalogue* from the Apex Novelty Company.

Andrea used the following company guidelines to prepare the letter to Apex Novelty:

- Open your first sentence with words such as *Please send* or *Please ship.*
- Include all the necessary order details such as quantity, item number, size, price, color, special engraving, and so on.
- Indicate the method of payment you plan to follow.
- Include shipping instructions.
- Indicate your expected delivery date.

Notice that Andrea tabulated the ordered items. In this case, a table is much clearer than the same information in paragraph form.

She also checked her figures and item numbers very carefully and determined the applicable sales tax rate, the method of delivery, who will pay the freight charges, and the expected delivery date. All of this information was provided in the supplier's catalogue.

Requests for Appointments

Requests for appointments with people who are nearby are often handled by telephone. If, however, you are requesting an appointment with someone who is in a distant city or even another country, you will probably handle this request with a letter. Your request should include the proposed date, time, and purpose of the appointment, as well as the length of time you expect it to take. It is also a good idea to include a number at which you can be reached prior to the appointment in case it must be changed. Figure 39-3 shows a letter written by Rochelle Gardner, guest relations director of WXCZ Television, in preparation for her business trip to Chicago.

Requests for Reservations

Although you can make hotel reservations by telephone, you may prefer to write a letter. By doing so, you will have a record of the reservation information you have provided and you can be sure that the hotel has received the same information. Of course, if time is short or many individuals will be requesting accommodations at the same time (as for a large conference), you will want to call for the reservation.

**Guest Relations Office
126 Pierre Avenue
New Orleans, Louisiana 70116-7575**

July 12, 1988

Apex Novelty Company
Attention: Marketing Manager
867 Bloomington Drive
Franklin Lakes, NJ 07417-8880

Dear Marketing Manager:

Please send us the following items from your Guest Relations Specialty Catalogue.

Quantity	Item	Description	Unit Price	Total
25 dozen	650-L	Keychains	6.50 dozen	162.50
22 boxes	722-G	Name Badges	12.00 (Box of 100)	264.00
14 dozen	555-W	T-Shirts	35.75 dozen	500.50
8 dozen	976-T	Coffee Mugs	27.50 dozen	220.00
			Total	$1,147.00

Each item should be printed with the WXCZ Television logo. Please prepare the T-shirts in your standard size assortment. I have added a color code letter, as specified in your catalogue, to each of the item numbers. An art sheet containing camera-ready copies of our logo in assorted sizes is included with the order.

I understand that there is no sales tax for items shipped to other states and that your company will pay the shipping charges. Please bill us using your standard 2/10, net 30 terms.

Your catalogue indicates that deliveries will be shipped via United Parcel Service within six weeks. If for any reason we will not have delivery by September 1, please call me at (504) 555-1986. We look forward to offering your quality novelty items in our WXCZ Gift Shop for the fall tour season.

Sincerely yours,

Andrea Cohen

Andrea Cohen
Guest Policy Coordinator

Enclosure

Figure 39-2 Request for order.

Guest Relations Office
126 Pierre Avenue
New Orleans, Louisiana 70116-7575

December 15, 1988

Mr. Charles Williams
Guest Relations Office
WPON Television
144 North Michigan Avenue
Chicago, IL 60608-3939

Dear Mr. Williams:

On January 19 and 20 I will be in Chicago and would like to talk with you
about your station's efforts to improve guest relations. Your exciting new
viewer participation program also interests me greatly.

Would it be convenient for you to see me at 2 p.m. on Thursday, January 19?
An hour of your time would be much appreciated. You can reach me at the
above address until January 18; I will be staying at the Blake Hotel while I
am in Chicago. I shall appreciate it if you share your experience with me.

Sincerely,

Rochelle Gardner

Rochelle Gardner
Guest Relations Director

Figure 39-3 Request for appointment.

A good reservation letter includes the following items:

- the name of the person needing accommodations
- the dates of arrival and departure
- the type of accommodations needed

You may also include the expected price of the room and the time of arrival.

Reservations are usually held only until 6 p.m. unless the first night's accommodations have already been paid for. If the room should be held for "late arrival" (after 6 p.m.), specify this in your letter, and enclose a check or provide a credit card number.

If the traveler has any special needs or preferences—such as a double room or accommodations on the ground floor—you should describe them in the letter. This may be especially important if you must reserve a room that has been equipped for the disabled.

When Andrea Cohen reserved a room at the Blake Hotel for Rochelle Gardner, she wrote the following information in the body of her letter:

> Ms. Rochelle Gardner, the guest relations director of station WXCZ, would like a single room for the night of January 17, with a January 18 departure date.
>
> She will arrive at 8 p.m. and would like the reservation held for late arrival. Ms. Gardner will charge the room to American Cheque Card Account No. 8722 511298 91006.
>
> We look forward to your confirmation of this reservation and the price of $69 per night. Thank you.

WRITING RESPONSES TO REQUESTS

You may also be asked to answer requests that have been sent to your office. These requests should be answered as quickly as possible—within a day or two of receipt—because your prospective customer may lose interest in your product or service if the answer is delayed.

State the answer to your customer's request at the beginning of the letter and express appreciation for the inquiry. Then provide necessary details. The tone of your letter should be helpful and sales-minded.

Paul Pulaski was recently asked to answer a letter from the author of *Fun on a Shoestring*, a book of inexpensive activities in and around New Orleans. The letter asked for information about the studio tours and free guest tickets to the taping of television talk and quiz shows. The following excerpt shows the body of Paul's response:

> Thank you for including WXCZ Television in *Fun on a Shoestring*. We offer complete studio tours at 10 a.m., 2 p.m., and 4:30 p.m. Monday through Friday. The price of the tour is only $2.50, and when the tour is completed, each guest receives a coupon worth $2.50 at our WXCZ gift shop.
>
> Tickets are available for all of our local shows at no charge. A complete list of shows is enclosed with this letter, together with information on how to order tickets.
>
> Thank you for listing us as an interesting activity in *Fun on a Shoestring*.

WRITING LETTERS OF TRANSMITTAL

Letters of transmittal, which are also known as cover letters, are written to accompany checks, advertising pamphlets, price lists, catalogues, reports, and any other items that are sent by a business. When you write a transmittal letter, you let the recipient of the letter know what you are sending, why it is being sent, and what you expect the person to do in response.

For example, WXCZ has published a catalogue of the novelty items that are featured in its gift shop. In answer to a letter asking how to order WXCZ coffee mugs and T-shirts, Paul Pulaski wrote this to accompany the gift catalogue:

> Thank you for your letter requesting order information for WXCZ gift shop items. The enclosed catalogue lists all our merchandise, including the WXCZ coffee mug (page 14) and T-shirts (page 27) that you specifically asked about.
>
> We are delighted that you like our novelty items and look forward to receiving your order. An order form and a stamped, addressed envelope are included on page 32 of the catalogue for your convenience.

WRITING LETTERS OF ACKNOWLEDGMENT

The guest relations office at WXCZ Television, like other business offices, is in the habit of acknowledging the receipt of much of its incoming correspondence. The office makes it a practice to acknowledge appointments, requests, oral agreements, orders, and group tour reservations.

In sending such letters, the office creates a record that indicates incoming correspondence has been received and acted upon. Copies of acknowledgment letters provide documentation to help the station avoid misunderstandings.

Organizing the Acknowledgment Letter

Acknowledgment letters begin with a statement of appreciation for the reader's actions. This statement is followed by supporting details. If the letter acknowledges the receipt of money, it indicates the amount and purpose. If it acknowledges an order, the letter identifies the order (by number, if it is submitted on a numbered order form) and specifies the time and method of delivery. As with all business letters, the acknowledgment letter ends with a statement designed to promote goodwill.

The letter that follows acknowledges the receipt of a group tour reservation form.

> Thank you for selecting WXCZ Television as one of your tour stops while you are in New Orleans. We have arranged a special 11 a.m. tour exclusively for your group of 25 students on Tuesday, February 16.
>
> Please assemble the group at the information desk of the fourteenth floor of our building at 126 Pierre Avenue at 10:50 a.m. The tour will last approximately 80 minutes, and I have made special arrangements for your students to meet talk-show host Craig Lewins at the conclusion of their tour.
>
> We look forward to seeing you on the morning of February 16.

Acknowledging Letters for Your Manager

Some correspondence can be handled only by managers. When they are out of town, it is still important to acknowledge receipt of incoming mail. Letters of this type should be courteous and brief. In addition, they should be non-committal, avoiding any statements that might be read as official reactions to the content of the letter. It is not usually necessary to state exactly where the manager has gone or what he or she is doing there. As a matter of fact, many managers caution against giving out such information.

When Rochelle Gardner was out of the office for two weeks, a letter and catalogue arrived from Jacob Malestrom, sales representative of a specialty gift company. The catalogue illustrated items that the station might add to their gift shop offerings. Impressed with the products, John Suneski wrote:

> Thank you for your letter and catalogue.
> Rochelle Gardner, the guest relations director of WXCZ, will be out of the office until March 1. You will hear from her as soon as she has had an opportunity to review your catalogue.

This letter told Mr. Malestrom all he needed to know without committing the company to an order or revealing Ms. Gardner's personal business.

WRITING PRINTED RESPONSES

If you expect thousands of responses to an offer, you might consider constructing a printed response in advance. The printed response will not be addressed personally to your customer, but it should be written in a friendly manner that will retain goodwill.

The guest relations office at WXCZ created a special offer to stimulate interest in audience participation. Every viewer who submitted the rating form that was widely published in local newspapers received a free coffee mug and an opportunity to be chosen as a contestant on *Dollar Dynamics.* The following letter went to every respondent:

> Dear WXCZ Viewer:
> Thank you for submitting your completed rating form. Your comments will help us to produce the type of programming you most enjoy. In appreciation for your help, we are sending you a colorful ceramic WXCZ coffee mug by separate mail this afternoon.
> As a participant in our survey, you will have the opportunity to appear as a contestant on *Dollar Dynamics.* The winning contestant will be notified by mail on Monday, May 2.
> Thank you for watching WXCZ Television and for helping us to make it your kind of station.

Note that even though this same response goes to many individuals, the strong "you" focus of the letter personalizes the message for each reader.

EDITING EXERCISES

Each of the following is an excerpt from a piece of routine correspondence. Rewrite each excerpt to give it stronger "you" focus.

1. I have always enjoyed staying at the Blake Hotel in the past and I am sure I will continue to do so.

2. We certainly appreciate the kind words about our new children's program, *Wee Workout.*

3. We have been very happy with the products we have used in the past and look forward to a continuing relationship.

4. I am very pleased to be able to send our *Telethon Premium Catalogue.* I think that the items on pages 10 through 25 will be of particular interest.

5. We are grateful that the questionnaire we sent was returned so quickly.

6. I am very interested in discussing the "viewer enrichment program" that has been developed by your station. May I come at 10 a.m. on Wednesday, August 10, to discuss the program?

7. We will be glad to send a free copy of our publication *Broadcasting and You.* We hope it will help with career decisions.

8. The tour of our station will begin in the outer lobby. We will finish in the *Dollar Dynamics* taping area, Studio B.

PROBLEMS

A. Suppose that you are working for Rochelle Gardner at WXCZ Television. She has asked you to write a request letter to Mr. Jacob Malestrom, Guest Gift House, 347 Jackson Avenue, Janesville, WI 53534-6212. Mr. Malestrom sent a letter and catalogue of specialty gifts to the office in Rochelle's absence. She has now returned and would like to take advantage of an offer that Mr. Malestrom made in his letter. Rochelle would like Guest Gift House to send samples of three products in the catalogue: the leather coin purse shown on page 3, the pen on page 7, and the notepad on page 8.

   WXCZ will return these items within one week and will pay return postage. Write an appropriate request letter to Mr. Malestrom. Sign your own name to the letter.

B. Assume that Rochelle wants to order the three items she has seen from Guest Gift House along with one additional item. She would like you to write an order letter to Guest Gift House at the address shown in the previous exercise.

   Order 8 dozen leather coin purses (item 4356) at a price of $15 per dozen; 24 dozen pens (item 5112) at a price of $10 per dozen; 30 boxes of notepads (item 1336) at $20 per box; and 5 dozen clipboards (item 9732) at a price of $25 per dozen.

Indicate that the WXCZ Television logo should be printed on each item and that you have included an art sheet containing camera-ready copies of the logo in assorted sizes.

Calculate the total price for each item and the total price for the order. (There is no sales tax charged for shipments outside Wisconsin.) Guest Gift House pays shipping costs, uses standard 2/10, net 30 terms, and ships via United Parcel Service within eight weeks. Write your letter following an accepted letter arrangement format.

C. Assume that Rochelle is out of the office for two weeks, and you must acknowledge her mail. This week she is in London attending a special broadcasting workshop. Next week she will be on vacation in Ireland and Scotland.

The office has received a letter from Mr. Damian Chen of New Orleans Community Charities, 2356 Bonbon Avenue, New Orleans, LA 70118-4141, asking the guest relations office to help organize and run the usher service at the annual charity telethon. The telethon will be broadcast on another local television station, but there is still a need for qualified help.

You think aiding the telethon would be a good idea, but the decision will have to be made by Rochelle and her superiors at the studio. Write an appropriate response.

D. Suppose that you are working in the business office of WXCZ Television. You must compose a transmittal letter to accompany a check (number 14657) for $1,000 paid to Mr. Geoffrey Cecil (300 South 10 Street, Philadelphia, PA 19107) for appearing as a guest on *Idle Chatter*, one of the station's celebrity talk shows. Your station hopes to invite Mr. Cecil again as a guest in the future. Sign your own name to the letter.

PROJECTS

Talk to several secretaries or administrative assistants about their roles in writing routine correspondence. Find out about the following:

1. Do they do much drafting of letters and, if so, are they given extensive guidance about what should be included?

2. What are their supervisors' policies on acknowledging correspondence in their absence? Are employees to give information about the supervisors' whereabouts? If so, under what circumstances? If not, why not?

3. Do they make use of boilerplate material? If so, how do they personalize it for individual readers?

40
Developing Diplomatic Refusals

How do you say no to a friend? In most cases it isn't easy. You must be a skillful diplomat to accomplish the tricky task of presenting the bad news without making the person angry, creating hurt feelings, or even jeopardizing your friendship.

Businesses frequently have to say no to requests. Refusing these requests without losing goodwill is as difficult as saying no to a friend, and it requires the same sensitivity. Typically, businesses have to say no to the following:

- requests for products that are out of stock or discontinued
- requests for jobs when there are no openings or when applicants are unqualified
- requests for inappropriate or classified information
- requests for salary increases which are not deserved or which cannot be approved for financial reasons
- requests for donations to charitable causes that are beyond the company budget
- requests for credit by unacceptable credit risks

Tactless refusals by a company will lose many potential customers and loyal employees. In this chapter, you will learn the basic techniques for developing diplomatic refusal letters. First, you will look at the ways in which refusal letters differ from other business correspondence. Next, you will examine the outline of an effective refusal letter and the characteristics it should have. Finally, you will look at some attitudes and actions to avoid when trying to say no diplomatically.

A well-written refusal letter resembles other types of business letters in that it is courteous and prompt, thereby promoting goodwill toward the company. But a refusal letter differs from a routine letter because it presents the key idea *last*. Rather than stating the purpose in the first paragraph, a refusal letter places the actual refusal after an explanation that helps the reader understand why the company must say no. If the refusal statement comes too early in the letter, the reader may become discouraged or angry and read no further.

A successful refusal letter, therefore, should be written in the following manner:

1. Begin with a neutral comment as an introduction.
2. Explain the situation in a positive light.
3. State the refusal, along with alternatives.
4. End positively without mentioning the refusal.

You can see how these elements would work in a refusal letter to Roberta Giles, who has applied for a position with the product-testing laboratory of the Homan Company, a manufacturer of health and beauty care products.

The Neutral Introduction

The letter opens with a neutral statement that both the writer and the reader can agree upon. The opening comment should indicate the subject of the letter but should imply neither a yes nor a no decision.

> Thank you for applying for the laboratory technician position at Homan Company's La Cienega branch.

Ms. Giles is eager to find out whether she has been hired; this beginning introduces the subject of the letter—her application—and keeps her reading further.

The Positive Explanation

The neutral introduction is followed by a positive explanation of the background for the refusal. Presenting the reasons before stating the actual refusal will be more likely to convince the reader that the company has carefully considered the application or request and has said no with justification.

> As we discussed last Friday, we are still in the process of reviewing both the personnel requirements and the organization of the product-testing laboratory.

The Statement of Refusal

The next segment of the letter includes the statement of refusal. If possible, this statement of refusal should also suggest an alternative. Perhaps the statement of refusal can even offer the reader some hope for the future.

> We have decided not to hire new personnel for our product-testing laboratory until this period of reorganization is complete. We will, however, keep your application in our active files and review it seriously when we are ready to hire.

The Polite Conclusion

The conclusion of the refusal letter should be positive and should avoid mentioning the refusal. Its purpose is to keep the goodwill of the reader.

> We wish you success in your career and look forward to talking with you again when our personnel needs change.

CHARACTERISTICS OF AN EFFECTIVE REFUSAL

Effective refusal letters maintain the goodwill of both customers and employees when they are prompt, positive, and supply good reasons (not an apology) for the refusal.

Promptness

Recipients of refusal letters deserve the same courtesy that is extended to other readers. It is discourteous to be late. A late response makes readers feel ignored; their goodwill will be diminished before the letter is opened. In some cases you may do great harm. For instance, your delay could keep job applicants from seeking employment with other companies that might hire them.

A Positive Attitude

Sometimes writers of refusal letters find it difficult to send a negative message in a positive way. There are several specific techniques, however, for being positive in a refusal letter. The following sections illustrate two important methods.

Stress the Positive Aspects of the Situation. You might compliment an unsuccessful job applicant on having impressive credentials, even though the individual's background is not right for the job with your company. If you must tell a customer that an order will be incomplete, stress the fact that part of it is being sent. Estimate when the remainder should arrive. Even if you cannot grant a request, show appreciation for the person's efforts in making it. In rejecting a suggestion, you might comment that the individual's idea shows ingenuity and an understanding of your company, even though it cannot be used at the present time.

ON THE JOB
Managing Your Time

Wayne Nelson manages a toy store. Although he has a full staff and works extra hours himself, he can't seem to keep up with his work. The overtime he puts in also leaves him little time for his personal life.

There are many orders for popular toys that Wayne has not yet sent to the manufacturers. At the same time, his storeroom is filled with boxes of new toys that haven't yet been put on the store shelves. How can Wayne improve his job efficiency?

He could learn from effective managers who practice a few simple rules of time management. Effective managers set aside some time at the beginning of each day during which they work undisturbed. During this time, they may catch up on correspondence or do other paperwork. Good managers also set aside time to make and receive phone calls. Although much business communication and paperwork are routine, making sure that they get done promptly is a vital aspect of any business. This practice helps managers ensure that they will not fall behind

in their orders and that customers, suppliers, and others who deal with the company will not be neglected.

Good managers achieve efficiency partly by sharing responsibilities with other workers. They make effective use of their employees' time as well as their own. By doing so, they avoid long hours of overtime, which can have a negative effect on productivity; a tired worker can make costly errors.

Wayne wants to use some of these time-management tips to both increase his work output and decrease extra hours on the job. He plans to arrive at the store at eight in the morning, two hours before it opens. He will use this quiet time to write orders and to place and receive telephone calls. Instead of trying to stock the shelves himself, he is going to assign the task to two of his employees, giving him enough time to handle customer questions and complaints.

Using these techniques, Wayne should be able to leave the store when it closes at 5 p.m., with enough energy left to enjoy his free time.

Reject the Request, Not the Person. If Marianna Rose has submitted a proposal that your company cannot use, be careful to reject the proposal— not Ms. Rose. This can be done by stating that your company will consider future proposals from her. Be aware, however, that while it is good to leave the door open for future transactions between your company and the reader, you should not give false hope. This will only prolong the reader's disappointment and cause the loss of goodwill.

The Homan Company buys boxes from Delmar Products, Inc., a paper manufacturer in White Plains, New York, for Homan's after-shave and deodorant products. Barbara Delucia, president of Delmar Products, has written to Loretta Nero, vice president of packaging at Homan, offering to supply boxes for Homan's complexion soap, Babyface.

Ms. Nero must refuse Ms. Delucia's offer because the current manufacturer of boxes for Babyface does the job at a lower cost than the one quoted by

Ms. Delucia. Ms. Nero's refusal must say no but return Ms. Delucia's goodwill so that their future business dealings will continue smoothly.

After careful thought, Ms. Nero wrote a letter of refusal, which rejected Delmar Products' price, but not the company itself. In addition, Ms. Nero stressed the positive aspect of the relationship between the two companies by complimenting Delmar's service. This approach will be more likely to retain Ms. Delucia's goodwill.

> The Homan/Delmar Association during the past two years has been a fortunate one for the Homan Company. We appreciate your fine service as our supplier of boxes for our El Toro after-shave lotion and No Question deodorant.
>
> I have considered with interest your proposal to supply packaging for our Babyface soap. Unfortunately, we are not able to make a change from our current supplier of boxes for that product because the price you quoted is somewhat higher than theirs.
>
> Thank you for your good service to us. We look forward to a continued productive relationship with Delmar in the future.

Reasons, Not Apologies

Apologies for a refusal generally sound weak and unconvincing. If you give honest reasons for your decision, you do not need to apologize. A full explanation of the situation should lead the reader to understand that your decision was the only feasible one under the circumstances. You may even help your reader to feel as if the two of you have talked it over.

When you give reasons instead of apologies, there is less chance that your reader will feel brushed off. Your reader can also respond to your refusal knowing the facts, rather than emotionally reacting to your no and wondering what happened.

TECHNIQUES TO AVOID Certain behaviors—whether exhibited by a friend or in a business communication—repel people. Few people like to be treated in a condescending way or to hear meaningless excuses about company policy to support a refusal, and no one feels good about being refused merely with a curt no. The following section will describe how to avoid these three negative approaches when writing refusal letters.

Exhibiting a Condescending Attitude

A condescending letter—one that talks down to the reader—can destroy goodwill very quickly. An attitude of superiority shows lack of respect. When you represent a company, you must keep in mind that *every* reader is a potential customer or employee. Without them your company would be out of business and you would be out of a job.

Hiding Behind Company Policy

If you blame company policy for a refusal without telling the reader what that policy is, you will sound insincere. You have not really given the reader a reason for the refusal at all. Avoid problems by stating what the policy is.

Being Too Brief

A refusal letter that is too brief probably does not include an adequate description of the reasons for the refusal. This deprives recipients of their only solace: the belief that the company considered their request carefully and that the reasons for the refusal were justified.

EDITING EXERCISES

Each of the following excerpts from a refusal letter is potentially harmful to the reader's goodwill. Rewrite each excerpt (creating and adding appropriate facts as necessary) to make it more diplomatic.

1. Certainly you will understand that such a large company as Homan cannot accept proposals from just anyone who sends one in.

2. Sorry. We cannot refund your money because of company policy.

3. I'm really sorry that we cannot hire you. I feel very bad about it.

4. Yours is one of hundreds of applications we receive each day from inexperienced applicants who have no chance of getting a job with us.

5. I apologize for the fact that your idea was not accepted.

PROBLEMS

A. Suppose that you are Albert Purdy, production manager of Howard Stores, a large chain of department stores with headquarters in Pittsburgh, Pennsylvania (Box 1316, Pittsburgh, PA 15259-6767).

   You have received a letter with the following message from a disappointed customer.

   I have had my "Little Estate" lawn mower for four years now and it has been repaired an average of two times each summer.

   Personally I think your product is a lemon and want to get my money refunded. Furthermore, I will never buy a Howard mower again.

   If I cannot get my money back, the least you could do is pay for the repairs since the measly 30-day warranty has long since expired.

Although you cannot grant the customer (Ms. Nina Frielle) what she asks, you are authorized to offer the following alternatives:

- You can have a local Howard Stores mower specialist check the mower free of cost to determine whether there is a weakness in the product or an error in the way Ms. Frielle is operating it.
- If the specialist finds a defect in the machine, you can offer to have it fixed free of charge or offer a generous trade-in on a new mower.
- If you think Howard Stores will lose more money than goodwill in either of these ways, you can offer nothing.

Write the rough draft of a letter refusing the refund to Ms. Nina Frielle, 6 Jason Street, Arlington, MA 02174-3121.

B. Assume that you are Mrs. Samantha Ruggles, personnel director for Van Doren Company (Box 1500, Lubbock, TX 79410-4440).

Christopher Keller has written to you to obtain a job in your company's payroll department. The requirements for the job he wants are a six-month course in computer maintenance and a minimum of two years' experience in the field. The body of his letter follows.

I would like very much to work as a computer maintenance technician in your payroll department.

I have just completed a six-month course at Lubbock Community College in computer maintenance, graduating second in my class.

In the last two years, I have worked as a piano tuner, ranch hand, and checkout clerk at Quick Foods Supermarket on Main Street.

I look forward to meeting you and discussing my future with the Van Doren Company.

Write a response addressed to Christopher Keller, 4 West Street, Lubbock, TX 79401-7271.

PROJECTS

Suppose that you are Nicholas Christo, owner of Nick Nacks, Inc., a novelties manufacturer in Albany, New York (19 Van Buren Avenue, Albany, NY 12228-8899). You manufacture a line of delicately carved wooden and porcelain animals. Your factory produces 300 of each animal in its line every month. The line includes wooden lizards, rattlesnakes, armadillos, and gophers. The porcelain figures include bluebirds, eagles, horses, and cats.

You receive a letter from Ms. Gretchen Stein, president of the Wildlife Lovers of America, asking for 500 carved teak lizards to be used as donation incentives for the organization. You must refuse to honor a portion of her request because of your company's production capacity. There are, however, many alternatives you can offer. What are they? Ms. Stein's address is Wildlife Lovers of Ameria, 42 Middle Street, Phoenix, AZ 85031-1111.

41
Developing Sales Letters

Wayne Ferguson works for Black Bear Sports, Inc., a well-known sporting goods manufacturer in Milwaukee, Wisconsin. His supervisor has just asked him to write a sales letter introducing customers to a revolutionary new type of shoe. This exciting new product, called Foot-Ease shoes, was developed by the company's designers and a leading podiatrist.

THE ROLE OF SALES LETTERS

Wayne's assignment calls for something other than the routine and refusal letters you have been studying. The letter Wayne has been asked to write falls into a category called direct-mail advertising. Advertising through the mail is big business—according to the Direct Marketing Association, consumers bought about $44.4 billion worth of goods and services by mail in a recent year.

Despite their popularity, direct-mail letters are not the only type of sales letters you will write. Businesses produce many other types of sales correspondence. Often companies send sales letters to other companies to introduce themselves and their line of products or services. Sales letters also go out to current clients or customers—individuals and businesses alike—when a new product must be showcased. In a sense, all business letters are sales letters, because their aim is to create goodwill that will result in increased business.

Although this chapter will focus on writing direct-mail sales letters, the techniques discussed here will be helpful in writing other types of sales letters.

THE ADVANTAGES OF SALES LETTERS

Sales letters may not have the sound and action of television commercials or the potential distribution of print ads in national magazines, but they have selling strengths that other advertising media lack. Well-written sales letters can be more personal and can reach a specific group of buyers. It is also possible to measure their effectiveness with greater accuracy.

The Personal Approach

What's in a name? A lot, if the name is your reader's. Addressing a letter to the receiver by name is an effective sales tool. The person will have to handle the sales letter, even if it's just to toss it into the wastebasket. If your letter succeeds in attracting attention, it will be read, and the reader may even buy your product.

A Selected Audience

For the advertiser, choosing an audience can be very important. Many forms of advertising reach large groups of diverse people, only a fraction of whom would be likely to buy any one product. Sales letters, on the other hand, can be sent only to those people—known as the target market—who would be most interested in the product. If you are selling tractors, for example, you can save advertising dollars by sending letters only to farmers, not to big-city apartment dwellers or owners of suburban condominiums. Since they are not part of your clientele, there is no point sending your letter to them.

An Easily Measured Audience

It is difficult to measure exactly how many viewers have seen a television commercial, heard a radio ad, or read a newspaper or magazine ad. It is much easier to assess how successful your sales letters have been in reaching prospective customers. You know how many you have sent. If they have not been returned, you can be fairly sure your target audience has received them.

An Easily Measured Response

It is easy for businesses to determine the effect of properly planned sales letters. If you ask for some type of specific response, you can simply count the replies you receive.

What kind of response does the typical direct-mail letter receive? According to recent figures from the Direct Marketing Association, a return of from 1 to 6 percent is considered good for direct-mail campaigns. Although this percentage may seem very small, it must be considered in light of the huge volume of letters sent. If you calculate, for example, 1 percent of 1 million you get 10,000—a significant number of sales.

HOW TO FIND YOUR TARGET MARKET

To whom should you send a sales letter? What should you say? To answer these questions, you must know your product thoroughly, determine what kind of people are most likely to buy it (your target market), and select a mailing list that includes the names and addresses of those people.

Learning About Your Product

A thorough knowledge of your product will help you determine who would be most likely to buy it. This knowledge also gives your letter an authoritative tone that will encourage your readers to trust you and, therefore, to make a purchase.

The following is a list of questions that your sales letter should answer about your product. (Of course, not all questions apply to every product.)

- What can it do?
- From what material(s) is it made?
- How does it compare to its competition?
- How much does it cost?
- What are its uses?
- What special features does it have?
- What type of care and maintenance does it require?
- What are the terms of its warranty?

Developing a Target Market

When you have learned about your product, you should determine your target market(s)—those people most likely to buy it. Wayne's company has decided that Foot-Ease shoes have two distinct target markets. The first is made up of serious athletes who are concerned about both preventing injury and performing well. The second market consists of people who are not athletes, but who nonetheless appreciate the value of well-constructed and comfortable shoes that are also fashionable.

Because direct-mail marketing is big business, many companies invest a great deal of money and time in researching their target markets. During this research process, they attempt to determine answers to the following types of questions about people who are most likely to buy their products.

- What is their income level?
- What is their marital status?
- If married, how many children do they have?
- What are the ages of their immediate family members?
- What occupations are represented in the family?
- What is the level of education attained by family leaders?
- What are their hobbies and interests? Are they members of any clubs or organizations?
- Do they own or rent their homes?
- Do they live in rural or urban areas?
- What luxury items do they own (such as sports cars, boats, or second homes)?

After determining what type of consumer is likely to buy your product, you must develop a tool that helps you reach those people: a mailing list.

Securing a Mailing List

The most valuable list of names a company has is its own list of customers. A company can also obtain lists of names from other businesses called mailing list brokers, service bureaus, compilers, or managers. These companies usually rent lists of names on a one-time basis at a cost of from $35 to $60 per thousand names. The more specific the list, the more it costs to rent it. For example, a list of married suburban couples, aged 30 to 50, whose income is between $25,000 and $50,000 a year is less specific (and less expensive) than a list of single parents, aged 30 to 40, whose income is over $60,000 a year and who race sports cars for a hobby.

A mailing list of specific customers may cost more, but it will help you avoid making costly and possibly embarrassing mistakes such as trying to sell homes in a retirement village to young newlyweds or meat thermometers to vegetarians.

Wayne has been asked to address his sales letters to Black Bear's two primary mailing lists. One list includes the names of serious runners, and the other is made up of regular customers who do not consider themselves athletes. Both lists are up-to-date and consist mainly of charge account customers and customers who have asked to be notified of store events such as sales.

HOW TO APPEAL TO YOUR READERS

Suppose you already know specific information about your product, understand its target markets, and know where those people can be found. Now you need to know how to appeal to that audience.

A number of years ago, Abraham Maslow, a well-known behavioral psychologist, developed a theory that helps define the needs of individuals. His theory sheds light on ways businesses can appeal to prospective buyers.

Maslow theorized that people have five categories of needs, which he structured in a hierarchy. The needs on the lowest level must be satisfied (or at least partially satisfied) before those on the next level can be fulfilled. Basic survival needs such as food and shelter are on the lowest level. Self-actualization needs, which have to do with personal fulfillment, are at the top. In between are safety needs, belongingness needs (friendship, acceptance), and esteem needs (prestige, recognition).

The following sections show how Maslow's hierarchy can be applied to writing sales letters, with examples from varied businesses and specific application to the Foot-Ease shoes sales letter that Wayne Ferguson must develop.

Physical Needs

The products that fill these needs are basic ones. They include low- or medium-priced items such as small rental apartments, modest houses, beds and other basic furniture, standard foods, and simple clothing to protect the body from the elements.

You would address these physical needs if you were writing a sales letter for new, low-priced homes aimed at a target market of young singles or couples. The following excerpt from a sales letter speaks to these needs:

> Like everyone, you need a place to live—a place to call your own. But how do people just starting out—people like you—find quality homes at affordable prices? Your search can begin and end at Birch Run Farms, a residential development built by Allen and Steven Rubinstein. Birch Run Farms provides you with a home you can live in at prices you can afford.

Some buyers—like the young singles and couples targeted in the excerpt—are just beginning to accumulate the basics. Even people who have already satisfied their basic needs must continue to meet minimum physical goals (housing, food, clothing, and so on), though they may choose products that also satisfy their need for esteem (level four in Maslow's hierarchy). Thus, although few consumers would consider a pair of $64.99 Foot-Ease shoes to be a basic need, some people at higher income levels might buy Foot-Ease shoes because they are comfortable for everyday wear.

Safety Needs

Products such as property, health, and life insurance; burglar alarms and guard dogs; vitamin pills; and savings plans can satisfy safety, or security, needs. When addressing this type of need, a sales letter must clearly present the danger from which the product protects the reader.

> How would your family cope if the major source of household income were suddenly taken away—by job loss, prolonged illness, or even death? Would you have to sell your home because you could no longer meet your monthly mortgage commitment? With the Rushmore Mortgage Insurance Plan, you can rest in the knowledge that your mortgage commitment will be met should tragedy strike.

Foot-Ease shoes could appeal to a serious runner's need for safety by emphasizing that these shoes are designed to prevent injury.

Belongingness Needs

Maslow placed these needs third on his list, on a higher level than basic survival needs. However, it could be argued that the need to belong is almost as basic as the need for food. Many people who buy products do so because they want to belong to or already are a part of a certain group. Most products have "belonging" built in.

There are some products whose sales appeal can be defined as satisfying the need to belong more than others. For instance, beauty and youth products such as cosmetics, diet aids, alluring clothes, and recreational activity items appeal strongly to this need.

Notice how the following excerpt appeals to the young businesswoman's need to belong.

> Being part of today's business world takes a lot of style, personal style that is reflected in the way you choose and wear your clothes. The woman who shops at Walton's feels at home in the world of business because she knows her clothes are right.

Foot-Ease shoes could appeal to a customer's need to belong if, for example, popular students at a certain college began to wear them. Other students who purchased the shoes to "follow the leader" would be doing so to fulfill their need to belong.

Esteem Needs

The need for esteem or status is closely related to the need to belong; many products appeal to both at the same time. However, products that satisfy esteem needs are often high-priced variations of products that meet basic survival needs. Level-four products could be fancier versions of level-one goods. People satisfying level-four needs would buy an estate, not merely a roof over their heads. They would buy a designer coat, not just something to protect them from the weather. They would buy prime cuts of meat and exotic fruits, not hamburger and apples. Status needs are also met by luxury products such as jewelry, boats, sports cars, summer cottages, exotic vacations, and high-priced entertainment items. The following sales letter excerpt appeals to the status needs of its readers in promoting a Caribbean cruise.

> To paraphrase the words of a famous writer: The rich are different—they go on cruises. To many, the Caribbean cruise is the epitome of the good life. Charisma Cruises offer princely pleasures at prices that will not make you a pauper.

Foot-East shoes could fulfill the need for esteem and status if the customer who buys them is the only one among a group of friends to have a pair of custom-designed shoes.

Self-Actualization Needs

Products that satisfy self-actualization needs are those that help people advance in a profession or become more knowledgeable in an area of personal interest. Sporting goods, musical instruments, art supplies, and how-to books are products that can satisfy needs for achievement or fulfillment.

Notice how the following excerpt from a promotional letter for a technical institute appeals to the reader's desire for career growth.

> Have you ever wondered if further education would help you obtain the promotion you want? The skills you will gain at Swann Technical Institute can mean the difference between a dead-end job and a bright future.

A pair of Foot-Ease shoes could fill a serious runner's self-actualization needs in that they might help him or her achieve faster running times.

Most successful sales letters share a similar format that includes four basic themes.

THE BASIC FORMAT OF A SALES LETTER

1. *Attention*. You must grab the reader's attention.
2. *Interest*. You must spark the reader's interest.
3. *Desire*. You must convince the reader he or she desires your product or service.
4. *Action*. You must spur the reader to action.

The following section will show how Wayne might use this basic format for writing his Foot-Ease shoes sales letter.

Attention

As a writer of sales letters, you have two major opportunities to gain the reader's attention: through an attractive envelope and through an enticing introduction to your letter.

The Envelope. The first thing readers will notice about your sales letter is its envelope. There are only two kinds of envelopes for sales letters—those that are opened and those that are tossed unopened into the wastebasket.

Advertisers and writers of sales letters have developed many techniques designed to make recipients open envelopes. These techniques include using colored stationery, printing sales messages (such as "Free Sample Enclosed") on the front, and sending envelopes with windows that show a portion of a check made out to the reader. Creativity is important, as is design of an envelope that suits your audience and your products.

What kind of envelope can Wayne's Foot-Ease shoes letter have? He might use an ordinary business envelope with the following challenge written on it: "Don't open this letter if your feet have never hurt." He might, instead, design an envelope in the shape of a foot and address it to:

The Feet of John Smith
230 Main Street
Milwaukee, WI 53266-1553

The possibilities are endless. Of course, success in getting readers to open an envelope is only half the battle. After that, you must get them to read the letter.

The Introduction. There are at least six successful techniques used by writers of sales letters to get the immediate attention of readers and make them want to read the entire letter. In the following list you will read about each of these techniques and see how they can be applied to Wayne's goal of promoting Foot-Ease shoes.

1. *Ask a Rhetorical Question.* This type of question is one that is asked merely for effect; it does not require an answer. The question should be appropriate for both your audience and your product. For example, Wayne could pose this rhetorical question: "Your feet have stood by you all these years. Isn't it time you supported them?" Another might be "Are your feet running into trouble?"

2. *Present a Startling Fact.* This information will be readily available to you if you know your product well. A trip to the library will also yield useful facts. In addition, product trade associations usually have dramatic facts and figures.

   Here are some fascinating facts for the Foot-Ease shoes letter:

   Americans spent over $22.2 billion on shoes last year. But did any fit properly? The most expensive sports shoes you can buy are mink-lined golf shoes with 18-karat gold trim and ruby-tipped gold spikes. They retail for $8,800. But do they fit properly?

3. *Mention a Relevant Current Event.* Here is a recent current event that would be appropriate for the Foot-East shoes letter:

   Mickey Pendergast won the Chamber of Commerce Marathon last month. He was testing the first pair of Foot-Ease shoes. Now he won't even walk to the corner without them.

4. *Offer a Bargain.* Give the reader an incentive to buy your product.

   If you sign this card and bring it to our shoe department before February 1, you can get your first pair of Foot-Ease shoes for 10 percent off our low introductory price.

5. *Make a Challenge.* "If you don't try Foot-Ease shoes, you don't care about your feet."

6. *Tell an Anecdote.* Relate a story that will lead into a discussion of your product: "Every family has its resident expert, and Uncle George was ours. He used to say: 'If you want to live well, take good care of two things: your teeth and your feet. No one with a toothache or a sore foot can ever be truly happy.'"

Interest

After you have the reader's attention, you must stimulate his or her interest. A "you" focus is especially appropriate. The sales letter stimulates interest by addressing readers' needs directly. As a writer, you must relate your attention-getting statement directly to your audience and tell why they have been chosen as prospective customers. Use a detailed discussion of your product's features to tell how they can benefit from it. If you have chosen your target audience well, your readers will be interested in what you have to say.

Wayne's attention-getting statement to attract sports enthusiasts could be the story of Mickey Pendergast's winning of the Chamber of Commerce Marathon. The information in Wayne's second paragraph could be tied in with a "you"-focused statement like this one: "You're sure to agree with Mickey that Foot-Ease shoes are the only ones to wear when you run or play sports."

To continue to stimulate interest, Wayne might explain that Foot-Ease shoes may actually help wearers win sports events because they are so lightweight. Wayne could then tell his readers that Foot-Ease shoes are designed to prevent foot injuries.

The attention-getting statement for nonathletes could be the anecdote about Uncle George. Wayne would tie in his information with this statement: "You probably take good care of your teeth, but do the shoes you wear take good care of your feet?" Then he might continue to stimulate interest by stressing the fact that Foot-Ease shoes offer relief from common foot problems and keep feet feeling good. He could also mention that Foot-Ease shoes have a stylish look and come in a choice of colors and patterns.

Desire

Once you have the reader's attention and interest, you need to turn that interest into an active desire for your product. You can do this by appealing to one of your reader's basic needs through describing the rewards that will result from buying the product. This can be done with three types of appeals: emotionally positive, emotionally negative, and logical.

Emotionally positive appeals express the benefits that result from using the product. One such appeal might read, "Be a safer winner when you wear Foot-Ease shoes."

Emotionally negative appeals work in the opposite way, stating what will happen if the reader doesn't use the product. For example, if Wayne turns his positive reward for athletes who wear Foot-Ease shoes into a negative one, it becomes: "You shouldn't be risking foot injuries when you play to win."

Make sure the rewards that you promise relate to the information you have stressed. For example, Wayne should not promise, after praising the shoes' injury-reducing qualities, that they will provide athletes with the most stylish shoes in the game. Maintain a consistent approach with your messages to make them more effective.

The logical appeal is aimed at the reasoning ability, rather than the emotions, of the reader. Wayne might use this approach with the business person buying Foot-Ease shoes with company funds for use in an employee-incentive program. Since that person will have to justify the purchase to his or her supervisor, Wayne will want to stress the usual justifications for company purchases— economy and efficiency. Those items could be expressed well in a logical appeal:

> "Foot-Ease shoes cost 25 percent less than other custom-made shoes and give the wearer the benefits of design by a podiatrist."

Notice how this appeal is made effective by employing facts that can be verified. It aims to direct the recipient to make an objective evaluation of the product. No emotional factors are involved.

Action

Even if your readers are ready to buy, it is possible that they will lose their willingness because they are not in your store at that moment. This is less likely to happen, however, if you give them an easy way to respond to your offer. You could include a postcard to mail or a toll-free telephone number to call. To convince readers that *now* is the best time to respond, give them an incentive such as a special rate or a free trial period—but only if they respond within a limited time.

LETTER-WRITING TECHNIQUES

Now let's take a brief look at the special techniques that you should use in writing sales letters. Effective sales letters are written with an informal tone, addressing the reader by name or in the second person. Sales letters should be written as though the writer were a friend offering the readers a product they can use. Word processing technology makes it possible to personalize mass mailings for each reader.

Sales letters are written with informal punctuation, short chatty sentences, and extra space between paragraphs. Adding space between paragraphs emphasizes the ideas stated in each paragraph and encourages the reader to read on. Large blocks of type tend to be intimidating and difficult to digest so they are best avoided.

A sales letter can be longer than most other business letters, but, generally, it should not be more than a few pages. If the message runs longer, you risk boring the reader.

Let's see what Wayne's Foot-Ease shoes sales letter might look like if he used some of the ideas in this chapter to address the two target markets mentioned. The letter in Figure 41-1 is being sent to a mailing list composed of athletes' names and addresses. The letter in Figure 41-2 is being sent to individuals who do not consider themselves athletes. Notice the different appeals that Wayne used in each letter.

BLACK BEAR SPORTS INC.

January 14, 1988

Edward and Jill Norse
232 Nordica Drive
Milwaukee, WI 53201-6006

Dear Ed and Jill:

''I feel as if my feet had wings. I'll never wear any other shoes.'' That's what winner Mickey Pendergast said after testing Black Bear's revolutionary new shoes, Foot-Ease, in the Chamber of Commerce Marathon last month.

Foot-Ease shoes are custom-made to the unique shape of your feet and style of your gait according to a system developed by a leading podiatrist. Each shoe conforms to and cradles every part of your foot because it is adjusted to the height of your arch, the thrust of your heel, and the curve of your toes.

A pair of Foot-Ease shoes sells for only $64.99, far less than any other custom-made running shoes. Not only are these shoes custom-made, but they also come in an array of fabrics and colors.

Foot-Ease can give you the edge to help you win. They enable you to move more confidently, knowing that you are safer from ankle sprains, shin splints, and blisters whenever you wear them.

If you sign this card and bring it to our Shoe Department before February 1, you can get your first pair of Foot-Ease shoes for 10 percent off our regular price of $64.99.

We are eager to hear about your reaction to Foot-Ease shoes. Run to our Shoe Department today. Your feet will thank you for it.

Sincerely,

Wayne Ferguson

Wayne Ferguson
Director of Sales

1287 CAPITAL DRIVE MILWAUKEE, WISCONSIN 52367-7777

Figure 41-1 Sales letter directed at athletic market.

January 14, 1988

Kevin and Janet Washington
1824 Badger Drive
Milwaukee, WI 53225-4646

Dear Kevin and Janet:

You probably take good care of your teeth, but do the shoes you wear take
good care of your feet? Start pampering your feet with Foot-Ease shoes.

Foot-Ease shoes are a revolutionary new type of shoe made to fit the con-
tours of your feet. This individual fit helps prevent foot problems caused
by ill-fitting shoes. And Foot-Ease shoes are made to fit the fancies of
your imagination. You choose the style, from conservative tennis shoes to
chic running styles. You choose the fabric, from canvas to satin. You
choose the colors and patterns, from a classic navy blue to an eye-catching
light green with pink stripes.

Foot-Ease shoes will give you the latest styles and keep your feet healthy
for about the same amount of money you'd pay for ordinary shoes. You
couldn't ask for a better bargain.

If you sign this card and bring it to the Black Bear Shoe Department, our
consulting podiatrist will measure your feet and take your order. And if
you come in before February 1, you will save an extra 10 percent on your
first pair of Foot-Ease shoes.

Stop in today. Start taking care of your feet in style.

Sincerely,

Wayne Ferguson

Wayne Ferguson
Director of Sales

1287 CAPITAL DRIVE MILWAUKEE, WISCONSIN 52367-7777

Figure 41-2 Sales letter directed at non-athletic market.

EDITING EXERCISES

The following two excerpts from sales letters are written in a manner that is too formal. Rewrite each one to conform to the suggestions for writing sales letters in this chapter.

1. Perhaps the tents used by your family are getting a few leaks or the sleeping bags used by your family have many sewn-up slits. If so, you will be glad to know that Black Bear is having a Founder's Day sale on Saturday, March 12. All the brands of equipment that campers appreciate most will be sold at prices 25 percent off our regular low prices.

2. For a long time, mountain-climbing enthusiasts have known about the heat-conserving qualities of a lightweight fabric called Thermylon. Only now, however, is this revolutionary new fabric available to the general public in jackets, snowsuits, and other items of outerwear. Black Bear Sports has received a shipment of these items at prices that no intelligent consumer could reject.

PROBLEMS

A. Each of the following excerpts from a sales letter appeals primarily to one of the needs described by Abraham Maslow. Tell which need is being addressed by each excerpt.

1. Have you been wondering if you are the only person in your neighborhood without a videocassette recorder? The results of our poll say that you just may be, and there is no better time to join the electronics age.

2. If you are self-employed and are concerned that Social Security will not provide enough income for you in your retirement years, open a Keogh Plan at Kings Bank and be assured by the knowledge that your future is secure.

3. Everyone wears sunglasses, but only the most chic wear Lunettes—fashion jewelry for the eyes.

4. Are you looking for a house that is more than a home—one that reflects your affluent personal style and elegance? Visit Windsor Towers (by appointment only) and choose an estate that tells the rest of the world who you are.

5. You want to go away on vacation, but there has been a rash of burglaries in your neighborhood. Can you go without fearing that your belongings will be gone when you return? The answer is yes, if you install a Protect-All Alarm System today.

6. If you are a serious musician who wants your music to be all it can, visit Franz's Music Shop for all your instrument needs.

7. Do you have the desire to read the best in today's literature but not the time to search it out for yourself? A new magazine, *Literature Digest*, will provide you with the ideas and issues that will help you grow personally, all in an accessible monthly format.

8. If you want a winter coat that will keep you warm without putting you in debt, check out the Winter Clothing Sale at Top Flight Stores.

B. Suppose that it is your turn to write a sales letter for Foot-Ease shoes, or for some other product, using the techniques you have studied in this chapter. If you choose to write about Foot-Ease shoes, direct your letter to a target market made up of college-age runners who are members of the Collegiate Road Runners Club. If you choose another product, specify your own target market. Create ideas for your letter's envelope, and include suggestions for special action-generating incentives at the end of the letter.

C. Black Bear's managers are so pleased with your ability to write sales letters that they have asked you to help with the sales campaign for a new product, the Cozy Cup. This remarkable cup allows the user to have hot food or drink anytime anywhere. The cup is heated by a replaceable battery and can warm most food in less than five minutes. The built-in adapter plug allows the user to employ household electric current as well. The inside of the cup is made of an easy-to-clean nonstick surface. The clamp-on lid speeds the heating process and makes the cup ideal for storing leftovers.

Black Bear's managers would like you to write six different letter introductions so that they can choose the best one. Your six introductions should demonstrate each of the six successful techniques used by writers of sales letters to get readers' attention.

Assume that your target market is made up of customers who have previously purchased camping and cooking supplies from Black Bear.

D. Select the introduction you like best and use it to begin a complete sales letter for Cozy Cups. Be sure that your letter follows the format of a sales letter as described in the chapter—get the reader's attention, arouse the reader's interest, spark the reader's desire, and get the reader to take action.

PROJECTS

Collect several direct-mail sales letters and analyze them according to the points made in this chapter. Examine the needs they address. On what level or levels are they? How do the letters get attention, arouse interest, create desire, and promote action? Do they violate any of the rules described in this chapter? If so, how could they be improved?

42
Writing Social-Business Letters

The old adage "Don't mix business with pleasure" is almost as outdated in the modern business world as the manual typewriter. Employees of today's companies frequently *do* mix their business and social lives, because doing so can both increase company profits and enrich their personal lives.

Company personnel take clients to lunch. Clients entertain company representatives and their families at sports and cultural events. Many businesses encourage interoffice friendships by sponsoring company social events and providing recreational facilities. Today, people often meet lifelong friends and even marriage partners through their business activities.

Such social changes have broken down the barriers between private and business relationships. These new situations require a special type of correspondence—letters that are personal but appropriate for business occasions.

Social-business letters are used by business people to respond with good manners—friendliness, courtesy, tact, and sincere compliments—to social situations; they say "Thank you," "Congratulations," "I'd love to," or "I'm sorry." This type of correspondence is used to generate goodwill.

Business people have many opportunities to write social letters that represent themselves and their company. These communications fall into four general categories:

WHAT ARE SOCIAL-BUSINESS LETTERS?

- thank-you letters acknowledging gifts; service; courtesies; hospitality; business referrals; outstanding employee performance; and special favors from clients, associates, or staff
- letters of congratulation acknowledging promotions; pay raises; honors; and the family events of business associates, such as births, weddings, and graduations

- invitations to and announcements of business meetings, business dinners, company parties, gatherings introducing new product lines, and other events, along with replies to invitations
- letters of sympathy for financial setbacks, illnesses, deaths, and other losses suffered by business associates and their families

Social-business letters are different from other business letters in important ways. They do not convey business decisions in the way that routine or refusal letters do, and they do not sell the company's products in the direct way that sales letters do. However, social-business letters can be as important as other kinds of business correspondence because they are a company's special ambassadors of goodwill.

FORMAT OF SOCIAL-BUSINESS LETTERS

Except for formal invitations, the format of social-business correspondence differs from that of regular business letters in only four ways:

1. A comma, rather than a colon, should follow the salutation.
2. The inside address may be placed below the signature block, flush with the left-hand margin, instead of in its usual position above the salutation.
3. Small-sized (monarch or baronial) company stationery or good-quality personal stationery should be used.
4. A handwritten note may be appropriate, even preferable, especially for sympathy and thank-you letters.

RULES FOR WRITING SOCIAL-BUSINESS LETTERS

All types of social-business letters should use the same basic approach. In each type, you should aim to be direct, brief, friendly, sincere, and prompt. Your goal is to keep the reader in the spotlight.

Be Direct

Letters that thank, congratulate, invite, or console should start the same way that routine business letters begin, with the message stated in the first sentence. The following examples demonstrate the direct approach for each of the four types of social-business letters.

> Thank you for the silver rattle with your company logo engraved beside the initials of little Ernest.

> Congratulations on your recent election to the company's Advertising Hall of Fame.

DID YOU KNOW?
Special Mail Services

At your workplace, you will probably make use of many of the special services offered by the U.S. Postal Service. Descriptions of some of the most commonly used services follow:

- *Express Mail.* Express Mail is a guaranteed next-day delivery service for letters and packages weighing up to 70 pounds. If you take a package to a post office offering Express Mail service by 5 p.m., it will be delivered by 3 p.m. the next day. If the package does not arrive on time, you receive a full refund. The rate (based on weight) includes insurance, a shipment receipt, and a record of delivery at the destination post office.
- *Registered Mail.* The safest way to send something valuable is by registered mail. You receive a receipt when you mail the item, and its movement is carefully controlled at every point during its journey. Payment of an additional charge will provide you with a return receipt showing to whom the item was delivered and when and where it arrived.
- *Certified Mail.* When you send an item by certified mail, it goes through the usual postal channels, but you get a record of when you sent it and from where. You also know when it arrived at the destination post office. You have proof, should you need it, of the fact that the item was sent and the date on which it was sent.
- *Insurance.* You can insure any piece of mail against loss or damage. The fee depends on the value you place upon the item—the higher the value, the more costly the coverage.
- *Special Delivery.* Paying a special-delivery fee on top of regular postage guarantees that the mail will receive prompt transportation and delivery. When it arrives at the destination post office, a postal worker will attempt to deliver it right away.
- *Special Handling.* Special handling is for third- and fourth-class mail only. The fee is based on the weight of the item and is added to regular postage. Special handling means that your piece of mail will be handled and transported before all the other third- and fourth-class mail.

Mr. and Mrs. Andrew Douglas request the pleasure of Mr. and Mrs. Roland Dell's company at a celebration of Douglas Enterprises' twenty-fifth anniversary.

Accept my deepest sympathy for your loss in the death of your partner.

Be Brief

Social-business letters should not be long. Because these *are* business letters, they are often written and read during busy workdays or under trying circumstances, and brevity is appreciated at such times.

On the other hand, avoid making your letter so brief that it sounds **abrupt**. It should sound as if you wrote it because you wanted to, not because you had to.

Be Friendly

Friendship is the essence of social-business letters. With the exception of formal invitations, these letters should have an informal tone. As you write, choose the same words you would use if you were having a friendly talk with your reader.

Be Sincere

Social-business letters can backfire and cause more harm than no letters at all if the message sounds self-serving. Even with sincere intentions, you can convey a tone of insincerity if any of the following appear in your message:

- exaggeration
- false flattery
- a sales pitch, even a subtle one

Take care to make your compliments believable. For example, do not thank a client for "the best meal I ever ate." A more convincing compliment would be specific: "The medallions of beef were delicious."

Instead of saying that your host is the best in the country, simply say, "You made me feel welcome and at ease, as you always do."

Never include a sales message in a social-business letter unless you are conveying congratulations to a firm or writing a formal announcement. Sales pitches belong in sales letters. If you include a sales message in a social-business letter, you risk losing the goodwill of your reader because it will look as though you are using the occasion to promote your product.

Be Prompt

Promptness is just as important for social-business letters as it is for other types. When a social-business letter is late, the reader may get the impression that you were too busy or not concerned enough to respond when the event occurred.

Keep the Reader in the Spotlight

Social-business correspondence is used to respond to very personal events in the reader's life. If the message is to be direct, brief, and sincere, it must focus on the reader. Avoid using a social-business letter to talk about yourself or your company. Any language that might make the reader think you are using the occasion to try to promote your company is very inappropriate. Such a message will only alienate the recipient.

THANK-YOU LETTERS

A simple thank-you note is a strong builder of goodwill in any situation. It acknowledges the thoughtfulness of the reader. In the first sentences, you should express your gratitude and tell what the thank-you is for.

> Thank you for the flower arrangement celebrating the opening of our Fifth Avenue store.

The rest of the paragraph should personalize the thank-you in some way. A thank-you for hospitality might go on to mention a particularly enjoyable part of the stay. The thank-you for the flower arrangement could continue in this way:

> We have placed the bouquet on the receptionist's desk; the rose carnations are an attractive complement to the abstract painting in the lobby.

This paragraph, together with your friendly tone, makes the thank-you letter sound sincere and personal.

The ending of the letter should express appreciation one last time and encourage a continuing relationship. It can be as simple as saying "thank you" again.

> Thanks again; the arrangement is a very gracious gesture for our new expansion.

LETTERS OF CONGRATULATION

Business people have opportunities to write letters of congratulation to colleagues to acknowledge honors, promotions, pay raises, awards, and other measures of success. Letters of congratulation are important builders of goodwill because they show respect, recognition, and appreciation. In short, they make the recipient feel good.

Letters of congratulation can be addressed to an individual or to a company and can be formal or informal. Those addressed to individuals are formal if the person is only a business acquaintance and informal when the reader is also a personal friend. Congratulations addressed to companies are usually formal and can sometimes contain a sales message. Congratulations to individuals, however, must *never* include a sales pitch.

The following examples of effective formal and informal letters of congratulation were written by employees of Grant Valley Mills, Inc.

Michelle Romano, head of fabric design for GVM, has learned recently that her colleague and friend Chad Baker has been promoted to vice president of GVM's hosiery division. She immediately writes the following informal note:

> Congratulations on your promotion to vice president of our hosiery division.
> This promotion comes as no surprise—at least to me! Your experience in the field and ability to deal with clients are well known.
> I could not be more pleased. May your success continue.

While she is writing this note, Michelle decides it would be a nice gesture to welcome the new vice president of personnel, Claudia Szabo. Since Michelle does not know Ms. Szabo personally, she takes a formal approach. She uses the salutation "Dear Ms. Szabo."

> Welcome to Grant Valley Mills, Inc., and congratulations on your new position as vice president of our personnel department.
> I look forward to working with you on matters concerning fabric-design personnel and hope to extend my welcome to you personally in the near future.

At about the same time, Sebastian Grant, president and founder of GVM, has received an invitation from one of his new customers, Distinguished Look Fashions. Distinguished Look is opening a new branch, and its president, Elizabeth Lurie, has invited Mr. Grant to the grand opening ceremonies.

Since Mr. Grant cannot attend the opening, he combines his congratulations for the opening with regrets for his inability to attend. Because this letter is written to a company, a sales message is appropriate.

> Congratulations on Distinguished Look's expansion to the new wing of the elegant Davis Towers. It seems a fitting location and symbol of success.
> I regret that a scheduled business trip prevents me from attending the grand opening ceremonies next Thursday. My only consolation will be to tour the facilities when we have lunch to discuss our new fabrics for your spring line.

FORMAL INVITATIONS, ANNOUNCEMENTS, AND REPLIES

Business people must often send or respond to invitations. The events involved can be personal, such as an associate's fiftieth birthday celebration, or directly related to business, such as the preview of a new product line.

Events that are personal require a formal invitation; invitations that are more business-related may be sent in the form of an announcement.

Formal Invitations

All formal invitations contain the following information:

- the nature of the event
- the day of the week, date, and time of the event
- the location of the event

- the name(s) of the person(s) invited to the event
- the name(s) of the sponsor(s) of the event
- an address or phone number for reply concerning the event

In addition, formal invitations have the following characteristics:

- They can be handwritten or engraved.
- They address the recipient in the third person.
- They require a reply.
- They never contain a sales message.

Mr. Grant's secretary, Harold Whitley, sent the engraved invitation shown in Figure 42-1 to 75 of Mr. Grant's personal friends and business associates.

In another part of the city, Neil Sherman, administrative assistant at the Textile Marketing Association, is sending out handwritten invitations like the one in Figure 42-2 to the recipients of the prestigious TMA sales award. Although handwritten, this invitation is formal.

The letters *R.S.V.P.* used in both of the sample invitations shown below, are an abbreviation for the French expression *répondez s'il vous plaît,* which means "please reply."

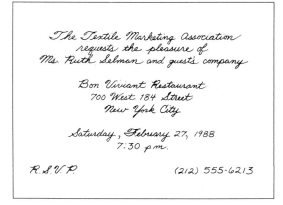

Figure 42-1 An engraved formal invitation.   **Figure 42-2** A handwritten formal invitation.

Announcements

People who are inviting colleagues to a business-related social gathering may do so by sending announcements. Announcements differ from formal invitations in the following ways:

- They may contain a sales message.
- They are usually typeset, not handwritten.
- They may not require a reply.

Chad Baker, vice president of the hosiery division, is having the following announcement typeset to introduce a new product line, High Steppers:

GRANT VALLEY MILLS, INC.,
makers of high-quality fabrics and hosiery, requests
the pleasure of your company at the introduction of
a stylish addition to its line

HIGH STEPPERS
Sheer Plaid Pantyhose

Monday, January 9, 1989
at 4:30 p.m.
First-floor boardroom
GVM Building

R.S.V.P.   (212) 555-9326

Figure 42-3 An announcement.

Replies to Formal Invitations

There are two kinds of replies to formal invitations—acceptances and refusals. The format is similar for both types except that a refusal must state the reason for declining the invitation. The following are the basic rules for replies:

- A reply to a formal invitation should not be typewritten. It should be handwritten on personal stationery, special note-sized stationery, or plain white notepaper.
- The reply should be brief.
- The reply should restate the important points of the invitation so there is no misunderstanding about what event the reply refers to.

Figure 42-4 is an example of a well-written acceptance.

---

*Ms. Ruth Selman and guest
accept with pleasure
the invitation to the awards dinner
on February 27.*

Figure 42-4 A handwritten acceptance to a formal invitation.

Misfortunes such as financial loss, sickness, and death are part of the human experience and, therefore, part of social communications in private and business life. When the loss you are responding to is great, a handwritten note or card is preferred, but typed letters are acceptable. If the loss or problem is not serious, perhaps a hospital stay for a routine procedure or a minor illness, the message of sympathy can be light or humorous.

LETTERS OF SYMPATHY

In all cases, the proper sympathy letter for a business associate should be brief—not more than two or three paragraphs, including the closing—in order not to dwell on the situation.

In an appropriate sympathy letter, the first paragraph expresses sympathy, and the second paragraph sets forth a calm and optimistic view of the future. If you are sending a letter of condolence for a death, use the word *dead* or *death*. Do not employ euphemisms for the truth, such as *passed on, departed,* or *at rest,* for they only prolong the discussion of the sad facts. In any sympathy letter, you should strive to be tactful without sidestepping the truth.

Sympathy letters should express genuine feelings. Only if you empathize with the reader's situation will you be able to write something comforting and appropriate.

> The news of Rockford's death deeply saddened me. I share some of the grief you must feel during this difficult time. Rockford was a close friend and an able businessman. His love for you and the children was very evident. He will be missed by many people.
>
> I know that his memory will inspire your life in the years to come.

EDITING EXERCISES

In each of the following excerpts from poorly written sympathy letters, the writer has used a euphemism instead of directly mentioning a business failure, illness, or death. Rewrite each excerpt so that it is tactful, but direct.

1. I was so sorry to hear of your little problem that resulted in a lengthy stay in the hospital.

2. Please accept my condolences for your company's recent difficult financial period.

3. I am glad that you have fully recovered from your recent indisposition.

4. I am so sorry to hear that Raymond has gone to his final rest.

5. It saddened me to hear of your company's stressful financial period of time.

6. The news of Erica's untimely departure both shocked and saddened me.

7. Accept my best wishes that you will soon cease being under the weather.

8. I know how difficult it can be to have a marriage partner quit this world.

PROBLEMS

A. Read the following thank-you letter, and explain why it is not an effective builder of goodwill. Then rewrite the letter, and discuss what you did to improve it.

Dear Ernie,

   It was heaven! How can I thank you? The food, the music, you—all superb!
   Take me to dinner again, and we'll discuss how we can supply you with high-quality paper for your secretarial staff.

Cordially,

B. Explain how the reader will probably feel after receiving the following letter. Then rewrite it to make it an effective goodwill builder.

Dear Pat:

   Congratulations on your new offices at 324 Park Street. We love ours. In fact, we're expanding to the 9th floor next month. Don't tell anyone—the news hasn't been officially released yet. The reason for the expansion is the tremendous amount of new business our account team has brought in over the past few months.

Cordially,

C. The following invitation violates some of the basic guidelines discussed in this chapter. Indicate which guidelines are not followed, and then rewrite the invitation in the correct format.

Mr. and Mrs. Alphonse Pease
request the pleasure
of the company of
Sally and Ed for dinner.

R.S.V.P.

D. Rewrite the following letter of sympathy. Then explain what you did to improve it.

Dear Ralph,

   It's too bad about your partner's passing into the big microchip in the sky. You can never really make up for his loss, especially since he was so important to your company and to the computer industry.
   The best you can do is try to forget him, though your offices won't seem the same without him.

Sincerely,

Draw up a chart describing the types of letters discussed in Part Six of this book: routine letters, diplomatic refusals, sales letters, and the various types of social-business letters. Create categories for the letter types, such as "outline," "tone requirements," "contribution to goodwill," and "techniques to avoid." The chart format will allow you to compare various types of correspondence and will help you remember the characteristics of each type of letter.

PART SEVEN
WRITING EFFECTIVE MEMOS, REPORTS, AND RELATED MESSAGES

43

Formats for Memos and Short Reports

Suppose you are one of five people assigned to work on an advertising campaign for Sun-Rich orange juice. Your group has had a meeting with the Sun-Rich people to discuss possible approaches to the campaign. After the meeting, you get a phone call from the client because they forgot to tell you to avoid the overused word *refreshing* in the campaign. What would be the most effective way of communicating this new information to the others in your group? You might call each of them, but this is time-consuming and repetitive. A more effective way might be to hold a meeting, but a meeting to transmit just one piece of information does not make good use of everyone's time. The most efficient way of sharing the new information would be to write a memorandum, or memo.

THE ADVANTAGES OF A MEMO

Memos help business people share information. As a valuable way of communicating, they have many advantages over other forms of office communication, such as phone calls, informal talks, and more formal meetings.

- A memo can reach many people at the same time. A memo gives all who receive it equal access to the information it contains. If the same information were relayed by word of mouth, some people would hear it much later than others, and some might not hear it at all.
- A memo can clearly present complicated or technical material that might be confusing if presented orally. In a memo, figures can be presented visually in chart form. Hearing these same numbers would probably overwhelm listeners and confuse rather than enlighten them.

- A memo can provide documentation of a plan, proposal, agreement, or some other type of decision. When two employees iron out a difficult policy matter in discussion and decide on a plan of action, a memo provides a written record of their solution and the specific methods they agreed upon for implementing it.
- A memo can promote consistency in company policy. For example, a memo from the general manager explaining the procedures for interviewing job applicants can lessen the chance of unfair hiring practices.

The memos you write serve many purposes within the company. In addition, they tell others something about you. A well-written, clearly presented memo accomplishes your purpose and lets others know that you are an effective communicator. In a large company with many employees, the memos you write may be the only way some people can evaluate you. Sometimes copies of memos are sent outside the company. Only a well-constructed memo is appropriate for outside circulation.

MEMO FORMATS

Most companies insist on a particular format for their interoffice correspondence. However, though details may vary slightly, most memo formats are similar because they serve the same purpose: to present needed information in a consistent and efficient way that saves time for both writer and reader.

Using Preprinted Forms

Many companies use preprinted forms for their memos, similar to the one in Figure 43-1. Preprinted forms usually include the company name, a designation such as *Interoffice Memo,* and the headings *TO, FROM, SUBJECT,* and *DATE.* The specific information is typed in each time as needed.

```
GREENLINE TRAVEL SERVICES, INC.



                          Interoffice Memo


   DATE:      June 30, 1987

   TO:        Gordon Chu, Ray Messina

   FROM:      Lauren Shelmire

   SUBJECT:   More Efficient Buying Procedures
```

Figure 43-1 An interoffice memo on a preprinted form.

Some businesses use memo sets that include several sheets and carbons that are perforated at the top. These sets provide an original for the recipient and two or more copies, which may be color-coded. Printed memo forms may also include an area for reply by the recipient, as shown in Figure 43-2.

Typing Your Own Memo Form

In some companies, you must create your own memo form on a blank sheet of paper. Because the arrangement for headings can vary, check with your supervisor or look in a company procedures manual before typing a memo form to make sure that it follows company style.

Unlike letters, memos are informal, working documents. The text of your message should appear in block paragraph style, single-spaced to save room, and close to the top of the page. In Figure 43-3, notice that the memo begins with a clear statement of purpose, that format is used to facilitate understanding of the information, and that the memo ends with a clear request for reader action.

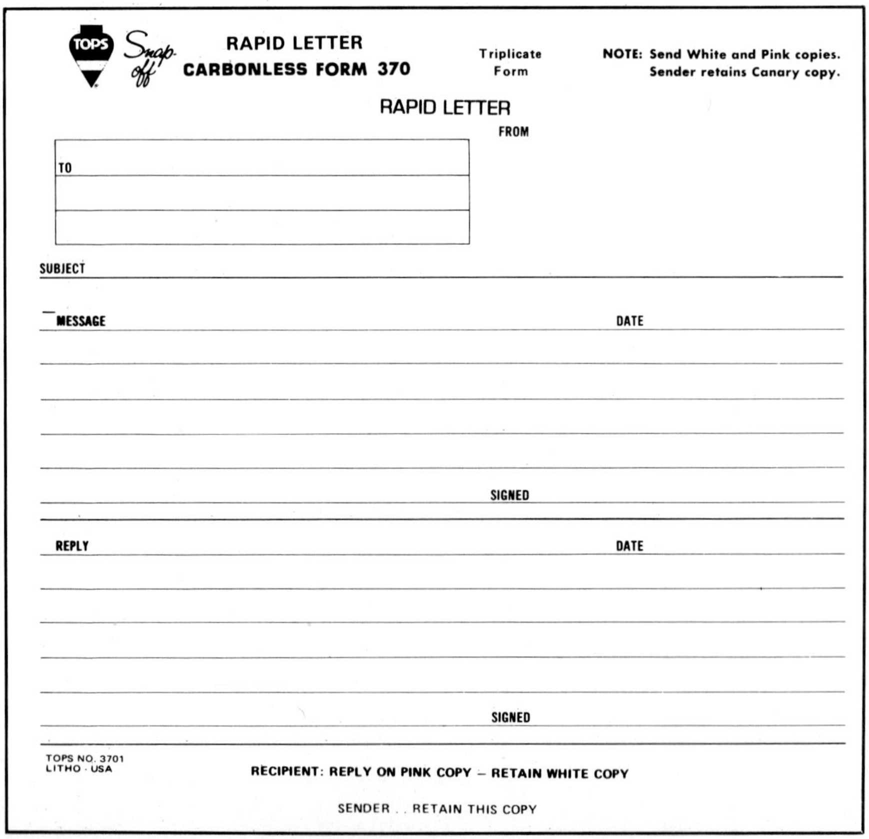

TOPS Snap-off RAPID LETTER CARBONLESS FORM 370

Triplicate Form

NOTE: Send White and Pink copies. Sender retains Canary copy.

RAPID LETTER

FROM

TO

SUBJECT

MESSAGE DATE

SIGNED

REPLY DATE

SIGNED

TOPS NO. 3701 LITHO · USA

RECIPIENT: REPLY ON PINK COPY – RETAIN WHITE COPY

SENDER . . RETAIN THIS COPY

Figure 43-2 Printed memo form supplying area for recipient's reply.

```
                      ARTISAN TOOLS, INC.

                     Interoffice Memorandum


     TO:       Philip Calderone        FROM:    Rufus Washington

     SUBJECT:  New Warehouse Procedures  DATE:    July 15, 1987


     Below I have outlined the new procedure for warehouse operations. It should
     take effect immediately.

     1.  Supervisor distributes pick tickets to individual pickers, noting in
           log the ticket numbers distributed to each picker.
     2.  Picker locates items in warehouse, places them in tub with pick ticket
           attached, and places full tubs on the conveyor.
     3.  Tubs arrive at checkpoint. Checker checks tickets and items. If tickets
           and items are correct, tub is placed on conveyor to sorter. Checker
           notes any errors on log sheet according to ticket number and sends
           tickets back for repicking.
     4.  Sorter takes tubs and places items on platforms according to order num-
           ber. When order is complete, sorter signals forklift operator to con-
           vey platform to packer.
     5.  Packer packs order, securely attaching mailing label, and places boxed
           order on conveyor to shipping department.
     6.  Shipping department prepares order for immediate shipment.

     After two weeks of operation, please submit an evaluation of the efficiency
     of the new procedure.
                                       RW


     lrn
```

Figure 43-3 A completely typewritten memo.

Filling in the Form

The following generally accepted guidelines will help you prepare memos in a variety of situations.

Recipient. After the word *TO,* type the name of the person(s) who will receive the memo. The form of the name depends on the purpose of the memo and its degree of formality, as well as your relationship with the recipient. For example, although courtesy titles, such as *Mr.* and *Ms.,* are rarely used, you might use a courtesy title for the president of a company. A job title is frequently used to make sure the appropriate person receives the memo. The larger an organization is, the more important it will be to clearly identify organizational responsibility along with the name of the person who can take action in response to your memo.

In smaller companies, a first name or an initial and last name may match the more informal workplace relationships.

> TO: F. Munoz, P. Androutsos, Personnel
> FROM: N. Reivers, Operations

Notice that a memo to more than one person should list all the names in the heading. When all the names will not fit, type *See below* or *Distribution* on the *TO* line. Then, at the bottom of the memo, type the recipients' names, arranged alphabetically or by rank, as shown in Figure 43-7.

Sometimes a memo, especially one from upper management or one that describes procedures affecting many workers, has a general *TO* line that includes all workers affected without naming them.

> TO: All Artisan Tools Staff
> FROM: Advertising Department

Writer. The name of the writer of the memo goes on the *FROM* line, usually without a courtesy title, unless the writer holds a high position in the company. Use a job title if it is necessary for identification or if its use clarifies the purpose of the memo.

Subject. On the line marked *SUBJECT,* state briefly what the memo is about. Use key words that describe the subject and purpose of your memo as clearly and concisely as possible. The description should fit in one or two lines.

Date. Type the date on the *DATE* line in standard form: *April 12, 1988,* or *12 April 1988,* if European style is preferred.

Heading Arrangements. Headings are usually arranged in a single column, as in Figure 43-1. Some companies, however, use a two-column format, as shown in Figure 43-3. The typed words are aligned in two columns, beginning each column two spaces after the longest guide word.

Text Placement. Begin the text of your message, or the body, on the third line below the last line of the heading; in other words, leave two blank lines. The body of the memo can be aligned with the far left margin, under the heading, as in Figure 43-3. It also can be aligned with the first letter of the recipient's name, as in Figure 43-4. Use the format set by your company as a guide for all memos and letters.

Unless the memo is a draft, it will generally be single-spaced with blocked paragraphs. Drafts can be typed double-spaced to allow the writer to edit the text with ease.

Writer's Name or Initials. Type the writer's name or initials, if used, two lines below the last line of the body. If the heading of the memo is arranged in one column, begin typing the writer's name or initials at the center. If a two-column heading is used, align the initials with the first letter of the typed name in the *FROM* line, as in Figure 43-4. Some writers prefer to add their handwritten name or initials to the end of a typed memo. For a signed or initialed memo, type the writer's initials on the fourth line below the text.

Reference Initials and Notations. At a later time, you may need to know who else saw the memo or who prepared the memo. The typist's initials should be placed at the left margin on the fourth line below the text, above any enclosure and copy notations, as shown in Figure 43-4. Adding the typist's initials here is the same as placing them at the bottom of a letter. These initials should be in lowercase letters.

WHY MEMOS ARE WRITTEN

The reasons for writing memos are as varied as the people who write them. Yet, most memos are written for one of the following reasons:

- to give directions
- to request information or action
- to provide information
- to provide confirmation
- to serve as a cover memo for another document

Memos That Give Directions

A memo may give directions about a new company procedure or policy. Frequently, a memo that gives directions includes a list of steps to follow, as shown in Figure 43-3.

Memos That Request Information or Action

Some memos are written to obtain information or assistance. A well-written memo makes the request clear early in the memo. Supporting information is provided as needed. Figure 43-4 shows such a memo.

ARTISAN TOOLS, INC.

Interoffice Memorandum

TO: Shelly Franco   FROM: Gabe Roth

SUBJECT: Slow-Moving Stock   DATE: July 17, 2987

Please provide me with the following sales and inventory information to facilitate planning next year's spring catalogue:

1. Catalogue numbers and descriptions of any items that have had
   sales of fewer than ten units a year for the last three years.
2. Present inventory of these items and unit costs.

Since we plan to offer special anniversary discounts on these items
as part of our 50th anniversary promotion, these figures should be
submitted by July 24.

                                        GR

aba
c Muriel Baker
  Carlos Valdez

Figure 43-4 A memo requesting information.

Memos That Provide Information

Companies often need to inform employees of events and situations of general interest. An internal memo is one of the main ways information of this type flows through a company. Plans for a company softball league or the arrival of a new vice president might be the subject of such a memo. The memo is usually widely distributed and may also be posted. Figure 43-5 is an example.

Memos That Provide Confirmation

When important agreements are reached at company meetings, it is a good idea to summarize the agreements in a confirmation memo so that everyone is sure of the decisions made.

To be effective, the memo must clearly describe the major points of each agreement and describe any specific strategies for implementing these agreements. A list format organizes the material well, as shown in Figure 43-6.

ARTISAN TOOLS, INC.

Interoffice Memorandum

TO: All Staff   FROM: Olivia Moss, President

SUBJECT: New Sales Office   DATE: July 27, 1987

I am pleased to announce that, because of unprecedented sales in fiscal 1986,
we are opening a new sales office to better serve the Eastern Sales Region.
Eunice Roberts will head the new office located at 417 Everly Boulevard.

I wish to thank each of you personally for your contributions in making this
company what it is today. The current expansion is directly attributable to
the hard work of all our employees. To show our gratitude, the company is
awarding end-of-year bonuses to all employees this year. In more immediate
recognition of your hard work, a company dinner and dance will be held on
August 5 at 6 p.m. at the River's Edge Restaurant. Please contact Anita
Barnes in Personnel (ext. 516), so we can determine how many people will attend. We look forward to seeing you there.

                                    OM

rds

Figure 43-5 A memo providing information.

ARTISAN TOOLS, INC.

Interoffice Memorandum

TO: B. Lambert, M. O'Neill   FROM: Ike Immelman

SUBJECT: Anniversary Catalogue   DATE: August 4, 1987

At the August 3 meeting regarding the anniversary edition of the catalogue,
we agreed to make three major changes:

1. Include three to five ''Anniversary Specials,'' full-page ads offering
   low prices on our most popular tools.
2. Offer ''Anniversary Closeouts'' on items that have had poor sales records for the last three years.
3. Include personal interest inserts highlighting individual employees,
   their present positions, and their histories with the company. Betty
   Lambert will interview five employees for this purpose and prepare a
   tribute to Rex Bradley, who retires this year.

I think this catalogue will be our best yet!

cem

Figure 43-6 A comfirmation memo.

Cover Memos

A memo will frequently accompany a report, study, or similar document to introduce the document to the reader with a brief explanation of its contents. The memo may highlight important points about the document but does not provide details. If appropriate, the memo gives credit to sources that the writer used to prepare the report or study. Figure 43-7 is a cover memo.

ARTISAN TOOLS, INC.

Interoffice Memorandum

TO: Distribution   FROM: Alison Galupo

SUBJECT: Sales Report   DATE: August 5, 1987

Enclosed are the results of the study on seasonal fluctuations in the sales of certain tools. As you know, we are taking up room in each season's catalogue to display tools that do not sell well during that season. With the information in this report, the catalogue can now be trimmed to exclude these seasonally unpopular items. These items can be displayed only during the seasons in which they sell well.

Please read the report carefully, and check the accuracy of the information. Any inconsistencies should be reported to me, in writing, by August 15. Information should be put in my mailbox (#43).

                          AG

pfg
Enc.

Distribution:

R. Fortunato
B. Lambert
S. Miles
M. O'Neill
J. Polachek

Figure 43-7 A cover memo.

THE SHORT REPORT

Business people are frequently called upon to write short reports. The basic purpose of any business report is to provide information that helps managers remain aware of what is happening within the company and gives them data to make decisions about policy changes. The memo format is a convenient way to present a short report that will be read and used inside the organization.

Short reports are somewhat more rigidly structured than routine memos. Most short reports have the following parts:

- an introduction, which states the purpose of the report
- a body, which includes the essential content of the report, along with the supporting details and relevant data
- a conclusion, which summarizes the main points of the report (and may include recommendations of future action)

Short reports generally fall into three broad categories: periodic reports, progress reports, and persuasive reports.

Periodic Reports

Periodic reports are submitted according to a set schedule; they may be prepared daily, weekly, monthly, quarterly, or yearly. Reports giving weekly overtime and monthly production statistics are two examples of periodic reports. By their nature, periodic reports include much specific information. A conclusion may not always be appropriate. Often, only an accurate reporting of data is necessary. Figure 43-8 shows a typical periodic report.

ARTISAN TOOLS, INC.

Interoffice Memorandum

TO: Carl Lopez   FROM: Kelvin Jones

SUBJECT: July Shipping Report   DATE: August 3, 1987

Below are the shipping figures for July. Also shown are the number of items on back order in each category.

	Shipped	Back Orders
Lawn and Garden	8,642	21
Storage and Organization	2,404	6
Non-Power Tools	2,289	18
Power Tools	2,053	–
Security	2,109	5
Household Gadgets	1,049	15
Automotive	833	–
Energy Savers	655	–
Gift Items	392	–

Total Pieces Shipped: 20,426
Total Orders Shipped: 3,853
Total Back Orders: 65

mpk

Figure 43-8 A periodic report.

Progress Reports

Progress reports tell the reader how well a particular plan or project is moving forward. Rather than merely stating what has occurred (as a periodic report does), a progress report tracks the development of a project over a period of time. A progress report may also provide key findings or predict when a project will be completed. Reports that communicate the results of a study fall into this general category as well. Figure 43-9 is an example of a progress report. Notice that the writer provides all the relevant information so that the recipients can gauge the status of the project.

ARTISAN TOOLS, INC.

Interoffice Memorandum

TO: Wilhelmina Montgomery   FROM: Roy Kirkpatrick

SUBJECT: Southwest Regional Sales   DATE: October 5, 1987

A study completed in November 1986 by Lester Wilson Associates predicted that a change in marketing strategies could double our sales in Nevada, Texas, Arizona, and New Mexico from 4,500 orders (approximately $200,000 annually) to over 9,000 orders (approximately $400,000).

In January 1987, we began direct mail advertising and telephone sales, and we increased sales calls. As of September 30, Southwest regional sales totaled 6,542 orders, or $352,609.

Since November and December sales are typically high, we forecast 9,500 and 11,000 orders for total yearly sales of approximately $500,000.

It would seem that our advertising efforts have been a success.

ajp
c Matthew Lepo

Figure 43-9 A progress report.

Persuasive Reports

Some reports are written to convince the reader of something, such as the need for a new piece of machinery or a change in procedures. Rather than merely giving information, these reports use facts and figures to persuade the reader to follow a particular course of action. Figure 43-10 shows a persuasive report in memo style.

ARTISAN TOOLS, INC.

Interoffice Memorandum

TO: Steven Mancuso   FROM: Gail Randall

SUBJECT: Adoption of New Tool Line   DATE: September 8, 1987

Proposal

In your memo of June 8, you asked me to look into the initiation of a new line of tools. I propose that in our 1989 catalogue we offer a line of ''antique'' tools, built in the manner of and with the same materials as tools made 50 or more years ago. While these could legitimately be used as tools, most buyers would purchase them for their nostalgic and decorative value.

The results of the survey recently completed by Hook & Clark Research Corp. suggest that these tools will sell well. I can furnish you with a copy of this report if you are interested.

Reasons for Adoption of Antique Tool Line

1. More and more people are looking to the values and fine craftwork of the past as a model for today. These tools would reflect this respect for years past.
2. Next year marks our 50th anniversary. We will be looking back to our roots. What better time to begin advertising a new line of tools ''just like the ones in your granddad's tool chest''?
3. Our present customers are the very people who are most likely to want to purchase these tools. The Hook & Clark survey indicates that 70 percent of our customers would be interested in antique tools. The survey also shows that 25 percent of noncustomers would be interested.
4. I have the names of several manufacturers who produce tools such as these. Most are located near farming communities in western Pennsylvania and in the Midwest. For orders over 500 units and with 6 months' lead time, they could provide excellent reproductions at a cost of approximately 10 percent more than our currently listed prices for similar ''new'' tools.

Conclusion

I recommend that we offer a new line of authentically reproduced ''antique'' tools in our spring 1989 catalogue. In the spring 1988 catalogue, I propose that we place a half- or full-page advertisement announcing this new line of tools. Please call me to set up an appointment to discuss this further.

ytr

Figure 43-10 A persuasive report.

SHORT REPORT FORMATS

Different types of reports require different formats. As a report writer, you must decide which format will best fit the report you are writing.

Paragraph Format. The paragraph format is narrative in style. It is appropriate for reports that state facts or present arguments that do not require many figures as supporting data. The report in Figure 43-9 displays paragraph format.

List Format. The list format is a good choice for reports that enumerate reasons, recommendations, individuals, products, and so on. Each item listed should begin on a separate line and may be preceded by a number, letter, or symbol. Figure 43-10 displays a typical list format.

Table Format. The table format is the clearest format for reports containing statistics or a large number of figures broken into several categories. A table helps the reader to organize the information visually. It also allows the reader to compare pieces of data. Refer to Figure 43-8 for an example of the table format in a short report.

Letter Format. Short reports, especially those directed outside the company, are often presented in letter format. All the standard parts of a letter are present, and the report is written on letterhead stationery. The body of the letter is the report.

Since a report in letter format is usually sent outside the company, its introduction may be more formal than that of other short reports. The introduction should explain the purpose of the report and may also describe the circumstances under which it was commissioned. Occasionally, letter format is used within a company.

The body of the report contains the details that carry its message. If the discussion requires a number of paragraphs, headings will help the reader to digest the material.

The conclusion of a report in letter format may offer further help or give instructions if there are questions. Figure 43-11 is a letter report by a research firm summarizing the results of a marketing survey.

Preprinted Forms. Certain reports are prepared so frequently that companies provide preprinted forms for them. Sales reports, expense reports, and production reports may fall into this category. The preprinted form helps the writer record the necessary information easily and quickly. The reader can obtain needed information at a glance. Often, preprinted forms include several color-coded carbons for the convenience of the writer. Figure 43-12 shows a sample preprinted form.

Hook
  & Clark Research Corp.
  4000 Woodlawn Avenue
  Spokane, Washington 99208

September 8, 1987

Ms. Gail Randall
Artisan Tools, Inc.
P.O. Box 999
Spokane, Washington 99208

Subject: Market Survey for ''Antique'' Tool Line

Dear Ms. Randall:

We have analyzed the market potential of your proposed line of ''antique''
tools. We find that not only is there a strong market, but you are also already in touch with the very customers who are most likely to purchase these
items.

Summary of Results

- Nostalgia and early Americana are popular concepts today. Of people we
  surveyed, 62 percent were more receptive to promotional themes of country life, family, and home than they were to more futuristic themes and
  slick advertising.

- Of those surveyed, 72 percent believed that the ''antique'' tools you
  propose to market will be of higher quality and last longer than other
  tools currently available.

- Artisan Tools, Inc. currently has access to many potential customers for
  this new line of tools. Of your current catalogue customers, 70 percent
  expressed interest in the antique tools. Of noncustomers surveyed, 25
  percent expressed interest.

- Because of your advance promotional work, 93 percent of your customers
  are aware that you are approaching your 50th anniversary. Of those questioned, 51 percent indicated that they anticipate special offers from
  Artisan Tools as part of the celebration.

If you have any further questions concerning the details of our research,
please call me at 555-8962.

Sincerely yours,

Sylvester Rzepnicki

Sylvester Rzepnicki
Market Analyst

Figure 43-11 A letter report.

CARBONLESS FORM 3878

NO CARBON REQUIRED

EXPENSE REPORT

DUPLICATE

EXPENSE REPORT

(ATTACH RECEIPTS IF POSSIBLE)

TO ______________________ FROM ______________________

FOR PERIOD ENDING	SUN. CITY	MON. CITY	TUES. CITY	WED. CITY	THUR. CITY	FRI. CITY	SAT.	TOTALS	
1 HOTEL MOTEL									1
2 BREAKFAST									2
3 LUNCH									3
4 DINNER									4
5 PLANE-RAIL BUS FARE									5
6 LOCAL TAXIS BUS FARE									6
7 AUTO EXPENSE-RE-PAIR-TIRES-SUPPLIES									7
8 GAS AND OIL									8
9 LUBRICATION AND WASH									9
10 GARAGE PARKING									10
11 TOLLS									11
12 PHONE TELEGRAMS									12
13 TIPS									13
14 ENTERTAINMENT									14
15									15
16									16
TOTALS									

STATE BUSINESS PURPOSE—PEOPLE ENTERTAINED—PLACE OF ENTERTAINMENT AND TIME—LIST CALLS MADE

I HEREBY CERTIFY THAT THE ABOVE EXPENDITURES REPRESENT CASH SPENT FOR LEGITIMATE COMPANY BUSINESS ONLY AND INCLUDES NO ITEMS OF A PERSONAL NATURE.

SIGNED ______________________

DATE	REPAYMENT RECAP	AMOUNT	MILEAGE RECORD		APPROVAL	CASHIERS MEMO
	ADVANCE RECEIVED		END OF TRIP			
	REIMBURSED					CHECK NO.
	TOTAL		LESS START			
	EXPENSE FOR WEEK		MILES PER TRIP			
	OVER OR SHORT					DATE AMOUNT

TOPS FORM 3878 LITHO IN U.S.A.

Figure 43-12 A preprinted report form.

EDITING EXERCISES

A. The memo that appears below has five format errors. List the five errors, and tell how the item should appear.

ARTISAN TOOLS, INC.

Interoffice Memorandum

TO: All Staff   FROM: Olivia Moss, President

SUBJECT: New Head of Advertising   DATE: August 24, 1987

    Artisan Tools is pleased to announce the promotion of Ian Cumpstone to the position of Head of Advertising. Ian will take the position held by Rex Bradley, who will retire at the end of this month.

When Ian came to our company five years ago, his task was to build a small telephone sales department into an effective advertising network. His success with telephone sales assures us that the Advertising Department is in good hands.
Please take time to congratulate Ian on his promotion.

OM

rds

B. Descriptions of eight memos follow. For each memo, note whether it gives instructions, requests information, provides information, provides confirmation, or serves as a cover memo.

1. Levi Rose, biology department chairman at Ramsey University in Sioux City, Iowa, has been offered a grant to study at Oxford University for one year. Rose has been given a one-year leave of absence. The administration wants to inform all staff members of Professor Rose's honor.

2. Yesterday Helen Grabowski and Sloan McGlade of National Wholesale Furniture, Inc., met in Louisville, Kentucky, to discuss a plan for marketing their furniture to nursing and convalescent home facilities. Helen wants to send a memo to Sloan, detailing the plans they made and who will be responsible for implementing each part of the plan.

3. The management at Coastal Bottling Company in San Francisco, California, has instituted a new procedure for storing soft drink ingredients. The management wishes to inform the receiving department members of the details of the new procedure.

4. Allen Oliveri, production supervisor at Lasting Plastics Company in Bridgeport, Connecticut, has written a report investigating several methods for disposing of waste from the production process. He needs to write a memo to send with his report to the company president.

5. David Howard, a vice president at Unity Gas and Electric, needs to find out how many customers call the recently installed Energy Hotline with questions about ways to conserve energy through home improvements. He writes a memo to the public relations director, Lily Tang, who supervises this project.

6. The vice presidents at First Federal Savings and Loan in Grand Rapids, Michigan, recently met to review plans for several new branch offices in Battle Creek. Norman Jackson, who attended the meeting, must draft a memo documenting the agreements reached.

7. Richard Sanchez, the head of consumer relations at Global Laboratories in Dallas, Texas, needs to find out from plant supervisors what precautions are being taken during drug manufacture to prevent tampering.

8. At Au Revoir Travel Services, a new policy of customer follow-up has been instituted. President Renata Shelburn wants to give details of the new procedure by memo.

PROBLEMS

Each item that follows describes the contents of a short report. Tell which format (paragraph, list, or table) you think would be most appropriate, and why.

1. for a sales report by an employee of Industrial Gauge, Inc., figures showing dollar sales of pressure gauges by month for the years 1984, 1985, 1986

2. from the personnel director to the head of the accounting department of KinderBooks, Inc., the names, addresses, and telephone numbers of recent applicants for an open position

3. from the head of receiving to the payroll director of National Trucking, a report of employee overtime hours (includes name of employee, hourly wage, total overtime hours worked, and overtime pay due)

4. a memo reporting the status of plans for a Christmas fund for the needy, on which an employee committee has been meeting weekly

5. a short memo justifying the use of temporary clerical help during a busy period in the word processing department of Safety Insurance Company

6. a memo presenting a series of recommendations for redesigning the art studio at Morley Graphics

You are the assistant to Raoul Fuentes, marketing director of Excel Sportswear. Mr. Fuentes has given you the task of summarizing data from a recent marketing study. You do not know exactly how the study will be used. Using the data supplied below, write a cover memo to accompany the report you will give to Mr. Fuentes. Organize the data logically, and choose the best format for the memo. Be sure to set up the memo with the correct headings in the correct placement. Also include closing notations.

Data for memo:

- Of all our customers, 63% prefer natural fiber clothing to synthetic fiber clothing.
- Women whose ages are 18 to 35 make up 69% of our market.
- Of all athletic shoes, running shoes account for 51% of sales, tennis shoes for 25%, aerobic shoes for 19%. Golf, basketball, and other specialized shoes make up the remainder.
- Of all our male customers, 12% buy clothing as gifts for their girlfriends or wives.
- Of all our customers, 2% are over 75 years old.
- For tennis clothing, 86% of our customers prefer white over all other colors.
- Athletic shoes account for 40% of all sales.

44
Planning and Writing Memos and Reports

Good business writing does not happen accidentally. Rather, it is the result of careful planning and effective use of communication skills. This chapter will help you plan and write influential memos and short reports.

TONE AND STYLE

The tone of any memo depends on the identity of the recipient and the subject of the memo. Notice how the tone of each of the following excerpts matches its subject.

> Once again it's time for the annual company blood drive. Last year almost three-quarters of us here at Smythe & Smythe donated blood. Let's see if we can reach 100 percent this year! The drive will take place during the week of February 11. Make sure to mark the date on your calendar; we need all the help we can get. Call Hannah Clarke anytime before then to give her an idea of how many people will be participating. Our large staff can make a real difference in the emergency blood supply of this community. Thanks for your help, support, and generosity in this endeavor.

> Enclosed is the report you requested on projected enrollment at McKittrick University for the years 1988 to 2000. As you will see, we expect steady growth through the end of the century. This growth will necessitate expansion of both housing and teaching facilities.

The tone of the first excerpt is conversational because the subject is an announcement about an optional event. A formal tone is appropriate for the second excerpt, which is part of a memo introducing a formal report.

No matter what type of memo you write, first you must organize your thoughts. A memo that wanders from the subject or one that is confusing may not even be read, let alone acted upon. The following simple framework can be helpful in organizing memos:

- statement of purpose
- supporting data
- follow-through

The first or second sentence of a memo should clearly state the purpose of the memo. Often, a reference to a previous letter, memo, meeting, or conversation will help provide a brief background and state the purpose.

Data pertinent to your request, recommendation, or report should make up the major part of the memo. State your main points clearly and briefly. Visual aids such as lists, tables, charts, graphs, or headings will often help clarify the presentation.

Your memo should conclude with a very clear statement about what you want the reader(s) to do in response to the memo. The follow-through of a memo will depend on the specific subject of the memo. Thus, the follow-through can vary in its purpose.

- It may detail future action that will, or should, be taken.
- It may make recommendations.
- It may request information or other help.
- It may summarize the main points of the memo for emphasis.

Generally, when you sit down to write a memo, you should attempt to organize your thoughts into categories such as those just described. Certain types of memos, however, will benefit from less direct presentations.

Always keep your purpose in mind, and organize the memo to accomplish that purpose. Suppose you need to write to several department heads announcing budget cuts. Rather than announce the cuts immediately, it might be best first to explain the financial pressures that have led to the decrease in funds. Think about how you organize your thoughts whenever you want to persuade someone to follow an unpopular course of action. You probably explain your reasoning first, then suggest your alternative. This approach lessens resistance to your suggestion.

When you write a memo that requests action, you are a salesperson, making a pitch for your request. You must support the request well, especially if it will cost money. To write this type of memo, follow five important steps:

1. Make a request; do not give an order. People are more likely to respond positively to a polite request than to a brusque demand.

2. Tell why the recipient should grant the request. Be factual. This part of the memo gives the reader supporting reasons for your request. When you summarize more than one reason, organize your ideas in logical order. Consider using an organizational pattern that presents information consistently in most to least important order, or least to most important order, or by category.

3. Detail the probable costs. Inform the recipient of the costs as fully as possible. By this time, your reader should be convinced of the merit of your proposal.

4. If appropriate, mention what you have done to try to avoid the expenditure. People are more willing to grant a costly request if they believe that less costly options have been explored.

5. Summarize your request, and clearly present your recommendations for carrying it out. Briefly restate your request, including all major points. If appropriate, detail what action will be taken—how the request, if granted will be carried out.

USING YOUR WORD PROCESSOR
Formatting Reports

Word processors can make report preparation much easier by taking care of many format considerations for you. Here are some examples:

- Like typewriters, word processors will maintain margins throughout a document. You can easily create special indentions, as for a binding on the left. With a word processor, margins can be reset or adjusted after you have inputted the material but before you print it. For example, even though you have inputted the material with a 65-character line, you can print it out at any line length without retyping.
- Some word processors will keep track of multilevel heading structures. Placement, spacing, and capitalization are taken care of by the word processor when you indicate the level of the head.
- Most word processors will paginate a report for you, placing the page number at the top or bottom of the page. (For title pages and other front matter, you will need to cancel this command.)
- Many word processors can format footnotes. All you need to do is indicate where the superscript should be and type the footnote. The machine will automatically reserve the proper number of lines at the bottom of the page.
- You can use a word processor to create an endnotes page. As you type the manuscript, type in the notes as well. The machine will save them to be printed out as correctly formatted endnotes.
- A word processor can be programmed to help with the format of bibliographic entries, which can have many variations. This capability reduces the chance for error.

Different hardware and software options have different capabilities, of course. Be sure you know how your machine can help you before you type a document.

Another type of memo is one that seeks information from the recipient. This type of memo should contain three main elements.

1. Provide a clear statement of the request in the first paragraph. Suppose the dean of McKittrick University wants to find out which students have not yet paid their yearly tuition, so that the university can send out reminder notices.

    Please provide me with the following information on all students from whom you have not received a 1987–1988 tuition payment.

2. Provide additional information that clarifies the request. Be specific about exactly what information you need or in what form it should appear. For example, a list format may be useful for the tuition information.

    1. Student name, university address, and telephone number.
    2. Parents' names (if applicable), address, and telephone number.

3. Restate the request and any other necessary information in the last paragraph. Tell when the information is needed, where it should be sent (if not to you), and so on. Include any request for follow-up information.

    I would appreciate having the information on late-paying students by September 15. I will send you copies of my correspondence for your files and would appreciate updates on payment as appropriate.

As you learned in the previous chapter, a confirmation memo has a very specific purpose: to document decisions made verbally. If necessary, you or others can refer to a confirmation memo to refresh your memory about specifics. When writing a confirmation memo, keep these points in mind:

1. State the purpose of the memo, and specify the meeting or conversation it documents. Make clear that this memo confirms the agreements of a particular meeting.

2. Clearly restate agreements or decisions reached verbally. Be specific about the main topics and decisions. A list format is best when more than one topic is represented.

3. Include a follow-through paragraph. This paragraph should, when appropriate, ask the reader to respond with any questions or corrections.

A memo that provides information must be well organized and clear. The main goal is for the reader to be able to understand and use the information.

Sometimes you will use the memo format to make suggestions to improve your workplace. When you write this type of memo, you must keep a balance between persuasion and tact. Refer to Figure 44-1 as you read the following tips.

1. Do not apologize for your ideas, but avoid sounding like a know-it-all.

2. Suggest improvements, pointing out deficiencies in the present system or procedure. Avoid extreme negativism, however. Whenever possible, acknowledge the merits of the existing system. Although you want to support your case for improvement, you need not attack the present system or procedure unmercifully. Also, avoid intimidating or browbeating the reader. These strategies will only alienate your reader.

3. Be specific and clear. Present your ideas logically and coherently.

McKITTRICK UNIVERSITY
Interoffice Memorandum

TO: Harrison Lewis   FROM: Ruth Vandever

SUBJECT: Dormitory Expansion   DATE: May 4, 1987

I have been thinking about our present plans for dormitory expansion and believe that we can save time and money by approaching the problem in a different way. Here are my thoughts:

1. Hiring a consultant firm to do a study of projected needs would serve our purpose, but it would cost thousands of dollars. Why not discuss with the statistics and economics departments the possibility of paying some of our best students to conduct research and draw conclusions? I have discussed the idea informally with Mort Aarons, and he feels the idea is feasible as long as we choose the most gifted juniors and seniors, whose abilities are proven.

2. Although a consultant could offer many kinds of experience, missing would be an understanding of the university atmosphere and the living trends of the student body. Who would be better qualified than our own students to assess these important factors?

3. Finally, I believe that as we save money we will also give invaluable experience to students here at McKittrick. With our own professors (who themselves act as consultants to local businesses) overseeing the project, we will conserve resources and increase profits, both financial and personal.

Your thoughts on this suggestion would be appreciated. If the idea seems feasible, let's meet with Mort Aarons and Ed Strykowski as soon as possible.

                        RV

jnm

Figure 44-1 A suggestion memo.

As you learned in Chapter 43, progress reports differ from periodic reports. Periodic reports simply present data; progress reports usually analyze the data. When writing a progress report, keep these suggestions in mind:

PROGRESS REPORTS

1. Briefly remind the reader of the scope of the project. If appropriate, summarize the progress made.

   The construction of a six-story, 120-unit dormitory is well underway. So far, excellent weather has permitted us to progress beyond our goals for this date.

2. Describe the progress in as much detail as necessary. Make sure your report fully informs the reader. If progress is inadequate, give an explanation.

   The foundations for the entire building have been poured, and most of the steel framework for the structure is in place. However, the flu epidemic has kept many workers off the job in recent weeks and has slowed down progress temporarily.

3. Summarize development and forecast progress. Summarize the progress made so far and give a realistic forecast of further progress and completion of the project. Avoid the temptation to predict a better rate of progress than is probable.

   Despite the flu epidemic, progress has put us three weeks ahead of schedule. Therefore, we should easily have the building enclosed by the time the rainy season begins. I believe the building will be fully completed for the opening of the 1990–1991 academic year.

The term *formal report* is really just another way of saying "long report." Formal reports usually run to ten or more pages. They cover subjects of greater complexity than those covered in short reports. For example, a formal report might explain the findings of a group researching several data processing systems and recommend one system based on these findings.

FORMAL REPORTS

Because of their complexity, formal reports may take many months to complete. Generally, many people contribute to a formal report: some do the research; others write the report. Secretaries or administrative assistants are often closely involved in the writing phase of a formal report, which typically has many parts:

1. *Covering Document.* As you learned in Chapter 43, a cover letter or memo tells what the report is and why it is being submitted. Figure 43-7 shows a cover memo. Other covering documents may go into greater detail than that example, telling more about the report or stating the sources of the information used in its preparation.

2. *Cover.* A cover attached to the front of a formal report gives it a finished look. The cover may be a special binder or simply an extra sheet of paper bearing the report title.

3. *Title Page.* A typical title page displays the full title of the report, including the subtitle if one exists; the writer's name, title, and department; the name of the person for whom the report has been prepared; and the date on which the report is being submitted.

4. *Table of Contents.* This page lists the main divisions of the report along with the page number where each division begins. Sometimes main headings within chapters are also included in the table of contents.

5. *Lists of Tables, Figures, or Illustrations.* If a report has many tables, charts, or other illustrations that people need to consult, these items should be included in a separate list (or several lists, if there are many groups of items). Similar in style to a table of contents, this list gives the table or illustration number, the title, and the page number.

6. *Summary or Abstract.* A sort of "minireport," the abstract summarizes the contents, giving the main points and recommendations.

7. *Body.* This is the main part of the report and the longest section. It presents the "meat" of the report—the findings. It may also give an analysis of those findings.

8. *Conclusions and Recommendations.* Most reports include the writer's conclusions as well as recommendations made by the writer based on the information presented.

9. *Appendix (or Appendixes).* Supplementary material, called an appendix, may be placed at the end of a report. Writers frequently place technical graphs, charts, questionnaires, and drawings in an appendix. These items support the text but are not appropriate within the body of the report. The text refers the reader to these items in the appendix. If there is more than one appendix, each is labeled with a letter (starting with Appendix A) and identified that way in the text.

10. *Endnotes.* Endnotes are textual notes that are placed together at the end of a report. They credit the sources used for specific pieces of data or give further explanation of particular points.

11. *Bibliography.* This is an alphabetical listing of the references used to prepare the report.

WHAT A FORMAL REPORT CAN ACCOMPLISH

Formal reports are valuable business documents. What can they do?

- Reports supply data to executives that enables them to make informed decisions. A report analyzing information about markets for a new product can help executives to decide whether or not that product should become part of the company line.

- Reports help company planners distribute work so that all resources are used and deadlines are met. A report that analyzes procedures at a book publishing company helps management devise systems for smooth and efficient work flow.

- Reports allow experts in a variety of areas to collaborate in solving complex problems. A report containing contributions by health experts, equipment specialists, and chemical engineers can help managers at a chemical plant find ways to protect employees and local residents from toxic leaks.

These three examples also illustrate the three basic types of reports: informational, interpretive, and problem-solving.

The informational report is the most basic type. Its purpose is to present detailed information on a particular subject. It presents information with a minimum of analysis and interpretation. An informational report might, for example, tell which industries in the Northeast might use a company's new product.

An interpretive report takes the informational report one step further. It reports data and then analyzes it in terms of a particular purpose. For example, an interpretive report might describe what types of data processing systems are available in a particular price range and which is the best for the company.

A problem-solving report collects and interprets data with a view to solving a particular problem. Businesses often ask employees to prepare and write such reports to determine such things as how efficiency on a production line can be increased.

PLANNING A FORMAL REPORT

As you plan your formal report, keep in mind that it is just as important to decide what will *not* be included as what will. Like a photograph, a report must have a clear focus. Otherwise, the important points you have to make will not come through to the reader.

The planning of a formal report can be broken into seven stages.

Establish the Purpose

Once you have chosen your topic, you must still establish your purpose before you can plan effectively. For example, suppose that the topic of your report is the high rate of absenteeism among workers. Is your purpose merely informational? If so, you will plan to collect data on which employees were absent when and for what stated reasons. Or is your purpose interpretive—do you need to speculate on why absenteeism is so high? In this case, you will not only have to do the research, but also perhaps interview employees and supervisors. If your purpose was to suggest solutions for the problem, in addition to the research and interviews, you might need to talk to other employers about their experiences.

Consider the Audience

During the planning stage of your report, you must think about your audience. Are your readers familiar with the situation, or do you need to provide a lot of background information? Are they well versed in the subject, or must you define terms carefully and simplify the language? Are your readers biased for or against your proposal, or are they neutral? Do they have the authority to act on your recommendations?

Conduct the Research

Research can take many forms, depending on the type of report you need to write. You may need to consult published works, unpublished studies, company correspondence, or other company records. You may need to distribute questionnaires or do in-person or telephone surveys.

Whatever your sources of information, it is important to acknowledge them. Sources can be divided into two types: primary and secondary. Primary sources are firsthand sources—information from interviews, questionnaires, conversations, and firsthand accounts. Secondary sources include information already developed and published by someone else. Books, magazines, and newspapers are secondary sources.

Evaluate the Results

Once your research is complete, you must organize and edit the data, and then interpret it. Unorganized data is of little or no use to a report reader.

Be sure to keep your purpose firmly in mind. Organize the data around the key points you need to make. Whittle down the data, removing information that is redundant or unrelated to your point. Once you have done this, you can begin analyzing the data and choosing how you will organize and present it to support your point.

Prepare the Outline

The outline you prepare will be the skeleton on which you build the body of your report. A well-thought-out outline will reduce the time you spend writing the actual report. When writing an outline, be thorough, making sure that you include every point you want to make. Do not, however, write the report at this time.

Organization of Writing

A well-organized report will be easier to read and more convincing than one that is poorly organized. There are many ways to organize information when you write. Different methods may be appropriate for different parts of the same report. Let's briefly examine four common methods.

Chronological Order. Chronological order is arrangement according to time of occurrence. This order is especially helpful when tracing the development of a process or explaining how to perform a task. The paragraph that follows is ordered chronologically:

> In January 1986, a questionnaire concerning interest in on-site day care was distributed to all employees. A surprising percentage of employees responded by the end of February, expressing interest and offering useful suggestions. In March, a ten-member committee was formed to study and report on on-site day care in other companies.

Spatial Order. This type of organization concerns the physical location of objects. You might organize from bottom to top (as when describing a building), near to far, left to right, and so on. The paragraph that follows describes a floor plan from left to right, referring to an illustration included in the report but not shown here.

> As you will see on the floor plan in Figure 5.3, the entrance at left opens into a cloakroom/storage area. A movable screen separates this area from the group play area at center. A smaller room, shown at far right, has tables for drawing, painting, and clay modeling.

This organization is the best for describing the relationship of objects in a space.

ON THE JOB
The Undocumented Source

Suppose that you have been helping your supervisor, Scott Kimball, with a report. You have done much of the research, making library trips and recording the information on note cards. You passed these on to Scott, who read, edited, and shaped the material to write the report. Now, as you begin typing it, you notice that, in at least three places, Scott has used information from outside sources but has failed to credit them. What should you do? Ignore the matter? Tell Scott about it—but how?

Whenever you use previously published information in a report or other document, whether you quote it directly or just use the ideas, you must acknowledge the source with a footnote, endnote, or some other form of credit. Not to do so is plagiarism, which is literary theft. You are stealing someone else's ideas or words by using them and implying that they are your own. In this situation, you do not know whether Scott is plagiarizing on purpose or whether he has merely been careless. The latter is the more likely possibility. It would be at best tactless and at worst unfair to accuse him of plagiarism.

You should approach Scott by asking if there are footnotes missing. You could explain that you remembered from your research that certain pieces of information came from particular sources. As you talk to Scott, keep your comments in the context of being a careful and thorough employee, not of accusing Scott of wrongdoing.

Chances are, Scott will realize that he has made a mistake and thank you for helping him create an accurate report. A good supervisor will welcome your thoroughness.

Order of Importance. Another common way to organize is by order of importance—either from least to most or from most to least important. The following paragraph uses the least-to-most format.

> Having parents help out in the center for two to four hours per week is recommended for several reasons. First, the children will be more cooperative if they see their parents as part of the program. Second, this system will cut costs. Third, parents will gain a feeling of genuine involvement.

Comparison/Contrast. Another organizational scheme involves comparing and/or contrasting two or more items, systems, or plans. Sometimes, all the characteristics of one item are given, followed by all the features of the other. Another way is to compare or contrast one quality at a time, as done below.

> The Kinderplay chairs are sturdy, well supported, and made of molded plastic. The Childtime chairs, on the other hand, are painted wood. Although attractive, they are slightly wobbly. The Kinderplay table is made of molded plastic with a washable, laminated top. The Childtime table is made of wood with a varnished surface, which could be damaged or stained.

Choice of Style

Formal reports are generally written in a formal (third-person) style rather than in an informal (first-person) style. Note the difference between the two:

> To meet the day-care needs of its employees and to promote better employee morale and productivity, Gardner Electronics should institute an on-site day-care facility that will be operational by September 30, 1988.

> We need to start an on-site day-care facility, which should be going full steam by September 30, 1988. Our study suggests we'll see a good increase in employee morale and productivity. Let's do it!

For most reports, a more formal style is preferred. The first-person style of the second excerpt may be easier and more interesting to read, but it loses some of its power because of its informal tone.

FORMATTING A FORMAL REPORT

Earlier in this chapter, you learned about the elements of a formal report—what their purposes are and how to write them. This section discusses how the elements should be presented in finished form.

Cover. Center the title of the report horizontally on the top half of the page. If the title is longer than one line, double-space in inverted pyramid style.

Title Page. Title page material is usually grouped in two or three blocks of type, with at least one inch of space at the top and bottom. The title of the report should be entirely in uppercase letters. The remainder of the page should be in uppercase and lowercase letters. See Figure 44-2.

ON–SITE DAY CARE AT
GARDNER ELECTRONICS

A Feasibility Study

Prepared by

Joseph M. Rodriguez
Assistant Director
Personnel Department

Submitted to

Nathan O. Mandel
Director of Personnel

July 27, 1987

Figure 44-2 Title page.

CONTENTS

Figure 44-3 Table of contents.

Table of Contents and Other Tables. Beginning about one-quarter of the way down from the top of the page, type *CONTENTS* or *TABLE OF CONTENTS* in uppercase letters. This line should be centered horizontally. Three lines below this, begin typing the table of contents. The items that are usually included are front matter, chapters, and end matter. Within those sections, double-space between different items. Between the sections, triple-space. For an item that will not fit on one line, single-space and go down to the next line to complete the item. If you include a breakdown by parts, center the part title horizontally and set it in all-capital letters. Leave two blank spaces above the part title and one space below.

After each item, skip one blank space and then type a leader (a solid row of periods with no spaces between them) to carry the reader's eye across the page to the page number. The ends of all leaders should align. Type all page numbers so that they line up at the right margin. See Figure 44-3.

Body. For the actual text within the body, use double-spacing. Leave a top margin of 12 lines and a bottom margin of 6 lines on opening pages. On other pages, leave top and bottom margins of 6 lines each.

When numbering text pages, do not number the first page. On all other pages, type the page number on the seventh line from the top at the right margin. You may use just the numeral or place the word *Page* before it. Begin the text on the third line below the page number.

Endnotes. Center the word *NOTES* in uppercase letters on line 13 as shown in Figure 44-4. Begin the first note on the third line below the title, using these guidelines:

- Single-space within notes, but double-space between them.
- Indent the first line five spaces.
- Use commas to separate elements such as author, book or article title, and publisher.
- Underscore book, magazine, and newspaper titles.

```
                              NOTES

     1. Morley Peters, ''Working Mothers Breathe a Sigh of Relief,'' New
York Journal, January 5, 1987, p. 14, cols. 1-2.

     2. Donald Zuccarelli, ''Taking Your Child to Work,'' Working, February
1987, p. 20.

     3. Ibid., p. 21.

     4. Benjamin Moskowitz, Working in a New Age, Apex Press, New York,
1986, p. 19.

     5. Ibid., p. 22.
```

Figure 44-4 Endnotes.

```
                          BIBLIOGRAPHY

Lu, Nancy, Women in the Work Force, Apex Press, New York, 1987.

Moskowitz, Benjamin, Working in a New Age, Apex Press, New York, 1986.

Peters, Morley, ''Working Mothers Breathe a Sigh of Relief,'' New York
     Journal, January 5, 1987, p. 14, cols. 1-2.

Reed, Stephen K., Management Techniques, Apex Press, New York, 1985.

Spain, Mildred, ''On-Site Day Care--Insurance Considerations,'' Manage-
     ment, June 1986, pp. 3-6.

Timko, Theresa S., ''On-Site Day Care Can Work!'' Women at Work, December,
     1986, pp. 11-16.

Zuccarelli, Donald, ''Taking Your Child to Work,'' Working, February 1987,
     pp. 18-22.
```

Figure 44-5 A bibliography.

Bibliography. Center *BIBLIOGRAPHY* in uppercase letters on line 13. On the third line below the title, type the first entry. Arrange entries alphabetically by the first word (usually the author's last name) of the entry. Single-space entries and double-space between them. Begin the first line at the left margin, but indent all turnover lines five spaces. Again, check a business procedures or standard office manual for more detailed information. Figure 44-5 shows a bibliography in accepted business format.

Heading Structure

Headings serve many purposes in a report. They break up the page and make it more readable. They summarize sections of text, thereby organizing and previewing material for the reader. By reading over the headings, a reader can get an idea of what the report covers. Three levels of headings are usually sufficient.

First-Level Headings. Center these headings with two blank lines above and one blank line below. Type them in uppercase letters.

Second-Level Headings. Begin second-level headings at the left margin with two blank lines above and one below. Type them in uppercase and lowercase letters and underscore them.

Third-Level Headings. Third-level headings are not placed alone on a line but appear on the same line as the text that follows. Leave one blank line above and indent five spaces, as you would any paragraph. Type third-level headings in uppercase and lowercase letters, underline them, and follow them with a period.

Quoted Material

Quoted material of more than four typewritten lines should be indented. Indent the entire quotation five spaces from both the left and the right margin. Single-space the material and leave one blank line above and below it.

Meryl Bittner gave the following assessment of child-care trends:

> More and more companies are offering child care at the place where the parent works. Employers have found that this decreases absenteeism and builds employee morale by making workers feel that they are important.

EDITING EXERCISES

A. Rewrite the following memo excerpts to make them clearer, more concise, or more appropriate.

1. It is unfair that Jane has an editorial assistant and I don't. No human being could possibly be expected to complete this project on time and remain sane! It's not my fault.

2. The figures in this report are the same as always. We sell more of some things and less of others, depending on the market.

3. I know you will find it in the goodness of your heart to give me time off to be with my sick mother. When can I arrange for my week off?

B. Type a bibliography of at least six entries, in proper format, on the subject of office manuals and secretarial handbooks. Make use of a standard office manual to help you correctly type the bibliographic entries.

PROBLEMS

A. Each of the following memo descriptions is followed by an excerpt from that memo. Each excerpt is inappropriate in one or more ways. Identify weaknesses in its tone, style, or format.

1. A shop supervisor is suggesting a new shop arrangement:

I know that I've only been shop supervisor for three years, but it seems that there might be a better way to arrange the production line. This is just an idea, and maybe it is not a good one, but I'll explain it.

2. A production manager is explaining recent increases in accidents:

I believe that there are at least five factors involved in the recent increase in work-related injuries. One is that new workers are trained inadequately in safety procedures. Another is that plant morale is poor, leading to sloppy work habits. Also, there is a serious lack of communication between departments. Another reason is that several key pieces of machinery are in poor repair. Also, production quotas are much too high to allow workers to take the proper safety precautions.

B. Tell which of the four methods of organizing information (chronological, spatial, order of importance, or comparison/contrast) would be best for each paragraph described.

1. an explanation of a diagram shown in the text telling how a piece of machinery works

2. a description of reasons for bringing out a new product line now rather than later

3. a discussion of advantages and disadvantages of one management style over another

4. a brief overview of the progress of a building program over the last three months

5. a discussion of contributions of a particular department to the company's profits

PROJECTS

A. Using the information provided, write a well-planned memo or report that fits each of the following descriptions. Use your own name as writer. Make sure the format is correct.

1. Send a memo that requests action to Maria Mendez, dated October 18, 1988. As the manager of the small secretarial staff at Clinical Medical Supplies, Inc., you wish to request three Avanti electronic typewriters to replace the old electric models currently in use. The new typewriters, which will cost a total of $1,500, should eliminate the current typing backlog. The typewriters are compatible with the data processing system used in other parts of the company. Renting the equipment would cost about the same as buying after three years. If you buy, you will have the equipment and be able to depreciate the equipment cost on tax returns. Recommend that the typewriters be purchased before the end of the year.

2. Send a confirmation memo to Skip Hanson, Stan Kusick, and Julia McClain, dated November 4, 1988. The memo confirms decisions made at a November 1 meeting (Perfect Paper Products), which you and the three memo recipients attended. At the meeting, which concerned new product lines, the group decided to pursue the following new products: insulated paper cups (Stan Kusick will explore various designs and weights); holiday paper placemats (Julia McClain will identify holidays to be represented and contact artists); paper coffee filters to fit all major brands of coffeemakers (Skip Hanson is responsible for designing one or more filters after study of major coffeemaker brands).

45
Preparing Minutes and Telecommunications

Rae Carson sat in the management committee meeting and listened carefully to the lively discussion about annual salary increases. She was the secretary for the group and was responsible for recording and typing a record of each meeting—the minutes. It was an important job, involving listening, note taking, writing, and secretarial skills. Her co-workers depended on her to document agreements and discussions correctly because they might be needed for future reference.

Minutes are one of the two types of business correspondence you will study in this chapter. The other is telecommunications, or messages that are sent electronically. Both types of correspondence are vital parts of business communication.

Although minutes and telecommunications have very different purposes and formats, they are alike in that both must accomplish a lot in very few words. In a telecommunication, in fact, every word costs money. Unnecessary words mean money spent unnecessarily.

To write effective minutes and telecommunications, you must extract the essence of a discussion or message and communicate it in a way that is easily understood by your audience. Too many words are wasteful. Too few will make a message unclear.

CONCISENESS COUNTS

Meetings are an inevitable part of business. They are held for a variety of reasons: to discuss problems, to make recommendations, to facilitate communication between individuals or departments, and to share information.

MEETINGS AND MINUTES

499

Meetings range from gatherings of informal work groups to highly structured, scheduled events with rules and protocol that must be followed.

The Importance of Agendas and Minutes

Before most formal or informal meetings, an agenda is prepared and often distributed to all who will participate in the meeting. An agenda is a list of subjects to be discussed. It helps the leader of the meeting to remember to cover all scheduled items and also keeps the discussion focused.

Proceedings of a meeting need to be recorded and distributed to those who attended the meeting and to other employees. Later, these minutes can be referred to as a permanent record of key decisions or events that occurred at the meeting. It is essential, then, that minutes be accurate and complete.

Taking the Minutes

If you are chosen to record and prepare minutes for distribution, you must pay constant attention to the proceedings of the meeting. Even informal work groups may require careful, well-documented minutes. To take complete minutes, you must do the following:

1. Record the date, time, and location of the meeting.

2. List the name of the person presiding.

3. Indicate who is attending. For small meetings, list the names of those who are present and, if applicable, those who are absent. For large meetings, give the number of people who are in attendance.

4. Refer to the minutes of the previous meeting. This is not always required, but when it is, note whether the minutes of the previous meeting were read and approved, read and revised, or not read at all.

5. Give a capsule account of all important points discussed, reports submitted, and agreements made. Include not only the subject discussed but any important supporting details.

6. List agenda items and the date, time, and location of the next meeting, if known.

Do not be afraid to ask to have something repeated if you have trouble recording the information the first time around. Minutes are useful only if they are accurate.

Meetings Run by Parliamentary Procedure

Sometimes meetings are held according to parliamentary procedure. Parliamentary procedure is a set of formal rules for conducting a meeting. The minutes of such a meeting should reflect this level of formality. Any motions or resolutions must be recorded word for word. You must name both the person who made the motion and the person who seconded it. Sometimes, when one or more subjects are voted on, the voting record of the members is included in the minutes.

The precise format for minutes varies depending on the type of meeting and company policy. The following are general guidelines. Be sure to check with your supervisor for any specific format instructions before typing minutes on the job.

FORMATS FOR MINUTES

The Heading

The heading identifies the group holding the meeting, often the company as well, and the date the meeting was held. Begin the heading 10 to 13 lines from the top of the page, and center it. Leave two blank lines after it, then begin the body. Figure 45-1 shows one format for minutes. Note that the heading specifies the body that met and the date of the meeting. This information is important for company records.

DID YOU KNOW?
Facsimile Transmission

Telegrams and telexes are two ways that you can send messages almost instantaneously from one place to another. Some offices use another method of telecommunication—facsimile transmission. You might think of facsimile transmission as long-distance photocopying. It combines photocopying technology with the features of a telex machine. A facsimile is a likeness. With facsimile transmission, you place a letter or other document into a special machine in your office. As the machine "reads" the document, it encodes information electronically that describes exactly how the document looks. This encoded information travels over telephone lines to another office, where there is a similar machine. There, the information is "decoded," and

a document is printed that is an exact copy of the one in your office. All this happens almost instantaneously.

Facsimile transmission has many different applications. You might transmit to a supplier a complicated order that could easily be garbled over the telephone. You could send to a different branch of your company long, involved instructions that would cost a fortune to send in a telegram.

Various types of visual documents—charts, graphs, drawings, and plans, for example—are especially suited to facsimile transmission. As more companies purchase facsimile equipment, this technology will take on more and more importance.

PREMIER EQUIPMENT COMPANY, INC.

MINUTES OF THE MANAGEMENT COMMITTEE MEETING OF JUNE 24, 1987

DATE, TIME,
ATTENDANCE

The monthly meeting of the management committee was held on June 24, 1987, at 9 a.m. in Conference Room B. President Ian McKenzie presided. Also attending were Rae Carson, Hector Gomez, Drew Russo, Blanche Strycharz, and Donna Waters. Absent were John Muhlheisen and Sol Stein.

MINUTES OF
PREVIOUS
MEETING

The minutes of the last meeting were read and corrected as follows: The new evaluation procedure will go into effect in July, not June.

OLD
BUSINESS

Blanche reported that the memo concerning personal telephone calls had been circulated to the staff and seemed to have solved the problem. Personal calls were at an all-time low so far this month.

Donna Waters reported that Phil Takats accepted the sales position and will begin actual sales on July 1.

NEW
BUSINESS

Drew Russo suggested we send two inside salespersons——Ernestine Walker and Lane Weir——to the Ferguson Controls, Inc., sales school in Houston in September. The group agreed to appropriate the funds. Drew will inform Ernestine and Lane.

NEXT
MEETING

The next meeting of the management committee will be on July 29 at 9 a.m. in Conference Room D.

Respectfully submitted,

Rae Carson, Secretary

Figure 45-1 Format for minutes.

The Body

The body of the minutes contains the record of attendance and the documentation of the meeting proceedings.

Display each major topic of discussion in a separate paragraph. Side headings, as shown in Figure 45-1, are one way to organize these paragraphs effectively and attractively. Identify the person who presents the topic as well as each speaker who contributes an important point. Briefly summarize each point made. In topic summaries, avoid using personal pronouns unless they are within a direct quotation.

The Closing

The traditional closing for minutes is the phrase *Respectfully submitted,* followed by the writer's signature (written) and name and job title (typed). Increasingly, however, minute formats dispense with the traditional closing and include merely the writer's signature and title. Check with your supervisor to find out your company's policy.

As we noted at the beginning of this chapter, the chief skills in recording minutes are extracting the main points of a discussion and summarizing them in an understandable way. Let's look at a few meeting excerpts and possible ways of summarizing them.

Suppose that the following is a verbatim account from a part of a meeting at Premier Equipment Company, Inc., of Denver, Colorado.

EXTRACTING THE MAIN POINTS

> Ian: I'm proposing that we split Deirdre's territory in half and hire another sales representative. Deirdre originally made this suggestion to me, so I know she's in favor of it.
> Hector: We could let Deirdre keep the Denver metropolitan area and give the new person the region to the north: Boulder, Fort Collins, and so on.
> Donna: You know, Phil Takats has told me several times that he would like to go out on the road. Do you think he could handle the job?
> Ian: Probably. Phil is a good inside sales rep and is already well known in the area because of his sales expertise. Since you're his supervisor, Donna, would you please check with him to see if he's interested?
> Donna: I'd be happy to.

The main points here are the proposal to split Deirdre's territory and the discussion of Phil's suitability for the open sales position.

Here is how this discussion might be summarized in the minutes:

> Ian proposed that Deirdre's sales territory be split, with Deirdre keeping the Denver metropolitan area and a second sales representative taking the area to the north. Donna proposed that Phil Takats be offered the job. Ian agreed that Phil might do well and asked Donna to approach him about it. Donna agreed.

How would you summarize the points in this example of a verbatim account from the same meeting?

> Blanche: As office manager, I'm distressed about the amount of time certain employees spend on the phone taking personal calls. Since the problem, as I see it, is limited to a few individuals, it seems unfair to ban personal calls for everyone. Maybe I should just talk privately to the employees who are causing the problem.
>
> Drew: Maybe. But how can you be sure that the employees you see are the only ones who are abusing the privilege? If you just talk to them, they might feel they are being singled out unfairly. And even if you talk privately, these things have a way of getting around.
>
> Ian: How about this? We'll send a memo around saying that some employees are abusing telephone privileges and that this practice cannot continue. At the same time—and we'll mention this in the memo too—let's have the receptionist keep a log of incoming personal calls for *all* employees. If the abuse continues, we can talk to individuals with the weight of documentation behind us.
>
> Blanche: I'll write the memo and have you approve it, Ian.

The main points of this discussion are the introduction of the problem, which is too many personal telephone calls; Drew's warning; Ian's solution; and the steps Blanche will take.

In the minutes of this meeting, all the important information should be included in a summary written as follows:

> Blanche brought up the problem of excessive personal telephone use by a few employees and proposed discussing the problem with them. Drew cautioned that talking to just a few might be unfair since abuse may be more widespread. Ian suggested that a memo be distributed stating the problem and asking that employees limit personal calls. The memo would also state that the receptionist is beginning a log of incoming personal calls for each employee. Ian suggested that if the situation did not improve, individuals could be approached. Blanche agreed to draft the memo and show it to Ian for approval.

Notice that this summary recalls the discussion without giving it verbatim. Blanche will be able to look at the minutes and know what her memo should include.

TELECOMMUNI- CATIONS

Telecommunications are messages transmitted electronically, such as the telegram, the cablegram or telex, and the mailgram.

Telegram. A telegram can be sent instantly at any time of day or night. Generally, the message is relayed over the telephone to the transmitter. The standard rate is based on a 15-word minimum, with a charge for every additional word. Telegrams get people's attention and are appropriate when the message must be received immediately. An overnight telegram can be used when the message is to be sent after-hours to a place of business. The message is delivered on the following morning. Overnight telegrams cost less than regular telegrams.

Cablegram or Telex. A cablegram or telex is a message transmitted directly from a special piece of equipment in one office to a similar piece of equipment in another. The recipient receives a printed copy of the message. When the equipment is in place in both the sending and the receiving office, a cablegram or telex can be sent and received any time during the business day.

Mailgram. Mailgrams are telecommunications sent via the postal service. The sender calls a telecommunications company and dictates a message. (The call must be made before 7 p.m.) The message is transmitted electronically to the post office, printed out, and delivered in the following day's mail. The cost is based on a 100-word minimum and is less than the cost of a telegram. A mailgram is appropriate when a message must be sent quickly, but not immediately.

Guidelines for Writing Telecommunications

Two goals—conciseness and clarity—should be uppermost in your mind when you write telecommunications. Because the cost of such messages is based on the number of words they contain, conciseness is very important. Any words that do not contribute to a clear meaning should be omitted. On the other hand, a message that is short but unclear is equally undesirable. To achieve clear and concise messages, keep the following guidelines in mind as you write telecommunications.

1. Remember that there is no charge for the inside address, the date, or punctuation. Effective punctuation aids clarity. Avoid the outmoded use of *STOP* for a period. Your company would not be charged for the period, but *would* be charged for the word *STOP*.

2. Use only necessary words. You need not write telecommunications in complete sentences as long as phrases are clear. You may also omit some of the courtesies that are part of regular letters, such as *please* and *thank you.*

3. Omit explanations and background information unless clarity is affected. For example, if you want to make a hotel reservation and have it confirmed, you would need to give only the appropriate dates and ask for confirmation. No explanation is necessary.

4. Use clear abbreviations to reduce word count. A two-word place name such as *New York* or *New Jersey* will be counted as two words. Therefore, *NY* or *NJ* would be better ways to convey these words. A list of standard state-name abbreviations is available at any post office. Make use of other common abbreviations as well: *PO* for *purchase order* and *COD* for *cash on delivery.* However, do not abbreviate single words—*Phil.* for *Philadelphia* or *imm.* for *immediately.* You will be charged for one word in either case. Since abbreviations allow for the possibility of misinterpretation, use them only when they will save money and will not affect the clarity of the message.

5. Use figures rather than words for numbers. Use the figure *125* rather than the words *one hundred twenty-five.* Every five characters of a number are considered a word. Therefore, *125* is one word; *125,000* is two words.

6. In a name with a separate prefix, omit the space. Names with separate prefixes are considered two words. Omitting the space saves a word. For example, write *Du Barry* as *DuBarry.* (Never do this in a letter or memo, however. These rules apply only to telecommunications.)

The two example messages that follow show how to reduce a message to its shortest clear form. The unedited version is given first, followed by a shortened version that is suitable for telecommunication.

> Please send the following items: 6 outdoor thermometers with the model number 8163; 6 thermometer brackets with the model number 4562; and 10 pressure gauges with the model number 9120. A plant accident damaged about half our equipment, and we need to replace it as soon as possible. Thank you.

> Send immediately 6 thermometers, #8163; 6 brackets, #4562; 10 gauges, #9120.

The courtesy phrases *please* and *thank you* have been left out in the second version. Also, since model numbers are provided, only the sketchiest parts descriptions are necessary. Commas and semicolons clarify the message, making it unnecessary to repeat words such as *with the.* Also omitted is the explanation of why the parts are needed. For the purpose of this message, it does not matter.

Here are two more messages, the first showing an unedited version and the second showing its telecommunication form.

> There has been a change in the car rental reservation for your sales trip to New York City. Rather than having a car waiting for you at Kennedy International Airport, the car will be waiting for you at your hotel, the De Mille, in New York City.

> Change in car rental for NYC trip. Pick up car at DeMille, not airport.

Here, unnecessary words such as *There has been a* have been deleted. The message is not written in complete sentences. *New York City* (three words) becomes *NYC* (one word). And the hotel name, *De Mille,* has been made into one word by omitting the space.

You should have the following information available to you when you are transmitting a telecommunication:

1. the account to be charged for the message

2. the full address and telephone number of the recipient

3. your full address and telephone number

4. the date of the message

Be sure to keep a copy of every telecommunication you send. You may also want to make additional copies for distribution within your company or to send as a confirmation copy to the recipient.

EDITING EXERCISES

Each of the following messages is complete but is not appropriate for use as a telegram, telex, or mailgram. Condense the message into the smallest number of words that will still convey a clear message.

1. Because of heavy snow conditions, my flight was not able to land at La Guardia Airport and landed at Newark Airport instead. I will, therefore, be unable to speak at the meeting of ski equipment retailers in New York City at 8:00 this evening. I am sorry for such late notice. I hope that this does not inconvenience you.

2. Here is a last-minute addition to the advertising copy for the Speedy Five Hundred Typewriter. The last line of the advertisement should read as follows: "Comes in black, blue, or green." I hope this arrives before you go to press. Thank you.

3. I have found that I need two additional documents for my meeting tomorrow afternoon. Please send a copy of the Leonard Williamson contract and the royalty statement for 1986 for Williamson's book. Send the documents by Air Express to me at my hotel. Thank you.

4. I would like to order the following items to arrive immediately. A broken water main destroyed our stock of these items: 40 Jiffy Toasters with the model number AK13; 80 Goldbrew Coffeemakers with the model number ML562; and 40 Le Mixers with the model number PN73. We will place another, larger order in several weeks. Please confirm this order by telephone. Thank you.

5. Please cancel Purchase Order 65023 for various office supplies. We recently discovered sufficient stock of these items in our warehouse. We hope that this cancellation will not inconvenience you.

PROBLEMS

In each set of excerpts, choose the one (a or b) that would be most appropriate to record as official minutes of a meeting. Write a brief sentence explaining your choice.

1. a. Janis gave a brief report on her trip to Ferguson Controls, Inc., of Houston, Texas. She received a tour of the facility and five days of classes concerning the Ferguson line. She felt the trip was well worth her time and suggested that it become a regular part of our trainee program.
   b. Janis told about a trip she took to Texas where she learned about the way another company conducts its business. She enjoyed herself immensely.

2. a. Sales figures and strategies for summer of 1986 (January through March) were compared with sales from the same period of 1985. Sales were up in 1986.
   b. Sales figures and strategies for the period of January through March of 1986 were compared with sales from the same period of 1985. Sales were up 5 percent in 1986 over 1985.

3. a. Blanche accused Donna of nagging when she reminded her that time sheets for her department had not been handed in yet. Donna complained that Blanche never listens to her.
   b. Blanche raised the issue of lateness in turning in personnel time sheets. The sheets for Donna's department are one week overdue. Blanche and Donna were told by Steve that they must work together to solve the problem.

4. a. The meeting recessed at 12:15 for lunch. Bill, Dana, Julie, and Audrey remained to discuss plans for the upcoming trip to Toronto. They agreed that a representative from each department should attend the convention and that department heads should select the people who would go. When the meeting reconvened at 1 p.m., Bill told the rest of the group what he and Dana, Julie, and Audrey had agreed upon.
   b. The meeting recessed at 12:15 for lunch. Bill, Dana, Julie, and Audrey remained to discuss plans for the upcoming trip to Toronto. The group ordered a pizza from Tony's Pizzeria on Broadway. When the meeting reconvened, Bill told the rest of the group what his group had agreed upon during lunch.

PROJECTS

A. Write a memo to your instructor, using proper format, giving guidelines for writing telecommunications.

B. Write a short report comparing the rates and services offered by local telecommunications companies.

PART EIGHT
WRITING EFFECTIVE EMPLOYMENT COMMUNICATIONS

46
Planning and Writing Résumés

If you are a recent college graduate or expect to be one soon, you are probably about to look for a job. You want to put your education to work so that your investment of time, energy, and money will gain rewards. However, even if you have done extremely well in your college work, you may not be successful at getting the job you want. It's not enough to be well qualified for a job; you must also know how to sell your qualifications to a prospective employer. Your first selling tool is your résumé.

The word *résumé* is derived from a French word that means "to summarize." A résumé is a brief summary of certain aspects of a person's life that are pertinent to the world of work. It is a selective personal history. A résumé (sometimes spelled without the accents) may also be called a personal data sheet, personal qualification sheet, personal profile, vita, or curriculum vitae.

Your résumé sells you in much the same way a sales letter sells a product. It has the job of convincing a prospective employer to interview you—and to hire you.

You must plan your résumé the way you would plan a sales letter, as described in Chapter 41. You are the product, and you know yourself very well. You must also know the buyer—a company with a desirable job opening—thoroughly. Then you must write a résumé that matches your qualifications with the needs of the company.

An effective résumé is important because, like other sales letters, it must make a good impression on your reader in a very short time. It's estimated that your résumé has just 20 seconds in which to make an impression on a prospective employer. In less than a minute, you can become one of the applicants asked to come in for an interview, or one who receives a rejection— all on the strength of your résumé.

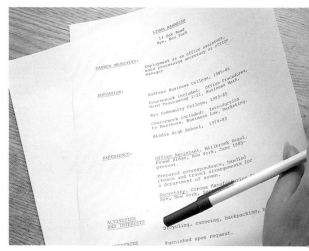

Getting Hired

Looking for work is not easy. In fact, many people believe that finding a job can be more difficult than actually doing the work. How do you go about finding such a job? What steps are involved in a successful job search? Let's take a look at one young woman's effort to find work.

Linda is a recent business school graduate with some previous office experience. Her first step is to meet with an advisor from her school's placement office, who gives her some general tips on job hunting as well as a few specific job leads. Linda is also using school and local libraries to research the job market in her area (*top left*). She makes notes on potential employers, including their addresses and telephone numbers.

(*Top right*) At home, Linda puts together a résumé that summarizes her education and work experience. The résumé lists the schools she has attended, the companies she has worked for, and the positions she has held. After Linda finishes typing her résumé, she proofreads it for typographical errors and mistakes in spelling, punctuation, and grammar. Once Linda perfects her résumé, she has it printed on good-quality, conservatively colored bond paper, so that the final product looks professional and presents her qualifications in an attractive and easy-to-read format.

(*Bottom right*) Linda's next step is to approach a variety of employment sources. Using names and addresses she found through her research, Linda sends her résumé, along with a cover letter, to a number of nearby companies. Linda is as careful with her cover letter as she was with her résumé: she makes sure it is brief, neat, and error-free.

(*Top*) Linda also brings her résumé to an employment agency and discusses her career goals with a staff member. He, in turn, describes job openings that the agency is trying to fill for various employers. Linda learns that if she obtains one of these jobs, the employer will pay the agency's fee. Some agencies require the job seeker to pay the fee. Fees are often based on a percentage of the job's yearly salary and can be as high as one month's salary; it is important to find out who will pay.

Like many employment agencies, the one Linda visits wants to test her office skills, particularly her typing speed (*bottom*). After several minutes of practice to familiarize herself with the agency's typewriter, Linda takes a timed test, typing for both speed and accuracy. Some employment agencies also have equipment available to test their applicants' skills on a variety of word processing machines. In addition, some agencies may test an applicant's ability to take dictation, add figures, spell, and proofread. Agencies use the results of these tests to match an applicant's skills with available positions. If there is a match, the agency will send the applicant to interview for the position.

(*Top*) Another way to obtain job interviews is by reading the classified section of the newspaper. While many companies rely on employment agencies to provide them with prospective employees, others prefer to do their own screening and hiring. Such companies are likely to advertise job openings in the classified sections of newspapers. Such advertisements usually describe the position and the firm in a few sentences, list the qualifications applicants should have, and tell whom to contact at the firm and whether to do so in person, by phone, or by mail.

(*Bottom*) This particular advertisement appeals to Linda because she is an excellent typist but does not know stenography. She has never worked for a law firm, but thinks she might want to, especially if the office is congenial and the salary is acceptable.

3

(*Top*) Linda answers the ad by calling the law firm. She knows that some companies ask applicants to phone them so that they can use the phone call as a screening device. If the applicant sounds personable and well spoken, the firm will ask them to submit a résumé or come in for an interview. If the applicant comes across poorly during the initial phone call, he or she may be told that the position is filled. Linda, who takes care to speak clearly, distinctly, and politely, is offered an interview with the law firm.

(*Bottom*) Linda now takes time to select the appropriate clothes for her interview. Her past employers were informal. Employees wore casual clothes, such as sweaters and slacks. Because this is a job interview—and a job interview with a law firm—Linda decides that those clothes just won't do. Instead, she selects her most businesslike outfit, a simple dress and jacket. A suit or a skirt, blouse, and blazer would also be appropriate.

(*Top*) To make sure her entire appearance is businesslike, Linda applies very little makeup and avoids strong perfume and excessive jewelry. She wears plain pantyhose and neat, polished shoes. After all her preparations, Linda feels she will make a good first impression by being well dressed and well groomed.

(*Bottom*) Another way to make a good impression is to arrive for a job interview on time, or even a bit early. Linda makes a point of getting directions in advance and allowing ample travel time. She arrives a few minutes before her scheduled appointment, makes one last check in a mirror, and enters the law office.

(*Top*) Once inside, Linda fills out an application form. Since she has brought along her résumé, she is able to refer to it for dates, addresses, and other items that need to be filled in on the application.

(*Bottom*) Linda is then called in to meet the law firm's personnel manager. Linda begins by shaking hands and introducing herself. She is nervous, but she tries to appear as calm and poised as possible. She makes her handshake firm and her voice steady. The manager offers Linda a seat, and the interview begins.

(*Top left*) The manager describes the company to Linda, explaining how long the firm has been in business, the kind of work it does, and how the work load is handled. Then the manager talks about the position that is available, telling Linda what a typical day's work is like for secretaries in the firm. She mentions how many people the secretary will work for and the kinds of office support they require. She also notes that some overtime work is required and describes the company's policy regarding new employees. Next, she lists the benefits the company offers. Finally she mentions the starting salary but explains that it is flexible. As part of the interview, the manager then asks Linda whether she has any questions. Linda has several: What is the starting date? How much overtime is involved? What is company policy about overtime compensation? How long is the trial period for new employees? How frequently does the company review its employees' job performance after the trial period ends? How flexible is the starting salary, and what factors might make it higher or lower?

(*Top right*) Then the manager begins questioning Linda about her work background, skills, and interests. She asks the following questions: What were your favorite classes in school? What do you like to do in your spare time? What interests you about working for a law firm? Do you work well under pressure? What were your responsibilities in your previous position? What makes you think you can handle this job? Linda answers each question thoughtfully and presents herself as a capable and competent individual with the right skills for the job. She backs up her claims with examples drawn from her school and work experience. The manager tells Linda that she is impressed by her résumé, her background, and her composure. She says that if Linda has no more questions, she will take her on a brief tour of the office and introduce her to the staff. Linda asks when the company will reach a decision on whom to hire. The manager explains that she will be interviewing applicants for several days and will make a decision the following week. She assures Linda that she will certainly be considered for the job.

8

(*Above*) Linda has several other job interviews that week, but no position appeals to her as much as the one at the law firm. She is delighted when the firm's personnel manager calls to offer her the job. She accepts the offer and confirms several important items with the manager, such as the date and time she will begin working for the company, her starting salary, the length of her trial period, and the approximate date of her first performance review.

(*Below*) Linda arrives for her first day on the job well rested, well dressed, and ready to work. Her job search is over, and her career is about to begin.

The following sections of this chapter will explain which of your assets and qualifications are of interest to employers and need to be in your résumé.

A prospective employer expects to find six points in a résumé:

1. the heading, which includes the applicant's name, address, and telephone number

2. career objectives

3. educational background as it relates to the company

4. work experience

5. relevant personal data

6. references

In this section you will examine the standard parts of a résumé and see how they apply to different kinds of work and educational backgrounds.

The Heading

The heading of a résumé is the part that contains your name, address, and telephone number. The applicant's name usually becomes the title of the résumé; it is often centered at the top of the page. An alternate title is the word *résumé* itself, but this style is quickly becoming obsolete.

If you use your name as the title of your résumé, your present address and telephone number should appear below your name, placed on the left or the

```
                           ANN SALENO
(address through June 15, 1987)     (address after June 15, 1987)
324 Fairfield Road                  65 River Road
Stamford, Connecticut 06901         Derby, Maine 04463
(203) 542-8293                      (617) 668-2317



                           JOHN CHU
                       237 Joliet Street
                     Chicago, Illinois 60601
                        (312) 876-2910



                           Résumé
                        Sandra Wilson
                      655 Jackson Avenue
                  Wauwatosa, Wisconsin 53213
                       (414) 555-6734
```

Figure 46-1 Three formats for a résumé heading.

right or in the center, depending on the format you have chosen. If you will be graduating from school shortly and living at a different address, also indicate that address and telephone number and the date when you can be reached there.

It is not necessary to include a picture of yourself with your résumé. In fact, because federal law prohibits discrimination based on race, sex, and age, it is better for both you and your prospective employer if you do not send a picture.

Figure 46-1 gives examples of résumé headings.

Career Objectives

Career objectives, which state the kind of job you are applying for, are placed a few spaces below the heading.

There are two basic rules for writing a career objective. First, be specific. Second, be concise.

Be Specific. Employers have job openings with detailed job descriptions. They need applicants whose qualifications and career objectives match these job specifications. Usually, applicants state general career objectives, such as "editor" or "sales manager." Although these general objectives might be specific enough for many employers, it is better, when possible, to state the exact title of the job opening you are applying for. For example, use "Editorial Assistant, School Division" instead of the generic "editor," or "Director of Sales, Software Division" instead of "sales manager."

Be Concise. When describing your career objective, avoid lengthy descriptions. For example, if you want a job as an editorial assistant, do not state your career objective this way:

> INCORRECT: to improve the educational process in general and the elementary school experience in particular by providing higher-quality textbooks for elementary students

If you are applying for a sales manager position, do not state your career objective in this way:

> INCORRECT: I want to play a part in American consumerism and help the economy grow.

Both of these descriptions would leave prospective employers wondering exactly what kinds of jobs you are applying for.

A well-stated job objective will include the specific title of the job being applied for; the career path being taken (ultimate goal); and the field or industry, if appropriate. Two well-stated job objectives are illustrated in Figure 46-2.

```
CAREER OBJECTIVE:   Editorial Assistant, leading to position as Project Ed-
                    itor in elementary school textbook division



OBJECTIVE:  Director of Sales in software division of a major computer
            software developer
```

Figure 46-2 Job objective section of a résumé.

Educational Background

Most recent college graduates place the education section immediately after the career objective on their résumé. This makes sense when a person does not have a great deal of work experience. When listing your educational background, you should emphasize those courses or degrees that qualify you for the job you are seeking. If you are applying for a job as a sales manager in a company that manufactures photography equipment, you would list any courses in photography in addition to your degree(s). You might not mention these courses in a résumé you send to an insurance company when you apply for a job as a claims adjuster. In this résumé, you would mention the courses you took in automotive repair or perhaps an introductory course in a pre-law program.

You should list the basic information in your education section in reverse chronological order. That is, place the most recent course or degree first, and work your way backwards.

The information in the education section should include the following items:

1. the degree you received or expect to receive and the date earned or expected

2. the institution that granted the degree

3. your major or field of concentration

4. the title or contents of job-related courses

5. your grade point average, if it is high, along with an explanation of the rating system used by the school

Normally, it is not necessary, or recommended, to list high school graduation information. If you have a college degree, it is assumed that you received a high school diploma first. The exception to this would be if you took special courses or graduated from a special high school, such as a vocational-technical school, and completed a special course of study relevant to the job you are pursuing. Then it would be appropriate to list this information in your education section.

The following is an example of the education section of a résumé.

```
EDUCATION:  Bachelor of Arts, University of New Mexico, Albuquerque, New
            Mexico, June 1985. Major: Business Administration. GPA: 3.1 on
            a 4-point scale.
```

Figure 46-3 Education section of a résumé.

Work Experience

When you are a recent high school or college graduate, an employer will expect your work experience to be that of a student and to consist of summer employment and part-time or volunteer jobs.

List as many jobs as you wish, no matter how varied they seem to be, because each job you held imparts a good impression of you. These jobs show that you are willing to work, have acquired different skills, and can be independent.

List your work experience in reverse chronological order as you did with your educational background, and include the following information:

1. the beginning and ending dates of your employment

2. your job title

3. the name and address of your employer

4. a brief description of your responsibilities

5. your accomplishments, or the positive results of your work

Here is an effectively organized example of a work experience section.

```
WORK EXPERIENCE:  Camp Counselor. Kiwi Camp, Somers, New York. Summers
                  1983-1985. Taught tennis and guitar, managed cabin of
                  seven nine-year-old campers. Established Camp Kiwi
                  Strummers, a camper group of performing musicians.

                  Landscaper. Ridgefield, Connecticut, Parks Department.
                  Spring and fall, 1982-present. Designed planting areas;
                  bought and planted variety of plants; pruned shrubs and
                  trees; maintained lawns. Earned one year's college tui-
                  tion and expenses.
```

Figure 46-4 Work experience section of a résumé.

Personal Data

The personal information section is an important part of your résumé. It tells a prospective employer something about your character and personality.

The personal data section can include activities, hobbies, interests, honors, achievements, special skills, military service, memberships in organizations, and offices held. If you wish, information such as age, race, religion, or national origin can be included; you are protected by the Fair Employment Practice Law against discrimination on the basis of this information. Be aware, however, that many employers believe such information will bias their consideration of you, and they may have a negative reaction if you provide it. This type of information is best provided only when it is directly related to the job for which you are applying. For example, if you are seeking a job as a Spanish translator, your Spanish heritage and ability to speak Spanish fluently would be an asset, and would therefore be worth mentioning.

Other personal data, such as height, weight, marital status, date and place of birth, health status, and willingness to relocate, may also be included if you think the information is related to the job you want. Most employers, however, attempt to make a hiring decision without considering personal data, so including this information may simply serve to distract the person's attention. Again, this information is best provided only when it will help you get the job.

If you have three or more items in any category in the personal data section, you can create a special section to highlight them in your résumé. For instance, if you have three or more honors, you can include a special honors category. You may choose to subdivide all your personal data under separate headings, such as "Interests," "Activities," and "Personal."

Employers can learn a great deal about you from your personal data section. Try to list interests and activities that present you as a balanced person who

USING YOUR WORD PROCESSOR
Simplifying Your Job Search

As a conscientious job seeker, you will find your word processor a very useful tool. You can use it to take notes, make letter writing easier, and tailor your résumé to apply for specific positions.

Use your word processor to take notes about companies to which you have applied. Whenever you learn something new about one of them, update your notes. Before going to an interview, print out your notes on that company, and take them with you. A five-minute review in a personnel manager's outer office may provide just the information you need to get the job.

Although you must write a different application letter for every ad you answer, you need not start from scratch every time. Write your first letter very carefully on the word processor, and save it on a disk. Use a spelling checker to help you proofread. For future letters, use the add, delete, and other features of the word processor to modify your original until it is ready to send to another prospective employer.

Changing your résumé to meet the needs of specific employers can get you the interview you want. If you know a company is growing rapidly, you could begin your job objective, "To serve a growing company ..." If a job requires a knowledge of marketing, list your marketing courses in the education section.

You can even change the whole emphasis of your résumé. If your previous experience makes you the right candidate for a job, put the experience section immediately under your name and address. If education will be more important to the employer, use the block command mode to move your education information above your experience section.

enjoys doing things alone as well as with others. For example, list activities such as writing poetry or painting watercolors as well as playing softball or bridge. Also, by including membership and offices you've held in volunteer organizations, you can show your capacity for social responsibility and leadership.

Be sure to state the percent of your college expenses you yourself paid for by working. This information shows you have good character, determination, and independence. This information **can be added to** your personal data section or to the education or experience sections.

The items in the personal data section, like those in the education and experience sections, should be listed in reverse chronological order as they are in Figure 46-5.

```
PERSONAL DATA:

Activities:   Big Brother to child in Newark, New Jersey, 1983-present;
              member of local computer club; avid nature photographer.

Honors:       Graduated college with honors, 1986; Member Pi Gamma Mu, Na-
              tional Honor Society for Superior Scholarship (college);
              Outstanding Spanish Student (high school), 1981 and 1982

Personal:     single      170 lb      5'11"
              Excellent health; willing to relocate
```

Figure 46-5 Personal data section of a résumé.

References

You may list references on your résumé, or you may omit them and include a line at the bottom of your résumé stating that references are available upon request. If you list references, you save a prospective employer the extra step of having to call or write you to find out how to contact your references. On the other hand, if you do not list references, you have the advantage of changing them as needed to fit the position for which you are applying or to reflect changes in your experience.

Many employers will not bother to contact the people you give as references because they assume your references will speak favorably of you. Some employers, however, will contact your references to verify the facts you have stated on your résumé.

It is standard practice to list three people as references. A person from each of these three categories should be included:

1. someone in your career field, such as a former employer, who can evaluate your performance on the job

2. an educator who can substantiate your performance as a student

3. a community member who can assess your character and personality

Select the most prominent person in each category who is willing to give you a good recommendation. Be sure to ask permission to include the person's name, address, and telephone number on your résumé.

Do not list friends, relatives, or anyone else who could be suspected of giving a biased or unknowing assessment of your qualifications. References should be qualified to comment on your educational or employment experience.

The next section of this chapter will explain how to arrange the various parts of a résumé into a form that presents your qualifications in the strongest way.

There are three basic ways to arrange the data on a résumé. They include the following:

1. the traditional, or basic, format

2. the chronological format

3. the functional format

Each one has certain advantages.

FINDING THE RIGHT RESUME FORMAT

Traditional, or Basic, Format

The traditional, or basic, format is widely used for entry-level jobs by applicants who do not have a great deal of work experience. This format stresses the education section and can contain a full description of course work as well as information on degrees earned. The education section can be placed before or after the experience section.

The standard design of the traditional, or basic, résumé calls for the section headings to be placed at the left-hand margin in capital letters. The corresponding information is placed to the right of the heading in block form. Each section is separated from the others by white space. This design makes it easy to find specific information and is easy to read. Figure 46-6 gives an example of a traditional, or basic, résumé.

The Chronological Format

This format and the functional format, which will be discussed in the next section, are used by applicants with extensive work experience.

In the chronological format, work experience usually is placed before the education section and describes each position in detail. The education section is usually brief and less detailed.

The chronological résumé can be arranged on the page with the dates of each position at the left margin and the job description to the right of the dates in block form. Figure 46-7 is an example of a chronological résumé.

ALLEN RICHARDS
19 Old Post Road
Pleasantville, New York 15432
(914) 555-3487

CAREER
OBJECTIVE: Research zoologist

EDUCATION: Bachelor of Science, Pace University, Pleasantville, New
York. Major in biology. Minor in statistics. Twenty hours of
course work in the area of animal behavior. GPA: 3.6 on a
4-point scale. Graduated with honors, June 1985. Earned 50
percent of college expenses.

WORK
EXPERIENCE: Veterinarian's Assistant, Peekskill Animal Hospital,
Peekskill, New York, 1984 to present. Responsibilities: to
assist in examination, treatment, grooming, and general care
of animals. Accomplishments: helped establish special
treatment and boarding facility for pet and wild birds.

Zoo Tour Guide. New York Zoological Society, Bronx, New York,
1983-1984. Responsibilities: giving tours of the zoo with
informational monologues. Accomplishments: led publicity
campaign to increase public awareness of zoo's importance in
preserving wildlife.

Pet Store Assistant, The Zoo Store, Peekskill, New York,
1977-1982. Responsibilities: cleaning cages and feeding
animals and fish. Accomplishments: successfully managed the
store for several weeks during owner's absence.

HONORS: Awarded Humane Society's Friend to Pets Scholarship of $500,
1980

ACTIVITIES: College: Swimming team for four years, baseball team for
three years

REFERENCES: Professional
               Dr. Jan Sutens   Dr. Betsy Blare
               Biology Department   Resident Veterinarian
               Pace University   New York Zoological Society
               Pleasantville, NY 15432   Bronx, NY 10026
               (914) 555-6172   (212) 555-2358

               Character
               Mr. Bruce Paulsen
               The Zoo Store
               14 Main Street
               Peekskill, NY 12674
               (914) 555-4071

Figure 46-6 A traditional résumé.

```
                        CAROLYN NIEVES
                       7896 North Broadway
                      Arnold, Maryland 21012
                         (301) 555-1334


    AVAILABLE:      Immediately


    OBJECTIVE:      Responsible and challenging position in bank
                    administration


    EXPERIENCE:

    September 1982  Assistant Manager, North Side Savings Bank, 950 South
    to Present      Broadway, Yonkers, New York.
                    Responsibilities:
                    • Supervising tellers
                    • Checking loan applications and credit references
                    • Participating in policy meetings
                    • Assisting manager with all phases of banking operations
                    Accomplishments:
                    • Increased productivity of tellers by 30 percent with
                      improved check-recording methods
                    • Improved hiring of disabled and minority workers

    Summers of      Bank Teller, Peoples Savings Bank, 501 White Plains Road,
    1978-1982       White Plains, New York.
                    Responsibilities:
                    • Accepting and recording cash transactions
                    Accomplishments:
                    • Increased salary by 15 percent each year


    EDUCATION:      Bachelor of Science Degree, University of Delaware,
                    Newark, Delaware, 1980.
                    Major: Economics    Minor: Business Administration



    COMMUNITY
    SERVICE:        Yonkers League of Women Voters, Treasurer, 1983 to present
                    Big Brothers and Big Sisters of Yonkers


    INTERESTS:      Scuba diving, softball, photography, reading


    REFERENCES:     Available upon request
```

Figure 46-7 A chronological résumé.

The Functional Format

When people work for several different companies over a short period of time or when they want to emphasize what they can do rather than for whom they have worked, the functional résumé can be useful. This résumé format serves to emphasize the applicant's expertise in different areas of work.

In a functional résumé, experience is arranged under job title headings. For example, a functional résumé can show that an applicant has expertise in many aspects of the same business and is therefore qualified to be a general administrator or manager. Notice how the sample functional résumé shown in Figure 46-8 guides the reader to focus upon the different facets of the applicant's work history and the skills the applicant possesses.

BASIC RULES FOR WRITING RESUMES

The language used in a résumé is of supreme importance. Choose your wording carefully, making all information brief and specific. Complete sentences are not necessary. A clipped, telegraphic style presents data simply and cleanly. Read this excerpt from a résumé:

> I took dictation each day. I also typed the company's proposals, editing them as I typed.

This information would be more effectively presented as follows:

> Responsibilities: took dictation, typed and edited proposals

It is also important to choose words that are positive rather than negative, active rather than passive. Consider the following examples:

> INCORRECT: In three years at JVR, Inc., I never let a single deadline be missed.

> CORRECT: Accomplishments: met or beat every deadline

The first passage states the accomplishment using negative, passive language. The second passage, which uses a positive, active voice, sounds more forceful and would be much more effective.

The design and appearance of your résumé are also very important. The arrangement of data should be attractive and visually pleasing, which basically means it should be well balanced on the page. If you are using a centered format, be sure all sections—not just some—are centered. If you have your headings off to the left side, make sure the sections that follow balance them by extending fully to the right margin. Whichever format you choose, arrange your headings so that they stand out and are easy to find, which can be accomplished through underlining and/or using all capital letters. If your résumé is professionally prepared or if you prepare it on a computer, you might choose colored headings or boldface or italic type to make headings stand out. Remember, however, that consistency counts: Choose one style for headings and sections and use it throughout the résumé.

Normally, your résumé should not be longer than one page. Sometimes, however, people with many years of work experience feel it necessary to use

```
                              SHELDON B. STEIN
    232 East 32nd Street      Home: (212) 555-3498
    New York: New York 10003  Work: (212) 555-4734


    OBJECTIVE:      Art Director for an advertising agency, with responsibility
                    for creative direction of ad campaigns.


    EXPERIENCE:

    Group Head      Responsible for visual ideas and execution, TV and print
                    campaigns for Angel Face Tissue, Sharp Eye Cameras, Fast
                    Haul Truck Rental, and other national accounts. Supervised
                    staff of six graphic artists. Worked with copywriters and
                    account executives to develop campaigns. Accomplishments:
                    Winner of three graphic design awards, 1984 and 1985.
                    Responsible for bringing the Luxury Swimming Pool account
                    to agency for billing of $1 million.

    Graphic         Designed box and print ads for Good Morning breakfast
    Designer        cereal, worked on layouts and storyboards for Fresh Face
                    cosmetics, No-Run Panty Hose, and Toughie Sportswear.
                    Accomplishments: Doubled salary in first three years.

    Paste-Up        Prepared dummies and mechanicals. Responsible for laying
    Artist          out type, making stats, designing boards, and making final
                    corrections on boards.


    WORK HISTORY:

    1984-present    Group Head, Schwartz and Miller Advertising, Inc., 350
                    Third Avenue, New York, New York.

    1982-1984       Graphic Designer, Picone and Beldman Agency, Chicago,
                    Illinois.

    1980-1982       Paste-Up Artist, Lawrence Chester Associates, Rockford,
                    Illinois.


    EDUCATION:

    January 1980    Master of Fine Arts, Rochester Institute of Technology,
                    Rochester, New York.

    June 1978       Bachelor of Fine Arts, Alfred University, Alfred, New York.


    INTERESTS:      Filmmaking, sculpting, camping, basketball.


    REFERENCES:     Available upon request.
```

Figure 46-8 A functional résumé.

two pages in order to cover everything. Exceed one page only if you really believe doing so will help you get the job. Remember that prospective employers will be looking at dozens, perhaps hundreds, of résumés; they will not react favorably to any résumé that is unnecessarily long.

The résumé should be typed or photocopied on white, beige, or ivory paper. For extra effect, some people choose light yellow or light blue paper. Regardless of color, the paper should be a good-quality smooth or textured bond, $8\frac{1}{2}$ by 11 inches. The envelope and cover letter should be of the same paper.

Before sending your résumé, be absolutely certain that it contains no content errors or typographical mistakes. Even one mistake can disqualify you for a job. To be safe, proofread your final draft carefully, and then have at least one other person proofread it as well.

EDITING EXERCISES

The following résumé was given to you by your friend Donna Jackson. She is unhappy with the results it has been getting. Try to help her by drafting a revised (and improved) version of the résumé.

DONNA JACKSON
143 Sixth Avenue, Apt. 775
Tuscaloosa, Alabama 35643
(205) 555-7109

OBJECTIVE: To earn enough money to move into an apartment of my own.

EDUCATION: Asrociate of Arts degree from Tuscaloosa Junior College in secretarial science. Graduated 1986 with a 3.2 average.

EXPERIENCE: Worked at school library in High School shelving books. Worked for Adams, Jones, and Westfall, Attorneys at Law summers of 1984–1986 and part time during school year while in college. They're located at 335 Birmingham Avenue in Tuscaloosa. I was a secretary but filled in for legal asst. when she was out sick or on vacation. They offered me a job, but I need more money.

PERSONAL
DATA: I'm 18 and am healthy I like to read, was secretary of the Sophomore class at Tuscallosa Jr. College, and have had experience with word processing at the lawyer's office. I won the Future Business Leader of the Year award in high school my senior year and have a pin to prove it.

Your friend Neil Walker has asked you to help him write his résumé. He has written you a note with the information he considers important. Use the appropriate information from Neil's note, and draft a résumé for him.

Hi--

Thanks for offering to help me with my résumé. I was born in Waukegan, Illinois, on November 8, 1963. I'm a Scorpio and I like skiing and archery. I graduated from Waukegan High School in 1982 and from Northern Illinois University in 1986. In high school I took both college prep and business courses and was elected to the National Honor Society. I was also a violinist in the high school orchestra.

In college I majored in marketing and minored in political science. I got my B.A. in 1986. I had a 3.5 average out of 4 points. During my sophomore, junior, and senior years, I worked at Danert's department store in Sycamore, Illinois, to help earn my way through college. I did mostly sales work, but I also got some experience in advertising, display, and inventory. I think I actually earned about 60 percent of my tuition, fees, and expenses.

I want a job in retailing. Eventually I want to be a buyer, but I guess I need to start in one of those executive training programs that the big department stores have. I'll probably work in Chicago, but I sure wouldn't mind moving to New York.

My zip code is 60087 and my phone number is (312) 555-7145. I live at 565 Lewis Avenue in Waukegan. I'm 6'1" and weigh 175 lb.

When I was a junior at Northern, I won the Student Marketing Association's award for my market segmentation study. I studied the buying habits of 16- to 21-year-olds in Rochelle, Illinois, and how they related to the target markets identified by the DeKalb-Ogle Market Research Association.

On a blank piece of paper, write the six major points to be included in a résumé:

1. Heading
2. Career Objective
3. Education
4. Work Experience
5. Personal Data
6. References

Then list all the important information that you will place in your résumé. Be sure to include dates, relevant school courses, and all the other information that might be important to your future career.

Next, decide which format you should use for your résumé. Finally, design and write your résumé.

47

Writing and Answering Application Letters

If you have written your résumé, you have one half of your job application package put together. Now you must gather the other half—your application letter. Once you have a job, you may be in the position of answering application letters sent by others, which means you will need to know how to respond appropriately. Whether you are writing application letters or answering them, you will have to be aware of the characteristics of an effective application letter.

This chapter will first explore how to write successful application letters and then discuss the sometimes difficult situations that can occur when you are in a position that requires you to answer application letters.

HOW TO WRITE AN APPLICATION LETTER
An application letter is a cover letter for your résumé. It introduces the services that you want a prospective employer to buy. It is important that you focus your letter on your prospective employer rather than on yourself. Concentrate on what the employer will gain by hiring you, not on what you will gain. For example, do not use this type of introduction:

> I am seeking a job with your firm because I think the salary will be better and I will enjoy working with top-notch attorneys.

An employer would much rather know how you will help the company, as in the following:

> My efficient filing methods will keep the information in your office well organized and neatly stored. Also, my average typing speed of 80 wpm will ensure that your attorneys are not kept waiting for their materials.

An important thing to note here is that your application letter should not be a repeat of the information in your résumé. It should merely highlight the information that is most relevant to the position, underscoring the reasons that the experience listed in your résumé will be of value to the employer.

Because you are essentially selling your skills, you should write your application letter using the same guidelines that you would use to write a sales letter. First, the letter must get the attention of the reader and arouse interest in you as a prospective employee. Next, the letter must make the reader want your services as an employee. Finally, it must enable the reader to act with ease.

An application letter should be brief but powerful. A good application letter usually consists of three paragraphs, each with its own purpose. The three paragraphs should be arranged in a basic letter format that runs no longer than one page. A busy employer does not want to read pages and pages of material from each job applicant.

THE FORMAT OF AN APPLICATION LETTER

The First Paragraph

Use the first paragraph to do the following:

1. Get the attention of the prospective employer.
2. State the position for which you are applying.
3. Explain how you found out about the job.
4. Describe how your qualifications fit the job description.

Getting Attention. Just as with a good sales letter, an application letter must make a prospective employer want to read the entire letter as well as the accompanying résumé. Therefore, it is important to capture the employer's attention at the very start of the letter. There are five opening techniques that have proved to be successful attention-getters in application letters.

1. *The Referral.* If you can, mention that someone the employer knows of or knows personally has suggested that you apply for the job.

   Judge Harold Hawkins suggested I apply for the legal secretary's position in your firm. Judge Hawkins was my employer during the last three summers at the Dubuque district attorney's office.

2. *The Question.* Ask the employer a thought-provoking question.

   Wouldn't it help to hire a camera salesperson who not only knows your cameras but has also taken award-winning photographs?

3. *The Summary.* Write an opening sentence that summarizes those qualifications on your résumé that would be the most useful to the employer.

   My three summers of keeping the books for Jackson & Weber would make
   me a valuable addition to your accounting department.

4. *The New Development.* Mention a current event that involves the company to which you are applying. Tie the information to a reason for hiring
   you.

   Your new microfiche system, as described recently in *The Bulletin,* sounds
   very exciting and is one with which I am familiar; I worked with a similar
   system at the Seven Oaks Public Library last year.

5. *The General Fact.* Relate a common fact or belief held by people in your
   career area, and tie it in with a reason to hire you.

   Most business managers expect the first six months of a recent college graduate's employment to be a training period. That will not be the case if you
   hire me. While preparing for my degree in journalism, I worked part-time and
   summers as a journalist for the *Tribune.*

Stating the Title of the Job for Which You Are Applying. Your application letter and résumé will have a better chance of being directed to the
right department or division if you indicate the specific job for which you are
applying. If you do not include this information in your first attention-getting
sentence, be sure to state the job title somewhere in the first paragraph.

If you do not know if there is a specific opening, give a general job description
of the position you want.

Indicating How You Learned About the Opening. Your first paragraph
should also indicate where you read or heard about the job opening. This
information will help your prospective employer gauge what you have already
learned about the job.

Stating Why You Are Suited for the Job. This part of the first paragraph
should describe your strongest qualifications for the job opening. It should
never express dissatisfaction with your current job.

The following is an example of a first paragraph that includes all the required
facts and uses one of the attention-getting techniques—the referral statement.

Cecil De Merle, owner of the French Quarter Restaurant on La Salle Street in
New Orleans, suggested I apply for the chef's assistant position in the New
York branch of Le Pomme. Your advertisement in the *Times* on May 3 asked
for someone with the type of cooking experience that matches mine almost
exactly. I am a 1983 graduate of the Culinary Institute in Hyde Park, New
York, and my chef's experience in French cuisine has been extensive.

DID YOU KNOW?
Networking

Many people begin searching for their first job by reading the want ads in the daily paper. Others sign up with an employment agency. Most jobs, however, are filled neither through want ads nor through employment agencies. The most important source of job leads in modern business is personal contacts.

Using personal contacts—also called networking—may seem reserved for top executives, but it isn't. If a student sitting in the library lounge says, "I'd like to find a job in an insurance company," another student might reply, "Well, my aunt works at the Safe Haven Insurance Company, and she mentioned last week that the personnel manager was looking for management trainees." This kind of personal contact is available to everyone.

Whether you realize it or not, you know people who can help you get a job. If you list all the people you know, you could probably think of at least 200 names. Someone on your list will either have information that can help you or know someone who does.

Your first step is to let as many people as possible know you are looking for work. You may be pleasantly surprised at who can provide you with a lead. When you talk to people, ask for advice, not a job. Do not ask them to set up appointments for you. A network of acquaintances is not an employment agency; you still need to write the application letters yourself.

Once you get a lead, follow it up. Do not be afraid to telephone strangers; people are usually willing to be helpful, and you have nothing to lose. If you do get a job, tell the good news to the person who gave you the tip. He or she will surely be pleased by your success.

The Second Paragraph

After the first paragraph has aroused the interest of an employer, the second paragraph must convince the person that you are a serious candidate for the job and that you should be interviewed.

The second paragraph shows the employer that you know something about the company—an important attribute, as it demonstrates initiative, interest, and drive on your part. You should also use the second paragraph to explain how your particular qualifications can help the company's business. Do not, however, give your life story—simply highlight your qualifications, referring the reader to the specific information listed on the résumé you have enclosed.

In order to appear knowledgeable about the company to which you are applying, you will probably have to do some research. Information on the size of organizations, their annual sales and profits, the kind of business they do, and other vital statistics is available through a number of sources.

- Annual reports from companies can be obtained in libraries, stockbrokers' offices, or directly from the firms.
- The *Business Periodicals Index* lists articles published about companies in various business magazines.

- Dun and Bradstreet's *Million Dollar Directory* lists American-based companies with net earnings that exceed $500,000. The names of executives, subsidiaries, services and products, annual sales, and number of employees are among the facts listed in this reference.
- *Standard & Poor's Corporation Records* lists information similar to that given in the Dun and Bradstreet directory, in addition to giving brief histories of the companies and any plans for expansion.
- *Everybody's Business: An Almanac,* subtitled *The Irreverent Guide to Corporate America,* lists companies' sales and profits, number of employees and main employment centers, services and products, sales and marketing strategies, reputation, the presence—or absence—of minorities and women on boards of directors, and past histories and likely future direction.
- *Forbes* Annual Directory Issue is a special issue (usually published at the end of April) listing 400 to 500 of the largest companies.
- The May and June issues of *Fortune* magazine list 500 of the largest corporations in the United States, according to sales.
- *Moody's Industrial Manual* and *Moody's OTC Industrial Manual* offer an extensive stock survey of various corporations.
- Indexes for major newspapers such as *The New York Times* and *The Wall Street Journal* list any articles that have appeared regarding companies.

Information about small companies, which are not listed in the sources for large or national companies, can be obtained from local chambers of commerce, newspapers, libraries, or the companies themselves.

Always assume a positive, respectful tone when referring to a company. When you indicate how you can help the company, do not imply that it is in trouble or needs your help to save it. Also, avoid the hard-sell approach. You should present yourself simply and politely as someone who will further the company's current success or plans for the future.

Here is an example of how the second paragraph can be written. Its goal is to convince a prospective employer to invite the chef to come for an interview.

> I am especially intrigued by the innovative Le Cunard chain of French restaurants because of the variety of French pastry served. As my enclosed résumé shows, I specialized in French pastry at the Institute, and I believe your patrons would be pleased with the fine quality of my pastries. You will also notice that I have had experience preparing all types of French cuisine while working in New Orleans for the last two years. I have been complimented by the head chef at the French Quarter and by professors at the Institute for my flamboyant style while cooking, which would lend itself well to your custom of preparing food in booths in the center of the dining room.

The Third Paragraph

The purpose of the third paragraph is to make it easy for employers to arrange an interview with you. Inspiring employers to take immediate action may prevent them from forgetting to contact you while under the pressure of having to read many other résumés.

The French cook might end her application letter this way:

> I will be in New York the week of March 14 and would like to meet with you then. If you are interested in adding my skills to those of your fine staff at Le Cunard, please call me to arrange a mutually convenient time to meet. During the day on Monday through Saturday, you can reach me at (504) 555-7101. After 5:30 p.m., the number to call is (504) 555-8969. I look forward to meeting you.

WRITING THE LETTER

An application letter may seem like a mere cover letter to your résumé, but if the letter is not convincing or is sloppily written, the employer may not bother to read your résumé.

There are three basic rules to use when writing an effective application letter:

1. Revise your letter until the language and tone convey exactly what you wish.

2. Proofread your application letter as carefully as you did your résumé. A typo, a misspelling, an error in fact or grammar, or even a blemish such as a fingerprint smudge can create a negative impression and may disqualify you from final consideration.

3. Do not use company letterhead stationery unless you own the company. Also avoid using casual personal stationery. White or off-white bond that matches the paper color and quality of your résumé is the appropriate choice. The paper size should also match your résumé: 8½ by 11 inches.

The following letter obeys the guidelines for writing a good application letter, as outlined in this chapter. It is respectful and informative and has a self-assured, but not pushy, tone.

> I read the news of your expansion into custom-made furniture in the <u>Waco Record</u>, February 6, with great interest. I have had my own custom-made furniture business for the last five years in Waco. Recently, I have expanded into larger quarters and acquired more equipment and workers. Your ad in the February 17 <u>Record</u> for custom furniture makers comes at a time that could prove to be mutually beneficial.
>
> You might consider whether it would be advantageous for you to merge with my already established company, rather than to hire designers for new furniture and workers whom you would then have to train to make the furniture. My line of furniture comes with a proven track record and an established, loyal clientele. You would be investing in a popular line that you know will sell.
>
> I have a portfolio of the furniture I have created and reference letters from

my clients. I would like very much to meet with you at your convenience and discuss in greater detail what we can offer one another. I will call you Monday, February 22, to arrange a meeting. If you want to contact me before then, you may call me anytime at (817) 555-1121.

ANSWERING APPLICATION LETTERS

When you are on the job, one of your responsibilities may be to answer application letters. Depending upon the applicant and the job-opening situation, there will be four basic categories of response:

1. answering qualified applicants when a position is open
2. answering qualified applicants when no position is open
3. answering unqualified applicants when a position is open
4. answering unqualified applicants when no position is open

The simple guidelines for each of the four situations will be discussed in greater detail in the following section. However, the general rule for every type is to tell the truth tactfully.

Suppose you are in Mrs. Rubin's position, and you are receiving applications in response to your ad in local newspapers, including the *Waco Record*, for custom furniture makers. The following section can help you write responses to the four basic types of job applications you will receive.

Qualified Applicant/Position Open

Your letter of response to an applicant who seems to be qualified for a job that is available requires you to express appreciation for the application and invite the applicant to come in for an interview, suggesting a date, time, and place.

If you were responding to Mr. Alvarez, you might write the kind of letter shown here:

Thank you for your letter regarding the ad I placed for custom furniture builders in the Waco Record. I had not considered the possibility of merging with a preexisting furniture company, and I am not sure that this is the direction I want to pursue. Your suggestion did sound interesting, however. I am familiar with your line of furniture and think that it might work well with the current New World Elegance line.

I would like very much to discuss the matter further with you. Can you meet with me and the president of the company, Mr. Charles North, at my office on the third floor at 10 a.m. on February 25? If I do not hear from you to the contrary, I will expect to see you then.

Qualified Applicant/No Opening

It sometimes happens that qualified people apply for a job for which there is no opening. In this situation, the first thing you should do is express appreciation for the application. Then explain to the applicant that he or she is qualified for the job but that there are no openings. Offer to keep the applicant's résumé on file in case an opening does occur, but don't give false hope about something opening up soon. It is important to be honest in dealing with such a situation.

Here is a situation that Mrs. Rubin might encounter. Along with applications for the advertised position of custom furniture maker, she is receiving unsolicited applications for management positions in the new division—positions not open at the present time. Mrs. Rubin drafts the following letter to send to qualified applicants for management positions.

> Thank you for applying to New World Elegance, Inc. Your background in all phases of the furniture business is very impressive and well worth consideration.
>
> Unfortunately, there are no supervisory positions open at this time. When an opening does occur, our company policy specifies that we first consider qualified applicants from within the company.
>
> If we look for applicants outside the company, I will surely call you. In the meantime, I will keep your résumé in my active file. Thank you for considering New World Elegance, and good luck with your job search.

Notice how Mrs. Rubin effectively employs some of the techniques for writing refusals that were covered in Chapter 40.

Unqualified Applicants/Position Open

When unqualified people apply for a job that is open, you should tell them in a tactful manner why their experience does not meet the qualifications for the job opening. Start by expressing appreciation for the application. If possible, compliment the applicants on the positive aspects of their experience, and tell them why their credentials do not qualify them for the job. A carefully worded and tactful letter may help direct their job searches in more appropriate directions. The following letter is a good example of this type of reply.

> Thank you for responding to our ad in the <u>Waco Record</u> for a custom furniture maker.
>
> Though your background as a wood carver is impressive, applicants for this position must have at least three years' experience building furniture. Thank you again for considering New World Elegance.

Unqualified Applicant/No Opening

The response for an applicant in this category is the same as for an applicant who is unqualified when there is an opening. Every position has certain minimum requirements, and applicants whose backgrounds do not meet these requirements need to be told so in a polite but straightforward manner, as shown in the following letter.

> Thank you for applying for the position of salesperson in our young person's furniture department.
>
> Unfortunately, there are no sales openings at the present time. While your experience as a shoe salesman is impressive, applicants must have at least two years' experience selling furniture to be considered for a position in any of our departments. For this reason, we cannot encourage you as a prospective employee with Blake Furniture. Thank you, however, for considering our company.

Whether you are sending your own application letters or writing responses to application letters you have received on the job, always be sure that the tone of your letters is polite, respectful, and tactful. Be direct and to the point, and in the case of your own application letters, present yourself in a positive, self-assured way.

EDITING EXERCISES

A. Help this job applicant rewrite the following letter of application, using the rules you learned in this chapter.

Dear Mr. Shapiro:

I'd like to arrange an interview at your earliest convenience.

I read your ad in the *Milwaukee Sentinel* last week for a receptionist/secretary. I know I'd be an asset to Royale Books because I like to read and I can't think of anything more interesting than working with people who write books. I never worked for a publishing company before, but I have worked for three summers as a receptionist at Smith, Mason, and Furer, the brokerage house. My filing skills are top-notch, and I type a fairly respectable 55 wpm.

My credentials may not seem like much, but I know I'd do a good job if you'd just give me a chance. Maybe all your company needs is a receptionist with a warm smile to greet its customers and clients! Call anytime. My number's on my résumé.

Sincerely,

B. François Dubonnet, manager of the French restaurant Chez Moi, has received many applications for the chef's position since it was advertised.

He is tired of responding to unqualified applicants and is getting a bit careless with his replies. Rewrite the following reply to an unqualified applicant.

Dear Mr. Peabody:

Please! Do you think that we could run a reputable establishment if we hired people with your background? I'm sure your experience as chief cook on the breakfast shift at Bea's Diner in Santa Fe will qualify you for something, but it sure isn't this job.

As our advertisement indicated, Chez Moi requires a degree in French cuisine from an accredited culinary institute or cooking school and at least three years' experience.

Sincerely,

François Dubonnet

PROBLEMS

Below are the first and second paragraphs of three unsolicited application letters for a position as a fashion buyer trainee at a large department store. All the applicants are recent college graduates with approximately equal levels of experience. Which one would you respond positively to? Why? What is wrong with each of the letters you would reject?

1. I read your ad in the *Post* and, since my qualifications fit, I thought I'd apply for the job. I've been out of college for only one month, and I'm not sure exactly what I want to do yet.

   I think I would be good for the job because I have worked for two summers as a clerk in Benson's department store. I like clothes and have been told that I have an eye for fashion. I also have a personal flair in the way I dress. This may or may not be a good trait for a fashion buyer, but I guess I'll find out.

2. I read your ad in this Sunday's *Post* and decided that you really need someone like me ... so here I am—loaded with qualifications.

   I'm sure you could use someone with style, personality, and poise, and someone who's a self-starter on top of everything else. You won't have to worry about me staying in the background. I'm a take-charge person, and I'll be running the show before you know it. I worked for a couple of years in Charms, a downtown boutique—maybe you've heard of it? Within a few months, I was promoted from cashier to counter girl, and it wasn't long after that that I was helping the owner choose the new fall line. I left because she wouldn't agree to give me a piece of the business. That's my ultimate aim.

3. In response to your ad in the *Post* of June 24, I present the following qualifications for the position of fashion buyer trainee.

   For the last two summers of college, I worked full-time in the stock and inventory division of Ratchett's department store in Middletown. Your store is very similar to Ratchett's, and I have spoken with some of the personnel in your inventory department: your procedures are almost identical to the ones with which I am familiar. This gives you the advantage of hiring someone who will not need as long a training period as an inexperienced person might require. Also, fashion buyers are typically very clothes-conscious, and I am often complimented on my wardrobe and taste in clothes.

PROJECTS

Select a company for which you would like to work. Use three of the resources mentioned in this chapter to obtain information about the company. Write an effective letter of application based on your qualifications and the information you learned about the company.

48
Reference and Follow-Up Letters

Looking for a job used to require pounding the pavement. In today's business world, job hunting demands pounding a keyboard instead in order to write the various letters required for a successful job search.

You will need to write several kinds of letters besides application letters. These include letters asking for references and letters expressing appreciation for references after you get a job.

You will also need to write follow-up letters to thank employers for interviews, accept a position, reject a position, respond to a rejection, inquire about a company's decision, and delay your decision about accepting a position. In addition, you may be asked to provide references for other job seekers after you have a job. This chapter will describe the basic techniques for writing these different types of letters.

Most people only think in terms of getting a reference. It is, of course, important to know how to ask for one. However, you should also know how to give a reference. Both giving and getting references are important parts of the job-hunting process, and each has its own etiquette and set of rules.

REFERENCE LETTERS

Asking for a Reference

As discussed in Chapter 46, three recommendations—one each from an educator, an employer, and a community member—are usually requested by employers. These references should not be close personal friends or family members but should know you well enough to be able to speak about you with authority. The educator should be knowledgeable about your academic performance; the employer should be aware of your performance on the job;

the community member should be familiar with your general character and community participation.

Before you use a person's name as a reference on your résumé, you must ask permission to do so. You can ask directly, telephone, or write a request letter. If you choose to make your request in writing, the following are good examples to use as models. This letter simply asks permission to use the person's name.

> I am looking for a job with more responsibility and higher pay in the computer sales field.
>
> If you consent, please reply by signing the bottom of this letter and returning it in the enclosed envelope.
>
> As a former employer, you have known me professionally for several years. I would be most grateful if I could use your name as a reference.
>
> Thank you for your consideration.

This letter asks for an actual letter of recommendation. In both letters, the writers make it easy for the readers to comply with the requests.

> I was interviewed last week at Waller, Hicks, and Hillman for a position as a legal secretary. Ms. Waller asked me to provide a character reference. I would be most appreciative if you would write one for me.
>
> You have been pastor of our church since I began Sunday School when I was five years old. You might recall that I was on the committee to revise the Sunday School curriculum five years ago, and I have also taught Sunday School for the last three years.
>
> If you consent to writing a recommendation for me, please sign the bottom of this letter and return it to me. The recommendation itself should be sent directly to:
>
> Ms. Ann Waller, Partner
> Waller, Hicks, and Hillman
> 17 Grandview Avenue
> St. Louis, MO 63144
>
> Thank you.

Notice that in the second letter, which asks for an actual recommendation, the writer has supplied the person with some specific information that could be mentioned in the letter. This is a helpful strategy, particularly if it has been a long time since you had regular contact with the person. It is also a good idea to ask the people who write references to send their letters directly to employers. This practice enables the person giving the reference to feel free to be truthful without worrying about your reaction. Such recommendations have greater credibility than those first submitted to the applicants themselves.

Expressing Thanks for a Reference

When you get a job, it is good business manners to write thank-you notes to the people who agreed to act as references for you. The notes should be gracious acknowledgments of their efforts, as is the following.

> You will be pleased to know that I was offered, and have accepted, the position as legal secretary with the law firm of Waller, Hicks, and Hillman. I'm looking forward to working for such a prestigious organization; your letter of recommendation most surely helped secure the position for me.
>
> I am very grateful for your efforts on my behalf, and I'll see you next time I visit my family. Thank you again.

Writing a Reference

If you are in a supervisory or managerial role, you may be asked to provide references for other employees. If you feel you know an individual well and can write a positive recommendation, you can of course say yes to the request. If you are not knowledgeable about the person's performance or cannot recommend the person for the job, you have the right to decline graciously.

There are three basic types of references you can write:

- a positive reference
- a reference that mentions both positive and negative features
- a negative reference

When your reference is positive, the letter will be fairly easy to write. When you have negative comments to make, though, the task becomes difficult. The following sections contain guidelines for writing the three types of references.

Writing a Positive Reference. When you have a high opinion of the applicant and believe the individual would be a good candidate for the job, you should do the following:

- Express pleasure at writing a reference for the candidate.
- Describe the qualities you observed in the candidate that make the individual a good choice for the company to hire.
- Include any personal observations you think might strengthen the candidate's chances of getting the job.

The following is an example of a positive reference letter.

I am delighted to be asked to recommend Alex Kandell for the accountant's position with your company.

Alex came to Lewis & Coe three years ago as a clerk in the mailroom. He went to business school at night and was promoted within a year to Junior Accountant with our firm. We will be sorry to see him leave.

Alex's diligence, maturity, and enthusiasm made him one of our best young employees. These qualities, together with his mastery of accounting, will make him a valued member of your company.

We are also sorry to lose him from our softball team. For the last two seasons, Alex has been our star pitcher and has helped us win the city's corporate softball championship. We wish Alex all the best with your firm.

Writing a Mixed Reference. When you have positive and negative comments to make about a candidate, use the following guidelines:

- State the dates the person worked for the company.
- Express in detail, with specific backup information, the positive comments you have about the candidate.
- Express the negative briefly, with an emphasis on areas that need development, not on weak areas.
- End with a positive statement about the person's capabilities.

The following is an example of a mixed-review reference letter.

Mary Peck worked as an assistant buyer for Sweet Dreams Sleepwear from April 1982 to February 1985. She was always pleasant and fulfilled her duties satisfactorily.

Mary's one weak area was punctuality. Her supervisor reports that she was often late, apparently because she had an unusually long commute.

Mary is well liked by employees, employers, and clients because of her easy-going personality, which enables her to work well with all kinds of people. She also has a natural sense of fashion.

Writing a Negative Reference. There are essentially four ways to respond when asked to write a reference for a person who you believe was not a satisfactory worker. Because this is a difficult problem, with possible legal ramifications, it must be handled carefully. Before you decide how to deal with the situation, you should weigh the consequences of each option.

Your first option is to decline the request, perhaps on the grounds that you are not familiar enough with the person's qualifications. Bear in mind, however, that if you decline to give a reference, the implication may be negative for the applicant.

A second possibility is to give a positive recommendation that misrepresents the person. If you give a good but false reference, however, you place your credibility in jeopardy if the applicant gets the job and then cannot perform the work satisfactorily.

The third option is to write a negative letter. If you do so, you must be absolutely certain that your negative comments are objective and can be supported by other people or by actual evidence, such as poor evaluations or time sheets that show chronic lateness or absence. You should know that legal action may be taken against you if the applicant is rejected for a job based on your negative letter.

Finally, you can attempt to be honest while protecting the applicant as much as possible. This option allows you to uphold your credibility and integrity. At the same time, your actions may not hurt the applicant as much as a refusal to write the reference.

Consider the following examples of each type of negative reference letter for Robert Kearne, manager of the toy department in a small department store. Robert has applied to Toys Unlimited, a growing chain of toy stores in the western United States. He has worked at Rathbone's for two years under the supervision of John Hennesey, who is not entirely pleased with his performance. While Mr. Hennesey considers Robert very good at ordering toys that sell well, he is greatly disturbed by Robert's lack of patience with customers who have complaints. Some customers have filed written complaints about Robert's behavior. Still, Mr. Hennesey likes Robert because he is bright and knowledgeable.

Which letter should Mr. Hennesey send to the Toys Unlimited personnel office?

Declining the Request

Although Robert Kearne did work for Rathbone's from June 1985 to August 1987, I don't feel familiar enough with his work to give a fair evaluation.

Giving a Misrepresentative Positive Reference

Robert Kearne was a fine employee during the two years he worked at Rathbone's. I recommend him highly and believe he will be a good worker for your company.

Writing a Strictly Negative Reference

Robert Kearne has been manager of the toy department at Rathbone's for two years. During this time, we have received a number of complaints from customers regarding his impatient attitude. Mr. Kearne has been spoken to about these complaints and has not changed his behavior. While he does have some redeeming qualities as a buyer, I cannot recommend him for a position with your company.

Writing an Honest but Protective Reference

Robert Kearne has been manager of the toy department at Rathbone's for two years. During this time, he has been an aggressive and astute toy buyer. He has anticipated every major trend in the industry and has always had the shelves stocked to meet the demand.

In reviewing his file, I did find some complaints regarding his impatient behavior with customers. Mr. Kearne is in a position of extremely high pressure and has been told at his evaluations that he needs to work on being patient with all customers in all situations.

Mr. Kearne knows the market well and has an excellent, seemingly intuitive, sense of the toy business.

THE POST-INTERVIEW LETTER

Writing a letter to thank a prospective employer for an interview can be much more than a courteous gesture; it can give you an edge over the competition when the final decision is made.

What the Post-Interview Letter Can Do

You can impress an employer favorably with a letter of appreciation. A post-interview letter shows unusual courtesy and interest because most interviewees do not bother to write one. The letter will also remind the interviewer of you. In addition, you can use the letter to express enthusiasm for the job and add or reemphasize reasons why the employer should hire you.

The Format of a Post-Interview Letter

The post-interview letter should consist of three paragraphs.

1. The first paragraph should express appreciation for the interview and indicate that you are more interested in the position than ever.

2. In the second paragraph, add anything important about yourself or the company that you forgot to mention during the interview. You can also call to mind an important point you made during the interview.

3. The third paragraph of the letter should state your willingness to answer further questions. This paragraph should end with the statement that you are looking forward to hearing from the company.

The following is an example of a post-interview letter.

I want to thank you for the lively and informative interview last Thursday. Your analysis of the company's recent growth and development as a prime mover in the industry was particularly enlightening.

I neglected to tell you that I have enrolled in an evening course in employee relations at Washington University. The course work, along with my experience this year in personnel, should make me an even stronger candidate for your management position.

Bellman Laboratories is one of the most interesting and vital companies in the business today. I look forward eagerly to hearing from you about this position. Please contact me at 555-2777 if you have any further questions.

After the interview, you will have to wait for the employer's decision about hiring you. This process requires you to write another letter or two. Depending upon the action the employer takes, you may need to write any of the following kinds of letters:

RESPONSE TO AN EMPLOYER'S DECISION

- an inquiry, if you have not been told of the decision within the promised time
- an acceptance of a position offered to you
- a refusal of a position
- a response to a letter informing you that you have not been selected
- a letter delaying your decision to accept a position offered to you

A Letter of Inquiry

If an employer has not informed you about the decision when promised, wait several days to a week after the promised date and write a letter of inquiry, which simply asks the employer the status of your application. It can act as another sales letter too.

A letter of inquiry should include three segments:

1. a reminder of the specific position you interviewed for, the date you were interviewed, and the promised date of reply

2. an expression of your eagerness to learn of your status and the reason why you need to be informed

3. a statement of appreciation for the interview (Be sure to hide any annoyance at the delay, or you will turn a possible acceptance into a definite rejection.)

Note the courteous tone in the following letter of inquiry.

Since you interviewed me on May 19, I have received my degree and am now even more prepared for a position as bank teller. It was my understanding at the interview that you would inform me of your decision by early last week.

While I am most eager to receive a positive response, I would be grateful to know your decision either way as soon as possible. My lease is expiring, and I must make new housing arrangements by the end of the month.

Your time and consideration are greatly appreciated.

A Letter of Acceptance

When the good news arrives and you are offered a job you wish to accept, you will need to write a letter. It should include the following items:

1. acceptance of the position
2. confirmation of the details of the job, such as salary, starting date, and the person to whom you report
3. assurance that you are the right person for the job

   The following is an example of an acceptance letter.

   I was delighted to receive your offer for the position of horticulturist in the Miami branch of Blooming Gardens. I happily accept the position.

   Your offer of a starting salary of $15,500 a year is fine, and I will report to Mr. Gleason on March 1 as mentioned in your letter.

   Your confidence in me is well placed, and I look forward to a long and rewarding experience with your company.

A Letter Refusing a Position

When you are offered a position you do not wish to accept, you should write a letter of refusal, stating solid reasons for your decision. Since it is possible that you will reapply to this company in the future, strive to maintain good relations. A diplomatic refusal letter should contain the following four segments:

1. appreciation for the offer
2. a positive statement about the company or the interviewer
3. the refusal itself and an explanation of the reasons for your decision
4. a closing statement of appreciation

Here is an example of a refusal letter:

Your offer of a position as a sales trainee is greatly appreciated, and I am honored that you feel I am qualified to work for your company. Raymond Books publishes some of the finest titles in the field each year.

I regret that I must refuse the offer because I have accepted a position with DBI Publishing. Their offices are close to my apartment and accepting this position will not require me to move.

Thank you for your time and consideration.

A Letter Responding to a Rejection

You may also want to write a letter to a company after you have received a rejection, because you may be reconsidered if the first choice doesn't work out or because you may be offered another position in the company when one becomes available. You may also decide to reapply in the future.

A response to a rejection should include the following elements:

1. appreciation for being considered

2. acknowledgment of something specific that you learned during the interview

3. an indication that you might apply again when you have stronger credentials

Here is an example of a letter responding to a rejection.

> Your letter indicating that I would not be offered the position of executive secretary arrived this morning, much to my disappointment. Hathaway Inc. is a superior company, and it will continue to be a goal of mine to work there someday.
>
> The interview you granted me was extremely informative. You gave me valuable information that I will be able to use in future job pursuits. Your encouragement regarding my future prospects when I gather more experience was greatly appreciated.
>
> When my qualifications are stronger, I intend to reapply, and I hope to see you again at that time. Thank you for your time.

A Letter Delaying Your Decision

What should you do if you have been interviewed by more than one company and you receive an offer from one while waiting for another's decision? Do not be pushed into making a choice you are not ready to make. Instead, write a letter that delays your decision. Such letters are entirely acceptable in the business world.

The letter you compose should contain the following elements:

1. appreciation for the offer

2. a statement that your goal is to find the best match you can for yourself and a company

3. a request for an extension because your job search is not complete

4. an expression of your interest in the position and the company

The following is an example of a letter that postpones a decision.

Thank you for offering me the position of pediatric nurse. It would be an honor to work at Springfield General Hospital. My decision to accept or decline is complicated by the fact that I have an opportunity to become head nurse of pediatrics at a nearby hospital. The personnel director assures me that I will be notified within the week.

I would like to wait for that decision before answering your kind offer. I will call you immediately when I hear.

If you can allow me this time, please let me know.

In some cases, you may feel that a letter is too formal or too impersonal and may jeopardize your chances of getting the job. If so, you may want to call the person who interviewed you and discuss the matter in person. Be sure to follow the same guidelines in your conversation that you would follow in a letter. Stress that you are interested in the offer but that circumstances require you to postpone making a final decision. If the person who interviewed you is extremely busy or if you know that many people have been interviewed for the position, it is also a good idea to confirm your phone conversation in writing, briefly reminding the person of the agreement you reached on the telephone.

ON THE JOB
What Is *Your* Employability Quotient?

Gloria Silbert, the personnel director of Finch's department store, has just interviewed two candidates, Jim Wilfong and Fred Sanchez, for the buyer's job in the menswear department.

Like many employers, Ms. Silbert will consider the employability quotient, or EQ, of each candidate in making her decision. An applicant's EQ consists of the four A's—application, appearance, attendance, and attitude.

First, Ms. Silbert reviews each man's job application form. A neat and accurate application suggests that a candidate will be thorough and careful at work. Both Wilfong and Sanchez have filled out their forms carefully.

Ms. Silbert also considers the appearance of the two men. Dressing up for an interview shows high self-esteem and respect for the employer. Both candidates were well dressed.

Next, Ms. Silbert telephones both applicants' previous employers to check on their attendance because she knows she must rely on the person she hires to show up regularly. Both men have excellent attendance records.

When Ms. Silbert thinks about the attitudes of the two men, however, she begins to see an important difference between them. Wilfong acted in a superior manner toward Ms. Silbert's receptionist, and he showed no sense of humor during the interview. Sanchez, on the other hand, was courteous to everyone and was at ease during the interview, which indicated that he could deal with stressful situations without becoming upset.

When Ms. Silbert adds up the components of each man's EQ, who will be offered the buyer's job?

A. The following letters ask for references. Rewrite them so that they conform to the guidelines given in this chapter. Feel free to supply facts where necessary to make up for deficiencies in the letters.

1.

Dear Professor Tandy:

I took one of your courses in college several years ago. Maybe you remember me: I have red hair, am about 5′4″, and usually wore jeans and a sweater to class. Anyway, I'm applying for a job as a management trainee at Public Utilities Gas & Electric in Windham County. I was hoping you could tell them that I was a good student. Wish me luck!

Yours truly,

2.

Dear Ms. Hayward:

In the summer of 1982, you and I worked together on a day-care project in Howell. Because you are town supervisor, I thought your name would look good as a reference for me. Would you mind? I'm applying for a position with the town of Lakehurst as a clerk in the municipal building.

Maybe you could remind these people how I stayed up around the clock to cover for the people who lost interest halfway through the project. I really want this job.

Sincerely,

B. Wendell Harcourt is a former employee of Fox Electronics. He was fired after one year on the job because he spent too much time listening to the stereo equipment instead of testing and repairing it. Below is a letter written by his former employer in response to a request for a recommendation. Rewrite it in a way that you think is fair to Wendell, his former employer, and his future employer.

Dear Mr. Jackson:

Wendell Harcourt worked for Fox Electronics from February 1984 to March 1985. He had had some previous experience in working with high-tech stereo equipment before coming to Fox, but you'd never know it from the way he worked. After sitting with a problem for a week or two, he was able to find a way to fix it when others may have been baffled. Usually, though, the customers were so irate because of the wait that they never came back. Maybe he'll work out better for you than he did for us.

Sincerely,

C. Below is a follow-up letter turning down a job offer. Briefly describe what is wrong with the letter.

Dear Mr. Bender:

Many thanks for the job offer to work as an assistant to the executive secretary at Bender, Smythe, and Crepsac. I had fun at the interview.

I might have considered accepting your offer, but in the meantime a much better job has been offered to me. It pays better, has better hours, and is with a much better company. Besides, I always envisioned myself as being something better than a mere assistant to a secretary.

Thanks anyway, and good luck finding someone else whose qualifications are as good as mine.

Yours truly,

PROBLEMS

A. A company has asked you for a reference letter regarding Raymond Johnson, a former employee. Write a mixed reference letter based on Raymond's employment experience with you.

Raymond Johnson worked for four years as a camp counselor in your summer camp, Lake Knickerbocker, until he graduated from a nearby community college. He was talented as an instructor in most camp activities, especially swimming, tennis, and shuffleboard. He maintained a good relationship with campers and their parents, but he was argumentative with other camp counselors and with his superiors.

He is applying for a position as assistant social director on the luxury liner *Bermuda*.

B. Write a letter thanking Mr. Theodore Basil, personnel director of Bailey Brothers Accountants, for a recent interview. You are applying for a job as an accountant, and you forgot to tell him during the interview that you kept the books for your family's business when you were in college.

C. You have just had interviews with several insurance companies for a claims adjuster position.

You have been offered a job with Freedom Insurance Company. You are waiting to hear from Haverhill Insurance Company, where the pay and prospects of advancement are better. Surety Insurance has hired someone else for the job of claims supervisor. You were underqualified and hope to reapply when you have more experience.

1. Write a letter delaying your decision to accept the job offered by Freedom Insurance because you want to wait for Haverhill Insurance to reply.

2. Write a response to your rejection from Surety Insurance.

3. Write an acceptance letter to Mrs. Juanita Voquero, Supervisor, at Haverhill Insurance, which has offered you the job of claims adjuster.

4. Write a letter refusing the job with Freedom Insurance Company.

PROJECTS

You have been offered a position as junior accountant at Dawson & Rowe, Inc. The salary is $20,000 a year. Binckley & Caruthers has also offered you a position as a junior accountant, but you would have to relocate because the latter firm is in another city. At Binckley & Caruthers, your salary would be $23,500. Choose which job you want and write two letters: one to accept the job you do want, the other to reject the job you do not want.

PART NINE
READING BUSINESS COMMUNICATIONS

49
Efficient Reading

"Ms. Springer? I've brought the mail."

"She's stepped out, I guess," said Charlie Williams to himself. "I'll just leave this packet of letters on her desk." On approaching his manager's work area, however, he found very little room for the mail. Her desk was piled high with books, magazines, newspapers, and the annual reports of several corporations. In addition, a large stack of memos was lying in Ms. Springer's "In" basket. Charlie could see that several memos were marked "Urgent."

"Wow!" said Charlie. "How does she find time to read all this stuff? At the rate I read, I'm lucky if I have time to finish the sports pages in the daily newspaper. If being an executive means reading this much, I'd better not apply for a promotion. Does Ms. Springer have a secret system, or is she just smarter than I am?"

Ms. Springer has no secret system for reading, nor is she necessarily smarter than Charlie. She has simply become an efficient reader through practice. In addition, what she has learned through reading has given her a good background in business, and this, in turn, has made her an even better reader. She has learned that some material can be skimmed quickly, while more important or difficult texts must be read slowly and carefully. She has learned to recognize and remember key ideas and to grasp quickly how books and articles are organized.

READING SKILLS   If you are a good reader, you already possess a combination of skills. The ability to comprehend and interpret enables you to distinguish the main ideas in a book or article from the details supporting them. A good memory enables you to remember and think about what you have read, and the habit of reading critically enables you to distinguish facts from opinions.

Good reading skills are important for success in business, as Ms. Springer knows and Charlie Williams is just beginning to understand. But the same skills are also important in many aspects of daily life.

Many adults cannot read at all. To imagine what their lives are like, picture yourself in a foreign country where you cannot understand anything you read. Ordering food in a restaurant, deciphering street signs, or reading labels on medicine bottles would be very difficult or even impossible. Filling out a job application would be out of the question. You would quickly become confused by the simplest situations and might even be fearful that you could not obtain help in an emergency. This is the way life is for people who cannot read.

People can also be handicapped by reading deficiencies in less obvious ways. Those whose reading skills are not well developed may not be able to follow written instructions included with toys and appliances requiring assembly. They may be able to read daily newspapers but not the kind of books that could help them advance in their work.

You may think that with the development of television and computers, reading skills are less important nowadays. In fact, more people are reading now than ever before. Bookstores and libraries are doing a brisk business. People are increasingly aware that there is a whole world open to them through books—if they acquire and use good reading skills.

THE ROLE OF READING

Good reading skills will be valuable to you in business even before you find a job, and they will grow in importance as your career progresses. Reading is one of the best ways to find out what fields offer the best job possibilities now and in the future.

On the job, good reading skills can enhance your chances for advancement. If you read and remember vital information about your line of work, you will be recognized as knowledgeable by clients and co-workers alike. Employers notice—and reward—workers who make the effort to learn about their field.

READING IN BUSINESS

Average readers read at about 250 words a minute. Since people speak at about 150 words a minute, reading at an average rate is a more rapid way to learn than listening. In addition, people can skim for information about twice as quickly as they read, which can make reading an even more efficient way to gather facts and ideas.

Although reading at an average rate is obviously useful, improving your reading speed even moderately could substantially increase the amount that you will read during your lifetime. Suppose you are already someone who likes to read. If you read about an hour each day at an average speed, you would read about three books a month. In 5 years, your total would be an impressive 180 books. But if you could increase your reading speed to 350 words a minute, you could read about 250 books in the same 5 years.

IMPROVING READING SPEED

Such an increase is relatively easy to achieve. You have probably already improved your reading speed in the last few years because of the reading you have been required to do on the job or at school. You can do still better, though, if you believe that you can read faster and if you practice regularly.

Motivation is crucial to improving reading speed. Believing that you can read faster helps you concentrate so that you are reading as fast as the material allows. Even with the best motivation, however, reading speed does not increase without regular practice. If you are in school now, the amount you must read and the pressure of your class schedule make this an excellent time to work on increasing your reading speed. Start by reading everything assigned to you. Then look for supplementary reading—additional books and articles related to your assignments.

Of course, reading more quickly is worthless unless you remember what you read. Many textbooks allow you to check your comprehension by providing review questions at the ends of chapters. If a summary of important ideas is also provided, test your comprehension by first writing your own summary and then comparing it to the one in your book.

A good way to increase your reading speed is to practice reading different magazine articles of similar length. Choose a magazine that is easy to read, and set up a regular reading schedule. Daily practice is best, but do not give up if you cannot work on your reading that often. When you start to read, tell yourself, "I will read as fast as I can, understanding as much as I can." Time yourself, and keep track of how long it takes you to finish each article. A written record will motivate you to continue your efforts to increase your speed because it will give you concrete evidence of your progress.

Once you have increased the speed with which you read magazine articles, look for more challenging reading. Try to make a gradual switch to more difficult reading rather than struggling with reading that is much too hard. As you train yourself to read and remember increasingly difficult material, you will feel more and more comfortable with challenging reading. Think of reading as providing nourishment for your mind, just as food provides nourishment for your body. Very easy reading is much like bubble gum for the mind— pleasant, but nothing that can actually nourish your mind and spirit. More challenging books and articles, in contrast, are far more satisfying.

As you read more, your general knowledge will increase, resulting in a further increase in your reading rate. A good general background will help you to make sense of reading matter in a shorter time. Reading is like a psychological guessing game in which your mind constantly interprets what you are reading and predicts what will come next. The more you read, the more skillful at predicting your mind will become. To see how this works, try reading the following sentence:

The nomination ＿＿＿＿＿＿＿ Geraldine Ferraro for vice president supports ＿＿＿＿＿＿ idea that roles for ＿＿＿＿＿＿＿ are changing in this country.

Can you fill in the missing words? As you become a better reader, your mind is likely to fill in gaps more quickly, pushing you forward more and more rapidly. There are a number of mental and physical techniques that will help you read even more profitably.

THE PHYSICAL ASPECTS OF READING

If your general health is not good, you may have trouble concentrating on your reading. A healthful diet, adequate sleep, and regular exercise will help you read at top efficiency. Research suggests that scheduling reading and studying during daylight hours is most efficient, because people are most alert during that time. Doing your most difficult reading first will also increase your reading efficiency.

One important warning: Don't do important reading in bed. A soft, comfortable bed and the dim lighting usually supplied by bedside lamps will naturally make you sleepy. Instead, be sure you are reading in a setting that is conducive to staying alert. Adequate ventilation and comfortable seating with good back support are important.

USING YOUR WORD PROCESSOR
Becoming a Better Reader

You will usually use word processing for writing, but your word processor can also help you increase your reading speed and become a more active reader.

Speed-Reading. You may be able to transform your word processor into a reading pacer by changing the rate at which lines of text scroll by on the screen. Setting the scrolling speed at a faster rate will give you a chance to practice reading more quickly. First, find a comfortable rate at which to read a scrolling document. Then, gradually increase the scrolling speed each time you practice reading. Work on moving your eyes across the lines more rapidly and moving smoothly down and to the left to start each new line. Remember, concentrate on understanding and remembering ideas, not just increasing reading speed.

Active Reading. Try using word processing to get yourself actively involved in your reading. When you survey something you plan to read, try composing questions at the word processor. Then, after you have finished reading, word processing will make it easy for you to go back and fill in answers to your questions.

Word processing also makes writing summaries much easier. After you finish reading a chapter or article, summarize it at the word processor. Aim to get the main ideas in the same order the author used. Then look back to see whether your summary is accurate. With word processing, it is easy to change your wording and add any ideas you left out. Save your summary so that you can use it as the basis for a quick review later. You could also use your word processor to prepare an outline of the main ideas.

Reading requires some essential equipment: your eyes. Treat them well when you read. Make sure that you have enough light and are not sitting in your own shadow. If you are reading a video display screen, adjust the lighting in the room to avoid glare, and experiment with the brightness controls until you find settings that do not strain your eyes.

Many people neglect signs of eye problems, missing the chance to correct their vision and improve their reading. Often people who get glasses or contact lenses for the first time comment on how much easier and more pleasant it is for them to read. They had not realized the extent to which their vision problems had affected their attitudes toward reading. Their motivation, reading rate, and concentration all increase once they can see more clearly.

If you have difficulty reading, get your eyes checked. Signs of possible eye problems include headaches, dizziness, frequent eyestrain, and fatigue. Double vision and blurred vision are indications that you should see an eye specialist promptly. The best protection for your eyes is a regular checkup every two years or as often as your eye specialist recommends.

BASIC TECHNIQUES FOR EFFICIENT READING

Good readers generally move their bodies very little when they read. In contrast, poor readers often move their heads and their lips as they read. They may also point at words in order to keep their place on the page.

Moving your head or other parts of your body as you read tires you and slows you down. If the back of your neck aches after you have read for a short time, you may be moving without realizing it. Ask someone to watch you as you read to see whether you are making unnecessary movements. Working to limit body movement as you read helps you build better reading habits.

Good readers do not say each word to themselves, one word at a time. Keeping your lips and tongue motionless as you read will increase your reading speed and help you focus on the meaning of what you are reading. Try to process words only through your eyes and brain, not through your mouth. If you are consciously or unconsciously saying each word, you are limiting your reading speed to the speed of talking, about 150 words a minute. Avoid this trap by trying to read faster. Rather than concentrating on separate words, focus on the ideas represented by groups of words. When proofreading, pointing at each word is a good technique because it slows down reading and focuses attention on individual syllables and letters. However, pointing at the page during regular reading will limit your pace. You should also avoid moving your hands or a pencil down the page, or placing a ruler or a sheet of paper under each line.

As you read, you should try to keep your eyes moving from left to right and quickly sweeping to the left to start each new line. As you read, your eyes actually pause for a fraction of a second at a time. During each pause, they focus and take in information. Your brain interprets this information, allowing you to recognize the words you have read.

Sometimes you may need to look back to clarify a point, but constantly moving your eyes back to something you have already read is a poor habit. It slows you down and leads to confusion about what you have read because you lose the flow of ideas. Consider the following sentence:

> All over America, BestWay Investments is saving people time and money while providing a host of other benefits.

This is not a particularly difficult sentence. Now look at the same sentence as it is read by someone who habitually looks back at what he or she has already read.

> All over America over America, BestWay BestWay Investments is saving people is saving time and money while providing while providing a host of other host of other benefits.

No wonder people who read this way read more slowly and have trouble understanding what they read.

As you learn to concentrate on the meaning of what you are reading, you will be able to read longer phrases at a time rather than reading word by word. To see how slow reading one word at a time can be, try reading the following sentences, which have been printed so that you must read from right to left.

> you Can .example an is This
> are or phrases in this read
> ?word by word read to forced you

Do you ordinarily read as slowly as you read this example, or do you usually read more rapidly? Of course, you may want to slow down at times in order to comprehend something very difficult. You may, for example, want to break down an unfamiliar word into parts by looking at each syllable. When you are working with numbers or checking spelling, you may want to stop and look at each number or letter at a time.

Reading in meaningful phrases, rather than word by word, is a key technique for increasing speed and comprehension. Verb phrases, such as *have been selling* and *would have remembered*, are one type of meaningful phrase; prepositional phrases, such as *in my desk* and *after work*, are another kind. These kinds of phrases are used so often that you are already familiar with the way they work. As a result, you can predict what will come next and jump to the next idea. If you have a good background in the subject you are reading about, you will be able to take in larger chunks of information at a time. You can see how this method works by looking at the following passage, which is divided into meaningful phrases the way a good reader would process it.

> A recent trend / in the construction industry / is Victorian styling. Buyers will pay / top price / for the steep roofs, / large porches, / and gingerbread trim / on Victorian homes.

As you can see, reading groups of words that fit together makes reading easier and more meaningful.

EDITING EXERCISES

In each of the numbered items that follow, a phrase or number occurs twice. Proofread the phrase on the right against the phrase on the left. Correct any errors you find in the phrase on the right. Use the letter-by-letter proofreading technique.

1. AK693 Shetland   Ak693 Shetland
2. 482-52-6873   482-52-6873
3. $45,000 @ 9½% $45.00 @ 9½%
4. 101654000045982   10165499945982
5. June 27, 1945   June 27, 1945
6. ISBN 0-03-062762   ISBN 0-03-06272
7. (609) 555-1136   (609) 555-1136

PROBLEMS

A. In the following passage, check your ability to predict what will come next as you read by filling in the missing words.

At some shopping malls, clusters _____ fast-food restaurants offer customers convenience _____ variety. These clusters, known _____ food courts, may include as many _____ 20 _____ . Food courts _____ very popular because people like _____ variety _____ foods _____ offer, such as Italian, Chinese, and Mexican _____. After choosing foods _____ several restaurants, customers _____ in a central area that is shared all _____ restaurants and enjoy _____ meals.

B. Watch someone else read, and record approximately how many times the person's eyes stop per line. Do the eyes sweep smoothly and rapidly to the left to start a new line? Ask the person to begin to read and then to go back to reread a section without telling you when he or she is doing so. Can you see the eyes move back? Then ask the person to continue reading, and record the number of times that you see the person's eyes return to something already read. If the person often goes back over material already read, ask if he or she is aware of that habit.

C. Select a magazine article or a chapter from this book, and use slash marks (/) to divide it into meaningful phrases. Then read the article or chapter, concentrating on speed and retention.

PROJECTS

A. Begin a book you have been planning to read, and keep a record of how many pages you can read in an hour. Before you start to read, tell yourself, "I will read as quickly as I can, understanding as much as I can." Check your comprehension by summarizing what you have read at the end of each session.

B. Keep a log in which you record the total amount of time you spend reading in one week. Record the name of each magazine, newspaper, or book you read, and categorize it as easy, average, or difficult to read. Also, take notes on your reading comprehension and speed.

   Experiment to see if your reading rate varies depending on the time of day or the presence of distractions such as music.

50
Active and Critical Reading

Reading requires an active mind. You need to make a conscious effort to read in a searching way so that you can retain and respond to what you are reading. Any kind of reading is more rewarding if you become involved, make an effort to remember main ideas, and reflect on what you are reading.

READING STRATEGIES Preparing yourself to read is an important part of active reading. Previewing, predicting, and questioning are among the strategies that will help. Previewing gives you an overview of main ideas and their relationships to each other, predicting provides a chance to guess what will be covered, and raising questions equips you with a clear purpose for your reading.

Previewing

Glancing through an entire article or chapter before you start to read it familiarizes you with its content and its organization, giving you a clear overview of the material you will be covering.

One goal of previewing is to classify the type of material you are reading. For example, is it fiction or nonfiction, theoretical or practical? For information that will help you determine the kind of material you are reading, look at the book jacket (if there is one), and read the introduction or preface of a book or the introductory paragraph and summary of an article. These ready-made previews can provide important clues to the author's subject and intentions.

To find clues to the main ideas, look at headings, words printed in boldface or italics, and topic sentences. Try reading the first sentences of some of the paragraphs. If they seem to be topic sentences (sentences that state the main points in the paragraphs), read all first sentences in order to get a sense of the important ideas and their relationships to each other.

Previewing gives you a sense of the overall plan—the skeleton of the whole book or article. Part of understanding this skeleton is recognizing which parts are absolutely crucial and which are not so important. Later, when you read the whole thing carefully, your sense of the relative importance of the ideas will make your reading easier and quicker. Still, previewing is only a first step in preparing to read effectively. Subsequent steps give you the chance to flesh out the skeleton of main ideas with details and examples that give it deeper meaning.

Predicting

You can also begin at once to predict the author's purpose. At work, you will often read material written by people you know either personally or by reputation. Your knowledge of the writer should help you predict what he or she will have to say. You may already know whether or not the author is likely to be straightforward in his or her approach, and you might be able to identify personal beliefs or external pressures that could influence the content of the material or approach to the subject.

Predicting helps you guess the meaning of unfamiliar words too. Because you are actively trying to guess what will be coming next, you have a better chance of understanding new words in context.

Questioning

The questions you raise as you read will help motivate you and guide your reading. After you have raised questions about the title, you can make up questions based on the headings found within the chapter or article. If no headings are provided, base your questions on topic sentences. If questions do not occur to you, try using the standard question openers; who, what, when, where, how, and why. If questions are provided at the end of a chapter, read them before you read the chapter so that you are actively reading with some clear goals in mind.

Taking Notes

By taking notes, you can stay active while you read, remember what you have read, and, later, review the material much more easily. Some people are reluctant to mark up books because they regard writing as the author's job while their task is only to absorb what they find on the printed page. This detached attitude leads to passive reading.

Intelligent note taking can greatly enhance a book's value to its owner. Many books require at least some rereading. But to reread a book completely when you only need to find a few key ideas is a waste of time. Underlining, highlighting, and jotting notes in the margin should help you focus on crucial ideas and details. In addition, jotting notes in a notebook will help you crystallize your thinking and provide a further memory aid.

INCREASING COMPREHENSION

In order to understand a book or article quickly, you need to find clues to main ideas and see at a glance how ideas were organized. You can do so by using the aids to better comprehension that writers and editors provide.

Clues to Main Ideas

A logical place to begin a book or a long report is the table of contents. This aid presents an outline of all the material to be covered and provides some idea of how the chapters are related to each other. For example, indented chapter titles under a bold heading show that all the chapters contribute to one main idea.

Within chapters, headings and subheadings provide more information. When you preview, try reading only the heading to get an overview of the outline of a chapter. The headings may be printed in a second color, making it easier for you to locate the important points. Often, different type sizes and styles are used to help you distinguish the most important headings from the less important ones. Paragraphing is another important visual clue to main ideas. Each paragraph is likely to contain a different main point.

Other graphic aids and print devices provide further clues to main ideas. Charts, graphs, maps, and pictures are important because they provide another pathway to learning, a visual way of understanding the topic.

In many books, special types of print, such as boldface and italics, indicate important words and ideas. Underlining and capital letters may also provide clues to main ideas. Look, too, for lists and boxes that add to the text.

Organizational Patterns

All organizational patterns have one thing in common: a general idea supported by details. Certain words signal the relationship between thesis and evidence and between one piece of evidence and another. *For example* nearly always suggests that a general idea has been stated and evidence to support it is about to be offered. *In addition* and *also* are used to signal that details are about to be presented that add to those already listed. *However* and *on the other hand* are clues that contradictory ideas will be introduced.

Within the basic pattern of generalizations followed by details, several variations are possible. A chronological arrangement, which lists events in the order in which they happen, is easiest to understand and remember.

Listing details spatially, or by location, is also a simple scheme.

Listing details in order of importance is also a common practice.

Another straightforward way to organize details is by classification, or division of a topic into categories.

Other organizational patterns are harder to follow but may be best for certain kinds of material. Comparison and contrast, for example, require the reader to move back and forth, focusing on separate pairs of ideas or details in turn.

Another order that requires careful reading is cause and effect.

Good readers vary their reading rate according to the kinds of materials they are reading and their reasons for reading them. Sometimes they scan the material quickly to locate information or to get a general idea of its contents. Other times, they read slowly and carefully. Within a book or an article, readers may increase their reading rate when the material is familiar, and they may slow down when something is particularly interesting or difficult.

To become a more flexible reader, you must recognize that you need not read everything in its entirety or at the same speed. You should be able to skim for general ideas about twice as fast as you normally read and scan for information even more quickly. Speeding up at appropriate times could even give you more time to concentrate on the material that you must read slowly.

When to Read Quickly

No one reads an entire telephone book or encyclopedia from cover to cover. Many reference books are designed so that people can find what they need in a hurry and ignore everything else. When you know your purpose in reading, you can skip over material that you do not need. This technique enables you to scan for specific information very rapidly.

You can skim rapidly when you recognize that a book or article is not important enough to read thoroughly. You probably often flip through a newspaper or magazine just for enjoyment. You can take the same approach to an entire book.

VARYING READING SPEED ACCORDING TO PURPOSE

DID YOU KNOW?
The Effect of Computers on Thinking and Reading

In the Middle Ages, a book was a manuscript, laboriously copied by a scribe writing with a quill pen. Libraries often chained these valuable manuscripts to tables so that readers would not steal them.

In 1456, Johannes Gutenberg of Mainz, in Germany, invented printing. Gutenberg's invention meant that books could be produced more cheaply and in much greater numbers.

The invention of printing changed the world in many ways. As information became more easily available, people began to think more and more for themselves. Instead of passively accepting authority, they began to challenge it. Soon new ideas were winning acceptance. Developments in religion, science, and government after 1500 were partly due to the rapid spread of knowledge that printing had made possible.

Just as the invention of printing changed the world in the 1500s, the invention of computers is changing the world today. Now any person with a home computer and a modem has access to whole libraries of information.

People can now read directly from computer screens. Although computers will probably never replace print entirely, people will have greater freedom to choose how to get the information they need, and computer technology will help make their tasks easier and more enjoyable.

You can also move rapidly when you read material a second time. Your prior knowledge should make the second reading quicker and easier. Also, even if you have not read a particular book or article before, you can absorb it quickly if you have background knowledge in the subject. Your general knowledge will make it easy to predict what is coming next, and you will need to slow down less often to figure out unfamiliar words and ideas.

Unfortunately, you may also have to read in a hurry at times when your general goals and the nature of the material call for slow, careful reading. If you are required to read an overwhelming amount of material, it may be better to skim all of it rather than read only a small amount carefully.

When to Read Slowly

Slow reading is not necessarily poor reading, but when you reduce your reading speed, you should do so for a reason. If a general understanding of the material is not sufficient, you must read more slowly for better comprehension.

A slower reading rate is also necessary if the material is densely written, full of abstract ideas, or in a difficult-to-follow style. If the subject matter is new to you, you will need extra time to make sense out of unfamiliar ideas and vocabulary. Specialized technical writing requires this kind of approach.

You should also slow down to savor any writing that you enjoy. Taking the time to appreciate new ideas or an effective writing style will add to your reading pleasure.

READING FOR INFORMATION

When you scan to locate information, you are actually doing more looking than reading. To find information quickly, you must determine exactly what you are looking for. Try stating your purpose in a question, such as "What kinds of stocks did JKG Growth Fund invest in during 1986?" Making your question explicit will help you skip across other headings in the JKG annual report, such as "Planning Your Portfolio" or "How to Use the Fund." Headings such as "About the Fund" and "JKG's Ten Largest Holdings" are more likely to contain the information you need.

Once you find the right section, move your eye quickly down a narrow column or, if the column is wider, across and down the page in a zigzag pattern. Look for clues to the kind of information you want. Capital letters and numbers are easy to find at a glance. If you are familiar with your subject matter, you can also anticipate key phrases that might be found with the information you want, such as *growth stocks* and *common stocks*.

Skimming, like previewing before you do more thorough reading, is selective reading. You will often do this kind of reading at work as you glance through memos, letters, and proposals to find the main ideas. To skim, read the title and headings, look for a statement of the main idea, and study the summary if one is provided. Read the first sentence in each paragraph and glance at words in bold print and at illustrations. Slow down to read more closely if something that seems interesting or important catches your eye.

When skimming, you should skip most examples unless you can see that they cast a new light on main ideas. Your goal is to read for main ideas and skip the rest.

READING TO STUDY

When you must understand and remember what you read, you should add additional steps to the reading process: rereading, reciting, and reviewing. Without following these steps, you are more likely to forget what you have read.

Much of what you read will have to be read more than once. Having to reread material is not a sign of poor reading skills; most people do considerable rereading. However, concentrate on understanding and remembering as much as you can each time you read. Once you understand what you have read, underline or take notes to simplify later review. When you do reread, look closely at the way ideas are connected. Having read the material before puts you in a better position to examine the pattern of evidence.

Another important part of study reading is reciting, which is a form of immediate review in which you answer your own questions about what you have been reading. Stop now and then to repeat key ideas to yourself either silently or out loud and to jot them down. Speaking aloud and writing have the added advantage of involving other senses, increasing your chances of remembering important ideas.

Reciting key ideas forces you to select important information and shows you immediately how well you have read. It is also a way of testing yourself before an instructor, customer, or supervisor at work questions you.

Rereading and reciting should be linked with regular review. Repetition is an important key to improving your memory. Your review of what you have read may be brief, but to be effective it must be a regular part of your study schedule.

Taking Notes

Taking notes simplifies reviewing. Some of the techniques you can use are making notes in margins, highlighting or underlining key ideas, and outlining and summarizing what you have read.

Notes in a Book. The most common way to take notes is to underline or highlight key ideas. Underline only key ideas. Some people make the mistake of underlining so much that they might as well reread the entire text. Underlining too much defeats the purpose: to see at a glance what is important.

Taking notes in the margin enables you to begin a dialogue with the author. Use the margin to write questions and responses to the author's ideas.

Outlines and Summaries. Outlining and summarizing are useful ways to test your grasp of the author's key ideas. Neatness is not important; understanding the relationships between ideas is your goal. A good outline will help you see which ideas are most important and how ideas are related to each other. Try making a summary of a chapter or section without looking back. If the book contains a summary, compare it with your own.

Outlines and summaries should never become ends in themselves. Quickly listing a chapter's most important ideas to test your comprehension is the best form of review. Reciting the main ideas aloud, even without writing any notes, can help provide necessary reinforcement.

Careful reading and note taking are not enough. Although the temptation to plow ahead can be great, occasional review sessions pay big dividends. Along with previewing, predicting, and questioning, reviewing will ensure that you remember what you need to know.

READING CRITICALLY

To do a good job of assessing and evaluating information, you need to question everything you read. You should always be asking whether information is true, logical, and useful. Part of your task is to look for contradictory ideas and outdated information. The most important question you should ask is "Why?" Asking this question forces you to evaluate the evidence an author provides.

Understanding Inferences

Sometimes writers merely suggest ideas rather than state them directly. Have you ever wondered why writers do not state all their ideas in an obvious manner? One reason you may have to read between the lines for an author's implied meaning is that the author may assume the reader is familiar with the subject and write to that level.

Moreover, an author may decide that letting readers draw their only conclusions is more effective than expressing opinions directly. Once readers have drawn a conclusion on their own, they are more likely to understand and remember it.

One way to do a better job of reading between the lines is to use what you have read up to a point as the basis for making a reasonable guess about what is intended. Your first step is to understand what is directly stated. Then, once you understand a passage at a literal level, ask yourself: "What does it all mean? What does this add up to?" When you have some guesses about the implied meanings, look for words and phrases that verify your hunches.

Identifying Bias

All authors necessarily write from their own viewpoints. An author's beliefs always affect the choice of details and the manner in which they are presented.

As a reader, you may have to do some detective work to determine an author's bias. For example, the author's background and experiences often provide clues to his or her point of view.

Having a point of view does not necessarily mean that a writer distorts the truth or attempts to manipulate readers in a dishonest way. A writer does not have an obligation to present all sides of an issue. Indeed, the author's intention is to present only one side. Understanding the writer's purpose will help you be aware of bias and prompt you to look elsewhere for opposing viewpoints.

Evaluating Faulty Arguments

In order to spot a faulty argument, you must be able to distinguish between a general idea and its supporting details and then make sure that enough evidence is offered to support the generalization. An incomplete analysis is one reason for rejecting an author's ideas. However, you should not be misled by an abundance of details. Instead, make sure that the details provided are typical and that the source of information is reliable.

Another kind of faulty argument is one in which the main ideas are over-simplified. This often happens when one situation is compared to another. The same kind of mistake is often made when a writer claims that one event or situation caused another. Remember, just because one event happened after another one, the first one is not necessarily a cause of the second one.

PROBLEMS

A. Test your scanning skills by seeing how quickly you can find information in this book on the following topics:

using apostrophes   listening on the job
writing minutes   avoiding wordiness
speaking on the telephone   writing topic sentences
using periods with abbreviations   forming noun plurals
expressing percentages in figures   distinguishing between *it's* and *its*

B. For each article title listed below, write at least three questions that could help guide your reading. Base your questions on key words in the titles.

1. "New Desserts for Special Occasions"
2. "Minimizing Flood Damage"
3. "The HMO Approach to Health Care"
4. "'Morphy, Fischer, and the U.S. Chess Hall of Fame"
5. "The Captivity of Cambodia"
6. "Major Guidebooks to Europe"
7. "The People's Judge"

8. "The New Immigrants"

9. "Untying the Knots of Metropolitan Traffic"

C. Identify the sentences below as facts or opinions.

1. John Steinbeck won the Nobel Prize in 1962.

2. Receiving the Nobel Prize was responsible for Steinbeck's publishing nothing in the last six years of his life.

3. Most Americans use mouthwash because of the fear of offending others with their bad breath.

4. Most mouthwashes contain alcohol.

5. The parking brake is usually attached to the rear wheels of a car.

6. You should never put off working on your car's brakes.

7. Every woman looks better with makeup.

8. In the summertime, women should choose lipstick that is a shade darker than the lipstick they usually wear.

9. In 1930, one out of every five Americans owned an automobile.

10. The Irish Sweepstakes became very popular during the Depression because people needed something to hope for.

11. Coping with the long-term effects of becoming a parent may take a year or more.

12. Unrealistic expectations of what it means to be a parent may contribute to feelings of depression.

D. Use your detective skills to determine the main principles of organization used to put the lists below in order. Choose among the following: chronological order, spatial order, order of importance, comparison/contrast, classification, and cause/effect.

1. preview, predict, question, read, take notes, review

2. apples, bananas, peaches, carrots, broccoli, peas, chicken, hamburger, pork chops, eggs, buttermilk, yogurt

3. How qualified is the medical staff? What facilities are available? What extra benefits are offered? How difficult is the enrollment procedure?

4. San Francisco, Salt Lake City, Denver, Kansas City, St. Louis, Cincinnati, Pittsburgh, Washington, D.C.

5. in-use light, automatic redialing, type and loudness of ring, convenience of push buttons, memory capacity, durability, voice quality

6. The igniter often does not work. You have to crouch with your face near the grill. Closing the lid can blow the flame out. Sometimes igniting the gas causes a large flame to flare up. Gas can drift away from the igniter. An unsuspecting user faces serious hazards.

PROJECTS

A. Select a chapter from this book. Prepare to read it by predicting the main points it will cover, previewing it, and asking questions based on the title and headings. As you read, underline key points, and stop from time to time to check your recall of the main ideas. Conclude by writing a 75- to 100-word summary and comparing it to the summary at the end of the chapter.

B. Choose a book that you would like to read but that you consider too difficult. Use the following checklist to identify aids to understanding provided in the book: book title, table of contents, introduction or preface, statement of purpose, headings and subheadings, boldface, italics, study questions, pictures, maps, charts or graphs, vocabulary list or glossary, summaries or a summarizing chapter. List any additional clues to main ideas that the book provides. Write a one-paragraph statement of the main ideas in the book as you understand them after studying the aids that you found.

PART TEN
LISTENING AND SPEAKING EFFECTIVELY

51
General Listening Skills

Perhaps when you were young you played a game called "Telephone" or "Whisper Down the Lane." One person whispered a message in the ear of another, who whispered it to another, and so on. The last person to get the message said it aloud. You may recall that, most of the time, what the last person said was quite different from what the first one had said.

How did this happen? Perhaps the people did not hear correctly, were not paying attention, or failed to remember what was said to them. In any case, they listened poorly. While the consequences of poor listening in a child's game are of little importance, poor listening in business can cause serious problems.

LISTENING: THE MOST NEGLECTED COMMUNICATION SKILL

The majority of your on-the-job communication time will be spent listening. Does that surprise you? Almost half—a full 45 percent—of your communication time consists of listening (as opposed to 30 percent speaking, 16 percent reading, and 9 percent writing). Even though people spend so much time listening, most do it remarkably badly. Immediately after listening to someone speak, individuals remember, on the average, only half of what they heard even when they believe they have listened closely. Two months (some researchers say two weeks) later, they remember only one-quarter of what they heard. Clearly, a great amount of information is lost because of poor listening. You may say, "That's not a listening problem. That's a *remembering* problem." Yet, listening and remembering cannot be separated.

Misconceptions About Listening

Many people think hearing and listening are the same thing. Hearing is merely the passive receiving of sound waves into the ear. Listening, however, involves paying attention, understanding, and remembering—as well as hearing. Listening requires an active stance.

A mistaken idea about listening is that it automatically improves as reading skill improves. Perhaps this is one of the reasons that educators have in the past neglected to teach listening skills. Although reading and listening both involve attention and understanding, they demand different skills.

The reading you do is done alone and at a pace set by you; listening must be done with at least one other person, the speaker, and he or she—not you— sets the pace. To improve your listening skills, you will need to concentrate on the act of listening.

THE BENEFITS OF GOOD LISTENING SKILLS

What will improving your listening skills do for you? How will it help you both in your daily life and in your job performance? There are four major benefits of effective listening.

1. Good listening is the best way to improve your general language ability. Just as reading books that are well written will help you become a better writer, listening to effective speakers or good conversationalists will help you use language more skillfully. Listening is, in fact, a painless way to expand your vocabulary. Instead of looking up words and memorizing definitions, through listening, you can learn the meanings of new words in context. An expanded vocabulary aids effective communication.

2. Good listening increases your general knowledge. Successful business people have a broad general knowledge. They can converse intelligently on a number of subjects. Listening to others helps you add to your store of general knowledge. Listening is an especially effective way to gain knowledge because the speaker—assuming she or he is well versed in the subject—has already compiled the facts and put them into a logical order. In essence, your "research" has been done for you—all you have to do is *listen.*

3. Good listening helps you become a better conversationalist. Doing business today requires conversing with people not only about work but about a number of other matters as well. People who can carry on an intelligent conversation are looked upon as more capable (and more interesting) than those who are less-skilled talkers. Listening to others can help you develop this important skill.

4. Good listening will improve your on-the-job performance. Listening to your supervisor as he or she gives directions will allow you to follow those directions accurately. Listening closely during an interview will help you make a better impression on a prospective employer. Listening well during a meeting or conference will allow you to participate intelligently and make the most of your time. Listening to your co-workers will help you get to know your workplace better and move about within it with greater ease.

These are just a few ways that good listening skills can help you do your job better and advance more quickly. As you become a better listener, you become a more valuable employee.

DIFFERENT KINDS OF LISTENING

Make a list of the various types of written material you have read in the last week. It might include textbooks or administrative information (exam schedules, announcement sheets, and so on); a magazine or book you enjoy; or a friend's letter. You read each of these for a different reason: to gain information, to improve your grades, or purely for enjoyment. Just as there are different kinds of reading, there are different kinds of listening. Listening can be broken down into two broad categories—serious listening and social listening—each of which includes different types of listening.

Serious Listening

When you engage in serious listening, you listen to understand, to evaluate, to analyze, or to remember. Serious listening is "practical listening." You engage

ON THE JOB

Handling Hard-to-Understand Callers

Have you ever received a telephone call at home from someone whose speech was difficult to understand? An individual who speaks very quickly or very softly or who has a marked accent or a speech impediment (such as a stutter or a lisp) may be difficult to understand. Because you are not face-to-face with the person, you cannot make use of facial expressions or body language, which frequently aids comprehension. How do you handle this situation when it is crucial to take the message correctly and also be tactful? Here are some guidelines:

- If an individual speaks very quickly or very softly, politely request that he or she speak somewhat slower or louder. Use "I" language as much as possible. For example, say "I'm having a little trouble keeping up. Could you repeat that a little more slowly?" rather than "You're talking too fast. Talk more slowly, please."
- You might ask a person with an accent to repeat a phrase or to speak more slowly as

well, explaining that you did not quite catch the last bit of information. Most individuals with accents are aware that others may have trouble understanding them and will speak more slowly and distinctly. Avoid implying that the accent is annoying or makes the speaker seem unintelligent. The more exposure you have to various kinds of speakers, the more easily you will be able to understand different types of accents.

- Extreme sensitivity is necessary when a person has a speech problem. Such a person may be very self-conscious already; a tone of criticism or derision from you will be painful and may make the impediment worse. In such a situation, concentrate hard, and ask for clarification only when absolutely necessary. If the person stutters, be patient. Never finish a word or a sentence for a stutterer—wait for him or her to complete it.

in serious listening when you listen to a lecturer to gain and retain information, when you listen to a persuasive speaker to analyze the validity of his or her argument, and when you listen to several experts on a subject to evaluate the sum of their information.

On the job, you will spend much of your time doing serious listening, which requires skills such as attention, discrimination, the ability to distinguish a main point from supporting data, and the capacity to retain information for future use.

Social Listening

Social listening is listening for pleasure, to be courteous, or to express respect and concern. It includes listening to your favorite music, listening to friends at a party, or listening to a person who is in trouble. While serious listening is primarily practical and task-oriented, social listening is personal and people-oriented. Social listening will be part of your job no matter what your position in the company.

Determining Your Listening Purpose

Part of being an effective listener is deciding what type of listening is required in a given situation and responding appropriately. For example, calling the weather information number merely involves listening closely to the recording and jotting down the necessary information. However, listening to a co-worker describe a personal problem would involve a sympathetic and emotional response on your part.

COMMON BARRIERS TO EFFECTIVE LISTENING

To avoid the common barriers to effective listening, follow the rules given in this section.

- Do not allow differences in speaking and understanding rates to block communication. In some ways, verbal communication is a tortoise-and-hare race with the tongue as the tortoise and the brain as the hare. While people speak at a rate of about 125 to 150 words per minute, they can understand at several times that speed. Listeners, then, have "spare time" while they listen. Poor listeners use this time to think about other things; good listeners think about the speaker's message.
- Do not just pretend to pay attention. Many individuals become extremely good at acting as if they are listening. They fix the speaker with an earnest stare while tuning out the message entirely. This kind of acting becomes a hard habit to break. Even when such a person wants to listen, force of habit may cause the mind to wander.
- Do not prejudge a subject as uninteresting or too difficult. Sometimes people decide a subject is boring almost as soon as—or even before—a speaker begins talking, and they tune the speaker out. Keep in mind that

you can learn valuable information even if you find the subject uninteresting.

A related problem involves discarding a message because it seems difficult. This type of poor listening has a snowball effect: the less one works on listening to complex messages, the less practice one has and the more difficult such listening becomes. Over time, the ability to listen to any but the most unchallenging messages is lost.

- Do not listen for "just the facts." Some people think good listening means listening for facts. By concentrating on isolated facts, however, these listeners usually miss the main points. Someone listening to a presentation might, for example, focus upon the fact that one machine costs $3,500 and another costs $3,000 but miss the main point that the $3,500 machine has features which make it more cost-effective than the less expensive one.

- Do not dismiss the speaker before hearing the message. Everyone knows that you cannot judge a book by its cover, yet some people use superficial characteristics such as an unattractive appearance or a speech impediment as an excuse for not paying attention to the message. This is not a valid way of thinking. We can all think of times when we had important things to say even though our appearance or method of delivery was open to improvement.

- Do not let emotions block communication. Sometimes, if people are very involved emotionally in what a speaker says, their emotions keep them from listening well. This barrier can work in two ways. Negative emotions can make one shut the speaker out and refuse to listen to the message objectively. Positive emotions can make one swallow everything a speaker has to say without critically evaluating its worth. Sometimes particular words—especially negative ones—make listeners stop paying attention because of the anger the words arouse.

- Do not succumb to distractions. Sometimes people let distractions take their attention from the message at hand. Environmental distractions, such as noise, or internal distractions, such as a personal problem, can keep individuals from listening effectively.

IMPROVE YOUR LISTENING EFFECTIVENESS

Fortunately, it is possible to improve your listening ability and, as a result, to increase your effectiveness at work and in your personal life.

Learn to Concentrate

This is the most important listening improvement technique. To listen well, you have to increase your powers of concentration. Whenever possible, help your concentration by eliminating distractions. Close a window that creates a draft. Move nearer to the speaker or ask the person to speak louder if you

Training for the High-Tech Office

(*Left*) Traditionally, office workers have relied on business tools such as the typewriter. Many of today's offices, however, are replacing typewriters with desktop computers. As the cost of computers has decreased, the number of businesses using them has increased dramatically. According to one survey, more than 3 million businesses will have electronic office systems in place by 1990. The high-tech office is not just the office of the future; it is the office of today.

(*Below*) In order to function in the high-tech office, employees must have certain specific skills, including the ability to work with computers. The ability to use a computer on the job is sometimes called computer literacy. Many educators and business people believe that in order to survive in the job market of the future, individuals will need to be not only competent at reading, writing, and mathematics, but also computer-literate. Because computers have been introduced into the workplace relatively recently, many people still are neither familiar nor comfortable with them. In fact, a number of people are actually intimidated by computers and fear that they may never be able to use them. The best way to overcome computer anxiety is to learn how to use computers.

(*Top*) Computer education can begin at any age. Elementary schools through-out the country now introduce their students to computers in the first or second grade. As these students progress through high school, their computer education will continue. In addition, many families have home computers or computer games that help familiarize children with computers. As a result of the growing use of computers at home and in school, many young people know more about computers than their parents do.

(*Bottom*) Adults who have never had any formal education in computers need not worry, however. Most adult education centers offer introductory courses in computers. Some are specifically geared to home computer users. Others are designed for people who use computers at work. Some introductory courses provide a general overview of computers, while others concentrate on a par-ticular brand of computer hardware or software.

(*Left*) Many people prefer courses that offer hands-on experience with a computer because such courses allow them to learn by doing.

(*Right*) People who do not have other access to computers will particularly benefit from a hands-on course. However, not everyone who learns about computers is enrolled in a course.

(*Top*) A great deal of computer education occurs right in the workplace. Many companies provide on-the-job training for workers without computer experience. This training may take place in corporate classrooms, or it may consist of one-on-one instruction in the office itself.

(*Bottom*) An employee who is already familiar with the company's equipment and programs will often help a new employee learn how to use them.

(*Left*) Besides the help of other employees, trainees may turn to manuals published by the various computer manufacturers for users of their products. These guidebooks are often referred to as the computer's documentation. Depending on the type of equipment, the documentation could range from one thin book to a multivolume series. Documentation is especially helpful for trainees when they begin working with computers on their own.

(*Below*) A number of computers are designed to help beginners by providing prompts and by posing questions to help users operate hardware and software. Some computers even feature a button that allows new users to ask for and receive help. Computers that offer such assistance are sometimes called user-friendly.

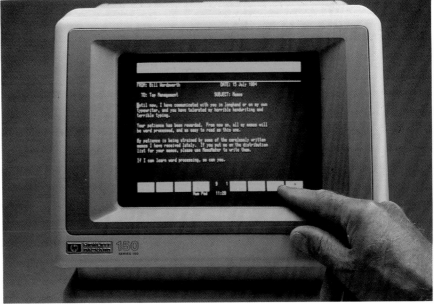

(*Top*) Although different computer systems have greatly varying components and programs, some features are fairly standard. For instance, most microcomputers have one or two disk drives that read and write data. To begin operating the computer, users generally need to insert a program disk, which contains the computer software, and a data disk. The program disk is already written and usually cannot be altered. The data disk is a blank that is made to be written on; that is, it stores whatever information the user places upon it.

(*Bottom*) In order to get information onto the disk, users need to input it, generally by using the computer's keyboard. Computer keyboards contain the same basic key arrangement as the typewriter, with some additional keys located on either side.

(*Left*) A light pen provides another method for inputting information. Light pens allow users to select one item from a group shown on the computer screen, request additional information, or create a graphic image.

(*Below*) Along with learning how to input information, computer users need to learn how to have the computer output that information. The most common output device is the printer, which converts electronic data on disk to printed words on paper. Computer users do not always need or want paper copies of their work, but when they do, they need to know how to operate a printer.

(*Above*) How long does a trainee need in order to learn the ins and outs of a computer system? The amount of time will vary depending on the system and the individual. Simply learning how to use equipment may require as little as several hours or as much as several weeks. A thorough understanding of a system and its capabilities might require months of day-to-day use. Even after employees master their company's computer system, their computer education should continue. Computer hardware and software are constantly being updated and improved. As a result, what is in the forefront of technology this year may be obsolete next year. In order to keep computer skills current, employees will occasionally need reeducation and retraining. The more individuals know about computers, the more access they will have to information, and the greater their ability will be to express themselves. Computer literacy will open doors for job applicants who want to work in the high-tech offices of today, and it will help them pursue their careers in the high-tech offices of tomorrow.

cannot hear. Then focus on listening. The more you practice concentrating, the better you will be at it.

Take a Positive Attitude

Before the speaker even begins, decide that the message will be worthwhile and will benefit you. Effective listening will not just happen—you must be motivated. You will be surprised at how much more you gain from a message when you are prepared to learn something from the outset.

Determine Your Purpose for Listening

You will also increase your motivation if you designate a particular purpose for listening. Your purpose may be as specific as "to learn how to use this machine properly" or as general as "to convince my supervisor that I want to do a good job." You will find that establishing a reason for listening also helps you to concentrate.

Control Your Emotions

Avoid letting your emotions overpower your intellect in subject areas about which you feel strongly. Self-knowledge will help you identify areas in which your emotions are in danger of taking over; self-control will help you keep these emotions in check. Try to withhold judgment on emotional subjects until the speaker has finished. If a speaker uses words that offend you, avoid focusing on those particular words and concentrate instead on the overall message.

Use Your Brain's Spare Time

Remember that you can receive messages several times faster than people can speak them. Use the extra time to advantage. Try to anticipate what the individual is getting at and what he or she will say next. Ask yourself questions about the message to identify main points. Periodically summarize the main ideas to yourself to be sure you have listened and remembered.

Be Empathetic

To empathize is to put yourself in someone else's place. As you listen, try to see what the speaker is getting at from his or her point of view. This will also help you control your emotions by focusing your attention on the speaker and the message rather than on your own feelings.

Analyze the Speaker's Message

Concentrate on the concepts the speaker is putting across. How well does he or she support these ideas? Is the speaker's reasoning logical or faulty? Does the speaker's tone of voice or body language tell you anything the words themselves do not? For example, suppose you are listening to a co-worker talk about her working relationship with her supervisor. She tells you that things are going well, but her voice is louder and higher in pitch than normal, and her hands are clenched. You might, on the basis of her body language, conclude that she is not telling you the truth and that tension does exist.

Take Notes

Effective notes can greatly improve your ability to concentrate and can help you retain material. When taking notes, keep them clear and brief. Avoid concentrating so completely on the act of note taking that you lose track of what the speaker is saying. Review your notes as soon as possible to be sure they help you recall the message.

Give Feedback

Feedback turns listening into communication. Feedback can involve as little as giving the speaker your undivided attention or as much as asking questions and summarizing main points aloud. Feedback is discussed in greater depth in Chapter 52.

EDITING EXERCISES

A. Each of the following statements includes a word or phrase that is likely to create negative emotions in a listener. Identify that word or phrase.

1. The competitors' claims for their products are nothing short of lies.

2. This book will appeal primarily to the eggheads in the audience.

3. Rockwell fashions are created exclusively for fat men.

4. This company's management style is quickly moving from hands-on to dictatorial.

5. It is hard to believe that anyone could think of such a stupid plan.

B. Identify each of the following statements as either a statement of fact or a statement of principle.

1. People tend to work more effectively when they are self-motivated.

2. Leon Brooks has increased his output since he has been allowed to budget his own time.

3. Several workers have complained that their supervisors hound them to get work done.

4. Workers like to feel that their supervisors trust them to get their work done.

5. One supervisor keeps a log of how many times his workers visit the coffee machine and bathroom.

A. Choose a partner for each of the following exercises. Take turns following the directions.

1. Choose a short incident from your life that you wish to tell your partner about. Tell the story, and then have your partner write down as precise a summary as possible of what you have said. Read over the written summary and point out discrepancies.

2. Draw three shapes (for example a square, a trapezoid, and an oval). Orally direct your partner in drawing each shape without mentioning the name of that shape or any other shape. For example, for a rectangle do not say "Draw an elongated square." Observe how well your partner listens to directions.

3. Write down three 2- to 3-sentence statements of opinion or feeling. (For example: I feel that my older brother understands me very well. He knows what I am going to say before I say it.) After reading each statement to your partner, have him or her paraphrase it. Discuss the accuracy of the paraphrases.

B. The underlined word in each of the following sentences is a nonsense word. You should, however, be able to deduce its general meaning from the context. Give a brief definition or synonym for each nonsense word.

1. I found that the new employees were not at all polite; in fact, they were extremely caftatory.

2. Patience, compassion, and empathy—all these banfils are important in a teacher.

3. Gail wandered about fruptiously, like a lost child who had nowhere in particular to go.

4. Jenny Lio's alapenishness is beginning to cause trouble. She can't seem to talk to anyone without getting into an argument.

5. Unlike Vince, who is quite open with everyone, Martin is orfaculistic.

C. List three original examples (not ones given in the text) of ways that poor listening could affect on-the-job performance negatively. Then give three examples of how effective listening could improve performance or facilitate promotion.

D. Deciding on a purpose for listening is, as you know, one way to improve listening effectiveness. Following are five short descriptions of possible listening situations. For each situation, give a plausible purpose for listening. Be specific.

1. You have been given the opportunity to attend a seminar on management techniques although you are not currently in a management position.

2. A co-worker, under emotional strain, is telling you about his family troubles.

3. On your first day on the job, your supervisor is explaining the organizational chart of the company.

4. A client is explaining how she wants a particular job done.

5. One of the employees you supervise is talking about personality conflicts with others in the department.

PROJECTS

Choose a news-analysis or news-and-opinion broadcast on television or radio. (Public radio and television stations offer these, as do commercial stations in the news magazine format.) Take fact/principle notes on three story segments of the broadcast. Were you able to separate facts from principles? Were you able to take notes and listen effectively at the same time? When you look back at your notes, do they help you remember what was said?

   Take summary notes on three different segments from the same type of broadcast. Were you able to discover when the speaker had concluded a main point? Were you able to take notes and listen effectively at the same time? When you look back at your notes, do they help you remember what was said? Which type of notes seemed more helpful when listening to a news-analysis broadcast?

52
Using Listening Skills

Jill Giordano lowered herself wearily into the chair by Yvonne Powell's desk.

"I just finished talking to Ed, my supervisor, about the problems in my department. What's the use?"

"What's the matter?" said Yvonne. "Did he refuse to help you?"

"Worse, almost," said Jill. "He didn't even *listen*. I poured out my story, and he sat there fiddling with the papers on his desk and looking at his watch."

"Look, it's time for lunch," said Yvonne. "Let's go out to eat today. You can tell me about the problem. I may not be able to solve it, but I know it helps to talk."

"That would be great," Jill said with a smile. "Thanks for listening."

It's true that Yvonne may not be able to help Jill work out a solution to her problem. At the very least, however, she will ease Jill's tension and help her feel more hopeful. Listening to co-workers is an important aspect of communicating on the job—something Jill's supervisor needs to learn.

Studies show that the most important messages in business settings are sent orally. Oral messages must pass through several channels:

COMMUNICATION CHANNELS AT WORK

1. the mind of the speaker (the message as it is thought)
2. the words of the speaker (the message as it is spoken)
3. the mind of the listener (the message as it is interpreted)
4. the memory of the listener (the message as it is remembered)
5. the words of the listener (the message as it is passed on)

In what specific ways can a message be changed?

- The listener underplays or leaves out certain information. Because of personal prejudices or in an attempt to simplify a message, a listener may subtly—or not so subtly—distort the original message when recalling it or when passing it on.
- The listener overstates or overdramatizes certain information. This technique can be a companion to the distortion just described. By overemphasizing certain parts of a message, the listener underemphasizes others.
- The listener changes a message to fit his or her expectations or attitudes. This modification is commonly known as "hearing what one wants to hear." A listener unconsciously alters a message to make it match his or her expectations or reflect his or her attitudes.

Feedback

Feedback—the verbal and nonverbal response that the receiver of a message gives to a speaker—is a vital part of the communication process. The ability to give effective feedback is one of the qualities of a good listener.

The amount and type of feedback you give will affect the amount and type of communication you receive. For example, suppose you are one of a group of people listening to a speaker who is presenting her ideas in a disorganized way. If you merely sit and feign interest, the speaker will continue in the same confusing way, and the message will be lost. If, however, you reveal your confusion through facial expressions or questions, the speaker is likely to try to be more lucid. The chances are that the message will be delivered effectively.

Judgmental Feedback. Judgmental feedback evaluates and attempts to affect the direction of a message. The listener offers an opinion about what is being said. Opinions, of course, can be either positive or negative. Positive judgmental feedback will encourage a speaker to keep communicating in the same way. If you nod and smile and sometimes interject "I agree" and "That's true," a speaker will continue to present his or her ideas, perhaps even more forcefully.

Negative judgmental feedback is designed to change the direction or quality of communication. The most effective type is called formative feedback, because it attempts to form or shape communication rather than block it through negativism. The key to effective formative feedback is timing. Rather than provide formative feedback immediately after or during communication (the best time to give positive feedback), provide it right before communication is repeated. This timing helps a speaker view the feedback as guidance rather than as criticism.

Probing Feedback. Probing feedback is an attempt to obtain more information through gentle questioning. You show interest in the message while helping the speaker clarify his or her thoughts and feelings. For example, suppose a co-worker comes to you and says that she feels that her supervisor disapproves of her. To use probing feedback, you might ask: "What does she say or do that makes you think that?" Your co-worker will have to examine the problem more closely and provide fuller information.

Understanding Feedback. Understanding feedback is an attempt to comprehend fully what is being said and to assure the speaker that you are listening and understanding. It consists mainly of restating the speaker's words. Suppose, for example, that an employee you supervise complains, "Nobody around here cares about my problems!" You might ask, "Are you saying that you feel that others aren't sensitive to the things that are bothering you?" Understanding feedback will help you check the accuracy of your version of the message, while assuring the speaker that you are giving your full attention to the conversation.

Supportive Feedback. Through supportive feedback, you agree with a speaker that his or her problem has significance. Rather than attempting to solve the problem at this point, you merely assure the speaker that you recognize the importance of what is being said. Suppose a co-worker comes to you upset because he feels he did a task poorly and may be fired. If you say, "Oh, don't be silly—they wouldn't fire you over that," you will not have made him feel

DID YOU KNOW?
Subliminal Messages

In the late 1950s, Vance Packard wrote a book called *The Hidden Persuaders*. It discussed psychological techniques used by merchandisers to persuade consumers to buy. Among other things, Packard discussed what he called subthreshold effects, now frequently referred to as subliminal advertising. Such methods introduce messages to people in a way that bypasses the conscious mind. By doing so, advertisers can lower the resistance of potential customers to a sales pitch. Packard cited the example of a movie theater that flashed an ice-cream advertisement on the movie screen too quickly for people to recognize it but long enough for the message to reach the subconscious mind. If people had recognized the ad, they would have had the opportunity to accept or reject it. As it was, they may have gone to buy ice cream without really knowing how they got the idea.

In recent years, there have been reports of stores that place barely audible messages in their taped music. These hidden messages say such things as "Don't shoplift," "Don't steal," and "Be a good customer."

Workplaces could, potentially, use such methods to their advantage by playing messages such as "Work harder" and "Take shorter breaks" at low levels behind office music.

How do you feel about subliminal messages such as these? Are they valid, or are they a form of brainwashing? Is the technique open to abuse and, if so, how? Is this method appropriate in advertising, in the workplace, or in stores?

any better. He will only conclude that you do not understand the seriousness of the problem. Supportive feedback would involve a response such as, "I can see that you're very upset. Tell me about it, and I'm sure we can think of something to do to correct the mistake."

"I" or "We" Statements. A fourth type of feedback involves the use of "I" (or "we") statements rather than "you" statements. "I" statements convey your feelings without passing judgment. They are especially helpful when a conflict arises in a work situation. For example, suppose two workers have come to you because of a personality clash that is affecting the department's output. You might be tempted to come out with such statements as, "You must be more understanding" or "You can't keep acting this way." These statements, however, accuse the employees and put them on the defensive. A better tactic is to say, "I can see that there is a personality conflict here, but if we are going to succeed as a department, we have to work together. Let's try to overlook individual differences so that we can work as a team." In addition to being more positive, this response describes your feelings and thoughts about the situation without assigning blame.

Nonverbal Feedback

So far, this section has discussed only verbal feedback. Nonverbal feedback is just as important. There are several techniques you can use.

- Make eye contact. It is not necessary to stare unblinkingly at a speaker, but looking at a speaker with interest tells him or her that you are listening.
- Body language, such as leaning forward slightly, assures a speaker that you are interested in, rather than bored by, the message.
- Touch is not always appropriate, but it can provide effective support. When a person you know well is expressing grief or pain, touch can comfort, calm, and show concern.
- Appropriate facial expressions, such as smiles to show approval or agreement, also give a speaker useful feedback.

LISTENING TO LEARN When you are trying to learn a skill or a fact on the job, you have to listen to understand and to retain. In any business situation in which you listen to learn, you can benefit from the following guidelines.

- If possible, prepare for listening by reading appropriate material before the speaker begins. You will listen more effectively if you have some familiarity with the subject.
- Establish at once the speaker's purpose in communication. This knowledge will, in turn, enable you to establish your own purpose in listening. The title of a talk or an outline, as well as the speaker's opening statement, can help you direct your listening.

- If a concept, principle, or procedure is unclear, do not be afraid to ask for further explanation. Neglecting to clear up confusion early in a presentation may make the rest of the talk difficult to understand.

Taking Messages

Feedback is a vital part of accurate message taking. It allows you to confirm the accuracy of your version of the message. Correcting a mistake during transmission is much less costly—and usually less embarrassing—than doing so later. When you take messages, whether they are simple or complex, follow these guidelines to ensure accuracy.

- Ask questions and restate message elements during the message. Ask for clarification immediately if any element is not clear. Read the description back to the speaker so that any errors can be corrected immediately.
- Ask for spellings of names.
- Make sure you record the message in the proper sequence. Changing the order of message elements can radically transform a message. Even something as simple as a telephone number, recorded in the wrong sequence, becomes meaningless.
- Take notes. Making written notes as you listen will help you record message elements and their sequence accurately. Write neatly and clearly— a 7 for a *1* or the name *Morton* mistaken for *Norton* will create an inaccurate message.
- Repeat the entire message for verification. Even if you have followed each of the previous guidelines, it is possible to make an error. By reading the complete message back to the speaker, you provide one final chance to correct any errors.

Listening to Instructions

A fair amount of your listening time at work will be spent listening to instructions and directions. As with most listening on the job, you will be listening to understand and to remember.

Listening to Understand. To understand well, you must concentrate on what is being said. If you give yourself a purpose for listening, you will be able to focus on the instructions or directions more easily. Remember these tips:

- Be sure you hear the sequence correctly. Sequence is crucial to understanding instructions or directions. Finding logical links between the steps of a sequence will help you remember their order. For example, suppose you are told to proofread a memo, photocopy it, and then distribute it. Proofreading first makes logical sense. If you photocopied the memo and then found an error, you would have wasted time and paper.
- Be alert for the same idea expressed in different ways. Listen for ideas as well as for facts. Look for the main points within instructions or directions.

- If an unfamiliar word is not clear from context, question the speaker. Do not be afraid to ask questions about any aspect of the instructions or directions. Intelligent questions usually impress both superiors and co-workers by showing them that you are listening well and want to understand.
- Be prepared to answer questions. The speaker may ask you to repeat the instructions or want to check your understanding of a particular point. If you are concentrating, you will have no trouble answering such questions.

Listening to Remember. Of course, understanding instructions or directions would do you little good if you did not remember them long enough to carry them out. Here are some helpful guidelines for retaining such information.

- Use visualization and other memory tricks to increase retention. When you visualize, you form mental images as you listen.
- Take notes if possible. Taking clear notes will remind you of the proper sequence of the instructions or directions.
- Review the instructions or directions as soon as possible after receiving them. You may want to repeat the instructions to the speaker, as you would a message, to be sure you have them right. Always review any notes you take as soon as possible to be sure they give you clear and complete recall. You may also find it helpful to talk them over with someone else, such as a co-worker who understands the procedure or even another individual who received the instructions at the same time you did.

CRITICAL LISTENING SKILLS

To be a good critical listener, you should develop these skills.

- Distinguish between fact and opinion. Critical listeners can discriminate between statements that are verifiable facts and those that merely express the beliefs or ideas of the speaker. Some speakers slip their own opinions into an otherwise factual discussion. Whenever possible, check a speaker's statements in another source.
- Distinguish between emotional and logical arguments. Effective persuasive speakers know the emotional vulnerabilities of their audience. They may present arguments built, not on facts and logic, but on fear, insecurity, or pride. If you are an effective critical listener, you can put your emotions—positive or negative—aside and concentrate on the facts and logic of an argument. Look for fallacies and circular logic, as in "This product is effective because I say so, and I say so because it is effective." Avoid being swayed by a pleasant manner or an attractive appearance.
- Detect bias and prejudice in the speaker if it exists. Ask yourself this question about every speaker who tries to persuade you: "What does she or he stand to gain from my acceptance of the message?" The answer will help you be alert to biases or prejudices held by the speaker and passed on to you through the message.

Weaknesses of Listeners

The difficulties of critical listening cannot be attributed entirely to the oral method of transmission. Some are rooted in basic human qualities such as the desire to be accepted or to get the "inside story." Have you ever found yourself affected by a speaker in one of the following ways?

- You may agree to gain approval. Deep down, most people want others to think well of them. When listening to a persuasive speaker, you may unconsciously be moved toward agreement because of a desire to be liked and accepted.
- You may be flattered by believing that a speaker is confiding in you. Printed messages are generally available to many readers. In a one-on-one conversation, though, you may be convinced that a message is for your ears only. If so, you are likely to be uncritical of its content. Clever communicators may use this to their advantage, implying that you are receiving information not available to others.
- You may be impressed by a speaker's status. When a speaker gives a group talk, he or she is usually introduced by someone who lists the speaker's position and accomplishments. This "status report" tells listeners why they should pay attention to the speaker. As a critical listener, however, you must take care not to let respect or admiration for a speaker stop you from evaluating what the person has to say. Critical listening sets the same standards for validity no matter what the position of the communicator.

Recognizing that these difficulties exist for you as a critical listener will help you overcome the barriers formed by oral methods of communication or your own weaknesses. In addition, you must be aware of common methods of persuasion used by many speakers.

Common Methods of Persuasion

If you want to listen critically, you must be alert to common devices used by persuasive speakers to win you over to their causes. Generally, these methods are designed to persuade you before you have thought through the speaker's argument. Whenever you recognize one of these methods, be aware that the speaker is probably trying to manipulate you.

Using Name-Calling. A speaker who uses name-calling will discredit an individual, group, or product by attacking it on a personal level instead of presenting sound evidence against it. Usually, such words are designed to evoke negative emotions in the listener. For example, suppose a salesperson is comparing her company's typewriters with those of another firm. Rather than giving concrete information on the advantages of her firm's machines, she refers to the competition's typewriters as "Stone Age equipment." She has not proved that her product is more sophisticated or more up-to-date, but instead has tried to bring down your opinion of the competing product.

Transferring Prestige. This method involves mentioning one or more prestigious figures or institutions without really tying them to the issue at hand. The speaker does not *say* that the figure or institution supports his or her argument, but implies that it does. The careless listener assumes that the product or service is backed by that person or institution.

Presenting Biased Information. Another persuasive technique used by speakers is the careful shaping of evidence to support a point of view. All positive evidence, no matter how flimsy, is used, while negative evidence is ignored. The result is an unbalanced presentation that distorts the issue.

Sprinkling Glittering Generalities. The term *glittering generalities* has been coined to described generalized terms that evoke positive emotions in listeners, causing them to accept an argument on the basis of these emotions.

Suppose a fund-raiser comes to your office asking for a donation for a particular charity. She describes the fund-raising in terms of "moral duty" and "democratic ideals." As a critical listener, you must ask yourself what relation these terms actually have to the issue. You must look beyond them to the reality of the proposal, the person, or the issue.

Invoking the Bandwagon. A popular fast-food chain uses the bandwagon technique when it announces periodically how many billions of its sandwiches have been sold to date. In addition to being a source of pride for the company, this information is a subtle message which tells you that since billions of people are eating this food, you should too. When using this technique, speakers give no evidence about the quality of the products or services they are promoting; you are supposed to buy them because so many others have. The implication is that so many people could not be wrong.

Using Testimonials. Advertisers often hire a show business or sports personality to give a testimonial on behalf of a product. This persuasive technique counts on your respect for the person's qualifications in the entertainment or sports field. You are expected to believe that since the individual is qualified in one area, he or she is qualified to advise you about another.

Using Flattery. Flattery is a persuasive technique that feeds upon your desire to see yourself as bright, attractive, or competent. The persuasive power of flattery is at work when a sales representative tells you that any intelligent, competent business person will choose the word processor she is selling. If you are taken in by this technique, you will purchase the equipment in order to prove that you have the qualities she has mentioned.

Questions to Ask Yourself

As a critical listener, you must be aware of both the problems characteristic of oral communication and the manipulative techniques used by certain speakers. As you listen to a persuasive speaker, you must concentrate on content and evaluate it continually. There are four categories of questions you should ask about any persuasive message:

- What is the speaker's motive? Good listeners always try to establish a speaker's purpose immediately. Doing so is particularly important when listening to a persuasive speaker. Ask yourself what the speaker wants and whether this desire could prejudice the presentation. The simple awareness that a speaker may not be completely objective will prevent you from accepting uncritically everything that is said.
- Does the speaker support all statements with up-to-date facts? Any speaker can make claims to persuade you to buy a product or use a service. However, can the speaker back up these claims with facts that can be verified? If he or she provides statistics or study results, find out whether they are current. Out-of-date statistics can be misleading.
- Does the speaker use appropriate sources? Watch for techniques such as transferring prestige and using testimonials. If an outstanding baseball player says that you should buy a certain home computer, ask yourself whether the player is qualified to judge the merits of the computer.
- Does the speaker tell the whole story? When you listen to a persuasive speaker, be alert for any important areas that are being ignored. Also note whether the person is reluctant to answer certain questions.

Critical listening may sound like hard work—and indeed it is. Yet without it, your decisions will be made on the basis of who got to you first or who manipulated you most effectively. By listening critically, you will be able to make judgments based on logic and reason. Employers value workers who can evaluate what they hear and use their analyses to make good business choices.

EDITING EXERCISES

In each of the following items, the original message is given first, followed by the message as recorded by the listener. In each case, the recorded message includes one or more errors. Correct the recorded message so that it is accurate. (You need not repeat the first message verbatim.)

1. (a) Please send 27 copies of *Speaking for Success* to the Corner Bookstore at 2500 N. Whittlesey Ave., Wallingford, CT 06492. (b) Send 72 copies of *Speaking for Success* to the Corner Bookstore, 2500 N. Whittlesey Ave., Wallingford, CT 06492.

2. (a) Please call Jeffrey Tini at (609) 555-1861 by 2 p.m. (b) Call Jeff Freytini at (609) 555-1861 by 3 p.m.

3. (a) First disconnect the machine from its power source. Then carefully remove cover A, lift lever 1, and pull out the damaged sheet. (b) First disconnect the machine from its power source. Carefully remove cover A, pull out the damaged sheet, and lift lever 1.

4. (a) Stan Rabinowitz will arrive on Open Airways Flight 261 at 6:10 a.m. (b) Stan Rabinowitz to arrive Open Airways Flight 261 at 1:06 a.m.

5. (a) Home Products, Inc., will send 30 individuals to the sales seminar on June 5 to 9. (b) Home Products, Inc., will send 13 individuals to the sales seminar on June 5 to 9.

PROBLEMS

A. Each of the following statements might be made by a co-worker. Write a response that provides the type of nonjudgmental feedback listed after the statement.

1. I don't like to go to departmental meetings. I never seem to have anything to add to the discussion. (Understanding)

2. I have too much work to do! I can't handle it all! (Probing)

3. The idea of moving to another state really depresses me. I'll have a hard time making all new friends. (Understanding)

4. The person I share my apartment with is really taking advantage of me. She never does her share of the housework. (Probing)

5. Next week I take my first solo business trip. I'm worried that I'll make a poor impression on the client and lose the account. (Supportive)

B. Choose a partner. Prepare a message that fits each of the following descriptions. Read the message to your partner as he or she listens (without taking notes). Then have your partner repeat the message accurately (not necessarily verbatim) to you. Switch roles. After the exercise, discuss possible reasons for inaccuracies.

1. directions from the high school you attended to your home

2. instructions on how to operate a washing machine in a home or landromat

C. Choose a partner. Each of you should make up three imaginary orders of five items each for various products—office supplies, industrial supplies, and so on. Simulate a telephone conversation, and read your orders to your partner as he or she follows the guidelines for taking messages. After recording all three messages, check their accuracy. Then switch roles.

D. Identify the method of persuasion used in each of the following items.

1. All the other businesses in this area have subscribed to our magazine. You don't want to be the only one left out in the cold.

2. Believe me, this charity is one to which you should contribute. I'm a member of several civic organizations such as the Lions Club and the YMCA. This is the type of cause that many such groups support.

3. I knew as soon as I began talking to you that you were a successful business owner. That is why I am offering you this particular insurance package—because you will understand its advantages.

4. You want a photocopier that works more quickly and more cheaply than your present one. This model is for you. It can make more attractive copies than any other, and it is the newest on the market.

5. I'm Vivian Dubell, star of the TV series *New York, New York.* Let me tell you about the best word processor that money can buy.

6. Going with our competitor, the Noreika Advertising Agency, is fine if you are content with the conceited image they project to their customers. Even their company logo is pretentious.

7. I suppose you have tasted some of the repulsive excuses for breakfast entrées that our competitors are offering.

8. It's a relief to talk to someone with such sensitivity to the directions of the market today. You have pinpointed the major areas to watch.

9. Our belief in freedom and democracy leads us to ask for your help at this crucial time.

10. Our company is very interested in pleasing the consumer. We believe that this personal computer is right for you. We are very much in favor of the product tests done by organizations such as Consumers Union, which publishes *Consumer Reports* magazine.

PROJECTS

A. In a group listening situation (a class lecture, a speech, and so on). Observe the people in the group to examine the nonverbal feedback they give. What types of feedback did you observe? What did this feedback tell you about their level of listening? Did the speaker seem to be aware of the feedback? If so, how did it seem to affect the direction of his or her message?

B. Select a documentary on television or radio. Listen for main points and supporting data, taking notes that will help you remember program content. Was it difficult to separate main points from supporting material? Did taking notes distract you or help you listen? Were your notes clear to you later? Did they help you understand and remember the program.

C. Watch several commercials on network television over the course of several days. Note the use of the following items:

1. nonverbal elements that make the products more acceptable (attractive speakers, for example)

2. any of the methods of persuasion discussed in this chapter

3. any other methods of persuasion you notice

4. factual product information

Which methods were used most often? Were they used effectively? Did you discover any new methods? Now that you have completed this chapter, do you feel you will be less susceptible to persuasive methods?

53
General Speaking Skills

Suppose that for the rest of the day, as you go about your daily routine, no one will be able to speak.

On this day without oral communication, it may seem as if everyone has walked onto the set of a silent movie. People may use the exaggerated body language of a game of charades. They may do a great deal of pointing; and, for the same reasons captions underline scenes in silent movies, they may write signs to each other.

Without speech, people would spend far more time and energy trying to communicate. Their communications would probably be basic, with little opportunity for subtlety; and their meanings would be subject to a wide margin of misinterpretation. As a day of silence would illustrate, speech is an integral part of all our relationships.

Effective speaking is essential for conducting most business transactions. Surveys indicate that approximately 75 percent of the workers in an average company take part in discussions, present oral reports, give oral instructions to subordinates, and speak with clients. Effective speaking skills often make the difference between doing a job well and doing it poorly. Good speaking techniques are necessary for advancement in most career areas.

PURPOSES OF BUSINESS SPEAKING

When you speak with people in business, you are communicating for one of four basic purposes:

- to inform
- to instruct
- to persuade
- to explain or report

As the following examples show, a day on the job may require transmission of all four types of messages.

Sarah Stone is a social worker in a nursing home. Her caseload includes 78 patients and their families. She also supervises a student intern.

By following Sarah through part of a normal day, you can see how she uses the four basic kinds of speaking.

To Inform

Ira Higgins has an appointment with Sarah to discuss the possibility of moving his mother from the hospital floor to a well-patient room on the twelfth floor.

Sarah informs Mr. Higgins about the basic requirements for assignment to the well-patient floor. She explains what his mother's health condition must be to permit her to leave the hospital floor. She also tells him about the cost of the room and the social activities available to well patients.

Informing is one of the essential functions of a business person. Salespeople and other representatives must inform customers or prospective buyers about the nature of their products or services. To transmit information effectively, you need to be knowledgeable, logical, and capable of answering questions.

To Instruct

After Ira Higgins leaves, Sarah Stone is scheduled to meet with Amy Pierce, her student intern. She will instruct Amy in some of the techniques used to record the physical therapy received by patients as well as their progress toward specific therapy goals.

Like many skilled workers, Sarah Stone is responsible for instructing beginners about various aspects of the field. Experienced workers in many businesses or professions may be called upon to instruct customers in the use of products or services. They may also need to give instructions to co-workers about on-the-job procedures.

To Persuade

Sarah Stone has an early afternoon meeting with her supervisor, Rachel Standish. She plans to discuss the case of Nels Ferguson. She wants to persuade Ms. Standish that Mr. Ferguson should leave the nursing home and participate in the home care program. This program would permit him to live with his family yet receive medical help from the nursing facility.

Ms. Standish believes that Mr. Ferguson would require too much physical care to be at home. Sarah will try to persuade Ms. Standish that the emotional satisfactions Mr. Ferguson will gain from being at home with his family will benefit his health. She also wants to suggest that a part-time health care worker would ease the burden on Mr. Ferguson's family. She will try to persuade Ms. Standish to try the home care for a month to see whether it will work.

Persuasive speaking is necessary for success in every profession. Job seekers persuade prospective employers to hire them. Salespeople persuade customers to buy a product. Teachers persuade students to learn their subject matter. Lawyers persuade judges or juries that their clients' claims are justified.

To Explain or Report

Sarah must use her oral skills in yet another capacity still later in the afternoon, when she explains to one of her patients, Mr. Hartwell, why he can't have a toaster oven in his room. She plans to tell him that while she wants him to have as many of the comforts of home as he can, it is against the safety code of the nursing facility to allow hot plates or burners to be in operation in the rooms. She plans to explain the dangers posed by such appliances. Sarah will then report the outcome of her meeting with Mr. Hartwell.

Explanations and reports are a common form of oral communication in business. These interactions help prevent misunderstandings, thus promoting and maintaining goodwill among business associates and the public. They can also help bring about solutions to problems.

THE QUALITIES OF EFFECTIVE SPEAKING

The key to effective speaking in any situation is to have something important to say. However, your manner of speaking is equally important. No matter what your message, you may lose your audience if your delivery is ineffective.

The way in which you speak involves voice qualities such as volume, pitch, tone, and tempo, as well as the skills of pronunciation and enunciation. The following section will explain how these qualities can be developed to allow you to deliver your message in the clearest, most compelling way.

Volume

Oral communications must be heard to be received and understood. Therefore, the volume of your voice must be loud enough so that your audience can hear every word, but not so loud that their ears feel assaulted.

Your volume should be appropriate for your audience. You would speak more softly if you were making a report to your supervisor in an office than you would if you were trying to teach math to a group of fifth graders who were more interested in a classmate's live frog.

The acoustics of the area in which you speak also affect the volume of your voice. You may, for example, need more volume when speaking to colleagues about a business matter in a large conference hall than if you were in a small office.

When you know what volume you want to maintain in a speaking situation, you can learn to control the loudness of your voice by practicing the methods of deep breathing used by singers. Breathe deeply to fill your lungs with air. Then use your diaphragm and abdominal muscles to release air evenly.

Pitch

Pitch refers to how high or low your voice is. A moderate pitch—somewhere in the middle of the voice range—is best for normal speech. However, you should vary the pitch of your voice when speaking to avoid monotony and to give emphasis.

Raising and lowering pitch is called intonation. Speakers of English automatically drop their pitch at the end of a sentence, unless the sentence is a question. Then English calls for a rise in pitch.

You can greatly alter the meaning of a sentence by emphasizing certain words. For example, notice the change in the meaning of the sentence repeated below as you emphasize the italicized word in each case.

Judy parked this truck. (Judy, not someone else, parked it.)

Judy *parked* this truck. (Judy parked it rather than doing something else.)

Judy parked *this* truck. (Judy parked a particular truck.)

Judy parked this *truck*. (Judy parked the truck rather than some other vehicle.)

Tone

The tone of a voice includes not only volume and pitch but also emotions, attitudes, and the personality of the speaker. The tone of your voice should match the content of what you have to say.

For example, you would use a serious and sad tone of voice when consoling a person on the death of a family member. On the other hand, you would have a happy tone of voice when congratulating a friend who has just announced he is getting married.

Tempo

Tempo refers to speaking speed. A good speaker talks slowly enough for the audience to understand each word, but not so slowly that the audience gets bored.

Tempo can be used for emphasis just as pitch can. Effective speakers often emphasize important words and phrases by saying them more slowly than less important ones. This technique also makes speaking patterns more interesting to listeners.

Pronunciation and Enunciation

Correct pronunciation means saying a word correctly. Correct enunciation means saying the word distinctly. Correct pronunciation and enunciation are important tools for effective speaking. Incorrect pronunciation and enunciation lead to misunderstanding and create the impression that the speaker is careless or uneducated.

Pronunciation. If you are unsure about how to pronounce a word, look it up in a dictionary. Be sure you have a thorough understanding of pronunciation symbols, which vary from dictionary to dictionary.

When speaking, be especially wary of common mispronunciations, such as "irrevelant" for *irrelevant,* "nick" for *niche,* "bidness" for *business,* and "compareable" for *comparable.*

Enunciation. There are few people who enunciate properly all the time. Most people often run words together, saying, for example, "Jeet?" for "Did you eat?" It is also common to drop consonants and vowels, saying "feelin' " for *feeling* and " 'specially" for *especially.*

Enunciation can be improved by slowing the tempo of your speech. Speak slowly and carefully so that you can pronounce each word distinctly and not run one word into the next.

HOW LOOKS AND MANNERS AFFECT SPEAKING

Effective speaking in a business situation depends upon more than what you have to say and how you speak. Your appearance also affects how your audience perceives your message. Your physical appearance and mannerisms can either inspire confidence or detract from what you are saying and create a negative impression.

Many aspects of your appearance combine to make an impression. Your hair and clothing, as well as your grooming, posture, facial expression, hand movements, and body language, deliver a message to your audience as you speak. The following sections will describe how you can make sure these factors are working in your favor.

Clothing and Grooming

If you want people to have confidence in what you say in a business situation, they must see that you can take care of yourself on a personal level. When you are speaking to them, they will notice if you are clean, well groomed, and appropriately dressed. If you create a good impression in these areas, they will have a good feeling about you and be able to concentrate on what you are saying.

In general, you should dress conservatively for work because in most businesses, clothing is not the focus of attention—business is. Unusual or conspicuous dress can cause distractions that have a negative effect on conducting business.

Be sure to dress appropriately for your age and position. Your clothes should be in keeping with those of your colleagues. The object of business dress is to be appropriate and serve your needs, yet not to make your appearance more important than what you have to say.

Posture and Body Movement

You must move with self-confidence, not self-consciousness. Good posture is a must. Not only does a straight back help you appear sure of yourself, but it also helps you project your voice. When you speak, avoid excessive body movement. Some movement, of course, is natural and helps punctuate your message; too much movement distracts from it. If you are standing, remain in one place with your weight balanced evenly. Shifting your weight from leg to leg makes you look ill at ease or even bored. If you are sitting, keep your knees together and your back straight in order to look graceful and alert.

As a rule, you should not use your hands to speak unless you are using sign language. Otherwise, your hands may be speaking a language of their own to your listener—and you may not like what they are saying.

Hand movements are usually an unnecessary distraction to what you are saying. Many hand movements are done unconsciously, so you must make yourself aware of your actions. Distracting hand movements include fixing your hair, shuffling papers, and tapping a pen or pencil on a table.

If you are standing while you speak, keep your hands at your sides most of the time. An occasional appropriate gesture can help get your message across, but only an occasional one. If you are sitting, keep your hands in your lap or rest them on a table or the arms of a chair.

Facial Expressions

When you speak, the expression on your face communicates a great deal. Your facial expressions should generally mirror the emotional content of your words. In a business situation, your face should be pleasant, attentive, and confident.

You should smile easily and appropriately and look at your listeners as much as possible. Eye contact inspires confidence, sincerity, and goodwill.

COURTESY IN BUSINESS EXCHANGES

In business, as in other speaking situations, you do not talk at, but speak with, other people. Part of a general speaking situation will involve other interactions with your listeners, who must be made to feel they are respected partners in the business exchange.

Listening Attentively

Don't do all the talking. After you have said what you need to say, encourage your listeners to respond.

When your listener is speaking, look the person in the eyes attentively. Don't look at your watch or the ceiling. Don't fidget, which can distract the speaker and make him or her feel that you are bored.

Using the Person's Name

When you are introduced to a business associate, try to use the person's name after you hear it. For instance, you might say, "It's nice to meet you, Mr. Nelson." If you don't understand the name, ask immediately. Say, "I'm sorry, but I'm not sure I heard that correctly. Did you say your name was Melson?" You could also say, "How do you pronounce [or spell] your name?"

During the conversation, try to use the person's name occasionally; and when you say good-bye, use the person's name again. Adding the person's name to the conversation personalizes the interaction and helps you remember the name.

Meeting the Public

When you are in a position to meet the public in a business capacity, follow the guidelines suggested in the previous sections regarding effective speaking. In addition, be sure to act in a friendly yet professional manner.

Greet each person pleasantly, and answer questions thoroughly but concisely. Do not give more information than is requested or give away company secrets. The idea is to be warm and courteous but not overly friendly.

EDITING EXERCISES

A. In each of the following sentences, the word *only* appears in a different position. Explain the differences in meaning among the sentences.

1. Only Ms. Graves is permitted to operate the new computer.

2. Ms. Graves is only permitted to operate the new computer.

3. Ms. Graves is permitted only to operate the new computer.

4. Ms. Graves is permitted to operate only the new computer.

5. Ms. Graves is permitted to operate the new computer only.

B. In the following items, the same sentence is repeated with a different word underlined in each case to show that it receives special emphasis when the sentence is read or spoken aloud. Explain the differences in meaning among the sentences.

1. <u>We</u> should buy five cases of stationery now.

2. We <u>should</u> buy five cases of stationery now.

3. We should <u>buy</u> five cases of stationery now.

4. We should buy <u>five</u> cases of stationery now.

5. We should buy five <u>cases</u> of stationery now.

6. We should buy five cases of <u>stationery</u> now.

7. We should buy five cases of stationery <u>now.</u>

C. Pauses are crucial elements in conveying meaning. Each of the following sentences requires one or more commas to indicate important pauses. Insert the missing commas.

1. Think Mr. Alonzo about your expanding insurance needs.

2. If Carol stops the project will be in trouble.

3. Model 276 is now available in blue green red and white.

4. The auditor will arrive at noon if I recall the time correctly.

5. Remember the special price will last only until midnight.

PROBLEMS

To check on your pronunciation, look up the following words in a dictionary. Say each word aloud according to its correct pronunciation. If possible, tape-record your pronunciation to check for errors.

aluminum	height	dessert
roof	burglar	desert
exhalation	theater	derisive
tomato	homogeneous	long-lived
mischievous	library	imprudent
censure	peremptory	calm
codicil	strength	literally
column	prerogative	relevant
denunciation	athlete	incomparable
gist		

PROJECTS

A. Interview a professional in your chosen career. Ask the person what types of speaking he or she does on a typical workday. Following the guidelines for effective speaking given in the chapter, give a talk to your class explaining how each speaking situation fits one of the four basic purposes of business speaking.

B. Keep a diary for two or three days of the types of speaking you do (informative, persuasive, and so on). Using the information you have learned in this chapter, evaluate each instance of speaking. Indicate both your strengths and the areas in which you would like to improve.

54

Speaking on the Telephone

The telephone is an indispensable tool in today's business world. Employees use the telephone to place and receive orders, discuss ideas, reach agreements, make appointments, and solve problems. Because modern business depends so much on the use of the telephone, it is essential that business employees have good telephone skills and manners. Employees with poor telephone techniques can reflect negatively on the company they represent.

Business calls require different techniques for effective speaking than do face-to-face conversations or personal telephone calls. In this chapter, you will learn how to use the telephone effectively, how to exercise good telephone manners, how to be sure that you are transmitting and receiving accurate information, and how to use discretion in your telephone business conversations.

EFFECTIVE USE OF THE TELEPHONE

The following suggestions for use of the telephone can help ensure accurate and effective communication.

Keep Your Voice Loud and Clear

The telephone receiver is a sensitive instrument and requires special speaking techniques.

- Speak directly into the receiver. Keep your lips about an inch from the mouthpiece. Keep the mouthpiece in front of your lips—not under your chin or behind your hand. If the mouthpiece is not directly in front of your mouth, your words will be muffled.

- Speak more loudly than normal. If the telephone is working properly, you should not have to shout into the receiver to be heard. However, you do need to speak in a voice that is slightly louder than your normal speaking voice.
- Enunciate. Clear enunciation is especially important when you are speaking on the telephone. A telephone listener usually hears your words with only one ear. Further impediments may be caused by background noises or by distortions on the telephone line. Be sure, then, to say unusual, difficult, or easily misunderstood words and phrases slowly and clearly.

Avoid Unnecessary Noise

Try to hold telephone conversations in a quiet place, and never eat or drink while talking on the phone. Even chewing gum can distort your words.

If you have to cough, sneeze, or clear your throat while you are talking, excuse yourself and move the phone away from your mouth. You might even cover the mouthpiece to muffle the sound. Then thank the other person for waiting, and resume your conversation.

If you need to put the receiver down during the conversation, do not let the receiver fall, thus causing your listener to hear annoying sounds. Place the receiver on a book, magazine, or other object that acts as a shield. When you have finished your call, replace the receiver in the cradle gently and quietly.

Transfer Calls Efficiently

Know how to use the call-transfer system in your office, and use it courteously. Callers can get the impression that your company is careless and inefficient if their calls are not transferred to the right person or are inadvertently disconnected in the process.

Be sure to tell callers when you are going to transfer the call. They will then know the reason for any delay or silence on the line. A courteous way to transfer someone is to say, "If you will hold the line for just a moment, I will have your call transferred." Tell the caller the name and number of the person to whom the call is being transferred so that he or she will know whom to ask for when the call reaches its new destination.

When people speak on the telephone, they receive and send only their voices. There is no body language or facial expression to help transmit or interpret signals. Voice does it all. Therefore, be sure your voice sounds friendly, interested, and positive at all times when speaking in a business capacity. One way to help personalize a speaking situation that has been made less than personal by lack of visual contact is to use the other person's name occasionally during the conversation.

BASIC TELEPHONE MANNERS

The Informative Greeting. Whether you place a call or receive it, good business telephone manners require you to identify yourself immediately. If you are the caller, identify yourself, and state the purpose of your call.

The Courteous Conversation. When you converse on the telephone, answer questions pleasantly and promptly. Be as helpful as possible. If the caller has a complaint, follow these steps:

1. Listen carefully.
2. Take notes if necessary.
3. Express concern for the customer's or colleague's problem.
4. Tell the caller what action you plan to take or to whom you will refer the caller for assistance.

If you are receiving a call, greet the caller, and state your name. If you are answering someone else's phone, an appropriate greeting would include both the name of the person being called and your name, as in "Wendy Patrulo's office, Anthony Lennon speaking." Offer any help you can give if the person called is unavailable. If you cannot be of assistance, take the caller's name, telephone number, and message, and leave it for the person called.

If you must leave the telephone temporarily for any reason—to answer another call or to get information for the caller—tell the caller you are leaving the telephone. Also, let the person know why you are leaving and approximately how long you will be gone.

The Positive Farewell. End a business telephone conversation as you would a business letter—on a positive note.

- Personalize the farewell by using the caller's name at least once.
- End the conversation with a positive remark, such as "Thank you for calling, Mr. Billings. I look forward to talking with you again soon."
- The final courtesy is to allow the caller to hang up first.

ACCURACY ON THE TELEPHONE

When you speak on the telephone, there may be a lack of visual aids to help you receive or transmit messages accurately. The person on the other end of the line may, for example, not have access to the same price list to which you are referring. The following methods can ensure precision in relaying and receiving information in such situations.

Write Down Important Information

Recording information on paper is a major aid to accuracy. In addition to requesting the correct spelling of names, be sure to ask for the spelling of any word you are unsure of. After you write down any piece of information, read it back to the caller to check its accuracy.

Write Down What You Want to Say

You can make the most of any call you place by preparing beforehand. If you make a list of the topics you wish to discuss, you will be a more effective speaker because you will have the confidence of knowing what you want to say. Your questions and statements will also be more accurate, and you will be saved the inconvenience and embarrassment of calling the person back because you have forgotten to discuss an important item of business.

During a business call, you must remember to protect your co-workers and your company by avoiding indiscreet statements. Remember the following points:

TELEPHONE DISCRETION

- Never discuss confidential or negative information with callers.
- When you answer another person's telephone, do not disclose the person's whereabouts. Simply say that the individual is not near the telephone, but that you will take a message.
- Never promise to do something for a caller that is beyond your authority. Just say you will try to help the caller; then either transfer the call to someone who can give assistance or call back when you have an answer.
- When you leave your desk, tell co-workers what to say to callers in your absence, and ask them to take messages.

EDITING EXERCISES

Mindy Harris takes notes during every telephone conversation with a client. Correct the errors in spelling, grammar, and punctuation in the following excerpts from business documents that were generated from her notes.

1. Neither the client or we want to discuss the matter further.

2. Ms. Otlowski demands to no whom will pay for the ruined equipment?

3. Has Mr James asked for an extension.

4. Well need they're social security numbers.

5. The book "Last Chance to Finish First" is selling more better then expected.

6. All the true facts, appear in the book.

7. Send the package to 12 jefferson Street, Peoria Illinois, 62310.

8. Only customers with charge accounts are aloud to deduct 10 %.

9. Do not stack boxes, be sure to keep them off of the floor.

10. Will you please ask all staff members to report to me at once?

11. Smoothie pens now come in red, black and, blue.

12. Find out weather the personal department is interviewing applicants now.

13. Swipe does a real through job of cleaning.

14. Each person must keep their expense account up to date.

15. The key to the locker was laying on the desk; making a forced entry unnecessary.

16. Mr. James and myself planned the entire ad campaign.

17. The number of workers who smoke have decreased dramatically.

18. Every dog and cat need a Flee flea collar in hot whether.

19. Sales representatives should know when they have wore out their welcome.

20. Him and I are responsible for the Darby account.

PROBLEMS

Tell how you would handle each of the following situations involving telephone use in the office.

1. Bob Riley, who shares your office, has decided to get a haircut on company time. He tells you to explain to callers that he is across town at a meeting.

2. Your supervisor has told you that she must finish a report by noon and does not want to be disturbed for any reason. Her son calls and says he needs to speak to his mother immediately.

3. Jack Donato has called Ms. Maxwell, the head of your division, for the third time this afternoon. You know that she does not want to speak to him again—ever.

4. A customer calls to complain about a product. The information she needs can be supplied by someone in another department. Before you have time to transfer the call, however, the customer becomes extremely abusive.

PROJECTS

Contact different telephone companies to find out what special services they offer customers who have impaired vision or hearing or physical disabilities. Report your findings to the class, concluding with a discussion of improvements you think could still be made.

55
Speaking in Groups

In the last few decades, many modern business managers have dispensed with the conventional business practice of making all decisions and then handing them down to staff through memos or general announcements. Instead, they now employ the technique of participative management, which calls for small group discussions that involve employees at all levels of the organization in decision making.

Participation in small group discussions requires both speaking and listening skills. You will need the skills that make possible the informal give and take of reaching group decisions. You will also need the skills required to present an oral report.

The general discussion format used in many groups is based on John Dewey's Reflective Thinking Process. This process is designed to develop the group members' analytical skills so they can reach the best possible resolution of a problem. The Dewey process consists of six segments or steps, which are discussed in this section.

THE FORMAT OF SMALL GROUP DISCUSSIONS

1. Define the problem. The leader begins the small group discussion by explaining the problem and its probable causes. This information will focus the group's thinking.

2. Establish requirements for a solution. The leader next explains the requirements for an acceptable solution. In business, there are usually budget and time requirements that the solution must meet.

3. Brainstorm for possible solutions. Following three basic guidelines will make the brainstorming step as productive as possible. First, group members should express every idea they have without worrying about their

quality. Second, group members should not criticize ideas during the brainstorming stage. Third, members should feel free to develop or combine the ideas to form another solution.

4. Evaluate the possibilities. During this stage, group members review the solutions offered in the previous stage. During the review, they weigh proposed solutions against the requirements outlined in the second step.

5. Select a solution. The group next narrows down the various possibilities to those that meet the requirements for a solution. The participants do not have to choose any of the solutions offered if they do not believe they are worth implementing. If the group decides to explore the ideas recommended, it should appoint people to be in charge of determining the benefits of each possibility.

6. Plot a course of action. The final step focuses on how to put the solution into action. The group may agree to meet again to hear and discuss the findings of the solution committee. The group then makes final decisions on which solutions to implement.

HOW TO BE A GOOD SMALL GROUP PARTICIPANT

In addition to generating ideas, participants in small group discussions must observe the courteous manners that apply to any form of group activity. The key to being a good group member is to participate in discussions. Group discussion is an active process that requires thoughtfulness and knowledge. You can be an active group member by following several guidelines.

- Be prepared. Being prepared is important for strong participation. If you know the topics of discussion in advance of the meeting, you can offer more appropriate suggestions and respond more constructively to the suggestions of others.
- Be tactful. When you are asked for your opinion of an idea or you volunteer a response, express yourself positively and with consideration for the feelings of others. This rule is especially important if you disagree with an idea. Never object with negative comments. Always find something to compliment about the idea before expressing your thoughts.
- Be a good listener. When others are speaking, listen attentively and use positive body language to show that you are interested and alert. Allow the speaker to talk without interruption, and refrain from talking with others in the group at the same time. Take notes; they provide positive reinforcement for the speaker, help you pay attention, and provide documentation if you need to refer to something a speaker said.
- Be a good speaker. Business meetings need to be conducted efficiently, so it is important to make the most of your speaking time. Make suggestions or comments only when they are pertinent to the discussion, and be brief.

A simple set of guidelines will help you lead small group discussions success-fully. First you must realize your role is that of a moderator or guide, not a dictator or expert.

Before the meeting, prepare the agenda and have copies sent to each par-ticipant. You will need to make arrangements to reserve the room where the meeting will be held and inform the participants of the time and place.

During the meeting, speak as little as possible yourself and follow these rules for leading effective small group discussions:

- Stop digressions tactfully. When a person with a dominant personality begins to take over the discussion or when one of the participants begins to digress, the leader must redirect the discussion firmly but gently.
- Encourage quiet members to talk. Just as leaders must stop digressions and quell overbearing participants, they must also try to draw out quiet members of the group. This task can be accomplished with encouraging words.
- React positively to suggestions. Never react negatively to a suggestion, because it will not only discourage the speaker but can also keep other members of the group from expressing their ideas freely.

HOW TO LEAD A SMALL GROUP DISCUSSION

USING YOUR WORD PROCESSOR
Creating and Using Visual Aids

If you need to use overhead transparencies as visual aids in oral reports or formal speeches, you can produce them with your word proces-sor and a dot matrix printer. You can create the graphics or display type for each transparency on your computer. Then you can produce a quality transparency on your dot matrix printer.

You just insert a plain paper copier film in your printer. If you have a color printer, your transparency can be in color. If you have a stand-ard printer, your transparency will match the color of the ribbon you are using. The film is available to produce tinted background and re-verse-image displays.

Overhead transparencies are a popular visual aid for both oral reports and formal speeches because they are convenient, versatile, and at-tractive. They are small—usually the size of an 8½-by-11-inch sheet of paper—and therefore easy to carry.

When the transparency is displayed during a presentation, it has many positive features.

- It is clear because it is magnified by the projector. If one part is obscured, simple repositioning makes it easy to read.
- You never have to turn your back to your audience when you use a transparency as you would to write on a blackboard.
- You can combine several transparencies, laying one on top of the other, to produce a step-by-step illustration of the concept you are presenting.
- Whenever necessary, you can write on the transparency to add to your concept. Then, if you wish, you can erase what you added.

- Summarize the proceedings frequently. The leader should keep the discussion centered on the ideas most members agree would be most fruitful.
- Conclude the meeting with a summary. One of the rules of concluding a small group discussion is to end the meeting on time. A few minutes before the end of the meeting, summarize the group's consensus. Then ask the members if they need another meeting. If so, suggest ways to set up the next discussion. After the meeting, arrange to have the minutes typed and sent to participants. You may also need to draft a memo to be sent to members who were selected to perform tasks and to the rest of the group as well.

ORAL REPORTS

In business, the oral report is often the most appropriate way to relay information. Oral reports require the use of the same good speaking habits and skills as are needed when giving a public speech (see Chapter 53). Both oral reports and public speeches also reflect upon the speakers and upon the cause or company they represent. In both speaking situations, the time allotted is brief, so the content must be concise, well organized, and adequately rehearsed. There are, however, several key areas in which oral reports differ from public speeches: audience, topic and presentation, and question format.

Audience. A public speech is often made to an audience of diverse people with diverse interests. The speaker often does not know the members of the audience personally. In contrast, the audience for an oral report in business is usually made up of co-workers and other people known to the speaker.

Topic and Presentation. The public speaker usually tailors the speech to the particular audience, considering age, education, gender, occupation, and other factors that would affect the audience's response to the speech. The subject of an oral report most often concerns company business. Therefore, the speaker does not need to create ways to make the speech interesting to the audience, as is common practice for a public speaker. Members of the audience for an oral report are already concerned with the subject matter because it affects their work.

In addition, the oral report is often the oral presentation of a written report rather than a speech that exists on its own. The speaker's goal is to present the information from the written report in a way that facilitates understanding. The information given in an oral report will probably be used on the job by members of the audience after the meeting.

Question Format. The audience for an oral report does not have to wait until the end of the presentation to ask questions, as is the case with a public speech. When interjected during an oral report, questions can affect its content.

The first step to take in preparing an oral report is to gather research materials. The research process does much to determine the quality of the report.

PREPARATION

Good researchers always try to have more information than necessary by the time they are ready to organize their material. An abundance of research material provides a wealth of ideas from which to create an interesting, informative presentation. It is up to the speaker to decide which specific pieces of information will best support the main ideas of the report. The additional information can be useful when answering questions posed by the audience.

Common sources of reliable data for oral reports are described below.

On-the-Job Sources

Many business speakers use their own expertise as material for an oral report. Because of their knowledge, they may not need other sources of information. Firsthand experience has the added value of helping to make a report come alive. Business people can also get information from colleagues in their own or other companies.

The Library

When speakers need information on a subject that is outside their experience, they may look for books and articles written on the subject. Public, college, and university libraries often have special business sections. Large companies may have their own libraries as well.

Once you have completed the research, you must organize the information into a presentation that will be interesting and understandable to the audience. The basic structure of an oral report is made up of three parts: the introduction, the body, and the conclusion.

The central theme of an oral report is the one idea a speaker wants the audience to remember. The central theme should be stressed in the introduction or opening remarks of an oral report. The idea should be presented in an attention-getting manner to stimulate the members of the audience and encourage them to be attentive to the body of the presentation. The audience's attention can be captured through the appropriate use of one or more of the following devices:

THE INTRODUCTION

- a visual aid
- a quotation from an authoritative source
- a dramatic fact or statistic
- a comparison or contrast
- a humorous anecdote
- a simple statement

THE BODY   In the body of the speech, you will flesh out the ideas you presented in the introduction. Each point you make requires at least one form of support, or evidence, to convince your audience of its validity. The following categories of support are commonly used:

- examples
- statistics
- quotations
- comparisons and contrasts
- audiovisual aids

In all cases, the support you select must be valid, current, and logical. The success of your presentation will depend in part upon support and in part upon the way the main points are organized.

Organizing the Main Points

The appropriate way to arrange the main points in an oral report depends on subject matter. Some effective types of organization are the following:

- chronological
- topical
- spatial
- cause and effect
- problem/solution

THE CONCLUSION   The conclusion to your speech should be a combination of a summary and a call to action. Remind the audience of the main points of the speech and make a closing statement that explains how the audience should respond. As with the introduction, brevity is called for in the conclusion.

THE PRESENTATION   As with almost any kind of performance, success in giving oral reports requires rehearsal. Experienced speakers time themselves during rehearsals to make sure their material fits the time allotted. Videotaping or recording the rehearsal can help speakers make sure they are using the principles of good voice control, pronunciation, and enunciation, as described in Chapter 53. Listening to the speech can also reveal awkward language or ideas that need clarification, and it can show whether audiovisual aids are understandable and interesting. Three guidelines can help ensure the effectiveness of these aids.

- Make graphics large enough for everyone in the audience to see easily.
- Keep visual presentations simple.
- Check equipment to make sure it is operating properly.

The Delivery

Whether you are giving a public speech or an oral report, you will deliver your message effectively only if you are heard by all members of the audience. Be sure, then, to speak loudly enough for all to hear.

You must also be aware of your audience. Make eye contact with various members, and gauge the mood of the audience, so you will know whether you need to make your presentation shorter or to expand upon certain parts.

Handling Questions. When you give an oral report, you must be prepared for comments from the audience during the presentation. Often, such comments are welcome, since the answers to thoughtful questions can help clarify the subject matter. Questions may open important new areas for discussion and can change the way the speaker presents the material.

During rehearsal, it is important to be alert for places where questions are likely to occur and to prepare answers.

EDITING EXERCISES

A. Each of the following is an excerpt from a written report that is the basis of an oral presentation. Each one contains a number of errors in grammar, style, spelling, and punctuation. Rewrite the excerpts, correcting the errors.

1. When Cronar Corp. first began us employees had no idea it would become the most large solar panel producer in north America. With annual sails of fifty million dollars, in nineteen eighty seven, Cronar dwarfs it's competitors. To quote President Charles Seal; "We have'nt reached our zenith yet.

2. Studys indicate that 50 of the participants prefer the floral sent; 25 the pine; and 15, the unscented version. None of the participants were attracted to the citrus scent. The marketing director Jane Fields, beleives we should discontinue testing that scent. Would you please raise your hands if you agree?

3. The accident was caused by a lose wheel. Let me insure you that economics are not an issue in dealing with the problem. The company of Baker Bro's. are determined to rectify the situation: no matter what the cost.

B. Below is an excerpt from the first draft of a memo that Helen Meyers is preparing to send to the general manager of Carver Publishing to explain the outcome of the small group discussion regarding the future of the children's book division. In her haste, Helen has made a number of spelling and capitalization errors. Rewrite the paragraph, correcting Helen's mistakes.

Several possibilities for acheiving our goals were recomended. Our principle plan may be to begin an intern program with outstanding english majors from a local college. Their are several benefits to this idea. We would not excede our budget because, as interns, the students would not be payed. These beginers would acquire sound knowledge of publishing while fullfilling our need for editorial assistance. Articles on similar programs at other companys state that student interns definitly lesson the work load of permanent employees, thus improving moral. Some interns were actually termed "indispensible" by their supervisers. Three members of my division will analyse our needs so we can make a final judgement about weather to procede.

PROBLEMS

A. For each of the following oral report topics, identify the most appropriate method of organization (spatial, chronological, topical, cause-and-effect, or problem/solution).

1. a report on the growth of a company's holdings during the past decade

2. a report on the effectiveness of a new line of lawn fertilizers and weed killers

3. a report on ways to decrease vandalism in county parks

4. a report on the current status of various departmental projects

5. a report on the proposed plans for a new shopping mall

B. Which of the following decisions or problems would be best discussed in a small group discussion, and which would be best decided independently by the person in charge? Explain why.

1. which car rental agency to lease company cars from

2. which brand of napkins to purchase for the cafeteria

3. how to promote a new product line

4. the company's new salary structure

5. an increase in theft of company supplies

6. the establishment of a company day care center for employees with young children

7. the problem of poor employee morale

PROJECTS

A. Write an outline for a brief oral report on one of the following subjects. Suggest the type of research that would be suitable for the subject. Then create an introduction, a body with several main points, and a conclusion.

1. You are a building contractor giving a presentation to a group of town officials. The object of your oral report is to convince them to sell you land to develop according to your view of housing of the future.

2. As the inventor of robot pets, you will be giving a presentation to a group of executives from a large robot manufacturing company. Your aim is to convince them to produce your idea because you believe there will be a large market for the product.

3. You are a sporting goods manufacturer who is going to try to persuade a group of major league baseball coaches to buy your new safety equipment for their teams.

B. Think of a problem in school, at your job, or at home that could be solved by a small group discussion. Write a one- to two-page essay explaining why the problem could be solved in this manner. Suggest some of the solutions that might result from such a meeting.

Appendix

Proofreading Symbols

Correction	Symbol	Example of Marked Copy	Example of Corrected Copy
Insert character	∧	th̭re (e)	there
Insert word	∧	it∧true (is)	it is true
Insert space	# ∧	How#can	How can
Insert period	⊙	to me⊙	to me.
Add on to word	‿	present‿s	presents
Delete letter	ℓ	why∮not	why not
Delete word	ℓ	now ~~now~~ or	now or
Delete and close up space	ℓ	plain℮ly	plainly
Delete space	⌒	on‿to	onto
Capitalize letter	≡	t̲w̲ice	Twice
Capitalize word	≣	d̲a̲n̲g̲e̲r̲	DANGER
Lowercase letter	/	W̸hite	white
Lowercase word	⌐	C̸AUTION	caution
Transpose letters	⌣	t⌣he	the
Transpose words	⌣	of⌣process	process of
Change word	— or ∧ℓ	three / ~~two~~	three
		three / ∧~~two~~ℓ	three
Change letter	/	afflu̸nt (e)	affluent
Align vertically	‖	‖Raymond / Joseph	Raymond / Joseph

615

Picture Credits

Front cover *Left cube:* (Top) Hewlett-Packard Company; (Left) Hewlett-Packard Company; (Right) Tom Hollyman/J.P. Morgan & Company. *Right cube:* (Top) Tom Dunham; (Left) Tom Dunham; (Right) Hewlett-Packard Company

Back cover (Top) Hewlett-Packard Company; (Left) Hewlett-Packard Company; (Right) Tom Dunham

Frontmatter (Page vii) Rockwell International Corporation; (Page viii) Hewlett-Packard Company; (Page ix) Hewlett-Packard Company; (Page xi) Burroughs Corporation; (Page xiii) Tom Hollyman/J.P. Morgan & Company; (Page xiv) Hewlett-Packard Company; (Page xv) Tom Dunham © 1986; (Page xvi) Hewlett-Packard Company

Part One opener (page 3) *Left cube:* (Top) Sperry Corporation; (Left) Sperry Corporation; (Right) BankAmerica Corporation. *Right cube:* (Top) Hewlett-Packard Company; (Left) BankAmerica Corporation; (Right) NCR Corporation

Part Two Opener (page 29) (Top) Hewlett-Packard Company; (Left) NCR Corporation; (Right) Hewlett-Packard Company

Part Three Opener (page 175) (Top) Hewlett-Packard Company; (Left) Hewlett-Packard Company; (Right) Hewlett-Packard Company

Part Four Opener (page 303) *Left cube:* (Top) Jim Anderson/Woodfin Camp & Associates; (Left) Tom Hollyman/J.P. Morgan & Company; (Right) Lynne Jaeger Weinstein/Woodfin Camp & Associates. *Right cube:* (Top) Michal Heron/Woodfin Camp & Associates; (Left) Jim Anderson/Woodfin Camp & Associates; (Right) Intergraph Corporation

Part Five Opener (page 353) *Left cube:* (Top) Jim Anderson/Woodfin Camp & Associates; (Bottom) Jim Anderson/Woodfin Camp & Associates. *Right cube:* (Top) Intergraph Corporation; (Left) Tom Hollyman/J.P. Morgan & Company; (Right) Lynne Jaeger Weinstein/Woodfin Camp & Associates

Part Six Opener (page 395) (Top) Timothy Eagan/Woodfin Camp & Associates; (Left) Intergraph Corporation; (Right) Sepp Seitz/Woodfin Camp & Associates

Part Seven Opener (page 463) *Left cube::* (Top) AMP, Inc.; (Left) Jim Anderson/Woodfin Camp & Associates; (Right) Sylvia Johnson/Woodfin Camp & Associates. *Right cube::* (Top) Michal Heron/Woodfin Camp & Associates; (Bottom) Rockwell International Corporation

Part Eight Opener (Page 511) (Top) Michal Heron/Woodfin Camp & Associates; (Bottom) Sepp Seitz/Woodfin Camp & Associates

Part Nine Opener (page 551) *Left cube:* (Top) Leif Skoogfors/Woodfin Camp & Associates; (Left) Sepp Seitz/Woodfin Camp & Associates; (Right) Timothy Eagan/Woodfin Camp & Associates. *Right cube:* (Top) Sylvia Johnson/Woodfin Camp & Associates; (Left) Hewlett-Packard Company; (Right) Tom Hollyman/J.P. Morgan & Company

Part Ten Opener (page 571) *Left cube::* (Top) Will Rhyins/Woodfin Camp & Associates; (Left) Sepp Seitz/Woodfin Camp & Associates; (Right) Sepp Seitz/Woodfin Camp & Associates. *Right cube:* (Top) Sepp Seitz/Woodfin

Camp & Associates; (Left) Hewlett-Packard Company; (Right) Sylvia Johnson/Woodfin Camp & Associates

Business and Technology photo essay (between pages 64 and 65) *Page 1:* (Top) Tom Hollyman/J.P. Morgan & Company; (Bottom) Tom Hollyman/J.P. Morgan & Company. *Page 2:* (Top Right) Tom Hollyman/J.P. Morgan & Company; (Bottom Left) Tom Hollyman/J.P. Morgan & Company. *Page 3:* (Top Left) Hewlett-Packard Company; (Bottom Right) Michal Heron/Woodfin Camp & Associates. *Page 4:* (Top) Hewlett-Packard Company; (Bottom Left) Hewlett-Packard Company; (Bottom Right) Hewlett-Packard Company. *Page 5:* (Top Left) Hewlett-Packard Company; (Top Right) Hewlett-Packard Company; (Bottom Right) Hewlett-Packard Company. *Page 6:* (Top) Hewlett-Packard Company; (Bottom Left) Honeywell, Inc. *Page 7:* (Left) Hewlett-Packard Company; (Right) Hewlett-Packard Company. *Page 8:* (Top Left) Compaq Computer Corporation; (Bottom Right) Compaq Computer Corporation.

The High-Tech Office photo essay (between pages 320 and 321) *Page 1:* (Top Left) Hewlett-Packard Company; (Bottom Right) Hewlett-Packard Company. *Page 2:* (Top Left) Honeywell, Inc.; (Bottom Left) Bernard Gotfryd/Woodfin Camp & Associates. *Page 3:* (Top Left) Hewlett-Packard Company; (Top Right) Jose Fernandez/Woodfin Camp & Associates; (Bottom Right) Sperry Corporation. *Page 4:* (Top) Hewlett-Packard Company; (Bottom) Hewlett-Packard Company. *Page 5:* (Top Left) Hewlett-Packard Company; (Top Right) Hewlett-Packard Company; (Bottom Left) Hewlett-Packard Company. *Page 6:* (Top Left) Hewlett-Packard Company; (Top Right) Hewlett-Packard Company; (Bottom Right) Hewlett-Packard Company. *Page 7:* (Top) Hewlett-Packard Company; (Bottom) Hewlett-Packard Company. *Page 8:* (Top) Tandy Corporation; (Bottom Right) Sepp Seitz/Woodfin Camp & Associates.

Getting Hired photo essay (between pages 512 and 513) All photos by Tom Dunham © 1986

Training for the High-Tech Office photo essay (between pages 576 and 577) *Page 1:* (Top Left) Steelcase, Inc.; (Bottom Right) ITT Corporation. *Page 2:* (Top) Hewlett-Packard Company; (Bottom) Hewlett-Packard Company. *Page 3:* (Top Left) Sepp Seitz/Woodfin Camp & Associates; (Bottom Right) Sepp Seitz/Woodfin Camp & Associates. *Page 4:* (Top Left) Hewlett-Packard Company; (Bottom Left) Sepp Seitz/Woodfin Camp & Associates. *Page 5:* (Top Left) Hewlett-Packard Company; (Bottom Right) Hewlett-Packard Company. *Page 6:* (Top) Steelcase, Inc.; (Bottom) Hewlett-Packard Company. *Page 7:* (Top Left) Tom Hollyman/J.P. Morgan & Company; (Bottom Right) Hewlett-Packard Company. *Page 8:* Hewlett-Packard Company.

Index